Teaching Infants and Preschoolers with Disabilities

SECOND EDITION

Donald B. Bailey, Jr.
University of North Carolina
at Chapel Hill

Mark Wolery
Allegheny-Singer Research Institute

Merrill,
an imprint of Prentice Hall

Englewood Cliffs, New Jersey   Columbus, Ohio

Library of Congress Cataloging-in-Publication Data
    Bailey, Donald B.
        Teaching infants and preschoolers with disabilities/Donald B.
Bailey, Jr., Mark Wolery. - 2nd ed.
       p. cm.
       Rev. ed. of: Teaching infants and preschoolers with handicaps, c1984.
       Includes bibliographical references and indexes.
       ISBN 0-675-21390-8
        1. Handicapped children-Education (Preschool). I. Wolery, Mark.
II. Bailey, Donald B. Teaching infants and preschoolers with
handicaps. III. Title.
LC4019.2.B35   1992
371.9'0472--dc20   91-38387
                                                      CIP

Cover art: © Clare Wood
Editor: Ann Castel
Production Editor: Sheryl Glicker Langner
Art Coordinator: Ruth A. Kimpel
Cover Designer: Cathleen Norz
Production Buyer: Patricia A. Tonneman

This book was set in Melior by Compset.

 © 1992 by Prentice-Hall, Inc.
A Simon & Schuster Company
Englewood Cliffs, New Jersey 07632

Printed in the United States of America
10 9 8 7 6 5 4 3

ISBN   0-675-21390-8

Prentice-Hall International (UK) Limited, *London*
Prentice-Hall of Australia Pty. Limited, *Sydney*
Prentice-Hall Canada Inc., *Toronto*
Prentice-Hall Hispanoamericana, S.A., *Mexico*
Prentice-Hall of India Private Limited, *New Delhi*
Prentice-Hall of Japan, Inc., *Tokyo*
Simon & Schuster Asia Pte. Ltd., *Singapore*
Editora Prentice-Hall do Brasil, Ltda., *Rio de Janeiro*

Preface

Much has changed in early intervention since we wrote the first edition of this book. Public Law 99–457 made early intervention a national priority and provided a framework around which services for children and families are to be provided. The movement toward family-centered services accelerated and has emerged as a guiding theme for early intervention programs. Furthermore, the goals for early intervention have expanded, requiring professionals from multiple disciplines to examine current practices to determine how consistent they are with these goals and philosophical principles. These factors, along with the changing data base for early intervention practices, meant that the second edition of this text could not be a simple update of references and language; rather, it is a major rewrite in which we have attempted to accomplish several objectives.

First, we have described major legislative changes and their impact on service delivery systems. These changes have necessitated the inclusion of chapters on the goals of early intervention and the ecology of early intervention. Although the text is written primarily for teachers and other child care providers, it is essential that teaching activities be conducted in ways that are consistent with the goals and ecologies in which children, families, and programs exist.

Second, we have increased the infancy focus of the text. Part H of Public Law 99–457 has stimulated the rapid growth of services for infants and families. It has also prompted a recognition of the uniqueness of the infancy period and the importance of designing programs and procedures that are consistent with the needs and characteristics of very young children.

Third, we have tried to infuse a family-centered approach throughout the text. Families have needs, resources, priorities, and concerns, all of which must be considered in planning intervention goals and services.

Fourth, we have attempted to present information about teaching methods and procedures that is consistent with both data and philosophy about best practice. These in- clude practices that are important for all children as well as those that are likely to be effective for children with special needs.

Finally, we recognize the rapid increase in specialized knowledge about work with young children over the past five years. This led us to ask a number of experts to assist in the preparation of selected chapters.

It is impossible for any one text to provide all of the information one needs to work with young children with disabilities and their families. Here we have attempted to provide a synthesis of what we feel are the most important considerations. We encourage readers to consult the references for more detailed presentations and to keep abreast of changes in the field by reading professional journals, books, and attending professional conferences related to early intervention.

We would like to acknowledge the support of numerous students, colleagues, staff, and family members who helped with this edition of the text. We especially appreciate the many constructive and supportive comments made by readers of the first edition of the text. We have tried our best to listen and respond accordingly. We hope that readers of the second edition will continue to provide feedback to us about the usefulness of this text.

We are grateful to S. L. Odom, M. A. McEvoy, and D. M. Sainato for providing "in press" documents for chapter 9. We would also like to thank the following reviewers for their invaluable suggestions: Blanche Glimps, Marygrove College; Jeanette McCollom, University of Illinois; Tandra Tyler-Wood, West Georgia College; M. Diane Klein, California State University, Los Angeles; Sarah Rule Salzberg, Utah State University; Mary Ellen Pearson, Mankato State University; Elanor W. Lynch, San Diego State University; William Glenn Morgan, Southeastern Louisiana University; John Richardson, Clemson University; and Dean A. Zoerink, Kent State University.

We dedicate this book to our wives, Pam and Ruth, and our children, Lara, Rebecca, Nathaniel, Steve, and Tim.

Contents

1

Fundamentals of Early Intervention

The term *early intervention* has been used to describe a variety of services for young children with special needs and for their families. Recent years have witnessed a significant growth in services offered, a federal mandate for preschool programs, national incentives for infant programs, an expansion of early intervention to work with diverse populations and in a variety of settings, and new ideas about the goals of early intervention as well as the methods by which those goals are to be achieved.

But what does it mean when professionals say that they provide early intervention services? One type of early intervention is teaching or providing therapy for young children with disabilities; but instructional and therapeutic activities must be conceived broadly as integrated into the ecologies of family and community. The purpose of this chapter is to establish the historical as well as the current context for early intervention. We present an overview of the diversity of early intervention settings, professional roles, and philosophical perspectives. We review the research that has been conducted on the effectiveness of early intervention, and we discuss the implications of this research for future early intervention services.

HISTORICAL PERSPECTIVE

The most visible events shaping early intervention programs for infants and preschoolers who have, or are at risk for, disabling conditions are recent legislative acts and mandates. These events, however, are embedded within a broader historical context; over the years society has changed its view of children as well as its view of equity (Shonkoff & Meisels, 1990).

Broad Historical Themes

Three broad historical themes form the background for the current status of early intervention programs. First, society has become concerned about the care and welfare of young children. Early reflections of this concern included the passage of laws prohibiting child labor and requiring public education. More recently, parents and professionals have recognized that the early years are critical to the child's physical, emotional, social, and cognitive development. Thus increased attention has been focused on the quality of early experiences for all children. Furthermore, as more mothers of young children are returning to work shortly after childbirth, greater attention is being paid to promoting high-quality options and national standards of quality for out-of-home care for young children.

A second major theme is society's concern for the rights and needs of individual citizens and of minority groups. History has provided ample evidence of discrimination against minority groups, women, and persons with disabilities. However, as minority groups began to fight for and secure their rights, the views of the nation began to change. The leaders of the civil rights, individual rights, and women's rights movements were not necessarily directly involved in advocating early intervention programs, but they helped set the stage for society's receptiveness to the needs of various minority groups. The parents of children with disabilities, and professionals interested in the care and education of such children, made up one such group. They were successful in initiating lawsuits and in motivating legislators to pass laws that improved services for children with disabilities. The most visible example of this effort was the passage of Public Law 94–142 in 1975. For the first time, children with disabilities were recognized as having the same rights as all other children to a free and appropriate public education. Embedded within the increased recognition of the rights of all citizens has been the recognition of a need to provide programs or services to help compensate for disability or for minority status. Thus there has been an increased societal commitment to providing specialized services for persons with disabilities.

A third societal trend is an increased focus on support for both individuals and families as a primary goal of human service programs. Increasingly it is being recognized that services often are provided in a way that creates dependency on the part of recipients. Health and human services across a variety of state, federal, and private agencies are being evaluated in terms of the extent to which they promote independence and self-determination.

Historical Notes on Early Intervention

Given these broad societal trends, several key events have shaped the nature and ex-

tent of current early intervention services and practices. The first public commitment to young children with special needs was the initiation of Head Start in 1965. Head Start's overarching goal was to break the cycle of poverty, based on the assumption that the best way to do this is to intervene in the early years. Designed for 4- and 5-year-olds from low socioeconomic families, Head Start attempted to address the goals of improving health and social-emotional development, increasing cognitive skills and self-confidence, and encouraging responsibility. A description of the Head Start program is provided in Box 1.1.

In 1968 a national network of model early intervention programs for children with disabilities was established by the Bureau of Education for the Handicapped of the U.S. Department of Education. Known as the Hand-

---

BOX 1.1   Head Start at a glance

Head Start was established in 1965 to serve young children (ages 3 to 5 years) from poverty environments. Since that time more than 11 million children have received an array of services, including day care, developmental enhancement, nutritious meals, medical and dental screening, and family support.

Currently there are more than 1,300 Head Start programs serving more than 450,000 children. Most of the children are 3 (25%) or 4 (60%) years of age. Approximately two thirds of the children are from minority groups, primarily Black (38%) and Hispanic (22%).

In 1972 the Economic Opportunity Act mandated at least 10% enrollment of children with disabilities in Head Start. Current figures indicate that more than 13% of the children served have some type of disability. Most (66%) of these are classified as having a speech impairment. Very few children with severe or profound disabilities are served in Head Start.

As of 1988 Head Start employed nearly 80,000 people. More than 30% of the paid staff are parents of current or former Head Start children. In addition to the paid staff, there are approximately 615,000 volunteers, mostly parents.

In 1990 the Head Start Expansion and Quality Improvement Act reauthorized the Head Start Program through 1994 and significantly increased funding for this program. Priorities for additional funding included staff benefits, transportation, reduced staff-child ratio, and staff training. The 1990 act requires increased coordination with other agencies, including local and state educational agencies. By 1994, each classroom must have one teacher who has either (a) a child development associate (CDA) credential, (b) a degree in early childhood education or a related degree plus certification, or (c) a state certificate that equals or exceeds the CDA. Also being considered is a downward extension of Head Start to cover infants and toddlers.

icapped Children's Early Education Program (HCEEP), its purpose was to develop and demonstrate the feasibility of alternative models for serving young children with disabilities and their families. Since its inception, more than 500 model demonstration programs have been funded nationwide. A summary of this network is provided in Box 1.2. In 1972, the first national mandate to serve young children with disabilities was issued when the Economic Opportunity Act required that Head Start programs devote at least 10 percent of their enrollment to children with disabilities.

In 1975, Congress passed Public Law 94–142, the Individuals with Disabilities Education Act. This landmark legislation had its primary impact on school-aged children by establishing the following important provisions.

- *Zero reject*—Children have a right to a free appropriate public education regardless of the type and severity of their disabilities.
- *Individualized and appropriate education*—Educational programs should be designed to meet the particular needs of particular children.
- *Nondiscriminatory testing, classification, and placement*—The procedures used to assess, label, and place children in educational programs must be free of bias and must be conducted with parental notification and consent.

BOX 1.2   The Handicapped Children's Early Education Program

In 1968, Congress passed Public Law 90–538, the Handicapped Children's Early Education Assistance Act. This act created the Handicapped Children's Early Education Program (HCEEP) to establish models for providing early intervention services. Because there was at that time no mandate for early intervention, the program was intended to develop multiple models for serving children and families, demonstrate that they could be implemented, train others in how to implement them, and evaluate their effectiveness.

Twenty-four projects were funded in 1969. Since then nearly 600 demonstration projects have been funded, addressing a wide range of topics and children. Some have addressed specific groups of children, such as those with visual impairment or fetal alcohol syndrome. Others have demonstrated special models or components of services, such as rural service delivery, integration into day care, interagency collaboration, or family-centered services.

Karnes and Stayton (1988) conducted a survey of 96 HCEEP projects that focused on children ages birth through 2 years. They found that the projects operated within a variety of agencies, most frequently universities or public schools. Most reported a developmental learning model, but program practices were not always consistent with the model. Most (70%) used a home–center combination model and were staffed by professionals from a wide array of disciplines.

The network has been highly successful, with nearly 80% of the demonstration projects continuing to operate after federal funding ended. Many assessment instruments and curriculum packages have been developed by HCEEP projects.

In 1990, Public Law 101–476 (the Individuals with Disabilities Education Act) renamed the program The Early Education for Handicapped Children Program. Increased emphasis was placed on identifying and serving infants and toddlers in need, facilitating the transition from medical to early intervention services, promoting the use of assisting technology, and serving children exposed prenatally to maternal substance abuse.

• *Children must be placed in the least re-strictive appropriate environment*—Children with disabilities must be placed, to the maximum extent possible and appropriate, in regular educational settings with nonhandicapped children.

• *Rights to procedural due process*—Parents have the right to question and challenge actions, intended by the school, that would affect their disabled children's education.

• *Shared decision making*—Parents are to be involved in planning and developing state and local educational policy regarding their children and in developing and implementing the children's educational programs.

Public Law 94–142 recognized the importance of early intervention and was designed to apply to children ages 3 to 21. It provided, however, that states did not have to serve children ages 3 to 5 if such services were inconsistent with state law. Although a small financial incentive was built into the legislation to encourage the provision of preschool services, states generally were reluctant to pass legislation mandating preschool programs. By 1985, 31 states had passed some form of preschool legislation, but many were not comprehensive mandates and provided services only to particular groups of children with special needs.

In October 1986, Congress passed Public Law 99–457, amending P.L. 94–142. This legislation extended all of the rights and protections of P.L. 94–142 to 3- to 5-year-old children with disabilities. Specifically, by school year 1991–92 states will have to demonstrate that they are providing a free and appropriate public education to all 3- to 5-year-old children with disabilities. The legislation also provides incentives and a framework for states to provide services for infants and toddlers with disabilities and for their families. This component of the law recognizes that working with infants is dif-ferent from working with preschoolers, and it puts particular emphasis on early intervention as a family-centered service rather than as just a child-focused service. The most obvious example of this emphasis is the requirement for an Individualized Family Service Plan that is to include, if the family so desires, a statement of family resources, priorities, and concerns and a description of family goals and of the services to be provided. In addition, a case manager is to be assigned to assist families in gaining access to and coordinating early intervention services.

A summary of some of the major landmarks in legislation for early intervention services is provided in Box 1.3.

WHAT DO WE KNOW ABOUT THE EFFECTIVENESS OF EARLY INTERVENTION?

Is early intervention effective? As we shall see, this is not a simple question. For example, how early is early? What constitutes intervention? By what markers will we determine effectiveness? In this section we briefly review the research on early intervention effectiveness and discuss the implications of this research for practice.

A Historical Study

In the early part of this century, assumptions about intelligence focused on its heritability, with little attention paid to environmental influences. A small, but significant study by Skeels and Dye provided evidence of the powerful influence of environmental conditions on children's development. In 1939, Skeels and Dye took 13 children under 3 years of age out of an orphanage and placed them in a ward for older retarded women in an institution. They left 12 other children in the orphanage. At that time, orphanages were frequently understaffed and were poor

---

BOX 1.3   Major landmarks in early intervention services

1965   Project Head Start was established to serve 3- and 4-year olds from poverty environments.

1968   The federal government established the Handicapped Children's Early Education Program to fund model preschool programs for children with disabilities.

1972   The Economic Opportunity Act required at least 10% enrollment of children with disabilities in Head Start.

1975   Public Law 94–142, The Education for All Handicapped Children Act, established services for some preschoolers with disabilities ages 3 to 5 years.

1986   Public Law 99–457, amending P.L. 94–142, mandated free and appropriate public education for children with disabilities ages 3 to 5 years. This law also established incentives and a framework for serving infants and toddlers.

1990   The Head Start Expansion and Quality Improvement Act (part of Public Law 101–501, the Human Services Reauthorization Act) reauthorized the Head Start Program through 1994, significantly increased appropriations for programs, reduced to staff–child ratio, and raised requirements for staff qualifications.

1990   Public Law 101–476 reauthorized the Education for All Handicapped Children Act (P.L. 94–142) and renamed it the Individuals with Disabilities Education Act (IDEA).

1990   Public Law 102–119 reauthorized an extended Part H (the infant component) of Public Law 99–457 and made several amendments regarding how services are to be provided.

---

environments. All children were pretested for IQ when the 13 were transferred to the institution. They were also tested 18 months to 3 years later when they were placed in foster homes. The 13 children who had been placed on the ward with older retarded women had gained an average of 27 IQ points while those who remained in the orphanage had lost an average of 26 IQ points.

In 1966, Skeels reported on a 21-year follow-up of the children. The findings from the follow-up study indicated that all the children who had been placed in the institution were self-supporting and none were wards of the state. Of the 12 who stayed at the orphanage, 1 had died in an institution for children with mental retardation as an adolescent and 4 others were wards of the state and were in institutions for persons

with mental retardation. Half were working, but all except 1 were unskilled laborers. The median school year completed by the institutionalized group was more than 12th grade, whereas the orphanage children received an average of less than a 3rd grade education.

Skeels and Dye's methodology has received considerable criticism; but the study did demonstrate that environmental conditions influence development, and it remains as one of the few truly longitudinal studies of intervention effectiveness.

Research on Children From Low-Income Families

The evaluation studies of intervention programs for children from low-income families represent an important body of research related to young children with disabilities. Although the results of these studies do not necessarily generalize to early intervention for children with disabilities, the studies provide an important methodological and conceptual framework.

An early report on the effects of Head Start was the Westinghouse Study (Cicirelli et al., 1969). This study prompted considerable discussion and debate (cf. Cicirelli, Evans, & Schiller, 1970; Smith & Bissell, 1970). Following are four of the Westinghouse Study's major findings.

1 Summer Head Start programs do not produce cognitive or affective gains that persist into the early elementary grades.
2 Full-year Head Start programs do not appear to influence affective development, but have marginal effects on cognitive development which can still be detected in grades one, two, and three.
3 Head Start children are below national norms on the Stanford Achievement Test and the Illinois Test of Psycholinguistic Ability—although their Metropolitan Readiness scores approach national norms.
4 Parents liked the program and participated in it. (Smith & Bissell, 1970, pp. 52–55)

As might be expected, these studies prompted a range of reactions. Although some argued that Head Start should be abandoned, three ideas emerged that have continued to shape early intervention efforts today. First, it was argued that one year of preschool experience could not be expected to produce long-term effects (Zigler & Hunsinger, 1979), and that interventions should begin earlier. A program called Home Start was initiated under Head Start and began to enroll younger children (Deasey, 1978). Second, in recognition of the long-term needs of children living in poverty, it was argued that intervention should not stop when children enter elementary school. Follow Through was initiated as a federally supported pro-

gram to assist children in making the transition to public school (House, Glass, McLean, & Walker, 1978; Stallings, 1975). Finally, the fact that parents liked and participated in Head Start provided an early indication that child progress alone was insufficient as an indication of the effectiveness of early intervention, and served as one stimulus behind the broader family focus of early intervention. A later review of early intervention by Bronfenbrenner (1975) reinforced the family focus by suggesting that parent involvement was necessary if children's gains were to endure.

Since the Westinghouse Study, hundreds of other studies of Head Start and other preschool programs have been conducted. Several recent reviews have summarized this vast body of research (Collins & Kinney, 1989; Haskins, 1989; Schorr, 1989; Slaughter, Washington, Oyemade, & Lindsey, 1988). Haskins (1989) points out that the research can be divided into two types of studies: those based on well-run model preschool programs, such as those reported by the Consortium for Longitudinal Studies (Lazar, Darlington, Murray, Royce, & Snipper, 1982), and those based on Head Start programs. In reviewing both types of studies, he drew the following conclusions.

1 Both model programs and Head Start produce significant and meaningful gains in intellectual performance and socioemotional development by the end of a year of intervention.
2 For both types of programs, gains on standardized IQ and achievement tests as well as on tests of socioemotional development decline within a few years (or even less in the case of Head Start studies).
3 On categorical variables of school performance such as special education placement and grade retention, there is very strong evidence of positive effects for the model programs and modest evidence of effects for Head Start programs.
4 On measures of life success such as teen pregnancy, delinquency, welfare participation, and

employment, there is modest evidence of positive impacts for model programs but virtually no evidence for Head Start. (Haskins, 1989, p. 278)

This review suggests that early intervention can have both immediate and lasting effects for children from low-income families, *especially when a high-quality early intervention program is provided.* An example of a longitudinal study demonstrating a wide range of lasting benefits is the Perry Preschool Program (Berrueta-Clement, Schweinhart, Barnett, Epstein, & Weikart, 1985), described in Box 1.4. Schorr (1989) argues that effective programs are those that (a) are comprehensive and intensive, (b) have well-trained staff who have the time and skills needed to develop positive and trusting relationships

with children and families, (c) view the child as part of a family and the family as part of a unique ecological system, and (d) "are prepared to offer a wide variety of services, in nontraditional settings, including homes, and at nontraditional hours" (p. 369). In other words, the successful program attempts to meet the individual needs of children and families in ways that are acceptable to them.

Research on Children at Risk Due to Low Birth Weight or Prematurity

A second group of children who have served as the focus of early intervention effectiveness studies are those children who are believed to be at risk due to low birth weight

---

BOX 1.4   A longitudinal study of early intervention

The Perry Preschool study examined the immediate and long-term effects of preschool education on the lives of low-income children and their families and on the community as a whole. Subjects consisted of 123 children who shared similar background characteristics and were at-risk for educational failure. Children in the experimental group experienced one or two years of preschool education directed at intellectual and social development, as well as weekly home visits. Children in the control group had no preschool experience.

Follow-up of youths in the Perry Preschool Project has occurred on a regular basis to evaluate the effectiveness of the program. Initial follow-up studies revealed that preschool education improved the performance of children on IQ tests. Although this effect did not persist over time, children in the preschool group attained higher levels of academic achievement than did their counterparts throughout the elementary and middle school years.

More recent follow-up studies have documented the effects of preschool on school achievement, socioeconomic success, and social responsibility in adolescence and young adulthood. When compared to their counterparts, those who attended preschool earned higher grades, spent fewer years in special education classrooms, performed better on a test of competence in daily living skills, and expressed more positive attitudes toward high school. In addition, those in the preschool group were found to have higher levels of employment, less unemployment, higher earnings, fewer occurrences of delinquent behavior, and were less likely to receive public assistance than those who did not attend preschool.

Note: Adapted from "Changed Lives: The Effects of the Perry Preschool Program on Youths Through Age 19" by J. Berrueta-Clement, L. Schweinhart, W. Barnett, A. Epstein, and D. Weikart, 1985, *Monographs of the High/Scope Educational Research Foundation, 8,* Ypsilanti, MI: High/Scope.

or prematurity. Many of these children spend considerable time in the hospital and suffer neurological or respiratory problems that could lead to subsequent delays in development, although our ability to predict the children in this group most likely to have later problems is limited (Cohen, 1986).

A variety of studies have investigated the effects of different treatment alternatives, both within the hospital and after hospitalization is over (Bennett, 1987; Resnick, Eyler, Nelson, Eitzman, & Bucciarelli, 1987). One of the largest studies was reported in 1990 as part of a multi-site collaborative study (Infant Health and Development Program, 1990). The study involved 995 infants of low birth weight or prematurity who were randomly assigned to receive either an educational curriculum or pediatric follow-up only. The children were in eight sites distributed across the country. The intervention consisted of weekly home visits for the first year of life and the provision of health and developmental information and of specially developed curricula for families to implement at home. A center-based program was then provided until 36 months of age.

In terms of cognitive development, those children in the intervention group weighing more than 2000 grams at birth had IQ scores that were 13.2 points higher than the control group children, who received pediatric follow-up only. The intervention group children who weighed less than 2000 grams at birth only scored 6.6 IQ points higher than the control group children. Both of these comparisons were statistically significant. The intervention group children also had fewer behavior problems.

Research on Children with Disabilities

Evaluating early intervention for young children with disabilities is difficult. An effective intervention program must produce results that are better than those when no intervention is used. To make such compar-

isons, control groups traditionally are used, but several factors make it difficult to obtain a control/comparison group similar to the group that receives intervention. First, many persons consider it unethical to withhold intervention from one group of children while giving it to another. Second, few programs provide different levels of the same intervention services to the same type of children. If two programs are located that provide different levels of the same intervention services, we are no longer trying to determine whether early intervention is effective, but rather which of the levels of intervention is more effective than the other. Third, when comparisons across children in different programs are made, it is difficult to have equal groups. Obviously, comparing the effects of intervention programs having 4- and 5-year-old children with the effects of another program dealing with infants is invalid. Likewise, interventions would be difficult to compare across different types of disabling conditions. We cannot validly compare the effects of an intervention program for children who are blind to the effects of an intervention program for children who have mental retardation. But even when we limit our study to children experiencing the same disabling condition we cannot validly compare the effects of intervention programs on cases exhibiting varying levels of severity; certainly a child with profound deafness will respond differently than a child with a mild hearing impairment, or a child with a severe case of cerebral palsy will respond differently than a child experiencing only mild motor delays. These evaluation problems are chronic because of the relatively small number of children in most intervention programs; thus, evaluators must usually construct their comparison groups from small numbers of diverse children (Dunst & Rheingrover, 1981; Simeonsson, Cooper, & Scheiner, 1982).

One solution for this problem may be to compare a child's performance before intervention to his or her performance during and after intervention (White, 1980). By comparing the performances of the same children under different conditions (with no intervention and with intervention) we may eliminate the need for comparison groups because the children serve as their own controls. However, we must proceed by alternately withholding and implementing the intervention; withholding then implementing; or we must withhold intervention from all the children and then initiate it on a staggered basis for different children at different times. We must also measure children's performance more than once under each condition.

Besides having problems making comparisons between situations of intervention and nonintervention, evaluation studies also have the problem of interpreting maturation. Most children with disabilities will make some progress despite their disabling conditions even when they do not receive intervention. When evaluating the effects of intervention, we have this problem: How much progress is due to the intervention program, how much is due simply to the maturation that would have occurred anyway, and how much additional progress is needed before the intervention is considered effective?

Another evaluation problem involves determining what measures should be used. Should children's developmental levels and gains be the primary criteria of effectiveness, and if so, which of many developmental scales should we use? Or, should we use IQ change, or the number of objectives children have met, or parental satisfaction, or changes in the rates of given behaviors (e.g., the number of words spoken per hour)? Bricker and Sheehan (1981) suggest that several measures should be used to determine effectiveness. While this recommendation appears logical, it prompts an additional question: How do we get the time and resources to use multiple measures with each child in an intervention program?

Despite these and many other problems, studies evaluating the effectiveness of intervention with young children with disabilities have been conducted. The results of early evaluation studies were reviewed by Dunst and Rheingrover (1981) and Simeonsson et al. (1982). Dunst and Rheingrover (1981) focused primarily on the strengths and weaknesses of the methods used in the evaluation studies rather than on the findings. They found that 35 of 49 studies (71%) used methods that essentially made the results scientifically uninterpretable. When taken together, the studies clearly showed progress; the question is whether the progress was a result of the intervention program or other factors. Dunst and Rheingrover recommended that the authors of the evaluation reports reexamine their studies to eliminate factors that made the results uninterpretable, and that future evaluation studies be carefully planned and implemented to control extraneous factors. Dunst and Rheingrover also suggested that there was not enough scientifically valid evidence to conclude that early intervention is effective.

Simeonsson et al. (1982) agreed that the majority of the evaluation reports lacked sufficient scientific rigor, but went on to state, "In spite of limitations from the standpoint of scientific criteria, the research does provide qualified support for the effectiveness of early intervention. Although only 48 percent of all studies yielded statistical evidence for effectiveness, this figure increases to 81 percent when the analysis is restricted to those studies that incorporate statistical procedures" (p. 638). They gave several reasons why the 48 percent figure underestimates the effectiveness of early intervention for children with disabilities: The small number of children used in each report would work against finding statistically significant results; children's progress may have occurred in developmental areas that were not assessed; children's progress may have occurred in areas of management rather than in developmental areas; changes may have occurred in only the family and living environments; and only a small percentage of studies utilized statistical procedures. One further consideration is the distinction between statistical and clinical significance (Kazdin, 1976; Wolery & Harris, 1982). Some changes may not be statistically significant but may produce worthwhile changes in the child's functioning. A child's learning to feed himself may not be a significant development statistically, because, for example, of the small number of children studied for the report; but clinically—in the child's own life—the development is quite significant.

Since the publication of these early reviews, a number of other reviews, summaries, and analyses of early intervention research have been published (e.g., Casto & Mastropieri, 1986; Ottenbacher, 1989; Shonkoff & Hauser-Cram, 1987). All have concluded that we still do not have a sufficient empirical base for evaluating the effectiveness of early intervention. Perhaps the most visible and controversial of these reviews has been the paper published by Casto and Mastropieri (1986). Using meta-analysis techniques (a statistical procedure that compares "effect sizes" reported by different studies using different measurement procedures), the authors integrated the findings from 74 early intervention studies. Overall, they found that early intervention programs resulted in only moderate benefits during the course of the program, with an effect size of just .68. This means that the average child in early intervention scored .68 of a standard deviation higher than the average child who did not receive early intervention. This effect dropped to .40, furthermore, if only studies using high-quality methods were included in the analysis. Casto and Mastropieri also concluded that intervention programs that utilize parents are no more effective than those that do not, that earlier treatment is no better than later, that effects are not related so much to the degree of structure in the pro-

gram as to the length and intensity of the program.

This study prompted two critical reactions (Dunst & Snyder, 1986; Strain & Smith, 1986) and has resulted in numerous discussions about the goals of early intervention as well as about the methodology of research into the efficacy of early intervention. A specific criticism was that the existing studies involved children with diverse disabling conditions, applied different intervention models and procedures, and incorporated a variety of outcome measures. Is it meaningful, therefore, to make summary statements about effectiveness based on such diversity? A further concern was the focus of most studies on change in children's intelligence test or developmental test scores. It is quite possible that these measures do not reflect other important outcomes for children; they certainly do not reflect family outcomes.

It could be argued that documentation of the effectiveness of early intervention became a moot issue once early intervention was mandated by Public Law 99–457. Clearly, however, early intervention programs will continue to be accountable, and valid studies of intervention effectiveness do need to be conducted. Of particular importance are studies that compare alternative strategies or approaches to treatment, that assess outcomes in a variety of domains, and that seek to determine strategies for maximizing the goodness-of-fit between child and family needs and early intervention services.

Current Knowledge About Early Intervention

Given this background of efficacy research, what do we really know about early intervention and its effectiveness? Shulman (1986) argues that *propositional knowledge* (broad-based, generalizable information) about children, families, and intervention strategies actually derives from three sources. Some knowledge, referred to by Shulman as *prin-*

ciples, is derived from empirical research and theory development. Other knowledge, referred to as *maxims*, exists as "the accumulated wisdom of practice" (p. 11). Finally, *norms* are "propositions that guide . . . not because they are true in scientific terms, or because they work in practical terms, but because they are morally or ethically right" (p. 11).

This framework acknowledges the diversity of sources of knowledge about professional practices. In early intervention, it is readily apparent that maxims and norms form the basis for many practices. For example, there are numerous approaches that have emerged because of the "accumulated wisdom of practice"; likewise, there are certain values or philosophical commitments (e.g., to mainstreaming, to providing family-centered services) that have been embraced prior to the establishment of a strong empirical data base. This experience does not mean that research is not needed; in fact, research has an important role to play in documenting the effects of these nonempirically derived practices. We should recognize, however, that early intervention is inherently both a value-laden and experientially driven endeavor. Examples of principles, maxims, and norms in the context of early intervention are displayed in Table 1.1.

CURRENT STATUS OF EARLY INTERVENTION

The practice of early intervention has come to consist of a diverse and expanding network of professionals, services, and consumers. In order to work effectively within this network, early interventionists must be aware of the diversity and must possess skills for addressing complex problems and needs. In this section, we describe the diversity and the challenges that exist today in early intervention.

Diversity in Children Served

Special educators serving elementary-aged and older children usually work with relatively homogeneous groups of children (e.g., children with learning disabilities or children with behavior disorders). Early intervention professionals, however, inevitably work with children and families who have a broad spectrum of disabilities and needs. In part this variability is due to the fact that early intervention programs and services are not usually categorical in nature. The variability is also a reflection of broadened legislative guidelines, particularly at the infancy level. For example, although P.L. 99–457 is a downward extension of P.L. 94–142 for children ages 3 to 5 years, states are not required to report those children by disability labels, and noncategorical approaches to identification are thus allowed. The guidelines are even broader for children from birth to three years of age. In this age group, states are required to provide services to children with documented developmental delays (the specific extent to be determined by each state) and to children who have a condition that typically results in delay or disability (e.g., Down syndrome). States may also elect to serve children who are at risk for delay for other reasons—such as being of low birthweight or having adolescent or low income parents—or children who are at risk for abuse or neglect.

This diversity in children requires that professionals have a sound knowledge of basic developmental processes and functions, a broad understanding of various disabilities and risk conditions, and familiarity with strategies for gaining new information when confronted with new cases. In this section we highlight some of the variability that will likely increase in the near future.

Newborns and Infants   Certainly one dramatic change in the last five years has been the increased emphasis on working with

TABLE 1.1
Descriptions and examples of propositional knowledge in early intervention

Propositional knowledge: The accumulated knowledge in a profession, based on research, theory, and clinical experiences

Principles		Maxims		Norms	
Knowledge derived from empiral research		The accumulated wisdom of practice, never confirmed by research		The values or ideological/philosophical commitments that we wish clinicians to incorporate and employ	
Well-Documented	Emerging Documentation	Generally Accepted	Somewhat Controversial	Generally Accepted	Controversial
1. The quality of a child's physical and social environment exerts a significant influence on the child's behavior as well as on the child's long-term development. 2. When handicapped children are taught skills under artificial training conditions, newly acquired skills are not likely to generalize to other contexts without planned generalization activities.	1. Interventions that build heavily on children's initiations are likely to result in greater acquisition and use of functional skills than interventions that are solely teacher-directed. 2. Speech therapy is likely to be more effective when conducted during natural routines, in typical environments, and in the context of ongoing interactions with peers and adults.	1. Early intervention is effective in reducing or ameliorating the effects of handicapping conditions. 2. Individualized assessment of children's abilities is a necessary prerequisite to effective intervention. 3. When teaching children with multiple impairments, clinicians should teach to the child's strengths rather than focusing on building the child's deficits. 4. Intervention must be developmentally based, teaching skills according to normal developmental sequences.	1. Home-based intervention is preferable for infants, whereas center-based services are preferable for preschoolers. 2. Physical and occupational therapy services significantly affect children's long-term development and functional status.	1. Parent involvement is essential to appropriate early intervention services. 2. Early intervention is most effective when professionals work together in an interdisciplinary team.	1. Early intervention should focus on parental, not professional, priorities for services. 2. All handicapped infants and preschoolers should be served in the least restrictive environment, with opportunities to interact with nonhandicapped children.

Note: From "Issues and Directions in Preparing Professionals to Work With Young Handicapped Children and Their Families" (pp. 121–122) by D. B. Bailey, 1989, in *Policy Implementation and P.L. 99–457: Planning for Young Children With Special Needs*, J. J. Gallagher, R. M. Clifford, & P. Trohanis (Eds.), Baltimore: Paul Brookes Publishing Co., P.O. Box 10624, Baltimore, MD, 21285-0624. Copyright 1989 by Brookes Publishing Co. Reprinted by permission.

newborns and infants. Just as we have recognized that working with 3- to 5-year-olds
is not just a downward extension of working
with elementary-aged children, so too must
we recognize that working with infants is different from working with preschoolers. Some
ways in which interventions with infants,
preschoolers, and elementary-aged children
vary are displayed in Table 1.2. Three dimensions are highlighted: characteristics of
the children, the nature of the intervention
context, and the role of families.

With respect to child characteristics, variable factors such as population parameters,
goals for intervention, schedule regularity,
endurance, and motivation all contribute to
the need for unique models of service delivery. The fact that infants are not generally
subject to adult schedules, have short attention spans, and are motivated primarily by
the inherent appeal of a person, material, or
activity (as opposed to adult expectations for
compliance) means that interventions must
be brief and highly motivating and must take
place during alert periods. Interventions will
most likely occur during the normal course
of caregiver–child interactions, during play,
or in the context of regular routines such as
feeding, bathing, and diapering.

Low Birth Weight and Prematurity   A tremendous increase has been observed in the
number of children born prematurely (before
38 weeks gestation) or low in birth weight
(usually less than 2500 grams, although definitions do vary). The increased number of
children in these categories is primarily due
to increased survival rates resulting from advances in the knowledge, techniques, and
technology of neonatal care. Often these
children are characterized as "medically
fragile," and much of the initial effort in the
hospital is focused on maintaining life rather
than facilitating development. For at least
two reasons, however, early interventionists
will need skills and knowledge related to
these children. First, hospitals are beginning

to recognize that family support, quality of
life, the regulation of behavioral states, and
the facilitation of development are important
concerns, even for the neonate who is medically fragile (Flynn & McCollum, 1989). Consequently, many hospitals now employ early
interventionists from a variety of professions
who have expertise related to working with
families, caring for the behavioral and developmental needs of neonates, or monitoring and adapting the hospital environment.
Wolke (1987), for example, has described a
new field called "environmental neonatology" which seeks to answer the question
"What is the environment of the special care
baby unit like today, and how can we best
provide for the bio-behavioural well-being
of the preterm infant?" (p. 987). A second
reason that early interventionists need to
know about low birth weight and premature
babies is that some (but not all) will have developmental delays, and many will be classified as high-risk. Thus many will enter
early intervention programs at discharge
from the hospital or will participate in
high-risk tracking and monitoring systems.
Some characteristics of the neonatal intensive care unit experience are described in
Box 1.5.

What skills should the early interventionist working with neonates or in hospital
environments have? Cooper and Kennedy
(1989) provide an overview of selected
skills. The early interventionist should have
basic knowledge about the organization and
staffing patterns of neonatal intensive care
units; about common medical complications, treatment procedures, and equipment
for emergencies as well as routine care; and
about methods for assessing behavioral cues
and states, environmental variables that influence newborn behavior, and support from
family members. Also important for the early
interventionist is the ability to support families in the hospital-to-home transition and
in the locating of necessary services following discharge.

Children with AIDS AIDS, or acquired immune deficiency syndrome, is a disease caused by HIV, the human immunodeficiency virus. The syndrome reduces the body's ability to resist infections and eventually results in death. The dramatic increase of AIDS cases in adults is paralleled by a similar increase in pediatric cases of AIDS. The rate of newly identified cases of pediatric AIDS has approximately doubled each year of the past decade (Dokecki, Baumeister, & Kupstas, 1989). Although some children contract AIDS through transfusions of contaminated blood or clotting factor, most cases are caused by perinatal transmission from an infected mother. In children, because of their underdeveloped immune systems, AIDS appears to take a more rapid course than in adults. The disease results in both medical problems and developmental delays. Thus children with AIDS usually qualify for early intervention services.

Pediatric AIDS poses a challenge for early interventionists because of the complex nature of the disease, the emotional issues surrounding it, and its terminal nature. Urwin (1988) paints a compelling picture of AIDS as a family concern, and outlines several major family and child needs that could be provided by early intervention programs: (a) information about the disease and available resources, (b) physical and practical support, (c) emotional support, (d) social support, (e) financial advice and assistance, and (f) counseling. Dokecki, Baumeister, and Kupstas (1989) emphasize the importance of the case manager's role in providing early intervention services to children with AIDS and their families, since they quite likely will need to work with multiple agencies. These authors also affirm the need for staff training and support in designing a sensitive program of services for children with AIDS.

Infants Exposed In Utero to Alcohol, Cocaine, or Other Drugs It is now well known that maternal ingestion of drugs usu-ally results in a negative effect on the fetus and the newborn infant. Alcohol has long been established as a cause of growth and developmental delays (Schultz, 1984). More recently, the dramatic increase in pregnant women who use cocaine has provided documentation that cocaine exposure in utero negatively affects state control, motor development, and behavioral organization; it also appears to increase the incidence of premature labor and delivery, intracranial hemorrhage, and sudden infant death (Hume, O'Donnell, Stranger, Killan, & Gingras, 1989).

As with AIDS, drug abuse during pregnancy is not a problem that affects only the infant. Early interventionists working with infants and preschoolers affected by maternal ingestion of drugs inevitably need to be family-centered in their orientation to providing services. Schneider, Griffith, and Chasnoff (1989), writing about such infants, suggest that early interventionists need skills related to prenatal education, the positioning and handling of newborns, the promotion of stability and the organization of states, and family support. Because of the complex nature of the infant's environment, case management skills are essential.

Diversity in Families

The stereotypic traditional family had two parents, two children, and a pet. The father worked and the mother stayed home to care for the children. The majority of families in today's society no longer fit this stereotype. One reason is that women are much more likely to be employed today, for economic and for personal reasons. Recent statistics indicate that more than 50 percent of all mothers of children under 5 years of age work, including mothers of children under 12 months of age. It is projected that this figure will rise to 65 percent by 1995 (Collins & Kinney, 1989). A second factor is that many children live in single-parent families, due to divorce, separation, or the fact that some

TABLE 1.2
A comparison of interventions with infants, preschoolers, and elementary-age children with special needs

Domain	Infants and Toddlers (0–36 months)	Preschoolers (36–60 months)	Elementary (5–12 years)
I. Characteristics of children			
Population parameters	Noncategorical; developmentally delayed, conditions that typically result in delay, at risk of substantial delay; results in wide range of ability levels and types of handicaps	Noncategorical; wide range of ability levels and handicaps (some states, however, will choose categorical descriptions)	Categorical; more restricted range of ability levels and disability types; formal eligibility criteria
Goals for intervention	Behavior and motor organization, differentiated responses to environmental cues, cause and effect, early communication and social skills, attachment	Cognitive, self-help, social, fine motor, communication, behavior, toy play, gross motor	Reading, spelling, mathematics, appropriate social behavior
Schedule regularity	Low–almost entirely determined by infant	Moderate—some adult determination of schedules, but requires flexibility depending on children's needs and interest	High—preset routine and time allocation for tasks; very little in the way of child-initiated activities
Endurance	Short—interactions typically last less than 2–3 minutes	Moderate—interactions may last 5–15 minutes	Long—interactions may last 30 mintues to 2 hours
Motivation	Must come from inherent appeal of material or activity; based on infant's interest	Begin to follow adult expectations, but high-interest toys and activities are critical	Based on adult expectations for compliance; reliance on self-regulation and response to rules

TABLE 1.2
(continued)

Domain	Infants and Toddlers (0–36 months)	Preschoolers (36–60 months)	Elementary (5–12 years)
II. The intervention context			
Context of teaching	Parent-child interactions; feeding, bathing, diapering, and dressing routines; object play	Object play, peer interactions, adult-child interactions, routines	Classroom instruction, written materials
Sites for intervention/ services	Homes, day care centers, family day homes, specialized developmental centers, developmental evaluation centers, hospital settings (NICU, pediatrics ward)	Specialized developmental center/classrooms, day care centers, homes, developmental evaluation centers, hospital settings	Elementary schools (regular classroom, resource room, self-contained classroom)
Responsible agencies	Mental health centers, hospital, public health services, private day care, specialized nonprofit agencies, public school	Public school, mental health, Head Start, day care	Public school
Team functioning	Often involves multiple professionals from multiple agencies; considerable role overlap, requiring extensive communication and coordination	Moderate blending of roles, but work in isolation is possible	Differentiated and specific roles; isolation likely
III. Family role			
Mandated family role	Essential and family-focused—IFSP requires documentation of family needs and strengths, a statement of family goals, and the provision of family services, including case management	Very important—IEP provisions pertain, all parents' rights protected, and parent training encouraged when necessary	Important—IEP provisions pertain, all parents' rights protected

Note: From "Issues and Directions in Preparing Professionals to Work With Young Handicapped Children and Their Families" (pp. 101–102) by D. B. Bailey, 1989, in *Policy Implementation and P.L. 99–457: Planning for Young Children With Special Needs*, J. J. Gallagher, R. M. Clifford, & P. Trohanis (Eds.), Baltimore: Paul Brookes. Copyright 1989 by Brookes Publishing Co., P.O. Box 10624, Baltimore, MD, 21285-0624. Reprinted by permission.

BOX 1.5   The neonatal intensive care unit

The family that finds itself with an infant in the neonatal intensive care unit (NICU) needs information and support. Special educators can assist the family by providing a multitude of services, including the behavioral and developmental care of the infant, information and support for the family itself, training and support of nursery staff related to developmental needs of the infant, and coordination with community programs. The following illustration describes some typical issues facing the family.

The preterm delivery was sudden and unexpected. The baby medical "swat team" rushed into the delivery room to save your baby and rushed him to the NICU. Because your baby was born 3 months early (born at 28 weeks gestation instead of 40 weeks), you know there are many serious problems possibly facing your baby, including death or a handicapping condition. Family and friends have not known how to help; you have had no baby showers; nothing at home is ready for the baby; you are not yet ready to leave work; you are in the middle of a possible tragedy. You are catapulted into contact with medical terms, procedures, and conditions that are completely foreign to you but may have critical meaning for your baby. You have seen your baby—very small, thin, and helpless-looking in the middle of wires, tubes, needles, and monitors of all kinds, with ventilator tubing taped to his face, and fingers barely able to wrap around the tip of your finger. You are scared to death and not even able to hold your baby yet. You have little idea how to distinguish the emergency and routine aspects of the situation.

Over the months of hospitalization, you learn what your baby likes, but you also fear entering the nursery. Although the staff is friendly, you dread the new issues presented each day— the baby is not gaining weight, the baby has stopped breathing and has had to be aroused, a new infection might or might not be dangerous, a newly discovered bleeding in the brain may be benign or may cause cerebral palsy (only time will tell), the baby is showing increased demand for oxygen or intolerance for food. Some days do bring hope and joy—there has been a whole ounce of weight gain, the baby is to have a trial period off the ventilator, for the first time ever you will see your 2-month-old baby without some tubing taped to his face, an exam shows no problems. You do not sleep well.

In the excitement of taking your baby home, your fears continue. Can you take care of this baby who needed the constant vigilance of highly trained experts? Will your baby have handicaps?

The family, trying to understand and cope, faces constant challenges. Someone—and often it is the special educator in conjunction with the physician and other specialists—needs to support the family, to help determine the child's behavioral and intervention needs and developmental status, and to help coordinate community services.

Note: Contributed by Jim Helm, PhD, Wake Medical Center, Raleigh, NC.

---

parents have never married. For these and other reasons, early intervention professionals must be prepared to work with diverse family systems. In this section, some examples and implications of this diversity are discussed. A major theme is the need for an individualized approach that reflects a respect for family diversity.

Cultural Diversity   The United States population is comprised of individuals from many different racial, cultural, ethnic, and religious backgrounds. These individuals have a wide range of educational backgrounds and their socioeconomic status ranges from extreme poverty to extreme wealth. Early intervention professionals, on the other hand, are primarily white, well-educated, middle-class Americans. They value child care, believe that education is important, and feel that professionals and agencies provide an important service for families and children. Inevitably, most early intervention professionals will work with families who have different backgrounds, experiences, and value systems. An example of how one culture's traditions and views of family life influence the provision of early intervention services is displayed in Box 1.6.

What skills are needed to ensure that interactions between professionals and families from diverse backgrounds are positive and facilitative? It is important to recognize that differences do, in fact, exist. Families from different cultural groups vary in child-rearing practices and parent–child interactions (Westby, 1986), values, the definition of family, the definition of problems, perceived solutions to problems, and attitudes toward seeking help (McGoldrick, 1983). McGoldrick suggests that the primary skill required of professionals who work with diverse families is to be "open to understanding values that differ from our own and no longer need to convince others of our values or give in to theirs" (p. 25). Winton (1988) emphasizes the ability to communicate with family members in a way that is respectful and clear.

Single-Parent Families   One of the more dramatic changes in today's society is the increasing divorce rate and the consequent increase in the proportion of children who live in single-parent families. Usually the parent living with the children is the mother. Norton and Glick (1986) report that half of all black children and one sixth of all white children live in single-mother homes, and

these proportions are expected to increase. Bristol, Reichle, and Thomas (1987) reviewed the literature on separation and divorce in families of children with disabilities. Although the evidence is mixed, there are some indications that the divorce rate is higher among these families. Thus it is quite likely that early interventionists will be working with many single-parent families.

What are the unique needs of single-parent families? Bristol, Reichle, and Thomas (1987) caution that single-parent families are not a homogeneous group; thus broad assumptions about their needs should be discarded in favor of an individualized approach. One major need that is likely to emerge, however, is finances. Divorce almost inevitably results in a substantial decrease in income; furthermore, mothers often have difficulty obtaining support payments from fathers (Haskins, Schwartz, Akin, & Dobelstein, 1986). Consequently many single-parent families live in poverty or certainly under stressful financial conditions. Many single mothers of young children must work. Assuming full responsibility for all family functions without the ongoing support of a spouse often means that single parents live with a high degree of stress. Being aware of this stress should help early interventionists appreciate the extra burdens they may be creating when they ask parents to assume teaching and therapeutic activities at home.

Adolescent Parents   Adolescent parents represent another significant and unique set of clients served by early interventionists, especially in states that include high-risk children in the groups that are eligible for services. Among the factors that often make these children high risk are low socioeconomic status, poor prenatal care, and increased medical problems at birth. Helm (1988) describes four additional factors that need to be considered when working with adolescent parents.

BOX 1.6   Working with Puerto Rican families

The **Ninos Especiales Program (N.E.P)** was funded by the Handicapped Children's Early Education Program to develop and disseminate a culturally sensitive model of early intervention for families who were of Puerto Rican heritage, had an infant with severe disabilities and were living in Hartford, Connecticut. The significant difference in services delivered by the N.E.P. from the services delivered by other early intervention programs was the cultural considerations which were imbedded throughout the program.

Learning about the individual's cultural context will help us better understand the individual. Variables such as the degree of acculturation, socioeconomic class, educational status, occupation, and geographic location will affect beliefs and behaviors among those who share a common cultural heritage. This consideration of the individual is especially relevant to Puerto Ricans; their migration has occurred over more than thirty years, and therefore, as individuals they demonstrate varying degrees of adaptation to the Anglo-American culture.

Listed below are some characteristics that are prevalent but not always present in families of Puerto Rican heritage.

Family Relationships: Puerto Rican families tend to be male dominated (when there is a father figure present in the home). The man assumes responsibility for important decisions, and the woman assumes responsibility for child rearing and running the household. The mother–child relationship is the primary relationship in the family. Children are expected to be dependent on adults.

Child Rearing: Child rearing practices foster dependence and sharing rather than competition. Structured guidance (for example, developing school readiness skills) often is not valued in the Puerto Rican culture; instead, children are allowed to grow and develop freely.

Support Networks: Puerto Rican families depend primarily on their extended families and neighbors for ongoing support. By relying on this personalized, bilingual, and bicultural support system, the families are able to access multiple supports twenty-four hours a day.

Sense of Time: Puerto Ricans often choose to "live in the present" rather than plan for the future. Long-range planning and preparation tends to be informal. Time frames are very flexible and punctuality is not highly valued.

Belief in Fate: Within the Puerto Rican culture, a common belief is that destiny or fate controls the outcome of individual lives. Thus, oftentimes one's condition of life is accepted without question.

Health-related Beliefs: Fate is a commonly used explanation for a child's disability. In some instances disease or disability is seen as a punishment, lowering a parent's sense of personal control. Families also tend to distrust any "expensive" toys or equipment brought to the house by professionals, choosing instead to ignore the child's special needs since it is felt the disability resulted from God's will. Many families will use the services of a spiritualist and folk healer.

***

Note: Contributed by Dr. Mary Beth Bruder, New York Medical College, Valhalla, NY.

1 They are experiencing a unique series of developmental stages in which they themselves are maturing and seeking to develop their own identity and individuality. Peer pressure is strong and frequently they are put in positions of having to choose between immediate gratification of needs and future planning. As Helm states, this means that "adults sometimes have expectations for them that exceed their ability" (p. 313).

2 They may feel frustrated because they perceive that they are not in control of life's events. When individuals feel that their behavior makes no difference in the outcome, they are more likely to follow their own wishes and less likely to respond to or to implement suggested changes.

3 Their skills and interests in interacting with their children may not match what many interventionists believe to be the best practices in child rearing. Interventionists should expect this discrepancy and should further recognize that adolescents may view early interventionists the same way they do their parents—as authority figures to be challenged rather than listened to.

4 They likely will be experiencing stress from multiple sources, including economic strain, lack of spouse support, parental pressures, and peer pressures.

Collectively, these factors indicate that work with adolescent parents will require interventionists to rethink their goals and the types of services they offer. Especially important will be the ability to understand what life is like for adolescent parents and to work within the constraints imposed by their age and their limited support systems.

Parents with Mental Retardation Fifty years ago, most adults with mental retardation, even mild retardation, were institutionalized. Providing services to children whose parents were mentally retarded was simply not an issue. Today, with deinstitutionaliza-tion and normalization, persons with mental retardation are able to participate more fully in the normal experiences of living; having children is one such experience, and consequently there is an increase in the number of children whose parents have mental retardation (Whitman, Graves, & Accardo, 1987). These children are likely to be labeled as at risk or may have disabilities themselves (Lynch & Bakley, 1989); thus they are likely to be referred for early intervention services.

What are the special needs of children whose parents have mental retardation? Lynch and Bakley (1989) describe several risk factors, most of which pertain to real or perceived limitations of the parents—their cognitive and social/emotional limitations, for example, and their limited teaching and parenting skills. Espe-Sherwindt and Kerlin (1990) argue that some of these problems may be due in part to the fact that persons with mental retardation have been treated as being incapable and have been taught in a directive or prescriptive fashion. The authors suggest that a model approach to services with parents who are mentally retarded is to focus on empowering these parents by reinforcing (a) their sense of control over life events and their awareness that their behavior can make a difference, (b) their self-esteem, (c) their social skills, (d) their comprehension of the roles they play or can play socially, and (e) their problem-solving skills. By responding to needs identified by the family, rather than imposing needs or solutions on the family, the interventionist can build a trusting and collaborative relationship, and goals related to family support will be more likely to be achieved. Box 1.7 describes a family in which a parent has mental retardation and one example of early intervention services for that family.

Diversity in Settings

Public school teachers usually work in classrooms located in public schools. Early interventionists, however, are likely to work in a

BOX 1.7   A parent with mental retardation

Effective early intervention for families in which parents have special needs as a result of mental retardation requires a collaborative network of support that provides continual opportunities for respectful partnerships, for successful problem solving, and for an increased sense on the part of the parents of having control over their lives and those of their children.

Susan and her 9-month-old son were referred to the early intervention program by a caseworker concerned about the baby's developmental delays. Background information described Susan as an inconsistent, uninvolved, unresponsive mother with mild mental retardation. Since previous children had been removed at birth, this infant represented Susan's first chance to raise a child on her own. Initially Susan made it clear to the EI staff that she herself did not need services, but she did identify that she wanted her son to learn to crawl and walk. The program staff began to build a trusting relationship with Susan by focusing nonjudgmentally on her immediate concerns about crawling.

Within three months, Susan was described as increasingly interactive with both staff and her young son. Nevertheless, shortly thereafter the baby was removed from Susan's care because of the many safety hazards in Susan's apartment, most of which stemmed from poor building maintenance and were beyond Susan's control. The intervention team now expanded to include not only Susan and the program staff but also a new caseworker, the case aide providing transportation, and the foster mother who served as a mentor to Susan during her visits in the foster home. The EI program staff continued to promote opportunities for competence through such strategies as asking Susan to choose activities for herself and her son, building on Susan's strengths (e.g., Susan enjoyed making toys for her son), asking Susan if she would like assistance in completing the complex application for new housing, and responding to Susan's need for emotional support during the long waiting period for an apartment. During this time, Susan attended consistently, demonstrated a warm and interactive involvement with her son, smiled and initiated conversations with staff, commented on how much she liked the program, and displayed problem-solving skills both within and outside the program. The long-awaited move to the new apartment (and, for the first time, a telephone) meant reunification for Susan and her son. Their involvement in the early intervention program continues, as many parents with special needs/mental retardation benefit most from long-term support. Most recently Susan requested the phone number of her pediatrician ("I'd like to call myself") and added the following outcome to the Individualized Family Service Plan: "Susan would like to read so that she can keep track of appointments and classes."

Note: Contributed by Marilyn Espe-Sherwindt, Project CAPABLE, University of Cincinnati, Cincinnati, OH.

variety of settings and programs. Knowledge of the unique characteristics of each setting is essential for effective work in each.

Center-based Programs   The most common setting for serving 3- and 4-year-olds with disabilities is the center-based program.

Center-based programs may be located in public schools, churches, private agencies, or other sites. Children typically spend sessions of between 3 and 6 hours in such programs, engaging in a variety of play, instructional, and therapeutic activities. The services provided in center-based programs usually are very child-focused. Professionals assess children's needs, provide therapy or instruction, supervise teacher aides, and monitor child progress. Therapists may work as part of the core staff or may serve as consultants to the teachers.

Center-based programs can offer a wide range of family services and supports. Sometimes these are provided by the teaching staff; in other cases, a special staff person is assigned family support as a primary responsibility. Parent involvement in center-based programs may include observing and participating in the center's activities, attending parent training sessions, and receiving training at home to ensure maintenance and generalization of the skills learned in the center. Centers are increasingly adding other types of family support services.

The center-based model has several distinct advantages, including the efficient use of staff time and the ease of supervision. Team members can work closely with one another because they are all in one location. For children, the center-based model provides increased opportunities for socialization with other children; and if their parents are unable to be involved in training, the children still receive services. By participating in group activities and learning to follow expectations, children in center-based programs are exposed to experiences that will likely facilitate their transition into kindergarten. Finally, center-based programs are a visible source of services—interested members of the community can come to the center, observe the program, become educated about the importance of early intervention, and perhaps be motivated to support the program through advocacy work, volunteering, or contributions.

At least three major disadvantages exist for center-based programs. The first is transportation. Public schools will need to provide transportation for preschoolers with disabilities if the parents need or desire it.

Transportation is expensive for all children but especially so for children with specialized needs, for often special equipment and extra personnel are required during transport. Transportation can also consume a great deal of professional time (e.g., coordinating routes and ensuring maintenance). Furthermore, because many early intervention programs are centrally located and serve wide geographical areas, children may spend long periods of time each day in transport to and from school. A second disadvantage of center-based programs is the cost of the buildings and upkeep. Finally, although center-based programs are attempting to be more family-focused, the demands of planning and providing high-quality services for children often mean that professionals do not have the time needed to establish close working relationships with families or to focus on family support services.

Several key issues are confronting center-based programs today. One is how schools will provide preschool programs in the least restrictive environment (LRE). Although Public Law 99–457 mandates that schools adhere to the LRE provision, the fact that schools rarely serve normally developing 3- and 4-year-olds creates a substantial logistical problem. Some schools have begun to explore alternative strategies, such as expanding services to include normally developing children or placing children in regular day-care programs and providing specialized consultation and support to day-care staff. A second issue is how to ensure that preschool programs are not watered-down kindergarten classes, but rather that they are designed and arranged to meet the developmental needs of young children (Bailey & McWilliam, 1990). The National Association for the Education of Young Children (NAEYC) has established accreditation criteria for early childhood programs in order to ensure developmentally appropriate practice (NAEYC, 1984). Hopefully, schools will attend to these criteria, in addition to the usual school accreditation standards, as they establish center-based programs for preschoolers. Finally, center-based options for infants and toddlers with disabilities are desperately needed in many parts of the country. Many families work and need options for out-of-home care for very young children. However, the challenge for agencies and programs serving infants and toddlers is to provide high-quality programs—which means providing adequate staff wages—that are yet affordable for parents (Hartley, White, & Yogman, 1989).

Home-based Programs Under the home-based model, as the name implies, services are provided in the child's home. The frequency of visitation may range from once a month to one or two times per week. Home-based programs most frequently serve infants and children under 36 months of age, although some provide services to older children. Because of the small amount of direct contact with children, home-based programs usually focus their energies on work with parents. Some home-based models view time with parents primarily as an opportunity to provide parents with information about how to teach or play with their children. Other home-based models take a broader perspective, viewing the professional's role as one of providing family support. The professional meets with families and explores needs and priorities from a family perspective. As a result, professionals may spend less time in working with children and more in case management and other family support services.

The home-based model has a number of advantages. Young and medically fragile children and families without transportation can stay at home and still receive services. Also, these programs are relatively inexpensive because they do not require large facilities that cost a lot to build and maintain. In addition, the children remain in their natural settings,

so generalization should be less of a problem than in center-based programs. Further, because contact with families is more frequent, home-based programs may have more opportunities to be responsive to family needs.

Home-based programs have some disadvantages, the primary one being that many require parents to do a great deal of work, such as teaching children, implementing therapeutic activities, and keeping records of children's behavior. Many parents do not want these responsibilities or simply do not have the time to complete them, and the result is additional stress and feelings of guilt. Further, parents get fewer breaks from caretaking responsibilities because their children do not leave to go to school. Another disadvantage is that the programming may not be as broad as it is in center-based programs. As children get older and need more social interactions with peers, the home-based model may become restrictive. Finally, under the home-based model the professional is on the road a good bit of the time, and as a result valuable planning, teaching, and record-keeping time is lost.

Bailey and Simeonsson (1988) reviewed the literature on home-based programs and concluded that they have a number of potential advantages and limitations. The research to date is inconclusive, although studies with children from low-income families suggest that greater child progress is usually found in center-based programs. But this progress may come at the cost of a decrease in family-focused services.

Hospital-based Programs As we have indicated, improvements in medical technology have resulted in there being more chronically ill children and children with disabilities in hospitals—in neonatal intensive care nurseries, in newborn nurseries, and on pediatric wards. Realizing the importance of providing family support and considering children's developmental needs in the hospital setting, hospitals increasingly are hiring special educators, therapists, psychologists, and social workers to provide support and assistance to families and children.

Gilkerson (1990) and Gilkerson, Gorski, and Panitz (1990) have described six dimensions for contrasting hospital programs and community-based early intervention programs (see chapter 3 for a more detailed description of this framework). These authors argue that early intervention services will be most effective when each institution comes to understand the characteristics, needs, and assumptions of the other institutions and agencies involved. Professionals who work in hospital environments likely will focus heavily on supporting parents. They also will work collaboratively with medical personnel to ensure that the hospital environment and the interactions between staff and children or between staff and parents are maximally supportive and unintrusive.

Centers for Screening and Evaluation Professionals are also likely to work with infants and preschoolers with disabilities in programs that provide screening and developmental evaluations. These programs are essential from an institutional perspective in order to respond to referrals and identify children who are eligible for early intervention services. The programs are of great importance for families, because often they are the family's first contact with early intervention. Often it falls to professionals in such programs to be the first to inform parents of their children's developmental status. Skills needed for work in such an environment include a broad understanding of normal early development, knowledge of various disabling conditions, assessment and diagnostic skills, the ability to work with other professionals in an interdisciplinary fashion, and the ability to communicate effectively with families.

Diversity in Philosophical Perspectives

Early intervention is a field characterized by diverse philosophical perspectives. For many practitioners, arguments among proponents of different theories may seem irrelevant to daily decisions regarding intervention practice. Yet the assumptions one makes—about children and family life and about the role of professionals—will shape the focus and direction of one's early intervention efforts. Throughout this text, we refer to and discuss various theories and how they influence professional decision making. In this chapter, we briefly highlight three broad perspectives: developmental, behavioral, and ecological.

The Developmental Perspective One inescapable conclusion is that children grow and develop over time. The developmental perspective attributes this growth primarily to maturational factors. Children are born with certain physical and cognitive abilities and limitations. As they grow and mature, their bodies become physically capable of doing more. Likewise, the brain itself matures through the process of myelinization, allowing for more complex and integrated intellectual functioning (Anastasiow, 1990). Piaget's (1963) model of cognitive development demonstrates the effects of cognitive maturation on the abilities of children to master increasingly complex concepts. Many developmentalists also believe that children are born with an intrinsic motivation to explore and master the environment (Brockman, Morgan, & Harmon, 1988; White, 1959). Experiences obviously play a role in facilitating development. From the developmentalist perspective, however, development is first a product of maturation. Competence is gained through self-initiated play, exploration, and practice.

The Behavioral Perspective The behavioral perspective focuses on learning as central to children's growth and development (Bijou & Baer, 1961; 1965; 1978). Children are born with the capacity to learn, and the skills that they display emerge as the result of experiences with the environment. Antecedents and consequences serve to shape behavior. Children learn behaviors through repeated reinforcing interactions with the environment.

The Ecological Perspective   The ecological perspective encompasses a number of different yet related views of children and families. The transactional model (Sameroff & Chandler, 1975; Sameroff & Fiese, 1990) emphasizes the fact that children and caregivers influence each other, interdependently, over time. For example, an infant's being difficult to feed might lead to feelings of incompetence on the part of the parent. These parental feelings might then generalize to other areas of interaction, such as playing or talking with the child, and result in an altered caregiving environment for the child. From the transactional perspective, intervention programs must consider the reciprocal and ongoing nature of relationships. Focusing on just one aspect of the system—on just the child or just the caregiver—is not likely to be effective.

Another ecological perspective is systems theory, which views children as part of the broader family system. Bronfenbrenner's (1977) ecological model extends systems theory to view families as embedded within broader neighborhood and community systems. It is assumed that all systems within the systems, but especially families, incorporate basic value assumptions about what is desirable for children and families. From an ecological perspective, interventions will only be effective to the extent that they achieve a fit with the value framework and eco-cultural milieu of each individual family. Thomas and Chess (1977) refer to this concept as "goodness-of-fit"; the outcome of an intervention, they write, is best predicted by studying the fit between the unique characteristics of the child, the family, and the ecology within which they live. Thurman (1977) has employed a similar construct,

"ecological congruence," to describe the extent to which individuals and environments are mutually tolerant.

Implications of the Theoretical Perspectives   Formerly, there was much contention between the developmental and behavioral perspectives, particularly regarding assessment. The developmentalists held that assessment should proceed by documenting the extent to which the child has attained specific developmental milestones, while the behaviorists looked for assessment to identify the functional skills needed by the child to increase the likelihood of success in current and future environments. The trend among researchers and practitioners today, however, is toward acceptance of an ecological perspective in early intervention. The aim of assessment should be the determination of the child's skills, the characteristics of the caregiving environment, and the family's needs, resources, expectations, and aspirations. This trend does not mean that the developmental or behavioral perspectives are inaccurate. Few people would deny that maturation occurs, nor would they disavow the role of learning and teaching. The ecological perspective simply states that these processes cannot be examined or applied in isolation. Table 1.3 lists some major characteristics of each theory along with assessment and intervention implications. Further discussion of each theory is provided throughout this text.

Diversity in Professional Roles

Twenty years ago, professionals working in early intervention needed to be prepared for one primary role: caring for and teaching children. Today, because of the diversity in settings, children, and families, professionals must be prepared to work in at least three areas: child services, family support, and consultation.

TABLE 1.3
Three theoretical perspectives and their implications

Theoretical Perspective	Basic Assumptions About the Nature of Children	Basic Assumptions About Learning and Development	Assessment Implications	Intervention Implications
Developmental	Children are born with an intrinsic motivation to explore and master the environment. Skills emerge in a relatively predictable sequence.	Development is primarily a result of physical maturation. Competence is gained through self-initiated exploration and play.	Document the extent to which the child has attained specific developmental milestones.	Arrange the environment and provide materials that are highly interesting to children and are most likely to facilitate competence in developmentally appropriate skills.
Behavioral	Children are born with the capacity to learn. The skills that a child displays emerge as a result of experiences with the environment. Biological and physiological processes also are acknowledged as important.	Antecedents and consequences serve to shape behavior. Children learn behaviors through repeated reinforcing interactions with the environment.	Identify the functional skills needed by the child to increase the likelihood of success in current and future environments.	Provide experiences and supports that promote success; identify and use effective reinforcers to ensure rapid and efficient learning.
Ecological	Children influence and are influenced by the environment. Children inevitably are a part of a family system. Likewise, families are embedded within larger neighborhood, community, and institutional systems.	Development results from the complex interactions or transactions between children and the environment over time. Development cannot be examined in isolation, but rather must be examined over time and in the context of systems within which children and families function.	Determine the child's skills, the characteristics of the caregiving environment, and the family's needs, resources, expectations, and aspirations.	Provide services that support families and children in ways that are congruent with their ecology and are consistent with expressed family goals.

Child-related Services Professionals caring for children must perform a number of specific tasks, including assessing children's abilities and needs, developing and writing individualized plans, providing stimulating environments, designing appropriate experiences to facilitate competence in a range of developmental and functional areas, and evaluating the effectiveness of intervention strategies. In order to perform these tasks, professionals must possess several forms of knowledge. First, early interventionists must know about normal as well as atypical child development. A basic understanding of normal child development is essential for planning appropriate educational environments and experiences. Second, a knowledge of the principles and procedures of learning theory provides essential information about the relationship between children's behavior and variables such as the physical environment, instructional procedures, and the consequences of behavior. Third, early interventionists must know how to design and provide environments that are appropriate for the normal developmental needs of infants and preschoolers and then how to modify these environments for children with specialized learning or caretaking needs.

Family Support Services One of the most significant shifts in early intervention in recent years has been a refocusing of efforts from the child alone to the child in the context of the family system. In fact, Dunst (1985) has called for a rethinking of early intervention in which the ultimate goal is to enable and empower families of young children with handicaps. Professionals working with families should be trained to understand the ecological and systemic nature of families, to assess family needs and resources, to use effective listening and interviewing techniques, to negotiate values and priorities, and to provide case management services (Bailey, 1987). Ultimately, the effectiveness of family support services will depend on the extent to which professionals can establish trusting and collaborative relationships with families and provide services in ways that enable families to make decisions for themselves (Dunst, Trivette, & Deal, 1988).

Consultation Because of the interagency nature of service delivery systems and the multiple needs of many young children and their families, most professionals either will need to rely on the services of consultants to address specialized intervention needs or will themselves be called upon to provide consultation in their areas of expertise. Consultation is a complex activity that requires a unique set of professional skills. Tindal, Shinn, and Rodden-Nord (1990), for example, describe three types of factors that influence the success of the consultation process:

1 characteristics of the people involved in consultation, including the consultant, the consultee, administrators, and the client
2 process variables, such as the problem-solving relationship, agreement on theoretical or philosophical perspectives, prior history of collaborative/consultative work, and the type of consultant activity
3 procedural implementation variables, such as the type of data collected, the development of recommendations, and outcome evaluation

Tindal et al. emphasize that effective communication skills are important for serving as a consultant and for working with consultants.

Phillips and McCullough (1990) suggest that the key to effective consultation is the establishment of a "collaborative ethic" in school and intervention programs, and they offer several prerequisites to collaborative efforts.

(a) colleagues must be able to identify important problems that are commonly appreciated and for which joint problem solving is necessary and appropriate; (b) an appreciable body of knowledge or repertoire of skills must be held in common; (c) involvement must enable participation of primary constituencies at a level which facilitates a sense of ownership in the problem-solving process; (d) specific, organizational structures and routines must be established to ensure that formally sanctioned consultation occurs; and (e) collegial problem solving must be valued and espoused as a tool for the concerned and dedicated educator instead of viewed as a last resort for the singularly incompetent (p. 295).

Of great importance is the need for administrative support for collaborative consultation and an appreciation by the consultant of the unique needs, resources, and goals of the individual or organization receiving consultation services.

SUMMARY

Early intervention is a growing and diverse enterprise. In part, this growth has been stimulated by research documenting the importance of early supports for children with disabilities and for their families. Perhaps more significantly, however, is an increased societal commitment to young children and federal legislation mandating services.

In this chapter we have presented examples of the growth and diversity in early intervention, and discussed implications for skills needed by early intervention professionals. In subsequent chapters, issues that have only been highlighted here are discussed in greater detail. Perhaps the most important message from this chapter is the importance of an individualized approach to providing early intervention services. Because of the diversity in children, families, and professionals, it is impossible to prescribe a single curriculum or intervention model that meets the needs of all clients or all service delivery systems. Only by seeking to understand the individual needs, resources, values, and priorities of families,

and by providing services matched to those individual characteristics, can early intervention efforts be maximally successful.

REFERENCES

Anastasiow, N. J. (1990). Implications of the neurobiological model for early intervention. In S. J. Meisels & J. P. Shonkoff (Eds.), *Handbook of early childhood intervention* (pp. 196–216). Cambridge: Cambridge University Press.

Bailey, D. B. (1987). Collaborative goal-setting with families: Resolving differences in values and priorities for services. *Topics in Early Childhood Special Education, 7*(2), 59–71.

Bailey, D. B. (1989). Issues and directions in preparing professionals to work with young handicapped children and their families. In J. J. Gallagher, R. M. Clifford, & P. Trohanis (Eds.), *Policy implementation and P.L. 99–457: Planning for young children with special needs* (pp. 97–132). Baltimore: Paul Brookes.

Bailey, D. B., & McWilliam, R. A. (1990). Normalizing early intervention. *Topics in Early Childhood Special Education, 10*(2), 33–47.

Bailey, D. B., & Simeonsson, R. J. (1988). Home-based early intervention. In S. Odom & M. Karnes (Eds.), *Early intervention for infants and children with handicaps* (pp. 199–216). Baltimore: Paul H. Brookes.

Bennett, F. C. (1987). The effectiveness of early intervention for infants at increased biologic risk. In M. J. Guralnick & F. C. Bennett (Eds.), *The effectiveness of early intervention for at-risk and handicapped children.* Orlando, FL: Academic Press.

Berrueta-Clement, J. R., Schweinhart, L. J., Barnett, W. S., Epstein, A. S., & Weikart, D. P. (1985). Changed lives: The effects of the Perry Preschool Program on youths through age 19. *Monographs of the High/Scope Educational Research Foundation, 8.*

Bijou, S. W., & Baer, D. M. (1961). *Child development: Vol. 1. A systematic and empirical theory.* Englewood Cliffs, NJ: Prentice-Hall.

Bijou, S. W., & Baer, D. M. (1965). *Child development: Vol. 2. Universal stage of infancy.* Englewood Cliffs, NJ: Prentice-Hall.

Bijou, S. W., & Baer, D. M. (1978). *Behavior analysis of child development.* Englewood Cliffs, NJ: Prentice-Hall.

Bricker, D. & Sheehan, R. (1981). Effectiveness of an early intervention program as indexed by measures of child change. *Journal of the Division for Early Childhood, 4,* 11–27.

Bristol, M. M., Reichle, N. C., & Thomas, D. D. (1987). Changing demographics of the American family: Implications for single-parent families of young handicapped children. *Journal of the Division for Early Childhood, 12,* 56–69.

Brockman, L. M., Morgan, G. A., & Harmon, R. J. (1988). Mastery motivation and developmental delay. In T. D. Wachs & R. Sheehan (Eds.), *Assessment of young developmentally disabled children* (pp. 267–284). New York: Plenum.

Bronfenbrenner, U. (1975). Is early intervention effective? In B. Friedlander, G. Sterritt, & G. Kirk (Eds.), *Exceptional infant: Assessment and intervention* (Vol. 3, pp. 449–475). New York: Brunner/Mazel.

Bronfenbrenner, U. (1976). The experimental ecology of education. *Educational Researcher, 5*(9), 5–15.

Bronfenbrenner, U. (1977). Toward an experimental ecology of human development. *American Psychologist, 32,* 513–531.

Casto, G., & Mastropieri, M. A. (1986). The efficacy of early intervention programs: A meta-analysis. *Exceptional Children, 52,* 417–424.

Cohen, S. E. (1986). The low-birthweight infant and learning disabilities. In M. Lewis (Ed.), *Learning disabilities and prenatal risk* (pp. 153–193).

Cicirelli, V., et al. (1969). *The impact of Head Start: An evaluation of the effects of Head Start on children's cognitive and affective development.* Report to the U.S. Office of Economic Opportunity by Westinghouse Learning Corporation and Ohio University. Washington, DC: Government Printing Office.

Cicirelli, V., Evans, J., & Schiller, J. (1970). The impact of Head Start: A reply to the report analysis. *Harvard Educational Review, 40,* 105–129.

Collins, R. C., & Kinney, P. F. (November, 1989). *Head Start research and evaluation: Background and overview.* Technical paper prepared for the Head Start Evaluation Design Project, Collins Management Consulting, Inc., Vienna, Virginia.

Cooper, C. S., & Kennedy, R. D. (1989). An update for professionals working with neonates at risk. *Topics in Early Childhood Special Education, 9*(3), 32–50.

Deasey, D. (1978). *Education under six.* New York: St. Martin's Press.

Dokecki, P. R., Baumeister, A. A., & Kupstas, F. D. (1989). Biomedical and social aspects of pediatric AIDS. *Journal of Early Intervention, 13,* 173–182.

Dunst, C. (1985). Rethinking early intervention. *Analysis and Intervention in Developmental Disabilities, 5,* 165–201.

Dunst, C., & Rheingrover, R. M. (1981). An analysis of the efficacy of infant intervention programs with organically handicapped children. *Evaluation and Program Planning, 4,* 287–323.

Dunst, C., & Snyder, S. (1986). A critique of the Utah State University early intervention meta-analysis research. *Exceptional Children, 53*(3), 260–265.

Dunst, C., Trivette, C. M., & Deal, A. G. (1988). *Enabling and empowering families: Principles and guidelines for practice.* Cambridge, MA: Brookline Books.

Espe-Sherwindt, M., & Kerlin, S. L. (1990). Early intervention with parents with mental retardation: Do we empower or impair? *Infants and Young Children, 2*(4).

Flynn, L. L., & McCollum, J. (1989). Support systems: Strategies and implications for hospitalized newborns and families. *Journal of Early Intervention, 13,* 173–182.

Gilkerson, L. (1990). Understanding institutional functioning style: A resource for hospital and early intervention collaboration. *Infants and Young Children, 2*(3), 22–30.

Gilkerson, L., Gorski, P., & Panitz, P. (1990). Hospital-based intervention for preterm infants and their families. In S. J. Meisels & J. P. Shonkoff (Eds.), *Handbook of early childhood intervention* (pp. 445–468). Cambridge: Cambridge University Press.

Hartley, M., White, C., & Yogman, M. W. (1989). The challenge of providing quality group child care for infants and young children with special needs. *Infants and Young Children, 2*(2), 1–10.

Haskins, R. (1989). Beyond metaphor: The efficacy of early childhood education. *American Psychologist, 44*, 274–282.

Haskins, R., Schwartz, J. B., Akin, J. S., & Dobelstein, A. W. (1986). How much child support can absent fathers pay? *Policy Review, 14*, 201–222.

Helm, J. M. (1988). Adolescent mothers of handicapped children: A challenge for interventionists. *Journal of the Division for Early Childhood, 12*, 311–319.

House, E., Glass, G., McLean, L., & Walker, D. (1978). No simple answer: Critique of the Follow Through evaluation. *Harvard Education Review, 48*, 128–160.

Hume, R. F., O'Donnell, K. S., Stanger, C. L., Killan, A. P., & Gingras, J. L. (1989). In utero cocaine exposure: Observations of fetal behavioral state may predict neonatal outcome. *American Journal of Obstetrics and Gynecology, 161*, 685–690.

Infant Health and Development Program (1990). Enhancing the outcomes of low-birth-weight, premature infants. *Journal of the American Medical Association, 263*, 3035–3042.

Karnes, M. B., & Stayton, V. D. (1988). Model programs for infants and toddlers with handicaps. In J. B. Jordon, J. J. Gallagher, P. L. Hutinger, & M. B. Karnes (Eds.), *Early childhood special education: Birth to three* (pp. 67–108). Reston, VA: Council for Exceptional Children.

Kazdin, A. E. (1976). Statistical analyses for single-case experimental designs. In M. Hersen & D. Barlow (Eds.), *Single case experimental designs: Strategies for studying behavior change* (pp. 265–316). New York: Pergamon Press.

Lazar, I., Darlington, R., Murray, H., Royce, I., & Snipper, A. (1982). Lasting effects of early education: A report from the Consortium for Longitudinal Studies. *Monographs of the Society for Research in Child Development, 47*(2–3, Serial No. 195).

Lynch, E. W., & Bakley, S. (1989). Serving young children whose parents are mentally retarded. *Infants and young children, 1*(3), 26–38.

McGoldrick, M. (1983). Ethnicity and family therapy: An overview. In M. McGoldrick, J. K. Pearce, & J. Geoidano (Eds.), *Ethnicity and family therapy* (pp. 3–30). New York: Guilford Press.

National Association for the Education of Young Children (1984). *Accreditation criteria and procedures of the National Academy of of Early Childhood Programs.* Washington, DC: NAEYC.

Norton, A. J., & Glick, P. C. (1986). One parent families: A social and economic profile. *Family Relations, 35*, 9–17.

Ottenbacher, K. J. (1989). Statistical conclusion validity of early intervention research with handicapped children. *Exceptional Children, 55*(6), 534–540.

Phillips, V., & McCullough, L. (1990). Consultation-based programming: Instituting the collaborative ethic in schools. *Exceptional Children, 56*, 291–304.

Piaget, J. (1963). *The origins of intelligence in children.* New York: Norton.

Resnick, M. B., Eyler, F. D., Nelson, R. M., Eitzman, D. V., & Bucciarelli, R. L. (1987). Developmental intervention for low birth weight infants: Improved early developmental outcome. *Pediatrics, 80*, 68–74.

Sameroff, A. J., & Chandler, M. J. (1975). Reproductive risk and the continuum of caretaking casualty. In F. D. Horowitz, M. Hetherington, S. Scarr-Salapatek, & G. Siegel (Eds.), *Review of child development research* (Vol. 4, pp. 187–244). Chicago: University of Chicago Press.

Sameroff, A. J., & Fiese, B. H. (1990). Transactional regulation and early intervention. In S. J. Meisels & J. P. Shonkoff (Eds.), *Handbook of early childhood intervention* (pp. 119–149). Cambridge: Cambridge University Press.

Schneider, J. W., Griffith, D. R., & Chasnoff, I. J. (1989). Infants exposed to cocaine in utero: Implications for developmental assessment and intervention. *Infants and Young Children*, *2*(1), 25–36.

Schorr, L. B. (1989). Early interventions to reduce intergenerational disadvantage: The new policy context. *Teachers College Record*, *90*, 362–374.

Schultz, F. R. (1984). Fetal alcohol syndrome. In J. A. Blackman (Ed.), *Medical aspects of developmental disabilities in children birth to three* (pp. 109–110). Rockville, MD: Aspen System.

Shonkoff, J. P. & Hauser-Cram, P. (1987). Early intervention for disabled infants and their families: A quantitative analysis. *Pediatrics*, *80*(5), 650–658.

Shonkoff, J. P., & Meisels, S. J. (1990). Early childhood intervention: The evolution of a concept. In S. J. Meisels & J. P. Shonkoff (Eds.), *Handbook of early childhood intervention* (pp. 3–31). Cambridge: Cambridge University Press.

Shulman, L. S. (1986). Those who understand: Knowledge growth in teaching. *Educational Researcher*, *15*(2), 4–14.

Simeonsson, R. J., Cooper, D. H., & Scheiner, A. P. (1982). A review and analysis of the effectiveness of early intervention programs. *Pediatrics*, *69*, 635–641.

Skeels, H. (1966). Adult status of children with contrasting early life experiences: A follow-up study. *Monographs of the Society for Research in Child Development*, *31* (Serial No. 105).

Skeels, H., & Dye, H. (1939). A study of the effects of differential stimulation on mentally retarded children. *Proceedings and Addresses of the American Association on Mental Deficiency*, *44*, 114–136.

Slaughter, D. T., Washington, V., Oyemade, U. J., & Lindsey, R. W. (1988). Head Start: A backward and forward look. *Social Policy Report*, *111*(2), 1–19.

Smith, M. S., & Bissell, J. S. (1970). Report analysis: The impact of Head Start. *Harvard Educational Review*, *40*, 51–104.

Stallings, J. (1975). Implementation and child effects of teaching practices in Follow Through Classrooms. *Monographs of the Society for Research in Child Development*, *40* (Serial No. 163).

Strain, P., & Smith, B. J. (1986). A counter-interpretation of early intervention effects: A response to Castro and Mastropieri. *Exceptional Children*, *53*(3), 260–265.

Thomas, A., & Chess, S. (1977). *Temperament and development*. New York: Bruner/Mazel.

Thurman, S. K. (1977). The congruence of behavioral ecologies: A model for special education programming. *Journal of Special Education*, *11*, 329–333.

Tindall, G., Shinn, M. R., & Rodden-Nord, K. (1990). Contextually based school consultation: Influential variables. *Exceptional Children*, *56*, 324–336.

Urwin, C. A. (1988). AIDS in children: A family concern. *Family Relations*, *37*, 154–159.

Westby, C. (1986). Cultural differences in caregiver–child interaction: Implications for assessment and intervention. In L. Cole & V. Deal (Eds.), *Communication disorders in multicultural populations*. Rockville, MD: American Speech, Language, and Hearing Association.

White, O. R. (1980). Practical program evaluation: Many problems and a few solutions. In M. J. May (Ed.), *Evaluating handicapped children's early education programs*. Seattle: WESTAR.

White, R. W. (1959). Motivation reconsidered: The concept of competence. *The Psychological Review*, *66*, 297–333.

Whitman, B. Y., Graves, B., & Accardo, P. (1987). Mentally retarded parents in the community: Identification method and needs assessment survey. *American Journal of Mental Deficiency*, *91*, 636–638.

Winton, P. J. (1988). Effective communication between parents and professionals. In D. B. Bailey & R. J. Simeonsson (Eds.), *Family assessment in early intervention* (pp. 207–228). Columbus, OH: Merrill.

Wolery, M., & Harris, S. R. (1982). Interpreting results of single-subject research designs. *Physical Therapy*, *62*, 445–452.

Wolke, D. (1987). Environmental neonatology. *Archives of Disease in Childhood*, *63*, 987–988.

Zigler, E., & Hunsinger, S. (1979). Look at the state of America's children in the Year of the Child. *Young Children*, *34*, 2–3.

2

Goals of Early Intervention

The provision of early intervention services is based on four fundamental assumptions.

1 Children who have disabilities or are at risk for having disabilities need and have a right to specialized services to maximize their development and the likelihood of success.
2 Families of children with disabilities often experience special needs and stresses.
3 The provision of *earlier* services can mean the achievement of optimal outcomes for children and families.
4 Because of the unique characteristics, needs, and resources of each child and family, no one curriculum or set of services could be expected to meet the needs of all. An individualized approach to service planning and delivery, therefore, is essential.

Given these assumptions, what are the goals that we hope to achieve by providing early intervention services for infants and preschoolers with disabilities and for their families? Answering this question is an essential first step for any professional working in early intervention programs. By articulating the broad goals for early intervention, professionals and programs provide a clear direction for service delivery. Services can be ranked in priority order and program decisions can be guided by the extent to which they are likely to achieve program goals. A statement of goals makes clear to consumers (families and the public), professionals, and other agencies or programs the purpose of early intervention, and provides a set of standards for evaluating program effectiveness and progress.

Goals for early intervention may be found in the history of legislative initiatives, statements by professional organizations, and in professional literature. Head Start, for example, has been characterized as a program designed to "enable disadvantaged children

to cope better with traditional schooling and to help children and their families achieve economic self-sufficiency" (Slaughter, Washington, Oyemade, & Lindsey, 1988, p. 1). Collins and Kinney (1989), citing from the Head Start standards, suggest that the primary goal of Head Start is to foster social competence in children of low income families. Schorr (1989) argues that the goal of early intervention programs for poor children should be that of reducing "intergenerational disadvantage," thus focusing on the long-term effects in primarily economic terms. Haskins (1989) reviewed the research on effectiveness of early intervention for economically disadvantaged children and concluded that while the outcomes related to child achievement in school have not yet been adequately documented, other outcomes are evident. For example, about 70 percent of the teaching staff are from poor families; thus much of the money allocated for Head Start is received by people who need it. Head Start teachers also receive training and certificates, which ultimately should make them more marketable. Further evidence of beneficial outcomes is the fact that children in Head Start centers receive nutritional services and health screenings that otherwise may not have been available. Thus some forms of early intervention may have very broad goals.

Part H of Public Law 99–457 establishes the purposes of early intervention as follows:

The Congress finds that there is an urgent and substantial need (1) to enhance the development of handicapped infants and toddlers and to minimize their potential for developmental delay, (2) to reduce the educational costs to our society, including our Nation's schools, by minimizing the need for special education and related services after handicapped infants and toddlers reach school age, (3) to minimize the likelihood of institutionalization of handicapped individuals and maximize the potential for their independent living in society, and (4) to enhance the capacity of families to meet the special needs of their infants and toddlers with handicaps. (P.L. 99–457, 1986, Sec. 671)

BASIC SERVICE GOALS FOR EARLY INTERVENTION

The broad goals articulated for early intervention are important in formulating a program philosophy, determining program policies, allocating resources, and evaluating effects. They are also important at the individual child and family level as professionals attempt to provide individualized services. This chapter suggests seven goals for early intervention:

1 to support families in achieving their own goals
2 to promote child engagement, independence, and mastery
3 to promote development in key domains
4 to build and support children's social competence
5 to promote the generalized use of skills
6 to provide and prepare for normalized life experiences
7 to prevent the emergence of future problems or disabilities

The remainder of this chapter provides a rationale and description for each goal and suggests broad strategies by which each can be achieved.

Supporting Families in Achieving Their Own Goals

Fifteen years ago, when asked the primary goal of early intervention, professionals almost inevitably would suggest that providing specialized treatment for children was of utmost importance. Today the child still serves as the focal point for services. The characteristics of the child are used to determine eligibility for services; without the child, early intervention programs would never have occasion to interact with families.

Increasingly, however, professionals have begun to recognize that viewing young children as entities that are separate and apart from families results in a limited and fragmented perspective. Families have hopes for and concerns about their children. The child inevitably affects the lives of individual family members as well as the functioning of the family group as a whole. Likewise, the skills, values, and choices of family members inevitably exert influences on the child. Every family functions as a system with its own structure, subsystems, values, and functions (Aponte, 1985). These forces shape and influence each other in complex ways through repeated interactions and transactions over time (Sameroff & Fiese, 1990). When a professional begins working with a child, she becomes another factor in this complex family system, sometimes exerting a positive and supportive influence and sometimes adding to the stress and complexity of the system. Thus at one level, a goal of early intervention must be to serve the child in ways that are consistent with family structures, values, and functions.

At another level, however, is a recognition that the child is not the only client of early intervention services. In fact, many writers are now arguing that the family is the primary client, that the primary goal of early intervention should be family support (Dunst, 1985). This perspective is sometimes difficult to accept for professionals whose training and work has been almost entirely child focused. Yet the arguments for family-centered care are compelling, and programs throughout the country are now engaged in serious self-examination to determine the extent to which this philosophy can and should be incorporated in their work.

From a legislative perspective, the role of families of infants and toddlers (children up to 36 months of age) is most evident in the requirements for an Individualized Family Service Plan (IFSP), as compared to the traditional Individualized Education Plan. Specifically, the IFSP must include, if the family so desires, a description of family resources, priorities, and concerns, and a statement of goals and services for the family. A case manager must be provided to help ensure access to and coordination of services, and a transition plan must be developed to ensure that the move from infant to preschool services is smooth. Also, for preschoolers (children 3 to 5 years of age), the legislation encourages the establishment of family goals.

The legislation is reflective of broader perspectives on the role of programs in relation to the families they serve, regardless of the children's ages. Zigler and Black (1989), for example, describe America's family support movement, the ultimate goal of which is "to enable families to be independent by developing their own informal support networks" (p. 11). Dunst (1985) argued for a rethinking of early intervention such that the primary goal is parent empowerment. Brewer, McPherson, Magrab, and Hutchins (1989) describe a family-centered approach to services in the following way.

Family-centered care is the focus of philosophy of care in which the pivotal role of the family is recognized and respected in the lives of children with special health care needs. Within this philosophy is the idea that families should be supported in their natural care-giving and decision-making roles by building on their unique strengths as people and families. In this philosophy, patterns of living at home and in the community are promoted; parents and professionals are seen as equals in a partnership committed to the development of optimal quality in the delivery of all levels of health care. To achieve this, elements of family-centered care and community-based care must be carefully inter-woven into a full and effective coordination of the care of all children with special health needs. (p. 1055)

Bailey, McWilliam, Winton, and Simeonsson (1991) suggest seven themes that reflect the law and currently accepted best practices with regard to the role of families in early intervention. First, early intervention is changing from a child-centered to a *family-centered* endeavor. Families no longer are recognized merely as legitimate recipients of services; rather they become the focal point around which decisions about goals and services are made. Second, a family-centered approach is *enabling and empowering* (Dunst, 1985), designed to assist families in their efforts to make decisions and secure services for themselves. Third, a *needs-based approach* is supplanting the service-based approach to early intervention. This means that the program starts with the family's needs and asks how services can be provided to meet those needs rather than starting with the services a program has to offer and asking how family needs fit within those existing services. Fourth, a family-centered approach is *normalized*, helping families achieve what they would ordinarily define as a normal lifestyle. A related fifth theme is that a family-centered approach is *culturally sensitive*, recognizing the significant influence of culture on a family's expectations for themselves, their children, their relationships with service providers, and for making decisions. Sixth, family-centered services are *individualized*; instead of providing a single form of services, the program seeks to provide services that meet individual needs, resources, and preferences. Finally, *coordination of services* across agencies is an essential aspect of family-centered care. It should be clear that few programs by themselves can develop and implement all of these themes of meaningful family services. As a result, programs must work with other agencies and groups to assist families and to avoid wasteful duplication of effort and resources.

If family support is, indeed, a primary goal of early intervention, programs and individual professionals will need to examine their practices to determine the extent to which they are consistent with this perspective. Unfortunately, Bailey, Buysse, Edmondson, and Smith (in press), found that professionals consistently reported a discrepancy between typical and desired practices with respect to work with families, suggesting that substantial changes are likely to be needed in many programs. Bailey, McWilliam, Winton, and Simeonsson (1991) suggest that this will involve an examination of every aspect of early intervention services, including program philosophy, child assessment, family assessment, team meetings and decision-making, forms for intake and program planning, case management, service provision, and transitions. A list of questions for programs to consider related to many of these areas is displayed in Box 2.1. These questions may be useful on at least two levels. First, program personnel can use them as the structure for discussions about their program. By using the questions as a self-examination, programs should be able to identify areas where they can make their services more family-centered. Second, these questions can be used and adapted to get information from families about the program's operation and its progress toward the provision of family-centered services (Bailey, Buysse, Smith-Bonahue, & Elam, in press).

A widely-cited statement (cf. Roberts & Magrab, 1991; Rushton, 1990) of the principles of family-centered care is displayed in Box 2.2 (p. 40), and a study with implications for planning services for families is described in Box 2.3 (p. 41). We should note that although the text cited in Box 2.3 focuses on methods for working with children, the strategies and procedures described ought to be embedded within the context of a family-centered approach to services.

Promoting Child Engagement, Independence, and Mastery

A second goal of early intervention should be to promote the child's engagement, independence, and mastery. *Engagement* is de-fined as the involvement of situationally appropriate interactions with the physical environment, materials, or other persons. *Independence* is the ability to function while depending as little as possible on help from other people. *Mastery* is the acquisition of new skills or knowledge that results from specific forms of engagement. Risley (1981) characterized engagement as high-quality interactions between children and their environments and suggested that the amount of engagement indicates the quality of a program and presages its effectiveness.

Much research has focused on the outcomes of early intervention that extend beyond participation, such as enhanced developmental progress or a reduced need for special education services. Highlighting engagement, independence, and mastery as goals for early intervention programs suggests a more immediate outcome that is important for its own sake. Regardless of the long-term benefits of services, we ought to be able to show that children with disabilities are engaged in meaningful activities for an extended period of time and that they have become reasonably successful in mastering the demands of the environments in which they most frequently live and play.

The concept of engaged time first appeared in the literature on school-aged children. Numerous studies demonstrated that the amount of time spent in school tasks is positively related to academic achievement (Anderson, 1976; Wyne & Stuck, 1979). Carroll (1963) initially proposed a model in which the degree of learning was assumed to be a function of the amount of time spent on a given task relative to the amount of time needed to master the task. Although subsequent publications have pointed to different variables affecting time spent and time needed (Block, 1971; Carroll, 1971), the basic model remains applicable today.

The amount of time spent in an activity can be viewed from the perspective of allocated time, from the perspective of engaged time,

---

BOX 2.1   Key questions about family-centered practices in early intervention

  I. What is our philosophy about working with families?
- A. Is a family focus central to our program philosophy and shared by all team members?
- B. Have families been invited to collaborate in the development of our program philosophy?
- C. Are our interactions with families positive?
- D. Do we respect family diversity in beliefs, values, and coping styles?
- E. Are our services flexible enough to meet individual family needs?
- F. Does our IFSP process recognize and support informal support systems?
- G. Do we allow families to refuse help?

 II. How will we involve families in child assessment?
- A. Are we complying with all P.L. 99–457 regulations regarding child assessment?
- B. Do we try to determine family preferences about the purpose and format of child assessment, as well as their wish to be involved?
- C. Do we convey assessment information in a sensitive and jargon-free fashion?
- D. Does the family's perception of child needs determine the focus of child assessment?
- E. Do we listen to the family's preferences in determining settings, times, and parent roles in child assessment?
- F. Do we address children's strengths in the assessment process?
- G. Do we validate and check the results of our assessment activities against the views of families?

III. How will we identify family resources, priorities, and concerns?
- A. Are we complying with all P.L. 99–457 regulations regarding family assessment?
- B. Do parents know that we are responsive to family needs?
- C. Do we try to determine family preferences regarding family assessment?
- D. Have we agreed on a flexible model and alternative procedures for assessing family needs and strengths?
- E. Is family assessment recognized as part of each team member's role?
- F. Does each team member have the skills needed to communicate effectively with families?

IV. How will we involve families in team meetings and decision making?
- A. Are we complying with all P.L. 99–457 regulations regarding the team and family participation on it?
- B. Do we try to determine family preferences regarding their role on the team?
- C. Do families determine team membership?
- D. Do we employ strategies to make sure that families feel comfortable participating in team meetings?

---

and from that of mastery time. *Allocated time* refers to the amount of time within a given schedule devoted to specific activities. For example, the preschool teacher may allocate 20 minutes for snack, 30 minutes for free play, 15 minutes for story time, and so forth. Research in schools has generally indicated that although allocated time is necessary for learning to occur, it is not strongly related to academic achievement (Borg, 1980), probably because what occurs within allocated time varies substantially across teachers, children, and settings. *Engaged time* (also referred to as *time-on-task* in the school-

E. Do we function as a team or as individual specialists?

F. Do we hold our meetings in settings and at times convenient to the family?

G. Do we respect parents' decisions even if professionals disagree?

V. What will be the format of an IFSP or IEP?

A. Are we complying with all P.L. 99–457 regulations regarding the IFSP or IEP document?

B. Do we try to determine family preferences regarding their role in developing or writing the IFSP?

C. Have we agreed on an IFSP format that will work for us?

D. Do we write goals using words that are acceptable and understandable for families?

VI. How will we implement the IFSP and provide case management services?

A. Are we complying with all P.L. 99–457 regulations regarding service provision and case management?

B. Do we try to determine family preferences regarding their role in case management and service coordination?

C. Have we decided who will serve as case managers?

D. Have we determined the skills and training that will be needed by case managers?

VII. How will we involve families in transition?

A. Are we complying with all P.L. 99–457 regulations regarding transitions?

B. Do we try to determine family preferences about the transition process, as well as whether they wish to be involved?

C. Do we work collaboratively with other programs to identify a range of choices for families?

D. Do we work collaboratively with other programs to ensure that transitions are smooth and effective?

E. Have we developed and implemented procedures to prepare the child for changes in service delivery, including help to adjust to and function in a new setting?

F. Do we support families during the process of transition from our programs?

G. Have we established a mechanism for transmitting assessment and IFSP information to the child's next placement that is based on parental consent?

Note: From *Implementing Family-Centered Services in Early Intervention: A Team-Based Model for Change* by D. B. Bailey, R. A. McWilliam, P. J. Winton, & R. J. Simeonsson, 1991, Chapel Hill, NC: Frank Porter Graham Child Development Center, CB No. 8180, University of North Carolina.

age literature) refers to the amount of allocated time in which the student is actually engaged in the intended activity. For example, during a 30-minute gross motor period, how much time does the child actually spend in gross motor activities? A strong relationship exists between engaged time and student achievement (Anderson, 1976). *Mastery time* (also referred to as *academic learning time* in the school-age literature) refers to the amount of time a student is engaged with materials that are appropriate for his or her level of development and that maximize learning and development. A general as-

---

BOX 2.2   Elements of family-centered care

Elements of Family-Centered Care

1 Recognition that the family is the constant in the child's life while the service systems and personnel within those systems fluctuate.
2 Facilitation of parent/professional collaboration at all levels of health care:
   - care of an individual child;
   - program development, implementation and evaluation; and
   - policy formation.
3 Sharing of unbiased and complete information with parents about their child's care on an ongoing basis in an appropriate and supportive manner.
4 Implementation of appropriate policies and programs that are comprehensive and provide emotional and financial support to meet the needs of families.
5 Recognition of family strengths and individuality and respect for different methods of coping.
6 Understanding and incorporating the developmental needs of infants, children, and adolescents and their families into health care delivery systems.
7 Encouragement and facilitation of parent-to-parent support.
8 Assurance that the design of health care delivery systems is flexible, accessible, and responsive to family needs.

Note: From *Family-Centered Care for Children With Special Health Care Needs* by T. L. Shelton, E. S. Jeppson, and B. H. Johnson, 1987, Washington, DC: Association for the Care of Children's Health.

sumption is that engagement with moderately difficult toys or activities is optimally facilitative of mastery, although Yoder's (1990) review suggests that for children with disabilities this assumption may need to be modified such that the toy or activity provides only a *slight* challenge. There is a strong relationship between mastery time and achievement (Borg 1980), with research suggesting that variation in mastery time is more effective at explaining variation in achievement than is variation in engaged time alone. The relationship between allocated, engaged, and mastery time is displayed in Figure 2.1.

Considerable research has addressed the engagement and mastery behaviors of young children, although studies have not yet addressed the relationship between engaged or mastery time and developmental progress

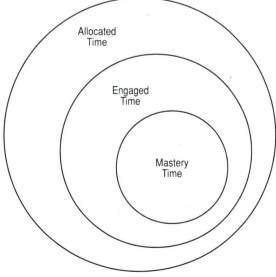

FIGURE 2.1
Relationship between allocated, engaged, and mastery time

BOX 2.3   The benefits and costs of trying to help families

In many early intervention programs professionals make too many assumptions about the services families want and need. Sometimes this well-intended effort is not only ineffective but also counterproductive. A study by Affleck, Tennen, Rowe, Rosher, and Walker (1989) reinforces this point.

The purpose of the study was to examine the effects of a support program for mothers of high-risk infants who had been in the neonatal intensive care unit (NICU). The support program was designed to assist in the transition from hospital to home care. Nurses made weekly home visits averaging 2 hours each for 15 weeks. The primary activities in the home visits included (a) listening to feelings and concerns, (b) providing information about typical and atypical development, (c) observing and describing the infant's development, (d) facilitating mutual problem-solving, (e) demonstrating therapy and other care-giving procedures, and (f) planning for the future.

The results indicated several positive outcomes, including greater feelings of competence, increased perceptions of control over life events, and greater responsiveness toward the infant. *But this effect was only observed for those mothers who, prior to discharge from the hospital, indicated a need for support.* The mothers who indicated that they did not need help, but who participated in the program anyway, felt less competent, had a lowered sense of control, and were less responsive than they were before the program started!

Affleck et al. speculate that "some program participants who had little need for support may have experienced threats to their adaptation because the information imparted to them, which they did not actively seek, disrupted their optimistic view of the child's condition and diminished their self confidence"(p. 499).

The study suggests that professionals should tailor programs more closely to the needs and priorities of families. Failure to do so may actually result in a negative effect for families.

Note: Summarized from "Effects of Formal Support on Mothers' Adaptation to the Hospital-to-Home Transition of High-Risk Infants: The Benefits and Costs of Helping" by G. Affleck, H. Tennen, J. Rowe, B. Roscher, and L. Walker, 1989, *Child Development, 60,* pp. 488–501.

(Yoder, 1990). Research on characteristics of young children with disabilities, however, reinforces the importance of focusing on engagement and mastery. Several studies have shown that children with disabilities are likely to be engaged with toys and other aspects of the environment at lower rates and for shorter episodes than normally developing children (Weiner, Ottinger, & Tilton, 1969). A study describing mastery motivation in young children with physical handicaps is described in Box 2.4. A more thorough discussion of engagement and mastery,

including procedures to assess and promote them, is provided in chapter 8.

Children may be engaged in a variety of ways, some of which promote independence and others which do not. For example, a child may be engaged in sand or water play, but if the teacher has to get all of the materials, place the child at the water table, and manipulate the child's hands, that engagement is heavily dependent on others. Of course, many young children with developmental delays and disabilities do have skill repertoires that make them dependent upon

BOX 2.4   **Mastery motivation in preschoolers with physical handicaps**

Do children with disabilities engage in mastery-related behaviors in ways similar to normally developing children? This question was the focus of a study by Jennings, Connors, Stegman, Sankaranarayan, and Mendelsohn (1985). In this study, 25 preschoolers with physical handicaps were compared with 44 normally developing children. Mastery motivation was assessed in both structured and free play settings. In the structured tasks the measures assessed persistence at solving difficult problems (e.g., fitting cutout animals in a small wooden box) and curiosity. In the free-play setting the observers coded children's attention span, complexity of play, degree of involvement, and level of social participation.

Results showed that the children with physical disabilities were less persistent at difficult tasks, less goal-directed, and gave up sooner. Also, in the free-play setting, the play of children with disabilities was less complex; they were also less likely to be engaged and played less frequently with peers.

The authors speculated that one reason for the findings is that the children with disabilities appeared to be more dependent on adults to help structure their activities. They further suggested that their observations of preschool programs indicated that many program practices may, in fact, reinforce overdependency on adults because of the lack of emphasis on free play and the high degree of adult-directed activities. Although this conclusion is only speculative, it is plausible. There is a need for further study, but an implication is that professionals should try to provide programs that help facilitate children's independent use of the environment and effective problem solving.

Note: Summarized from "Mastery Motivation in Young Preschoolers: Effect of a Physical Handicap and Implications for Educational Programming" by K. D. Jennings, R. E. Connors, C. E. Stegman, P. Sankaranarayan, and S. Mendelsohn, 1985, *Journal of the Division for Early Childhood, 9,* pp. 162–169.

others. Although infants are born highly dependent upon others for meeting many of their basic needs, as they grow they progressively become more independent. However, many children with disabilities are dependent because of skill deficits. For example, the child who is not toilet trained must depend upon someone to change diapers when an accident occurs. The child who cannot crawl, walk, or use an electric wheelchair is dependent upon someone else to move from place to place. A fundamentally important goal, therefore, is facilitating independence.

Promoting Development in All Domains of Importance

A third goal of early intervention is to promote the development of the child. Historically this has been viewed as the primary goal of early intervention, and its placement as third on this list is not to imply that it is no longer important. Many children in early intervention programs are referred to as developmentally delayed; thus a primary goal is to ameliorate or reduce the magnitude of delays in development. Working closely with families and providing engaging environments and activities, however, are necessary prerequisites to the facilitation of development.

What do we mean by "development"? An examination of much of the early intervention efficacy research would lead one to believe that development is synonymous with the acquisition of cognitive or intellectual skills, since IQ measures have served as the primary dependent variable for many of those studies. Child development theorists have offered various conceptualizations of development, some focusing on the functions of skill acquisition and behavior change, others examining the stages in physical and mental growth. For our purposes in this text, we define development broadly as including changes in behavior, thoughts, and feelings, and in competence in multiple areas of functioning. Development occurs in part from maturation and in part from interactions with the social and physical environment. The task of the teacher, parent, or other specialist is to design an environment and provide activities that maximize children's meaningful interactions with the environment and thereby promote their development.

Five or six key domains have typically been described in the context of children's development. *Cognitive skills* are associated with mental development. During the infancy period cognitive skills include imitation, behavior that begins to distinguish means from ends, the beginning perceptions of causal and spatial relationships, and an initial grasp of object permanence. During the preschool period cognitive skills that emerge include the development of concepts, the understanding of relationships between objects and people, and preacademic skills. *Motor skills* involve muscles and limbs and are distinguished as gross motor (involving large muscle groups in activities such as walking and throwing) and fine motor (involving small muscle movements

such as holding, cutting, and writing). The achievement of muscle tone and the development and inhibition of primitive reflexes are also classed as motor skills. *Communication skills* involve the exchange of information or feelings between two or more persons. *Play and social skills* involve both toy play and peer interaction. *Self-care skills*, such as toileting, feeding, dressing, and toothbrushing, are related to independent daily functioning.

Because of their importance, these skills and strategies to facilitate them are discussed in later chapters of this text. Despite considerable knowledge about them, there is still much to learn about how these skills develop naturally, about how children can learn them, and what the best teaching sequences and strategies are. The skills are complex, tending to include many interrelated strands and sequences that appear to build upon one another. Also, although these skills are described separately, relationships clearly exist across domains and subskills within domains. Most skills needed in everyday environments involve contributions from multiple domains. For example, communicating with another person involves not only communication skills but also cognitive, motor, and social skills. So professionals need to understand the sequences and the relationships of skills and be prepared to restructure the curriculum to meet each child's specific needs.

In addition to the basic skill areas that we have mentioned, Bredekamp (1986) suggests three other issues that should be attended to in programs for young children. Programs should be organized to encourage the development of self-esteem, to ensure that children perceive themselves as competent and worthwhile individuals who are liked and respected by all. Bredekamp suggests that this is accomplished by "expressing respect, acceptance, and comfort for children, regardless of the child's behavior" (p. 11). Programs should also attend to the issue of self-control. Dependent behavior—behavior that adults sometimes have promoted and reinforced—is one problem encountered in programs for young children. Bredekamp argues that the development of self-control should be a primary goal, one that can be accomplished by setting clear, reasonable limits on behavior, using mistakes or inappropriate behaviors as learning opportunities, and helping children learn to resolve conflicts in appropriate ways rather than avoiding them or responding aggressively. It must be recognized that this goal requires that the adult allocate sufficient time for activities so that the child can attempt to complete them with as little assistance as possible. For example, while it may be faster and neater to feed a child, allowing the time for self-feeding is critical to the development of self-control. Stress is still another issue. Programs should not impose undue stress on children through excessive demands or through routines that are too highly structured.

A sample set of developmental goals for all children recommended by the National Association for the Education of Young Children is displayed in Box 2.5.

Building and Supporting Social Competence

Of all the skills likely to facilitate success in life, the ability to interact appropriately with others is one of the most important. A fourth goal of early intervention, therefore, should be the building and supporting of social competence. Indeed one writer, Guralnick (1990), goes so far as to say that "understanding and promoting the social competence of young handicapped children may well be the most important challenge to the field of early intervention in the decade of the 1990s" (p. 3).

Research has clearly documented that young children with disabilities engage in lower levels of social play than do children of similar chronological ages. Guralnick and Weinhouse (1984) for example, found that both mildly and severely delayed children exhibited deficits in peer interaction skills and low rates of social interaction. Much play was alone, and when social bids were made, they were only responded to about half the time and did not often lead to longer and more elaborate interchanges. Guralnick and Groom (1987) also documented peer-related social deficits, even in children with only mild delays. These studies, combined with a substantial body of previous research, suggest that a defining characteristic of most children in early intervention programs is a deficit in social skills. As Raupp (1985) indicates, and as Box 2.6 demonstrates, social skills deficits also are likely to lead to problems in establishing and maintaining friendships.

Research with older children with disabilities suggests that social skills deficits not dealt with through early intervention are not likely to clear up over time. The school-age and adult literature provide convincing evidence of the persistence of social skills difficulties throughout life. Landesman-Dwyer and Berkson (1984), for example, reviewed the literature on the friendships and social behavior of adults with mental retardation and found loneliness and lack of special peer relationships to be among the more serious problems experienced. Other studies have shown that many failures in both sheltered and competitive employment settings are due not to the inability to perform the job but rather to the inability to get along with peers or supervisory personnel. Even small gains in social competence made through early intervention may evolve to prevent such problems for the adult.

What is meant by social competence and how can social skills be enhanced? Bailey and Simeonsson (1985) describe a variety of perspectives on social competence and con-

BOX 2.5 **A suggested set of goals for children recommended by the National Association for the Education of Young Children**

Responsible adults want children to:

Develop a positive self-concept and attitude toward learning, self-control, and a sense of belonging

Develop curiosity about the world, confidence as a learner, creativity and imagination, and personal initiative

Develop relationships of mutual trust and respect with adults and peers, understand perspectives of other people, and negotiate and apply rules of group living

Understand and respect social and cultural diversity

Know about the community and social roles

Use language to communicate effectively and to facilitate thinking and learning

Become literate individuals who gain satisfaction as well as information from reading and writing

Represent ideas and feelings through pretend play, drama, dance and movement, music, art and construction

Think critically, reason, and solve problems

Construct understanding of relationships among objects, people, and events such as classifying, ordering, number, space, and time

Construct knowledge of the physical world, manipulate objects for desired effects, and understand cause and effect relationships

Acquire knowledge of and appreciation for the fine arts, humanities, and sciences

Become competent in management of their bodies and acquire basic physical skills, both gross motor and fine motor

Gain knowledge about the care of their bodies and maintain a desirable level of health and fitness

---

Note: From *Guidelines for Appropriate Curriculum Content and Assessment in Programs Serving Children Ages Three Through Eight* by the National Association for the Education of Young Children, 1990, Washington, DC: NAEYC.

clude that it is a complex construct that is heavily dependent on situational factors. Landesman-Dwyer and Berkson (1984) suggest that "social behavior always reflects the interaction of personal and environmental variables . . . and the interpersonal meaning of social acts cannot be interpreted independently of their context" (pp. 131–132). Bailey and Simeonsson (1985) define social competence as

the infant or preschooler's ability to engage with adults or peers in interactions that (a) either elicit nurturing environmental responses or achieve desired goals, (b) are mutually satisfying to both the child and the person with whom he or she is interacting, and (c) are consistent with the adult or peer's expectations for socially competent behavior. (pp. 21–22)

Factors contributing to social competence include the child's skills, temperament, so-

BOX 2.6   Friendships for young children with disabilities

Much of the research on social competence in young children with disabilities has focused on specific behaviors, such as initiations or responses to other children, or on social types of play, such as associative and cooperative versus solitary play. Likewise, most curriculum activities address specific social skills such as smiling, looking at a peer, or responding to a peer's initiation. Although studies have consistently shown that skills such as these can be taught, of interest is whether these skills lead to the development of friendships.

Guralnick and Groom (1988) studied the friendship patterns of 4-year-old mildly delayed boys in playgroups with 3- and 4-year-old boys without disabilities. The children were observed in free play and 14 categories of social behavior were coded. A *friendship* was identified if the focal child directed at least one third of all social interactions to a single child. A *reciprocal friendship* was identified if the friend reciprocated by directing at least one third of all his social interactions toward the focal child.

Results indicated that children without disabilities were much more likely to select other children without disabilities as friends. Only two of the 16 children with delays met the criterion for reciprocal friendships. The authors conclude that "as a consequence, on the basis of these friendship criteria, mildly delayed children must be considered as socially separate from the other children in the setting" (p. 602). They also observed that the children with disabilities were able to display "surface" friendship behaviors, but that these behaviors did not lead to the development of reciprocal friendship relationships.

This study raises the question whether the achievement of friendship formation requires a different approach to teaching social skills or whether it is merely an extension of basic social skills training. The authors suggest that one reason for the failure of children with disabilities to form friendships may be their inability to engage in *sustained* interactions.

Note: Summarized from "Friendships of Preschool Children in Mainstreamed Play Groups" by M. J. Guralnick and J. M. Groom, 1988, *Developmental Psychology, 24,* pp. 595–604.

cial cognition, and learning history, and environmental support for social skills, including the skills and attitudes of peers. Enhancing social skills is likely to involve a combination of factors, including skills training, environmental modifications, teacher support, and work with peers. A detailed discussion of guidelines and procedures for enhancing social competence is presented in chapter 9. As Raupp (1985) suggests, however, teaching social skills may not necessarily result in the development of friendships. Designing programs that facilitate both social competence and the development of friendships remains a challenge for early intervention professionals.

Promoting the Generalized Use of Skills

Another important goal of early intervention is to provide services in a way that ensures that children will be able to use what they have learned. *Generalization* occurs when a behavior that has been learned in one situation is observed in a different context (Kazdin, 1975). For example, Jesse's teacher helped him learn to wave goodbye when leaving the preschool at the end of the day.

Not only did he wave goodbye to the teacher; he also waved goodbye to other children. Furthermore, he waved goodbye when his grandparents left the next day. For Jesse, waving goodbye had generalized to other persons and other settings; it became a useful skill for him. When generalization does not occur, we can view early intervention efforts as having only limited success. If children only use skills in the settings in which they are taught, those skills are of little value.

Research in this area has resulted in two clear findings. The first is that children with disabilities often do not generalize well. Warren and Kaiser (1986) reviewed the literature on generalization of treatments for language and communication problems and found that the greater the difference between the intervention environment and other settings in which the skills could be used, the less likely generalization was to occur. Similar findings have been reported in a variety of other developmental domains, such as social skills (Odom, Hoyson, Jamieson, & Strain, 1985) and motor skills (Kirby & Holborn, 1986). A review of 115 studies by White, Leber, and Phifer (1985), concluded that the usual "train and hope" (Stokes & Baer, 1977) approach rarely resulted in generalized skill use.

A second general finding, however, is that a number of strategies can be used to help promote generalization. Wolery, Bailey, and Sugai (1988) identify four types of strategies. One is to examine and manipulate characteristics of the settings by (a) teaching in the natural environment, (b) ensuring similarities between the instructional setting and the generalization setting, (c) conducting intervention activities in varied settings, or (d) using a variety of adults and peers to teach and reinforce the same skills. An example of a study in which similar toys were used to enhance generalization across play settings is described in Box 2.7.

A second type of approach is to teach multiple examples of the skill using appropriate materials. These examples should be distributed throughout a play or activity session rather than presented in a single block of "trials." A third approach is to teach only those skills and behaviors that are functional; that is, they are likely to be useful in a variety of settings and will result in increased feelings of success and positive feedback. Finally, skills are most likely to generalize if functional rather than contrived reinforcers are used and if real rather than artificial materials are used. Throughout this book, strategies for ensuring generalized skill use are described. A general rule of thumb is that intervention with respect to and teaching of a particular skill should not stop until the child readily uses it when and where it is needed. Otherwise, why teach the skill?

Providing and Preparing for Normalized Life Experiences

A sixth goal for early intervention is to help children with disabilities and their families live lives that are as normal as possible. Historically, persons with disabilities were institutionalized or otherwise isolated from society. Gradually, over the past three decades, however, we have realized the importance of providing normalized life experiences for all persons. The deinstitutionalization movement of the 1960s and 1970s, undergirded by the normalization principle, formed the basis for this change. Two different views of the normalization principle have been offered. Nirje (1976) stated that

the normalization principle means making available to all mentally retarded people patterns of life and conditions of everyday living which are as close as possible to the regular circumstances and ways of life of society. (p. 231)

Wolfensberger (1972), on the other hand, defined normalization as using means that are

---

BOX 2.7   Helping preschoolers with hearing impairments learn and use social interaction skills in multiple settings

Children with hearing impairments often display impairments in social skills. Research has shown that a variety of techniques can help children learn social skills, but only a few studies have shown that this training generalizes to other settings. A study by Kreimeyer and Antia (1988) was conducted to address this issue.

The subjects were 12 children with hearing impairments. The children were divided into three groups and a multiple baseline design was used. The intervention consisted of a variety of activities to teach and practice eight social skills: greeting, sharing, assisting, making appropriate refusals, conversing, complimenting and praising, cooperating with peers, and responding appropriately to peers' affective behavior. The children were observed in the intervention setting and in a free-play setting where training had not occurred. The free-play setting was varied each day, so that some days it included the toys found in the intervention setting and other days it contained only new toys.

Results indicated that all children increased their social skills as a result of the training, especially in sharing and conversational skills. In the generalization setting (the free-play area), however, the increases were only seen when toys were present that had been used in the intervention setting.

This is an example of "programming common stimuli," a generalization technique described by Stokes and Baer (1977) in which the intervention and generalization settings share common physical properties. The study provides further documentation that learning can be situation specific, especially for children with disabilities, and provides an example of one of the many strategies that teachers and specialists can use to help children use new skills in a variety of settings.

Note: Summarized from "The Development and Generalization of Social Interaction Skills in Preschool Hearing-Impaired Children" by K. Kreimeyer and S. Antia, 1988, *Volta Review, 90*, pp. 219–231.

---

as culturally normative as possible to teach behaviors that are as "normal" as possible. Although Perrin and Nirje (1985) are critical of Wolfensberger's definition, claiming that it overemphasizes making persons with disabilities seem normal, both they and Wolfensberger do argue for the value of normal life experiences and for the use of intervention strategies that will promote such experiences. It is important to remember that the movement toward normalization has developed from values about how people should be treated rather than from laws about how they should behave.

Mainstreaming   The normalization principle is partly reflected in Public Law 94–142, which states that to the greatest extent possible, children with disabilities ought to be educated with children who do not have disabilities. Known as the *least restrictive environment* provision, the law implies that integration—defined by Odom and McEvoy (1988, p. 242) as "the active process of mixing the two groups of children"—should be the usual mode of services unless it can be shown that segregated services are needed. Unfortunately the reverse rule is often applied, and children with disabilities are placed in segregated settings until they can demonstrate the skills needed to function in mainstream environments.

The legal basis for *mainstreaming* infants and preschoolers—that is, for getting those with disabilities as involved as possible in the flow of life with those without disabilities—is found in Public Law 99–457, in recent court decisions, and in documents from the U.S. Department of Education (Turnbull & Turnbull, 1990). A memorandum from the Department of Education (see Box 2.8)

makes it clear that the least restrictive environment provisions of P.L. 94–142 also apply to preschoolers, although the memorandum recognizes the special challenges this application may pose for schools that do not serve normally developing preschoolers. Part H, the infant and toddler component, of P.L. 99–457 speaks to this issue.

It is important that efforts be made to provide early intervention services in settings and facilities that do not remove the children from natural

---

BOX 2.8   Answers to some questions about the *least restrictive environment* (LRE) provision for preschoolers

1 Do preschool programs have to mainstream?

Any preschool child with a handicap who is provided special education service is entitled to all the rights and protections guaranteed by Part B. of the Education for All Handicapped Children Act, including placement in the least restrictive environment.

2 How can schools that do not serve preschool programs for normally developing children provide services in the least restrictive environment?

Some alternatives include (a) providing opportunities (even part-time) for participation in other preschool programs operated by public agencies, such as Head Start, (b) placing children in private school programs for nonhandicapped children, or (c) locating classes for preschoolers with handicaps in regular elementary schools.

3 If a child is placed in a local nursery school, what costs must the school pay?

Parents may not be charged any costs associated with the special education or related services contained in the Individualized Education Plan (IEP). The agency is not responsible for services not contained in the IEP, such as tuition for full-time day care. Transportation must be provided if the site provides a related service.

4 What are the state's responsibilities if the child is placed in a private program?

The state is still ultimately responsible for ensuring a free *and appropriate* public education. The state agency must monitor private programs for compliance with all state standards.

5 Are home-based programs appropriate for preschoolers?

Although home-based services may be best for a particular child, it should not be the only option available for a particular age or handicapping condition.

Note: From Memorandum to Preschool Coordinators from Nancy Treusch, Early Childhood Branch, Special Education Programs, Office of Special Education and Rehabilitative Services, U.S. Department of Education, August 1, 1989.

environments (e.g., the home, day care centers, or other community settings). Thus it is recommended that services be community based, and not isolate an eligible child or the child's family from settings or activities in which children without handicaps would participate. (*Federal Register*, 54(11a), p. 26313)

Although the law allows segregated *settings* (Turnbull & Turnbull, 1990), there is a clear legislative mandate for integrated early intervention *services*. Once programs begin considering options, securing mainstreamed situations for 3- to 5-year-old children may be easier than it first seems. Well over half of the preschool programs (i.e., Head Start, private and community child care programs, and public school prekindergarten and kindergarten programs) from across the nation report that they enroll preschoolers with disabilities (Wolery, Fleming, & Venn, 1990).

Several recent reviews of the research on mainstreaming all have concluded that mainstreaming can be implemented successfully and almost always results in positive outcomes (Bailey & McWilliam, 1990; Buysse & Bailey, 1991; Guralnick, 1990a; Odom & McEvoy, 1988; Strain, 1990). In general, the following conclusions may be drawn.

1 The developmental progress of children with disabilities seems to be about the same in both mainstreamed and segregated programs.
2 When children with disabilities are mainstreamed, they usually display higher rates of social behavior and play more constructively.
3 No negative outcomes have been shown for normally developing children participating in mainstreamed settings.
4 The adults in the classroom play critical roles in facilitating social interactions among children.

However, it seems clear that simply enrolling in a mainstreamed program will not en-

sure a positive outcome. Mainstreamed programs must also attend to the individual needs of children and ensure that the most appropriate practices are used. Clearly the most substantial benefits documented thus far are in social interaction skills and behavior (Buysse & Bailey, 1991; Strain, 1990), especially when teachers play an active and facilitative role. A sample study documenting these outcomes is described in Box 2.9.

Other Dimensions of Normalization   Bailey and McWilliam (1990) argue that early intervention programs, in addition to providing mainstreamed options for children, need to ensure that other dimensions of normalization are also addressed, including normalized environments, normalized teaching strategies, and normalized family involvement. Environments should be as normal as possible and eliminate unnecessary restrictions. With respect to normalization, Bailey, Clifford, and Harms (1982) found that segregated environments for children with disabilities differed substantially from those provided for normally developing children in typical child care programs; the environments for children with disabilities received significantly lower ratings on an environmental rating scale. Unfortunately, many of the teachers in this study felt that children with disabilities would not profit from time spent in play environments similar to those found in many typical child care programs. Environments should also be organized and equipped in ways that do not stand as barriers to children with sensory or motor impairments. Examples of various types of restrictive practices are displayed in Table 2.1.

A continuum of teaching strategies is described in chapters 4 and 5 of this text. The normalization principle argues that the most normal (and least intrusive) means possible should be used to teach skills or decrease inappropriate behaviors. For example, the National Association for the Education of Young Children has written several docu-

---

BOX 2.9   The social benefits of mainstreaming

Proponents of mainstreaming have argued their case from legal, humanitarian, and empirical perspectives. Research clearly documents that the greatest benefits of mainstreaming are social. A study by Guralnick and Groom (1988) illustrates this point.

The subjects were 11 mildly delayed boys who ranged in age from 49 to 59 months. They were observed in free-play situations in both mainstreamed and self-contained settings. Play behavior was coded according to the amount and quality of social participation as well as the cooperative level of play.

Results indicated that the children's rates of social interaction in the mainstreamed settings were more than double those observed in the segregated settings. Also the children engaged in more constructive play in the mainstreamed environments. However, the children engaged in more adult-directed activities in the segregated settings.

The authors suggest that the presence of nonhandicapped peers accounted for the higher levels of social play in the mainstreamed settings; the responsiveness of the nonhandicapped children provided more opportunities for entry into social activities. The peers in the specialized settings were less responsive and interactive, and the children thus turned to adults rather than to peers for interactions.

Note: Adapted from "Peer Interactions in Mainstreamed and Specialized Classrooms: A Comparative Analysis" by M. J. Guralnick and J. M. Groom, 1988, *Exceptional Children, 54,* pp. 415–425.

---

ments describing "developmentally appropriate practices" for adults who care for young children (Bredekamp, 1986; 1991). These practices, described in chapter 5, ought to be in place in every program, although some children will require additional specialized interventions. Giangreco, York, and Rainforth (1989) argue for a normalized approach to providing therapy and other related services by integrating them with other disciplines and incorporating them in the context of daily learning situations rather than in isolated therapy rooms.

Finally, family involvement should be normalized. Families of children with disabilities should be given the same respect and should have the same rights that other families have, especially when it comes to making choices for their children. It should also be a goal of early intervention to help families achieve lifestyles that are normalized, according to their own definitions of

normality. Programs may end up addressing intervention goals that are different from those that professionals working alone might have identified. For example, going out to dinner one night a month might be very important for a couple, but they might not feel comfortable leaving their child with a babysitter because of their child's seizures. An important family support activity might thus be to help them locate and train a babysitter so that they could achieve their personal goal of being able to go out.

Preventing the Emergence of Future Problems or Disabilities

Yet another goal of early intervention is prevention. Teachers working in programs with elementary- and secondary-school-aged children usually deal with already manifested problems and delays. In early intervention, however, many children identified as having

TABLE 2.1
Examples of restrictive practices in early intervention

	Availability	Accessibility	Organization	Scheduling & Use
Space	No outdoor play space for gross motor and movement activities	Books area is located in a loft that is not independently accessible by motorically impaired children	Boundaries for activity areas not clearly specified, resulting in frequent shifts from area to area, toys and materials distributed across the room	No scheduled time for use of outdoor play space
Materials/ Equipment	Inadequate number of blocks in play area to encourage complex constructions or play by more than one child	Housekeeping materials are stored in high cabinets accessible only to teachers and not visible to children	Blocks, fine motor materials and dolls all placed on the same set of shelves, with no organizational pattern or cues for proper storage	Sand and water play equipment available, but no designated time for use or no teacher support to promote appropriate engagement with sand and water materials
Persons	No nonhandi-capped peers available	Nonhandicapped peers in building, but cared for in separate classes	Nonhandicapped peers in same classroom, but grouping children by ability for instructional activities results in infrequent opportunities for interaction	Nonhandicapped peers present, but no systematic strategies employed to foster social-communicative exchanges between handicapped and nonhandicapped children

Note: From "Normalizing Early Intervention" by D. B. Bailey and R. A. McWilliam, 1990, *Topics in Early Childhood Special Education, 10*(2), p. 36. Copyright 1990 by PRO-ED, Inc. Reprinted by permission.

certain conditions may not yet have substantial problems; still the likelihood for future difficulties is high. For example, an infant identified as having Down syndrome may not be delayed at six months of age; yet because she will likely experience delays when she gets older, early intervention is provided in hopes of reducing them. Likewise, a child with cerebral palsy may show some delays and abnormalities in motor movements; early intervention and therapeutic services are provided in hopes of reducing contractures and other problems likely to emerge over the years.

The prevention literature distinguishes among three types of risk and prevention (Pianta, 1990; Simeonsson, 1991). *Primary prevention* is intended to prevent problems or disabilities from occurring. Prenatal nutrition programs, counseling regarding use of alcohol or cocaine during pregnancy, genetic screening, and restricted intake of prescription medications are examples of primary prevention programs. Simeonsson (1991) argues that services for children who are at risk (e.g., children born prematurely or with low birth weight) is an example of primary prevention, since the likelihood of developmental delay often is uncertain. With these children, the goal of early intervention is to prevent delays from occurring.

Secondary prevention involves providing services to children who have a high probability of having a particular problem but may not evidence all of the signs at the present time. Early intervention for the nondelayed child with Down syndrome is an example of secondary prevention. Although some delays are expected in the future and special education services will likely be needed, the goal of secondary prevention is to minimize delay and reduce the need for specialized services.

Tertiary prevention refers to services provided after a problem has already manifested itself. The goals of early intervention for a 3-year-old child referred because of a language delay would likely be to reduce the magnitude and effect of this delay and to prevent secondary or related problems. A child who cannot communicate needs and wants effectively through typical communication modes (e.g., through speech or gestures) may use whatever behavior is available to carry out communicative functions, and sometimes others may perceive the behavior as inappropriate (Donnellan, Mirenda, Mesaros, & Fassbender, 1984). The child who wants to stop an activity but cannot communicate that desire will quickly learn that if he bites whoever is involved, the activity will stop. Or the young child who does not want to do something may throw a tantrum that results in escape from the task. And another child, unable to ask for a desired toy, may resort to grabbing for it. Tertiary prevention would aim at preventing such resultant behaviors by dealing constructively with the communicative problems.

It has been argued that the entire early intervention effort is really a prevention effort (Simeonsson, 1991; Upshur, 1990), with goals such as the prevention of school failure and institutionalization. In many ways prevention is a positively oriented perspective in that it focuses on strengthening the child or family and maximizing the possibilities for success rather than addressing identified failures or delays. Despite this perspective, however, many children in early intervention will have substantial delays that need to be addressed immediately.

OTHER GOALS FOR EARLY INTERVENTION

The goals already described in this chapter focus on family and child services. Many intervention programs and early intervention professionals have other goals as well. They have goals for society at large, and they have personal/professional goals.

Goals for Society

The passage of P.L. 99–457 has made the provision of widespread, public services for infants and young children and their families a potential reality. It is important to remember, however, that these services have not always existed. Until recently, many communities in the nation did not have comprehensive intervention services for preschoolers with disabilities, and even fewer had appropriate services for infants who were at risk for or displayed developmental delays and disabilities. Chapter 1 of this text and other sources (Garwood & Sheehan, 1989; Smith, 1988) have documented the slow and incremental process involved in establishing appropriate services. Why were services not always available? For one thing, few individuals recognized the need for and the possibility of such services, and even fewer individuals advocated them.

Early intervention professionals should have the goal of increasing the awareness on the part of the public about individuals with disabilities and about the need for and the nature of intervention services. An increased community awareness and a basic understanding and acceptance of individuals with disabilities are important factors in the achievement of normalization for the children and their families. For example, if a family with a young child who has obvious and visible disabilities goes to a local restaurant, their experience will be more comfortable, rewarding, and hence normalized, if they can avoid being a spectacle. If the staff of the restaurant are hesitant to seat and serve them, if other patrons stare at them, or if others make ill-informed comments, then this simple attempt to be a typical family in the community may be impeded. With ap-

propriate information and understanding, the general public can increase the ease with which families adjust to living with a child who has disabilities while simultaneously participating in the community at levels and in ways they find desirable. The informed goodwill of the general public is also needed in the form of votes and support for decisions to devote resources at the local, state, and national level for intervention services. The early intervention community—children, parents, professionals—by itself simply does not have the votes to secure the resources needed to provide appropriate and quality services.

Many mechanisms can be used to inform the public—to increase their general awareness and acceptance of individuals with disabilities and to describe the need for intervention services. The mass media can be used, individuals and groups can be invited to visit programs, presentations can be made to local service groups, basic information can be disseminated by word of mouth. The point is that most intervention programs and professionals should engage in efforts to educate and inform the general public. Care must be taken in such efforts, of course, to preserve the dignity and confidentiality of families and to create appropriate and positive images.

Again, the early intervention community is a voting minority, and further, society has relatively limited resources but almost unlimited needs (Strain, 1984). Needs clearly exist for better roads and mass transit systems, for more effective and available substance abuse treatment programs, and for better health services for children from low income families, for better detection and treatment of child-abuse cases, for better health and social services for economically disadvantaged elderly people, for more and better treatment of juvenile law offenders, for a more effective criminal justice system, for more effective and humane public schools, and for additional funding of health and social service research efforts. Early intervention services must compete with numerous legitimate and worthy causes such as these for the limited funding resources that are available. Still, in this country the needs and aspirations of minority and underrepresented groups frequently are addressed and advanced by eloquent, vocal, persistent, and visible advocates. The eloquence of Dr. Martin Luther King called attention to the injustices experienced by African-Americans; the vocal and persistent work of Ralph Nader has called attention to many safety and consumer issues; the visibility and work of Eunice Schriver has resulted in the widespread establishment of Special Olympics. The point of these examples is that if early intervention services are to compete well for needed resources, then vocal, informed, and effective advocates are necessary. *Early intervention professionals must play a role in informing potential advocates, in providing decision makers with accurate and objective information, in assisting advocates in their efforts, and in supporting politicians and others who advocate for the needed services.*

Personal/Professional Goals

Appropriately, professionals from many different disciplines are engaged in providing early intervention services to infants and young children with developmental delays and disabilities and to their families. This chapter has listed the goals shared by most early intervention professionals. Shared goals aside, however, most experienced early interventionists will readily acknowledge that there is a wide discrepancy in the quality of services provided across and sometimes within programs. Thus, some programs may provide more responsive services to families, promote higher levels of meaningful engagement and mastery in children, and generally meet the listed goals more completely and appropriately than other programs which do relatively poor jobs. In fact, there may be programs in which knowledgeable interventionists would not enroll their own children.

This variability in the quality of services suggests an important goal for early intervention professionals and programs: *We should continually and consistently attempt to improve the quality of services provided.* To meet this goal, intervention teams and programs must (a) be aware of what constitutes quality services, (b) systematically examine the extent to which their services reflect those quality characteristics, and (c) make adjustments and modifications to their services to increase their quality. In part, this book is designed to describe what constitutes quality services; many other documents also serve this function (e.g., Bailey & Simeonsson, 1988; Bailey & Wolery, 1989; Bredekamp, 1991; Bricker, 1989; Dunst, Trivette, & Deal, 1988; Hanson & Lynch, 1989; Jordan, Gallagher, Hutinger, & Karnes, 1988; Meisels & Shonkoff, 1990; Odom & Karnes, 1988; Thurman & Widerstrom, 1990; Wachs & Sheehan, 1988). Early intervention professionals should become and remain informed about the best practices in the field. They must also engage in evaluation of their efforts to determine how well they are meeting their goals and to understand the extent to which quality practices are reflected in their programs. Such evaluation efforts are not designed to understand the impact of programs, but to understand how well programs are doing in meeting their goals and conforming to best practices (Wolery & Bailey, 1984). The evaluation requires self-examination and systematic collection of information related to questions about how well the program in question is doing (Wolery, 1987). However, being aware of best practices and evaluating how well an intervention program is meeting its goals and using best practices are only the first steps in ensuring quality services. Program leaders must also adjust and modify the services when it is clear that better practices should be used. Program modification can be a difficult task, but involving all relevant persons (e.g., all team members and families) in the evaluation process may lead to more efficient changes in service patterns and practices.

Most experienced early intervention professionals will also acknowledge that we are still learning how best to provide intervention services. What we know now is very different from what we knew 23 years ago when the Handicapped Children's Early Education Program funded the first model demonstration projects. What we know now is quite different from what we knew in 1975 when P.L. 94–142 was passed. In fact, what the authors of this text knew when the first edition was written in 1983 and 1984 is quite different from what we know now. Indeed, there are many things we still do not know (Wolery, 1991). This situation exists for many reasons—the complexity of the issue, the diversity of the needs and problems being addressed, the relative youth of the field, the relative shortage of early intervention research funds, and the effects of changes in society on the manner in which services are provided.

So to amplify the personal/professional goal for early interventionists, let us add that *we should consistently seek to understand better ways to provide services and should communicate them to other members of the profession.* Because we have much to learn about providing early intervention services, each practicing professional has the potential for learning new and useful information. As Bailey (1989) has articulated, each early intervention professional makes many decisions about the services he or she provides. To do this well, the professional must have decision-making skills that allow for recognizing and evaluating the complexities, realities, and possibilities that are presented by

the problem or issue and its context. In addition, the professional needs both propositional knowledge and case knowledge to make these decisions. *Propositional knowledge* includes information derived from research, from the collective wisdom of the field, and from ideals and values that guide practice. *Case knowledge,* on the other hand, includes information about how propositional knowledge can be implemented in different contexts. However, as many practicing professionals know, they are faced regularly with situations where two or more potential options seem viable.

In such situations, the practicing professional has a responsibility to select, implement, *and* evaluate the most defensible option(s)/solution(s). Evaluating interventions requires professionals to have basic applied research skills; and personnel preparation programs are required in turn in order to train early interventionists in research competencies (cf. Heward, Heron, & Cooper, 1990; Kaiser & McWhorter, 1990). The professional who participates in this process is in a position of generating new information about how to provide intervention services, information that must then be communicated to other professionals. Communication can occur at the level of telling other team members about new or improved strategies, providing training to other interventionists, presenting at professional conferences, or writing for publication in newsletters and professional journals.

WHY BE CONCERNED ABOUT THE GOALS OF EARLY INTERVENTION?

When goals are discussed in the context of early intervention, the focus is usually on individual goals for children or families. In this chapter, we have argued that professionals need to be aware of the broader goals of early intervention. Such an awareness

> **BOX 2.10   Some questions for evaluating the extent to which individual service plans reflect the broad goals of early intervention**
>
> I. Family support and involvement
>   A. Does the plan reflect family priorities for their child?
>   B. Does the plan address the broad array of needs expressed by the family?
>   C. Did the process of developing the plan help family members feel valued and respected as knowledgeable participants in the planning process?
>   D. Does the plan draw on and reinforce informal support networks?
> II. Engagement and mastery
>   A. Does the plan include goals related to engagement with toys and environments?
>   B. Are engagement goals related to developmental as well as environmental expectations?
>   C. Have the demands for behavior expected in current environments been specified?
>   D. Have the expectations for the future environments been identified and incorporated in the plan when appropriate?
> III. Development
>   A. Does the plan include goals related to the development of cognitive, motor, communication, play, social, and self-care skills?
>   B. Are the goals developmentally appropriate, yet functional?
>   C. Does the plan reflect an attempt to build self-esteem and self-control?
> IV. Social competence
>   A. Is social competence highlighted as a primary goal for services?
>   B. Does the plan reflect a recognition of the complex and interactive nature of social competence?
>   C. Are social goals integrated with those of other domains, especially communication?
>   D. Besides social skills, does the plan seek to facilitate the development of friendships?
> V. Generalization
>   A. Does the plan include a statement of goals for both acquisition and generalization?
>   B. Are skills expected and taught in multiple contexts?
>   C. Are the goals functional as well as developmentally appropriate?
> VI. Normalization
>   A. Does the plan include opportunities to interact with normally developing children in typical environments?
>   B. Are the intervention strategies selected "least intrusive" yet effective?
>   C. Have families identified goals that they consider to be normal for them?
> VII. Prevention
>   A. Does the plan support and strengthen children and families?
>   B. Have future needs been identified?

means that for each child and family served, questions need to be asked regarding the variety of possible goals. Although resources will always be limited, an important assumption is that the more narrowly focused the goals, the smaller the ultimate effect. An intervention program that focuses only on child engagement, for example, would likely be much less successful than one that considered family needs and planned a prevention component. In reality, the seven goals proposed in this chapter all are important and each will likely require attention in planning individualized services for most children and families. Some questions related to each goal that might be considered in evaluating a service plan are displayed in Box 2.10. As with the questions in Box 2.1, these can be used in the self-examination and self-evaluation of early intervention programs and services.

SUMMARY

In this chapter, we have suggested that there are some broad common goals for the provision of early intervention services to infants and young children who are at risk for or display developmental delays and disabilities and to their families. Early intervention professionals should (a) support families in achieving their own goals; (b) promote infant/child engagement and mastery of current environments; (c) promote development in key domains; (d) build and support children's social competence; (e) promote the generalized use of skills; (f) provide and prepare infants, children, and families for normalized life experiences; and (g) prevent the emergence of future problems or disabilities. These seven goals focus on the provision of services. We also have proposed that early interventionists should have goals for society at large—that they should aim at increasing the knowledge and general awareness of the public about individuals with disabilities, the need for services, and the nature of services, and that they should develop and support advocates for individuals with disabilities and for the needed services. Further, we have proposed that early interventionists should have personal/professional goals—that they should attempt to improve the quality of their services and that they should communicate improvements to their colleagues.

REFERENCES

Affleck, G., Tennen, H., Rowe, J., Roscher, B., & Walker, L. (1989). Effects of formal support on mothers' adaptation to the hospital-to-home transition of high-risk infants: The benefits and costs of helping. *Child Development, 60,* 488–501.

Anderson, L. W. (1976). An empirical investigation of individual differences in time to learn. *Journal of Educational Psychology, 68,* 226–233.

Aponte, H. J. (1985). The negotiation of values in therapy. *Family Process, 24,* 323–338.

Bailey, D. B. (1989). Issues and directions in preparing professionals to work with young handicapped children and their families. In J. J. Gallagher, P. L. Trohanis, & R. M. Clifford (Eds.), *Policy implementation & PL 99–457: Planning for young children with special needs* (pp. 97–132). Baltimore: Paul Brookes.

Bailey, D. B., Buysse, V., Edmondson, R., Smith, T. M. (in press). Creating family-centered practices in early intervention: Professionals' perceptions of typical practices, ideal practices, and barriers to change. *Exceptional Children.*

Bailey, D. B., Buysse, V., & Smith-Bonahue, T. (in press). The effects and perceptions of family involvement in program decisions about family-centered practices. *Evaluation and Program Planning.*

Bailey, D. B., Clifford, R. M., & Harms, T. (1982). Comparison of preschool environments for handicapped and nonhandicapped preschoolers. *Topics in Early Childhood Special Education, 2*(1), 9–20.

Bailey, D. B., McWilliam, R. A. (1990). Normalizing early intervention. *Topics in Early Childhood Special Education, 10*(2), 33–47.

Bailey, D. B., McWilliam, R. A., Winton, P. J., & Simeonsson, R. J. (1991). *Implementing family-centered practices in early intervention: A team-based model for change.* Chapel Hill, NC: Frank Porter Graham Child Development Center, CB No. 8180, University of North Carolina.

Bailey, D. B., & Simeonsson, R. J. (1985). A functional model of social competence. *Topics in Early Childhood Special Education, 4*(4), 20–31.

Bailey, D. B., & Simeonsson, R. J. (Eds.) (1988). *Family assessment in early intervention.* Columbus, OH: Merrill.

Bailey, D. B., & Wolery, M. (Eds.) (1989). *Assessing infants and preschoolers with handicaps.* Columbus, OH: Merrill.

Block, J. H. (1971). *Mastery learning: Theory and practice.* New York: Holt, Rinehart, & Winston.

Borg, W. R. (1980). Time and school learning. In C. Denham & A. Lieberman (Eds.), *Time to learn.* Washington, DC: U.S. Department of Education.

Bredekamp, S. (Ed.). (1986). *Developmentally appropriate practice.* Washington, DC: National Association for the Education of Young Children.

Bredekamp, S. (1991). *Guidelines for appropriate curriculum content and assessment in programs serving children ages three through eight.* Washington, DC: NAEYC.

Brewer, E. J., McPherson, M., Magrab, P. R., & Hutchins, V. C. (1989). Family-centered, community-based, coordinated care for children with special health care needs. *Pediatrics, 83,* 1055–1060.

Bricker, D. D. (1989). *Early intervention for at-risk and handicapped infants, toddlers, and preschool children.* Palo Alto, CA: VORT.

Buysse, V., & Bailey, D. B. (1991). Mainstreamed versus specialized settings: Behavioral and developmental effects on young children with handicaps. Chapel Hill, NC: University of North Carolina.

Carroll, J. B. (1963). A model of school learning. *Teacher's College Record, 64,* 723–733.

Carroll, J. B. (1971). Problems of measurement related to the concept of learning for mastery. In J. H. Block (Ed.), *Mastery learning: Theory and practice.* New York: Holt, Rinehart, & Winston.

Collins, R. C., & Kinney, P. F. (1989). *Head Start research and evaluation: Background and overview.* Vienna, VA: Collins Management Consulting, Inc.

Donnellan, A. M., Mirenda, P. L., Mesaros, R. A., & Fassbender, L. L. (1984). Analyzing the communicative functions of aberrant behavior. *Journal of The Association for Persons with Severe Handicaps, 9,* 201–212.

Dunst, C. J. (1985). Rethinking early intervention. *Analysis and Intervention in Developmental Disabilities, 5,* 165–201.

Dunst, C. J., Trivette, C., & Deal, A. (1988). *Enabling and empowering families: Principles and guidelines for practice.* Cambridge, MA: Brookline Books.

Garwood, S. G., & Sheehan, R. (1989). *Designing a comprehensive early intervention system: The challenge of PL 99–457.* Austin, TX: PRO-ED.

Giangreco, M. F., York, J., & Rainforth, B. (1989). Providing related services to learners with severe handicaps in educational settings: Pursuing the least restrictive option. *Pediatric Physical Therapy, 1,* 55–63.

Guralnick, M. J. (1990a). Major accomplishments and future directions in early childhood mainstreaming. *Topics in Early Childhood Special Education, 10*(2), 1–17.

Guralnick, M. J. (1990b). Social competence and early intervention. *Journal of Early Intervention, 14,* 3–14.

Guralnick, M. J., & Groom, J. M. (1987). The peer relations of mildly delayed and non-handicapped preschool children in mainstreamed play groups. *Child Development, 58,* 1556–1572.

Guralnick, M. J., & Groom, J. M. (1988a). Friendships of preschool children in mainstreamed play groups. *Developmental Psychology, 24,* 595–604.

Guralnick, M. J., & Groom, J. M. (1988b). Peer interactions in mainstreamed and specialized classrooms: A comparative analysis. *Exceptional Children, 54,* 415–425.

Guralnick, M. J., & Weinhouse, E. (1984). Peer-related social interaction of developmentally delayed young children. Development and characteristics. *Development Psychology, 20,* 815–827.

Hanson, M. J., & Lynch, E. W. (1989). *Early intervention: Implementing child and family services for infants and toddlers who are at risk or disabled.* Austin, TX: PRO-ED.

Haskins, R. (1989). Beyond metaphor: The efficacy of early childhood education. *American Psychologist, 44,* 274–282.

Heward, W. L., Heron, T. E., & Cooper, J. O. (1990). The masters thesis in applied behavior analysis: Rationale, characteristics, and student advisement strategies. *The Behavior Analyst, 13,* 205–210.

Jennings, K. D., Connors, R. E., Stegman, C. E., Sankaranarayan, P., & Mendelsohn, S. (1985). Mastery motivation in young preschoolers: Effect of a physical handicap and implications for educational programming. *Journal of the Division for Early Childhood, 9,* 162–169.

Jordan, J. B., Gallagher, J. J., Hutinger, P. L., & Karnes, M. B. (Eds.). (1988). *Early childhood special education: Birth to three.* Reston, VA: Council for Exceptional Children.

Kaiser, A. P., & McWhorter, C. M. (Eds.). (1990). *Preparing personnel to work with persons with severe disabilities.* Baltimore: Paul Brookes.

Kazdin, A. E. (1975). *Behavior modification in applied settings.* Homewood, IL: Dorsey Press.

Kirby, K. C., & Holborn, S. W. (1986). Trained, generalized, and collateral behavior changes of preschool children receiving gross motor skills training. *Journal of Applied Behavior Analysis, 19,* 283–288.

Kreimeyer, K., & Antia, S. (1988). The development and generalization of social interaction skills in preschool hearing-impaired children. *Volta Review, 90,* 219–231.

Landesman-Dwyer, S., & Berkson, G. (1984). Friendships and social behavior. In J. Wortis (Ed.), *Mental retardation and developmental disabilities* (Vol. 13, pp. 129–154). New York: Plenum Press.

Meisels, S. J., & Shonkoff, J. P. (Eds.). (1990). *Handbook of early childhood intervention.* Cambridge: Cambridge University Press.

National Association for the Education of Young Children. (1990). *Guidelines for appropriate curriculum content and assessment in programs serving children ages three through eight.* Washington, DC: NAEYC.

Nirje, B. (1976). The normalization principle. In R. Kugel & A. Shearer (Eds.), *Changing patterns in residential services for the mentally retarded.* Washington, DC: President's Committee on Mental Retardation.

Odom, S. L., Hoyson, M., Jamieson, B., & Strain, P. S. (1985). Increasing handicapped preschoolers' peer social interactions: Cross-setting and component analysis. *Journal of Applied Behavior Analysis, 18,* 3–16.

Odom, S. L., & Karnes, M. B. (1988). *Early intervention for infants and children with handicaps: An empirical base.* Baltimore: Paul Brookes.

Odom, S. L., & McEvoy, M. A. (1988). Integration of young children with handicaps and normally developing children. In S. L. Odom & M. B. Karnes (Eds.), *Early intervention for infants and children with handicaps: An empirical base* (pp. 241–268). Baltimore: Paul Brookes.

Perrin, B., & Nirje, B. (1985). Setting the record straight: A critique of some frequent misconceptions of the normalization principle. *Australia and New Zealand Journal of Developmental Disabilities, 11*(2), 69–74.

Pianta, R. C. (1990). Widening the debate on educational reform: Prevention as a viable alternative. *Exceptional Children, 56,* 306–313.

Raupp, C. (1985). Approaching special needs children's social competence from the perspective of early friendships. *Topics in Early Childhood Special Education, 4*(4), 32–46.

Risley, T. (1981). *Research on day care environments.* Paper presented at Frank Porter Graham Child Development Center, University of North Carolina at Chapel Hill.

Roberts, R. N., & Magrab, P. R. (1991). Psychologist's role in a family-centered approach to practice, training, and research with young children. *American Psychologist, 46,* 144–148.

Rushton, C. H. (1990). Family-centered care in the critical care setting: Myth or reality? *Children's Health Care, 19,* 68–77.

Sameroff, A. J., & Fiese, B. H. (1990). Transactional regulations and early intervention. In S. J. Meisels & J. P. Shonkoff (Eds.), *Hand-*

book of early childhood intervention (pp. 35–52). Cambridge: Cambridge University Press.

Schorr, L. B. (1989). Early interventions to reduce intergenerational disadvantage: The new policy context. *Teachers College Record, 90,* 362–374.

Shelton, T. L., Jeppson, E. S., & Johnson, B. H. (1987). *Family-centered care for children with special health care needs.* Washington, DC: Association for the Care of Children's Health.

Simeonsson, R. J. (1991). Primary, secondary, and tertiary prevention in early intervention. *Journal of Early Intervention, 15,* 124–134.

Slaughter, D. T., Washington, V., Oyemade, U. J., & Lindsey, R. W. (1988). Head Start: A backward and forward look. *Social Policy Report: Society for Research in Child Development, 3*(2), 1–15.

Smith, B. J. (1988). Early intervention public policy: Past, present, and future. In J. B. Jordan, J. J. Gallagher, P. L. Hutinger, & M. B. Karnes (Eds.), *Early childhood special education: Birth to three* (pp. 213–228). Reston, VA: Council for Exceptional Children.

Stokes, T. F., & Baer, D. M. (1977). An implicit technology of generalization. *Journal of Applied Behavior Analysis, 17,* 273–278.

Strain, P. S. (1984). Efficacy research with young handicapped children: A critique of the status quo. *Journal of the Division for Early Childhood, 9,* 4–10.

Strain, P. S. (1990). LRE for preschool children with handicaps: What we know, what we should be doing. *Journal of Early Intervention, 14,* 291–297.

Thurman, S. K., & Widerstrom, A. H. (1990). *Infants and young children with special needs: A developmental and ecological approach* (2nd ed). Baltimore: Paul Brookes.

Treusch, N. (1989, August 1). Memorandum to Preschool Coordinators. Early Childhood Branch, Special Education Programs, Office of Special Education and Rehabilitative Services. Washington, DC: U.S. Department of Education.

Turnbull, H. R., & Turnbull, A. P. (1990). The unfulfilled promise of integration: Does Part H ensure different rights and results than Part B of the Education of the Handicapped Act? *Topics in Early Childhood Special Education, 10*(2), 18–32.

Upshur, C. C. (1990). Early intervention as preventive intervention. In S. J. Meisels & J. P. Shonkoff (Eds.), *Handbook of early childhood intervention* (pp. 633–650). Cambridge: Cambridge University Press.

Wachs, T. D., & Sheehan, R. (Eds.). (1988). *Assessment of young developmentally disabled children.* New York: Plenum Press.

Warren, S. F., & Kaiser, A. P. (1986). Generalization of treatment effects by young language-delayed children: A longitudinal analysis. *Journal of Speech and Hearing Disorders, 51,* 239–251.

Weiner, B. J., Ottinger, D. R., & Tilton, J. F. (1969). Comparison of the toy-play behavior of autistic, retarded, and normal children: A reanalysis. *Psychological Reports, 25,* 223–227.

White, O. R., Leber, B. D., & Phifer, C. E. (1985). Training in the natural environment and skill generalization: It doesn't always come naturally. In N. Haring, K. Liberty, F. Billingsley, V. Lynch, J. Kayser, Y. F. McCarty (Eds.), *Investigating the problem of skill generalization* (3rd ed.) (pp. 63–79). Seattle: Washington Research Organization.

Winter, E. A., & Weiner, B. J. (1974). Differentiation of retarded and normal children through toy-play analysis. *Multivariate Behavioral Research, 9,* 245–252.

Wolery, M. (1987). Program evaluation at the local level: Improving services. *Topics in Early Childhood Special Education, 7,* 1111–1230.

Wolery, M. (1991). Instruction in early childhood special education: Seeing through a glass darkly . . . knowing in part. *Exceptional Children, 58,* 127–135.

Wolery, M., & Bailey, D. B. (1984). Alternatives to impact evaluations: Suggestions for program evaluation in early intervention. *Journal of the Division for Early Childhood, 9,* 27–37.

Wolery, M., Bailey, D. B., & Sugai, G. M. (1988). *Effective teaching: Principles and procedures of applied behavior analysis with exceptional students.* Boston: Allyn and Bacon.

Wolery, M., Fleming, L., & Venn, M. (1990). *10 Year Report: Research Institute as Preschool Mainstreaming.* Pittsburgh, PA: Allegheny-Singer Research Institute.

Wolfensberger, W. (1972). *The principle of normalization in human services.* Toronto: National Institute on Mental Retardation.

Wyne, M. D., & Stuck, G. S. (1979). Time-on-task and reading performance in underachieving children. *Journal of Reading Behavior, 11,* 119–128.

Yoder, P. J. (1990). The theoretical and empirical basis of early amelioration of developmental disabilities: Implications for future research. *Journal of Early Intervention, 14,* 27–42.

Zigler, E., & Black, K. B. (1989). America's family support movement: Strengths and limitations. *American Journal of Orthopsychiatry, 59,* 6–19.

3

An Ecological Framework for Early Intervention

Historically, early intervention focused primarily on the infant or preschooler with a disability. Professionals working in early intervention programs spent most of their time assessing children and designing instructional activities to enhance children's development. Although such an emphasis will always be a primary focus of early intervention, recent trends have made it clear that we need a broader perspective on the factors that influence children as well as in our views of what constitutes "intervention." The purpose of this chapter is to describe a way of conceptualizing these factors and to provide guidelines to assist professionals in maximizing intervention efforts through a comprehensive and integrated program of services. The chapter is organized around Bronfenbrenner's (1976, 1977) ecological model of education and human development. We begin the chapter with an overview of systems theory and its implications for intervention planning and service delivery.

SYSTEMS THEORY

Although knowledge about the interactive nature of systems has been developing for centuries, von Bertalanffy (1968) is generally credited with conceptualizing the theoretical framework known as general systems theory. According to this perspective, individuals, families, organizations, and agencies are viewed not as independently functioning units but rather as components of an "organized whole." This "whole" is a hierarchical and orderly system of interrelated and interdependent components. A system changes constantly as its components adapt to information, feedback, and stressful or supportive stimuli. The early interventionist working from a systems perspective will be aware of the need to take into account multiple components, some of which influence

and some of which are influenced by the infant or preschooler with a disability (Ramey, Yeates, & MacPhee, 1984).

Key Aspects of a Systems Approach

Powers (1988) suggests that three characteristics form the basis of a systems approach to service delivery. The first is referred to as *ecological sensitivity.*

There must be explicit recognition that proposed change in one part of the organizational system will reverberate through other parts of the system, creating imbalance and, in some cases, transitional crises. Predicting these imbalances, recognizing the system's natural tendency toward homeostasis (that is, to resist imbalancing by exerting pressure to return to an earlier form of behavior), and proactively intervening to support change and rebalance the system are crucial issues for professionals to address prior to implementation. (p. 7)

For example, a parent asked to conduct therapeutic activities at home with his child may then have reduced time for his other children, argue with his spouse, or develop feelings of personal frustration at not achieving other goals or of guilt if he fails to implement the activities regularly. Another parent, on the other hand, may develop feelings of efficacy, may receive increased positive regard from her spouse, and may find her whole family taking an increased interest in the child with a disability.

The second characteristic discussed by Powers is *attention to organizational process.* Although established to be supportive systems for children and families, organizations can often serve as barriers to change, especially when individuals are not aware of organizational structures, rules, and modes of response. Professionals, for example, may not understand the values, structures, and resources that a family perceives to be normal and important for them. On the other hand, families may perceive agencies as cold and impersonal entities unwilling to be flexible enough to meet individual family needs. Also, professionals themselves may have a range of feelings about the systems in which they work. For example, Bailey, Buysse, Edmondson, and Smith (in press), found significant discrepancies between professionals' reports of typical and desired practices in working with families. When asked to identify factors that kept them from implementing ideal practices, they most frequently mentioned systems barriers—such as lack of administrative support, inadequate resources, the difficulty inherent in changing established patterns of practice, and inconsistency between the philosophical perspectives of administrators and practitioners. An awareness of and attention to organizational processes is essential if effective services are to be provided.

The third characteristic of a systems approach, as discussed by Powers, is *an awareness of the interrelationships between individual behavior and the environment.* Such an awareness requires a knowledge of general principles of environmental design and specific dimensions of environmental planning as well as the ability to match environments to individual needs, styles, and preferences. Thomas and Chess (1977) suggested the concept of "goodness of fit" and argued that the best outcome occurs when there is a fit between the child's and the family's characteristics and the services provided. Sprunger, Boyce, and Gaines (1985) found, for example, that family adaptation to an unpredictable infant varied according to the predictability of other family routines. Families who preferred predictable routines were less able to adapt to an unpredictable child than were families with greater variability in family schedules.

Bernheimer, Gallimore, and Weisner (1990) describe "ecocultural theory" as an important foundation and context for developing the Individualized Family Service Plan. Each family, they claim, adapts to a niche within a given ecology, a niche that includes factors of culture, materials, and place. This niche can only be understood by an examination of (a) the objective components of the family's ecology and (b) the family members' *perceptions* of their own circumstances. The ecology provides both constraints and opportunities for the family, and these must be viewed from the family's perspective rather than the professional's. The professional must learn to view the family's needs within a hierarchical framework based on such an examination.

Our understanding of systems theory is enhanced by two related theoretical frameworks. Bronfenbrenner's (1976; 1977) ecological model clarifies the hierarchical relationships among multiple levels of a system. And Sameroff and Chandler's (1975) transactional model demonstrates the nature of interactions and the directions of influence in the context of systems theory.

An Ecological Model of Education and Development

Bronfenbrenner (1977) defined the ecology of human development as

the scientific study of the progressive, mutual accommodation, throughout the life span, between a growing human organism and the changing immediate environments in which it lives, as this process is affected by relations obtaining within and between these immediate settings, as well as the larger social contexts, both formal and informal, in which the settings are embedded. (p. 514)

Central to his model is the notion that the ecological environment is "a nested arrangement of structures, each contained with the next" (p. 514). Drawing on earlier work by Brim (1975), Bronfenbrenner identified four levels of the environment, as displayed in Figure 3.1. The *microsystem* is the setting in which the child spends a significant portion

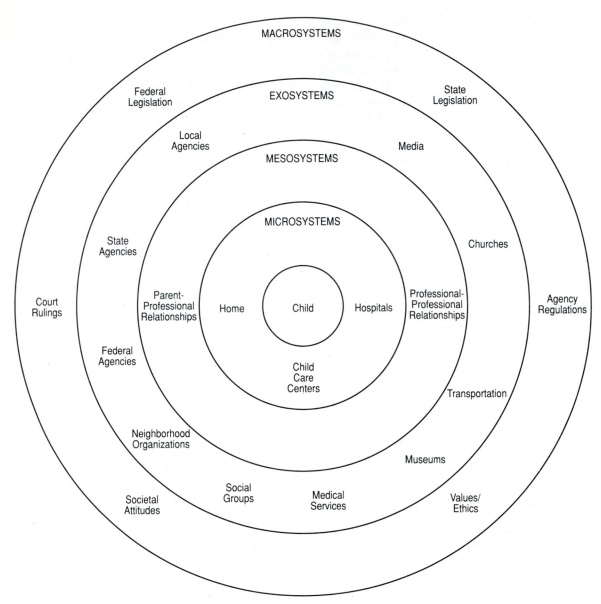

FIGURE 3.1
Four nested levels of the environment

Note: Figure form and content by D. B. Bailey. Based on concepts presented in "The Experimental Ecology of Education" by U. Bronfenbrenner, 1976, *Educational Research, 5*(9), 5–15, and in "Toward an Experimental Ecology of Human Development" by U. Bronfenbrenner, 1977, *American Psychologist, 32,* 513–531.

of time. Young children spend most of their time in homes, with friends, neighbors or relatives, in family day care homes, or in child care centers. Some children also spend considerable time in hospitals or other institutional settings. The *mesosystem* consists of relationships among those microsystems of which the child is a part at a particular point in his or her life—relationships between parent and teacher, therapist, or physician, and interactions of professional with professional. The *exosystem* consists of concrete societal structures such as local and state agencies, advocacy groups, neighborhood and community organizations, and churches. Early intervention programs probably fit best within this level of the hierarchy. Finally, the *macrosystem* consists of the cultural and legislative/judicial contexts in which the micro-, meso-, and exosystems operate. Because of the mandate it gives for the education of 3- to 5-year-old children with disabilities and for services for infants and toddlers, Public Law 99–457 is probably the most powerful example of a macrosystem element within the context of early intervention. Bronfenbrenner argues that it is of minimal use to treat a problem in isolation without an understanding of systems factors that contribute to the problem, the likelihood that the system will support the desired change, or the potential "ripple effects" of any intervention on other aspects of the system (Gabarino, 1990).

Transactional Theory

Bell's (1968) research helped practitioners in the field begin to see that behavior is rarely unidirectional, that usually behavior is bidirectional. Early research on parent–child interaction, for example, had emphasized the influence of the mother in shaping the child's behavior. Bell argued that infants, in turn, shape the behavior of their parents. Sameroff and Chandler (1975) extended this ar-

gument and proposed a *transactional model* in which the individual and the environment are interdependent and constantly interacting. Sameroff and Fiese (1990) illustrate the model by describing a complicated childbirth that caused a mother to become quite anxious about her child. Her anxiety led to inconsistent patterns of care-giving which, in turn, resulted in disruptions in feeding and sleeping patterns. These disruptions were obviously not enjoyable for the mother, and so she tended to spend less time with her child, to such an extent that a language delay was observed in the child at age four. This example illustrates that "the child's outcome at any point in time is neither a function of the initial state of the child nor the initial state of the environment, but a complex function of the interplay of child and environment over time" (Sameroff & Fiese, 1990, pp. 122–123). Not only is the child's outcome a cumulative product of a series of interactions and transactions, it also is a function of how the individual (in this case the mother) perceives, defines, and interprets experiences. Sameroff and Fiese (1990) suggest that adoption of this model means that the professional must also apply a transactional model for intervention, that the professional must view "problems" (e.g., delayed development, poor feeding skills, difficult behaviors) as the products of series of experiences and the perceptions of the participants regarding those experiences. From the point of view of this model, quick fix interventions are not likely to be very effective, with the possibility of a few exceptions. Effective intervention takes into consideration multiple effects and perspectives and applies strategies at multiple levels of a system, strategies that are consistent with the beliefs, values, and perceptions of key players within the system.

Given this overview, how can early interventionists use systems theory, ecological models, and transactional theory in their

TABLE 3.1
Levels of an ecological system: Implications for early intervention

System Level	Definition	Examples	Interventionist's Tasks
The Child	Infants and preschoolers who have or are at risk for disabilities.	Premature or low birth weight Chromosomal anomalies Motor or sensory impairments Delayed development Chronic health problems or illnesses Effects of maternal drug use	Know infant and preschool development and characteristics Know handicapping conditions and effects Assess child strengths and needs Design and implement learning activities for young children
Microsystem	A setting in which the infant or preschooler spends a significant portion of time	Home/family Child care center (specialized or mainstreamed) Family day care home Hospital	Be familiar with the array of typical environments Understand the influence of environments on behavior and development Work with and within typical environments Modify environments to meet children's needs Help child adapt to environmental demands Communicate effectively with adults in typical environments Assess family needs and resources Provide consultation
Mesosystem	The interrelationships among the microsystems of which the child is a part at a particular point in his or her life	Parent–physician relationship Parent–teacher relationship Parent–therapist relationship Professional–professional interactions	Recognize and address problems frequently encountered across disciplines, across settings, or when parents and professionals attempt to communicate Know and use effective communication strategies Participate in and work to enhance the performance of interdisciplinary teams Serve as advocate for children and families

System	Definition	Structures/Contexts	Skills
			Facilitate family participation on teams and in decision making
			Facilitate transition from one program to another
Exosystem	Concrete societal structures that influence activities of the microsystem	Local, state, and federal agencies	Know and adhere to agency regulations; work to improve agency guidelines
		Advocacy groups	Provide case management services, helping families gain access to various components of the exosystem
		Neighborhood and community organizations	Understand how societal structures influence family functioning
		Transportation system	Analyze the array and coordination of services at local, state, and federal levels
		Media	Be aware of the array of programs and services available
		Churches	Involve families in decisions about program policies and practice
		Mental health, public health, and public school systems	Recognize and use the powerful effects of informal support systems
Macrosystem	The cultural and legislative/judicial contexts in which the micro-, meso-, and exosystems operate	Legislation	Justify services to the population
		Court decisions	Serve as advocate for services
		Prevailing societal attitudes	Evaluate services within their social context and according to the extent to which they correspond to broader societal mandates
		Ethical/moral principles and issues	Provide leadership in the development of new services and the renewal of existing services
			Understand the broader context within which families must function
			Understand the broader context within which day care centers, hospitals, and other microsystems must operate

Note: Adapted from "Preparing Infant Interventionists: Interdepartmental Training in Special Education and Maternal and Child Health" by D. B. Bailey, A. M. Farel, K. J. O'Donnell, R. J. Simeonsson, and C. A. Miller, 1986, *Journal of the Division for Early Childhood, 11,* 67–77. Copyright 1986 by the *Journal of the Division for Early Childhood,* now the *Journal of Early Intervention.* Adapted by permission.

work? The remainder of this chapter is organized around Bronfenbrenner's (1976; 1977) ecological model. Each level of the model is described in greater detail, and examples of intervention principles and strategies at each level are discussed. A summary of the key points to be made is displayed in Table 3.1.

THE CHILD WITH A DISABILITY

The first level of the system is the child with or at risk for a disability—for example, the premature or low birth weight infant, or the child with chromosomal anomalies, motor or sensory impairments, delayed development, chronic health problems, or a variety of other risk factors. To work at this level the professional needs a knowledge of infant and preschool development and characteristics; a knowledge of handicapping conditions and their effects; the ability to assess child characteristics, strengths, and needs; and the ability to design and implement learning activities for young children. Because much of this text focuses on this level of intervention, this chapter addresses how to provide this intervention in the context of a systems approach. Here we treat four important characteristics of young children: (a) their rapid growth and development; (b) their developing social awareness, social competence, and social connections; (c) their learning through experience; and (d) their motivation to learn. In this section we also discuss the concept of behavioral covariation.

Rapid Growth and Development

The most obvious and continually amazing characteristic of children in infancy and the preschool period is their rapid rate of growth and development. In the first 12 months alone, the typical infant develops from a neonate into a toddler who is walking, communicating in many ways (including saying a few words), smiling at others, and self-feeding, with a relatively predictable daily schedule. Over the next 4 years the typical child stops taking naps, becomes toilet trained, learns to ride a tricycle, becomes very interested in peers, watches lots of television, develops basic writing, drawing, and cutting skills, learns to tie shoes, develops sophisticated concepts about the world, and engages in many activities related to the emergence of literacy. These rapid changes are due both to maturation and to experience.

The early intervention professional should have knowledge of both typical and atypical patterns of development, in order to know those skills that are reasonable to expect and those that are not. Because children with disabilities often do not display typical patterns of development, this information becomes even more essential, especially given Yoder's (1990) suggestion that the optimal learning activity for a child with a disability is one that is just slightly ahead of the child's current skills.

Development as a Social Being

The infancy and preschool period is characterized by a central focus on the development of social awareness, social relations, and social competence. This process begins very early with the development of an attachment relationship between infant and parents, and it rapidly expands to include siblings, grandparents, and other significant persons in the infant's life. Gradually, peer relations and friendships begin to emerge, and the preschooler learns many social conventions, identifying the contexts and situations in which specific social skills are needed, expected, or appropriate.

The central nature of social development means that early intervention professionals need to be aware of the powerful nature of the bond between children and their families. Also, many children with disabilities may be delayed in social skills, and will need supportive environments and activities that will enhance social competence. Finally, it is important to recognize that much learning occurs in social contexts, and their importance as opportunities to teach, reinforce, and build on multiple skills should not be overlooked.

Learning Through Experience

Physical maturation accounts for much of the development observed in young children. However, it is through interactions with the environment that learning occurs. As we describe in the remaining chapters of this text, learning can occur in multiple ways; but two fundamental aspects are common to all learning contexts: (a) repeated opportunities to be engaged with stimulating and appropriate learning materials and situations and (b) meaningful feedback. Young children need concrete materials that they can manipulate, explore, and use—materials that are developmentally appropriate, safe, and interesting. Children also need to know that their behavior has an effect and whether it is appropriate. This feedback can occur in many forms, and it can come from things as well as from people. The toy makes a noise when shaken, the puzzle looks completed, the pants stay pulled up, the adult smiles, the other child complies with the request. Adults working with young children with disabilities need to be aware of the critical importance of designing environments in which children receive frequent and appropriate feedback. Ideally feedback comes from the natural results of behavior; but in working with children with disabilities, early intervention professionals also need to use more direct forms of both instruction and feedback. Examples and strategies are discussed in chapters 5 and 6.

Motivation to Learn

Most children seem to be highly motivated to learn and to become proficient at activities. Some have argued that children are born with an intrinsic need or desire to master the environment (e.g., White, 1959) or that they are innately curious. Others have suggested that children's behavior is a function of experience, that it is imitative, for example. At any rate, many children certainly appear to be motivated by the desire to master activities or tasks. A good example of this is the child who puts together a six-piece puzzle, claps or smiles when it is done, dumps it out, and puts it together again.

Adults working with young children should be aware of and capitalize on children's motivation to learn, and should be aware that such learning—frequently initiated by the child—takes time and that feedback is often a crucial element for success. Adults should also recognize that many children with disabilities may not be so strongly motivated to learn, may have had more failure experiences, and may initially need support in both engaging in activities and successfully completing them.

Behavioral Co-variation

The ecological model assumes and predicts that changes in one part of a system will produce changes in other parts of the system. The child's behavior is part of such a system (Rogers-Warren, 1984). Learning a new behavior, for example, may lead to a decrease in problem behaviors—learning to play independently may lead to a decrease in disruptive and stereotypic behaviors. Or learning a maladaptive or problem behavior may lead to decreases in adaptive patterns of responding—learning that tantrums are a successful means of escaping difficult situations may result in a decrease in persistence and a loss of the disposition to take on difficult tasks. Or increasing adaptive behavior may lead to increases in other adaptive responses—learning to play with toys and initiate social interactions may lead to increased interest in and longer interactions with peers. Or changing some problem behaviors (e.g., decreasing self-injurious behaviors) may lead to increases in other problem behaviors such as aggression, crying, and other emotional reactions. Or learning some behaviors may set the stage for learning many other behaviors—learning to imitate the behavior of peers may lead directly to the acquisition of a number of interactive and communicative behaviors.

Such relationships hold important implications for intervention. Teams should recognize that the behaviors they teach children may have positive and negative benefits in other areas of the children's behavior. Professionals should be sensitive to the broad effects of their interventions and should attempt to teach behaviors that will have far reaching positive effects. For example, teaching a child to explore, become engaged with, and master some materials may lead to a durable pattern of responding to new situations. In such cases, the benefits of the instruction exceed the initial objectives in positive and desirable ways.

MICROSYSTEMS

Bronfenbrenner (1977) defines a microsystem as "the complex of relations between the developing person and environment in an immediate setting containing that person" (p. 514). Probably the most common microsystem for young children is the home. However, many young children spend a considerable portion of their time in other settings, such as child care centers or family day care homes. Some children who have or are at risk for disabilities spend a considerable amount of time in hospital or clinic settings. Other settings (e.g., churches, grocery stores,

neighborhoods, playgrounds) are less frequently involved, but still are important in the lives of some children and families. Settings may be distinguished according to their location, the amount of time the child spends in them, the activities they support and materials they provide, and the role the child plays in them (e.g., family member, student, patient) (Bronfenbrenner, 1976).

Knowing that children spend time in a wide array of microsystems adds several skills to the list of qualifications for early interventionists. Here we discuss (a) understanding the influence of environment on behavior; (b) being familiar with the array of typical environments and their characteristics; (c) working with adults in multiple environments to assess their needs and, when appropriate, make environmental modifications; and (d) helping children adapt to environmental demands.

Understanding the Influence of Environment on Behavior

It is an obvious but essential principle that the environment shapes our behavior, thoughts, and feelings in many important ways. The environment dictates the kinds of behaviors that are appropriate and inappropriate, invites or discourages exploration, provides feedback on behavior, and can establish a mood or tone that may range from exciting and enjoyable to boring or scary. A key to effective intervention by any professional is understanding this relationship and recognizing that the environment is both a tool that can be modified for intervention purposes and a factor that must be taken into consideration when setting realistic expectations for change.

Thus, assessment and intervention activities must take into account children's preferences for materials and activities and their styles or patterns of interacting with the environment. They must also consider how variations in environments will influence children's performance and learning. For example, the child's learning to initiate interactions and play cooperatively with peers who have been trained to assist with the child's disabilities may or may not generalize to the family day care setting where peers do not have such training.

Being Familiar with the Array of Typical Environments

A second important skill at the microsystem level is familiarity with the array of typical environments for young children, including an understanding of characteristics shared across settings and those unique to specific settings. As we described in chapter 1, the typical environments within which professionals work include child care centers, homes, developmental and diagnostic evaluation centers, clinics, and hospitals. Chapter 7 presents a more detailed discussion of environmental planning, and environmental considerations are integrated into other chapters of this text as well.

An important point to be made here is that with different environments come different expectations and philosophies with which the professional must seek to establish congruence by modifying her own behavior. This point is illustrated by Gilkerson (1990) in a comparison of institutional functioning style in hospital and early intervention settings. Six variables are suggested to differentiate the two settings. This framework is summarized in Table 3.2. In brief, Gilkerson describes hospitals as settings that have tremendous community respect and support. They are self-contained and set all their own rules for how they will function, and the physician is in charge. They provide an acute, short-term orientation to care, reacting to immediate needs and focusing on the individual patient. Early intervention programs, in contrast, have a longitudinal approach to services, focusing on the individual within the context of the family and

other systems. Early intervention programs must work with multiple agencies and programs to coordinate services, and are based on a symmetrical relationship between professional and client. This example clearly suggests that the hospital and early intervention environments differ in substantial ways and that the skills needed to work in one setting likely will be different from those needed in the other.

Assessing Aspects of Microsystems and Facilitating Change

A third important skill at this level is the ability to assess critical aspects of microsystems and work to facilitate changes that might be needed or desired. The professional might need to assess the environment itself or to document the needs of individuals within the environment. Bailey (1989a) describes considerations, guidelines, and selected strategies for assessing dimensions of home, child care center, and hospital environments. The purpose of such an assessment might be to determine the extent to which an environment is developmentally facilitative, comfortable, and "least restrictive" or normalized. Using this information to change an environment is likely to be a challenging task, however, a task that is best accomplished when it is desired by the adults within the environment and conducted in a collaborative and facilitative fashion (Dunst, McWilliam, & Holbert, 1986).

Another task related to this skill might include the assessment of family needs and resources. Issues and considerations related to family assessment are addressed briefly in chapter 4 and extensively in Bailey and Simeonsson (1988b). However, it is essential to realize that family assessment is likely to be appropriate in the context of early intervention only when it focuses on determining family members' priorities for services or outcomes to be achieved (Bailey, 1991).

TABLE 3.2

A comparison of selected aspects of institutional functioning style in hospitals and early intervention programs

Setting	Orientation and Goals of Care	Management Style	Focus of Services	Basis for Care and Status of Caregivers	Relationship to Other Agencies	Professional-Client Relationship
Hospitals	*Acute,* short-term, medically focused care. Primary goal is to preserve life and physical health.	*Reactive* style that allows for flexible scheduling and immediate responses as needs arise.	The *individual patient* who is ill.	*Medical science* basis for care. Physicians have high social status, social distancing, and high prestige. High degree of technology.	*Vertical* framework; the hospital is a self-contained system that sets its own rules. Stratified, with clearly defined roles and relationships.	A *symmetrical* relationship between professionals (physicians) and patients. Patient has the problem, physician has the solution.
Early Intervention Programs	*Chronic,* long-term, developmentally focused care. Primary goal is to promote development and prevent delays or other problems.	*Proactive* management, long-term approach to problems and needs. More predictable schedule of planned services.	Although the child is the reason early intervention is provided, a *broader systems* approach is emerging.	*Social science* basis for care. Professionals have lower status in the public eye and services are not likely to be "high-tech."	*Horizontal* framework; the program cannot provide all of the needed services, and so interagency collaboration becomes essential.	A *symmetrical* relationship is promoted, with parents serving as primary decision makers.

Note: Summarized from "'Understanding Institutional Functioning Style: A Resource for Hospital and Early Intervention Programs" by L. Gilkerson, 1990, *Infants and Young Children, 2*(3), 22–30.

Finally, professionals may need to assess the needs of other professionals within a specific dimension of a microsystem. For example, a teacher in a day care center may need information from the physical therapist about appropriate positioning techniques for a child with cerebral palsy, or a physician may need information from the social worker about working with families in a culturally sensitive fashion.

Helping Children Adapt to Environmental Demands

In the previous section, the emphasis was on modifying the environment to meet the needs of the child. In some cases, however, the environment cannot realistically be changed, and thus the professional's task becomes one of identifying skills, equipment, or coping strategies to help the child adapt to environmental demands. For example, Jack may need to learn to stay in a center for 15 minutes because that is the standard expectation for all children. Marcellus may need to learn to crawl up a set of stairs if he wants to get to the reading area, because his wheelchair will not fit.

MESOSYSTEMS

The mesosystem consists of "the interrelations among the major settings containing the developing person at a particular point in his or her life" (Bronfenbrenner, 1977, p. 515). For the purpose of this discussion, two major aspects of the mesosystem are critical: intersetting connections and ecological transitions (Brenfenbrenner, 1979). *Intersetting connections* are the linkages that occur within and between the microsystems that influence young children with disabilities and their families. The relationship between parents and professionals is the most common example of such linkage. Other examples are communications among professionals, both within a single microsystem (e.g.,

communication between therapists and teachers in a center-based child care program) and across multiple microsystems (e.g., communication between a diagnostic clinic and the home-based infant intervention program). *Ecological transitions* are the movements from one setting to another. The ease with which such a transition can be made is a function of the quality of the intersetting connections between the systems.

What professional skills are needed at the mesosystem level? Here we describe (a) recognizing potential problems in communicating with parents or other professionals (b) working to establish linkages within and across systems, (c) serving effectively as a team member, (d) facilitating family participation on teams and in decision making; and (e) working to ensure that transitions are smooth and effective.

Recognizing the Potential for Communication Problems

Perhaps the most important skill related to mesosystems is the realization that communication problems between various systems are almost inevitable. Teachers often have difficulty finding out about important events that occur in children's lives outside of the early intervention program. Parents are usually interested in the activities provided in early intervention programs, but they may not have the time or resources to monitor them on a regular basis.

Parent–professional communication often is one of the biggest barriers to collaborative work. Numerous professional behaviors standing in the way of good communication have been identified, some of which are described by Roos (1977) and displayed in Box 3.1. Roos (1977) recommended the following to facilitate productive parent–child interaction.

1 Consider parents as full members of the interdisciplinary team.

BOX 3.1   Some examples of counterproductive parent–professional interactions

Roos (1977) identified eight types of "professional mishandling" that lead to counterproductive parent–professional interactions:

Professional ignorance	Lack of basic information about the child's condition or disability
Professional hopelessness	Communicating a defeatist attitude
Referral ad infinitum	Repeatedly referring the child to yet another specialized assessment
Veil of secrecy	Withholding from parents information believed to be too threatening or uncomfortable
Deaf ear syndrome	Ignoring ideas, requests, or suggestions made by parents
Professional omniscience	Staunch defense of professional opinions and expertise
Professional omnipotence	Assuming that professionals have the wisdom to make important decisions about the destinies of others
Parents as patients	Viewing most parents as being in need of therapy to "accept" their child's diagnosis or alleviate depression

Note: Adapted from "A Parent's View of What Public Education Should Accomplish" by P. Roos, 1977, in *Educational Programming for the Severely and Profoundly Handicapped* (pp. 72–86), E. Sontag (Ed.), Reston, VA: Council for Exceptional Children.

2 Accept and try to understand parents' perspectives through good listening skills.
3 Share all relevant information.
4 Allow families to determine goals for services.
5 Minimize professional jargon.
6 Provide support and encouragement.
7 Don't compete with parents.

Communication problems are also likely to occur for professionals both within and between the various settings that serve children and families. For example, therapists would like to know whether therapeutic goals are being addressed in the classroom, but may not have the time to meet regularly with teachers to discuss possible difficulties implementing therapeutic recommendations. For parents, it is an especially frustrating situation to learn that professionals are not communicating effectively with each other. Parents expect a coordinated system of services, a system that is interactive, communicative, and consistent—a system in which the participants are mutually supportive.

Working to Establish Linkages Within and Across Systems

Given the likelihood that communication problems will occur, what should be done to enhance linkages? This is a challenge because factors such as excessive time demands, limited resources, poor communication skills, territoriality, and distance can serve as significant barriers. Bronfenbrenner (1979) suggests that one key component is the establishment of *supportive links* between systems based on "the growth of mutual trust, positive orientation, goal consensus between settings and an evolving balance of power responsive to action in behalf of the developing person" (p. 214). A variety of means can be used to achieve such links, but three key factors are the frequency, ease, and acceptability of strategies. Communication must be frequent, but also it should be done in the easiest and most natural way possible. Winton and Turnbull (1981) found that parents often preferred informal times and strategies (e.g., arrival and pickup time) rather than formal meetings for communicating about their child's work and progress. Teachers and specialists have developed a variety of creative and informal strategies for sharing information with parents, including exchanging daily journals, sending home sample materials related to activities completed, using a weekly photograph album, and placing lunchtime phone calls. An important guideline is to use procedures that are doable for the professional and that the parents find interesting and useful. Many of the communicative exchanges that occur between families and professionals, dealing as they do with problem situations, can become charged with negative feelings. To alleviate such situations, intervention teams can make concerted and regular efforts to report to parents about positive events and accomplishments in addition to making general comments. Hearing positive things about their children, parents are more likely to entertain positive attitudes toward the communications of professionals. A study by Cadman, Shurvell, Davies, and Bradfield (1984), summarized in Box 3.2, documents the importance of a number of aspects of the decision-making process that enhance the likelihood of good communication and follow-up.

Serving Effectively as a Team Member

Most professionals working in early intervention programs receive very little training in working with team members from other professions (Bailey, Simeonsson, Yoder, &

Huntington, 1990). Yet such work is both mandated by law and necessary if comprehensive and integrated services are to be provided. Serving as an effective team member requires good communication skills, an understanding of group process and group dynamics, and a willingness to listen to and (when appropriate) challenge recommendations or offer alternatives to suggestions raised by others. An effective team has a workable structure and takes an advocacy orientation toward children and families; the members of an effective team engage in regular communication, discussing problems and issues openly, with mutual respect, and sharing decision making.

Involving Parents on Teams and in Decision Making

An important strategy in building linkages between systems is the facilitating of family involvement in decisions about practices that affect their child and that affect the program as a whole. The importance of such an approach has been described in chapter 2, and strategies for involving families in team meetings and decision making related to their own children are described in chapter 4. When encouraged to participate in the decision-making process, parents can gain a broader understanding of the rationale behind goal selection and service delivery and can help shape those decisions in ways that are consistent with their own needs, values, and priorities (Nash, 1990). Such involvement should also reinforce families' feelings of competence and worth.

Ensuring Smooth and Effective Transitions

Bronfenbrenner (1977) discusses the importance of understanding the magnitude of the importance of transitions in the lives of children and families.

Research from many areas suggests that transitions are difficult times for most in-

BOX 3.2   Factors about the decision-making process that facilitate follow-through

What factors influence the extent to which parents or professionals follow through on recommendations made by interdisciplinary teams? This question was the focus of a study by Cadman, Shurvell, Davies, and Bradfield (1984). The study involved a regional consultation team for a 700-square-mile region of Canada. The team conducted comprehensive assessments of children and provided written recommendations to parents and professionals in the children's home communities.

In analyzing compliance, or follow-through on recommendations, the researchers found that the characteristics of the professional, the family, and the child and the content of the recommendations had little effect upon the extent of the follow-through. More influential were the *aspects of the decision-making and consultation process*, such as the following:

• the care the consultant took in listening to the client at assessment
• the adequacy of the consultant's explanation of the reason for the therapy
• the amount of time taken for discussion of the recommendation
• belief in the efficacy of the prescribed therapy
• clarity of roles of other individuals working with the child
• the client's perception of his own adequacy at implementing the specific therapy
• the feasibility of the recommendation
• overall agreement with the perception

This study shows that attitudes and beliefs about intervention goals and strategies play a key role in determining whether they will be implemented. If clients feel that they have been listened to and that their unique perspectives have been considered, they are more likely to follow through.

Note: Adapted from "Compliance in the Community with Consultants' Recommendations for Developmentally Handicapped Children" by D. Cadman, B. Shurvell, P. Davies, and S. Bradfield, 1990, *Topics in Early Childhood Special Education,* 9(4), 91–105.

dividuals, and the research supports Bronfenbrenner's assertion that transitions often have "ripple effects" within systems. For example, when infants leave the home to enter center-based programs, they need to learn new skills, meet and become acquainted with new children, and interact with adults they do not know. Parents may be faced with new transportation responsibilities and meetings about school services, and they may need to be available to support their children during such transitions. The children's school entry may represent a time when some mothers who have stayed at home with their children are forced to begin thinking

about the possibility of returning to work or starting a new career. Hains, Rosenkoetter, and Fowler (1991) describe several commonly expressed concerns about transitions, including the loss of or changes in friendships, changes in services, new labels or eligibility requirements, and concerns about social acceptability. Worthington (1987) suggests that the extent to which transitions disrupt schedules or routines and the number of new decisions they lead to are directly related to the amount of stress they cause.

The significance of transitions is acknowledged by Part H of Public Law 99–457 when it requires that a transition plan be included

---

BOX 3.3   P.L. 99–457 Regulations regarding transition

The Individualized Family Service Plan (IFSP) must describe the steps to support transition at age 3 to preschool services available under Part B or to other appropriate services.
  Steps required include:

• discussions with and training of parents regarding future placements and other matters related to transition
• procedures to prepare the child for changes in service delivery, including help to adjust to and function in a new setting
• with parental consent, transmission of assessment and IFSP information to the local education agency

P.L. 99–457 stresses the importance of flexible interagency agreements, especially if the (*Part H*) lead agency for infant and toddler services differs from the (*Part B*) lead agency for preschool services, to ensure that gaps in services will not occur.

---

as a part of the Individualized Family Service Plan for infants and toddlers with disabilities—although this requirement only relates to the child's transition at age 3 from infant to preschool program. A summary of the regulations regarding this component of the IFSP is included in Box 3.3. In reality, a number of other transitions may occur during the infant and preschool period, transitions from hospital to home (Bruder & Walker, 1990), into the handicapped service system, for home-based to center-based programs, from preschool to kindergarten (Conn-Powers, Ross-Allen, & Holburn, 1990), and from specialized to mainstreamed programs (Rule, Fiechtl, & Innocenti, 1990) or (in the other direction) from mainstreamed to specialized programs. The importance of transitions *within* a program also should not be overlooked, such as when a child moves to a new class, begins with a new teacher, changes schedules or routines, or simply changes from one activity to another.

Thus transitions are critical times for children and families, and professionals need skills that will ensure that such transitions are as smooth and effective as possible. We provide some further suggestions regarding support during transitions in Box 3.4 and in the following listing.

1 The professional should view transitions as processes involving multiple components, and thus requiring multiple support strategies. Fowler (1980) suggests eight strategies for the early intervention professional—using a transition coordinator, visiting the public schools, observing in the new classrooms, meeting with the preschool staff, meeting with parents, working with placement specialists, encouraging flexible and gradual transitions, and providing ongoing support services.

2 Parents should be involved in the transition process, with a special focus on identifying their concerns and providing services to help answer their questions and satisfy their needs. (Winton, Turnbull, & Blacher, 1984)

3 Interagency agreements and transition policies should be developed and supplemented by a formal, individualized transition plan for each child and family. (Noonan & Kilgo, 1987)

4 The professional should identify the skills children will need for success in subse-

BOX 3.4   Some suggestions regarding support during transitions

1 Some form of anticipatory assessment is important in order to identify recent critical events, upcoming transitions, and the extent to which families want assistance or support.
2 How family members *perceive* an event is perhaps more important than the event itself.
3 Exercise caution to prevent assessment activities from actually creating a problem.
4 Transitions usually are extended processes rather than one-time events.
5 Parent involvement in planning and implementing a successful transition plan maximizes its success.
6 An individualized approach to transition planning is needed.
7 Interagency cooperation will be needed at many different levels.
8 Part of transition planning may include new skills or information for children and families.
9 Be careful not to be completely future-oriented in providing services for young children.
10 Evaluate the effectiveness of decisions made and strategies tried.

quent environments and, further, should assess each child's readiness to perform those skills and the extent to which transition environments are willing and able to accommodate to each child's special needs. (Polloway, 1987; Salisbury & Vincent, 1990; Vincent et al., 1980)

EXOSYSTEMS

Bronfenbrenner (1977) defines an exosystem in the following manner.

An exosystem is an extension of the mesosystem embracing other specific social structures, both formal and informal, that do not themselves contain the developing person but impinge upon or encompass the immediate settings in which that person is found, and thereby influence, delimit, or even determine what goes on there. These structures include the major institutions of the society, both deliberately structured and spontaneously evolving, as they operate at a concrete local level. They encompass, among other structures, the world of work, the neighborhood, the mass media, agencies of government (local, state, and national), the distribution of goods and services, communication and transportation facilities, and informal social networks. (p. 515)

Any number of examples of important elements of the exosystem can be identified in the context of early intervention—the various local, state, and federal agencies that could provide services, advocacy groups, neighborhood and community organizations, churches, and informal supportive networks of friends, neighbors, and extended family members. For the early intervention professional, we can describe four skills related to work at the level of the exosystem: (a) being aware of the array of programs and services; (b) providing case management services; (c) recognizing and using informal support systems; and (d) involving families in decisions about program practices. Finally in this section we discuss the importance of interagency collaboration.

Being Aware of the Array of Programs and Services

By definition, the exosystem encompasses a potentially broad array of programs and services. It is hard enough for professionals to be aware of these services; it is a virtually impossible task for families. One of the needs most frequently expressed by families is for information about services currently available for their children as well as for services their children might receive in the future (Bailey & Simeonsson, 1988a; Bailey, Blasco, & Simeonsson, in press). Thus professionals have a special responsibility for learning about existing resources and services. Because of the potentially broad array of programs, interagency coordination is a mandated component of Part H of Public Law 99–457. The law also requires that each state maintain a central directory that includes a description of the early intervention services that are available and a listing of other resources (including subject-matter experts) and of any demonstration projects being conducted in the state. This directory, according to the law, should be accessible to parents and professionals and should be updated on a regular basis. Also, such a directory should facilitate long-term planning by identifying gaps in resources or instances of service duplication (Mayfield-Smith, Yajnik, & Wiles, 1990).

At the local level, several types of resources are worth mentioning. Many families, for example, have needs for babysitting, respite, or day care services, and finding a program that will serve a child with special needs, especially one with a severe disability, severe behavior problems, or substantial medical needs, can be a challenge. Resources that professionals should be aware of include typical day care centers, family day homes, respite care programs, home-health nurses, and capable and willing baby-sitters.

The early intervention professional should also know about providers of social-emotional support. Many families would like opportunities to discuss their feelings and frustrations with others besides early intervention professionals; and besides friends, neighbors, or extended family members, several other resources may be available. Specialized support groups and parent organizations can often fulfill families' needs,

especially when their children have diagnosed syndromes. Such organizations include the Association for Retarded Citizens, the Learning Disability Association, and the Down Syndrome Association. Although many of these organizations have local chapters, often such groups are not readily accessible. A large national movement today centers on parent-to-parent programs. Professionals should be prepared to help families start such groups; and professionals should realize that once started such groups usually function better if they are run by and for parents. Reading material about other children and families in similar circumstances is also helpful for many families, and professionals may provide families with or refer them to, for example, newsletters from parent organizations, magazines such as *Exceptional Parent,* or books describing personal family experiences. Some families may have a need for professional counseling services, and early intervention professionals should be aware of local psychologists, psychiatrists, social workers, and other counselors who are trained and experienced in working with families of children with special needs.

Also at the exosystem level are other professional programs and services besides those provided directly by the early intervention program. Depending upon the community, providers of such programs and services may include local parks and recreation departments, public transportation systems, public health services, libraries, physicians, dentists, therapy clinics, musical organizations, and museums. Increasing awareness of the special needs of persons with disabilities has forced many such service providers to examine the accessibility of their services and to provide special services for persons who need them.

Finally, professionals should be aware of the array of support programs and services available for families whose financial resources are limited—for example, food stamps, public housing, Head Start, job counseling programs. Services specialized for children with disabilities are provided by Medicaid and by sources that pay for equipment such as wheelchairs, hearing aids, and glasses.

Providing Case Management Services

Being aware of existing programs, services, and financial resources is one component of a broader service generally referred to as *case management* or service coordination. Although case management involves a large number of possible roles, its fundamental purpose is to help clients gain access to services. The assumption underlying case management is that service delivery systems are extraordinarily complex and that access to services often is difficult to achieve. Recognition of the special challenges faced by the parents who have only recently learned of their child's disability or risk status and have had little if any experience with service systems led to the requirement in P.L. 99–457 that case management services be available at no charge under the Part H program for infants and toddlers. Case management is defined in the Part H regulations as an activity designed to "assist and enable a child eligible under this part and the child's family to receive the rights, procedural safeguards, and services that are authorized to be provided under the State's early intervention program" (Sec. 303.6 [a][1]). According to the regulations, case managers are responsible for the following activities:

1 coordinating the performance of evaluations and assessments
2 facilitating and participating in the development, review, and evaluation of Individualized Family Service Plans (IFSPs)
3 helping families identify available service providers
4 coordinating and monitoring the delivery of available services

5 informing families of the availability of advocacy services
6 coordinating with medical and health providers
7 facilitating the development of transition plans for children moving to preschool services

The success of service coordination depends upon several factors. The law requires that case managers know the eligibility requirements for infants and toddlers, know Part H and the regulations, and be aware of the services available and the system of paying for services. Weil, Zipper, and Rounds (1990) suggest that case managers must also value families, respect families' rights and capabilities, accept variation across families, be able to communicate well, and be able to facilitate interprofessional collaboration. Also, the system must be set up to ensure that case managers can operate effectively. Bailey (1989b) describes three aspects of the ecology of case management. First is the extent to which case management services are valued by clients and other professionals, as well as by case managers themselves. Second is the administrative support for and assignment of case management services. Often case managers are overworked and function with inadequate resources. In some communities multiple case management systems exist, creating yet another complex layer of bureaucracy. Finally, the authority or clout of case managers influences their ability to function (Schwartz, Goldman, & Churgin, 1982).

It is essential that states and local communities develop functional service coordination systems that are consistent with the needs of families and with the services that are potentially available. Likely to be required is a systematic planning process, such as the sample process, suggested by Weil, Zipper, and Rounds (1990), displayed in Figure 3.2.

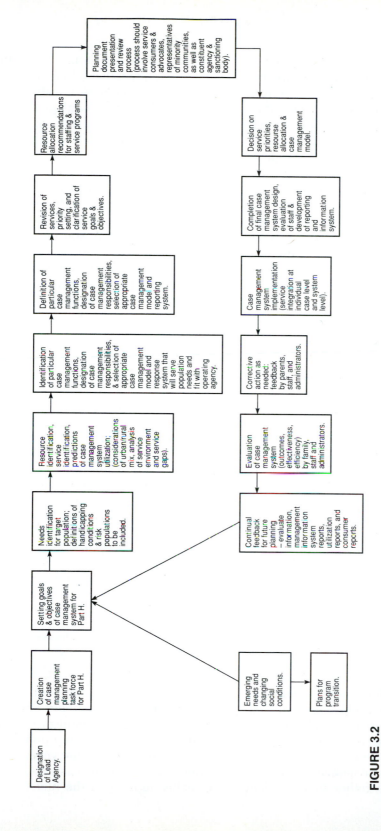

FIGURE 3.2

Process for developing a case management system
for Part H of P.L. 99–457

Adapted from Weil, 1985.

The law only requires that service coordination be available for families of infants and toddlers. The hope is that these services will be so good that by the time their children are three, families will be very familiar with the service delivery systems and will no longer need case management services. Such hope, however, will not always become reality. Thus early intervention professionals working in preschool programs should be aware that the principles and guidelines underlying service coordination may be useful across the age span—that is, also for preschoolers and older children.

Recognizing and Using Informal Support Systems

An important but often overlooked aspect of family and child support is the array of informal resources and supports available for many families. As professionals, we tend to think only about the services that professionals can offer. This is unfortunate—while professionals come and go, informal support systems are likely to be more enduring. Potential sources of informal support include spouses, in-laws, co-workers, social organizations, churches, and friends and neighbors.

One example of useful informal support services comes from the research on the role of religion and religious organizations in providing support for children with disabilities and their families. Religion can provide a framework for personal support as parents try to answer existential questions about their children's disabilities (Heifetz, 1987). Religious groups—primarily local synagogues or churches—can also provide families with social-emotional and instrumental support. Clergy may provide counseling, fellow members friendship, and staff child care during worship services and other activities. Recent studies have shown that religious parents are more likely to describe their children as opportunities rather than burdens

(Weisner, Beizer, & Stolze, 1991); the studies have also shown that religious beliefs and involvement in religious rituals are associated with positive coping strategies for many families (Pargament, Ensing, Falgout, Olsen, Reilly, Van Haitsma, & Warren, 1990). In a study of nearly 1,000 parents whose children have serious emotional disorders, Friesen (1989) found that religion was reported as an important source of coping for many families; in fact, 27 percent said that religion was their most important source of support.

Dunst, Trivette, and Deal (1988) argue for a model of early intervention that focuses on "enabling and empowering" families to draw on informal (and, when necessary, formal) supports to meet needs.

The help giver does not mobilize resources on behalf of the help seeker, but rather creates opportunities for the help seeker to acquire competencies that permit him or her *to mobilize sources of resources* and support necessary to cope, adapt, and grow in response to life's many challenges. (p. 44)

They provide a number of guidelines—displayed in Box 3.5—for help givers that are consistent with this model. They emphasize that this model is often difficult for professionals to implement because it requires that they structure services in a way that will lead to their not being needed anymore. But the fostering of independence is one of the ultimate goals of early intervention.

Involving Families in Decisions about Program Practices

A final skill useful for work at the exosystem level of the early intervention ecology is the ability to involve parents and other caregivers in decisions about program practices. Usually professionals and policy makers determine the policies that govern the services provided by public agencies. There is increasing support in the literature, however,

---

BOX 3.5   Guidelines for providing help

1 Help is most useful when the help giver is positive and proactive.

2 Help is more likely to be favorably received if the help giver offers help rather than waits for it to be requested.

3 Help is more effective when the help giver allows the locus of decision making to rest clearly with the help seeker.

4 Help is more effective if the aid and assistance provided by the help giver are normative and do not infer deviance or undue variations.

5 Help is maximally effective when the aid and assistance provided by the help giver are congruent with the help seeker's appraisal of his or her problem or need.

6 Help is most likely to be favorably received when the response costs of seeking and accepting help do not outweigh the benefits.

7 Help is more likely to be favorably received if it can be reciprocated and the possibility of "repaying" the help giver is sanctioned and approved but not expected.

8 Help is more likely to be beneficial if the help seeker experiences immediate success in solving a problem or meeting a need.

9 Help is more effective if the help giver promotes the family's use of natural support networks and neither replaces or supplants them with professional networks.

10 Help is more likely to promote positive functioning when the help giver conveys a sense of cooperation and joint responsibility (partnership) for meeting needs and solving problems.

11 Help is most likely to be beneficial if the help giver promotes the help seeker's acquisition of effective behaviors that decrease the need for help.

12 Help is more likely to be beneficial if the help seeker perceives improvement and sees him or herself as the responsible agent for producing the change.

Note: From *Enabling and Empowering Families: Principles and Guidelines for Practice* (pp. 94–96) by C. Dunst, C. Trivette, and A. Deal, 1988, Cambridge, MA: Brookline Books.

---

for consumer participation in decision making about agency policies and practices. In the public school literature, for example, some approaches are being tested in which parents are involved in decisions about how programs are run (Kowalski, 1986).

Bronfenbrenner (1979) argues that consumer involvement is necessary because it maximizes the likelihood that resources will be responsive to the needs of clients. Katan and Prager (1986) suggest that consumer involvement in decisions about program practices is warranted for at last four reasons. First, such participation fosters the notion of equality or symmetry between service providers and service recipients. Second, partic-

ipation in decision making may lead to greater ownership of change and increase the likelihood that change will occur. Third, those who participate in the process may have greater feelings of self-esteem if they feel their opinions are valued. Finally, Katan and Prager suggest that consumers have a right to influence the agencies that directly affect some aspect of their lives. As Burke (1968) argued, "citizens *should* share in decisions affecting their destinies. Anything less is a betrayal of our democratic tradition" (p. 287).

In early intervention, the focus of consumer involvement has primarily been on increasing the rights and roles of parents in

---

BOX 3.6   Consumer involvement in decisions about program practices

As early intervention programs attempt to become more family-centered in their work, they are undergoing a process of self-examination and a rethinking of program policies and procedures. Involving parents in this change seems logical, since they are the primary recipients of these services and will be most affected by any decisions.

What happens if parents are included in this process? To answer this question, Bailey, Buysse, Smith-Bonahue, and Elam (in press) evaluated two decision-making workshops, one that parents were invited to attend along with professionals and one attended only by professionals. The workshops were organized around the key questions described in Box 2.1. Parents attended all aspects of the one workshop, were encouraged to express opinions or concerns at any time, and were asked to participate in discussion related to setting goals for change in program policies and practices.

Data from four sources—pre- and post-workshop ratings of current and desired practices, the verbal behavior of participants during the workshops, surveys of participants' perceptions, and an analysis of decisions made during the workshops—were used to assess the effects and perceptions of consumer involvement in program-level decisions. Results indicate that parent presence influenced the extent to which professionals perceived a need for change in program practices. Parents and professionals who experienced parent presence were positive about the experience, and professionals who attended the workshop without parents felt strongly that parents should have been there.

Note: Adapted from "The Effect and Perceptions of Parent Involvement in Program Decisions About Family-Centered Practices" by D. B. Bailey, V. Buysse, T. M. Smith-Bonahue & J. Elam (in press), *Evaluation and Program Planning.*

---

making decisions about the services that they and their children receive. Involving parents in making decisions about broader program policies is still a challenging task. Recent research by Bailey, Buysse, Smith-Bonahue, and Elam (in press), however, demonstrates a number of positive outcomes that could result from greater parent involvement. A summary of that study is provided in Box 3.6.

Interagency Collaboration

Many different agencies have responsibilities for supporting children and families. Unfortunately, these services often are not very well coordinated. In recognition of this fact, Public Law 99–457, Part H, mandates that states develop a program of services that is statewide, coordinated, and interagency in focus. The law allows each state to choose a lead agency for its infant and toddler program, an agency that could be different from the state's department of education. Because federal funds will not cover the costs of early intervention services, collaborative pooling of resources and services is necessary.

Peterson (1991) suggests five critical aspects of a coordinated interagency system. First, the state's lead agency must establish a leadership style and procedures that facilitate and promote collaboration. A strong Interagency Coordinating Council and a commitment to trust and open communication are fundamental to this process. Second, a comprehensive child-find and referral system is needed so that children can be identified for any of the relevant programs offered by the state. Third, case management and IFSP development procedures must be developed so that children and families have access to the same array of coordinated services, regardless of the point at which they enter the system. Fourth, personnel policies need to be established in such a fashion as to facilitate rather than impede cross-agency service coordination. Finally, formal interagency agreements are needed in order to specify the goals, processes, and procedures for interagency collaboration.

MACROSYSTEMS

The final level of Bronfenbrenner's (1977) ecological model is the macrosystem:

A macrosystem refers to the overarching institutional patterns of the culture or subculture, such as the economic, social, educational, legal, and political systems, of which micro-, meso- and exosystems are the concrete manifestations. Macrosystems are conceived and examined not only in structural terms but as carriers of information and ideology that, both explicitly and implicitly, endow meaning and motivation to particular agencies, social networks, roles, activities, and their interrelationships. What place or priority children and those responsible for their care have in such macrosystems is of special importance in determining how a child and his or her caretakers are treated and interact with each other in different types of settings. (p. 515)

In the context of early intervention, macrosystem variables include legislation, court decisions, prevailing societal attitudes, and ethical/moral principles and issues. Here we describe four broad skills related to work at the macrosystem level: (a) knowing relevant laws and the rationale behind each; (b) recognizing the value base underlying early intervention; (c) resolving ethical dilemmas; and (d) serving as an advocate for appropriate and high-quality services.

Knowing Relevant Laws and the Rationale Behind Each

Federal and state legislation is heavily involved in shaping early intervention services, just as legislation is involved in shaping other special services for persons with disabilities. The laws are important because they stand as a statement of national or state policy (Gallagher, Trohanis, & Clifford, 1989). They also establish the right to services, provide financial support, specify who is eligible for services, and describe essential service system characteristics.

The most important federal legislation relevant to early intervention is, of course, Public Law 99–457. Every professional working in early intervention programs should be thoroughly familiar with this law and its provisions. Several comments are relevant, however. First, almost every law results in a set of regulations regarding how the law is to be implemented. Usually these regulations are written by the state or federal agency responsible for implementing the law. Thus knowledge of the law itself is insufficient, because the regulations provide the details necessary to clarify the law and facilitate implementation. All regulations pertaining to federal laws are printed in the *Federal Register*. For example, the final regulations for Part H of P.L. 99–457, pertaining to infants and toddlers with disabilities, appeared in the June 22, 1989 edition of the *Federal Register*.

Professionals should also be aware that federal legislation often mandates that state legislatures take some action. For example, P.L. 99–457 mandated that states had to assure that all children with disabilities ages 3 to 5 years must be provided a free and appropriate public education. Many states had to pass new laws in order to make this mandate a reality. Another example: In Part H, the law describes three categories of children that can be served but leaves it to the states to set specific criteria for each category. State laws, of course, are also likely to be insufficient for implementation; thus the relevant state agencies must develop regulations and procedures describing how the law is to be implemented.

Finally, professionals should be aware that despite the presence of federal laws, federal regulations, state laws, and state regulations, many aspects of professional practice in early intervention are subject to interpretation. Thus memoranda providing further clarification often are issued by departments. In some cases parents must go to the legal system to get a court ruling regarding interpretation of legislative acts. In reality, there is likely to be considerable variability at the local level in the implementation of laws and the provision of services. In some cases such variability is appropriate because it reflects an expression of services provided according to individual needs or local philosophy. In other cases, however, the laws may not be implemented as intended.

Recognizing the Value Base
Underlying Early Intervention

Sometimes an empirical justification is offered for providing early intervention services. We argue, for example, that early intervention should be provided because it reduces the need for future special services, prevents problems from occurring, enhances developmental progress, and supports families. The same arguments are used to support specific practices. For example, a particular therapeutic technique is suggested based on the assumption that it is more effective than another.

The empirical basis for early intervention is fundamentally important, but inadequate. More research is needed and we will continually be asking what is the best way to provide services. Professionals working in early intervention programs, however, should also recognize that there is a strong *value* justification for early intervention. From this perspective, services are provided and service decisions made in part on the basis of what we believe to be good or right, regardless of whether data exist to empirically justify our decisions.

This tendency is evidenced in the original decision to provide services for young children with disabilities. The decision was heavily based on the assumption that each infant, toddler, preschooler, and family has enough value to have the right to early intervention services. They have value simply because they are human, and this value is not tied to how much they can do for society or how little they take from it. The young child with profound mental retardation has the same value as a gifted child. These rights are evidenced in the Constitution, federal and state laws, and court decisions. Procedural safeguards exist to ensure that these rights not be denied, and professionals should be aware of parents' rights and should help parents be aware of them. Turnbull and Turnbull (1991) demonstrate that the guidelines and procedural safeguards for infants and toddlers may be different from those for preschoolers; thus professionals will need to be aware of the implications of these discrepancies and inform parents of them.

The value base for early intervention is also evidenced in some decisions about program practices. For example, mainstreaming and placement in the least restrictive environment are articulated as desirable goals for every child. Age-appropriate materials, normalized environments and experiences, parent involvement in decision making, and the provision of family support represent other decisions about service delivery that have a strong value base.

In many cases, when parents and professionals disagree, the source of that disagreement is a difference between the values of the professional and those of the family

(Aponte, 1985; Bailey, 1987). Kaiser and Hemmeter (1989) state that

Values are the basis of the critical constructs that influence the choices offered to families as well as the general approach taken toward family intervention. Values mediate the choices interveners make about the purpose, form, and desirable outcomes of family intervention. The operative values that shape the decisions about family interventions may be those of the intervener, of the agency employing the intervener, or some combination of both. (p. 75)

Resolving Ethical Dilemmas

Because of the value base for early intervention, it is inevitable that early intervention professionals will face questions about ethical practice. Bryant, Lyons, and Wasik (1990) provide a helpful discussion of ethical issues faced by professionals who provide home-based services. Drawing on Reamer's (1990) guidelines for resolving ethical dilemmas, they recommend that professionals recognize the inevitability of ethical dilemmas and prepare to address them. Most professional organizations (e.g., the Council for Exceptional Children, the American Psychological Association, the American Occupational Therapy Association) have developed standards for ethical professional practice. However, many situations will arise for which there are no clear answers. In such cases, Reamer's (1990) guidelines and the discussion by Bryant et al. (1990) should prove helpful.

The first guideline puts the well-being of the family above following rules or avoiding threats to "additive" goods (goods and services that go beyond basic goods such as life, health, food, and shelter). For example, if parents told a professional in confidence that they were not administering a needed seizure-control medicine to their child because they did not believe in it, then the professional could violate the parents' con-

fidentiality because the health and welfare of the child is more important. Reamer's second guideline, dealing with cases related to individual freedoms, states that a person's right to freedom is secondary in importance to another's (e.g., a child's) right to basic well-being. If the exercise of some freedom harms the basic well-being of another, then the right to freedom can be sacrificed. For example, a parent has the right to consume alcohol; however, if the entire paycheck is devoted to buying alcohol and the child is going hungry, then the professional has an obligation to act on behalf of the child. Reamer's third guideline balances an individual's right to freedom against his or her own right to basic well-being. A professional should allow a young adult who is in a treatment program for drug abuse to choose to terminate treatment, despite the fact that this might result in danger to her health and life. The professional could argue against the client's decision, but the client reserves the right to make the decision. The key element in such dilemmas is the extent to which the client is informed. Thus, it rarely applies to young children. For example, this guideline could not be used to justify allowing a child to engage in self-injurious behavior as a means of expressing his frustration. The preschool child is not considered an informed decision maker about rights of expression. The fourth guideline states that professionals who voluntarily submit to laws, rules, and regulations forfeit their right to disregard those laws, rules, and regulations. This applies to the codes of conduct of professional associations as well. For example, many programs have a regulation that all volunteers should have TB tests prior to working in the classroom. A teacher could not disregard this policy for the sake of getting help in the classroom. However, nothing in this guideline prohibits the professional from working to change the policy or decision. The fifth guideline gives the professional the freedom to disregard the laws, rules, regulations, and policies if they are in conflict with the well-being of the client. For example, a home-based professional may go to a home and find no adults present and a toddler with disabilities being supervised by her 6-year-old brother. The agency policy may prohibit the professional from entering the home without a parent present, and may prohibit a referral to protective services before the supervisor has been consulted. In this situation, the professional could violate the policy of not entering a home with the parents absent; the well-being of the child is at stake. Also, if the professional made repeated attempts to contact the supervisor, but was unsuccessful, then the policy that no referral be made without supervisory consultation also could be violated—particularly, if the parent was absent for several hours. The sixth guideline deals with the government's ability to tax its citizens to provide for the good of individuals. Bryant et al. (1990) suggest that it also applies to times when professionals use their personal money and property to deal directly with the needs of their clients; however, they suggest that this is not a good practice if it occurs repeatedly.

Professionals in early intervention should recognize that they will undoubtedly be faced with ethical dilemmas, which they should prepare themselves to deal with wisely and in reasoned ways. Personnel training programs should provide training to students in thinking clearly about and resolving ethical dilemmas. Program leaders should examine their policies for instances when the policies put staff members in unnecessary ethical dilemmas. Intervention teams should function as resources to individual team members who find themselves in potential ethical dilemmas. Time should be made available for discussing these issues with the team and for consultation with ex-

perts in ethics. Professionals should recognize that in some instances, rare, we hope, the ethical dilemmas in which they find themselves may involve their fellow team members. Most professional associations have procedures for dealing with these instances. It may be wise for early intervention teams to develop such procedures.

The guidelines articulated by Reamer (1990) provide a set of standards for judging the extent to which interventionists' behavior is ethically defensible. Early intervention programs should encourage discussions about ethics and the cultivation of awareness of the professional codes of ethics as a part of ongoing training.

Serving as an Advocate for Appropriate and High-Quality Services

Finally, we must accept the premise that all young children with disabilities and their families have the right to receive the best intervention services possible, delivered in the most competent manner. All professionals, first of all, have a responsibility for reading the literature and keeping up with best practices as defined by current theory and research. Then also, as we described in chapter 2, professionals have a responsibility to evaluate the services they provide, especially when two or more options seem possible. Finally, professionals need to serve as advocates for best practice rather than minimal services.

SUMMARY

Although this book is primarily about teaching, this chapter argues that to be effective teaching must be consistent with the ecology in which children and families live. Understanding this ecology and *how families perceive this ecology* is therefore an essential part of the process.

Bronfenbrenner's (1976; 1977) ecological model of education and human development was used as the organizing framework for this chapter. The model describes four nested layers of the ecology: microsystem, mesosystem, exosystem, and macrosystem. After looking at the child as in the center of this nest, we have, working outward, examined each layer in turn from the perspective of early intervention services, and we have discussed the professional skills appropriate for working at each system level. This ecological model adds to the complexity of the early interventionist's vocation; and training programs surely need to focus more sharply on understanding the child as a system participant and then on assessing the properties of systems and devising and cultivating approaches appropriate to those properties.

REFERENCES

Aponte, H. J. (1985). The negotiation of values in therapy. *Family Process, 24,* 323–338.

Bailey, D. B. (1987). Collaborative goal-setting with families: Resolving differences in values and priorities for services. *Topics in Early Childhood Special Education, 7*(2), 59–71.

Bailey, D. B. (1989a). Assessing environments. In D. B. Bailey & M. Wolery (Eds.), *Assessing infants and preschoolers with handicaps* (pp. 97–118). Columbus, OH: Merrill.

Bailey, D. B. (1989b). Case management in early intervention. *Journal of Early Intervention, 13,* 120–134.

Bailey, D. B. (1991). Issues and perspectives on family assessment. *Infants and Young Children, 4*(1), 26–34.

Bailey, D. B., Blasco, P., & Simeonsson, R. J. (in press). Needs expressed by mothers and fathers of young children with handicaps. *American Journal on Mental Retardation.*

Bailey, D. B., Buysse, V., Edmondson, R., & Smith, T. M. (in press). Creating family-centered services in early intervention: Perceptions of professionals in four states. *Exceptional Children.*

Bailey, D. B., Buysse, V., Smith-Bonahue, T. M., & Elam, J. (in press). The effects and perceptions of parent involvement in program decisions about family-centered practices. *Evaluation and Program Planning.*

Bailey, D. B., Farel, A. M., O'Donnell, K. J., Simeonsson, R. J., & Miller, C. A. (1986). Preparing infant interventionists: Interdepartmental training in special education and maternal and child health. *Journal of the Division for Early Childhood, 11,* 67–77.

Bailey, D. B., & Simeonsson, R. J. (1988a). Assessing needs of families with handicapped infants. *Journal of Special Education, 22,* 117–127.

Bailey, D. B., & Simeonsson, R. J. (1988b). *Family assessment in early intervention.* Columbus, OH: Merrill.

Bailey, D. B., Simeonsson, R. J., Yoder, D., & Huntington, G. S. (1990). Preparing professionals to serve infants and toddlers with handicaps and their families: An integrative analysis across eight disciplines. *Exceptional Children, 57,* 26–35.

Bell, R. Q. (1968). A reinterpretation of the direction of effects in studies of socialization. *Psychological Review, 75,* 81–95.

Bernheimer, L. P., Gallimore, R., & Weisner, T. S. (1990). Ecocultural theory as a context for the Individual Family Service Plan. *Journal of Early Intervention, 14,* 219–233.

Brim, O. G. (1975). Macro-structural influences on child development and the need for childhood social indicators. *American Journal of Orthopsychiatry, 45,* 516–524.

Bronfenbrenner, U. (1976). The experimental ecology of education. *Educational Research, 5*(9), 5–15.

Bronfenbrenner, U. (1977). Toward an experimental ecology of human development. *American Psychologist, 32,* 513–531.

Bronfenbrenner, U. (1979). *The ecology of human development: Experiments by nature and design.* Cambridge: Harvard University Press.

Bruder, M. B., & Walker, L. (1990). Discharge planning: Hospital to home transitions for infants. *Topics in Early Childhood Special Education, 9*(4), 26–42.

Bryant, D. B., Lyons, C., & Wasik, B. H. (1990). Ethical issues involved in home visiting. *Topics in Early Childhood Special Education, 10*(4), 92–107.

Burke, E. M. (1968). Citizen participation strategies. *Journal of the American Institute of Planning, 34,* 287–294.

Cadman, D., Shurvell, B., Davies, P., & Bradfield, S. (1984). Compliance in the community with consultants' recommendations for developmentally handicapped children. *Developmental Medicine and Child Neurology, 26,* 40–46.

Conn-Powers, M. C., Ross-Allen, J., & Holburn, S. (1990). Transition of young children into the elementary education mainstream. *Topics in Early Childhood Special Education, 9*(4), 91–105.

Dunst, C., McWilliam, R. A., & Holbert, K. (1986). Assessment of preschool classroom environments. *Diagnostique, 11,* 212–232.

Dunst, C., Trivette, C., & Deal, A. (1988). *Enabling and empowering families: Principles and guidelines for practice.* Cambridge, MA: Brookline Books.

Fowler, S. A. (1980). Transition from preschool to kindergarten for children with special needs. In K. E. Allen & E. M. Goetz (Eds.), *Early childhood education: Special problems, special solutions* (pp. 309–334). Baltimore: Aspen.

Friesen, B. J. (1989). *Survey of parents whose children have serious emotional disorders: Report of a national study.* Portland, OR: Research and Training Center on Family Support and Children's Mental Health, Portland State University.

Gabarino, J. (1990). The human ecology of early risk. In S. J. Meisels & J. P. Shonkoff (Eds.), *Handbook of early childhood intervention* (pp. 78–96). Cambridge: Cambridge University Press.

Gallagher, J. J., Trohanis, P. L., & Clifford, R. M. (1989). *Policy implementation and PL 99–457: Planning for young children with special needs.* Baltimore: Paul Brookes.

Gilkerson, L. (1990). Understanding institutional

functioning style: A resource for hospital and early intervention programs. *Infants and Young Children, 2*(3), 22–30.

Hains, A. H., Rosenkoetter, S. E., & Fowler, S. A. (1991). Transition planning with families in early intervention. *Infants and Young Children, 3*(4), 38–47.

Heifetz, L. J. (1987). Integrating religious and secular perspectives in the design and delivery of disability services. *Mental Retardation,* 127–131.

Kaiser, A. P., & Hemmeter, M. C. (1989). Value-based approaches to family intervention. *Topics in Early Childhood Special Education, 8*(4), 72–86.

Katan, J., & Prager, E. (1986). Consumer and work participation in agency-level decision-making: Some considerations of their linkages. *Administration in Social Work, 10,* 79–88.

Kowalski, T. J. (1986). The second coming of community education: Taking the first step. *Contemporary Education, 57,* 194–197.

Mayfield-Smith, K. L., Yajnik, G. G., & Wiles, D. L. (1990). Information and referral for people with special needs: Implications for the Central Directory of Public Law 99–457. *Infants and Young Children, 2*(3), 69–88.

Nash, J. K. (1990). Public Law 99–457: Facilitating family participation on the multidisciplinary team. *Journal of Early Intervention, 14,* 318–326.

Noonan, M. J., & Kilgo, J. L. (1987). Transition services for early age individuals with severe mental retardation. In R. N. Ianacone & R. A. Stodden (Eds.), *Transition issues and directions* (pp. 25–37). Reston, VA: Council for Exceptional Children.

Pargament, K. I., Ensing, D. S., Falgout, K., Olsen, H., Reilly, B., Van Haitsma, K., & Warren, R. (1990). God help me: (I): Religious coping efforts as predictors of the outcomes to significant negative life events. *American Journal of Community Psychology, 18,* 793–824.

Peterson, N. L. (1991). Interagency collaboration under Part H: The key to comprehensive, multidisciplinary, coordinated infant/toddler intervention services. *Journal of Early Intervention, 15,* 89–105.

Polloway, E. A. (1987). Transition services for

early age individuals with mild mental retardation. In R. N. Ianacone & R. A. Stodden (Eds.), *Transition issues and directions* (pp. 11–24). Reston, VA: Council for Exceptional Children.

Powers, M. D. (1988). A systems approach to serving persons with severe developmental disabilities. In M. D. Powers (Ed.), *Expanding systems of service delivery for persons with developmental disabilities* (pp. 1–14). Baltimore: Paul Brookes.

Ramey, C. T., Yeates, K. O., & MacPhee, D. (1984). Risk for retarded development among disadvantaged families: A systems theory approach to preventive intervention. In B. Keogh (Ed.), *Advances in special education* (Vol. 4, pp. 249–272). Greenwich, CT: JAI Press.

Reamer, F. G. (1990). *Ethical dilemmas in social service.* New York: Columbia University Press.

Rogers-Warren, A. K. (1984). Ecobehavioral analysis. *Education and Treatment of Children, 7,* 283–303.

Roos, P. (1977). A parent's view of what public education should accomplish. In E. Sontag (Ed.), *Educational programming for the severely and profoundly handicapped* (pp. 72–86). Reston, VA: Council for Exceptional Children.

Rule, S., Fiechtl, B. J., & Innocenti, M. S. (1990). Preparation for transition to mainstreamed post-preschool environments: Developments of a survival skills curricular. *Topics in Early Childhood Special Education, 9*(4), 78–90.

Salisbury, C. C., & Vincent, L. J. (1990). Criterion of the next environment and best practices: Mainstreaming and integration 10 years later. *Topics in Early Childhood Special Education. 10*(2), 78–89.

Sameroff, A. J., & Chandler, M. J. (1975). Reproductive risk and the continuum of caretaking casualty. In F. D. Horowitz, M. Hetherington, S. Scarr-Salapatek, & G. Siegel (Eds.), *Review of child development research* (Vol. 4, pp. 187–244). Chicago: University of Chicago Press.

Sameroff, A. J., & Fiese, B. (1990). Transactional regulations and early intervention. In S. J. Meisels & J. P. Shonkoff (Eds.), *Handbook of early childhood intervention* (pp. 119–149). Cambridge: Cambridge University Press.

Schwartz, S. R., Goldman, H. H., & Churgin, S. (1982). Case management for the chronic mentally ill: Models and dimensions. *Hospital and Community Psychiatry, 33,* 1006–1009.

Sprunger, L. W., Boyce, W. T., & Gaines, J. A. (1985). Family-infant congruence: Routines and rhythmicity in family adaptation to a young infant. *Child Development, 56,* 564–572.

Thomas, A., & Chess, S. (1977). *Temperament and development.* New York: Bruner/Mazel.

Turnbull, H. R., & Turnbull, A. P. (1991). Procedural safeguards under Part H: How judicial interpretations of Part B may affect Part H. *Journal of Early Intervention, 15,* 80–88.

Vincent, L. J., Salisbury, C., Walter, G., Brown, P., Gruenewald, L. J., & Powers, M. (1980). Program evaluation and curriculum development. In W. Sailor, B. Wilcox, & L. Brown (Eds.), *Methods of instruction for severely handicapped students* (pp. 303–328). Baltimore: Paul Brookes.

von Bertalanffy, L. V. (1968). *General systems theory.* New York: George Brazilles.

Weil, M., Zipper, I. N., & Rounds, K. (1990). *Case management for early intervention programs: Parents and professionals.* Chapel Hill, NC: Carolina Institute for Research on Infant Personnel Preparation, Frank Porter Graham Child Development Center, University of North Carolina at Chapel Hill.

Weisner, T. S., Beizer, L., & Stolze, L. (1991). Religion and families of children with developmental delays. *American Journal on Mental Retardation, 95,* 647–662.

Winton, P. J., & Turnbull, A. P. (1981). Parent involvement as viewed by parents of preschool handicapped children. *Topics in Early Childhood Special Education, 1*(3), 11–20.

Winton, P. J., Turnbull, A. P., & Blacher, J. (1984). *Selecting a preschool: A guide for families of handicapped children.* Austin, TX: PRO-ED.

White, R. W. (1959). Motivation reconsidered: The concept of competence. *Psychological Review, 66,* 297–333.

Worthington, E. L. (1987). Treatment of families during life transitions: Matching treatment to family response. *Family Process, 26,* 295–308.

Yoder, P. J. (1990). The theoretical and empirical basis of early amelioration of developmental disabilities: Implications for future research. *Journal of Early Intervention, 14,* 27–42.

4

Individualized Assessment and Intervention Planning

Jennifer has just turned two. She has been accepted into an early intervention program because she has some delays in speech and communication skills. Her motor development also is of concern, and her physician has made a tentative diagnosis of mild cerebral palsy. Her parents are especially concerned about her mealtime and eating skills. What kinds of experiences would help Jennifer achieve the goals for early intervention described in chapter 2? What should be the specific goals for Jennifer? Should she be in a center-based program or should she be provided home-based services? Who should be responsible for making decisions about intervention goals and strategies?

Questions such as these point to the need for individualized assessment and intervention planning. Such planning is essential for providing services that meet the unique needs of children and families. The purpose of this chapter is to establish the goals for child and family assessment and to describe models and procedures for gathering assessment information.

ASSESSMENT: CHARACTERISTICS AND PURPOSE

Assessment refers to the process of gathering information for the purpose of making a decision. The focus of this chapter is on gathering information in order to plan intervention services for children and families. The traditional approach to assessment is characterized by a reliance on formal testing of children under standard conditions. Testing is conducted exclusively by professionals; a primary emphasis is on determining children's developmental levels, indicated by scores and diagnostic labels. The process also usually focuses on the identification of children's deficits for remedial or therapeutic purposes.

This model of assessment evolved for some good reasons. Professionals possess a great deal of knowledge about the assessment process, developmental sequences, and handicapping conditions, and thus are in a strong position to make decisions about the focus of the assessment process. Tests can provide important information about a child's development relative to that of typical children. There are some advantages to assessment in a controlled setting, the main one being that the results are comparable across children. Also, labeling is necessary for making eligibility and placement decisions, and the identification of deficits is essential if appropriate planning is to occur.

Unfortunately, however, this model of assessment has several major drawbacks. While some of the goals of the assessment process may be achieved, others may be compromised. The process establishes a discrepancy between the knowledge and skills of professionals and those of family members, reinforcing the notion of parental incompetence versus professional expertise. Parents may feel disenfranchised by the process, and instead of a whole team approach to problem-solving, a we–they situation may result. The process may result in goals that are not functional, since professionals often are not aware of the typical environments of individual children and the expectations of those environments for competence. Reports are likely to contain very little information about children's strengths; consequently, intervention plans often focus on remediating deficits rather than building on or reinforcing strengths. Finally, parents may not follow through actively on recommendations, especially if they feel that they have not been a part of the planning process or that their concerns have not been listened to, or if they do not agree with the recommendations that have been made (Cadman, Shurvell, Davies, & Bradfield, 1984).

Solving some of the problems associated

with traditional approaches to child assessment requires that programs and professionals first be explicit about *why* assessments are being conducted and *what* might be achieved through the assessment process. We suggest that the assessment process ought to achieve eight fundamental goals.

1. *Determine eligibility for services and the appropriateness of alternative environments.* Because resources are limited, infants and children must meet particular eligibility criteria to receive services from intervention programs. The question being asked in such assessment is: Does this infant/child meet the criteria specified for receiving services? In many cases, these criteria include the diagnosis of a handicapping condition. For example, infants or toddlers may be eligible for services if they are diagnosed as having cerebral palsy. Diagnostic assessments ask, "Does this infant/child have 'X' disorder/condition, and if so, what is the nature and extent of the condition (e.g., mild vs. severe)?" In other cases, eligibility criteria may include factors related to the risk of displaying developmental delays or some disability (Harbin, Gallagher, & Terry, 1991). As a result, the assessment strategies and procedures are designed to provide information about whether the child has a given condition or whether particular risk factors are present. For example, it may involve a norm-referenced assessment if a language delay is suspected; it may require a neuromotor assessment if cerebral palsy is suspected; and it may require extensive audiological assessment if a hearing loss is suspected.

In addition to determining eligibility, initial assessment should also focus on determining the best placement for children. This decision will likely involve a combination of information about the child's needs and capabilities, the appropriateness of alternative settings, and parent needs and preferences.

Consider the following example. Missy and Justin are 2 years old, have the same diagnosis, have similar patterns of interacting with peers and toys, have similar communication and motor skills, and in many ways appear to be functional twins. This would seem to indicate that they need similar intervention placements. However, assessment of the home environment might lead to a different conclusion. Missy has two older siblings (one in kindergarten and one in fourth grade) and she lives with both her parents. Her father is a well-paid professional and her mother is not employed outside the home. They have frequent and harmonious interactions with both sets of grandparents and several uncles and aunts who live in the area. Further, they have a well established network of friends both from their neighborhood and church. Justin, on the other hand, has three siblings, all under the age of five. They live with their mother who is recently divorced and is the sole support of the family. She also has experienced recurring and draining health problems. She lives in a community far from her extended family, and reports being cut off from all friends and family. While she is eager to provide the most appropriate care and attention possible for Justin, she also reports that she needs a break from the care-giving demands he presents. A cursory assessment of these two family situations suggests that a center-based intervention program may be more important for Justin than for Missy.

2. *Identify developmentally appropriate and functional intervention goals.* Traditional approaches to assessment are likely to identify developmentally appropriate goals for children; they are less likely to identify goals that have a high probability of being useful within the context of specific environments. Strategies are needed that will help the team understand the expectations and requirements for successful adaptation in home, school, and community environments.

3. Identify the unique styles, strengths, and coping strategies of each child. Children vary in preferences for activities and in the ways they respond to environmental stimuli, affection, stress, social overtures, and changes in routines. Each child also has strengths. Sometimes those strengths are relative to the strengths other children (e.g., that of a 3-year-old who is unusually persistent when faced with a difficult problem); in other cases, the strengths may be relative to the child's own skills in other areas (e.g., the strength of a child with a motor impairment who is very sociable). Knowledge of such unique styles and strengths is essential in designing effective individualized intervention plans.

4. Identify parents' goals for their children and their needs for themselves. Traditional assessment often results in professionals telling parents what their child needs to learn or do. Current models emphasize the importance of involving families in the process of identifying goals for their children as well as goals for other family members. When parents are involved in the assessment process, when the focus is on parent-identified needs and priorities, and when all parties seek to understand the demands on and the expectations for the child in typical environments, then intervention goals and plans are more likely to reflect the child's real needs. By broadening the focus of assessment to include family needs, the program moves toward the accomplishment of one of the primary goals of early intervention: providing support for families.

5. Build and reinforce parents' sense of competence and worth. Raising a child is a very personal experience, one that inevitably affects a parent's self-concept. Having a child with a disability is often a challenging experience that tests a parent's sense of competence. The assessment process ought to build and reinforce parents' feelings that they are knowledgeable about their children and that their opinions about the form of assessment and the goals for treatment are valued by professionals. Powell (1981), for example, suggested that professionals frequently react to parents' questions and concerns by providing information. She suggests that this response, while helpful and appropriate to some extent, may foster dependence and reinforce the parents' notion that professionals possess the key to specialized knowledge about their children. As an alternative, Powell suggests helping families resolve their own concerns by suggesting ways for them to gather information about the concern. This tactic may be particularly useful during the assessment process, and may model problem-solving strategies and thereby increase independence and self-sufficiency.

6. Develop a shared and integrated perspective (across professionals and between professionals and family members) on child and family needs and resources. This goal is important because the nature of the assessment process is such that professionals from several different disciplines are involved. While this specialized expertise is important, some models of assessment result in several fragmented views of the child that do not come together in a natural synthesis. The assessment process ought to be structured so that all participants have a shared and integrated perspective that results in a conceptually consistent plan for services.

7. Create a shared commitment to intervention goals. Team members (both professionals and parents) are less likely to follow through on recommendations if they do not agree with them or are not aware of them. The effectiveness of interventions will be enhanced if all persons working with children integrate an array of intervention goals in the interactions they have with them (e.g., if the physical therapist reinforces communication goals, or if the teacher uses appropriate positioning techniques).

8. Evaluate the effectiveness of services for children and families. Finally, assessment ought to be conducted in ways that allow the information to be used as a reference point for evaluating program effectiveness. Goals should be clearly defined, and strategies for documenting their attainment should be specified.

The eight goals listed here represent a significant departure from traditional approaches to child assessment, especially with respect to the role of families in the pro-

cess. Also, these goals suggest that an appropriate assessment model is one that is individualized according to child and family needs, rather than the automatic use of a standard battery. Although many professionals will find it difficult to take this approach, it is likely to make the assessment process more acceptable for families and ought to result in service plans that are more integrated and useful. Some parent comments about the assessment process are displayed in Box 4.1.

Given the goals we have suggested for assessment, what processes, strategies, and procedures should be used? As displayed in Box 4.2, three broad steps are essential: (a) determining the specific goals of assessment for this particular child and family; (b) gathering the desired information regarding child and family needs, and (c) meeting to discuss perspectives, establish goals, iden-

---

BOX 4.1   What a parent says about assessment

Parents often share feelings about experiences they have had with professionals. The following comments are excerpted from an article entitled "Notes to the Experts from the Parent of a Handicapped Child."

• The most important suggestion I can offer is to put yourself in my place.
• See my child in more than one dimension. Remember that my child is a person whom I love. You evaluate along one scale, but I cherish things that are on no scale. Treat my child as a many-faceted human being, not just a one-dimensional problem with a single label.
• Judge my child in terms of his or her own progress.
• Value my comments about my child. In general, the parent is the real expert. Listen to me. Give me time to speak. Create an environment where I feel comfortable enough to speak.
• Speak plainly.
• Consider my child as part of a family.
• Distinguish between fact and opinion.
• Steer me toward solutions and resources. Do not just give me a diagnosis and send me on my way.
• Tell me about other families in similar situations.
• Provide me with some ray of hope.

Note: From "Notes to the Experts from the Parent of a Handicapped Child" by R. Alexander and P. Tompkins-McGill, 1987, _Social Work_, 361–362.

BOX 4.2   Steps in the assessment and intervention planning process

Step 1 Determine the goals for assessment.
   a. Decide what broad goals need to be achieved.
   b. Find out what parents want from the assessment process.
   c. Determine parent preferences about participating in assessment.
   d. Determine what professionals want/need from the assessment process.
   e. Conduct team-based planning to determine specific assessments needed.

Step 2 Gather desired information regarding child and family needs.
   a. Use multiple methods and procedures to get the picture of needs across settings.
   b. Use techniques likely to build a shared and holistic view of child and family rather than a fragmented view.

Step 3 Meet to discuss perspectives, establish goals, identify resources, and determine needed services.
   a. Use formats and procedures that encourage open discussion and parent participation.
   b. Integrate information and priorities across professions and between professionals and parents.
   c. Determine child and family needs and resources.
   d. Establish individual goals for child and family.
   e. Identify existing resources related to goals.
   f. Specify services needed to achieve goals.
   g. Design a service plan.
   h. Determine strategies for assessing goal attainment.

---

tify resources, and determine services. We devote the remainder of this chapter to a discussion of the issues and procedures related to each of these steps.

DETERMINING INDIVIDUALIZED GOALS FOR CHILD AND FAMILY ASSESSMENT

The first step in the assessment process is to determine what is needed from it. In other words, what do all of the participants want as an end result of assessment activities? The answer to this question ought to shape an individualized assessment plan. At least five activities are likely to be important in achieving this step: identifying the broad goals to be achieved, finding out what parents want from the assessment process, de-

termining parent/caregiver preferences for participation, identifying professional goals, and planning specific assessments.

Identifying the Broad Goals to be Achieved

The first activity is to determine the broad purpose of assessment *for this particular child and family*. The eight goals described above provide an important beginning for this process. It is likely that goals 5 and 6 (building parents' sense of competence and worth and developing an integrated perspective on child and family needs) will be important in the context of any assessment activity. The relative importance of the other goals might vary according to the child's age and previous history and the kinds of decisions that must be made.

For example, if a child has just been referred to a program, the primary goals would likely be determining eligibility for services, making a diagnosis, and possibly making some recommendations regarding alternative intervention environments. In this case, the team is likely to use screening procedures in some areas and diagnostic procedures in others. A *screening* procedure is a short, economical, easily administered measure designed to determine whether a more detailed evaluation is needed (Meisels & Provence, 1989; Wolery, 1989a). For instance, a set of simple procedures (e.g., ringing a bell, calling a child's name, etc.) might be used to screen for possible hearing impairment. If a problem is suspected, a more thorough diagnostic evaluation is needed. A *diagnostic* procedure refers to the verification of a particular problem or condition. Usually a diagnosis is made on the basis of norm-referenced tests, laboratory procedures, and clinical judgment. A *norm-referenced* test is one in which the child's performance in response to standardized procedures and materials is compared with a normative group consisting of other children of the same age.

For another child, the primary focus of assessment will be on determining the best intervention plan. The determination of goals and services is usually based broadly on observations of behavior, parent interviews, and the use of assessment instruments that are specifically designed to assist in the development of treatment programs. Screening tests are not appropriate for goal selection because they were not designed for that purpose. They are likely to include only a sampling of skills rather than a thorough coverage, and may include items that are not appropriate instructional targets. Despite widespread acceptance of the limitations of screening measures, however, Johnson and Beauchamp (1987), in a survey of preschool special education teachers, found that 20 percent of the respondents used screening tests to develop educational programs.

Although norm-referenced measures may be used to help plan educational programs, they were not developed with this as their primary function. Determining a child's developmental level requires the selection of test items that meet rather rigid statistical standards. The instructional relevance of items on norm-referenced tests necessarily has been only a secondary consideration in item selection, and thus these measures should be used with caution in specifying instructional targets. Their utility lies in the developmental milestones and sequences included; their limitations are lack of information about how the child functions in typical environments and inability to identify the skills needed in those environments.

If the broad goal of assessment is to evaluate the effectiveness of services for children and families, at least three strategies should be used. First, when appropriate, follow-up test data can show a child's developmental progress on a standardized measure relative to other children or relative to an established curriculum. Second, the extent to which child and family goals have been attained should be documented (Simeonsson, Bailey, Huntington, & Brandon, 1991). Finally, parent and professional satisfaction with the service options provided Miltenberger (1990) and the validation of treatment outcomes through clinical or social judgment (Wolf, 1978) are essential.

Determining Parent Goals for Assessment

Once the broad goals for assessment have been determined, the next activity should be determining what parents want or expect from the assessment process. Some families want diagnostic information, scores, or predictions about what their child will be able to do at some point in the future. Some may want to know why their child behaves in a certain way or cannot do specific skills. Some want to know about specific developmental domains and others simply want an overall intervention plan. In some cases, parents may not have positive feelings about the assessment process at all, resenting the time that it takes or its formality, or simply feeling uncertain what it may say about their child. Understanding how different families approach the assessment process would help professionals design approaches that are sensitive to family concerns and that seek answers to questions families are asking.

Determining parent goals for assessment is probably best done through discussion and exploration of concerns and priorities, although a rating scale or form such as those described by Kjerland and Kovach (1990) may possibly be used. In this context, professionals should begin by asking open-ended questions regarding parent goals for the assessment process. Also, professionals should explore family members' feelings about assessment, especially to alert the team to families who have serious misgivings. At this time it is important to explain and to give the rationale for the assessment procedures usually conducted. Although some assessments may be required by state or local regulations, others are usually optional; asking parents if they feel these optional assessments would be appropriate conveys a sense of trust and respect. In addition to determining parent goals for child assessment, the professional can also ask at this time about factors such as the best time and place to conduct assessments in order to ensure the child's optimal performance.

Parents should also be given the opportunity to express their preferences regarding family assessment. Although Public Law 99–457 only describes family assessment in the context of programs for infants and toddlers, it is an important activity for all early childhood specialists. Bailey (1991) defines *family assessment* as "the ongoing and interac-tive process by which professionals gather information in order to determine family priorities for goals and services." The activities described above fit within this definition of family assessment. Families may also have needs for or desire services that extend beyond specific goals for their children, and they should be given the opportunity to express those needs. Bailey and Blasco (1990), for example, found that parents were very positive in their ratings of a survey of family needs, but most (82%) felt that parents should be given the opportunity to share this information *only if they choose to do so.* Thus, at this point in the process, parents should be told that the early intervention program has a broad mission that includes family support as one component. Surveys, open-ended discussions, and other strategies described later in this chapter could be offered as options that parents might view as helpful either now or sometime in the future.

Determining Parent Preferences Regarding Roles in the Assessment Process

Typically assessments have been conducted by professionals. Yet many parents may want to play some role in the assessment process. Since families will vary in this regard, another important activity is to determine the types of roles they would like to play. At least four broad kinds of roles could be played by parents: receiver, observer, informant, and participant.

The traditional role for parents has been as *receiver* of information gathered by professionals. Some parents may prefer only this role, and few can avoid it. Parents can, of course, play an important role by identifying the kinds of information they would like to receive. Of critical importance is how that information is conveyed. Murphy (1990) characterizes the traditional informing conference as one in which professionals assume an authoritative role in telling parents about their children. Effective sharing of information with families requires good communication skills, a recognition that parents and professionals have different perspectives on the child, being sensitive to parents' feelings, sharing information in a clear and unbiased fashion, and offering multiple opportunities to discuss assessment results.

Care-givers can also be *observers* during child assessment. This role can offer several advantages. By observing the tasks presented children and how children react, parents get a sense of the strategies and procedures used by professionals to gather information. The observation provides a reference point for parents to decide whether their child's behavior under testing conditions was representative of typical behavior. Also, if a parent is present during the testing, the child may be more comfortable and may perform better.

As *informants*, parents provide information for professionals about their children's development. One way is to provide information about specific skills, usually based on measures developed by professionals. For example, a parent might be asked whether the child drinks from a cup or plays regularly with other children. Another way is to ask more open-ended questions, such as "What are mealtimes like with your child?" or "What does your child do when other children are around?" Open-ended questions usually provide more information about aspects of behavior that are important to parents. In this role, parents can confirm, refute, or modify conclusions that professionals have made based on their assessments.

Finally, as *participants*, parents and other family members may be involved in some aspect of gathering data. For example, they may keep records of sleep-wake cycles, nutritional intake, toilet accidents, or other behaviors that professionals may not be able to observe in a comprehensive fashion. Also, as we describe later, parents may participate in some forms of assessment alongside professionals, such as in the arena model or the play-based assessment model.

Determining Professional Perspectives on the Assessment Process

Professionals bring a different set of experiences and expertise to the assessment process than do parents. While parent needs and priorities should be respected in making assessment decisions, it is incumbent upon professionals to inform parents about assessment strategies likely to be of importance in the program planning process. These procedures should be fully described and the rationale for their use explained, so that an informed decision about assessment procedures can be made by parents and other team members.

Conducting Team-Based Planning to Determine the Assessment Plan

A final activity in the individualized goal-determination phase is to hold a team meeting to plan the assessment activities. Often this activity is viewed as unnecessarily time consuming, and so it is rarely practiced. Yet it can be essential because it provides a context in which every team member, including the parent, has an opportunity to share goals and concerns, as well as to make suggestions for assessment activities. The outcome of this meeting should be a shared and coordinated assessment plan that each team member believes will provide a realistic and useful portrait of the child.

METHODS FOR GATHERING INFORMATION ABOUT CHILD AND FAMILY NEEDS

Once the team has come to a consensus about the goals and procedures for child and family assessment, the process of gathering assessment information begins. In this section we describe five general methods for gathering information about child and family needs: testing, observation, checklists, interviews, and qualitative or judgment-based procedures. Because the focus of this text is on intervention strategies, this review of procedures discusses assessment within that context. The reader is referred to Bailey and Wolery (1989) or Wachs and Sheehan (1988) for a more complete discussion of assessment strategies and issues. The next section describes formats for conducting assessments such that an integrated rather than fragmented view of needs and resources is obtained.

Testing

Probably the most common method of assessing children's needs is the administration of one or more assessment instruments. For purposes of intervention planning, curriculum-based measures are most frequently used. According to Neisworth and Bagnato (1988), a *curriculum-based assessment* "traces a child's achievement along a continuum of objectives, especially within a developmentally-sequenced curriculum" (p. 27).

Some of the more common curriculum-based measures used in early intervention include the Learning Accomplishment Profile (Sanford & Zelman, 1981), the Early Intervention Developmental Profile (Schafer & Moersch, 1981), the Hawaii Early Learning Profile (Furuno et al., 1979), the HICOMP Preschool Curriculum (Willoughby-Herb & Neisworth, 1983), the Battelle Developmental Inventory (Newborg, Stock, Wnek, Guidubaldi, & Svinicki, 1984), the Carolina Curriculum for Infants and Toddlers with Special Needs (Johnson-Martin, Jens, Attermeier, & Hacker, 1991), the Carolina Curriculum for Preschoolers with Special Needs (Johnson-Martin, Attermeier, & Hacker, 1990) the Brigance Diagnostic Inventory of Early Development (Brigance, 1978), and

the Evaluation and Programming System (Bricker, Gentry, & Bailey, 1985). Although each of these tests is unique, most have several common characteristics. Skills are usually grouped into several broad domains, the most common being cognitive or preacademic, language, gross motor, fine motor, social, and self-help or adaptive. Items are sequenced developmentally and typically serve as instructional targets. Some curriculum-based measures also include suggested teaching activities related to items on the scale. Finally, although some tests, such as the Learning Accomplishment Profile, suggest ways to convert performance into a developmental level, most criterion-referenced tests simply summarize performance in terms of items passed. The Battelle Developmental Inventory (Newborg et al., 1984) is the only one of the commonly used curriculum-based measures for which scores are based on a normative sample of children.

In using curriculum-based measures, early intervention professionals should be aware of several key limitations. Displayed in Box 4.3 are selected items from two curriculum-based measures. The box demonstrates that the two measures contain very different sequences of items related to the same developmental domain. The items do not necessarily represent good teaching sequences, and the value of some items as intervention targets is questionable. Thus while curriculum-based assessments provide an invaluable resource, practitioners should evaluate the extent to which a given sequence or item is appropriate for each individual child assessed.

Naturalistic Observation

A second method for gathering information about children is *naturalistic observation*. Although a variety of techniques have been developed, the essence of the procedure is the recording of behavior as it occurs in a variety of settings. Naturalistic observation has

---

BOX 4.3   A comparison of the first 10 cognitive items beginning at the 12-month level of two curriculum-based measures

Portage Guide to Early Education	Hawaii Early Learning Profile
1. Individually takes out six objects from container	1. Hands toy back to adult
2. Points to one body part	2. Enjoys messy activities such as finger-painting
3. Stacks three blocks on request	3. Reacts to various sensations such as extremes in temperature and taste
4. Matches like objects	4. Shows understanding of color and size
5. Scribbles	5. Places round piece in form board
6. Points to self when asked "Where's (name)?"	6. Nests two then three cans (puts the smaller cans inside the larger ones)
7. Places five round pegs in a pegboard on request	7. Understands pointing
8. Matches object with picture of same object	8. Pulls string horizontally to obtain toy
9. Points to named picture	9. Makes detours to retrieve objects
10. Turns pages of book two or three at a time to find named picture	10. Looks at place where ball rolls out of sight

---

several advantages. It samples the child's typical behavior; it allows for the assessment of many important skills (peer interaction, inappropriate behavior, communication, independence) not covered in a testing situation; it can be used to look at the sequence of behaviors and the context in which they occur. Naturalistic observation can also be used in a wide variety of ways.

Several naturalistic observation strategies have been developed and the selection of one depends on the type of information needed. Three forms of observation are running records, event sampling, and category sampling.

The *running record* is an attempt to document everything that occurs within a given time period. An example of a running record is the language sample, a record of everything a child says. Another example is a record of every motor behavior the child performs during morning free play.

The running record is particularly useful when the teacher is interested in what generally occurs and the sequence in which

things happen. However, it can be very time-consuming and requires constant attention. It may also be difficult to interpret because the information is not organized in a meaningful fashion; the teacher must convert it to another form. For example, once the teacher has collected several running records of Tina's social behavior, he might conduct a secondary analysis to determine the percentage of time Tina responded when a peer spoke to her.

Event sampling involves the measurement of specific behaviors as they occur, either through frequency counts or through duration recording. A *frequency count* is used for behaviors that are relatively short in duration. For example, the teacher may keep a record of the number of times Jack hits another child, the number of toilet accidents Ben has, or how often Greg offers to share a toy with a peer. A *duration measure* is an indication of how long something occurs, and it is used for behaviors that vary considerably in length. For example, the teacher may keep a record of the length of time Pam plays alone or the number of minutes Kim cries each day.

When the teacher is interested in a broad category of skills that actually encompasses many different behaviors, *category sampling* is a useful technique. For example, a primary goal for Matt is to increase the number of times he initiates an interaction with a peer. Many different behaviors could be considered initiations, however, and it might not make sense to count each one of them separately. The category of "initiations" could then be defined as encompassing a variety of specific behaviors within a limited set of categories. Another example of such a category is "aggressive behavior," which could also include many different discrete behaviors (e.g., hitting, biting, pushing).

Once a system for event sampling or category sampling has been developed, the time and technique for gathering data must be determined. Usually we do not have the luxury of observing all the possible times a behavior occurs, so we must be satisfied with a representative sample of behavior. Since we can only take data for relatively short periods of time, observation periods should be selected carefully. For example, it would not make sense to observe Matt's initiations to peers during a structured work session. A free play setting would provide a more representative sample of this behavior. The structured work session might be a better setting for counting the number of times Matt responds to a direct request by the teacher, however. The teacher should also observe only when she can see and record behavior accurately. If the teacher has other responsibilities, many behaviors may be missed.

One solution is to set aside short periods of time for continuous observation and recording of behavior. In event sampling, this allows the teacher to count each instance of a specific behavior. Another solution is to use a systematic time-sampling procedure which involves brief periods of observation at regularly scheduled intervals. For example, the teacher might set the timer and every five minutes check whether Pam is playing alone or with peers.

Checklists

A third procedure for gathering information is the use of checklists. A *checklist* is simply a list of items that a rater usually classifies as needs, problems, or skills. Usually checklists do not provide specific criteria for observing or scoring items. One example of the use of checklists is reported in a study by Brinckerhoff and Vincent (1986). Parents completed checklists describing home routines and their children's skills prior to the Individualized Education Plan (IEP) meeting. Another example is reported by Murphy and Vincent (1989) who used a checklist to determine critical skills needed by children in day care settings.

Perhaps the most frequent use of checklists in early intervention is in the context of assessing family needs and resources. A number of surveys have been developed in recent years to provide a way for families to indicate their needs for services—such as the Family Needs Survey (Bailey & Simeonsson, 1988), the Parent Needs Survey (Seligman & Darling, 1989); the Family Needs Scale (Dunst, Cooper, Weeldreyer, Snyder, & Chase, 1988), and How Can We Help? (Child Development Resources, 1989). Although these measures vary to some extent, they all consist of lists of needs on which parents or other care-givers indicate whether particular items are needs for them and whether they would like to receive services related to those items. A sample checklist is displayed in Box 4.4.

Parent Interview

A fourth way to gather information is the parent interview. An interview may be structured and formal or unstructured and informal. A number of structured assessment procedures based on parent interviews have been developed for the assessment of young children with disabilities, such as the Carey Infant Temperament Questionnaire (Carey & McDevitt, 1978) and the Development Profile (Alpern, Boll, & Shearer, 1980). Tests that consist primarily of direct test procedures may allow some items to be scored through parental report. The Battelle Developmental Inventory (Newborg et al., 1984) contains several such items.

Although interviews can be used to gather information about specific skills, they are

---

BOX 4.4   A checklist for assessing family needs

Family Needs Survey
(Revised, 1990B)

Child's Name: _____   Person Completing Survey: _____
Date Completed: _____/_____/_____   Relationship to Child: _____

Dear Parent:

Many families of young children have needs for information or support. If you wish, our staff is very willing to discuss these needs with you and work with you to identify resources that might be helpful.

Listed below are some needs commonly expressed by families. It would be helpful to us if you would check in the columns on the right any topics you would like to discuss. At the end there is a place for you to describe other topics not included in the list.

If you choose to complete this form, the information you provide will be kept confidential. If you would prefer not to complete the survey at this time, you may keep it for your records.

TOPICS	Would you like to discuss this topic with a staff person from our program?		
	No	Not Sure	Yes
Information			
1. How children grow and develop			
2. How to play or talk with my child			
3. How to teach my child			
4. How to handle my child's behavior			
5. Information about any condition or disability my child might have			
6. Information about services that are presently available for my child			
7. Information about the services my child might receive in the future			
Family & Social Support			
1. Talking with someone in my family about concerns			
2. Having friends to talk to			

BOX 4.4 *continued*

TOPICS	Would you like to discuss this topic with a staff person from our program?		
	No	Not Sure	Yes
3. Finding more time for myself			
4. Helping my spouse accept any condition our child might have			
5. Helping our family discuss problems and reach solutions			
6. Helping our family support each other during difficult times			
7. Deciding who will do household chores, child care, and other family tasks			
8. Deciding on and doing family recreational activities			
Financial 1. Paying for expenses such as food, housing, medical care, clothing, or transportation			
2. Getting any special equipment my child needs			
3. Paying for therapy, day care, or other services my child needs			
4. Counseling or help in getting a job			
5. Paying for babysitting or respite care			
6. Paying for toys that my child needs			
Explaining to Others 1. Explaining my child's condition to my parents or my spouse's parents			
2. Explaining my child's condition to his or her siblings			
3. Knowing how to respond when friends, neighbors, or strangers ask questions about my child			
4. Explaining my child's condition to other children			
5. Finding reading material about other families who have a child like mine			

	Would you like to discuss this topic with a staff person from our program?		
TOPICS	No	Not Sure	Yes
Child Care 1. Locating babysitters or respite care providers who are willing and able to care for my child			
2. Locating a day care program or preschool for my child			
3. Getting appropriate care for my child in a church or synagogue during religious services			
Professional Support 1. Meeting with a minister, priest, or rabbi			
2. Meeting with a counselor (psychologist, social worker, psychiatrist)			
3. More time to talk to my child's teacher or therapist			
Community Services 1. Meeting & talking with other parents who have a child like mine			
2. Locating a doctor who understands me and my child's needs			
3. Locating a dentist who will see my child			

Other: Please list other topics or provide any other information that you feel would be helpful to discuss.

_____

_____

Is there a particular person with whom you would prefer to meet?

_____

_____

Thank you for your time.
We hope this form will be helpful to you in identifying the services that you feel are important.

_____

Note: The Family Needs Survey was developed by Don Bailey, Ph.D., and Rune Simeonsson, Ph.D. For further information, write the authors at the Frank Porter Graham Child Development Center, CB#8180, University of North Carolina, Chapel Hill, NC 27599 perhaps best used in a more open-ended format to gain understanding of parents' perceptions of their children's skills, strengths, and needs, and to determine parents' priorities for themselves and their children. Winton (1988a; 1988b) suggests that three characteristics describe an effective interview: (a) the use of effective communication skills including listening, the reflecting of feelings and content, and appropriate question-asking, (b) sufficient flexibility to allow families and professionals to pursue topics of interest that emerge in the course of the conversation, and (c) enough structure to ensure that the purposes of the interview are achieved. A sample model for conducting a family-focused interview is displayed in Box 4.5.

Judgment-Based Assessment

A fifth group of methods for assessing child and family needs has been referred to by Neisworth and Bagnato (1988) as *judgment-based assessment*, which "collects, structures, and usually quantifies the impressions of professionals and caregivers" (p. 36). Judgment-based assessment procedures emerged out of a recognition that some aspects of competence are not readily quantifiable or assessed through a test, and are best documented through the subjective impressions of informed clinicians or parents (Hayes, 1990)—although these procedures can also be used to assess more traditional developmental domains (Fleisher, Belgredan, Bagnato, & Ogonosky, 1990). LeLaurin (1990) also suggests that judgment-based assessment can be very useful in documenting subtle features of children's behavior or in trying to describe themes or patterns of behavior. The regulations for Part H of Public Law 99–457 reinforce the importance of a judgment-based approach.

Since standardized diagnostic instruments are generally unavailable for use with infants and toddlers with handicaps, the Secretary believes that the evaluation of children under this part must be based on informed clinical opinion. (*Federal Register*, June 26, 1989, p. 26333)

Judgment-based assessment differs from naturalistic observation in that the latter typically involves simultaneous observing and counting of behavior. Judgment-based assessment is based on observation, but does not usually involve behavioral counts; rather a subjective rating of competence or behavior is made based on overall impressions. In part, judgment-based assessment may be linked to growing interest in qualitative or ethnographic approaches to research, approaches that rely heavily on participant observation and interviews to form comprehensive views of children and situations (Lincoln & Guba, 1985). Salisbury, Britzman, and Kang (1989), for example, describe the use of qualitative methods to assess social-communicative competence through extended observations and field notes over a 2-month period. Their study documented the unique strategies each child used to initiate and maintain interactions with other children. Because of the unique features of each child's strategies, it is unlikely that a standard assessment tool would have been able to capture the variability in individual styles. The authors conclude that a combination of qualitative and quantitative methods is likely to produce the most useful set of information.

Judgment-based assessment strategies for use in early intervention have recently emerged in several different formats, all of which rely on individuals having sufficient observation opportunities to make informed ratings of the children under assessment. Displayed in Box 4.6 (p. 114) is an item from the Carolina Record of Individual Behavior (CRIB) (Simeonsson, 1979; Simeonsson, Huntington, Short, & Ware, 1982). The purpose of the CRIB is to document clinical impressions of children's behavioral characteristics, such as tolerance for frustration, task persistence and endurance, consolability, or reactivity, as well as the severity of stereotypic behaviors. The CRIB provides a 9-point scale for the rater to use in describing a child's consolability when upset.

A second example of judgment-based assessment is found in Linder's (1990) transdisciplinary play-based assessment model. In this approach, specific items are not listed as part of the assessment instrument. Instead, within each of four developmental domains (cognitive, social-emotional, communication, and sensorimotor), seven to 10 subdomains are addressed. For example, the subdomains within the social-emotional area include temperament; mastery motivation; social interactions with parents, facilitators, or peers; dramatic play; and humor and social conventions. For each subdomain, the observer makes a general rating of the child's performance as either " + " or " – ", based on observations of behavior in the context of play. A " + " is indicated if the child's skills are developmentally appropriate, typical, and of good quality, whereas a " – " is indicated if there is delayed development, deviation from normal behavior patterns, or performance that is of poor quality. What classifies this as judgment-based assessment is the focus on broad dimensions of development and the basing of ratings on professional judgment and expertise rather than on explicit criteria.

A third example of judgment-based assessment may be found in Bagnato and Neisworth's (1990) System to Plan Early Childhood Services (SPECS). In this model, each team member rates the child on 19 dimensions of child development embedded within six domains (communication, sensorimotor, physical, self-regulation, cognition, and self/social). Each dimension is rated on a scale of 1 to 5 based on the rater's best judgment of the child in that dimension. Behav-

ioral descriptors are provided to help guide the team member in assigning the rating. For example, within the self-regulation domain is a dimension for Attention. The ratings for Attention range from 1—"Rarely pays attention except briefly to loud or sudden events" (p. 13) to 5—"Typically pays and shifts attention as well as or better than most children of the same age" (p. 13). As is typical of judgment-based assessment, no specific administration procedures or other scoring criteria are provided. The rater makes an informed clinical opinion on the child's functioning within each area.

Selecting Assessment Procedures

Testing, naturalistic observation, checklists, parent interviews, and judgment-based assessments each have advantages and disadvantages as summarized in Table 4.1 (p. 115). A comprehensive assessment should use a combination of these procedures, drawing on the unique strengths of each. Some form of direct testing is usually needed because of the logistics in transferring and recording information about children. Parent interviews, checklists, judgment-based procedures, and naturalistic observation should then verify the results of direct testing and measure skills that cannot easily be assessed in a direct testing situation.

METHODS FOR CONDUCTING ASSESSMENTS IN AN INTEGRATED FASHION

Most early intervention and preschool programs involve professionals from multiple disciplines as well as parents in the assessment process. Such programs are usually *multidisciplinary*—that is, each team member conducts his or her own assessment independently. The team meeting then becomes the context in which information

BOX 4.5   Model for conducting a family-focused interview

Phases and Tasks of the Interview	Purpose of Phase
Preliminary Phase	
Summarize standardized assessment data	Prepare for family interview by identifying topics that could be covered
Identify family members who should be involved in planning and goal setting	Arrange family interview
Negotiate time, place, and who will attend interview	
Explain to family why it is important for as many family members as possible to meet with interventionist	
Introductory Phase	
Explain the purpose of the interview and why it is important to involve the whole family	Create an environment where family feels supported
Explain the role of the interventionist	Build rapport with family
Clarify logistical details (time allotted, format, how to handle interruptions)	
Discuss confidentiality	
Structure physical environment to facilitate communication	
Inventory Phase	
Ask each family member to share their perspective of life with the handicapped child; make special efforts to include family members who seem distant or uninvolved	Identify and clarify each family member's definition of family needs, strengths, and resources
Gather information, when relevant, in the following critical domains:	
• informal and formal support networks • parent-child interaction • critical events • child characteristics affecting family functioning • family values and beliefs regarding intervention and the child's handicap • family roles and functions	

Phases and Tasks of the Interview	Purpose of Phase
Utilize communication skills that will enhance understanding of the relationship between people, events, values and beliefs	

Goal Setting Phase

Summarize your understanding of the family's major needs and strengths for validation by family members	Establish child and family goals
	Prioritize goals
Utilize reflexive questions to involve the family in setting and prioritizing goals, generating outcome criteria and specifying objectives for reaching goals	Establish a plan of action for reaching goals
Incorporate existing family resources including informal support systems and problem-solving abilities into plans to accomplish goals	
Provide information on formal support services to add to family's knowledge in terms of matching needs and services	
Refer family or individual members to other professional resources when needs are beyond the interventionist's level of expertise	
Specify a plan of action for accomplishing goals in which each person's tasks are clearly defined	

Closure Phase

Express appreciation for family's contribution to helping interventionist understand family's situation	Recognize family's effort
Ask family members if they have any additional concerns or final thoughts	Provide an opportunity for family to bring up concerns about interview process, confidentiality, etc.
Confirm time and place for next meeting, if appropriate	

Note: Adapted from "The Family-Focused Interview: A Collaborative Mechanism for Family Assessment and Goal-Setting" by P. J. Winton and D. B. Bailey, 1988, *Journal of the Division for Early Childhood, 12*, 195–207.

BOX 4.6   Sample item from the Carolina Record of Individual Behavior

Consolability
The manner and degree of consolability when the child has become upset. (Circle one)

Specify cause of upset _____
(e.g., hunger, pain, frustration)

1 Not consolable—neither caretaker nor examiner can console child—must terminate session.
2 Child requires removal from stimulation and being left alone for specified length of time (e.g., 10 min.).
3 Child requires sustained (5 min.) physical contact: hugging, rocking, holding by caretaker.
4 Child requires brief close physical contact: hug, hold and/or kiss.
5 Child requires brief physical contact: touch, pat on head, tickle.
6 Child can be consoled by being presented with food or novel object/toy.
7 Child can be consoled by verbal reassurance and/or social smile.
8 Child able to console self after several attempts (three or more) by use of some technique, e.g., thumb in mouth, seeking favorite object (blanket, toy, etc.), other (specify)
_____

9 Child is able to console self right away.
  X— Not applicable.
_____

Note: From *The Carolina Record of Individual Behavior*, unpublished test, by R. J. Simeonsson, 1979, University of North Carolina, Chapel Hill. Copyright 1979 by R. J. Simeonsson. Reprinted by permission.

TABLE 4.1
Characteristics, advantages, and limitations of five assessment methods

Procedure	Description	Advantages	Limitations
Curriculum-based assessment	A continuum of objectives embedded within a developmentally sequenced curriculum	Provides a standard set of items for assessing all children Items are developmentally sequenced Ensures comprehensive assessment	Content of most measures lacks substantive validation Lack of reliability data Problems in summarizing performance Questionable instructional sequences Lack of functional skills
Naturalistic Observation	Observation and recording of behavior as it occurs in a variety of settings	Measures what children do in real world settings Is sensitive to changes over time Can be done in the context of ongoing activities and routines Can be individualized Allows assessment of difficult-to-test behaviors	Is time consuming Requires a certain amount of skill to design a good observation system Lack of standards by which data gathered can be interpreted
Checklist	A list of items which a rater can designate individually as needs, problems, or skills	Usually simple and efficient means of gathering data Useful as initial screening Can provide functional information Allows respondents to indicate priorities	Respondents must be able to read Statements need to be worded carefully, since they will be interpreted by respondents Some parents do not like checklists
Interviews	Face-to-face discussion with an informed respondent	Allows for elaboration of findings from other procedures Flexible Can build trust and rapport Helps assess feelings and personal perspectives	Requires considerable skill on the part of the interviewer Difficulties in quantifying results Subject to accurate reporting by the interviewee and accurate integration by the interviewer
Judgement-based assessments	Rating of competence on the basis of informed clinical opinion	Useful with low-incidence behaviors or those that are difficult to quantify Allows for the integration of multiple perspectives and considerations in completing a rating	Subjectivity of ratings is sometimes criticized Assumes that the rater is extremely knowledgeable about typical and atypical child behavior and development Requires substantial knowledge of the child Are subject to error if based on just a few opportunities for observation

from these multiple assessments is shared and findings compared. Several strategies have been suggested recently to help facilitate a more integrated approach by establishing a common point of reference for all team members, either through the use of a common assessment setting or a common assessment tool.

The *arena model* (Foley, 1990; Wolery & Dyk, 1984) is an example of one such procedure. In this model, a facilitator is assigned to coordinate the assessment activities for a given child. This person interacts with the child while other team members observe, record observations, and score relevant items or measures. Team members usually ask the facilitator to administer certain items or try to elicit specific behaviors. Parents are present and can serve as the facilitator or as observers. Foley (1990) suggests that such a model results in "achieving a more integrated understanding of function, dysfunction, and the contributions of development across domains" (p. 276). All team members see the child performing the same behaviors at the same time. Also, each team member gets to see the kinds of items and activities that other team members incorporate in their assessments. In a study comparing the arena procedure with the more traditional multidisciplinary assessment process, Wolery and Dyk (1984) found that parents felt the arena model provided a more accurate picture of their children and took less of their time. Professionals also felt the arena model provided a better picture of the children and facilitated team discussions and consensus building. Some experiences, however, suggest that the arena model may be more useful for infants and toddlers and for preschoolers with severe disabilities than for preschoolers with mild disabilities.

The *transdisciplinary play-based model* described by Linder (1990) incorporates many of the same procedures as the arena model. The primary difference is that this model employs a common set of assessment matrices for all team members, whereas the arena model allows each professional to choose a specialized measure. Further, with the transdisciplinary play-based model, judgment-based ratings are employed in the context of a play setting, whereas with the arena model specific items are presented for scoring.

In Bagnato and Neisworth's (1990) *SPECS model,* a common set of judgment-based ratings using "a set of mutually understood instruments and materials" (p. 3) is used to develop a more integrated perspective. All team members are not required to see the child at the same time. Rather, each draws on his or her cumulative observations and interactions with the child to rate the child on the 19 developmental dimensions. The team meetings are used to develop team consensus on each dimension.

CONDUCTING TEAM MEETINGS AND PLANNING GOALS AND SERVICES

The final step in the assessment process is to conduct a team meeting to discuss perspectives, establish goals, identify resources, and determine needed services. This final step requires a team that can engage in effective group interactions, integrate information and priorities across participants, identify high-priority needs, establish goals, specify resources and services, design a service plan, and determine strategies for assessing goal attainment. The result of the team meeting will be a written plan that addresses the unique needs of each child and family. For infants and toddlers, the plan is referred to as the Individualized Family Service Plan (IFSP). For preschoolers, the plan is referred to as the Individualized Education Plan (IEP). As displayed in Box 4.7, the two plans are similar in that each contains a description of the child's current status, a statement of the outcomes (goals or objectives) desired, a description of the services to be provided, and criteria by which goal attainment can be determined. The major differences lie in the added family components of the IFSP regarding family goals and services, case management, and transition planning. Although the law does not require these family components in the IEP, there is no theoretical or empirical justification for not including them. In fact, good practice suggests that they are likely to be equally important for preschool-aged children and their families.

Engaging in Effective Group Interactions

Sundstrom, DeMeuse, and Futrell (1990) define work teams as "interdependent collections of individuals who share responsibility for specific outcomes for their organizations" (p. 120) and use an ecological perspective in establishing a framework for understanding teams and how they function. They suggest that three main factors affect team performance: the organizational context in which teams function, the team's independence within the organization, and the various processes that make up team development, including interpersonal processes, establishment and adherence to group norms, the cohesiveness of the group, and the extent to which roles are adequately defined. In this model, team effectiveness is measured by two outcomes: performance (whether the team does its job to the satisfaction of consumers and management) and viability (whether team members are satisfied with the group and it is likely to continue to function effectively).

The goal of the team meeting—to engage in open discussion to identify the most important service goals and strategies—can only be realized if everyone feels comfortable participating, if each team member values the perspectives of others, and if all actively work together. The following strate-gies are likely to help facilitate effective team practices.

Work actively to facilitate family involvement in team meetings and decision-making. This process should begin before the team meeting. Choices should be offered for roles in child assessment and in the meeting itself. Helping parents anticipate what will happen in the meeting, who will be there, what different roles they can play, and what their rights and responsibilities are in this process—such efforts can facilitate parent participation and decision making (Brinck-erhoff & Vincent, 1986).

Develop and reinforce good communication skills on the part of each team member, including listening, reflecting, understanding, asking questions, and giving feedback on others' suggestions.

Establish a team philosophy and a set of goals for team performance. This does not have to be extensive, but should help facilitate decision making by setting some criteria by which decisions are made. For example, a team may state that working toward normalized early experiences is an explicit goal, or they may adopt a policy in which family priorities are respected when they differ from professional priorities.

Develop a structure or plan for decision making. The meeting should not be so structured that useful discussion is repressed. Research in the group process literature, however, suggests that when teams agree on the process by which decisions are made, they are more likely to reach effective solutions to problems.

Learn to disagree effectively. A team meeting characterized by continual argument and dissension is likely to be ineffective. If no disagreements occur, however, the team may not be critically examining alternative goals and services. Janis (1971) described a phenomenon called *groupthink* in which teams fall into such a rut that they reach consensus immediately without signif-

---

BOX 4.7   Required components of the IEP and the IFSP

Individualized Family Service Plan (IFSP)

1. A statement of the infant's or toddler's present levels of physical development, cognitive development, communication development, social and emotional development, and adaptive skills, based on acceptable objective criteria.

2. A statement of the family's resources, priorities, and concerns relating to enhancing the development of the family's handicapped infant or toddler.

3. A statement of the major outcomes expected to be achieved for the infant and toddler and the family, and the criteria, procedures, and timelines used to determine the degree to which progress toward achieving the outcomes are being made and whether modifications or revisions of the outcomes or services are necessary.

4. A statement of specific early intervention services necessary to meet the unique needs of the infant or toddler and the family, including the frequency, intensity, and the method of delivering services.

Individualized Education Plan (IEP)

1. A statement of the child's present levels of educational performance, including academic achievement, social adaptation, prevocational and vocational skills, psychomotor skills, and self-help skills.

2. A statement of annual goals which describes the educational performance to be achieved by the end of the school year under the child's individualized education program.

3. A statement of short-term instructional objectives, which must be measurable intermediate steps between the present level of educational performance and the annual goals.

4. A statement of specific educational services needed by the child (determined without regard to the availability of services), including a description of

   a. all special education and related services which are needed to meet the unique needs of the child, including the type of physical education program in which the child will participate, and

---

icant discussion of issues. Team members need to be free to suggest alternatives and evaluate those suggested by others in an open fashion so that the best plan can be developed.

Ensure effective leadership. A good group needs a good leader. A good leader, however, does not try to control or manipulate a group; rather, through the use of strategies such as delegation, effective questioning, and encouraging each team member to par-

ticipate, a leader plays an important role in facilitating team performance. Accomplishing these goals is likely to require ongoing discussion of the roles of each team member, joint development of the team's philosophy, and within-team training.

Integrating Information and Priorities

Somehow, the team needs to assimilate the mass of information gathered by team

Individualized Family Service Plan (IFSP)

5. The projected dates for initiation of services and the anticipated duration of such services.

6. The name of the case manager from the profession most immediately relevant to the infant's and toddler's or family's needs who will be responsible for the implementation of the plan and coordination with other agencies and persons.

7. The steps to be taken supporting the transition of the handicapped toddler to services provided under part B to the extent such services are considered appropriate.

8. A statement of the extent to which services will be provided in natural environments.

Individualized Education Plan (IEP)

   b. any special instructional media and materials which are needed.

5. The date when those services will begin and length of time the services will be given.

6. A description of the extent to which the child will participate in regular education programs.

7. A justification of the type of educational placement that the child will have.

8. A list of the individuals who are responsible for implementation of the individualized education program.

9. Objective criteria, evaluation procedures, and schedules of determining, on at least an annual basis, whether the short-term instructional objectives are being achieved. (*Federal Register*, 41[252], p. 5692)

members throughout the assessment process. This is likely to be best accomplished by first giving all team members an opportunity to briefly share overall impressions gained from the assessment activities. Following that, the meeting should be organized according to skill or developmental areas, giving parents the opportunity to select the first areas to be discussed. Within each area, first ask parents to summarize their children's needs and skills, using an open-ended question (e.g., "How would you describe Lenny's communication skills right now?"). If necessary, other team members can follow up with closed-ended questions to gather more specific information, such as "How does Lenny show you that he wants something?" Following the parental summary, professional team members provide additional observations within the area being discussed. Discrepancies among perceptions of various team members are acknowledged and discussed, with the emphasis not on who's right and who's wrong, but on how the different perspectives might have been achieved.

Once the child's status has been discussed, parents are asked if they have any goals or priorities for intervention within that area. These priorities should, whenever possible, become the focus of the intervention plan. Professionals, of course, should indicate their priorities as well, and all suggestions should be discussed until an agreed-upon set of goals is identified (Bailey, 1989).

Establishing Individual Child and Family Goals

The discussion and activities described above should result in the identification of priority areas and outcomes likely to be of importance for the child and the family. The next step is to write those goals so that they meet legal and administrative requirements, are clearly understood by all team members, are integrated across settings and contexts, and are functional. Usually this process will begin with a statement of *long-term objectives*, which almost invariably are annual goals as required in both the IFSP and the IEP.

Annual goals help set the direction for services, but they usually are insufficient because they are broadly stated and because a 1-year period is too long for practical planning purposes. Thus long-term objectives need to be broken down into more usable *short-term objectives*, statements of expected outcomes within a 1- to 3-month time frame. Sometimes short-term objectives are obtained by conducting a *task analysis* of long-term objectives. Task analysis involves breaking down a skill into small, teachable steps. The process of task analysis, described in Box 4.8, results in a product, a written series of objectives sequenced by difficulty and presented in the order in which they should be taught. Short-term objectives may also be obtained by identifying skills that are assumed to be prerequisites for the achievement of the annual goals.

The way that objectives are written is important, since the objectives become both the focus of instruction and the standard by which success is evaluated. A good objective should be both clearly stated and worthwhile. From the perspective of clarity, an objective should first describe the *behavior* the child is expected to perform. Behaviors are observable (i.e., we can see or hear them) and measurable (i.e., we can document the extent to which they occur) actions. Objectives must describe behaviors so that professionals and parents can determine whether the child performs the desired skill. Usually objectives contain action words such as *cuts*, *places*, *reaches*, or *tells*. Obviously, some goals extend beyond a single, specific behavior. For example, understanding that a hot stove should not be touched or learning how to cooperate with peers are functional goals that many parents might identify for their children. These should still be stated as desired outcomes for children because of their importance; however, team members should try to identify specific behaviors by which those goals can be documented. For example, being cooperative could include giving toys to other children at their request; following one-step requests such as "come here" or "stop"; standing on the ladder of the slide waiting for a turn; and doing what the group is doing. From this array of behaviors we can begin to measure how cooperative a child is, and we can also determine the effects of attempts to increase the rate of cooperative behaviors.

Conditions describe the situations under which the behavior is expected, including the materials used, the amount of adult assistance, the use of adaptive equipment or other supports, and the settings in which the

---

BOX 4.8   Steps in conducting a task analysis

Task analysis involves breaking down a skill into small, teachable steps. The assumption is that the target behavior is too large a skill to teach at one time. Dividing it into several smaller tasks should increase the probability of skill acquisition because it allows both the teacher and child to focus on a very small component of the more complex task. The process of doing a task analysis involves five steps.

1 *Specify the long-term objective and look for related resources.* The long-term goal must be stated clearly so that its components can be identified. Then look for resources related to teaching the objective. Many such sequences can be found in various curricula, and these should be consulted first rather than trying to do it from scratch.
2 *Break the long-term objective into steps.* This can be done by watching someone else do it, doing it yourself, logically analyzing the skill, or examining developmental sequences.
3 *Eliminate unnecessary or redundant steps.* The steps should only include necessary behavior. Some children will obviously need more detail and smaller steps than others.
4 *Sequence steps for teaching.* Tasks can be arranged in temporal order (the order in which they would be performed) or in terms of difficulty.
5 *Specify prerequisite behaviors.* Prerequisite behaviors, sometimes called entry behaviors, are necessary before the child can perform the easiest step in the task analysis. Although many behaviors are desirable before training is initiated, two or three are usually critical and should be listed and the child assessed. If the child cannot perform the prerequisites, then the task analysis should be delayed until the behaviors are mastered.

---

behavior is performed. The conditions ought to reflect a realistic assessment of what is possible and desirable for the child and an identification of the situations in which the behavior would likely be needed and reinforced. Several authors (e.g., Dunst, Lesko, Holbert, Wilson, Sharpe, & Liles, 1987; Holvoet, Guess, Mulligan, & Brown, 1980) have suggested the use of a matrix, such as the one displayed in Table 4.2, in which the goals are listed on one side and the various settings in which they would be needed or could be taught are listed on the other. A matrix such as this helps the team decide how generally useful a goal might be and can be used to identify variations in expectations for skill performance across settings and activities.

The *criterion* of the instructional objective tells how well the child must perform the behavior before the performance is considered sufficient. Criteria are often difficult to state,

and should vary depending upon the skill. For some behaviors, the criterion may be stated in terms of accuracy or percent of opportunities (e.g., "responds 90 percent of the time to peer initiations"). For other behaviors the criterion may reflect duration (e.g., "selects an activity area during free play and engages in play within that area for at least 5 minutes before switching to another area") or rate (e.g., "walks a distance of 20 feet in less than 30 seconds"). In most cases, the criteria ought to indicate a level of mastery or proficiency that reflects consistent performance of the behavior in the identified environments at levels that are likely to be used and reinforced, or at sufficient levels so the behavior can be used for performing or accomplishing other objectives.

In addition to specific behavioral criteria, *social validation* of goal attainment by parents (Dunst, Trivette, & Deal, 1988) and pro-

TABLE 4.2
Matrix depicting goals by setting

Intervention Matrix   From: 12 / 14 / 90   To: 3 / 14 / 91

Objective	Arrival	Free Play	Meals	Structured Activity	Circle	Music	Art	Outdoors	Transitions	Nap	Personal Hygiene	Home
Use tools (scissors, markers) to cut out & draw 2 simple shapes.		X		X			X					
Complete 4–8 piece puzzles, copy parquetry pegboard or other designs with 6–10 pieces and create objects (people, cars) from materials.		X		X			X					
Appropriately answer questions related to abstract reasoning/predicting & sequencing during 3 activities.	X	X	X	X	X	X	X	X				
Comply with a variety of directions (at least 5) when given no more than 2 prompts or reminders.	X	X	X	X	X	X	X	X	X			
Kick, or catch, a moving ball at least 5 times during a 10-minute game.				X				X				
Pump legs while swinging at least 2 consecutive times.								X				

fessionals or other significant adults (Wolf, 1978) is also important. Social validation is a logical extension of judgment-based assessment, and involves the subjective judgment by knowledgeable adults regarding the attainment of desired outcomes. For example, the child may demonstrate a number of the specific skills that had been identified as important components of cooperative play. Social validation might involve asking the day-care teacher or parents of other children in the neighborhood whether they believe that the child plays in a cooperative fashion. Social validation reflects a recognition that many desirable goals for children are a complex combination of skills, and that no one measure (or even combination of measures) may fully reflect the intent of the goal.

Objectives should also be worthwhile, and several criteria for judging the usefulness of goals have been suggested (Notari & Bricker, 1990; Wolery, 1989b).

1 Objectives should be *developmentally appropriate*; that is, they should address skills that are typical for other children the child's age and are matched to the child's current developmental abilities.
2 Objectives should be *functional*. Wolery (1989b) states that functionality refers to the immediate usefulness of the skill, and may be based on several criteria:
   • the skill should help the child be more independent
   • the skill may not be immediately functional, but will help the child learn a more complex skill that is functional
   • the skill helps the child move to or function in a less restrictive environment
   • the skill will help the family care for the child
3 Objectives selected should be those valued by parents and significant others.
4 Objectives should be realistic and achievable.
5 Objectives should attend to all phases of learning, including initial acquisition, mastery, and generalized skill use.

Special Considerations in Writing Family Goals

Most early intervention professionals are familiar with the basic aspects of writing goals and objectives for children. Writing family goals, however, may be viewed as more challenging. A family goal may be defined as any goal that involves a change in behavior or skill for a family member other than the child with a disability. Part H of Public Law 99–457 indicates that the IFSP must include, *if the family so desires*, a statement of major goals for the family or establishes a service to address a specific family need or concern. What does this mean? Should professionals be providing services other than those directly related to providing teaching and therapeutic services for children?

The legal mandates, theoretical underpinnings, and empirical support for a family-centered approach described thus far in this text suggest that a broader view of early intervention services is warranted. The inclusion of family goals that are directly related to the care of children with disabilities (e.g., parent teaching skills) as well as goals related to other aspects of family functioning (e.g., respite services, sibling concerns) is becoming accepted practice. So what are the implications with respect to writing goals? Do the principles and guidelines for writing child goals also pertain to family goals? Generally speaking, the rationale for family goals is similar to that for child goals, and the considerations in writing the goals are similar also. We offer some additional suggestions, however, for consideration in writing family goals.

First, because of the voluntary nature of family goals and services, goals certainly should not be imposed by professionals. Second, write family goals using the family's own words. Third, the family should generally be the judge of whether family goals have been achieved. Thus, while objective criteria for goal attainment may be specified, the ultimate evaluation of effectiveness is social validation by families. Finally, as with child goals, trivial goals should be avoided for families. Goals should be stated in a meaningful fashion and should reflect an effort to support families in making decisions and obtaining resources for themselves rather than relying solely on professionals. Also, goals should be established and written so that a variety of activities can be used to meet them, thus providing flexible options for goal attainment.

SUMMARY

Assessment is the foundation for planning services for infants and preschoolers with disabilities and their families. In this chapter, we have described eight goals of the assessment process: (a) determining eligibility and placements, (b) identifying intervention goals, (c) identifying children's unique styles and strengths, (d) determining family needs and priorities, (e) building and reinforcing parents' sense of competence and worth, (f) developing an integrated plan, (g) creating a shared commitment to goals, and (h) evaluating effectiveness. We have presented a model for accomplishing these goals, and we have described alternative strategies for collecting assessment information. The major strategies include curriculum-based assessment, naturalistic observation, checklists or rating scales, interviews, and judgment-based assessment. Of special importance is the identification and use of assessment models that provide an integrated view of the child and family across multiple disciplines and domains.

REFERENCES

Alexander, R., & Tompkins-McGill, P. (1987). Notes to the experts from the parents of a handicapped child. *Social Work*, 361–362.

Alpern, G. D., Boll, T. J., & Shearer, M. S. (1980). *Developmental Profile II*. Aspen, CO: Psychological Development Publications.

Bagnato, S. J., & Neisworth, J. T. (1990). *System to plan early childhood services: Administration manual*. Circle Press, MN: American Guidance Service.

Bailey, D. B. (1991). Issues and perspectives on family assessment. *Infants and Young Children*, 4(1), 26–34.

Bailey, D. B. (1989). Assessment and its importance in early intervention. In D. Bailey & M. Wolery (Eds.), *Assessing infants and preschoolers with handicaps* (pp. 1–21). Columbus, OH: Merrill.

Bailey, D. B., & Blasco, P. M. (1990). Parents' perspectives on a written survey of family needs. *Journal of Early Intervention*, 14, 196–203.

Bailey, D. B., & Simeonsson, R. J. (1988). Assessing needs of families with handicapped infants. *Journal of Special Education*, 22, 117–127.

Bailey, D. B., & Wolery, M. (1989). *Assessing infants and preschoolers with handicaps*. Columbus, OH: Merrill.

Bricker, D. D., Gentry, D., & Bailey, E. J. (1985). *The evaluation and programming system: For infants and young children*. Eugene: University of Oregon.

Brigance, A. (1978). *The Brigance Inventory of Early Development*. N. Billerica, MS: Curriculum Associates.

Brinckerhoff, J. L., & Vincent, L. J. (1986). Increasing parental decision making at the individualized educational program meeting. *Journal of the Division for Early Childhood*, 11, 46–58.

Cadman, D., Shurvell, B., Davies, P., & Bradfield, S. (1984). Compliance in the community with consultants' recommendations for developmentally handicapped children. *Developmental Medicine and Child Neurology*, 26, 40–46.

Carey, W. B., & McDevitt, S. C. (1978). Revision of the Infant Temperament Questionnaire. *Pediatrics*, 61(5), 735–738.

Child Development Resources. (1989). How can we help? In B. H. Johnson, M. J. McGonigel, & R. K. Kaufman (Eds.), *Guidelines and rec-*

ommended practices for the Individualized Family Service Plan. Washington, DC: Association for the Care of Children's Health.

Dunst, C., Cooper, C. S., Weeldreyer, J. C., Snyder, K. D., & Chase, J. H. (1988). Family needs scale. In C. J. Dunst, C. M. Trivette, & A. G. Deal, *Enabling and empowering families: Principles and guidelines for practice.* Cambridge, MA: Brookline Books.

Dunst, C., Lesko, J. J., Holbert, K. A., Wilson, L. L., Sharpe, K. L., & Liles, R. F. (1987). A systemic approach to infant intervention. *Topics in Early Childhood Special Education, 7*(2), 19–37.

Dunst, C., Trivette, C., & Deal, A. (1988). *Enabling and empowering families.* Cambridge, MA: Brookline Books.

Fleischer, K. H., Belgredan, J. H., Bagnato, S. I., & Ogonosky, A. B. (1990). An overview of judgment-based assessment. *Topics in Early Childhood Special Education, 10*(3), 13–23.

Foley, G. M. (1990). Portrait of the arena evaluation: Assessment in the transdisciplinary approach. In E. D. Gibbs & D. M. Teti (Eds.), *Interdisciplinary assessment of infants: A guide for early intervention professionals* (pp. 271–286). Baltimore: Paul Brookes.

Furuno, S., O'Reilly, K. A., Hosaka, C. M., Inatsuka, T. T., Allman, T. L., & Zeisloft, B. (1979). *Hawaii early learning profile.* Palo Alto, CA: VORT.

Harbin, G. L., Gallagher, J. J., & Terry, D. V. (1991). Defining the eligible population: Policy issues and challenges. *Journal of Early Intervention, 15,* 13–20.

Hayes, A. (1990). The context and future of judgment-based assessment. *Topics in Early Childhood Special Education, 10*(3), 1–12.

Holvoet, J., Guess, D., Mulligan, M., & Brown, F. (1980). The individualized curriculum sequencing model (II): A teaching strategy for severely handicapped students. *Journal of the Association for the Severely Handicapped, 5,* 337–351.

Janis, I. L. (1971). *Victims of group think.* Boston: Houghton Mifflin.

Johnson, L. J., & Beauchamp, K. (1987). Preschool assessment measures: What are teachers using? *Journal of the Division for Early Childhood, 12,* 70–76.

Johnson-Martin, N., Attermeier, S. A., & Hacker, B. (1990). *Carolina curriculum for preschoolers with special needs.* Baltimore: Paul Brookes.

Johnson-Martin, N., Jens, K. G., Attermeier, S. A., & Hacker, B. (1991). *The Carolina curriculum for infants and toddlers with special needs.* Baltimore: Paul Brookes.

Kjerland, L., & Kovach, I. (1990). Family-staff collaboration for tailored infant assessment. In E. D. Gibbs & D. M. Teti (Eds.), *Interdisciplinary assessment of infants* (pp. 287–298). Baltimore: Paul Brookes.

LeLaurin, K. (1990). Judgment-based assessment: Making the implicit explicit. *Topics in Early Childhood Special Education, 10*(3), 96–110.

Lincoln, Y. S., & Guba, E. G. (1985). *Naturalistic inquiry.* Beverly Hills, CA: Sage.

Linder, T. W. (1990). *Transdisciplinary play-based assessment: A functional approach to working with young children.* Baltimore: Paul Brookes.

Meisels, S. J., & Provence, S. (1989). *Screening and assessment: guidelines for identifying young disabled and developmentally vulnerable children and their families.* Washington, DC: National Center for Clinical Infant Programs.

Miltenberger, R. G. (1990). Assessment of treatment acceptability: A review of the literature. *Topics in Early Childhood Special Education, 10*(3), 24–38.

Murphy, A. (1990). Communicating assessment findings to parents: Toward more effective informing. In E. D. Gibbs & D. M. Teti (Eds.), *Interdisciplinary assessment of infants* (pp. 299–307). Baltimore: Paul Brookes.

Murphy, M., & Vincent, L. J. (1989). Identification of critical skills for success in day care. *Journal of Early Intervention, 13,* 221–229.

Neisworth, J. T., & Bagnato, S. J. (1988). Assessment in early childhood special education: A typology of dependent measures. In S. L. Odom & M. B. Karnes (Eds.), *Early intervention for infants and children with handicaps: An empirical base* (pp. 23–49). Baltimore: Paul Brookes.

Newborg, J., Stock, J. R., Wnek, L., Guidubaldi, J., & Svinicki, J. (1984). *Battelle Develop-*

mental Inventory. Allen, TX: DLM/Teaching Resources.

Notari, A. R., & Bricker, D. D. (1990). The utility of a curriculum-based assessment instrument in the development of individualized education plans for infants and young children. *Journal of Early Intervention, 14*, 117–132.

Powell, M. L. (1981). *Assessment and management of developmental changes and problems in children*. St. Louis: Mosby.

Salisbury, C. L., Britzman, D., & Kang, J. (1989). Using qualitative methods to assess the social-communicative competence of young handicapped children. *Journal of Early Intervention, 13*, 153–164.

Sanford, A. R., & Zelman, J. G. (1981). *The Learning Accomplishment Profile*. Winston-Salem, NC: Kaplan.

Schafer, D. S., & Moersch, M. S. (Eds.). (1981). *Developmental programming for infants and young children*. Ann Arbor: University of Michigan Press.

Seligman, M., & Darling, R. (1989). *Ordinary families, special children: A systems approach to childhood disability*. New York: Guilford Press.

Simeonsson, R. J. (1979). *The Carolina record of individual behavior*. Unpublished test, University of North Carolina at Chapel Hill.

Simeonsson, R. J., Bailey, D. B., Huntington, G. S., & Brandon, L. (1991). Scaling and attainment of goals in family-focused early intervention. *Community Mental Health Journal, 27*, 77–83.

Simeonsson, R. J., Huntington, G. S., Short, R. J., & Ware, W. B. (1982). The Carolina record of individual behavior: Characteristics of handicapped infants and children. *Topics in Early Childhood Special Education, 2*(2), 43–55.

Sundstrom, E., DeMeuse, K. P., & Futrell, D. (1990). Work teams: Applications and effectiveness. *American Psychologist, 45*, 120–133.

Wachs, T. D., & Sheehan, R. (Eds.). (1988). *Assessment of young developmentally disabled children*. New York: Plenum.

Willoughby-Herb, S. J., & Neisworth, J. T. (1983). *HICOMP Preschool Curriculum*. San Antonio: Psychological Corp.

Winton, P. J. (1988a). Effective communication between parents and professionals. In D. B. Bailey & R. J. Simeonsson (Eds.), *Family assessment in early intervention* (pp. 207–228). Columbus, OH: Merrill.

Winton, P. J. (1988b). The family-focused interview: An assessment measure and goal-setting mechanism. In D. B. Bailey & R. J. Simeonsson (Eds.), *Family assessment in early intervention* (pp. 185–206). Columbus, OH: Merrill.

Winton, P. J., & Bailey, D. B. (1988). The family-focused interview: A collaborative mechanism for family assessment and goal-setting. *Journal of the Division for Early Childhood, 12*, 195–207.

Wolery, M. (1989a). Child find and screening issues. In D. B. Bailey & M. Wolery (Eds.), *Assessing infants and preschoolers with handicaps* (pp. 119–143). Columbus, OH: Merrill.

Wolery, M. (1989b). Using assessment information to plan instructional programs. In D. Bailey & M. Wolery (Eds.), *Assessing infants and preschoolers with handicaps* (pp. 478–495). Columbus, OH: Merrill.

Wolery, M., & Dyk, L. (1984). Arena assessment: Description and preliminary social validity data. *Journal of the Association for the Severely Handicapped, 3*, 231–235.

Wolf, M. M. (1978). Social validity: The case for subjective measurement or how applied behavior analysis is finding its heart. *Journal of Applied Behavior Analysis, 11*, 203–214.

Strategies for Intervention: Teaching and the Teaching Process

5

As we described the goals of early intervention in chapter 2, we have done well as professionals if the infants and young children who are our charges display adaptive skills when and where the need arises. The fundamental question addressed in this book is: How can we provide early intervention so that infants and young children with developmental delays and disabilities are prepared for the environments in which they live? This question gives us a lofty but realistic goal—that is, to prepare the children to live in their communities. The question assumes that some ways of meeting this goal are better than others. As we described the process in chapters 1 and 3, this goal is accomplished through diverse means, such as working with other agencies to ensure that appropriate services are available; helping families secure the resources and support required to meet their needs and aspirations, an achievement that in turn provides a more growth-promoting environment for the families' infants and children; assisting families to interact with and care for their infants and children in ways that are satisfying and that facilitate development; and providing services directly to infants and young children. Chapters 5 and 6 focus on providing direct services to children and deal specifically with the teaching process. In addition, we treat several questions about teaching.

Prior to addressing the questions, however, it is important to understand the context in which teaching takes place. Focusing on teaching does not reduce the importance of working with other agencies or of working with families. These are central issues in the provision of early intervention services. Our best teaching is done when it is based on and sensitive to children's ecologies and when it is designed to assist families in meeting high-priority goals for their infants and children in ways that are congruent with their values. However, we recognize that many services for infants and young children will occur in group contexts—in classrooms, that is. This chapter and the next, dealing with the process of teaching, are written to ensure that those settings are good places for young children.

Teaching also occurs in a team context. Intervention teams are collections of members from different disciplines who have unique areas of expertise. Physical and occupational therapists have unique knowledge in dealing with motor development and disorders; speech/language pathologists have unique knowledge in communication development and disorders; social workers have unique knowledge about families and how to access human services; nurses and physicians have unique knowledge regarding health and medical issues; the list could go on. What is the role of the educator? Does the educator implement the interventions for other team members? Is the educator the person who provides the context in which others can implement their interventions and therapies? Is the educator's role that of pulling it all together? The educator may do these things, but he or she also has a unique role: The educator is the pedagogical expert on the team. The educator should know more about structuring environments to promote learning than any other team member. The educator should know how to implement instruction and assist other team members in getting their interventions in place in meaningful and efficient ways. The educator should be able to help other team members monitor the effects of their interventions and show them how to get the maximum benefit from their manipulations of the environment. Our intent in this chapter and the next is to provide the foundation for learning to assume this role and perform this awesome task.

LEARNING AND TEACHING

We define *learning* as the enduring change in behavior or performance that occurs as a result of experience (Wolery, Bailey, & Sugai, 1988). For learning to have occurred, performance or behavior must be changed—because the change is the learning. Changes that are due to factors such as fatigue, medications, and physiological maturation, however, do not qualify as learning. The experience that results in learning can consist of teaching or other interactions with the social and physical environment. Clearly, the experience may not be followed by the behavior change that demonstrates—that *is*—the learning. You may "experience" something from reading this chapter, but you won't have demonstrated your "learning" until you have, for example, talked about the experience or taken a test. *Performance* or *behavior* is a movement that has a beginning and end, is observable (can be seen, heard, felt), is repeatable (can be done more than once), and is measurable (two or more individuals can reliably agree when it occurs). To infer that learning has occurred, we must note whether behavior has changed.

Teaching is simply the process of manipulating the environment to organize experiences so that learning will occur. Teaching, viewed broadly, involves deciding which behaviors should be learned, how the schedule and the structure of the physical and social dimensions of the environment should be ordered, which materials should be used, how children can be motivated, which teaching strategies will set the stage for learning to occur, how learning opportunities can be found throughout the day, how to know when learning is occurring and when it is not, and how to ensure that important skills are applied when needed.

In structuring experiences to cause learning, it is helpful to characterize learning (performance) as involving four phases: acquisition, fluency, maintenance, and generalization (Wolery, Ault, & Doyle, in press; Wolery et al., 1988). *Acquisition* is learning the basic requirements of a skill; it is learning how to do something new. When a child

learns to put one foot in front of the other, shift his weight, lift the other foot and put it in front, and maintain his balance while doing this repeatedly, we say he has learned to walk. However, learning does not stop there. To be useful, walking must be done fast enough to meet the child's need to get from place to place. If you have observed children who are learning to walk, it is common to see them drop to their knees and rapidly crawl to some desired goal. In such instances it seems that walking is not good enough; crawling is a more efficient way to get there. The children know how to walk, but they do not know how to walk fluently. *Fluency* is doing the skill smoothly or rapidly—at a natural rate, that is; fluency is a synonym for proficiency. Thus, to be independent, children must acquire skills, then perform them fluently. Still, teaching cannot stop at this point. Children also must learn to do the behaviors in the absence of teachers and teaching situations—doing this is referred to as *maintenance*. Finally, *generalization* is doing a behavior outside of the context in which it was learned. For example, if the child learns to walk on a carpeted floor in the family room, then for the skill to be useful, it must also be displayed on the slick kitchen floor, in the gravel driveway, and going up and down inclines.

Three statements about the phases of performance are important and hold direct implications for intervention. First, each phase is promoted by different intervention techniques (Wolery et al., 1988). Acquisition is promoted by a motivated learner, provision of assistance or information about how to do the behavior, and feedback about the appropriateness and adequacy of the behavior. Motivation is necessary, but it is not sufficient. You may be highly motivated to understand calculus, but without information on its principles and operations, motivation is useless. On the other hand, unless there is some motivation, you probably will not learn it as well. Later in this chapter we describe procedures for motivating children; in chapter 6 procedures for providing assistance and information are described. The educator promotes fluency by providing opportunities to practice and ensuring that children are motivated to practice. Maintenance is promoted by thinning reinforcement schedules, ensuring that there are uses for acquired skills, and using reinforcers found in the natural environment. Generalization is promoted, for example, by selecting teaching examples and materials carefully, varying the instructional procedures, teaching children useful skills, delaying reinforcement, and using self-management skills (Horner, Dunlap, & Koegel, 1988; Liberty & Billingsley, 1988; Stokes & Baer, 1977). The second statement is that each phase of the learning performance process usually requires purposeful planning. Progression through the process does not occur automatically. A recurring theme in teaching is that students (including young children with disabilities) do not automatically use and apply skills they have learned. The third point is that although the four phases are presented as a hierarchical process, teaching related to any phase may occur before the preceding phase is completed. During the acquisition phase, for example, the use of natural reinforcers may promote maintenance in addition to motivating the child; simultaneously, the educator could promote generalization by varying the materials.

DECISIONS INVOLVED IN PLANNING, IMPLEMENTING, AND EVALUATING INSTRUCTION

In this chapter we present five questions related to the process of teaching: (a) What should children learn? (b) How should we organize the schedule, physical dimensions, and social composition of the environment? (c) What materials are appropriate? (d) How can we motivate children to learn? (e) How can we know if learning is occurring? In chapter 6, we deal with three other questions: (a) What teaching strategies can be used? (b) How can we organize instructional opportunities? (c) How can we extend learning so that it has benefits beyond the immediate instructional context and the skill being learned? Entire books can be written on these topics and the treatment here is cursory; thus, you should consult the sources cited and other chapters in this book. We begin with an important question: What should children learn?

What Should Infants and Children Learn?

Here is the simple answer to this question: Infants and young children should learn everything they need to function more adaptively in their communities. Our teaching prepares children for their futures. Holding to this longitudinal perspective assists us in teaching important skills.

The more complex answer to the question has been introduced in the chapter 2 treatment of the goals of early intervention, and we will expand this answer in subsequent chapters. To review, the goals of early intervention are to promote engagement and mastery of current environments (chapter 8), to facilitate development in key domains (chapters 9, 10, and 12–15), to build and support children's social competence (chapter 9), to promote generalized use of skills (chapters 6 and 8–15), to prepare children for normalized life experiences (chapters 8–15), and to prevent the emergence of future problems or disabilities (chapter 11). Accomplishing these goals is a big task!

In chapter 4 we discuss the assessment process for determining which specific skills are important (see also Bagnato, Neisworth, & Munson, 1989; Bailey & Wolery, 1989; Gibbs & Teti, 1990; Wachs & Sheehan, 1988). We can distinguish three different types of skills that are identified for instruction by the assessment process.

Discrete Skills *Discrete skills* are behaviors that have relatively obvious beginnings and ends and relatively short durations and that can be used adaptively alone or in combination with other discrete behaviors. Examples of discrete responses are saying "Hi," pointing to a cookie on the table, naming pictures, giving a toy to a peer, putting a piece in a puzzle, naming letters or reading words, writing your name, and throwing a ball.

Complex Skills *Complex skills* are sequences or chains of behavior that, when put together, produce more complex or adaptive behaviors. Much of the early childhood curriculum includes the teaching of such skills. Examples include taking off and putting on clothing, setting the table for snack, brushing teeth, eating a meal, speaking in sentences, buttoning a shirt, building a block house, and riding a tricycle.

Some complex tasks have steps that must be completed in a specific order. For example, going to the bathroom involves entering the bathroom, pushing down one's pants, sitting on the toilet, eliminating waste, wiping (if necessary), pulling up one's pants, flushing, washing hands, and returning to the next activity. Other complex skills have steps that can be successfully completed in a variety of orders. For example, setting a table for a snack involves putting out napkins, cups, and fruit (or other food), and pouring the juice in the cups. This task could be completed by putting out all the napkins, then the cups, then the food, and finally filling the cups. Or, each place setting could be completed one at a time. Other complex skills have some steps that must be completed in specific sequences and others that can be done in flexible sequences. For example, when washing your hands and face, you must follow some steps in order (e.g., the water must be turned on first, and rinsing soap off your hands must follow putting soap on your hands). Other steps you can do in a variety of orders (e.g., face could be washed first, hands could be washed first, etc.). Still other complex tasks, such as walking and riding a tricycle, have a small number of steps that are repeated many times. Finally, many complex tasks are done in *formats*—that is, in groups of steps; it may be necessary to perform each group of steps in sequence, but the specific behaviors within each group may be variable. For example, a number of syntactic formats exist (e.g., noun phrase–verb phrase, noun phrase–verb phrase–object phrase), and the specific behaviors that fit within each format can be highly varied. Many dressing skills involve, in sequence, getting clothing out, checking alignment, putting clothes on, and fastening and adjusting them; but variety is possible within each group of steps. Although it is clear that teaching multiple examples of certain morphological and syntactic forms (e.g., adding "s" to make words such as "cup" and "toy" plural) will result in generalization to untrained stimuli (e.g., the child can proceed to perform the same procedure with words such as "dog" and "cat") (Goldstein, Angelo, & Mousetis, 1987; Guess, 1969), little research has addressed the issue of teaching formats that would increase the efficiency of learning subsequent chains.

Response Styles Finally, besides discrete and complex skills, we are concerned with *styles or patterns of responding*—how children interact with their environments. Does the child, for example, willingly try new things? Does she persist in tasks despite being unsuccessful? Does she seek help when something is not working? Does she watch others and match her behavior to their behavior? Is the child inclined to be a leader? Is he inclined to be cooperative? Children are frequently described in these terms (e.g., "He is persistent," "He's uncooperative," "She's a leader."), but these skills are less frequently the focus of systematic instruction, despite the fact that they often represent some of the most important goals of early intervention. Much less is known about how to teach these skills than is known about teaching discrete and chained tasks, although styles or patterns of responding are comprised, in part, of discrete behaviors. Some of these styles may facilitate learning while others may impede learning. The question of the style of response deserves more study.

Because much of our instruction occurs in mainstreamed settings, we need to know the behaviors expected of children developing normally. A list of such abilities is included in Box 5.1

Form and Function   After the infant or child has been assessed, the assessment data must be analyzed in terms of the behaviors that were displayed and those that are desired. As we indicated in chapter 4, assessment should provide information on the child's behavior and on the effects of the child's behavior. Here we address what has been referred to as the form/function issue. *Form* refers to the behaviors of children, and *function* refers to the effects of those behaviors. For example, walking is a form, and the effect is to get from one place to another; patting a peer on the leg is a form, and the effect may be to start an interaction; saying "more" is the form, and the effect is that the child receives additional juice. Several assumptions are involved in using such information

---

BOX 5.1   Important skill areas for children with typical development

 1 Develop a positive self-concept and attitude toward learning, self-control, and a sense of belonging.
 2 Develop curiosity about the world, confidence as a learner, creativity and imagination, and personal initiative.
 3 Develop relationships of mutual trust and respect with adults and peers, understand perspectives of other people, and negotiate and apply rules of group living.
 4 Understand and respect social and cultural diversity.
 5 Know about the community and social roles.
 6 Use language to communicate effectively and to facilitate thinking and learning.
 7 Become literate individuals who gain satisfaction as well as information from reading and writing.
 8 Represent ideas and feelings through pretend play, drama, dance and movement, music, art, and construction.
 9 Think critically, reason, and solve problems.
10 Construct understanding of relationships among objects, people, and events such as classifying, ordering, number space, and time.
11 Construct knowledge of the physical world, manipulate objects for desired effects, and understand cause and effect relationships.
12 Acquire knowledge of and appreciation of fine arts, humanities, and sciences.
13 Become competent in management of their bodies and acquire basic physical skills, both gross motor and fine motor.
14 Gain knowledge about the care of their bodies and maintain a desirable level of health and fitness.

Note: From *Guidelines for Appropriate Curriculum Content and Assessment in Programs Serving Children Ages Three Through Eight* (p. 13) by the National Association for the Education of Young Children, 1990, Washington, DC: NAEYC. Copyright 1990 by NAEYC. Reprinted by permission.

for instruction. First, *each behavior (form) is thought to produce some effect.* Children's behavior is not random; rather it is related systematically to environmental contexts and events. Teachers who understand the relationships between environmental events and children's behavior can change those events to promote more adaptive and complex behavior. Also, understanding the intent of children's behavior can result in identifying "teachable moments," moments in which learning might occur. For example, if a young child is watching other children play and keeps looking at a toy on a shelf which is out of reach, this behavior could be viewed as a desire to play with the toy. The teacher can use this moment for teaching requesting. Capitalizing on such opportunities may result in rapid learning because the child is motivated, attention is easily secured, and a natural consequence can be supplied for adaptive behavior.

Second, *that behavior has an effect on the environment and on others is one of the most important concepts that the child learns during the early years.* Infants first learn that crying usually causes an adult to appear and pick them up and feed them. Later, they learn that specific movements or noises can produce interesting spectacles in the environment. Ultimately, we hope that children learn that their behavior has an effect on others; only after children truly realize this fact can they develop styles of responding that are considerate and respectful of others.

Third, *many different behaviors can produce the same effect.* Nearly all effects can be produced by multiple behaviors. For example, to get more juice, the child could do several things. She could look expectantly at the teacher; she could look expectantly and hold up her cup; she could say "juice"; she could sign "drink"; she could point to the juice container; she could take her peer's cup. Each of these forms may result in the same effect; that is, she may get additional

juice. The implications for teaching are twofold. We can build upon children's current forms to teach more adaptive, normative, and complex ways of producing the same effect. For example, the child who says "more" to obtain additional juice can be taught to say "more juice" and/or "more drink." Teaching multiple forms for the same effect also increases the probability of generalization and independence. For example, the child who uses patting a peer on the leg to start social interactions could be taught to use verbalizations, eye contact, giving toys, and other forms to cause the same effect. Knowing several behaviors for initiating interactions may increase generalization to other children (i.e., those who would not interpret a pat on the leg as a bid for interaction).

Fourth, *functions appear to be longitudinal and seem to be actualized by more complex and varied forms with the passage of time.* In some cases, functions performed by infants and young children also are used by their parents and teachers. For example, young infants initiate interactions by smiling, cooing, and eye contact. Toddlers may initiate by using smiling and eye contact, but may also use physical proximity (getting close to another person), physical contact (touching, tugging, pulling), and vocalizations. Preschoolers may use the forms displayed by toddlers but may also use such forms as offering toys to peers and verbally suggesting playing together. Their parents and teachers also initiate interactions and may use the same forms but in more complex ways. Many of the objectives for infants and children involve teaching more complex and varied forms for fulfilling functions currently performed by less sophisticated forms.

Fifth, *learning a new form <u>and</u> a new function is extremely difficult.* Many college students who are faced with writing a paper for a class using a new format (e.g., APA Style Manual) find it difficult. The difficulty of getting the paper written will be increased substantially if they also are writing about new subject matter. If you are using a new format, it is much easier to write about something you know. Similar things occur with young children. It is one thing to learn to say "more" to request more juice, but it is quite another if the child does not know how to request—that is, if he does not understand that he can do something that will result in the adult reacting. Therefore, in organizing our instruction, we must understand what forms children currently use and what functions those forms fulfill.

Given these five assumptions about form and function, two related guidelines are applicable to the task of organizing instruction. *(a) Use existing functions to teach new forms, and (b) use existing forms to teach new functions.* It is useful to view the forms and functions of a child as related within a matrix such as the one shown in Figure 5.1.

There, the ultimate goal is to teach the child to distinguish between an object and the possessor of the object—that is, to understand the possessor–possession relationship. Currently, the child uses one word statements to express possession ("mine"), expresses only his personal possession and not that of others (e.g., does not say "daddy's" or "John's"), and only expresses one-word labels of objects (e.g., "toy," "cup," "hat"). Although the goal may be to teach the child to use two-word labels to describe possessor-possession relationships (e.g., "Daddy's hat," "John's book"), this represents both a new function (labeling the possession of others) and a new form (using two-word phrases to express possession). Thus, instruction should start in one of two places. It could focus on using single words (old form) to express the new function (possession of others)—for example, "Daddy's," or "John's." Or, instruction

Instructional Goal:

Child will use two-word phrases to express the possessor-possession relationship

Current Performance:

1. Child uses one-word statements to express personal possession (e.g., "Mine");

2. Child uses one-word statements to express objects that are possessed (e.g., "toy," "cup," "hat");

3. Child *does not* use two-word statements; and

4. Child *does not* express the possession of others (e.g., "Daddy's," "John's").

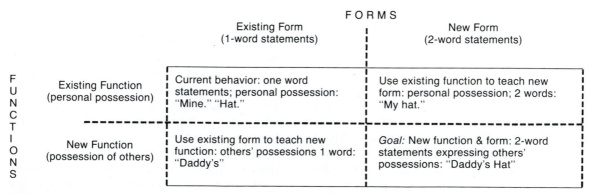

FIGURE 5.1
Example of analyzing assessment results by form and function

could focus on using the existing function (personal possession) to teach a new form, two-word phases (e.g., "My cup"). After either the new function or new form is learned, then the objective (two-word phases depicting the possession of others) can be addressed. By organizing instruction in this way, we take advantage of children's current repertoires and strengths—we make instruction more sensitive to children's needs and abilities.

In addition to identifying the forms and functions, the long-term benefits of the skills and the values assigned to skills by families (see chapter 4) must be determined. The high-priority skills are then established as objectives on the Individualized Family Service Plan (IFSP) or Individualized Educational Program (IEP). Understanding the types of goals (discrete, complex, and style) allows for more purposeful planning of instruction. We are led directly to the next question: How should we organize the schedule, physical dimension, and social composition of the environment?

How Should the Schedule and the Physical Dimension and Social Composition of the Environment Be Organized?

Structuring environments (homes and classrooms) for young children requires attention to many issues that are discussed in detail in chapter 7. Here we provide three guidelines.

First, *a time should be found in the daily schedule (home and/or class) to address each high-priority objective.* To implement this guideline, an activity-by-skill matrix frequently is used (Bricker, 1989; Guess & Helmstetter, 1986; Helmstetter & Guess, 1987). This involves identifying at least one time during the flow of daily activities when each skill can be taught. When infants and children are in classrooms, it is important to expand the matrix to include the home and other relevant environments (e.g., family day

care). The steps for completing such a matrix are presented in Box 5.2. When constructing such matrices for multiple children (e.g., three or four children with disabilities in a mainstreamed setting), the professional should superimpose each child's individual matrix on the classroom schedule. Careful attention must be given to the staffing patterns to ensure that the planned instruction can be implemented. Also, attention must be given to how data are collected to monitor learning (see Templeman, Fredericks, & Udell, 1989 for an example).

Second, *the physical environment should be arranged so that the targeted behaviors and functions (i.e., the high-priority objectives) are encouraged.* For example, an objective for Lisa (a young infant) was to increase her awareness of the fact that her behavior can produce an effect on the environment. Thus, the intervention team designed her crib so that it contained many things that would react when she moved. A mobile was placed above her, bells were suspended from the side of the crib and ribbons tied to the bells were pinned to the sleeve of her gown, and rattles were placed in her hands. An objective for Jeremy is to increase his exploration of his home environment. Since he is a mobile toddler who mouths "anything he can get in his mouth," his home environment must be checked for the potential danger he might encounter in his explorations; thus, a home safety checklist (e.g., Wolinsky & Walker, 1975) should be used, and the appropriate modifications should be made. An objective for Kisha is to elaborate her expressive language. The intervention team has decided to use the incidental teaching technique (Hart & Risley, 1975) which provides a teaching opportunity whenever she makes a request for materials, information, assistance, or permission. To increase the number of requests, the physical environment could be arranged so that her preferred toys were out of reach; that is, she would have to ask for

---

BOX 5.2   Steps for completing activity-by-skill matrix

1 List the events (activities, etc.) in which the child will participate during the day down the left-hand column of the matrix. The events should be listed in the order in which they occur daily.

2 List the location of each event below each listing in the left-hand column of the matrix. The listing should include the entire day, the purpose is to provide instruction in all relevant locations.

3 Also in the left-hand column of the matrix, list the time each activity will start and its expected duration each day.

4 Also in the left-hand column of the matrix list the name of the adult who is responsible for implementing the instruction; if peers also are used, then they should be listed here as well.

5 Across the top of the matrix list all of the skills that have been identified for instruction. Each column should include one behavior.

6 In the cells of the matrix list the materials and specialized instructional strategies that will be used. If a skill is not addressed at a given event/time, then that cell should be left blank.

7 Check the matrix to ensure that skills will be taught across adults, materials, and settings to facilitate generalization.

Note: Adapted from "Application of the Individualized Curriculum Sequencing Model to Learners with Severe Sensory Impairments" by E. Helmstetter and D. Guess, 1987, in *Innovative Program Design for Individuals with Dual Sensory Impairments*, L. Goetz, D. Guess, and K. Stremel-Campbell (Eds.), Baltimore: Paul Brookes.

---

them. Each request for those toys would represent an instructional opportunity. These modifications of the physical dimension of the environment were designed specifically for the objectives of each child. Although limits exist to the types and amounts of modifications possible (e.g., usually you cannot change the size of the rooms, etc.), modifications of the physical dimension are an underused resource.

Third, *the social requirements of each instructional procedure for each objective should be analyzed.* Relatively few instructional plans rely solely on the modifications of the physical environment and on materials (Yoder, 1990). Frequently, the modifications to the physical environment set the stage for the behavior to occur, but the actual instruction is implemented or mediated by another person. Plans such as the one just

described for Lisa are the exception rather than the rule. In fact, some data indicate that automated learning devices (e.g., microcomputers) used alone may be *ineffective* with young children who have disabilities (Richmond, 1983). As a result, efficient instruction frequently requires a "teacher." This role may be filled by the child's family (parents and siblings), a teacher, a therapist, a teaching assistant, or other children. Because child-to-staff ratios tend to be high in many preschool programs, there are limits to the availability of people who can fill this role. In homes, because of caregiving demands, household duties, work schedules, and many other issues, a shortage of "teachers" may exist as well. Thus, as each activity schedule is made, the person responsible for implementing it must be identified and assigned. Some ways of implementing instruction make better use of the social composition of the environment than others; these issues are discussed in chapters 6 and 9.

What Materials Are Appropriate?

As is the case with the physical environment, the materials used in teaching infants and young children should be individualized. They are selected based on their ability to cause learning opportunities to occur. For example, some materials/toys produce more social behavior than others (Odom & Strain,

1984). Thus, if social interaction is desired, those "social" materials should be used; if, on the other hand, independent play is desired, then materials should be selected accordingly. Considerable research has been done on the effects of toys and materials on children who are developing normally and, more recently, on young children with disabilities (Bradley, 1985; Rubin & Howe, 1985; Wachs, 1985). A summary of some of this literature is presented in Box 5.3. However, five general guidelines are presented here.

BOX 5.3   Summary statements about the relationship of play materials to children's development

1 If given the opportunity, young children tend to spend a considerable amount of time viewing and interacting with toys and other objects.
2 The availability of a variety of responsive toys is related to social-cognitive development throughout early childhood.
3 The association between play materials and development is partially a function of parental education and socioeconomic status, but is not solely a reflection of these influences.
4 The relationship between toys and development is bidirectional. More competent children tend to seek out a greater variety of appropriate play objects; appropriate play objects assist development.
5 Intrinsic motives of curiosity and mastery impel a child to explore and manipulate interesting toys and objects, thus providing an arena for learning.
6 Children's interest in toys leads them to social encounters with peers and adults; these are rich in cognitive and social learning opportunities.
7 Play materials sometimes act as catalysts for adult-child interactions (particularly mediated learning experiences) that help shape and support social-cognitive development.
8 Cognitive development in very young children is highly dependent on direct encounters with objects (including toys).
9 Toys and other realistic objects become useful hooks for the construction of spatio-temporo-causal scripts that characterize the infancy and preschool period.
10 As children become capable of representational thinking, objects are often used as pivots through which children transfer meaning from real objects in pretend play.
11 Toys sometimes serve as catalysts for imaginative play. They can serve to carry the meaning of the play situation to full realization. They may also help provide a link between learning derived from the imaginative world of play and the more concrete settings of the real world.

Note: From "Social-Cognitive Development and Toys" by R. H. Bradley, 1985, *Topics in Early Childhood Education,* 5(3), 11–30. Reprinted by permission.

Materials Should Be Responsive   As noted back in 1979, physically responsive environments (i.e., toys that provide feedback when activated) are positively related to cognitive growth (Wachs, 1979). The justification for using reactive toys is that they may allow the child to learn that what they do produces an effect and to learn what effects are possible. This awareness may lead to greater engagement with the environment, which in turn may lead to additional learning. A study evaluating the notion that greater responsivity leads to greater engagement was conducted with three children who had severe disabilities (Bambara, Spiegel-McGill, Shores, & Fox, 1984). The children were exposed in daily sessions to three toys that were reactive (i.e., that produced a sound when activated with a simple motor movement) and three toys that were nonreactive (i.e., that did not produce a sound when activated). The children were engaged more with the reactive toys than with the nonreactive toys, but the reactivity did not appear to influence their visual attention to the toy. It should be noted that this study did not mea-sure whether children learned additional behaviors or information from the increased engagement. Rather, it indicated that increased engagement occurred as a result of having reactive toys. This finding, in and of itself, is valuable and argues for including reactive materials.

Materials Should Be Age-Appropriate   Generally, the toys and materials for infants developing normally are appropriate for infants with disabilities; the same could be said for toddlers and preschoolers. The use of age-appropriate toys is justified by the fact that they are more normative and allow the child to appear less discrepant from his or her typically developing peers. Criteria for the selection of toys are displayed in Box 5.4.

Materials Should Be Adapted to Increase Use, Engagement, and Learning   The emergence of microcomputers and other electronic devices (e.g., switches) have led to considerable interest in adapting toys to allow children with physical disabilities and those with severe handicaps to engage in play (Musselwhite, 1986). Guidelines and

---

BOX 5.4   Criteria for the selection of toys

1 Toys and play materials should be *safe*.
2 Toys and play materials should be *durable*.
3 Toys and play materials occur on the continuum of *realism*; for toddlers, they should be quite realistic; for preschoolers less realistic toys may promote imaginative play.
4 Toys and play materials occur on a continuum of the extent to which they suggest a *structure* for play; with younger children toys should suggest ways for being played with, but for older children less structure may facilitate imaginative play.
5 Toys and play materials should be *responsive*; that is, they should react when they are activated.
6 Toys and play materials should have *motivational properties*; that is, they should be selected based on children's interest.

Note: Adapted from *Adaptive Play for Special Needs Children: Strategies to Enhance Communication and Learning* (pp. 36–38) by C. R. Musselwhite, 1986, Boston: Little Brown.

flow charts for making such adaptations have been proposed (Langley, 1985; Musselwhite, 1986; York, Nietupski, & Hamre-Nietupski, 1985). The primary purpose behind such adaptations is to find ways for children to interact meaningfully with the environment and thereby be more engaged, more inclined toward learning. An example of using a simulated microcomputer game to prepare young children for using a scanning augmentative communication device is described in Box 5.5.

Materials Should Include Naturally Occurring Objects A common report of parents and grandparents is that children frequently play less with new toys than the boxes in which they came. Parents also report that while they are in the kitchen cooking, their toddlers frequently play under their feet with

---

BOX 5.5   Example of a study using a simulated video game to teach preschoolers skills for using an augmentative communication device

Some children, for a variety of reasons, will never learn to use speech as a means of communication; however, they can learn to use augmentative communication devices. Augmentative communication devices frequently present a number of possible messages, and children must select the one they are trying to communicate. Children must scan the possible messages, and then select the one that matches their message. For the children to be efficient communicators, this scanning must be accurate and the selection must be rapid.

Horn, Hazel, and Hamlett (1991) conducted a study to teach children to make such selections. The purposes of their study were (a) to see if a video game with a microcomputer could teach scanning and selection skills, (b) to determine whether children would generalize scanning and selection skills to a specific communication device (i.e., to a Zygo 100), and (c) to assess the maintenance of the responses after training ceased.

The study involved three children (5–8 years of age) who had multiple disabilities. All three children had physical disabilities that made the use of speech unlikely, all had experience with on/off switches for activating electronic toys, and all had deficient skills in selection of messages on the communication device.

A microcomputer was adapted for use with a specialized video game. The game involved "catching" animals by pressing a switch as the animals passed across the screen. The number of boxes used to catch animals and the speed with which animals passed through the screen was individualized for each student. During training, a teacher prompted each child to activate the switch at the appropriate time. When the child activated the switch and "caught" one of the animals, the capture was noted on a scoreboard. Children also were praised for their performance.

The results of this study indicated that each child learned to play the video game, and that each child became more accurate in the selection of messages on the communication device. Also, each child was able to maintain the skill in the classroom after training stopped. This study is a good illustration of the application of microcomputers in teaching young children important and useful skills in a gamelike format.

Note: Adapted from "An Investigation of the Feasibility of a Video Game System for Developing Scanning and Selecting Skills" by E. Horn, A. J. Hazel, and C. Hamlett, 1991, *The Journal of the Association for Persons with Severe Handicaps, 16,* 108–115.

the pots and pans. Generally, the use of such "toys" is appropriate; given of course that they are safe. Such reports hold a couple implications for selecting materials. First, many things in the home environment can function legitimately as objects of play. Thus, families should be encouraged to use them. The growth promoting aspects of objects are based on children's interactions with them rather than the purposes identified by toy developers or others. If children are engaged extensively with safe materials that are found around the house, then those are probably appropriate play objects. Second, the child's preference for a particular object or toy is probably as important the toy's intended use. If children prefer to play in the pots and pans, then their engagement will likely be greater and additional skills may be learned. Perhaps this tells us something about the kinds of materials we should have available in child care centers.

Materials Should Be Selected to Promote Learning of Important Skills   We rarely rely solely on materials to provide children with experiences that will promote learning. However, careful selection of materials can increase the likelihood that experience with them will produce the desired outcome. A method for accomplishing this selection is general case programming. *General case programming* is a process used to select both the stimuli (materials) and the responses for structuring instruction to promote generalization (Albin & Horner, 1988; Horner, McDonnell, & Bellamy, 1986). Although the research supporting general case programming has occurred primarily with older students who have moderate to severe mental retardation (Sprague & Horner, 1984; Horner, Albin, & Ralph, 1986), the skills taught are similar to those needed by younger children, and the process is not bound by age. What is clear from the research is that some materials (stimuli) will result in much less generalization than others; general case program-

ming is a process that increases the probability that generalization will occur. Thus, it is seen as an important process for selecting teaching materials. The six steps of general case programming are displayed in Box 5.6.

Summary of Appropriate Materials   Materials should be selected based on the outcome that is desired from their use. The literature on typically developing children suggests that some types and uses of materials (toys) may promote positive social and cognitive development. Generally, we should use toys/materials that are responsive, age-appropriate, and naturally occurring. The general purpose is to select toys that capture children's attention, and encourage them to explore, use, and learn. When necessary, toys can be adapted to increase engagement. Finally, general case programming is a process that allows teachers to select materials that will promote generalization to other relevant stimuli and only to those stimuli.

How Can Children Receive Appropriate Feedback for Their Behavior and Be Motivated to Learn?

Ideally, we want infants and children to be intrinsically motivated to learn; and in fact, all appear to have some degree of motivation to learn. However, intrinsic motivation is often insufficient because children are young and human and have disabilities, and because the tasks being learned may be quite difficult (but necessary). Motivation is affected by many variables, including the child's history with similar tasks, the variety of tasks presented (Dunlap & Koegel, 1980), the choices of activities and reinforcers (Dyer, Dunlap, & Winterling, 1990), and degree of active involvement in activities. Still, however, these aspects will frequently not produce sufficient motivation for learning. A common and acceptable solution is to use reinforcement.

BOX 5.6 Steps for completing general case programming

1 Define the instructional universe—identify all the instances in the natural environment where the stimulus is present and where the response may be needed.
2 Define the range of relevant stimulus and response variation within the universe—describe all the ways that the stimulus appears in the instructional universe and all the ways that the response must be performed to fulfill its function.
3 Select examples from the instructional universe for use in teaching and probe testing—select the stimulus and the response variations that will be taught and probed; these should sample the range of variations that are found in the natural environment.
4 Sequence teaching examples—determine the order in which the various stimulus and response variations will be taught; also select examples that will not be taught but will be used for assessing generalization.
5 Teach the examples.
6 Test with nontrained probe examples—periodically test the child with stimulus and response variations that occur in the natural environment but have not received instruction; instruction can stop when generalization to these examples occurs.

Note: From "Generalization with Precision" by R. W. Albin and R. H. Horner, 1988, in *Generalization and Maintenance: Life-Style Changes in Applied Settings,* R. H. Horner, G. Dunlap, and R. L. Koegel (Eds.) (pp. 99–120), Baltimore: Paul Brookes.

What is reinforcement? Actually, two types exist: positive and negative (Cooper, Heron, & Heward, 1987; Wolery et al., 1988). *Positive reinforcement* is the process by which an event follows (occurs contingently upon) a behavior and produces an increase in the likelihood that the behavior will recur or continue to occur. For example, attention from family members increases the occurrence of the behavior, or the pleasant sound of a rattle increases the frequency with which the rattle is shaken. *Negative reinforcement* is the process by which an aversive event is removed contingent upon the occurrence of a behavior and produces an increase in the likelihood that the behavior will recur or continue to occur. Turning on a fan on a hot day removes the aversive stimulus of heat. This removal results in an increase in fan-turning-on behavior when it is hot. When your supervisor nags you to get your reports written on time, the nagging can

serve as an aversive stimulus. To remove it, you write and submit your reports on time and this stops the nagging.

The events that follow behaviors and increase their occurrence are called *reinforcers.* Positive reinforcers are used more frequently than negative reinforcers because we usually want to avoid presenting aversive stimuli to children. Two facts about reinforcers are well known and important. A reinforcer for one child will not necessarily be a reinforcer for others. And a reinforcer that worked at one time will not necessarily work at another. Thus, reinforcers must be selected individually, and the selection should be an ongoing process.

Selecting Reinforcers When selecting reinforcers, the professional should address five criteria, which we describe in the order of their importance. First, *the stimuli that are identified as reinforcers must truly be rein-*

forcers; they must increase the behaviors they follow. Too frequently, teachers use stimuli (e.g., praise) which are assumed to be reinforcers when in fact they have long since lost their reinforcing properties. Second, *when possible, activities should be selected and designed so that their accomplishment is reinforcing.* For example, if the goal is requesting objects, the reinforcement should be receipt of the requested object. Third, *reinforcers should be easily delivered.* Some things may be powerful reinforcers, but would be difficult for the teacher to deliver when and where they are needed. For example, playing a few minutes with a favorite uncle may be a powerful reinforcer, but it is not very useful unless that uncle is present. Fourth, *reinforcers also must be acceptable to the families, teachers, and program administrators.* Some programs prohibit the use of edible or tangible reinforcers; although the wisdom of such a policy is easily questioned, it represents a prevalent attitude, a reality that must be addressed (cf., Shevin, 1982). Thus, the acceptability of reinforcers is an important issue. Finally, *reinforcers should be selected that are likely to be present in the natural environment.* Use of such reinforcers is likely to increase the probability of skill generalization. However, when such "reinforcers" are not sufficiently reinforcing, then other more powerful reinforcers should be used in conjunction with them. This will allow the weaker but more natural reinforcers to acquire more value and be more effective when used alone. Many sources of reinforcers exist for most young children, including social interactions with adults and peers, food and drink, movement, toys, activities, and the sensory feedback of their own behavior.

Selection of reinforcers can occur through a four-step process. First, *use common reinforcers that appeal to most young children.* These include praise; pats; tickles; give-me-fives; smiles; enthusiastic facial expressions;

access to a variety of toys and objects, stickers, food and liquids; and the opportunity to move. These stimuli are assessed by trying them with skills the child can perform and seeing whether they result in increases in the occurrence of those skills. If these events do not appear to be reinforcers (i.e., if they do not increase the behaviors they follow), other reinforcers should be sought.

Second, *individuals familiar with the child should be asked about things or activities that might be reinforcing.* Parents frequently know what children like and dislike and thus what may be reinforcing. Ask about specific categories. "Does she have any toys she especially likes or plays with frequently?" "What are her favorite foods and liquids?" Such questions are more apt to prompt specific answers than general queries such as "What do you think she likes?" Once identified, these stimuli should also be tested.

Third, *observe the child and note any frequently occurring behaviors.* The observation should include two or three sessions of 10–15 minutes when the child is free to move about the room and do what she wants. The professional should note any frequently occurring behaviors and favorite objects; these can be used as reinforcers if access to the objects or the freedom to do the behaviors is made contingent upon the behavior you want to increase. Such arrangements are based on the Premack principle (Cooper et al., 1987; Wolery et al., 1988) which states that if behaviors that do not occur frequently are followed by behaviors that do occur frequently, then the low frequency behaviors will increase. For example, Darrin rarely engages in the circle time activities, but frequently plays with the trucks and blocks. If his teacher allows access to the trucks and blocks only after appropriate circle time behavior, then the circle time behaviors are likely to increase. Recently, investigators have begun to realize that some behaviors that are thought to be inappropriate, such as stereotypic behavior (repetitive movements such as rocking, gazing at the fingers, flapping the arms, and moving objects ritualistically), can be used to identify potential reinforcers (Lovaas, Newsom, & Hickman, 1987). These behaviors tend to occur at high frequencies, and following the Premack principle, can be used to increase adaptive behaviors that are less likely to occur. This increase in adaptive behavior has been accomplished by providing children with sensory stimulation similar to that received from their stereotypic behavior—for instance, by rubbing the arm of a child who frequently rubs his arms (Wolery, 1978); the increase in adaptive behavior has also been accomplished by providing children with opportunities to engage in the inappropriate behaviors for a few seconds, for example by allowing them access to an object they can manipulate in stereotypic ways (Charlop, Kurtz, & Casey, 1990; Wolery, Kirk, & Gast, 1985). Interestingly, use of those inappropriate behaviors as reinforcers does not appear to lead to increases in those inappropriate behaviors (Charlop et al., 1990; Wolery et al., 1985). Also, some evidence suggests that the effects served by inappropriate behaviors can be used to identify reinforcers (Durand, Crimmins, Caufield, & Taylor, 1989). For example, if a child appears to engage in a problem behavior to get adult attention (see chapter 11), then adult attention may be used as a reinforcer for adaptive behaviors. Thus, by carefully observing children's behavior, potentially powerful reinforcers can be identified.

Fourth, *if the above procedures do not result in useful reinforcers, you should conduct a reinforcer preference test.* Reinforcer preference testing involves providing children with a series of choices between stimuli that may be reinforcers (e.g., foods, drinks, stickers, toys, and sensory stimuli). If the child consistently selects one or two items,

then they will likely have reinforcement value. Mason, McGee, Farmer-Dougan, and Risley (1989) describe a systematic process of identifying reinforcers for young children with disabilities. At the beginning of the study, they presented children with choices of the following stimuli: "(a) olfactory (potpourri, coffee beans); (b) gustatory (juice, animal crackers, or cookies); (c) visual (flashing light, mirror); (d) tactile (vibrating windup toy, fan); (e) thermal (ice, heating pad); (f) vestibular (rocking, spinning); (g) auditory (touch-tone telephone beep, music); and (h) social (clapping, hugs)" (p. 173). Each stimulus was presented to each child 10 times, each time paired with a different stimulus from another group. Each time the child was allowed to select either stimulus. From this extensive testing, any item the child selected on 8 of 10 opportunities was then placed in a reinforcer pool. Each day before an individualized instructional session, a more limited test was conducted. Each child was asked to choose one of the preferred items, and the chosen item then became the reinforcer for the session. When such preferred reinforcers were used, the percent of correct responses increased and the occurrence of problem behaviors decreased.

Selection of reinforcers is critical because different stimuli (potential reinforcers) will have different effects with different children. For example, tickling appears to be a good reinforcer for Sandra, but Josh appears to avoid it. On the other hand, a small windup duck is an excellent reinforcer for Josh, but Sandra does not even look at it. Continual identification of reinforcers also is important, because some reinforcers will be very effective for a while and then they may begin to lose their value. Mason et al. (1989) found that children rarely selected the same reinforcer on consecutive sessions, despite the fact that the stimulus used in the first session appeared to have considerable power. Thus, reinforcers should be identified frequently.

Further, the decreases in problem behavior may occur without specific programming when specially identified reinforcers are used (Dyer, 1987; Mason et al., 1989).

Once reinforcers are identified, you must evaluate whether they can be delivered easily. For example, it is easy to give a child a small cracker or a small toy each time he responds correctly. It is very difficult to allow the child to play outside on the slide each time he does some adaptive behavior. If effective and easily delivered reinforcers are identified, then you should determine whether the reinforcers are acceptable to both the staff and family. If the reinforcers are acceptable, they should be used; if they are not, others should be identified.

Using Reinforcers   Reinforcers will be of little value in increasing motivation for skill acquisition and application unless they are used properly. *The response for which the reinforcer is to be given should be specified clearly.* For example, Jane's teacher wants her to use two words when making requests. If at snack time, Jane holds out her cup and says, "More, more," should the teacher give her more juice or should he say, "More what, Jane?" and attempt to get her to say, "More juice"? *The reinforcer also should be given immediately after the response.* If reinforcers are not given immediately after the desired behavior, then they will not increase that behavior. For instance, Brian is learning to sort objects by shape. When he sorts an object correctly, the teacher records his response, gives him another object, and a few seconds later hands him a reinforcer (a small piece of fruit). In the meantime, Brian begins to look out the window. If the teacher gives him fruit at that moment, she is likely to reinforce looking out the window rather than correct sorting.

When reinforcers such as food, drink, stickers, and toys are used, *the professional should pair those tangible items with social*

stimuli such as praise, touching, and hugs. Such pairing will result in the social stimuli becoming reinforcers. For example, if Gerald is learning to put a puzzle together and gets a sip of milk for each correct piece, the teacher should also say, "You put it in right, Gerald!" and pat him on the back. Social reinforcers are important because they can occur in a variety of situations and can be adapted to the natural environment. When praise is used it should include specific statements about the child's behavior, such as, "You put the puzzle together," rather than "Good work." Further, social reinforcers usually should be given with enthusiasm—except when working with children with high muscle tone that enthusiastic social reinforcement would tend to overstimulate.

When possible, *you should use a variety of reinforcers* (Egel, 1981), especially social ones. This will tend to increase motivation and help in keeping one or two reinforcers from losing their effectiveness. Variety in praise can be accomplished by using different words, animating facial and motor movements, and changing the volume and tone of your voice. Also, when edibles, toys, and stickers are used as reinforcers, children can be presented with a choice of these things (Cybriwsky, Wolery, & Gast, 1990). Presenting choices during instruction allows the child more control over the events of the session and reduces the possibility that a reinforcer will lose its power. Also, there is some evidence that allowing children to choose reinforcers and activities may result in decreases in problem behavior (Dyer et al., 1990; Mason et al., 1989).

Also, when possible, *use natural reinforcers* that occur as a result of the child's behavior or are in the child's typical environment. For instance, Emily and Catherine's teacher wants to increase the amount of time they play cooperatively. Giving them additional toys as a reinforcer is more natural than handing each a raisin and saying, "It's good to see you playing together." Giving toys to them may also prompt additional play and cooperative behavior. Likewise, if Jane says, "More juice," the natural reinforcer is to give her more rather than to say "You're talking so nicely" while giving her "five."

Determining the Best Schedule of Reinforcement The schedule of reinforcement refers to how frequently the reinforcer is given in relation to how frequently the behavior occurs. Usually during initial acquisition and when attempting to increase motivation, reinforcers are given each time the desired behavior occurs. Such a schedule is called a *continuous reinforcement schedule*. Once a skill has been acquired, the schedule can be changed, and the reinforcer is not given each time the behavior occurs. This is called an *intermittent reinforcement schedule*. Continuous reinforcement schedules help children learn the skill more quickly because the reinforcer is provided each time the behavior occurs. Intermittent reinforce-

ment schedules, however, help the child maintain the behavior longer, because they have to do more behaviors to get the reinforcer.

The steps for selecting and using reinforcers are shown in Box 5.7. For more detailed discussion of reinforcers and the procedures for selecting and using them, see Baer (1978), Cooper et al. (1987), and Wolery et al. (1988). It is clear from the literature that the appropriate use of reinforcers is an important part of instruction. Using children's preferred materials and activities as reinforcers, providing children with reinforcer choices, and using a variety of reinforcers can be combined with other external reinforcers, and are likely to result in the most effective learning.

Using Feedback Reinforcers are a special type of feedback; they follow behavior and increase the likelihood that the behavior will reoccur. There are other types of feedback. Some feedback tells children that what they are doing is not correct—that is, that it will

---

BOX 5.7   Steps for selecting and using reinforcers

Steps for Selecting Reinforcers

1 Test things and events which are reinforcers for most young children.
2 Ask the child's parents about specific types of things and activities which may be reinforcers.
3 Observe the child and identify behaviors which the child frequently does or objects the child frequently seeks.
4 Conduct reinforcer preference test by presenting the child with a number of objects which may be reinforcers and by allowing the child to choose from among the array.

Steps for Using Reinforcement Effectively

1 Precisely identify the behavior to be reinforced.
2 Give the reinforcer immediately after the behavior occurs.
3 Pair food, drink, and object reinforcers with social stimuli such as praise and touching the child.
4 Use a variety of reinforcers when possible.
5 Use natural reinforcers when possible.
6 Identify and use the most appropriate schedule of reinforcement.

not result in reinforcement. For example, Mario is playing with a plastic shape-sorting ball. He is trying to insert small shapes into the ball. He tries the round shape in the square hole, the star hole, the cross hole, but it does not fit; he tries it in the round hole, and it easily drops into the ball. He picks up the square block, tries it in the round hole, the triangle hole, the oval hole, but it does not fit; he tries it in the square hole, and it drops into the ball. With repeated experience with this toy, Mario will learn to put the round shape in the round hole and the square shape in the square hole quickly. This learning will occur because he is getting two important types of feedback: The round shape goes in the round hole, but it does not go in the nonround holes. Thus, he is getting information regarding when or under what conditions the behavior of inserting the round shape will be successful. He may also be getting feedback on a pattern of responding: if it does not work the first time, try another hole.

Several recommendations about using feedback can be made for teaching. First, *children should receive feedback on their behavior.* This feedback should tell them when they are correct—when they do a skill in the appropriate contexts and at the appropriate times, they should be reinforced. Similarly, when they perform skills in inappropriate contexts or at inappropriate times, they should receive feedback about this— they should not be reinforced. Nearly everything we learn is correct or acceptable in some contexts and not correct or acceptable in others. For example, counting is acceptable when you need to count; requesting is acceptable when you need information, permission, or assistance; interacting with peers is acceptable in low structure situations; dressing and undressing is acceptable when a change in clothing is needed. Each of these behaviors are legitimate goals of early intervention, but each of them must occur in spe-

cific situations to be considered adaptive. Much of our teaching involves establishing new behaviors and then teaching children when and where those behaviors should be used. One of the primary functions of feedback is to allow children to learn when and where (i.e., under what stimulus conditions) given skills should and should not be performed. This statement applies to the teaching of all types of content to all types of students; as teachers, we must learn under what situations to use which instructional procedures. Children's performance is our primary feedback for determining whether we have made the correct choices. However, with young children who are enrolled in their first group-care situation, there are many things to learn. Consider the situation from the child's perspective. On the first day in the classroom, the teacher greets you, gives you a hug, and helps you hang up your coat. He then encourages you to find a toy and play, and he has a lot of interesting toys. You start playing with a noisy toy, and he comes over, pats you on the back, plays with you a minute, and then goes to another child. Things are going all right; maybe school will not be so bad after all. In a few minutes, all the other children go over to a group of chairs situated in a semicircle. You follow them and take your noisy toy. You get in a chair and keep playing with the toy. The teacher takes it away from you. What is going on? The teacher was so pleased with you a couple minutes ago; why can you now not have the toy? Learning about behaviors being acceptable in some situations but not in others is a major task for young children. Providing feedback is one of the major ways of communicating this information, particularly with children whose language is not well developed.

Second, *the feedback should be provided consistently.* As noted earlier, reinforcement that is provided for every correct behavior will result in more rapid learning than reinforcement that is provided for some of the correct responses. This applies to all types of feedback. Therefore, our feedback should be consistent. For example, when Mario was playing with the shape ball, each time he tried to put the round shape in a hole that was not round he was unsuccessful. If the shape ball was poorly designed and allowed the round shape to fit in the square hole, then it would be quite difficult for Mario to learn that the round shape goes in the round hole (because it sometimes goes in the square hole too). Thus, provision of consistent feedback is critical for teaching children what to do and when and where to do it.

Third, *feedback should be provided immediately*. As we noted earlier, reinforcement will increase the behavior it follows, not the behavior we would like it to follow. The same is true of other types of feedback. For example, when you took your noisy toy to circle time, if the teacher let you play with it for a few minutes and then took it away, what would you learn? Most likely, you would decide that it is okay to take toys to circle time but that at some ill-defined point the teacher might take it away. Thus, if the teacher does not want you to play with noisy toys during circle time, he should take the toy away as soon as you arrive with it.

Fourth, *the feedback should be specific and salient*. To be useful, feedback should be presented in a manner that communicates with the child. The behavior for which feedback is being received should be identified, and it should be obvious to the child that he is receiving feedback. Research has shown that specific rather than general reinforcement will result in more rapid learning (Bernhardt & Forehand, 1975). Thus, when you are providing reinforcement or corrective feedback, it is appropriate to label the behavior that is being reinforced/corrected. For example, when praising a student for labeling a picture of a dog in a book, you should say, "Yes, that is a dog" rather than

saying, "Very good." Similarly, if when you took a toy to circle time, the teacher said, "No," you might decide that he meant you should not come to the circle but could go play, or that you were sitting in the wrong chair, or that you should have done some other behavior. If, however, he said, "Don't bring toys to circle time," you might understand what he was trying to communicate. By making feedback specific, it will also frequently be obvious. However, sometimes people give long explanations to children that decrease the salience of the feedback. For example, you may not understand the teacher's feedback if he said, "The purpose of circle time is to learn about the days of the week, to see what the weather is like, and to sing some fun songs. If we are all going to learn this, then everyone has to be quiet and has to listen real closely. It is inconsiderate of others when some children make too much noise. If we are too loud we can't hear what other children are saying." This type of explanation greatly reduces the salience of the feedback. Going beyond the use of verbalizations, feedback will be even more obvious if some action is required. If the teacher made you give him the toy or made you take it back and put it away, the feedback would have a tangible result.

Fifth, *feedback for incorrect responses should include information on how to do the behavior correctly*. Children can be highly motivated to learn, but if they do not receive information or assistance on how to do the behavior, then learning will not be likely. In chapter 6, we describe a number of procedures for providing children with information about and assistance in doing behaviors. It is important that feedback include information on how to do the behavior. For example, if your instructor gave you feedback about your writing skills, that feedback could be given in a number of ways. He or she could say, "Your writing needs to improve," or "You used too many awkward sentences"; or for each awkward sentence the instructor could write a clearer and less awkward way of writing the same thing. This latter type of feedback will provide you with more information on how to write clearly on the next paper. The same is true in our teaching of young children. If a child is learning to tie his shoes, saying "No, not that way" is not much help; providing some physical assistance may be more useful feedback. Similarly, if a child looks at a picture of a cat and says, "Dog," saying "No" will communicate that "dog" is not correct, but it will not tell the child what is correct. By saying, "No, that's a cat," you can provide feedback that "dog" is not correct *and* that "cat" is.

Sixth, *children should be taught to identify naturally occurring forms of feedback.* It is probably impossible for us to provide children with instruction that will prepare them to respond in all the situations in which they will find themselves. As competent adults, we frequently must make rapid decisions about our behavior based only on the feedback we receive in the situations we find ourselves in. The extent to which our behavior is perceived as acceptable and appropriate probably is related directly to the extent to which we identify and act on the feedback we receive. We need to teach children to identify and respond to naturally occurring forms of feedback. Having this skill is particularly useful in social situations, which frequently employ subtle forms of feedback. For example, with our peers who consistently interrupt us or who tell us the same old jokes or stories over and over, we rarely say, "Don't interrupt me anymore" or "You told me that story, and I don't want to hear it." Rather, we tend to ignore them by acting less attentive, to respond with longer latencies, or to laugh less enthusiastically. How can we teach children to respond to such subtle social cues? While research does not provide definitive direction, some recommendations are pertinent. The most basic element children must learn is that the be-

havior of others should influence their behavior. Fortunately, young children can and do provide fairly salient social cues to their peers. For example, when Casey decides he no longer wants to play with Wendy, he gets up, walks away, and finds something else to do. Or when Wendy wants to look at her book by herself rather than with Casey, she just pushes him away and says, "Don't." Thus, children should be engaged with other socially competent children who can provide them with salient and specific social feedback. In addition, teachers can use verbal explanations of social feedback. For example, when Casey walks away from Wendy and she looks bewildered or upset, the teacher can say, "Sometimes our friends want to play with other things," and then Wendy should be re-directed to play alone, or the situation could be used to teach Wendy to ask someone else to play with her. Similarly, when you are talking with a parent and another child interrupts, you are provided with an opportunity to say, "Wait a minute until I am done talking with Mr. Smith." These verbal explanations are probably most effective when they are coupled with reinforcement. For example, Wendy is most likely to learn that it is okay for Casey to go play elsewhere, if she becomes engaged in a fun task. The interrupting child will probably learn not to interrupt if she is attended to after a couple minutes of appropriate waiting. Similarly, on any occasion where you observe children reading the subtle social cues of other children, you should provide reinforcement and approval.

In summary, children should receive feedback for their behavior because it helps them learn when and where behavior should occur. That feedback can serve reinforcing functions or it can serve to reduce the occurrence of certain behavior. It should be given consistently and immediately after the behavior it addresses. The feedback should be specific—the behavior in question should be named—and obvious. Feedback for incorrect responses should include instructions or directions for doing the behavior correctly. Finally, we need to teach children to respond to naturally occurring feedback, particularly that in social situations. Then once we have motivated learners and ones who are receiving instruction and feedback for their behavior, we must ask, "How can we know if children are learning?"

How Can We Know if Children Are Learning?

Development is complex, the effect of various disabilities on development is multifaceted, children's skill repertoires are highly varied, their environments are quite diverse, and early intervention is a relatively new endeavor. As a result, it is *unlikely* that most intervention teams can devise instructional plans that will be totally accurate in terms of the skills being taught, the arrangements proposed for teaching them, and the strategies used to ensure efficient skill acquisition and use. Thus, the implementation and effects of instruction must be monitored regularly. This monitoring requires three things: (a) assessing whether instruction is implemented as planned, (b) assessing the effects of instruction on children's acquisition and use of high-priority behaviors and other desirable outcomes, and (c) making adjustments when instruction is not producing the desired effects.

Monitoring Implementation   The implementation of instruction should be reviewed and assessed to determine the extent to which correct use occurs (LeLaurin & Wolery, in press). Instruction can be implemented correctly, incorrectly, or inconsistently, or it can be developed but not implemented. If the level of implementation is not known, then it is impossible to make accurate judgments about the effects of the instruction. If instructional strategies have

not been implemented or if they have been implemented inconsistently or incorrectly, then the first step is to correct the problem. Only when correct implementation has occurred is it possible to make a determination whether instruction is successful, partially successful, or totally unsuccessful. Billingsley, White, and Munson (1980) describe procedures for assessing the implementation of instruction, procedures that involve observing the instruction directly and determining the extent to which it matches the plan. As examples, are the appropriate materials used, does the teacher provide the correct task directions, are children provided with an opportunity to respond, is the teacher using the instructional strategy correctly, is reinforcement used as planned? Although their procedures were developed for direct instructional activities, application is also possible to child-directed learning situations. For example, do children go to the appropriate activity areas, do children play with the materials that will allow them to learn the targeted skills, does the teacher reinforce their target behaviors, does the teacher respond to their initiations?

Monitoring the Effects of Instruction   Monitoring the effects of interventions requires some form of systematic data collection. Systems for collecting data on children's performance are well known and described in numerous sources (Bailey & Wolery, 1989; Billingsley & Liberty, 1982; Cooper, 1981; Cooper et al., 1987; Snell, 1987; White & Haring, 1980; Wolery et al., 1988). The results of survey data suggest that some experienced teachers collect data regularly, that they collect a variety of different types of data, and that they use rules for interpreting the data (Farlow & Snell, 1989). Teachers can frequently judge how well students are doing when no data are collected; but data collection does appear to help teachers make more accurate statements about how children's current performance compares to their past performance, and to make more accurate decisions about changes in instruction (Holvoet, O'Neil, Chazdon, Carr, & Warner, 1983).

To guide data collection efforts, we can provide some general guidelines. *Data should be collected on all of the high-priority objectives of each child.* This data collection is necessary to determine whether the instructional arrangements and strategies are producing learning. However, it is probably impossible—and even if it were possible, it would be impractical—to collect data on every instructional program and behavior every time it occurs. Thus, data can be collected on an intermittent basis. This can be accomplished by using probes (assessments) that occur every week or every two weeks. An intermittent probe may simply involve watching the child when a particular behavior is being taught or when it is needed and recording what the child does.

Using such probes, the team can develop a record of the child's learning, and they can then use the results to identify which behaviors and programs need more frequent monitoring. The implication of this latter function is that certain programs should be monitored more regularly than others. New programs on high-priority skills, programs that have been in place but for which no obvious progress is occurring, and programs in which the teacher is concerned about progress should be monitored more frequently and consistently. The purpose of this more frequent data collection is to use the data to make decisions about the changes that are needed in the instruction.

To implement data-based decision making, teachers must have skills in collecting, summarizing, and interpreting data. Although careful collection and use of daily data for decision making is a common practice in business and athletics, it occurs less frequently in education. Data should be collected and used with caution, however, and

teachers should use their common sense in evaluating instruction. For example, Ron's team is teaching him to initiate play with other children, and they are collecting data on the number of times he approaches others and begins to play with the same materials. The data indicate that over a 5-day period, Ron is initiating play more frequently. However, the team members notice that Ron is frequently aggressive toward the child with whom he is playing. Despite the fact that the data indicate he is acquiring the targeted skill, a sensible decision would be to change the focus of instruction to the initiating of play that is sustained and appropriately cooperative.

Teachers must make several decisions regarding data collection. When and how often should data be collected? What type of data should be collected? Sometimes frequent data collection is necessary. The more information the teacher has about a child's performance, the better the position she is in to make appropriate decisions. Frequent records of behavior can demonstrate trends in performance (Is the child learning, getting worse, or staying the same?) as well as variability in performance (Is the child consistent in his responses or are some days much better than others?). The less frequently data are collected, the longer the teacher has to wait to determine trends and variability and the longer an ineffective instructional program may be continued. One mark of excellent teachers is the frequency with which they evaluate and change children's instructional programs, continually adapting them to meet the needs of each child.

As a general rule, data relating to specific skills or behaviors should be collected when those skills are being taught, when the behavior is needed, and when it is likely to occur. For many skills that are receiving direct instruction, the teacher need not collect data during the entire instructional session. A probe consisting of a couple opportunities to do the behavior at the beginning of each session may be sufficient. For skills that are being learned in child-directed situations (e.g., cooperative play with peers), a short observation of a couple minutes at the beginning of a play session, a couple minutes in the middle of the session, and a couple minutes toward the end of the session may provide an adequate sample of the behavior. Data should be collected when behaviors are first being learned (i.e., during acquisition), and then again when fluency, maintenance, and generalization are being promoted.

Teams also must determine the type of data collection that is best for each behavior and program. The type of data that is collected depends upon the intent of the program (Wolery, 1989). Different data collection systems are required depending upon whether the intent is to increase the accuracy, or the frequency (proficiency), or the duration of a behavior. The intent should be expressed in the criterion statement of the child's objective. *Accuracy* refers to how well or how correctly a child does the behavior. It is frequently expressed in terms of the percent of correct responses. This figure is calculated by dividing the number of correct behaviors by the number of opportunities to do the behavior and multiplying by 100. In such cases, teachers should provide children with a specific number of opportunities to do the skill and record the number of times they are correct. The child's percent of correct responses can then be calculated.

Many times we collect data based on the *level of assistance* required to do the behavior. For example, if we are teaching a young child to brush his teeth independently, we might record how much assistance he needed on each step of the skill. We could record whether he did it independently, with verbal directions from the teacher, with the teacher demonstrating how to do the step, or with the teacher moving his hands in doing the correct behaviors.

Again, sometimes it is the *proficiency* or rate of the response that is important. This measure is frequently expressed in terms of the rate of responses per minute and is calculated by dividing the number of responses by the number of minutes the child had to do the behaviors. For instance, the teacher wants to increase Doug's rate of initiations during a 10-minute play period. The teacher would record the time Doug entered the play area and count the number of initiations he made in the next 10 minutes. If Doug made 15 overtures to peers during the 10-minute play period, his average rate of initiation would be 1.5 times per minute. Rate is a particularly sensitive measure during training for both acquisition and fluency. Rate data can be used equally with behaviors that occur correctly or incorrectly. For example, if we wanted to teach Tammy to go up stairs using alternating feet, we could count the number of steps on which she placed only one foot and the number of steps on which she placed both feet. If she went up 20 steps in 2 minutes, and placed only one foot on 12 steps and two feet on 8 steps, we would divide these numbers by two (i.e., the number of minutes). She would have a correct rate of .6 steps per minute and an error rate of .4 steps per minute. Such data are likely to be sensitive indices of children's learning.

Besides collecting data on accuracy, level of assistance, and proficiency, we also frequently collect data on how long behaviors last—on *duration*, that is. For example, you may want to record the duration of Jody's crying episodes, or the length of time it takes Tyrone to return blocks to the shelves. In such cases, you would start timing when the behavior begins and stop timing when the behavior ends. If Jody cried several times each day, you could summarize the data in terms of the total number of minutes of crying or by calculating the average duration of each crying episode.

Sometimes, of course, the professional is not interested in specific behaviors (forms), but in the effects (functions) or categories of behavior. For example, you may be interested in how frequently Ron initiates interactions, responds to the initiations of other children, and makes offers to share his toys. He could use several different behaviors to perform each of these categories of behavior and each of these functions. You would observe him and record any instances of his behavior representing one of these categories.

For each type of data collection we have discussed, the occurrence of the behavior prompts the teacher to record it. In many cases, however, teachers use time to cue them to record the behavior. For example, if you want to know how much time children in your class spend waiting for materials, waiting for their turn, or waiting for help from you, then you could use a time-sampling procedure. The day could be broken into various intervals, and at specified times you would observe and record the behavior. Such data collection can be done in at least three ways. A *momentary time sample system* can be used. Specific times can be identified (e.g., every 10 minutes) and at each time (e.g., at 9:00, 9:10, 9:20), the professional can observe and note which children are waiting *at that moment*. An alternative is the *partial interval system*, following which the teacher might observe from 9:00 to 9:01, then from 9:10 to 9:11, and then from 9:20 to 9:21, during each minute of observation, determining if selected children wait at all during that time. Finally, the *whole interval system* is implemented in the same manner as the partial interval system, with the difference that (to continue with the example) the teacher would record the children as waiting *only* if they waited for entire intervals.

Sample data collection sheets are shown in Figures 5.2 and 5.3. However, you should design your own data sheets to meet your own purposes. Each data sheet should in-clude identifying information (e.g., who was observed, who observed the child, the date, and the behavior being observed), a space for recording the data, and space for summarizing or totalling the data (Tawney & Gast, 1984).

To make the interpretation of data easier, teachers frequently use graphs, simple line graphs that display the value of the behavior being measured on the vertical axis and the passage of time on the horizontal axis. For additional information on graphing consult Parsonson and Baer (1976), White and Haring (1980), and Wolery et al. (1988).

Making Adjustments in Instruction Based on Data   The purpose of data collection on children's behavior is to identify adjustments that are needed in instructional programs. This frequently involves analyzing graphed data and applying data decision rules. Fuchs and Fuchs (1986) found that children learned more when their teachers use specific rules for interpreting their data. A number of data decision rules have been proposed (Haring, Liberty, & White, 1980; Liberty & Haring, 1990; Liberty, 1988). Data decision rules are used to analyze performance patterns and make decisions based on those patterns. A number of decisions and rules for acquisition and fluency are shown in Box 5.8; data decision rules for generalization are shown in Table 5.1 (pp. 156–157). These sets of rules move teaching from guesses about what should be done to more scientifically generated suggestions for potential changes that will correct inefficient skill acquisition and use.

SUMMARY

In this chapter, teaching was defined as the process of manipulating environmental events to organize experiences that will allow learning to occur. We described four phases of learning/performance: acquisition,

A. Rate

Name _____   Date ___/___/___

Behavior _____

    Start time __:__:__   Stop time __:__:__
    Total time __:__:__

    Occurrences

    [ ]

        Total number of occurrences _____

B. Duration

Name _____   Date ___/___/___

Behavior _____

    Start time   Stop time
    _____ | _____
    _____ | _____
    _____ | _____
    _____ | _____

    Total time _____

    Average time per occurrence _____

C. Time sample

Date ___/___/___   Behavior (or name) _____

                    Children's names (or behaviors)

Time						
9:00						
9:05						
9:10						
9:15						
9:20						
9:25						

    ✓ = Occurrence, X = Nonoccurrence

D. Interval sample

Date ___/___/___   Behavior (or name) _____

                    Children's names (or behaviors)

Time						
9:00–9:05						
9:10–9:15						
9:20–9:25						
9:30–9:35						
9:40–9:45						
9:50–9:55						

    ✓ = Occurrence, X = Nonoccurrence

E. Levels of assistance

Name _____   Date ___/___/___

Objective _____

	Trials				
Steps	1	2	3	4	5

FM = Full physical manipulation
PP = Partial physical prompt
M = Model
G = Gesture prompt
VP = Verbal prompt
I = Independent

FIGURE 5.2
Sample data collection sheets

A

Name________________ Date____/____/____
Behavior objective ______________________________

	Correct responses	Error responses	No responses
Total			

C

Name________________ Date____/____/____
Behavior objective ______________________________

Trial	Response	Trial	Response
1		6	
2		7	
3		8	
4		9	
5		10	

√ = Correct response
X = Error response
+ = No response

Total C ________
Total E ________
Total NR ________
Total trials ________

B

Name________________ Date____/____/____
Behavior ______________________________

Trial	C	E	NR
1			
2			
3			
4			
5			
6			
7			
8			
9			
10			
Total			

C = Correct, E = Error
NR = No response

D

Name________________
Objective ______________________________
____

Date____/____/____

Number correct	10	10	10	10	10
	9	9	9	9	9
	8	8	8	8	8
	7	7	7	7	7
	6	6	6	6	6
	5	5	5	5	5
	4	4	4	4	4
	3	3	3	3	3
	2	2	2	2	2
	1	1	1	1	1

– = Correct
X = Error
0 = Total number correct

FIGURE 5.3
Sample data collection sheets for percent data

fluency, maintenance, and generalization. In making the environmental manipulations to promote learning in each of these phases, teachers must first determine what skills need to be learned (e.g., discrete skills, chained tasks, patterns of responding). The specific skills for each child are identified through assessment and through analysis of the assessment information. In addition, teachers must determine how the schedule, physical space, and social dimensions of the environment will be organized. The general guideline is that these variables are organized based on the specific skills children

---

BOX 5.8   Data decision rules for acquisition and fluency

1 Is behavior at criterion?
>   YES - Go to next step/skill.
>   NO - Go to Question 2.

2 Are correct responses at zero?
>   YES - Go back to easier or prerequisite skill.
>   NO - Go to Question 3.

3 Are correct responses increasing and are correct responses higher than errors?
>   YES - Do not change; instruction is working.
>   NO - Go to Question 4.

4 Did previous compliance problems exist at this level?
>   YES - Go to Question 5.
>   NO - Go to Question 6.

5 Are correct responses increasing since previous compliance problems?
>   YES - Go to Question 6.
>   NO - Change to promote compliance—usually consequent events should be changed.

6 Are responses highly variable or has there been a sharp drop in correct responses?
>   YES - Change to promote compliance—usually consequent events should be changed.
>   NO - Go to Question 7.

7 Is the percent of correct responses above 83%?
>   YES - Change to promote fluency—provide practice and motivation to engage in practice.
>   NO - Go to Question 8.

8 Is the trend of correct responses decreasing?
>   YES - Go to Question 9.
>   NO - Change to promote accuracy—usually done through antecedent changes (e.g., add prompting procedures, etc.).

9 Did correct responses start higher than errors?
>   YES - Improve instructional format—change antecedent and/or consequent events.
>   NO - Change to promote accuracy—Usually is promoted through antecedent changes (e.g., add prompting procedure, etc.)

Note: Adapted from "Rules for Data-Based Strategy Decisions in Instructional Programs" by N. G. Haring, K. A. Liberty, and O. R. White, 1980, in *Methods of Instruction for Severely Handicapped Students* (pp. 159–192), W. Sailor, B. Wilcox, and L. Brown (Eds.), Baltimore: Paul Brookes.

---

need to learn. Teachers also must select and use materials that will provide children with the appropriate experiences for learning. In addition, children must be motivated to learn. With young children who have disabilities, motivation frequently requires use of positive reinforcement. Thus, teachers must be skilled in identifying and using rein-forcers. Finally, once instruction is implemented, teachers must collect data to determine whether learning is occurring and whether adjustments need to be made in the instruction. In the next chapter, we address other questions teachers face in providing instruction—which instructional strategies to use, how to organize learning opportuni-

TABLE 5.1
Data decision rules for generalization

Question	Procedures	Answer	Next Step/Decision
A. Has skill generalized at the desired level in all target situations?	Probe for generalization in all desired situations, then compare performance with criteria (IEP objective).	yes	1 SUCCESSFUL INSTRUCTION * Step ahead to a more difficult level of skill * Choose a new skill to teach EXIT sequence
		no	CONTINUE with question B.
B. Has skill been acquired?	Compare performance in instructional situation with criteria for acquisition or performance levels specified in IEP objective. Answer yes if student has met performance levels in training situation but not in generalization.	yes	CONTINUE with question C.
		no	2 SKILL MASTERY PROBLEM * Continue instruction EXIT sequence
C. Is generalization desired to only a few situations?	Analyze function of skill in current and future environments available to student.	yes	CONTINUE with question D.
		no	CONTINUE with question E.
D. Is it possible to train directly in those situations?	Are all situations frequently accessible for training so that training time is likely to be adequate to meet aim date in IEP objective?	yes	3 LIMITED GENERALIZATION SITUATIONS * Train in desired situation * Train sequentially in all situations (i.e., sequential modification) EXIT sequence
		no	CONTINUE with question E.
E. Is the student reinforced even though he/she does not do the largest skill?	Observe student behavior during probes and note events which follow appropriate, inappropriate, target, and nontarget skills. Determine if those events which should follow the target skill, or have been shown to reinforce other skills, are presented to the student, or available even if he does not respond, or if he does the skill incorrectly, or if he misbehaves.	yes	CONTINUE with question F.
		no	CONTINUE with question H.
F. Does the student fail to respond and is reinforced?	Answer yes only if the student is reinforced for doing nothing (i.e., accesses reinforcers for "no response").	yes	4 NONCONTINGENT REINFORCER PROBLEM * Alter generalization contingencies CONTINUE with question G.
		no	
G. Is the behavior reinforced by the same reinforcers as the target skill?	If misbehavior or other behavior accesses same reinforcer available for target skill, answer yes.	yes	5 COMPETING BEHAVIOR PROBLEM * Increase proficiency * Amplify instructed behavior * Alter generalization contingencies EXIT sequence

H. Did the student generalize once at or close to criterion performance levels and then not as well on other opportunities?

Consider performance in current and past probes. Compare student performance for each response opportunity with performance level specified in objective. If near criterion performance occurred on the first response opportunity, and performance was poor or nonexistent after that, answer yes.

- no →
  6 COMPETING REINFORCER PROBLEM
  * Alter generalization contingencies
  EXIT sequence

- yes →
  7 REINFORCING FUNCTION PROBLEM
  * Program natural reinforcers
  * Eliminate training reinforcers
  * Use natural schedules
  * Use natural consequences
  * Teach self-reinforcement
  * Teach to solicit reinforcement
  * Reinforce generalized behavior
  * Alter generalization contingencies
  EXIT sequence

CONTINUE with question I.

I. Did the student respond partially correctly during at least one response opportunity?

Analyze anecdotal data and observation notes from probe.

- no →
  8 DISCRIMINATION FUNCTION PROBLEM
  Vary stimuli:
  * Use all stimuli
  * Use frequent stimuli
  * Use multiple exemplars
  * Use general case exemplars
  EXIT sequence

- yes →
  CONTINUE with question J.

J. Did the student fail to perform any part of the target skill?

Analyze student performance during probe situation.

- no →
  9 GENERALIZATION TRAINING FORMAT
  * Increase proficiency
  * Program natural reinforcers
  * Use natural schedules
  * Use appropriate natural stimuli
  * Eliminate training stimuli
  EXIT sequence

- yes →
  STOP. You have made an error in the sequence. Begin again at Question A.

Note: From "Decision Rules and Procedures for Generalization" by K. Liberty, 1988, in *Generalization for Students with Severe Handicaps: Strategies and Solutions* (pp. 177–204), N. G. Haring (Ed.), Seattle, WA: University of Washington Press. Copyright 1988 by Washington Research Organization. Reprinted by permission.

ties, how to extend learning beyond the immediate instructional context.

REFERENCES

Albin, R. W., & Horner, R. H. (1988). Generalization with precision. In R. H. Horner, G. Dunlap, & R. L. Koegel (Eds.), *Generalization and maintenance: Life-style changes in applied settings* (pp. 99–120). Baltimore: Paul Brookes.

Baer, D. M. (1978). The behavioral analysis of trouble. In K. E. Allen, V. A. Holm, & R. L. Schiefelbusch (Eds.), *Early intervention—a team approach* (pp. 57–93). Baltimore: University Park Press.

Bagnato, S. J., Neisworth, J. T., & Munson, S. M. (1989). *Linking developmental assessment and early intervention: Curriculum-based prescriptions* (2nd ed.). Rockville, MD: Aspen.

Bambara, L., Spiegel-McGill, P., Shores, R. E., & Fox, J. J. (1984). A comparison of reactive and nonreactive toys on severely handicapped children's manipulative play. *The Journal of the Association for Persons with Severe Handicaps, 9,* 142–149.

Bailey, D. B., & Wolery, M. (Eds.). (1989). *Assessing infants and preschoolers with handicaps.* Columbus, OH: Merrill.

Bernhardt, A. J., & Forehand, R. (1975). The effects of labeled and unlabeled praise upon lower and middle class children. *Journal of Experimental Child Psychology, 19,* 536–543.

Billingsley, F. F., & Liberty, K. A. (1982). The use of time-based data in instructional programming for the severely handicapped. *Journal of the Association for the Severely Handicapped, 7*(1), 47–55.

Billingsley, F. F., White, O. R., & Munson, R. (1980). Procedural reliability: A rationale and an example. *Behavioral Assessment, 2,* 229–241.

Bradley, R. H. (1985). Social-cognitive development and toys. *Topics in Early Childhood Special Education, 5*(3), 11–30.

Bricker, D. (1989). *Early intervention for at-risk and handicapped infants, toddlers, and preschool children.* Palo Alto, CA: VORT.

Charlop, M. H., Kurtz, P. F., & Casey, F. G. (1990). Using aberrant behaviors as reinforcers for autistic children. *Journal of Applied Behavior Analysis, 23,* 163–181.

Cooper, J. O. (1981). *Measuring behavior* (2nd ed.). Columbus, OH: Merrill.

Cooper, J. O., Heron, T. E., & Heward, W. L. (1987). *Applied behavior analysis.* Columbus, OH: Merrill.

Cybriwsky, C. A., Wolery, M., & Gast, D. L. (1990). Use of a constant time delay procedure in teaching preschoolers in a group format. *Journal of Early Intervention, 14,* 99–116.

Dunlap, G., & Koegel, R. L. (1980). Motivating autistic children through stimulus variation. *Journal of Applied Behavior Analysis, 13,* 619–627.

Durand, V. M., Crimmins, D. B., Caufield, M., & Taylor, J. (1989). Reinforcer assessment I: Using problem behavior to select reinforcers. *Journal of the Association for Persons with Severe Handicaps, 14,* 113–126.

Dyer, K. (1987). The competition of autistic stereotyped behavior with usual and specifically assessed reinforcers. *Research in Developmental Disabilities, 8,* 607–626.

Dyer, K., Dunlap, G., & Winterling, V. (1990). Effects of choice making on the serious problem behaviors of students with severe handicaps. *Journal of Applied Behavior Analysis, 23,* 515–524.

Egel, A. L. (1981). Reinforcer variation: Implications for motivating developmentally disabled children. *Journal of Applied Behavior Analysis, 14,* 345–350.

Farlow, L. J., & Snell, M. E. (1989). Teacher use of student performance data to make instructional decisions: Practices in programs for students with moderate to profound disabilities. *Journal of the Association for Persons with Severe Handicaps, 14,* 13–22.

Fuchs, L. S., & Fuchs, D. (1986). Effects of systematic formative evaluation: A meta-analysis. *Exceptional Children, 53,* 199–208.

Gibbs, E. D., & Teti, D. M. (1990). *Interdisciplinary assessment of infants: A guide for early intervention professionals.* Baltimore: Paul Brookes.

Goldstein, H., Angelo, D., Mousetis, L. (1987). Acquisition and extension of syntactic repertoires by severely mentally retarded youth. *Research in Developmental Disabilities, 8,* 549–574.

Guess, D. (1969). A functional analysis of receptive language and productive speech: Acquisition of the plural morpheme. *Journal of Applied Behavior Analysis, 2,* 55–64.

Guess, D., & Helmstetter, E. (1986). Skill cluster instruction and the individualized curriculum sequencing model. In R. H. Horner, L. M. Meyer, & H. D. Fredericks (Eds.), *Education of learners with severe handicaps: Exemplary service strategies* (pp. 221–246). Baltimore: Paul Brookes.

Haring, N. G., Liberty, K. A., & White, O. R. (1980). Rules for data-based strategy decisions in instructional programs. In W. Sailor, B. Wilcox, & L. Brown (Eds.), *Methods of instruction for severely handicapped students* (pp. 159–192). Baltimore: Paul Brookes.

Hart, B., & Risley, T. R. (1975). Incidental teaching of language in the preschool. *Journal of Applied Behavior Analysis, 8,* 411–420.

Helmstetter, E., & Guess, D. (1987). Application of the individualized curriculum sequencing model to learners with severe sensory impairments. In L. Goetz, D. Guess, K. Stremel-Campbell (Eds.), *Innovative program design for individuals with dual sensory impairments* (pp. 255–282). Baltimore: Paul Brookes.

Holvoet, J., O'Neil, C., Chazdon, L., Carr, D., & Warner, J. (1983). Hey, do we really have to take data? *Journal of the Association for the Severely Handicapped, 8,* 56–70.

Horn, E., Hazel, A. J., & Hamlett, C. (1991). An investigation of the feasibility of a video game system for developing scanning and selecting skills. *The Journal of the Association for Persons with Severe Handicaps, 16,* 108–115.

Horner, R. H., Albin, R. W., & Ralph, G. (1986). Generalization with precision: The role of negative teaching examples in the instruction of generalized grocery item selection. *Journal of the Association for Persons with Severe Handicaps, 11,* 300–308.

Horner, R. H., Dunlap, G., & Koegel, R. L. (Eds.). (1988). *Generalization and maintenance: Life-style changes in applied settings.* Baltimore: Paul Brookes.

Horner, R. H., McDonnell, J. J., & Bellamy, G. T. (1986). Teaching generalized skills: General case instruction in simulation and community settings. In R. H. Horner, L. H. Meyer, & H. D. Fredericks (Eds.), *Education of learners with severe handicaps: Exemplary service strategies* (pp. 289–314). Baltimore: Paul Brookes.

Langley, M. B. (1985). Selecting, adapting, and applying toys as learning tools for handicapped children. *Topics in Early Childhood Special Education, 5*(3), 101–118.

LeLaurin, K., & Wolery, M. (in press). Research standards in early intervention: Defining, describing, and measuring the independent variable. *Journal of Early Intervention.*

Liberty, K. (1988). Decision rules and procedures for generalization. In N. G. Haring (Ed.), *Generalization for students with severe handicaps: Strategies and solutions* (pp. 177–204). Seattle, WA: University of Washington Press.

Liberty, K., & Billingsley, F. F. (1988). Strategies to improve generalization. In N. G. Haring (Ed.), *Generalization for students with severe handicaps: Strategies and solutions* (pp. 143–176). Seattle, WA: University of Washington Press.

Liberty, K., & Haring, N. G. (1990). Introduction to decision rule systems. *Remedial and Special Education, 11,* 32–41.

Lovaas, I., Newsom, C., & Hickman, C. (1987). Self-stimulatory behavior and perceptual reinforcement. *Journal of Applied Behavior Analysis, 20,* 45–68.

Mason, S. A., McGee, G. G., Farmer-Dougan, V., & Risley, T. R. (1989). Practical strategy for ongoing reinforcer assessment. *Journal of Applied Behavior Analysis, 22,* 171–179.

Musselwhite, C. R. (1986). *Adaptive play for special needs children: Strategies to enhance communication and learning.* Boston: Little Brown.

National Association for the Education of Young Children. (1990). Guidelines for appropriate curriculum content and assessment in programs serving children ages three through eight. Washington, DC: NAEYC.

Odom, S. L., & Strain, P. S. (1984). Classroom-based social skills instruction for severely handicapped preschool children. *Topics in Early Childhood Special Education, 4*, 97–116.

Parsonson, B. S., & Baer, D. M. (1976). The analysis and presentation of graphic data. In T. R. Kratochwil (Ed.), *Single subject research: Strategies for evaluating change.* New York: Academic Press.

Richmond, G. (1983). Comparison of automated and human instruction for developmentally retarded preschool children. *The Journal of the Association for the Severely Handicapped, 8*(3), 78–84.

Rubin, K. H., & Howe, N. (1985). Toys and play behaviors: An overview. *Topics in Early Childhood Special Education, 5*(3), 1–9.

Shevin, M. (1982). The use of food and drink in classroom management programs for severely handicapped children. *Journal of the Association for the Severely Handicapped, 7*, 40–46.

Snell, M. E. (Ed.). (1987). *Systematic instruction of people with severe handicaps* (3rd. ed.). Columbus, OH: Merrill.

Sprague, J. R., & Horner, R. H. (1984). The effects of single instance, multiple instance, and general case training on generalized vending machine use by moderately and severely handicapped students. *Journal of Applied Behavior Analysis, 17*, 273–278.

Stokes, T. F., & Baer, D. M. (1977). An implicit technology of generalization. *Journal of Applied Behavior Analysis, 10*, 347–367.

Tawney, J. W., & Gast, D. L. (1984). *Single subject research in special education.* Columbus, OH: Merrill.

Templeman, T. P., Fredericks, H. D., & Udell, T. (1989). Integration of children with moderate and severe handicaps into a day-care center. *Journal of Early Intervention, 13*, 315–328.

Wachs, T. D. (1979). Proximal experience and early cognitive-intellectual development:

The physical environment. *Merrill-Palmer Quarterly, 25*, 3–41.

Wachs, T. D. (1985). Toys as an aspect of the physical environment: Constraints and nature of relationship to development. *Topics in Early Childhood Special Education, 5*(3), 31–46.

Wachs, T. D., & Sheehan, R. (Eds.). (1988). *Assessment of young developmentally disabled children.* New York: Plenum.

White, O. R., & Haring, N. G. (1980). *Exceptional teaching* (2nd ed.). Columbus, OH: Merrill.

Wolery, M. (1978). Self-stimulatory behavior as a basis for devising reinforcers. *AAESPH Review, 3*, 23–29.

Wolery, M. (1989). Using direct observation in assessment. In D. B. Bailey & M. Wolery (Eds.), *Assessing infants and preschoolers with handicaps* (pp. 64–96). Columbus, OH: Merrill.

Wolery, M., Ault, M. J., & Doyle, P. M. (in press). *Teaching students with moderate and severe disabilities: Use of response prompting procedures.* White Plains, NY: Longman.

Wolery, M., Bailey, D. B., & Sugai, G. M. (1988). *Effective teaching: Principles and procedures of applied behavior analysis with exceptional students.* Boston: Allyn and Bacon.

Wolery, M., Kirk, K., & Gast, D. L. (1985). Stereotypic behavior as a reinforcer: Effects and side effects. *Journal of Autism and Developmental Disorders, 15*, 149–161.

Wolinsky, G., & Walker, S. (1975). Home safety inventory for parents of preschool handicapped children. *Teaching Exceptional Children, 7*(3), 82–86.

Yoder, P. J. (1990). The theoretical and empirical basis of early amelioration of developmental disabilities: Implications for future research. *Journal of Early Intervention, 14*, 27–42.

York, J., Nietupski, J., & Hamre-Nietupski, S. (1985). A decision-making process for using microswitches. *The Journal of the Association for Persons with Severe Handicaps, 10*, 214–223.

6

Strategies for Intervention: Teaching Procedures and Options

The teaching process, as described in chapter 5, includes identifying skills children need to learn; organizing the schedule and the physical dimension and social composition of the environment to promote learning; selecting appropriate materials; motivating children to learn; and monitoring whether they are learning. These issues are central to teaching, but they are not the entire process. We must ask three additional questions about the teaching process: (a) What teaching strategies can be used? (b) How can instructional opportunities be organized? and (c) How can we extend learning so that it has benefits beyond the immediate instructional context? Although we focus on these issues in this sep-arate chapter, they are integral with the process described in chapter 5.

WHAT TEACHING STRATEGIES CAN BE USED?

In the past 20 years, a lot of research has been devoted to developing and evaluating instructional procedures for teaching children with disabilities. In Box 6.1 ten types of strategies are listed. These strategies represent the range of environmental manipulations we make to organize experiences so that children will learn important behaviors. Many of these strategies are described in substantial detail in other chapters of this

---

BOX 6.1   Potential intervention strategies

1 Structuring the physical space and providing toys and materials that promote play, engagement, and learning.
2 Structuring the social dimension of the environment to include models and proximity to peers and responsive adults to increase engagement, interaction, and learning.
3 Using children's preferences for particular materials and activities to promote engagement and learning.
4 Structuring routines using violation of expectancy, naturalistic time delay, and transition-based teaching to promote interaction and learning.
5 Using structured play activities to promote interactions, communication, and acquisition and use of specific skills.
6 Using differential reinforcement, response shaping, and correspondence training to increase the complexity and duration of children's responses and engagement, and the display of appropriate behaviors.
7 Using peer-mediated strategies (i.e., providing specific training to peers) to promote social and communicative behavior in target children.
8 Using naturalistic or milieu teaching strategies (e.g., models, expansions, incidental teaching, mand-model procedure, naturalistic time delay) to promote communication and social skills.
9 Using response prompting procedures (e.g., most-to-least prompting, graduated guidance, system of least prompts, simultaneous prompting, progressive time delay, constant time delay) to ensure acquisition and use of specific skills from a number of domains.
10 Using stimulus modifications (stimulus shaping, stimulus fading, and superimposition) to promote acquisition of specific skills from a number of domains.

book; thus, in this chapter, they are discussed briefly. In this section, we describe these instructional strategies and discuss guidelines for selecting from among them.

Description of Instructional Strategies

Each strategy that we discuss here is designed to promote learning; however, the strategies are different from one another in some important ways. Some of the strategies are used to increase the likelihood that children will engage in the desired skills. Others are used to respond to children's behaviors and thereby promote learning. Again, some strategies are designed to provide children with assistance in performing and learning difficult behaviors, and other strategies are designed to make the stimuli to which children should respond more obvious (salient). (For a discussion of the process—establishing stimulus control—that drives these strategies, consult Wolery, Ault, and Doyle, in press.)

The strategies involve adjustments of setting variables (events), antecedent events, and/or consequent events. *Setting variables/events* are characteristics of the context or environment—the schedule (e.g., the type, sequence, length, and structure of the activities), the physical space, the materials, the number and type of persons present, the heat, the noise, and so forth. *Antecedent events* are stimuli, often specific behaviors of others, that occur before the child performs each behavior. The stimulus could be directions from an adult (e.g., "What are you doing?"), the behavior of a peer (e.g., giving a toy to the child and inviting him/her to play), or the antecedent step in some response chain (e.g., putting the toothpaste on the toothbrush is an antecedent for putting the toothbrush in the mouth). *Consequent events* are stimuli that occur after the child's behavior, stimuli that increase the occurrence of behavior (i.e., reinforcers), decrease

the occurrence of behavior (i.e., punishing stimuli), and those that have no effect on behavior (i.e., neutral stimuli). Again, the strategies work by making changes in the setting, antecedent, or consequent events.

The strategies also differ from one another in how they call for a teaching opportunity to be initiated. In some cases, the opportunity is to be initiated by the child's behavior. For example, during play time, Yancy's teacher noticed her intently looking and pointing at a picture in a book and then looking at the teacher. The teacher could use such a situation to provide Yancy with an opportunity to ask a question about the picture, to label the picture, or to describe it. In other cases, the opportunity for instruction may be signaled by an event. For example, when snack is completed, an opportunity exists for teaching children to clean their areas and throw away their napkins and cups. In still other cases, peers may signal opportunities for instruction. For example, when a peer initiates a social interaction, the child with disabilities has an opportunity to learn to respond to social bids. Or, the teacher may signal the opportunity, perhaps by asking direct questions (e.g., "How many blocks do you have?").

Structuring the Physical Space to Promote Engagement and Learning We briefly discussed the structuring of the physical space in chapter 5; and we will discuss this issue in more detail in chapters 7 and 8. Here we simply note this general guideline: *The physical environment should be structured to promote experiences that will cause children to learn important skills.* The professional must consider what skills the children need to learn *and* what effects various environmental arrangements will have on the children's behavior. Some ways of structuring the environment will increase the likelihood that children will perform important behaviors, and other ways will decrease this likelihood. The manipulation of the physical structure of the environment is important to the teaching process.

Structuring the Social Environment by Using Models, Proximity, and Responsive Adults to Promote Engagement and Learning

We discuss the structuring of the social environment in depth in chapters 7 and 8; and we discuss the effects and uses of peers in the environment in chapter 9. Here we consider the role of adults during child-directed learning. Dunst et al. (1987) identified five guidelines for promoting the interactive skills of young children, strategies which hold implications for other areas of instruction as well. First, the adult should be "sensitive to the child's behavior" (p. 29)—the adult (parent, other care-giver, teacher, therapist) should assume an observer or monitor role. The child's behavior should be watched to determine what secures the child's attention and what causes shifts in the child's focus of attention. The assumption is that attention is prerequisite to learning and that child-initiated attention (i.e., the child selects the focus of attention) sets the stage for optimal learning.

Second, adults should read "the child's behavior as intents to interact" (Dunst et al., 1987, p. 29). Although nearly all acts may carry different intents, instruction is probably best accomplished when the intent of the child's behavior is understood. The young infant who is being fed may look at the mother, coo, and smile. The intent of this behavior may be "I like what you are feeding me, give me more" or it may be, "I am full and ready to interact with you." To interpret the intents of children's behavior, the adult must have knowledge of the child, assess the context in which the behavior occurs, make a quick judgment about potential intents, select the most likely intent, respond accordingly, and evaluate the accuracy of the selection (i.e., did the child respond as though

you had understood or as though you had misinterpreted his cue?).

Third, the environment (physical and social) should be responsive to children's behavior (Yoder, 1990). Many infants with disabilities and many young children with severe disabilities need to learn "an awareness of control over the environment" (Brinker & Lewis, 1982, p. 38), an awareness that their behavior causes effects and that their behavior can be used to discover the range of effects possible. *Contingent responding*, a technique that has been used to teach this awareness, involves ensuring that some obvious response from the environment follows the infant's or the child's acts. The response may be social; for example, contingent upon each movement of the infant, the adult may provide animated facial expressions, exaggerated talk characterized by repetition, and physical contact (stroking, tickling, etc.). Or the response from the environment may be delivered mechanically through microcomputers and other specialized devices (Brinker & Lewis, 1982). Thus, being responsive to children's behavior can teach them to learn on their own and can be used to increase the behaviors that are important for more adaptive functioning.

Fourth, adults should encourage children's ongoing interactions. Daily activities (at home and/or in a class) should be structured to encourage high levels of engagement (see chapter 8) and child-initiated play and interactions. This guideline also emphasizes the importance of increasing the duration of children's engagement, play, interactions, and communicative exchanges. This goal is probably best achieved by providing additional materials, responding to children's behavior, suggesting expansions, and reinforcing longer durations or more complex behavior.

Fifth, adults should support and encourage children's attempts to display more complex behaviors. This guideline is slightly different from the fourth guideline. The focus is not on the content of children's play or interactions; rather it is on teaching children to try new things, to explore, to vary their responses, and to persist despite unsuccessful attempts to solve some problem. It is quite difficult to structure instructional sessions or activities that will cause children to learn such styles of responding. Thus, to ensure opportunities to support such skills, a challenging environment should be provided and the adult should be responsive to children's attempts.

Using Children's Preferences to Promote Learning   As with older children and adults, young children frequently display preferences for specific materials, activities, and other persons. Some preferences are quite durable, but others appear to change from day to day and sometimes within days (Mason, McGee, Farmer-Dougan, & Risley, 1989). When possible, teachers should honor children's preferences in terms of activities to be engaged in, and the reinforcers to be used for adaptive performance (see chapter 5). The underlying assumption is that if the child can learn the same important skill from more than one activity, then instruction probably will be more successful using the activity the child prefers. Children are generally more motivated to participate in activities they prefer than in low-preference activities. This notion does not mean that children should never encounter difficult situations or be encouraged to participate in low-preference activities; such an arrangement would be unrealistic. However, it does mean that children should be provided with as many choices as possible. Benefits other than increased motivation also appear to occur when children are provided with choices. For example, children appear to engage in less social avoidance behavior when in preferred activities (Koegel, Dyer, & Bell, 1987), and children appear to engage in less

inappropriate or problem behavior when given choices (Dyer, Dunlap, & Winterling, 1990). Thus, in structuring the environment, the educator should identify and endeavor to use children's preferences for particular materials, playmates, and activities.

Structuring Routines Using Violation of Expectancy, Naturalistic Time Delay, and Transition-Based Teaching   These strategies have been devised for use in routines and in transitions between activities. *Routines*, described in more detail later, are events that must be completed on a regular basis and frequently involve chains of responses. Examples of routines are getting dressed and undressed, entering the classroom and hanging up coats, preparing for snack, cleaning up and putting away materials after an activity, diaper changing and toileting, leaving for the day and getting in a car or bus. Routines are performed daily and in fairly ritualistic ways; thus, infants and young children begin to anticipate particular steps. This anticipation sets the stage for the use of *violation of expectancy*, which involves the adult doing some step incorrectly, doing a step out of sequence, or not performing a regularly completed step. In the case of dressing a young toddler, the adult could do a step incorrectly by attempting to put the shoe on the child's hand; a step out of sequence could be putting the shoes on the feet before the socks or putting the underpants on over the trousers; and not performing a step might involve putting the sock over the toes and stopping. Violation of expectancy can be used to (a) increase social initiations (e.g., the child initiates some social behavior because of an incorrect or out-of-sequence step or because of the adult's failure to complete a step); (b) increase communicative initiations (e.g., the child initiates some communicative exchange because the routine was violated); and (c) foster independence by setting the occasion for the child to complete the step on her own.

A procedure that is similar to violation of expectancy is *naturalistic time delay*, which is a variation of constant time delay (described later). Naturalistic time delay is used in routines or at other times to teach communicative behavior (Halle, Alpert, & Anderson, 1984; Halle, Baer, & Spradlin, 1981). Using the procedure, the adult may skip a step of the routine he usually performs. As that step arises in the routine, the adult stays in close proximity to the child, looks expectantly at her and withholds the materials or the opportunity to continue the routine for a fixed amount of time (e.g., for 5 seconds). If the child initiates a communicative response, the routine continues (e.g., materials are provided); if the child does not initiate, the teacher provides a model of the communicative behavior, the child imitates, and the routine continues. When implemented in routines and at other times throughout the day, this procedure has been effective in teaching children to make requests and in increasing the length of verbalizations, responsivity, and spontaneous communicative behavior (Schwartz, Anderson, & Halle, 1989).

A similar strategy is *transition-based teaching*, which involves the adult presenting a learning opportunity during transitions between activities (e.g., when going from the free play area to circle time, or from circle time to the bathroom). As an activity concludes, the teacher secures the child's attention, displays the stimulus and task direction (e.g., "What's this?"), and provides an opportunity for the child to respond. If the child's response is correct, the teacher praises the child and allows the transition to continue; if it is incorrect or if the child does not respond, then the teacher provides assistance; the child responds correctly; and the transition continues. This procedure is effective in teaching pre-academic content such

as naming letters, pictures, and shapes (Wolery, Doyle, Gast, Ault, & Lichtenberg, 1991).

Using Structured Play Activities As we have noted, the physical space and activities should be individualized based on the behaviors to be learned and the preferences of the children involved. The structure of play activities should also be individualized (see chapter 9). DeKlyen and Odom (1989) evaluated the effects of various levels of structure in play activities. They rated the amount of structure using the following rules.

Consider how the teacher structures the activity—by setting rules, defining what children can and can't do, etc.—especially but not exclusively before the children start playing. There are a number of tasks to be accomplished in social play: a) agreeing on the theme of play, b) assuming roles, c) managing the temporal structure of play (e.g., taking turns), d) handling interruptions, e) communicating, and f) changing the theme. To the extent that the teacher takes care of any of these, the structure score would be higher; to the degree that children are free to choose and perform these (e.g., deciding whether to play "shopping" or "family" in the dress-up activity), teacher structure would receive a lower score. (DeKlyen & Odom, 1989, p. 246)

This description provides a useful definition of the structure of play activities. Interestingly, these authors' findings indicated that increased peer social interaction occurred for both children with and children without disabilities as the structure of the play activities increased. Thus, if the goal is to increase the amount of interactions, then teachers should structure play activities. If more independent play is desired, then the structure (as just defined) should be low. Odom et al. (1988) describe a number of play activities of low and high structure in their *Integrated Preschool Curriculum*.

Affection training is a specialized strategy involving the structure of play activities

(McEvoy et al., 1988). In affection training, the teacher adapts frequently used preschool games to increase the amount of physical contact between children (touching, hugs, pats on the back, etc.), the amount of rough and tumble play, and the amount of discussions about "friends." McEvoy et al. (1988) used these procedures with three preschool children with autism to increase their interactions with peers during the affection training activities. For two of the three children, peer interactions also increased in a generalization free-play setting. For the third subject, verbal instructions to find a friend were required before peer interactions increased. The studies we have considered here indicate that the amount of structure and the nature of play activity can set the stage for interactions and learning.

Using Differential Reinforcement, Response Shaping, and Correspondence Training

Differential reinforcement, response shaping, and correspondence training are different from the previously discussed strategies, which involve the manipulation of setting events (e.g., of the structure of the physical space, the social composition of the environment, children's preferences, routines and transitions, and play activities). Differential reinforcement, response shaping, and correspondence training are manipulations of consequent events.

Differential reinforcement involves the presentation of reinforcement under defined conditions and the withholding of reinforcement under other conditions. Differential reinforcement is a powerful tool for increasing the occurrence of behaviors in nearly all types of populations, in subjects of all ages, and in highly varied settings. As we indicated in chapter 5, reinforcement can be used to increase children's motivation to participate in planned experiences. It can also be used to teach children when and under what situations particular behaviors should be displayed. This teaching is accomplished by reinforcing the desired behaviors when they occur in desired situations and by withholding reinforcement when the behaviors occur in other contexts.

Response shaping is a variation of differential reinforcement involving differential reinforcement of successive approximations of a target behavior (Cooper, Heron, & Heward, 1987). Following this strategy, the teacher can begin to reinforce the child for behavior that is quite inferior to the behavior eventually wanted. Over time, the teacher then shifts the contingency to reinforce progressively more accurate representations of the target behavior. For example, Hung rarely played with toys but sometimes touched them. At first her teacher reinforced her each time she touched a toy. After the frequency of touching increased, the teacher shifted the contingency and only provided reinforcement if Hung held a toy. Then after holding increased, the contingency was shifted to moving a toy. Over time, this process resulted in adaptive toy play. Initially, the toys communicated, "If you touch me, reinforcement is probable"; at the next level, the toys communicated, "If you hold me, reinforcement is probable, but it is not available for touching anymore." In this example, response shaping was applied to the complexity of Hung's play behaviors; progressively more complex manipulations of the toy were reinforced. Response shaping also can be used to increase the duration of behaviors (e.g., reinforcing Hung for playing longer with toys) and for increasing how fast (rate) behaviors occur (Wolery, Bailey, & Sugai, 1988). Thus, response shaping can be used to promote acquisition of more complex responses and to facilitate fluency.

Correspondence training involves reinforcing children for making verbalizations about their behaviors, or for matching their verbalizations and their behavior (i.e., for achieving a correspondence between their saying and doing) (Baer, 1990; Paniagua, 1990). Correspondence training can be implemented in several different ways (cf. Paniagua, 1990; chapter 11) and is based on the assumption that verbal behavior may influence nonverbal behavior. When using correspondence training, the professional first reinforces children for making verbalizations about their behavior. For example, a goal for Manuel is that he will play cooperatively with his peers. Prior to the play session, the teacher could stop Manuel, ask him what he is going to do, allow or prompt him to respond verbally, and provide reinforcement for his verbalization. Sometimes, simply reinforcing children's verbalizations will result in nonverbal behavior change (e.g., in Manuel's case, more cooperative play). At other times it may be necessary to shift the reinforcement contingency to reinforce verbalizations that match what children actually do. Frequently, reinforcing the correspondence between saying and doing will result in desirable behavior changes. For example, Manuel's teacher could ask him how he's going to play, secure his verbal response, observe his play, and provide reinforcement after the play session if Manuel's actual play matched his verbalization. Because of the relatively low effort involved in correspondence training, it is a viable strategy to use in child-directed learning situations.

Using Peer-Mediated Strategies   A number of strategies have been developed over the years that involve peers (Strain, 1981). Because of their implications for social skill development, these strategies are described in chapter 9. Kohler and Strain (1990) have identified four types of peer-mediated interventions. First, *peer management* (which they describe as nonacademic) "involves teaching a peer to prompt and/or provide

consequences of the nonacademic responses of the target individual" (Kohler & Strain, 1990, p. 4). An example of such a strategy is the peer social initiation technique (Strain & Odom, 1986). Following this procedure, the adult trains a peer (called a "confederate") by giving a verbal description of the social initiations desired and of their importance, by modeling the procedure, by encouraging the confederate to engage in role-play, and by giving verbal feedback. The confederate and the target child are then allowed to play with one another, and reminders and reinforcement are provided to the confederate for implementing the training (Strain & Odom, 1986). This procedure has been used successfully to increase the contact and interactions between young children with and without disabilities.

Peer tutoring (which Kohler and Strain refer to as academic) is a second type of peer-mediated intervention that involves a peer teaching a target child a skill (i.e., a particular physical, cognitive, or communicative skill, for example, not simply social skills). The peer learns to provide antecedent and/or consequent events and apply them with the target child. This strategy is exemplified in a study that taught 4-year-old children with typical and/or advanced development to engage their peers with disabilities in communicative exchanges (Goldstein & Wickstrom, 1986). Typical peers were taught to establish eye contact; obtain a joint focus of attention; describe their play and that of others; provide requests with a hierarchy of steps; respond to the target child's speech with imitation, expansions, requests for clarification; and redirect the play. The preschoolers with disabilities increased the frequency of their communicative responses and evidenced slight increases in their communicative initiations.

Peer modeling, a third type of peer-mediated intervention, involves having a peer perform the responses desired from the target child. Peer imitation training is an example of this strategy (Peck, Apolloni, Cooke, & Raver, 1978). Following this procedure, in a free play setting, the teacher will attempt during brief periods of time to increase one child's level of imitative behavior. When the child with disabilities is in close proximity to a peer model who is engaged in appropriate behavior, the teacher says, "Look! See what she is doing?" and points to the peer model. The teacher then cues the child to do the behavior (e.g., "You do it."). If the target child imitates, reinforcement is provided. If imitation is not forthcoming, the teacher verbally or physically assists the child through the action and provides reinforcement. Over time the assistance is slowly removed so that the child learns to imitate the behavior of his/her peers. This procedure has been effective in establishing frequent imitation in the training area and in non-training free play sessions (Peck et al., 1978).

The fourth peer mediated intervention identified by Kohler and Strain (1990) is the use of *group contingencies*. Pursuing this strategy, the teacher provides reinforcement equally for all group members but makes this blanket reinforcement dependent upon the performance of just one or a few of the group's members. There are several different ways to structure these contingencies, and frequently unplanned social initiations, interactions, and tutoring may occur (Greenwood & Hops, 1981). Group contingencies have been used without specific training of peers and also in combination with other peer-mediated strategies (Kohler & Strain, 1990; Kohler, Strain, Maretsky, & DeCesare, 1990).

The peer mediated interventions seek to use peers to provide children with experiences that promote learning. Specifically, the peer's behavior sets the occasion (e.g., through peer modeling) for the child with the disability to do the target behavior; or it prompts the occurrence (e.g., through peer

management or peer tutoring) of behavior and provides reciprocal responses and reinforcement; or it provides contingencies (e.g., group contingencies) to reinforce the target behavior. Although there is solid research evidence of the effectiveness of these procedures, some issues of practicality (e.g., the amount of adult effort and time required to use the procedures) need further investigation (Kohler & Strain, 1990).

Using Naturalistic or Milieu Teaching Strategies Efforts in the 1960's indicated that persons with disabilities could learn language when they were instructed systematically; however, the language skills that were learned often were not used when and where they were needed. Thus, naturalistic teaching or milieu teaching strategies were designed. Four strategies—*modeling, incidental teaching,* the *mand-model procedure,* and *naturalistic time delay*—comprise the milieu teaching procedures (Halle et al., 1984; Warren & Kaiser, 1988). These procedures involve relatively brief interactions between adults and children (usually in low-structure settings), provide instruction based on the child's focus of attention, and provide assistance as the child needs it (e.g., through models). The procedures have been effective in establishing a number of communicative behaviors and some other behaviors such as reading (McGee, Krantz, & McClannahan, 1986). They can be implemented in either classrooms and homes, by either teachers or parents. We discuss these strategies in detail in chapter 10; the basic procedural parameters of the strategies are displayed in Box 6.2.

Using Response Prompting Procedures A collection of procedures called response prompting strategies have been used extensively to teach children who have disabilities (Billingsley & Romer, 1983). Such a procedure involves five basic steps: (a) presenting the target stimulus, (b) providing a response prompt, (c) providing time for the

BOX 6.2   Procedural parameters of response prompting strategies

Error Correction   The teacher provides the target stimulus (discriminative stimulus) and presents an opportunity for the child to respond. Correct responses are differentially reinforced, and errors result in more prompts.

Antecedent Prompt and Test   The teacher presents a prompt simultaneously with the target stimulus before the learner responds, presents an opportunity to respond, and reinforces correct responses. In subsequent trials, the prompt is removed and a "test" is given to determine if the behavior occurs when presented with the target stimulus alone. During a test trial, an error response may or may not receive a prompt.

Antecedent Prompt and Fade   The teacher presents a prompt simultaneously with the target stimulus, presents an opportunity to respond, and reinforces correct responses. Over trials, the prompt is systematically faded until the learner responds to the target stimulus alone. Fading may occur on the dimensions of frequency and intensity.

Simultaneous Prompting   The teacher provides a prompt simultaneously with the target stimulus, presents an opportunity to respond, and reinforces correct responses. In daily probe trials, the target stimulus is presented alone.

Most-to-Least Prompting (Decreasing Assistance)   The teacher uses a hierarchy of prompts ordered from most to least intrusive. Initially the most intrusive prompt is presented simultaneously with the target stimulus, and correct responses are reinforced. This continues until the child attains a specified criterion level of performance. When criterion is reached with the most intrusive prompt, the next less intrusive prompt is provided until performance meets criterion. This process continues until the child responds to the target stimulus alone.

System of Least Prompts (Increasing Assistance)   The teacher uses a hierarchy of prompts ordered from least to most intrusive. On each trial, the teacher presents the target stimulus alone, and provides an opportunity for a response. If no response or an error results, the least intrusive prompt is presented as is an opportunity to respond. Again, if no response is forthcoming or an error occurs, the next most intrusive prompt is presented with an opportunity to respond. This process continues until the child responds correctly. Reinforcement is provided, and the trial is terminated when the child responds correctly to any level of the hierarchy.

Constant Time Delay   The teacher initially presents the target stimulus simultaneously with a controlling prompt followed by an opportunity to respond for a specified number of trials.

child to respond, (d) reinforcing the child for correct responding, and (e) removing the teacher assistance. *Response prompts* are teacher behaviors that assist the child in performing the desired behavior. They can come in several forms—as verbal cues (hints), as gestures, as models (demonstrations of the behavior), as pictorial prompts, as partial physical prompts (nudges, taps, etc.), as full physical manipulations (the adult places her hands over the child's and moves them through the behavior) (see Wolery, Bailey, et al., 1988, and Wolery, Ault, et al., in press, for a fuller explanation). The various response prompting procedures differ primarily in the way they call for the prompts to be presented and removed.

Some peer-mediated procedures (peer management, peer tutoring, and peer modeling) and all of the milieu teaching proce-

Correct responses are reinforced. For subsequent trials, the interval between the delivery of the target stimulus and presentation of the prompt is increased for a fixed number of seconds. Correct responses before and after the prompt are usually reinforced.

Progressive Time Delay   The teacher initially presents the target stimulus simultaneously with a controlling prompt followed by an opportunity to respond for a specified number of trials. Correct responses are reinforced. For subsequent trials, the interval between the delivery of the target stimulus and presentation of the prompt is *gradually* increased. Correct responses before and after the prompt are usually reinforced.

Graduated Guidance   The teacher begins each trial with the type and amount of prompt necessary, and as the child begins to perform the task the prompts are removed immediately. If the child stops or begins to perform incorrectly, the type and amount of prompts needed are immediately applied and withdrawn as appropriate. Reinforcement is provided if the child completes even a minimal amount of the task correctly; reinforcement is not provided if the child resists at the end of the task.

Incidental Teaching   The teacher arranges the environment to cause the child to initiate. When the child initiates, the teacher asks for an elaboration of the child's language and provides a response interval. If the elaboration is forthcoming, the teacher responds according to the child's initiation (e.g., supplies permission, materials, or information). If the elaboration is not forthcoming, the teacher provides a prompt and another response interval and provides consequences as described here.

Mand-Model Procedure   The teacher observes the child and notes his focus of attention. When the focus of attention is determined, the teacher provides a mand (a non-yes/no question) and provides a short response interval. If the child responds correctly, the teacher praises the child and terminates the interaction. If the child does not respond correctly, the teacher provides a model, a response interval, and consequences as appropriate.

Note: Some descriptions were adapted from "Review of Comparative Studies in the Instruction of Students with Moderate and Severe Handicaps," by M. J. Ault, M. Wolery, P. M. Doyle, & D. L. Gast (1989), *Exceptional Children, 55,* 346–356. For a complete description of the research with and use of these procedures see *Teaching Students with Moderate and Severe Disabilities: Use of Response Prompting Procedures* by M. Wolery, M. J. Ault, & P. M. Doyle (in press), White Plains, NY: Longman.

dures can also be classified as response prompting strategies. Several other response prompting strategies exist as well, strategies such as error correction, antecedent prompt and test, antecedent prompt and fade, simultaneous prompting, most-to-least prompting, system of least prompts, constant time delay, progressive time delay, and graduated guidance. The procedural parameters of all these strategies are displayed in Box 6.2. These procedures have been effective in teaching a broad range of skills to children with disabilities—communication skills, play skills, social skills (e.g., giving affection), pre-academic and academic skills, self-care skills, domestic and community living skills (janitorial skills, shopping), safety skills (cleaning up broken glass, resisting the lures of strangers) and others (Wolery, Ault, et al., in press). Further, many of the procedures are effective across domains and can be used with discrete and chained tasks. Summary statements about the effectiveness and efficiency of the procedures are displayed in Box 6.3.

From the literature, it is clear that these procedures can produce effective learning of many different behaviors in a variety of learners in a wide range of settings. Teachers of young children should be fluent in implementing these procedures, but five procedures are perhaps the most important. These are the constant time delay procedure (covered in chapters 14 & 15), because of its flexibility, effectiveness, and efficiency; the system of least prompts (see chapter 14), because of it effectiveness with a variety of different learners; the most-to-least prompting

---

BOX 6.3   Summary statements about the effectiveness and efficiency of response prompting procedures

1 The response prompting strategies produce effective learning (i.e., when they are used with minor adjustments, children learn) (Wolery, Ault, & Doyle, in press).

2 Some procedures are used more than others; the system of least prompts has been studied most extensively, particularly with chained tasks (See Doyle, Wolery, Ault, & Gast, 1988 for a review); however, the constant time delay has been evaluated extensively with discrete skills (Wolery, Holcombe et al., in press).

3 Antecedent prompting strategies (prompt is delivered before the child must respond) produce fewer errors than error correction and trial and error (See Ault, Wolery, Doyle, & Gast, 1989, for a review).

4 Stimulus modification procedures may produce fewer errors than response prompting procedures, but they require more teacher preparation time (Ault et al., 1989; Wolery, Ault, et al., in press).

5 Most-to-least prompting appears to be more efficient (i.e., produce more rapid acquisition) than the system of least prompts and, perhaps, constant time delay (Ault et al., 1989; McDonnell & Ferguson, 1989).

6 Constant time delay and simultaneous prompting appear to produce about equally efficient learning (on measures of the rapidity of acquisition) (Schuster, Griffen, & Wolery, in press).

7 Progressive time delay and constant time delay appear to produce about equally efficient learning (on measures of the rapidity of acquisition) (Ault, Gast, & Wolery, 1988).

8 Progressive time delay and constant time delay are more efficient (on rapidity measures) than the system of least prompts with discrete tasks (Ault et al., 1989); and constant time delay is more efficient than the system of least prompts on chained tasks (Wolery, Ault, Gast, Doyle, & Griffen, 1990).

9 Constant time delay, the system of least prompts, progressive time delay, antecedent prompt and test, and simultaneous prompting have been used in 1:1 arrangements and in small groups (Wolery, Ault, et al., in press; Wolery, Fleming, Venn, Domjancic, & Thornton, 1991).

10 Constant time delay is an efficient procedure that has been used extensively with preschoolers with minimal procedural modifications (Wolery, Holcombe, et al., in press); it has been used in small group instructional arrangements (Cybriwsky, Wolery, & Gast, 1990), in distributed trial formats such as during circle time (Fleming, Wolery, Venn, Boyko, & Harris, 1991), as a transition-based teaching procedure (Werts, Wolery, Holcombe, Vassilaros, & Billings, 1991), and in spaced trials throughout the day (Chiara & Wolery, 1991).

procedure and graduated guidance (covered in chapter 13), because of their effectiveness with children who have the most severe disabilities; and the simultaneous prompting procedure (see chapter 15), because of its apparent efficiency and simplicity.

Using Stimulus Modifications Stimulus modification, as the name implies, is a strategy that manipulates the stimulus to which we want children to respond. Let us compare stimulus modification with other strategies. In response shaping, successively more accurate approximations of the response are reinforced; thus, the stimulus to which children respond is always in its final form. The stimulus characteristics of a jack-in-the-box were not changed when Hung was taught (through response shaping) to play with it; rather the complexity of her behavior was changed. With the response prompting procedures, the stimulus to which children respond also remains in its final form, and the child is prompted (assisted) to display the response in its final form, and reinforcement is provided differentially. With stimulus modifications, on the other hand, the response is in its final form, but the stimulus is changed from some level where it will already produce the correct response to the final target level (i.e., the form of the stimulus to which we eventually want children to respond). For example, when teaching dressing, we frequently begin with loose fitting clothing. As children learn, we use more tight fitting clothing. The responses for putting on loose and tight fitting clothing are the same, but the stimulus (clothing) is changed from loose to tight. Or, in teaching children to put puzzles together, we start with puzzles that have a couple of pieces and a border, then we progress to puzzles with more pieces and borders, and finally we employ puzzles with more pieces and no border. The stimulus changes, but the responses remain the same.

Three types of stimulus modifications are used separately and in combination (Cooper et al., 1987; Etzel & LeBlanc, 1979; LeBlanc, Etzel, & Domash, 1978). These are stimulus shaping, stimulus fading, and superimposition. With *stimulus shaping*, the critical (defining) characteristics of the stimulus are changed over time; with *stimulus fading* a non-critical characteristic is changed over time; with *superimposition*, the target stimulus and some current stimulus are put on top of one another and their salience is change over time (i.e., the target stimulus becomes more obvious and/or the current stimulus becomes less obvious). For example, if we are trying to teach a child to select a set of objects greater in number than some other set, the defining characteristic is quantity (i.e., how many objects are in each set). With stimulus shaping, we must change the critical dimension of the stimulus (quantity in each set). Thus, we would begin our training with sets that had large differences in quantity (e.g., a set with 20 pennies and a set with 2 pennies). Over trials we would change the number of pennies in the sets so that they are progressively more equal (e.g., we would progress down to 8 pennies and 6 pennies). The response (identifying the set with the most pennies), would be the same throughout, but the stimulus is being changed on the critical dimension. With stimulus fading, a noncritical dimension would be changed. Since the discrimination is based on quantity, size and color are not critical. Thus, the set with more could have pictures of pennies that were enlarged; as training progresses, the size of the pennies would be changed to their real size. With stimulus fading, the child must make a shift in the basis on which the discrimination is made: in this example, the shift must go from the size of the pennies to the number of pennies. Thus, although stimulus fading programs frequently are easier to design, they may not be as effective because children must make this shift. With superimposition, both stimulus shaping and stimulus fading are frequently involved. For example, if the teacher wanted to teach a child to identify the written names of the children in his class, he might place pictures of the children over their names. As training progresses, the salience of the pictures would be decreased and/or the salience of the written names would be increased until only the written names were present.

Much of the research on and application of stimulus modification procedures has been done with academic tasks, sometimes academic tasks with older children. A couple factors limit the usefulness of these procedures. Since the stimuli have to be manipulated, the time and effort involved in the preparation of materials can be prohibitive. Also, some stimuli are difficult or expensive to modify. Nonetheless, these procedures can be used in combination with the response prompting procedures, and examples of their use appear in many preschool classrooms. In practice, these procedures are frequently conceptualized as adaptations of materials—modifying the looseness/tightness of clothing, the number of pieces in puzzles, the size of crayons and paint brushes, the ratio of pictures to words in books, the extent to which pictures represent the objects depicted.

Learning to Use Instructional Strategies

To be an effective teacher, you should understand how to use these different procedures and use them fluently. Perhaps, the best tactic for learning them is to acquire an understanding of their procedural parameters, and then begin to apply them. You should start with skills and children that are easy to teach, and then apply them to more difficult skills, more difficult children, and in more varied contexts. Pay particular attention to children's learning; this will give you feed-

back about how well you are doing. Given this array of available and effective procedures, teachers have the responsibility to implement instruction that produces rapid and near errorless learning.

Role of Errors in Learning   To err is human, but are errors good for learning? Consider these statements: "Adults recognize that children learn from trial and error and that children's misconceptions reflect their developing thoughts" (Bredekamp, 1987, p. 10). "Educators agree on the need to minimize students' errors" (Snell & Gast, 1981, p. 3). How can adult and educators reach such different conclusions? Do children learn from trial and error? Do errors reflect children's developing thoughts? Why should errors be minimized, or should they? Actually, these questions get at the heart of the philosophic differences that exist between early educators who work with typical children and those who work with children who have disabilities; thus, their answers deserve discussion.

Do children learn from trial and error? Actually, children with typical development do, and they appear to do so with relative ease and considerable regularity; perhaps that is why their development is progressing adequately. Children with disabilities can also learn through trial and error, but some qualifications are necessary. First, some children with disabilities who learn from trial and error do so inefficiently; they may eventually learn to communicate, to interact, to toilet, to feed themselves, but the process is slow and frustrating. Others learn from trial and error, but they learn the wrong things. For example, through trial and error they learn that screaming is an effective way to get others' attention, that aggression and self-injurious behaviors are effective ways to get people to stop working with them, and that taking toys from others is an effective way to get them to "share." Still other children with disabilities may learn nearly nothing through trial and error.

Perhaps the more important question is: Is trial and error a good way to teach? The answer clearly is: Not if you want efficient learning. Every new error interferes with learning in two ways: (a) An opportunity is lost to provide reinforcement for the target behavior in the appropriate contexts, and (b) the relationship between the stimulus and the target behavior is weakened.

Should children ever be allowed to use trial and error learning? Certainly, because in different situations we want to teach different things. Consider the following examples. When we provide children with free play opportunities, what are we trying to teach? Many goals are possible; one legitimate goal may be to have the stimuli of several toys and no demands for specific behavior result in sustained engagement (interaction and manipulation) with those toys. The "correct response" here is not the specific manner in which toys are to be manipulated, but simply the continued manipulation of them. Similarly, when we are trying to teach children problem-solving skills, the "correct behavior" is not the solution; the "correct behavior" is rather the very process of analyzing the problem, generating solutions, trying them, and evaluating their effects. Thus, when children are playing with a balance scale and objects of different sizes and weights (where large size is not always equal to more weight), the "correct behavior" is to keep trying a number of different comparisons of objects. The process of figuring out that weight does not equal size—the process of problem solving—is as important as what the process teaches in this case—that weight and size are not perfectly correlated.

The issue is not whether trial and error learning should be used for all skills; it clearly should not. If it were, then you

should not read this book or any other books on instruction, or listen to any lectures on the subject; you should just go out and learn how to teach by trial and error. We recognize, however, that this approach would be irresponsible and unethical. The real issue is what instructional procedures and arrangements should be selected for teaching what the child needs to learn. Perhaps it would be ideal for us to be able to structure the physical and social environment so that children learned everything on their own; however, our understanding of the necessary manipulations is so incomplete that this is currently impossible.

Do children's errors or misconceptions reflect their developing thoughts? Of course, and recognizing those misconceptions is important from at least two perspectives. First, many of their misconceptions will provide you with enjoyment and a source of humor as you go about the serious task of teaching children. This is illustrated nicely if you ask a young child who has little experience with money whether she wants a dime or three pennies. Frequently, the child will select the three pennies. In the child's view of the world, three is more than one; the respective values of the coins are irrelevant. Second, recognizing children's misconceptions will assist you in understanding their behavior. For example, it will tell you the rules they are following, the deductions they have made, and the assumptions they are using for interacting with the objects and people in their world. It will help you to design instruction that will dispel the misconceptions and allow the children to learn more about how the world is really structured. Again, the point is that all aspects of instruction (i.e., information about the child's current abilities, identification of important target behaviors and their functions, structuring the environment, and using instructional procedures) should be designed purposefully. Still, given this array of instructional strategies, how do you know which ones to use in which situations and for which children and behaviors? Guidelines for making selections among these procedures are presented in the following section.

Guidelines for Selecting Instructional Strategies

As Box 6.4 demonstrates, we propose two levels of guidelines for selecting instructional strategies. The guidelines in the first level are based on the nature of the outcomes that are sought, and those in the second level provide direction for selecting from among competing strategies. We discuss these guidelines in the following paragraphs.

Select Strategies that Do No Harm   The first guideline is that instructional procedures (and other interventions) should do no harm (i.e., *primum non noscere*—first not to injure). This guideline applies to interventions generally and to instructional strategies specifically. Teams have the responsibility of considering the potential harm that may come to the child and/or family from using any intervention. This guideline also is useful in evaluating exotic or unusual interventions. If a family comes to you and asks about a particular intervention or therapy and there appears to be little to no research literature on its effects, then a logical analysis of the potential harm of the intervention is appropriate. Harm can be thought of as physical injury, stigmatizing social exchanges, in-

---

BOX 6.4   Guidelines for selecting instructional interventions

First Level of Guidelines for Developing and Selecting Instructional Strategies

1   Interventions should do no harm.
2   Interventions should be used that promote acquisition, fluency, maintenance, and generalization of high-priority skills.
3   Interventions should be used that promote independence, but if independence is not possible, partial participation is preferred to total dependence or nonparticipation.
4   Interventions should be used that promote integration of skills across domains and environments.
5   Interventions should be used based on children's response patterns and learning histories.
6   Interventions should be used that result in efficient learning of the high-priority skills.

Second Level of Guidelines for Developing and Selecting Instructional Strategies

1   If child benefit in terms of learning (generalization, independence, integration, engagement, and efficiency) are equal, then more natural, more normalized, less restrictive, and less intrusive interventions and arrangements should be used.
2   If child benefit in terms of learning (generalization, independence, integration, engagement, and efficiency) are equal, then more child-directed interventions and arrangements should be used.
3   If child benefit in terms of learning (generalization, independence, integration, engagement, and efficiency) are equal, then parsimonious (simpler/simplest) interventions and arrangements should be used.

terference with learning and development, and the maintaining of states or conditions of dependency.

As a rule, instructional strategies present minimal risks to children. Still some strategies may prove harmful. For example, when physical prompts are used, then teachers must be careful to ensure that they do not inadvertently cause strains, sprains, or broken bones. Some children are weak, have brittle bones, and may be easily injured; so care should be taken when any procedure that involves physical contact with the child is involved. Thus, when possible, such prompting should be avoided. This example highlights the need to teach children to imitate, so that modeled prompts can be used.

Select Strategies that Address the Phases of Performance
This guideline states that instruction should promote acquisition, fluency, maintenance, and generalization. These terms were defined and statements about them were provided in chapter 5. This guideline has two implications for the selection of instructional strategies. First, different phases of performance may require different intervention strategies. For example, a peer-tutoring procedure may teach a child how to interact with his/her peers, but group contingencies may be needed to maintain those interactions and ensure that they are performed fluently. Thus, you must be aware of each phase on the hierarchy of each objective for each child; this information will guide you in selecting appropriate strategies or modifications of the one you are using. The second implication is that no instructional objective should be considered achieved until it is maintained by natural contingencies and exchanges with the environment and until it is fluently performed when and where it is needed (i.e., until generalization regularly occurs).

Select Strategies that Promote Independence
This guideline suggests that independent performance is highly valued and that intervention strategies should be selected to promote it. The general rule of thumb is: Do not do for children what they can do for themselves. This rule should be followed in our instructional sessions and when natural opportunities arise for learning. For example, if you are teaching a child to put on clothing, then a natural teaching opportunity is when she is leaving for the day and needs to put on her coat; however, if an opportunity arises for instruction (e.g., going out for a walk), then those opportunities should be used as well.

Occasionally, physical disabilities, lack of prerequisite skills, or lack of more complex skills may make independent behavior impossible. In such cases, partial participation in the activity or adapted and supported participation are preferred to total dependence (Baumgart et al., 1982). If a young toddler is incapable of moving a spoon to his mouth independently during feeding, it would be appropriate for the mother to let him hold her hand as she moved the spoon to his mouth. This would be better than having him keep his hands down. This approach allows some participation, although the behavior is completed by the mother. Similarly, a young child who is being toilet trained may be taught to push down and pull up his pants. However, because of weak hand/finger strength, it may be impossible for him to snap his pants. In such cases, the use of elastic waist-band pants (i.e., an adaptation) would allow more independence than snap or button pants. Similarly, a kindergarten child with severe cerebral palsy may have the cognitive skills to play bingo with her typical peers, but may not have the physical abilities to place the chip on the numbers of her card. Having a peer do this part of the game for her would allow her to participate in an age-appropriate game despite other limitations. Thus, in structuring our interventions, we strive for independent performance. Routines and activities where independence is impossible should be adapted to allow children to participate as fully as possible. A process for implementing this guideline is presented in Box 6.5.

Select Strategies that Allow Integration of Skills Across Domains and Environments (Berkeley & Ludlow, 1989)   This guideline is based on the recognition that children and their behavior cannot really be divided

---

BOX 6.5   Steps for implementing the principle of partial participation

Step	Description
1. Complete an inventory of a non-disabled person doing the skill.	Observe a non-disabled individual complete the target skill or activity in the designated environment and record the needed behaviors and their sequence.
2. Complete an inventory of the target student doing the skill	Observe the student perform the target skill or activity in the designated environment and record all behaviors that are performed independently and those which are not performed independently.
3. Identify the behaviors the student can be expected to learn independently	The teacher should meet with relevant persons such as the student's family and therapists to determine which skills the student can be expected to learn to do independently. A list of those skills should be made.
4. Identify the behaviors the student cannot be expected to do independently	The teacher should meet with relevant persons to determine which skills the student is unlikely to learn over a long period of time. A list of these skills should be made.
5. Develop hypotheses about adaptations that would allow participation	The teacher should identify adaptations that could be used to allow the student to participate in the activity.
6. Complete an inventory using the identified adaptation(s)	The teacher and/or other relevant persons should attempt to use the adaptation of the skill or activity in the designated environment. Data should be collected on the extent to which the adaptation is successful in promoting participation.
7. Decide which adaptation will be used	Over several opportunities, the adaptations should be used, and the most successful one should be retained.
8. Identify skills that will likely be acquired using individualized adaptations	The teacher and relevant others should identify the behaviors that are likely to be acquired if the adaptation is used. Systematic attempts to teach those skills should be employed.

Note: Adapted from "Principle of Partial Participation and Individualized Adaptations in Educational Programs for Severely Handicapped Students" by D. Baumgart, L. Brown, I. Pumpian, J. Nisbet, A. Ford, M. Sweet, R. Messina, and J. Schroeder, 1982, *Journal of the Association for the Severely Handicapped, 7*(2), 17–22.

into parts—social, cognitive, communicative, and so on. These abstract divisions are helpful in organizing our thoughts about children and their behavior; however, many of the children's skills require abilities from multiple developmental domains. For example, interacting with a peer is a social skill that also involves communicative, motor, and cognitive components. This guideline suggests that our intervention strategies should be implemented so that multiple components of skills are being taught during children's natural interactions with the environment. This strategy is generally preferred to isolated instructional or therapy sessions. It is particularly important with self-care, social, communication, motor, and early cognitive skills. Similarly, most useful behaviors for children will occur in multiple settings. Therefore, our instruction should be presented when children need skills *and* in all environments (to the extent possible) where those skills are useful.

Select Strategies that Attend to Children's Response Patterns and Learning Histories

One of the amazing things about children is how different they can be from one another. As a result, each child may respond differently to any given instructional strategy or to any given way of implementing a procedure. Making effective strategy and implementation decisions therefore requires knowledge of how the child tends to respond; the professional should also have knowledge of the potential impact of given instructional procedures when children have certain response tendencies. A number of examples of response patterns and their resulting implications for the selection of instructional strategies are displayed in Box 6.6; many other patterns and implications certainly exist.

Select Strategies that Result in Efficient Learning

Efficiency has two defining aspects. The first is effectiveness; that is, effi-cient instruction produces the outcomes that are intended. The second aspect of efficiency is superiority; efficient intervention produces better outcomes than inefficient intervention. How do we define "better"? At least five ways have been proposed for measuring instructional efficiency (Wolery & Gast, 1990). First, one procedure is thought to be more efficient than the other when it produces more *rapid learning*. Thus, if two procedures are compared, the one that results in children reaching criterion more quickly (i.e., with fewer instructional sessions, in fewer days, with less trials, with fewer minutes of instruction, and with fewer errors) would be considered more efficient. Both may result in the same amount of learning, but one procedure would produce faster learning. The second measurement method focuses on the *amount of generalization* that occurs. Two procedures could produce equally rapid acquisition, but one of them might produce greater generalization; the one that did would be considered more efficient. The third way of measuring efficiency deals with the *breadth of learning*, specifically with whether observational and incidental learning occur. Observational learning in this context refers to children learning what other children are being taught. For example, in small group instruction children have the opportunity to learn the behaviors their peers are learning; this cannot occur in 1:1 instruction (Cybriwsky, Wolery, & Gast, 1990). Incidental learning refers to children learning information that is in the instructional context but is not directly taught. In direct instructional situations, the extra information is inserted before each trial and after children respond (e.g., in praise statements) (Gast, Doyle, Wolery, Ault, & Baklarz, 1991). Thus, two procedures may produce equally rapid learning and equal generalization, but the amount of observational and/or incidental learning may be greater in one than the other. In this case, the one that pro-

BOX 6.6 "If . . . Then" recommendations about students' response patterns

If the Child,	Then the Teacher
IF physical contact with the teacher is a strong positive reinforcer,	THEN instructional strategies that involve physical prompts may be less successful than those that do not rely on such prompts (the physical prompt may lead to prompt dependency).
IF children withdraw from or react negatively to physical contact,	THEN physical prompts should be avoided.
IF children respond quickly to task directions without attending to the instructional stimuli or waiting for teacher assistance,	THEN (a) use of procedures that delay assistance may be contraindicated, (b) specific attentional responses (e.g., repeating the task direction or acting on the stimulus before responding) are warranted, and (c) waiting training is needed and appropriate.
IF children have a history of learning particular types of responses with a given procedure,	THEN use of similar procedures is indicated.
IF children have a history of 1:1 instruction,	THEN they may need specific instruction in group formats before new instructional procedures in group formats are attempted.
IF children become disruptive or work more slowly when errors occur,	THEN errorless teaching procedures should be used.
IF children become disruptive when required to wait for prompts,	THEN the system of least prompts may not be appropriate because the controlling prompt is presented at the end of a prompt hierarchy.
IF children have generalized imitative repertoires,	THEN models should be used as prompts.
IF children are not imitative	THEN model prompts should not be used.
IF natural contingencies, differential reinforcement, and error correction are ineffective or inefficient,	THEN response prompting strategies should be used.
IF response prompting strategies are ineffective or inefficient,	THEN stimulus modification procedures should be used.
IF children display overselective attention,	THEN stimulus shaping should be used.
IF children's performance is variable or deteriorates,	THEN changes in the reinforcers and reinforcement schedules should be attempted.
IF children remain prompt dependent,	THEN alternative methods of fading prompts should be used.

duced more extra learning would be considered more efficient. Fourth, efficiency has been measured according to the extent to which *untrained relationships emerge* (Gast, Van Biervilet, & Spradlin, 1979). Considerable basic research has focused on understanding the notion of stimulus equivalency, a concept that describes cases in which different stimuli produce the same response. For example, the numeral "5," the number-word "five," and a set of objects or combination of sets totaling five are all stimuli that produce the same response (e.g., an oral "five"). These stimuli are equivalent because they produce the same response. Some ways of teaching allow children to learn one or two of these stimuli through direct instruction, then allow the equivalent relationships to be comprehended without direct instruction. Thus, two procedures might produce equally rapid learning, equal generalization, and equal observational and incidental learning, but only one of the strategies—the more efficient strategy—would allow for the uninstructed comprehension of equivalent relationships. Fifth, efficiency can be measured by the extent to which current instruction positively influences *future learning* (Wolery, Doyle, Ault, Gast, Meyer, & Stinson, 1991; Holcombe, Wolery, Werts, & Hrenkevich, 1991). Two procedures may result in equally rapid learning, equal generalization, equal observational and incidental learning, and equal uninstructed comprehension of equivalent relationships; however, the more efficient strategy may cause the child to learn more rapidly and in a more generalized way *in the future*. A variation on this theme of influencing future learning is the notion of teaching keystone behaviors (Rincover, 1981). A *keystone behavior* is either the prerequisite to the acquisition of a large number of skills, or it allows the child to learn many skills in a new way. For example, attending to small differences in stimuli may be thought of as a keystone behavior because

it is a prerequisite for many types of learning; imitation may be thought of as a keystone behavior because it is a means of learning many different skills in a new way. Although little research has identified keystone behaviors, some of them are described in later chapters.

Second Level Guidelines These guidelines—doing no harm, focusing on the phases of instruction, promoting independence and partial participation, integrating instruction across domains and environments, attending to children's response patterns and learning histories, and using efficient procedures—provide clear direction for selecting instructional strategies. Sometimes, multiple strategies may meet these criteria. In such cases, the three guidelines in the second level are used to make selections among strategies. Each of the guidelines in the second level is prefaced by the statement: "*If child benefit in terms of learning (generalization, independence, integration, engagement, and efficiency) is equal, then . . .*" All strategies under consideration at the second level meet the guidelines of the first level. In other words, there is no justification for using interventions that do not result in generalization, do not promote independence, are not integrated into the child's day and across domains, do not promote engagement, and are inefficient. However, given that all the strategies under consideration meet these guidelines, then the more natural and normalized procedures should be used, so to approximate as closely as possible the instructional practices for children with typical development. The National Association for the Education of Young Children (NAEYC) has provided extensive descriptions of what it considers to be the best practices (called, developmentally appropriate practices) in early education programs (Bredekamp, 1987, in press); those would be considered normalized procedures. Again, given that all the strategies meet the first level guidelines, then the strategies should be chosen that are less intrusive and less restrictive. Restrictiveness refers to the extent to which procedures reduce children's freedoms, and intrusiveness refers to the extent to which procedures impinge upon children's bodies. For example, when teaching the child, a teacher may put his hands over the child's hands and move the child through the skill. Such assistance is restrictive (reduces the child's freedom to move) and intrusive (the teacher is physically moving the child). However, a partial physical prompt where the teacher nudges or taps the child is not restrictive (does not reduce freedom) but is somewhat intrusive (again, the teacher touches the child's body).

Another second level guideline is that, the first level guidelines having been met, child-directed arrangements and interventions are to be preferred. Child-directed arrangements are situations in which the child makes choices about what to do and how to do it, and in which the teacher serves as a monitor and consultant rather than a director of instruction. Generally, this type of arrangement also is normative (i.e., it is consistent with the developmentally appropriate practice guidelines). Procedures for structuring classrooms for child-directed learning are provided in chapter 7.

Finally, when different strategies fulfill the basic learning requirements equally, then teachers should use the simplest intervention possible. Experts generally believe that consistency in the implementation of instructional strategies is desirable; and it is a common perception that simpler procedures are more likely to be implemented correctly. So teachers are urged to employ simple procedures because they are more likely to use them consistently and correctly. Also, simpler procedures also require less work and fewer decisions on the part of the teachers. The task of teaching young children is suffi-

ciently difficult in and of itself; when learning is not sacrificed, teachers should opt for the simplest procedures available.

HOW CAN INSTRUCTIONAL OPPORTUNITIES BE ORGANIZED?

It is one thing to know what to teach and which strategy to use; it is quite another to find the appropriate opportunities to do it. In this section, we address the issue of implementation—first, by presenting the context in which learning opportunities occur, and second, by addressing procedures for structuring different types of learning opportunities.

Context for Presenting Learning Opportunities

The classroom experience of young children can be divided into four elements: routines, transitions, high-structure activities, and low-structure activities. The home experience can be characterized similarly, but it may involve fewer high-structure activities. Each of these elements presents, simultaneously, unique opportunities for and limitations of instruction.

Routines   Routines, as we have indicated, are events that must be completed on a regular basis and frequently involve chains of responses. Many routines involve caring for basic needs (e.g., diapering, toileting, dressing/undressing, eating); others are a matter of arriving at and departing from class, cleaning up after an activity, and so forth. The steps involved in completing routines tend to be relatively ritualistic, although sequences within some chains may vary. Adults may view routines from very different perspectives: They can see them as tasks that are best accomplished by adults themselves, or they can see them as rich opportunities for teaching independence and many other skills. For example, in preparing for snack, the teacher can set out the juice, food, napkins, and so forth, or the children can participate in setting these things out. The former approach gets the task done quickly; the latter provides opportunities for children to learn counting (i.e., count the children to be sure you have enough cups), assume responsibility, learn nonidentity matching (each cup must also have a napkin), cooperate with a peer (if two children help), and practice many other useful skills. Similarly, when children arrive for the day, the adult can take off each child's coat and hang it up, and check the lunch box for a note from the parents, or each child can do these things or at least participate to the extent possible.

Three general guidelines are provided for conducting routines. First, *to the extent possible, children should perform routines independently.* Some steps may be impossible for children and in such cases the principle of partial participation (Baumgart et al., 1982) should be applied (See Box 6.5 for guidelines). Second, *routines should be used for teaching skills.* As illustrated in the example of snack time above, a number of skills can be learned in some routines. Third, when appropriate, *routines should involve interaction rather than mechanical completion.* For example, when walking children to the bus, you should ask them what they are going to do that evening, point out things in the hallway, respond to their statements, and otherwise attend to them. Box 6.7 presents a study in which day care staff learned to interact with infants during diaper changing routines.

Transitions Another element of the classroom and home experience is transition. The transition encompasses completing one activity or routine, moving to the next activity or routine, and starting the new one. Transi-

---

BOX 6.7 Example of study for increasing interaction during diaper changing routines

The purpose of this study was to teach day care staff members who were paraprofessionals to engage in social interactions with infants while they changed their diapers. The study occurred in a mainstreamed daycare program.

The training of staff members involved a brief discussion of the importance of social interaction, a demonstration of interacting while changing a diaper, practice and goal setting for playing interactive games during diaper changing, and two sessions of interactive coaching. The entire training took less than 4 hours with each staff member. The training was implemented in a multiple probe design across three staff members.

Staff members were videotaped during diaper changing routines before and after they had experienced training.

The results indicated that the number of interactive game playing episodes (e.g., "This Little Piggy," "I'm Gonna Get You") increased after training; also, the amount of vocalizing and looking increased.

An interesting side effect of the training was that infants began to initiate games during diaper changing episodes. Also, the staff reported that they liked playing interactive games during diaper changing.

Note: Adapted from *Increasing Daycare Staff Members' Interactions During Caregiving Routines* by M. L. Venn and M. Wolery, in press, *Journal of Early Intervention.*

tions may occur between structured activities (e.g., when going from circle time to the snack table), between structured activities and unstructured activities or vice versa (e.g., when going from circle time to free play), and between unstructured activities (e.g., when going from the housekeeping area to the book area). Transitions can be initiated by the adult or the child.

Transitions are discussed more fully in chapter 7; here we present two guidelines. First, *for most transitions, children should assume as much responsibility as possible.* They should, for example, be encouraged to put away their toys and materials and make choices about which activity to do next. They also should be taught to get from one place to another as independently and quickly as possible. Second, *transitions, despite their confusion, can be viewed as teaching times.* As we have noted, the teacher may engage in transition-based teaching by presenting a brief learning opportunity as a child leaves an activity and begins a transition. Such learning opportunities usually take from 5 to 10 seconds per child, and they appear to result in rapid acquisition (Wolery, Doyle, Gast, et al., 1991) even when administered in as few as three transitions per day (Werts, Wolery, Holcombe, Vassilaros, & Billings, 1991).

High- and Low-Structure Activities The remaining elements of most young children's experience are *high- and low-structure activities.* In high-structure activities, teachers frequently assume the lead, direct the learning, and provide children with opportunities for responding. Examples are circle time, large group time, and small group instructional sessions. In low-structure activities, teachers frequently are less directive and children determine, at varying degrees of choice, what they will do, how they will do it, and how in general their time will be spent. Examples are free play, activity area

times, snack, and outdoor play. However, as we have indicated, the amount of structure within activities (e.g., play activities) can vary greatly (DeKlyen & Odom, 1989), and the roles teachers assume within activities also are highly varied (Fleming, Wolery, Weinzierl, Venn, & Schroeder, 1991).

High- and low-structure activities also are described more fully in chapter 7; and here again we simply present three general guidelines for instruction. First, *each activity in which a child participates should be designed so that learning can occur.* In chapter 5, we said each objective for the child should be pegged to specific times or activities identified for instruction. The guideline presented here is the inverse of that recommendation: all of the child's activities should be understood as learning opportunities. It is conceivable that all of the objectives for the child might be assigned to specific times and activities, but that there might be some activities of the child with no objectives assigned. Does this mean that the children are on break from learning during these times? Not at all; such times provide opportunities for practicing skills, extending them to new contexts, and integrating them across domains. Such activities may not involve direct teaching, and frequently will not; however, the time should not be wasted.

Second, *teachers should adapt their activities so that each one is an active learning time for children.* For example, circle time may involve identifying the day of the week, the nature of the daily weather, who is present and who is not, a time for singing some songs, and doing show and tell. However, it also is a time when trials using the response prompting procedures can be interspersed throughout the activity to teach high-priority objectives (Fleming, Wolery, Venn, Boyko, & Harris, 1991; Wolery, Fleming, Venn, Domjancic, & Thornton, 1991). Similarly, free play can be a time for playing as children wish, but it can also be a time for teaching communication skills with procedures such as incidental teaching or the mand-model strategy (Hart & Risley, 1975; Warren, Mc-Quarter, & Rogers-Warren, 1984), or it can be a time for using the peer-mediated strategies for teaching social interactions and cooperative play skills (Strain & Odom, 1986).

Third, when possible, *skills should be taught at natural times and in natural contexts*. If a goal is to increase interaction or communication skills with peers, then multiple, low-structure activities are needed when competent peers are present. If a goal is to increase independence in dressing and undressing, then multiple, naturally occurring events for needing these skills should be identified. The underlying assumption is that many skills are best learned when they are taught in a context where they are needed. This should not be surprising because nearly all learners (e.g., university students) state that they more readily learn and are more motivated to learn information that is relevant and skills that are needed. When attempting to place instruction in natural contexts, the teacher will find that the daily schedule frequently does not include sufficient opportunities for children to encounter the need to use all the targeted forms and functions. In such cases, the adult should adapt the schedule and activities to increase opportunities for instruction. For example, if a high priority objective is to teach a young child to dress and undress, the natural times for this would be when the child gets dressed in the morning and when she gets undressed in the evening. These times may not be easy times for parents to provide instruction, or these times may be of insufficient frequency for the child to learn the skills quickly. Thus, adapting the schedule is necessary. For example, the child could be required to change clothing before going outside to play (i.e., either at home or in school), when coming in from play, and before and after taking a nap. Further opportunities may

be presented at other times throughout the day, such as during toileting, when putting on a smock before painting in the paint area, or when taking off the shirt before playing at the water table. Such adaptations increase the opportunities to engage in the new skills, but are not as artificial and out-of-context as presenting several trials of dressing and undressing in the corner of the classroom.

Thus, in planning to implement instruction, adults should consider the existing routines, transitions, and high- and low-structure activities as contexts of the instruction. The primary recommendation is to ensure that all times have instructional value for each child. In addition to analyzing the elements of the classroom experience, it is important to understand how learning opportunities arise and how natural times can be identified for using teaching strategies.

Types of Learning Opportunities

Learning opportunities can be initiated by the child, by a peer, by some event, and by the teacher. *Child- and peer-initiated learning opportunities* occur most frequently in low-structure activities and in play activities. However, they also can occur during routines, transitions, and high-structure activities. For example, during circle time the child may say something that provides the teacher with an opportunity to implement an incidental teaching trial to expand the child's language. The peer-mediated interventions, incidental teaching, differential reinforcement, response shaping, and correspondence training are important interventions for child- and peer-initiated learning opportunities. *Event-initiated learning opportunities* usually occur during routines and transitions, as we described them earlier. *Adult-initiated learning opportunities* occur most frequently during high-structure activities in which the teacher is assuming an instructor role. However, they also can occur during transitions (e.g., in transition-based teaching) and during low-structure activities (e.g., following the mand-model procedure). The response prompting procedures are specifically designed for such learning opportunities.

Adult-initiated learning opportunities comprise a large percentage of the instructional exchanges that occur between children and adults. They usually are presented in three different ways. They can occur (a) between activities (e.g., using transition-based teaching or naturalistic time delay during routines), (b) interspersed throughout the day but not necessarily at transitions, and (c) within activities or sessions. We have just discussed learning opportunities between activities. The method of interspersing learning opportunities throughout the day, used less frequently by teachers, involves presenting children with opportunities to perform specific behaviors in low-structure situations. The opportunities should be provided when children appear to be unengaged or when they have just completed tasks (e.g., when the child has just finished working a puzzle) to avoid interrupting them. Although this distribution of adult-initiated learning opportunities has received little study, some data suggest it is effective with young children in mainstreamed programs (Chiara & Wolery, 1991).

When used within activities, adult-initiated opportunities can be provided in at least three ways (Helmstetter & Guess, 1987). First, teachers can use *massed trials,* providing repeated and rapid exposure to the same stimulus from the same instructional objective within a session. Second, teachers can use *distributed trials,* presenting trials on two or more skills within the same session but with the stipulation that no two consecutive trials are for the same behavior (Mulligan, Lacy, & Guess, 1982). Third, teachers can use *spaced trials,* including learning opportunities on the same program with oppor-

tunities between trials to engage in other behaviors (e.g., rest). Generally, distributed trials are recommended over massed and spaced trials (Helmstetter & Guess, 1987). However, when massed trials are used, it is clearly better to teach two or more behaviors (even from the same type of objective) than single behaviors in single sessions (Doyle, Wolery, Gast, Ault, & Wiley, 1989). Regardless of how the trials are distributed, ensuring child attention during teacher-directed learning opportunities is critical. Frequently, it is useful to have children show you in some active way that they are attending (e.g., by touching the stimulus) before presenting the trial (Doyle, Wolery, Gast, Ault, & Wiley, 1990). A variation of distributed trial presentation of adult-initiated learning opportunities is seen with the mand-model procedure. In that procedure, the teacher observes the child, notes his focus of attention, presents a learning opportunity, provides a chance for the child to respond, and if necessary provides a model and another chance to respond. Correct responses are praised, the trial is terminated, and the child continues with his play. Soon thereafter, the adult may repeat the process.

In instructional sessions, the decisions involved in adult-initiated learning opportunities are increased when groups of children are taught at the same time. For example, should each child get a turn in order, or should trials be randomly presented so that children cannot predict when they will occur. To date, the evidence suggests that either method will produce about equal learning in children who are familiar with small group instruction (Ault, Wolery, Gast, Doyle, & Martin, 1990). Another decision to make when conducting groups is whether children should learn the same behaviors or different behaviors. In short, the answer seems to depend upon the needs of the group members. Teaching the same thing increases the ease of presentation; teaching different things increases the opportunities for children to learn what is taught to other children (observational learning). Also, if learning the same thing, should children be taught chorally (all children respond on all trials) or individually (each child gets a turn). Again, the data are inconclusive as both approaches have been found to be effective (Collins, Gast, Ault, & Wolery, 1991). However, choral responding has been used to increase the number of opportunities for children to respond (Sainato, Strain, & Lyon, 1987). A list of questions for teachers to use in constructing small group instructional sessions is presented in Box 6.8.

Pulling It All Together   Although you may know what to teach, which strategy to use, and when you want to use it, that does not mean that it will actually work out that way. Many things can interfere with the implementation of individualized curricular programs. To assist the teacher in determining whether the planned individualization actually occurs and has the desired effects, ten questions are proposed in Table 6.1. Also presented are measures that can be used to secure the answers to those questions. Finally, to assist the teacher in identifying potential problems, a number of these are listed for each question.

Summary   Implementing instruction is more difficult than it may appear. It involves much more than taking a child to the table and conducting a session or allowing children to play in interesting areas. The entire day should be analyzed for potential opportunities for providing instruction. Also, adults should recognize that opportunities for learning may arise from other sources in addition to the teacher, sources such as the child and the classroom routines. Unfortunately, the task does not stop here; once instruction is implemented, you must determine how well it is working (see chapter 5)

and how to extend the benefits to the natural environment.

HOW CAN WE EXTEND THE BENEFITS OF LEARNING BEYOND THE INSTRUCTIONAL CONTEXT?

Our goal is to prepare children to function adaptively in their communities (i.e. outside the context in which intervention occurs); thus, we must ensure that our instruction is sensitive to their ecologies and that it promotes learning that extends beyond the teaching setting. Three different focuses assist teams in meeting this challenge. First, we must teach skills that will be useful to children and valued by their families. We have already treated this issue in depth in chapters 2, 4, and 5. Second, the phases of the hierarchy of learning performance—that is, acqusition, fluency, maintenance, and generalization—must each be promoted in systematic ways. A summary of some of the factors that promote each phase is presented in Box 6.9. In addition, throughout the book, procedures are discussed for facilitating each phase with different types of skills. Third, we must focus on improving the efficiency of instruction, so to extend learning. We must, for example, use instructional strategies and arrangements that produce rapid learning (see Box 6.3 for a summary of this research); and we must strive to increase the amount of generalization that occurs (see Box 6.9). As we have seen, efficient learning also means the promotion of observational and incidental learning. Observational learning is promoted by calling attention to the behavior of peers (as in peer-imitation training; Peck et al., 1978), by reinforcing peers for behaviors that are desired in the observer, by teaching in small group instructional arrangements (Collins et al., 1991), and by providing active attentional cues to individual children in the group and to the entire group

BOX 6.8   **Questions for use in planning group instructional sessions**

Group Composition

What skills do children need to be in the group (e.g., attending skills, waiting skills, absence of interfering behaviors)?

Will children in the group have different diagnoses?

Will children in the group be of different ages?

How many children will be in the group?

Will children be taught the same or different tasks?

Will children be taught the same or different behaviors/stimuli?

Will children interact (e.g., praise one another) during group sessions?

Will any children receive one-to-one instruction on behaviors as well as group instruction?

Instructional Procedures

Which instructional procedure will be used?

How many behaviors/stimuli will be taught each session?

Will an attending cue be used, and what will it be?

Will children respond individually or as a group to the attending cue?

What materials, if any, will be used?

What task direction, if any, will be used?

How many trials will be presented on each behavior to each child?

Will children respond individually or as a group to the target stimulus?

If children respond individually, will the trials be presented in a predictable or unpredictable order?

If children respond individually, how will each child know when it is his or her turn?

Will a massed, spaced, or distributed trial sequence be used?

What response will children make to each trial?

What consequences will be provided for correct, incorrect, and no responses?

What criterion will be used, and will there be an individual or group criterion?

Measurement and Evaluation

What data will be collected on children's learning?

How will the data be collected?

When will the data be collected?

How will the data be summarized (e.g., line graph, cumulative chart, or other)?

Will generalization data be collected?

If generalization data are collected, when and how will those data be collected?

Will maintenance data be collected?

If maintenance data are collected, when and how will those data be collected?

Group Management

How will problem behavior be addressed?

Will a group contingency be used?

If a group contingency is used, for whose behavior will it be applied?

Note: Adapted from "Small Group Instruction: Guidelines for Teachers of Students with Moderate to Severe Handicaps" by B. C. Collins, D. L. Gast, M. J. Ault, & M. Wolery, 1991, *Education and Training in Mental Retardation, 26,* 18–32.

(Cybriwsky et al., 1990; Wolery, Cybriwsky, Gast, & Boyle-Gast, 1991).

Although observational learning can be promoted by group instruction with discrete tasks, its use with chained tasks is more difficult. However, some initial attempts have been made. For example, teaching chained tasks in dyads (i.e., with pairs of children) where one child is taught and one child observes has resulted in both children learning the tasks (Schoen, Lentz, & Suppa, 1988; Schoen & Sivil, 1989); and teaching in dyads where one child does the first half of the chain and the second child does the second half also has resulted in both children learning the whole task (Wolery, Ault, Gast, Doyle, & Griffen, 1991). Also, teaching chained tasks in triads (i.e., with groups of three children) where one child is taught and two observe and follow along with picture cues has resulted in all children learning the tasks (Griffen, Wolery, & Schuster, in press). In all of these studies, the observers were cued to attend and/or they were reinforced for attending by the peer or teacher.

Two prerequisite skills appear necessary for observational learning: imitation and attention to the model. Thus, teaching imitation to many young children with disabilities is a valuable endeavor. Ensuring that children attend to the model is important in both low-structure situations where social behaviors are targeted, and in direct instructional situations where nonsocial behaviors are being taught. This can be accomplished by directing the attention of the observer (e.g., through verbal cues) to the peer's behavior, or by having observers deliver reinforcement to the peer for performing the behavior you want the observer to imitate.

Incidental learning has been promoted by adding additional information to instructional trials before children respond, and by adding additional information to the consequent events (e.g., to praise statements) after children respond (Cybriwsky et al., 1990;

Gast, Doyle, Wolery, Ault, & Baklarz, 1991; Wolery, Cybriwsky et al., 1991). In nearly all cases, children appear to learn some of this extra information despite the fact that it is not reinforced and they have not been asked to respond to it during instruction. Interestingly, they sometimes also learn the extra information taught to their peers (Wolery, Cybriwsky et al., 1991).

Finally, we can extend learning by pushing current instruction to influence future learning. Although this issue has received relatively little research, a couple studies have addressed this issue (Holcombe et al., 1991; Wolery, Doyle, Ault, Gast, Meyer, & Stinson, 1991). In these studies, children were taught four sets of stimuli, two sets at a time (e.g., sets "A," "B," "C," and "D"). Sets "A" and "B" were taught first in separate daily sessions, and sets "C" and "D" were taught after "A" and "B" were learned. While teaching set "A," correct responses resulted in the stimuli for "C" being displayed while children were being praised; when teaching set "B" only praise was provided for correct responses. The results indicated that sets "A" and "C" were learned more rapidly than sets "B" and "D." Thus, presentation of the future target behaviors in the consequent events for current instruction, seemed to cause more rapid learning of the future behaviors. Clearly, the task of extending learning beyond the behaviors being taught and beyond the immediate context of instruction requires careful attention to the way instruction is organized.

SUMMARY

In this chapter, three major questions about the teaching process have been addressed: what instructional strategies can be used, how can learning opportunities be organized, and how can the benefits of learning be extended to the natural environment?

TABLE 6.1
Ten tests for evaluating individualized curriculum endeavors

Question	Potential Measures for Answering Questions	Potential Difficulties in Mainstreamed Settings
1. Have important skills been identified?	Ratings of importance by parents and professional members of the intervention team. Description by team members of how each skill will increase developmental performance, independence, access to less restrictive placements, learning of more complex skills, and the ease with which families can care for the child.	Staff may perceive identification of specific skills as inappropriate and inconsistent with the developmentally appropriate practice (DAP) guidelines (cf. Bredekamp, 1987, in press). Staff may use inappropriate measures and measurement strategies to identify instructional targets. Staff may not have skills for conducting ecological inventories and for involving family members in assessments.
2. Are times scheduled for instruction to ensure acquisition of important skills?	Staff members can identify times each day when instruction can be provided for each skill. Instruction of each skill can be identified through direct observation of the classroom. Direct observation of child engagement in activities designed to promote acquisition of targeted behaviors.	Staff may view scheduling of instruction for specific skills as inconsistent with DAP guidelines. Staff may schedule time but fail to implement activities or the instructional strategies within the activities. Staff may implement strategies, but child may not attend or participate. Staff may not know how to schedule instruction for specific skills.
3. Are times scheduled to ensure use and application (generalization) of important skills?	Staff members can identify times when generalization of skills is appropriate. Opportunities for generalization can be identified through direct observation of classroom. Direct observation of child engagement in activities designed to promote generalization.	Staff may not understand the need to program generalization. Staff may view programming for generalization as incompatible with the DAP guidelines. Staff may not know how to program for generalization. Staff may schedule time and strategies for promoting generalization, but may fail to implement them. Staff may implement the strategies but the child may not participate.
4. Are times scheduled to train intervention agents to implement strategies?	Schedule of staff training that identifies specific strategies. Documentation that training is occurring. Direct measures (attendance, paper/pencil tests, direct observation) of staff members' participation in training.	There may be no skilled individual available to provide training. Staff may not attend/participate in training at scheduled times. Staff may not perceive the need for the training or the interventions.
5. Is the child engaged in instructional activities throughout the day?	Direct observation of randomly selected times using momentary time sampling. Staff members' ratings of child engagement.	Child may not have skills to be engaged in the activities. Activities may be too difficult/easy or too long/short. Child may be waiting for materials or adult direction.

Question	Methods	Possible explanations
6. Are staff using the strategies correctly?	Staff members' ratings of their use of the strategies. Direct observation of staff use of strategies.	Staff may believe reinforcement of engagement is inconsistent with DAP guidelines. Staff may view engagement as child rather than adult responsibility. Training may have been inadequate for staff to learn procedural parameters of strategies. Staff may believe strategies are inconsistent with DAP guidelines. Staff may have tried strategies, experienced failure, and stopped use. Lack of follow-up may lead staff to believe strategies are unimportant. Classroom demands may preclude use of the strategies. Strategies may be inconsistent with the roles staff use in the identified activities.
7. Is the child acquiring the important skills?	Staff and parents' ratings of child's acquisition. Collection of probe data on child performance. Collection of daily data on child performance.	Staff may not be implementing strategies or may do so incorrectly. Staff may view strategies as inconsistent with DAP guidelines. Staff may not be aware that acquisition is not occurring, and may not adjust interventions appropriately.
8. Is the child using and applying the important skills?	Staff and parents' ratings of child's skill use. Collection of probe data on child performance. Collection of daily data on child performance.	Staff may not be implementing generalization facilitating strategies, or may be doing so incorrectly. Staff may view generalization promoting strategies as inconsistent with DAP guidelines. Staff may be unaware that generalization is not occurring, and may not adjust interventions appropriately.
9. Are interventions adjusted when they are not working?	Staff reports of intervention adjustment. Documentation from review of records that interventions are adjusted.	Staff may be unaware of when to adjust programs; staff may need instruction in data decision rules. Staff may recognize need for adjustment, but may not know how to adjust program.
10. Are parents satisfied with the manner of instruction and its outcomes?	Parents' ratings of satisfaction with instructional procedures. Parents' ratings of satisfaction with outcomes. Comparison of outcomes with parents' previous statements of desired outcomes.	Staff may lack communication skills to describe methods to families. Staff may not involve families appropriately in selecting strategies or in developing adjustments. Staff may not communicate outcomes appropriately to parents.

BOX 6.9   Guidelines for promoting phases of performance

Phase of Performance	General Guideline
Acquisition	1. Ensure that the child has the prerequisite behaviors needed to learn the skill. 2. Teach skills that are useful (i.e., that perform some function for the child). 3. Provide information and assistance so the child can do the basic requirements of the skill, and fade or remove assistance as the child learns. 4. Ensure that children are motivated to learn by using their preferences and interesting activities and by providing choices and using positive reinforcement. 5. Make the stimuli to which children are to respond obvious and change them over time.
Fluency	1. Provide brief periods for practice of acquired skills. 2. Reinforce children for engaging in practice. 3. Reinforce children for improvements in the fluency of skills.
Maintenance	1. Provide children with situations where they need to use the acquired skills. 2. Thin reinforcement schedules to match those found in the natural environment and needed to maintain support for the skill. 3. Provide children with sufficient instruction so that skills are overlearned (i.e., so that the children become fluent and remain fluent). 4. Use natural reinforcers during training.
Generalization	1. Use general case programming to select stimuli and responses. 2. Use varied and multiple stimuli, materials, trainers, and training settings. 3. Provide opportunities for the skill to be used in generalization environments. 4. Reinforce the child for attempts to generalize; provide instructions for the child to use the skill when it is needed. 5. Delay and thin reinforcement for displays of the skill. 6. Teach children to manage their own behavior and use self-control procedures to promote generalization.

Several instructional strategies are available which manipulate setting, antecedent, and/or consequent events, and we have presented guidelines for selecting appropriate instructional strategies. The professional should select strategies that ensure that no harm is done; that children acquire, become fluent with, maintain, and generalize important skills; that independence is promoted; that integration across skill domains and environments is addressed; that children's response patterns are considered; and that efficient learning takes place. Then going beyond these guidelines, the professional should strive for strategies that allow for more natural, more normalized, less restrictive, and less intrusive interventions; that are more child-directed; and, finally, that are simpler. We have described various ways of organizing learning opportunities, and we have suggested some guidelines. Finally, to ensure true benefit of instruction, we have described procedures for extending learning. The extent to which teachers address the questions included in chapters 5 and 6 and carefully follow the various guidelines probably will have a direct effect upon the extent to which their infants and young children are prepared to perform adaptively in the communities in which they live.

REFERENCES

Ault, M. J., Gast, D. L., & Wolery, M. (1988). Comparison of progressive and constant time delay procedures in teaching community-sign word reading. *American Journal of Mental Retardation, 93*, 44–56.

Ault, M. J., Wolery, M., Doyle, P. M., & Gast, D. L. (1989). Review of comparative studies in instruction of students with moderate and severe handicaps. *Exceptional Children, 55*, 346–356.

Ault, M. J., Wolery, M., Gast, D. L., Doyle, P. M., & Martin, C. P. (1990). Comparison of predictable and unpredictable trial sequences during small group instruction. *Learning Disability Quarterly, 13*, 12–29.

Baer, R. A. (1990). Correspondence training: Review and current issues. *Research in Developmental Disabilities, 11*, 379–393.

Baumgart, D., Brown, L., Pumpian, I., Nisbet, J., Ford, A., Sweet, M., Messina, R., & Schroeder, J. (1982). Principle of partial participation and individualized adaptations in educational programs for severely handicapped students. *The Journal of Association for the Severely Handicapped, 7*(2), 17–27.

Berkeley, T. R., & Ludlow, B. L. (1989). Toward a reconceptualization of the developmental model. *Topics in Early Childhood Special Education, 9*(3), 51–66.

Billingsley, F. F., & Romer, L. (1983). Response prompting and the transfer of stimulus control: Methods, research, and a conceptual framework. *The Journal of the Association for the Severely Handicapped, 8*(2), 3–12.

Bredekamp, S. (Ed.). (1987). *Developmentally appropriate practice in early childhood programs serving children from birth through age 8.* Washington, DC: National Association for the Education of Young Children.

Bredekamp, S. (in press). *Appropriate curriculum and assessment in programs serving children, 3 through 8 years of age.* Washington, DC: National Association for the Education of Young Children.

Brinker, R. P., & Lewis, M. (1982). Contingency intervention. In J. D. Anderson, *Curricula for high-risk and handicapped infants.* Chapel Hill, NC: Technical Assistance Development System.

Chiara, L., & Wolery, M. (1991). *Comparison of small group and interspersed trials in a mainstreamed preschool program.* Unpublished manuscript.

Collins, B. C., Gast, D. L., Ault, M. J., & Wolery, M. (1991). Small group instruction: Guidelines for teachers of students with moderate to severe handicaps. *Education and Training in Mental Retardation, 26*, 18–32.

Cooper, J. O., Heron, T. E., & Heward, W. L. (1987). *Applied behavior analysis.* Columbus, OH: Merrill.

Cybriwsky, C. A., Wolery, M., & Gast, D. L. (1990). Use of a constant time delay procedure in teaching preschoolers in a group format. *Journal of Early Intervention, 14*, 99–116.

DeKlyen, M., & Odom, S. L. (1989). Activity structure and social interactions with peers in developmentally integrated play groups. *Journal of Early Intervention, 13*, 342–352.

Doyle, P. M., Wolery, M., Ault, M. J., & Gast, D. L. (1988). System of least prompts: A review of procedural parameters. *Journal of the Association for Persons with Severe Handicaps, 13*, 28–40.

Doyle, P. M., Wolery, M., Gast, D. L., Ault, M. J., & Wiley, K. (1989). Establishing conditional discriminations: Concurrent versus isolation-intermix instruction. *Research in Developmental Disabilities, 10*, 349–362.

Doyle, P. M., Wolery, M., Gast, D. L., Ault, M. J., & Wiley, K. (1990). Comparison of constant time delay and system of least prompts in teaching preschoolers with developmental delays. *Research and Intervention in Developmental Disabilities, 11,* 1–22.

Dunst, C., Lesko, J. J., Holbert, K. A., Wilson, L. L., Sharpe, K. L., & Liles, R. F. (1987). A systematic approach to infant intervention. *Topics in Early Childhood Special Education, 7*(2), 19–37.

Dyer, K., Dunlap, G., & Winterling, V. (1990). Effects of choice making on the serious problem behaviors of students with severe handicaps. *Journal of Applied Behavior Analysis, 23,* 515–524.

Etzel, B. C., & LeBlanc, J. M. (1979). The simplest treatment alternative: Appropriate instructional control and errorless learning procedures for the difficult-to-teach child. *Journal of Autism and Developmental Disorders, 9,* 361–382.

Fleming, L. A., Wolery, M., Venn, M. L., Boyko, D., & Harris, M. (1991). *Effects of constant time delay during circle time.* Manuscript submitted for publication.

Fleming, L. A., Wolery, M., Weinzierl, C., Venn, M. L., & Schroeder, C. (1991). Model for assessing and adapting teachers' roles in mainstreamed preschool settings. *Topics in Early Childhood Special Education, 11*(1), 85–98.

Gast, D. L., Doyle, P. M., Wolery, M., Ault, M. J., & Baklarz, J. L. (1991). Acquisition of incidental information during small groups. *Education and Treatment of Children, 14,* 1–18.

Gast, D. L., Van Biervilet, A., & Spradlin, J. (1979). Teaching number–word equivalences: A study of transfer. *American Journal of Mental Deficiency, 83,* 524–527.

Goldstein, H., & Wickstrom, S. (1986). Peer intervention effects on communicative interaction among handicapped and nonhandicapped preschoolers. *Journal of Applied Behavior Analysis, 19,* 209–214.

Greenwood, C. R., & Hops, H. (1981). Group-oriented contingencies and peer behavior change. In P. S. Strain (Ed.), *The utilization of classroom peers as behavior change agents* (pp. 189–259). New York: Plenum Press.

Griffen, A. K., Wolery, M., & Schuster, J. W. (in press). Triadic instruction of chained food

preparation responses: Acquisition and observational learning. *Journal of Applied Behavior Analysis.*

Halle, J. W., Alpert, C. L., & Anderson, S. R. (1984). Natural environment language assessment and intervention with severely impaired preschoolers. *Topics in Early Childhood Special Education, 4*(2), 36–56.

Halle, J. W., Baer, D. M., & Spradlin, J. E. (1981). Teachers' generalized use of delay as a stimulus control procedure to increase language use in handicapped children. *Journal of Applied Behavior Analysis, 14,* 389–409.

Hart, B., & Risley, T. R. (1975). Incidental teaching of language in the preschool. *Journal of Applied Behavior Analysis, 8,* 411–420.

Helmstetter, E., & Guess, D. (1987). Application of the individualized curriculum sequencing model to learners with severe sensory impairments. In L. Goetz, D. Guess, K. Stremel-Campbell (Eds.), *Innovative program design for individuals with dual sensory impairments* (pp. 255–282). Baltimore: Paul Brookes.

Holcombe, M. A., Wolery, M., Werts, M. G., & Hrenkevich, P. (1991). *Increasing the efficiency of future learning by manipulating current instruction.* Manuscript submitted for publication.

Koegel, R. L., Dyer, K., & Bell, L. K. (1987). The influence of child-preferred activities on autistic children's social behavior. *Journal of Applied Behavior Analysis, 20,* 243–252.

Kohler, F. W., & Strain, P. S. (1990). Peer-assisted interventions: Early promises, notable achievements, and future aspirations. *Clinical Psychology Review, 10,* 441–452.

Kohler, F. W., Strain, P. S., Maretsky, S., DeCesare, L. (1990). Promoting positive and supportive interactions between preschoolers: An analysis of group-oriented contingencies. *Journal of Early Intervention, 14,* 327–341.

LeBlanc, J. M., Etzel, B. C., & Domash, M. A. (1978). A functional curriculum for early intervention. In K. E. Allen, V. A. Holm, & R. L. Schiefelbusch (Eds.), *Early intervention—a team approach* (pp. 331–381). Baltimore: University Park Press.

Mason, S. A., McGee, G. G., Farmer-Dougan, V., & Risley, T. R. (1989). A practical strategy for ongoing reinforcer assessment. *Journal of Applied Behavior Analysis, 22,* 171–179.

McDonnell, J., & Ferguson, B. (1989). A comparison of time delay and decreasing prompt hierarchy strategies in teaching banking skills to students with moderate handicaps. *Journal of Applied Behavior Analysis, 22,* 85–91.

McEvoy, M. A., Nordquist, V. M., Twardosz, S., Heckman, K. A., Wehby, J. H., & Denny, R. K. (1988). Promoting autistic children's peer interaction in an integrated early childhood setting using affection activities. *Journal of Applied Behavior Analysis, 21,* 193–200.

McGee, G. G., Krantz, P. J., & McClannahan, L. E. (1986). An extension of incidental teaching procedures to reading instruction for autistic children. *Journal of Applied Behavior Analysis, 19,* 147–157.

Mulligan, M., Lacy, L., & Guess, D. (1982). Effects of massed, distributed, and spaced trials sequencing on severely handicapped students' performance. *The Journal of the Association for the Severely Handicapped, 7*(2), 48–61.

Odom, S. L., Bender, M., Stein, M., Doran, L., Houden, P., McInnes, M., Gilbert, M., DeKlyen, M., Speltz, M., & Jenkins, J. (1988). *The integrated preschool curriculum: Procedures for socially integrating handicapped and non-handicapped preschool children.* Seattle: University of Washington Press.

Paniagua, F. A. (1990). A procedural analysis of correspondence training techniques. *The Behavior Analyst, 13,* 107–119.

Peck, C. A., Apolloni, T., Cooke, T. P., & Raver, S. (1978). Teaching retarded preschoolers to imitate the free-play behavior of nonretarded classmates: Trained and generalized effects. *Journal of Special Education, 12,* 195–207.

Rincover, A. (1981). Some directions for analysis and intervention in developmental disabilities: An editorial. *Analysis and Intervention in Developmental Disabilities, 1,* 109–115.

Sainato, D. M., Strain, P. S., & Lyon, S. R. (1987). Increasing academic responding of handicapped preschool children during group in-

struction. *Journal of the Division for Early Childhood, 12,* 23–30.

Schoen, S. F., Lentz, F. E., & Suppa, R. J. (1988). An examination of two prompt fading procedures and opportunities to observe in teaching handicapped preschoolers self-help skills. *Journal of the Division for Early Childhood, 12,* 349–358.

Schoen, S. F., & Sivil, E. O. (1989). A comparison of procedures in teaching self-help skills: Increasing assistance, time delay, and observational learning. *Journal of Autism and Developmental Disorders, 19,* 57–72.

Schuster, J. W., Griffen, A. K., & Wolery, M. (in press). Comparison of the simultaneous prompting and constant time delay procedures in teaching sight words to elementary students with moderate mental retardation. *Journal of Behavioral Education.*

Schwartz, I. S., Anderson, S. R., & Halle, J. W. (1989). Training teacher to use naturalistic time delay: Effects on teacher behavior and on the language use of students. *The Journal of the Association for Persons with Severe Handicaps, 14,* 48–57.

Snell, M. E., & Gast, D. L. (1981). Applying time delay procedure to instruction of the severely handicapped. *The Journal of the Association for the Severely Handicapped, 6*(3), 1–14.

Strain, P. S. (1981). *The utilization of classroom peers as behavior change agents.* New York: Plenum Press.

Strain, P. S., & Odom, S. L. (1986). Peer social initiations: Effective intervention for social skills development of exceptional children. *Exceptional Children, 52,* 543–551.

Venn, M. L., & Wolery, M. (in press). Increasing day care staff members' interactions during caregiving routines. *Journal of Early Intervention.*

Warren, S. F., & Kaiser, A. P. (1988). Research in early language intervention. In S. L. Odom & M. B. Karnes (Eds.), *Early intervention for infants and children with handicaps: An empirical base* (pp. 89–108). Baltimore, Paul Brookes.

Warren, S. F., McQuarter, R. M., & Rogers-Warren, A. K. (1984). The effects of teacher mands and models on the speech of unresponsive language-delayed children. *Jour-*

nal of Speech and Hearing Research, 49, 43–52.

Werts, M. G., Wolery, M., Holcombe, A., Vassilaros, M. A., & Billings, S. S. (1991). Transition-based teaching: Acquisition of target and incidental behaviors. Manuscript submitted for publication.

Wolery, M., Ault, M. J., & Doyle, P. M. (in press). Teaching students with moderate and severe disabilities: Use of response prompting procedures. White Plains, NY: Longman.

Wolery, M., Ault, M. J., Gast, D. L., Doyle, P. M., & Griffen, A. K. (1990). Comparison of constant time delay and the system of least prompts in teaching chained tasks. Education and Training in Mental Retardation, 25, 243–257.

Wolery, M., Ault, M. J., Gast, D. L., Doyle, P. M., & Griffen, A. K. (1991). Teaching chained tasks in dyads: Acquisition of target and observational behaviors. Journal of Special Education, 25, 65–80.

Wolery, M., Bailey, D. B., & Sugai, G. M. (1988). Effective teaching: Principles and procedures of applied behavior analysis with exceptional students. Boston: Allyn & Bacon.

Wolery, M., Cybriwsky, C. A., Gast, D. L., & Boyle-Gast, K. (1991). Use of constant time delay and attentional responses with adolescents. Exceptional Children, 57, 462–474.

Wolery, M., Doyle, P. M., Ault, M. J., Gast, D. L., Meyer, S., & Stinson, D. (1991). Effects of presenting incidental information in consequent events on future learning. Journal of Behavioral Education, 1, 79–104.

Wolery, M., Doyle, P. M., Gast, D. L., Ault, M. J., & Lichtenberg, S. (1991). Comparison of progressive time delay and transition-based teaching with preschoolers who have developmental delays. Manuscript submitted for publication.

Wolery, M., Fleming, L. A., Venn, M. L., Domjancic, C. M., & Thornton, C. (1991). Effects of simultaneous prompting during circle time. Manuscript submitted for publication.

Wolery, M., & Gast, D. L. (1990). Efficiency of instruction: Conceptual framework and research directions. Manuscript submitted for publication.

Wolery, M., Holcombe, A., Cybriwsky, C., Doyle, P. M., Schuster, J. W., Ault, M. J., & Gast, D. L. (in press). Constant time delay with discrete responses: A review of effectiveness and demographic, procedural, and methodological parameters. Research in Developmental Disabilities.

Yoder, P. J. (1990). The theoretical and empirical basis of early amelioration of developmental disabilities: Implications for future research. Journal of Early Intervention, 14, 27–42.

7

Designing and Arranging Environments for Infants and Preschoolers with Disabilities

The preschool environment—in its design and use—plays an important role in teaching young children. Several aspects of the environment can be distinguished as affecting children's experiences: the materials and space provided; the scheduling, organization, and structuring of instructional activities; and the presence of other persons and the pattern and quality of interactions. In this chapter we review the rationale for environmental design, identify several considerations in environmental planning, describe factors to consider in classroom organization and scheduling, discuss the role of other persons (including peers without disabilities) within the environmental context, and describe considerations in planning spaces for young children with special needs.

WHY STUDY ENVIRONMENTS?

Diverse theorists have agreed that the environment is a major determinant of development. Skinner (1953) emphasized the role of environment in shaping *behavior,* suggesting that the consequences of our interactions with the environment affect the probability of our repeating given behaviors. Piaget (1952) emphasized the role of environment in the development of *knowledge,* suggesting that interactions with the environment confirm, deny, or challenge existing knowledge structures. Both Skinner and Piaget recognized that the critical element was not the environment alone but rather the individual's *interactions* with the environment.

From a teaching perspective, careful planning of the environment is important to skill acquisition, skill facilitation, generalization, and nurturance. *Skill acquisition*—learning new skills—is easier when the proper materials are available. For example, although

most children can learn to ride a tricycle, they must have access to one. Optimal development of expressive language skills requires an appropriate model, opportunities to talk with another person, and a variety of stimulating activities designed to elicit talking. When one or more of these factors is missing from the environment, the quality and rate of language development may be altered.

Skill facilitation is the arrangement of the environment to increase the probability that a previously acquired skill will be demonstrated. For example, Krantz and Risley (1977) found that the percentage of time preschoolers listened to a story could be increased when the group story time was preceded by a quiet activity or rest period. When group story time was preceded by an active session, the percentage of time that preschoolers spent listening dropped considerably. Another example: Siegel (1977) sought to reduce the frequency with which boys with mental retardation missed the toilet when urinating by simply placing an attractive floating target in the urinal. This environmental change dramatically reduced the number of misses.

Generalization means that a skill learned in one context is displayed in another. Making the training environment similar to the generalization environment should result in more generalization than when the two environments differ significantly. This observation was verified in a series of peer imitation training studies (Apolloni & Cooke, 1978; Apolloni, Cooke, & Cooke, 1977; Peck, Apolloni, Cooke, & Raver, 1978). Although training a preschooler with disabilities to imitate peers without disabilities was effective in both free play and structured one-to-one lessons, generalization was greater in the free play setting, presumably because this environment was similar to others where generalized imitation was measured.

Careful analysis and planning of the environment is also important for *nurturance*. Risley (1981) suggests every child has a right to live in a reinforcing environment. Even if environments have little effect on behavior change, teachers should provide warm and pleasant environments to meet the children's basic nurturance needs. Special education is based on the assumption that children with disabilities do not thrive in a so-called normal environment (Keith, 1979). However, Public Laws 94-142 and 94-457 and research (Wolfensberger, 1972) give us legal and ethical mandates to provide an environment that is as close to real life as possible.

David and Weinstein (1987) summarize these points by arguing that all environments should fulfill at least five basic functions for children. First, environments should foster personal identity, helping children define who they are in relationship to the world. Second, the environment should foster the development of competence by "allowing children opportunities to develop mastery and control over their physical surroundings" (p. 9). Third, the environment should provide opportunities for growth by providing rich and stimulating surroundings. Fourth, environments ought to foster a sense of security and trust by being safe, warm, inviting, secure, and predictible. Finally, environments ought to provide opportunities for both social contact with peers and for privacy.

The Importance of Environmental Design

There are many ways to facilitate learning. In most teaching situations we assess the child and identify desired behaviors that need to be taught or refined and inappropriate behaviors that should be reduced. The next step is to identify a teaching strategy (e.g., prompting, shaping, modeling, reinforcing, or punishing) to produce the desired changes.

Many times teachers overlook the possibility of environmental alterations that could result in the same changes with less effort. For example, take the example we just presented in which environmental alteration—the substitution of a rest period for an active session preceding group story time—resulted in increased preschooler attention. The same change could have been produced through an elaborate token reinforcement system; but a token system requires considerable planning and preparation and may be viewed by some as an unnecessary, artificial strategy.

A study by Bailey, Clifford, and Harms (1982) compared environments provided for preschoolers with disabilities with those provided for preschoolers without disabilities. The environments were similar in provisions for personal care routines, language-reasoning experiences, and adult needs; but the researchers found several differences that emphasize the importance of environmental design training in special teacher education. The programs for children with disabilities, in general, had fewer furnishings for relaxation and comfort; devoted less attention to room arrangement, child-related display, and artistic activities; had fewer blocks and facilities for sand/water and dramatic play, and less space for children to be alone; were less likely to encourage free play, or cultural awareness; and gave over space and scheduled time for gross motor activities.

The findings of this study raise many interesting questions regarding the nature of environments that *are* and *should be* provided for young children with disabilities. Why were the programs providing significantly different environments? Were these differences appropriate for the needs of the children involved? Did the programs provide other activities that fulfilled the same functions as sand/water play, blocks, and dramatic play? As Bailey et al. (1982) argue, the justification that children with disabilities require different activities lacks supporting data. On the contrary, such activities as sand/water and dramatic play appear to be appropriate for *all* young children—they fulfill meaningful functions and are enjoyable. The activities can also be adapted and structured for children functioning at widely differing developmental levels.

CONSIDERATIONS IN ENVIRONMENTAL PLANNING

At least one data-based study has addressed the question of quality in environments. Although the study dealt with the home, its implications for classrooms are readily apparent. Wachs (1979) studied 39 infants between 12 and 24 months of age. He found five dimensions of their home environments that were positively related to cognitive growth: physical responsiveness, presence of a stimulus shelter, lack of overcrowding, physical encouragement of exploration, and maintenance of temporal regularity; and he found one dimension, a high noise-confusion level, that was negatively related to cognitive growth.

A Physically Responsive Environment

The dimension found to relate most consistently with cognitive growth was the physical responsiveness of the environment. According to Wachs (1979), the importance of a physically responsive environment may lie in the child's awareness that her behavior can affect the environment; this may encourage the child to interact even more with the environment and thus facilitate other learning.

Olds (1979; 1987) considers responsivity to be essential for children to feel competent. One way of feeling competence is to experience success—your behavior affects other people or materials around you. Having re-

sponsive materials ought to increase the probability of a child being successful and feeling competent.

A physically responsive environment is particularly important for young children with disabilities. Historically, society has taken a protective attitude toward individuals with handicaps. Unfortunately this attitude frequently has resulted in adults doing everything for these individuals or exerting extensive control over their behavior. Such situations can easily lead to the children's perceiving that they lack control over their lives; they are taught helplessness (DeVellis, 1977; Seligman, 1975). A physically responsive environment provided during the early years may help to increase perceptions of control.

What is meant by a physically responsive environment? Wachs measured responsivity by counting the number of toys in the home that made an audiovisual response when activated. In a broader sense, a physically responsive environment allows success and independence, with materials *and* people who respond to the child's individual needs. A good environment should be socially as well as physically responsive. Elardo, Bradley, and Caldwell (1977) found emotional and verbal responsivity of the mother to be positively correlated with language development at age 3, and Bradley and Caldwell (1976) found the same responsivity factor to be positively correlated with mental test performance at age 4½.

The following strategies should be incorporated in designing a responsive environment: activities and materials should be appropriately challenging (frequently giving feedback) yet not so difficult that failure often occurs; the adults and children in the environment should learn to respond to verbal and nonverbal signals sent by others in that environment; and independence must be valued, encouraged, and facilitated through appropriate environmental design (such as adaptive equipment and child-size furniture) and expected by teachers.

Overcrowding and Stimulus Shelters

Two closely related dimensions identified by Wachs were the provision of sufficient space for the people in the environment and the provision of places where children can be away from people and noise; both of these dimensions were found to react with the general noise and confusion level within the environment. A number of studies investigating the effects of crowding and noise have been conducted with both animals and humans. Hutt and Viazay (1966) demonstrated that as group size within a given classroom space increased, both nonhandicapped and brain-damaged children exhibited increased aggressiveness. Kreger (1971) demonstrated that reduction of the stress from overcrowding in a residential institution resulted in decreased levels of aggression and other behavior problems. He suggested that the problems of persons with severe retardation may be as much a function of limited environments as they are of limited cognitive skills.

Nearly every state has established standards for square footage per child that must be available in programs for young children. The National Association for the Education of Young Children (1984) recommends a minimum of 35 square feet of usable indoor playroom floor space per child and a minimum of 75 square feet of outdoor play space per child. These guidelines may need to be adjusted in programs for children with disabilities if space is taken up by large pieces of special equipment.

Crowding is not merely a function of the number of people in a given space. Ittelson, Proshansky, Rivlin, and Winkel (1974) suggested that crowding results in frustration when others interfere with the individual's efforts to achieve some purpose.

Baker (1980) suggests that programs serving children with severe handicaps often contribute to maladaptive social and emotional behaviors by ignoring individual needs for territoriality and privacy. The Bailey et al. (1982) comparison of preschool environments reported that more than 75% of the preschool classrooms for children with disabilities provided no space especially set aside for children to be alone.

In reality, we all need some space and time to be alone. Although busy, active environments can be stimulating and exciting, quiet spaces are important for relaxation and concentration. Teachers should provide a balance between stimulation and opportunities for privacy and free choice.

Harms and Cross (1977) suggest that environmental provisions for play-alone spaces be created in a number of ways:

- Visual barriers, high enough to give children a feeling of privacy, but low enough for adults to see over, can be created by shelves and dividers.
- Enclosures can be made out of cardboard boxes, wooden crates, or cable reels.
- Lofts or platforms can be built above part of the room. (p. 22)

Scheduling, supervision, and careful planning of space may also be useful in reducing potentially negative effects of crowding. Krantz and Risley (1977), for example, found that children were more attentive to a story when they were spaced equidistantly from each other (either on chairs or sitting in assigned spaces) rather than when they were allowed to randomly sit together. Harms and Cross (1977) suggest that a system for taking turns in both activities and play-alone spaces can ensure sharing and reduce competition for space and materials.

Encouraging Exploration

Another aspect of the environment that Wachs (1979) found to be important was the degree to which the physical set-up of the environment permits exploration. As Appleton, Clifton, and Goldberg (1975) suggest, freedom to explore "allows the child to process stimulation at his own pace thus producing a great probability of a match" (Wachs, 1979, p. 31).

Weisler and McCall (1976) define exploration as "perceptual-motor examination of an object, situation, or event the function of which is to reduce subjective uncertainties" (p. 493). The child uses exploration to acquire information about the properties of objects, people, or situations. A relatively consistent sequence of behaviors appears to be associated with exploration, beginning with becoming alert to and attending to a new situation or object, and continuing with observing the new stimulus from a distance, motor-aided perceptual examination, and finally, active physical interaction.

According to Piaget (1963b), active interaction with the environment is a primary learning mode for both children and adults. Active interaction requires movement and high quality (as opposed to random) exploration. In fact, Olds (1979) suggests that "to deny activity is to halt development at its source" (p. 92).

The importance of exploration and the effects of inadequate exploratory skills become even more apparent when we consider young children with sensory or motor impairments that can reduce such opportunities. Such impairment of exploration results in the secondary handicap of deficits in experiences. How can a child in a wheelchair *really* understand the concept of "high" if he has never been able to explore heights through climbing?

Weisler and McCall (1976) suggest several considerations in encouraging and facilitating exploratory behaviors. First, teachers should attend to the stimulus properties of the objects or events in the environment, such as color and brightness contrasts, movement patterns, response to manipulation, and unpredictability. Second, children are more likely to explore novel stimuli. Thus some attempt should be made to vary the materials available for play. Third, children may be interested in exploring stimuli both similar and moderately discrepant with the previous stimuli. Weisler and McCall emphasize that infants may look at and explore only moderately unusual events; they cite Piaget (1963a), who suggested that children will not explore anything that is very familiar (because they are satisfied with their knowledge of it) or anything that is too discrepant (because it does not fit into their knowledge structure).

Children with sensory or motor impairments may need special adaptations or encouragement to facilitate exploratory behavior. In general, an environment should minimize the dangers of exploration, maximize the reward potential of exploration, and facilitate exploration through adaptive equipment and teacher structure.

Temporal Regularity

Finally, Wachs (1979) reported that the degree of temporal regularity in the home was positively related to cognitive development, although the only indicator used to measure temporal regularity was whether or not the child had a regular mealtime. Other authors, however, have also suggested the importance of temporal regularity. Harms and Cross (1977), for example, stress the importance of *predictable* environments. Predictability does not necessarily mean the same rigid schedule should be followed every day; but a relatively predictable schedule is important for children and adults to feel comfortable within a setting. Predictability would seem particularly important for children who come from unpredictable home environments.

CLASSROOM ORGANIZATION AND STRUCTURE

As we indicated at the beginning of this chapter, there are—besides the use of space and materials—several other aspects of environments that affect children's experiences. Of great importance are the scheduling, organizing, and structuring of activities.

Scheduling of Activities

Scheduling refers to deciding who will do what and when they will do it. Scheduling is important for both adults and children and can affect the behavior of both. A schedule provides a comfortable routine within which adults and children are able to identify a variety of needs and know that *sometime* during the day those needs will be met. A consistently followed schedule helps make a program a *predictable* setting. The best schedule specifies a sequence of activities, designates which children will be doing those activities, lists approximate time periods for the activities, and specifies responsibilities for each adult in the classroom (Hart, 1982). Several factors should be considered in planning a daily schedule.

Children are probably the most alert early in the day. Structured teaching activities requiring alert concentration should be planned early in the daily schedule.

Children usually arrive at different times. This fact makes conducting early structured activities difficult: the implication for scheduling is that structured play activities planned each morning and requiring minimal teacher supervision may be best. Teachers should wait to conduct structured teaching activities until most children have arrived. Such planning reduces interruptions and distractions, and frees the teacher to attend to arrival responsibilities.

Children need to be greeted appropriately when they arrive. Having independent activities available when children arrive does not mean the teacher is free to sit in the lounge and drink coffee. Children (and parents) need to be greeted when they arrive. Assign one or more staff members to greet children and parents each day (Harms & Clifford, 1980). Greeting time is especially important for young children. A familiar face, a smile, a directed welcome ("Hello, Mike! I am really glad to see you at school today!"), and a familiar routine at arrival time can serve to make school a pleasant experience. Here are some guidelines for the greeting procedure.

- Get down at the child's eye level and say, "Hello" or "Good morning," stating the child's name so that she knows you are talking to her.
- Assist the child as necessary in performing standard arrival behaviors such as taking off a coat or putting up a lunch box.
- Direct the child to a particular activity or present several optional activities from which the child may choose.
- Greet the parents as well, and use this time to talk and exchange information (Harms & Clifford, 1980).
- Children who have a long bus ride may need to go to the bathroom soon after they arrive at school.

Children need a carefully planned balance of activities. We all need and enjoy variety. Children need active as well as quiet times scheduled throughout the day. These activities should be interspersed so children will not burn out on tabletop activities or be too physically exhausted from motor activities.

Programs for young children must be planned to include time and space for both *acquisition* and *generalization* experiences. The environmental supports for each of these modes of instruction are somewhat different. Acquisition often requires individual or small group instruction that is teacher-directed and focuses on specific tasks. Generalization requires intrinsically motivating play and real-life activities that elicit and integrate a number of the acquired skills.

Many programs for children with disabilities currently use the acquisition mode almost exclusively, whereas most programs for children without disabilities emphasize the generalization mode. This difference accounts for the surprise that special education teachers feel when they see how much of the day normally developing children spend in noisy, active, hands-on play. Similarly teachers of preschool and kindergarten-age children are shocked to see young children with special needs sitting in chairs and being instructed for much of the school day. All children need an *appropriate balance* between instruction for acquisition and play for generalization (Olds, 1979; Piaget, 1963b). The effective early childhood special educator should combine the strengths of early childhood classrooms with those of special education classrooms. A truly nonrestrictive education environment for children with disabilities, according to Kenowitz, Zweibel, and Edgar (1979), must include activities to help prepare children to function to their capacity in the larger world.

Group Versus Individual Instruction

Grouping children for instruction and other activities can be difficult when working with those with very specific and diverse instructional needs. Given a large number of children, however, individual instruction may not always be possible. The issue of group versus individual instruction raises a variety of questions: Which procedure is the most effective method of teaching a skill? Which procedure is the most economical use of teacher time? Is it possible that some skills are best taught individually while others are just as easily taught in a group format?

Individual instruction is a primary strategy in many early intervention programs. Blank (1970) made a strong case for one-to-one instruction in preschool programming, particularly language intervention. She suggested that such an approach would be preferable for children with short attention spans and should result in more effective instruction by allowing the teacher to continually diagnose difficulties and adjust the lesson to make it appropriate for each child. "There is little opportunity in the group setting for the teacher to pursue the reasons for failure and then offer him the necessary experiences to help him understand the rationale for the correct answer" (Blank, 1970, p. 30).

There may be, however, some advantages to group instruction. Brown, Holvoet, Guess, and Mulligan (1980) suggest that in an individual lesson, the teacher has little recourse with the nonresponsive or "acting out" child—the problem must be dealt with directly. In a group lesson, however, the materials, cues, or feedback given to other children can serve as potential motivators for disruptive children. For example, if Johnny knocks his chair over, the teacher could praise Susie for staying in her chair and attending to the task rather than scolding or punishing Johnny. Group instruction also provides opportunities for learning by observing peers, opportunities that are impossible in one-to-one instruction. Group activities predominate in nonhandicapped preschool programs, and learning to function in such a setting may facilitate movement to less restrictive environments.

In some cases group instruction can be as effective as individual instruction, even for children with severe disabilities (Favell, Favell, & McGinsey, 1978; Storm & Willis, 1978). For example, Alberto, Jobes, Sizemore, and Doran (1980) found no significant differences in the effectiveness of group and individual instruction in tabletop activities involving receptive understanding of prepositions and in the discrimination of colors, even though there were more opportunities for responding in one-to-one instruction. Individual instruction did result in more effective acquisition of dressing skills, however.

Individualized instruction should be provided within the small group setting. For example, answering questions about a story may be an appropriate goal for Roy, Larry, and Emmy. Perhaps Roy needs to answer questions about what will happen next; Larry needs to figure out what the characters did; and Emmy needs to understand who did what. While each child has a different objective, they can listen to the same story as a group and answer questions appropriate to their individual objectives (c.f., Cybriwsky, Wolery, & Gast, 1990). A checklist for developing small group instructional activities is displayed in Box 6.8.

Children need not experience a lot of dead time waiting for other children to complete activities in group instruction. Activities involving children in meaningful experiences should be provided throughout the lesson. Children not directly involved with the teacher should have planned, concrete, and interesting work relating to instructional objectives. The children should be able to accomplish such activities independently.

Structure of Activities

Environmental structure provides a framework within which things can happen. In a broad sense, *any* program is structured by the nature of its setup and organization, which affect the behavior of both teacher and children. The real issue is whether the teachers are aware of the kind of structure they impose and its effect on children.

The structuring of programs for young children without disabilities rests heavily on principles and concepts articulated by Piaget. This model advocates self-initiated activity by children, with structure taking the

form of teacher selection of appropriate materials and options for activities. The basic premise is as follows.

The concept that children—or individuals of any age—learn best from self-initiated activity is perhaps the most important single proposition that the educator can derive from Piaget's work. . . . Piaget places major emphasis on the role of activity—both physical and mental—in intellectual development. In Piaget's view, "to know an object, is to act on it." . . . The essence of knowledge is activity. (Ginsburg & Opper, 1979, p. 224)

The child must act upon the environment to construct knowledge. She must be able to explore, manipulate, and change objects—in short, to investigate, test, retest, and question. Such activity, from Piaget's perspective, allows the child to discover knowledge and results in greater understanding and a more enduring change than knowledge we try to teach children. By providing the child with a wide range of environmental encounters, we allow the child "to come up with a variety of ideas, problems, and questions" and to "put objects and events into relationships and notice similarities and differences" (Kamii & DeVries, 1978, p. 40).

Organizing a preschool program based on these premises involves several steps. *The classroom environment must be arranged and equipped to invite and encourage activity.* The classroom materials should be appropriate to the children's abilities; just enough beyond their abilities to be challenging, but not frustrating. Children's products should be displayed and cultural/home environments reflected in the classroom (Elkind, 1976). The classroom should have space for movement and should include certain work areas, for example, block, housekeeping, construction, and sand and water areas (Hohmann, Banet, & Weikart, 1979). Hohmann et al. discuss arranging, organizing, and equipping the classroom in detail and provide suggestions for setting up the class-room for specific disabling conditions.

In organizing the Piagetian classroom, *the teacher must also provide inviting, interesting activities.* Hohmann, Banet, and Weikart (1979) maintain that "the overriding implication of Piaget's work for educators is that the teacher is a supporter of development, and as such his or her prime goal is to promote active learning on the part of the child" (Hohmann et al., 1979, p. 3). They have designed approximately 50 *key experiences* including using language, representing experiences and ideas, developing logical reasoning (classification, seriation, number concepts), and understanding time and space. The key experiences are not behavioral objectives to be mastered, but are central themes around which an endless variety of activities can be planned regardless of the child's developmental level. The activities can be initiated by either child or teacher, but a balance is desired. The key experiences allow children to constructively interact with the environment, provide the teacher with an awareness of children's cognitive processes, and serve as a means to expand activities for promoting development. The teacher is a supporter of development by doing the following:

Providing a rich array of materials and activities from which children are invited to select. Explicitly asking children to plan, in some way, what they are going to do and how they are going to do it. . . . Asking questions and making suggestions in order to set the stage for key experiences that stimulate the child's thinking processes, language development, and social development (Hohmann et al., 1979, p. 6).

Helping children plan daily activities is essential in implementing the key experiences of the book, *Cognitively Oriented Curriculum.* When children are involved in planning their activities, they begin to view themselves as capable of making and acting

upon decisions. Children may also begin to construct mental pictures of the activity they are about to do (Hohmann et al., 1979).

Initially, children must learn available options in work areas, materials, and human resources. The teacher assists children in planning what they are *going to do* rather than *where* they will be working or playing. Some children indicate their plans verbally, others may point to an area, bring materials to the teacher, or report they do not know what they are going to do. The teacher should recognize how children indicate their plans and assist them in making detailed, realistic, and varied plans.

Kamii and DeVries (1978) suggest that when *beginning* an activity, the teacher should "introduce the activity in a way that maximizes children's initiative" (p. 52). This principle is implemented "by putting out materials to which children will naturally gravitate, by presenting the material and saying, 'See whatever you can think of to do with these things,' and by . . . presenting the material and saying, 'Can you find something with which you can do X?'" (p. 53). Another principle for beginning activities is to "begin with parallel play" or "introduce the activity in such a way that cooperation is possible but not necessary" (pp. 53–54). Cooperation and social interaction are desirable for preschool children, but Kamii and DeVries suggest cooperation and social interactions occur as a result of children engaging in physical knowledge activities.

Kamii and DeVries (1978) also present principles for *continuing* activities. Initially, "figure out what the child is thinking and respond sparingly in his terms" (p. 54). Determining what children are thinking is not easy, and Kamii and DeVries suggest careful observation and educated guesses. Another difficult task is deciding what to do or say based on what you suppose the child is thinking. As we have suggested, intervene sparingly. Further, the teacher must decide when to say or do something. Teachers should provide opportunities for children to note relationships between objects and events. Kamii and DeVries (1978) suggest four types of questions to help children notice relationships.

1 What do you think would happen if you did (a *certain thing*) with your materials?
2 Can you do (a *certain thing*) or can you find something to accomplish (*with a certain thing*)?
3 Can you tell how you did (a *certain thing*), or how one way of doing it is different from another?
4 Can you explain why (a *certain thing*) happened? (This type of question should rarely be used.)

Teachers also can help children with lines of experimentation impossible (or unsafe) to do alone; they can offer more materials, and they can model different actions or possibilities with the same material.

Another principle for continuing an activity is to "encourage children to interact with other children" (Kamii & DeVries, 1978, p. 57). Ask the types of questions just listed, but encourage children to solicit peer assistance in acting upon the questions.

Still another principle is to "integrate all aspects of development in physical knowledge activities" (p. 59). Teachers should encourage growth in social, moral, and language development during physical knowledge activities.

After activities are completed, the teacher should ask questions which assist children in *reflecting on* what they did and saw other children do. Emphasize honest descriptions rather than one correct answer.

Another guideline for organizing the Piagetian classroom is that *children's spontaneous play must be allowed and encouraged* (Kamii & DeVries, 1977). Piaget believed that the child uses play to gain information about objects in the environment and thus con-

structs knowledge. When children play, they choose activities in which they are interested. This results in motivation for continued manipulations of the environment, manipulations being the acts through which intellect is constructed.

Forman and Kuschner (1977) propose guidelines for entering the child's play and assisting in constructing knowledge. Initially, the child is allowed to engage in free play. The teacher observes this and attempts to determine the specific type of knowledge the child is constructing. Based on the hypothesized explanation, the teacher makes a decision about how and when to enter the child's play. Typically, teachers enter by engaging in parallel play near enough to the child without giving the impression of forcing an interaction. Essentially the teacher is imitating the child's behavior from a "safe" distance.

The objective of imitating the child is to lead the child beyond her current knowledge. The teacher imitates what the child is doing: the child imitates the teacher's imitation of her; and then the child continues to imitate the teacher when the teacher presents novel variations on the theme of play. (Forman & Kuschner, 1977, p. 132)

These novel variations allow the child to construct new notions about objects and the actions possible with objects. This procedure appears very simple, but in reality involves considerable skill in rapid decision making by the teacher.

Research on Structure

The effects of various levels of structure in preschool programs for children without disabilities have been investigated in a number of ways. Johnson, Ershler, and Bell (1980) compared play behavior observed in a discovery-based preschool program with that in a formal education preschool program. The formal program emphasized Piagetian concepts but used a direct teaching approach to facilitate development. The discovery-based program focused more on the process of thinking and stressed spontaneous interactions with materials, peers, and teachers. The results suggested that the approach taken by the program could affect play behavior in a number of ways. Children in the formal program exhibited more constructive play and more transformations (changes in use of materials or the identity of people) than children in the discovery-based program. Discovery program children were observed in nonplay behavior (unoccupied or onlooking) more often than children in the formal program.

Huston-Stein, Friedrich-Cofer, and Susman (1977) compared highly structured (high percentages of adult-directed activities) Head Start classrooms with low-structure classrooms and found both positive and negative aspects. Children in high-structure classrooms were more attentive in circle time and helped to clean up more often after free play, but they did not show more independent task-oriented behavior.

Doke (1975) investigated the effects of formal versus informal activity periods in a day care treatment program for behavior-disordered preschoolers (aged 4 to 6 years). *Formal activities* were defined as those in which children remain in a group within a specified area and watch another person (usually the teacher) coordinate the activity. Manipulable materials are used simultaneously by all children and usually in the same way, as directed by the teacher. *Informal activities* were those in which children could obtain a variety of materials at any time and use them in a variety of ways. Formal activity periods included nursery rhymes, language lessons, and story time; informal activities included blocks, housekeeping, and manipulative play.

Doke measured the percentage of time all children were engaged in planned activities.

Results indicated the amount of engagement was consistently higher during informal activities than during formal ones. This finding was consistent over several days and for most of the children. As a result of these data, Doke (1975) concluded that

Informal activities appear to hold considerable promise. Children may be worked with individually while they request materials or assistance from the caregiver. These impromptu training episodes are ideal in that the caregiver does not have to vie for the child's attention or guess about what might be reinforcing for him. The child who approaches the caregiver with a request is specifying his reinforcer and is telling the teacher that he is ready to learn. In addition, well-stocked informal activities assure that children who are not interacting with the caregiver will stay busy. Formal activities are weaker in this respect, because they often require many children to wait while the caregiver interacts with one or two children. (p. 221)

Doke and Risley (1972) investigated required versus optional activities in organizing a day care environment. At the beginning of the school year the children followed an "Options" activity schedule. During this period at least two optional activities were always available throughout the day, and children were free to move from one area to another after meeting simple exit requirements such as putting away materials or cleaning up. Later a "No-Options" schedule was introduced. Under this structure only one activity area was open at any given time. When that area was closed, children completed their exit requirements and then moved on to the next area which had just opened.

Doke and Risley found no significant differences in overall percentage of engagement time between the Options and No-Options arrangements. This was only true, however, when children in the No-Options schedule left the activity area as soon as they completed their individual exit requirements. When they had to wait for all children to finish, the percentage of engaged time dropped dramatically.

LeLaurin and Risley (1972) investigated zone versus man-to-man staff assignment patterns. During the zone procedure, each teacher was assigned a specific activity area. Children were required to follow a basic activity schedule at their own pace. For example, at the beginning of lunch all four teachers were in the lunch area. As soon as the first child had finished his dessert, one teacher went to the bathroom and another to the shoe area to help children moving through those sections on their way to the nap area. As more children left the lunchroom, a third teacher went to the bed area to assist children who had gone through the bathroom and shoe areas. Children were free to move through each area as they finished their responsibilities. During the man-to-man procedure, each teacher was responsible for a group of 6 to 12 children. The entire group had to finish a given activity before anyone in that group could proceed to the next area.

The zone procedure clearly was the superior environmental organization. The percent of engagement in appropriate activities was considerably higher when children were allowed to move at their own pace rather than wait for other children. As LeLaurin and Risley suggest, a similarly high percent of engagement probably could have been achieved using the man-to-man procedure had supplementary procedures been used such as providing activities for waiting children. The zone staffing pattern provides a more natural structure, however, and may be more enjoyable for children and easier for staff to implement.

Structure in Programs for Preschoolers with Disabilities

The perceived importance of "low" structure in child care programs for young children is reflected in statements published by the National Association for the Education of Young Children describing what are assumed to be best practices (Bredekamp, 1986; NAEYC, 1984). For example, Bredekamp (1986) states the following:

Children's play is the primary vehicle for and indicator of their mental growth. Therefore, child-initiated, child-directed, teacher-supported play is an essential component of developmentally appropriate practice. (p. 3)

Does this statement also pertain to children with disabilities? The position of these authors is that "child-initiated, child-directed, teacher-supported" play is a goal to strive for in the context of early intervention for children with disabilities. When this model of services is effective, it should be the procedure of choice. However, we also believe (and know) that many children with disabilities do not learn efficiently if left to their own devices. They may explore less, interact with the environment less, and may not learn from subtle cues. Thus, in many instances, a more structured program is likely to be needed. This fact does not reduce the importance of play for children with disabilities, nor does it imply that teachers should not use play experiences as opportunities for teaching. Rather, a variety of types of activities should be provided in order to ensure that learning is facilitated.

DeKlyen and Odom (1989) examined this question in the context of a mainstreamed preschool program for children with disabilities. The authors defined *structure* as involving multiple meanings—the way the teacher introduces the activity, the rules that are established, the materials that are provided, the roles that are assigned. The study found that social interactions for children with *and* without disabilities increased when more structure was provided. In reality, the question is not whether structure should be used, but *how* structure can best and most appropriately be provided to maximize the goals intended for the children.

HUMAN DIMENSIONS
OF ENVIRONMENTS

In addition to physical space, scheduling, organization, and structure, a final relevant aspect of the environment is the human element. People are very much a part of the environment. The type, the number, and the relative status of the other persons present can affect the behavior of children and should be considered in planning early intervention programs.

The three major considerations regarding the human element in early intervention child care programs are the adult–child ratios, the availability of normally developing peers, and the presence of same-age versus mixed-age groupings. With respect to adult–child ratios, programs must attend to state requirements and national standards (e.g., NAEYC, 1984). In addition to professional staff, programs should also make use of volunteers when appropriate to ensure that children have ample opportunities for individual instruction, support, and feedback. The availability of normally developing peers and considerations regarding same-age versus mixed-age groupings of children are discussed in chapter 9, which treats the attainment of social skills.

ARRANGING THE PHYSICAL SPACE

Space and materials within a room can be arranged in many ways. The ideal space allows the teacher to observe ongoing activities in the classroom and yet reduces distractions across activity areas. The space should be functional, comfortable, and safe for both children and adults. Finally, the space should be designed to encourage and facilitate maximum independence for children with sensory or motor impairments.

Open Space Design

Most early childhood educators who work with children without disabilities advocate some form of open space design for infant and preschool centers. Unlike open education, which is an approach to teaching and learning focusing on self-directed learning, *open-space* refers to a large room without walls or high dividers (Rogers-Warren & Wedel, 1980). Open space architecture can be used with either an open or highly structured approach to early education. It can facilitate both staff supervision of children and children's movement to different activities and provide a context for development of care routines.

Twardosz, Cataldo, and Risley (1974) investigated the effect of an open space design on infant and toddler day care. A large room was separated by low dividers such as shelves. The experimenters used partitions to examine the effects of open or closed classroom designs on the visibility and supervision of children and staff, infant and toddler sleep patterns, and toddler preacademic activities (puzzles, beads, coloring). The studies demonstrated that an open environment made supervision much easier because it increased the amount of time a child could be seen by an adult, and staff persons by the supervisor; moderate levels of noise, light, and visibility of center activities had no adverse effects on the sleep patterns of infants and toddlers; and engagement in preacademic tasks was similar in both an open environment and in a separate room. The authors concluded that infant and toddler day care "definitely can and should be accomplished in an open environment" (p. 544).

Lining the walls with furniture and materials and leaving an empty area in the middle is not good use of open space, however. As Danoff, Breitbart, and Barr (1977) suggest, such a "child-sized toy cafeteria" (p. 60) may encourage children to keep moving from one activity to another without concentrating or becoming involved.

Another misuse of open space is encircling all activity areas with bookcases, storage units, or other furniture. Olds (1979) suggests that such an arrangement would make children "feel somewhat like rats in a maze, following defined pathways into enclosed, discrete boxes" (p. 109). Olds advocates increased use of *fluid* boundaries for some areas of the room. Examples of fluid boundaries include raising the floor level of an area; changing the level of the ceiling through use of canopies, streamers, or mobiles; creating a "pit" with low carpeted risers to enclose a space, or painting the work surfaces, display units, and dividers so that activity areas are defined by particular colors. An open space classroom should be attractively arranged into clearly differentiated, easily accessible activity areas, with sufficient dividers or boundaries to increase engagement but enough openness to allow ease of movement and adult supervision.

Moore (1987) suggests that a "modified open plan" may be the best way to arrange a child care program. A modified open-plan facility is defined as "the organization of space into a variety of large and small activity spaces open enough to allow children to see the play possibilities available to them while providing enough enclosure for the child to be protected from noise and visual distractions" (p. 52). This description contrasts with the open-plan facility, "unpartitioned space with few or no internal walls" (p. 51) and the closed-plan facility, "self-contained classrooms usually arranged along corridors or as in a house with several small interconnecting rooms" (p. 51). In a study comparing these three arrangements, Moore found that open-plan centers often resulted

in more random behavior and that closed-plan facilities resulted in more time spent in transitions as well as more withdrawn behavior. The modified open-plan facilities seemed to be best because they resulted in more use of activity settings, increased engagement in cognitively oriented behaviors, and more child-initiated behavior.

Making Space Comfortable

Olds (1979) mentions *variety* and *richness* as important in environmental planning. These qualities can be provided by intentional variation of dimensions such as scale, floor height, ceiling height, boundary height, visual interest, auditory interest, olfactory interest, textural interest, and kinesthetic interest. Brophy, Good & Nedler (1975) suggest that the floor should be carpeted since many activities take place there. The classroom space should have good lighting, adequate ventilation and temperature control, ample storage space, and effective sound absorption.

Appropriate furnishings are also important. Child-sized furniture, including tables, chairs, and toilets, should be provided. (A child-sized chair is one in which the child may sit and have his or her feet on the floor.) Each child should have a personal space, no matter how small. The locker, shelf, or cubby should be easily accessible and labeled with a name card and a photograph to help the child begin to recognize his or her name. If cubbies or lockers are too expensive or unavailable, use labeled dishpans, round ice cream containers, or large shoe boxes (Harms & Cross, 1977).

Another strategy for making space comfortable is the use of child-centered displays. Bailey, Clifford, and Harms (1982) found that child-centered displays for preschoolers with disabilities rarely included the children's own work. Display of children's work can be a basis for language interaction ("Tell me about this"), esteem building ("You did that"), or comparisons ("Look, the one you made today is a different color"). Displays can also remind children of the theme or concept (e.g., animals) being emphasized during a given time period. Commercial materials and teacher-made displays facilitate some of the same functions, so perhaps a balance between child-produced and teacher-made/commercial displays can be reached.

Keep several factors in mind when designing and planning displays. When you set them up, consider each child's eye level. This requirement may be complex in programs for children with disabilities, because eye level may vary considerably—some children are in wheelchairs, others may only crawl, still others might be unusually small. Vary the levels of display to meet the children's needs. Also, display each child's work, regardless of the quality. Progress will be reflected as skills are developed. Materials should be changed frequently, with the display being related to the subjects currently discussed.

Comfort considerations should not just be limited to children. The adults in the environment should also be comfortable. Regular furniture and a bathroom and lounge, an adult meeting area, and personal storage spaces should be separate from the children (Harms & Clifford, 1980).

Setting Up Activity Areas

One of the keys to designing a preschool environment is the effective establishment of activity areas or centers. *Activity areas* are spaces within the room designed to accommodate different types of activities for children and adults. Activities range from one-to-one tutoring or small group instruction to independent undertakings such as blocks, toy play, or art. Hildebrand (1975) suggests that organized space can serve as a stimulus for certain activities. Children can use the

centers to learn how different behaviors are expected in various settings and how one changes behavior to meet changing demands.

Moore (1987) emphasizes the importance of "well-defined behavior settings":

Well-defined behavior settings [are] areas limited to one activity, with clear boundaries from circulation space and from other behavior settings, and with at least partial acoustic and visual separation. Typically they are sized to accommodate two to five children and one teacher and include storage, a surface area, electrical connections for equipment, and display room for the activity.

Essentially a setting should define and support the types of activities and behaviors expected in that setting.

Selecting Activity Areas   Room arrangement should provide an appropriate balance of activity areas suited to the age, skills, and interests of the children. The room should be designed to fit the routine; for example, if many structured lessons are concurrently conducted, several activity areas with tables and chairs may be needed. Such a design will limit the number of specialized activity centers, so spread the structured lessons out over the morning, and try to provide variety in activity centers designed for independent use and skill generalization.

Harms and Cross (1977) suggest that by age 3, most children can manage an environment with a wide variety of activity areas. However, little data exist on the ability of infants and preschoolers with disabilities to respond to a large number of choices. It may be more appropriate to provide a smaller number of activity areas and focus on advanced skill development in those areas.

In any case, several activity areas should be included in any preschool program, for activities such as playing with blocks, dramatic play, art work, playing with manipulative toys, reading/language work, and sensory stimulation activities. At least six types of activity areas should be provided: a quiet, calm area, a structured materials/activities area, a crafts and discovery area, a dramatic play area, a large motor area, and a therapeutic area (Olds, 1979).

Arranging Activity Areas Placement of activity areas within a classroom can affect the amount of use any area receives and also the level of child engagement. Brophy, Good, and Nedler (1975, pp. 140–142) suggest the following guidelines for arranging activity centers:

1 Classroom traffic should be minimized and should flow freely. Controlling traffic patterns reduces safety problems such as jostling and bumping along with wasted time. Efficient traffic management requires storing materials and equipment near the areas they will be needed, avoiding cross traffic, and suggesting routes for travel.
2 Consider the noise levels typically generated in a given activity center when determining its placement in the classroom. For example, the small group lesson area should not be located next to noisy activities such as the block/construction area of the role playing/make-believe area. Centers requiring concentration, such as the book area, should also be in quieter places in the room.
3 Consider lighting when locating classroom areas. Areas requiring close, visually demanding activities should be placed near windows or lights.

Promoting Independent Use of Activity Areas As teachers, we want children to use centers independently. This goal requires the appropriate manipulation of materials and the return of no-longer-needed materials to their proper locations. Although many preschoolers have difficulty with these skills, several environmental manipulations can be incorporated so they can be learned.

Direct teaching within a given activity area may be necessary. This may involve a combination of shaping and fading strategies designed to teach independent use of mate-

rials. Or the use of a competent peer model may be a more appropriate strategy. Simply providing a competent peer model may be insufficient, however. The model may have to provide instructions/suggestions or reinforce the target child for appropriate imitation of modeled behavior.

Display and Storage of Materials How materials are displayed and stored may affect their use and replacement. A neat, straight, and clean center is more likely to invite use and prompt replacement.

Display and visibility of materials are critical and must stimulate the child's interest. Numerous classrooms for children with disabilities have closed or empty shelves or materials stored out of reach. Access is provided by the adults. The rationale for this practice is that the children do not know how to make choices, select materials, or appropriately use the items. Although this may initially be true, children need to learn appropriate use by experimentation with materials and activities.

Store large items such as blocks or trucks on open shelves; place small items such as beads, cubes, or crayons in containers. Montes and Risley (1975) compared the use of shelves versus toy boxes for storing and display of materials. They found that storing manipulative toys in boxes increased the amount of time children spent selecting toys, thus reducing actual play. No difference was observed in the amount of time spent cleaning up when using either shelves or boxes. These data suggest the use of open shelves to increase the amount of time for meaningful engagement with materials.

Accessibility is a major consideration. Materials that are easy to take out and store are more likely to be used and returned than less accessible items. Materials that get dirty, such as paint brushes, are more likely to be cleaned if the sink is next to the art area than if it is on the other side of the room.

An organized center that clearly indicates to children where materials belong is important. Visible storage and display are necessary for many exceptional children who need "unambiguous physical surroundings for orientation and limit settings" (Olds, 1979, p. 116). Clearly label shelves to ensure proper placement of items. The level of representation used in labeling will depend upon the developmental level of the children. For some advanced children working on beginning reading skills, the shelves can be labeled with words or can pair words with pictures. For others, pictures or symbols alone may be more appropriate.

Setting Up Specific Activity Areas

Each activity area should be carefully planned and organized to meet the needs of the children using it. This requires a knowledge of the functions a given activity fulfills for children of different ages; an awareness of available materials; and the ability to plan, organize, and structure the center so it will maximally benefit all children.

Block Areas   Block areas can provide opportunities to learn numerous scientific concepts (height, size, weight, etc.) and problem-solving skills, along with appropriate outlets for aggressive behaviors such as banging items or knocking down constructions. They can also encourage dramatic play, social interaction and cooperation, and language development. In addition, blocks facilitate muscle and eye–hand coordination, and offer a set of multisensory experiences. The occurrence of these behaviors depends upon both the ability of the children and the teacher's planning and organization.

Block-building is an activity nearly all children enjoy. The materials are simple and can be used in many different ways from infancy to the early primary grades. Children can learn by chewing, crawling over, or dropping and banging blocks; they can also

decide, for example, how many short blocks equal the same distance as three long blocks.

Block building is a noisy activity and thus should be located away from activities requiring concentration. It is often placed next to the housekeeping area, which is also noisy. A carpet (flat nap) may be helpful in reducing the sound. Frost and Kissinger (1976) suggest that the block area be kept away from animal cages since the blocks might injure or the noise might frighten the pets.

Solid wooden unit blocks and larger hollow blocks are generally found in activity centers. Each type has advantages and both should be provided. The solid unit blocks are good for small scale construction and are useful in learning "scientific" concepts, because they are carefully designed to be mathematically proportionate to one another. The large hollow blocks are better for dramatic play or role playing; children can actually create new environments to act out certain parts. Place large and small blocks in separate areas as they are used in different ways. When the two are combined, children may be less likely to appreciate the mathematical properties of the smaller units (Olds, 1979).

A sufficient number of materials in any activity area is important. Bender (1978) found that when a small number of blocks (20) were available, only one or two children used them for construction. Little cooperative conservation was observed; most comments by children were directed toward another child in an effort to maintain control of the available blocks. When the number of available blocks was increased to 70, more children were able to be actively involved in the building process and conversation primarily centered on the ongoing play rather than competition for the available blocks. Although the teachers had to settle many disputes when children were playing with 20 blocks, no disputes were observed with 70. Bender suggests that 60 to 80 blocks should be provided in any large area designed to accommodate more than two or three children.

A block-building area is incomplete without additional toys for children to use during constructive and dramatic play. These toys should at least include vehicles, such as cars, trucks, and airplanes, and figures of people and animals.

Housekeeping/Dramatic Play Areas   Another activity area found in almost every preschool allows children to act out real life roles. Frequently this area takes the shape of a housekeeping center, with props such as a stove, sink, refrigerator, table, pots and pans, dishes, and so forth. Providing the opportunity for dramatic play assists children in learning and practicing appropriate societal roles, allows them to explore various roles, encourages cooperative behavior, and gives the children a chance to apply language skills. Brophy, Good, and Nedler (1975), viewing dramatic play from more of an inner perspective, suggest such activity can "help a child to fulfill some of his wishes symbolically, to work through some of his fears and negative emotions, and to reduce egocentrism by allowing him to assume the perspectives of persons other than himself" (p. 137). Some of these processes are readily inferred from observing any dramatic play setting, when children become parents or teachers or assume other community roles they have observed.

Because dramatic play is a noisy activity, the area should be located in an appropriate section of the room. Many teachers place the dramatic play area next to the blocks. Dramatic play furnishings should never be lined up against a wall; a small enclosed space more closely approximates a room and facilitates fantasy (Olds, 1979). A loft area, appropriately enclosed to ensure safety, may be ideal for such activity. Unless a ramp is available or the teacher is willing to lift chil-

dren, however, a loft may not be appropriate for a classroom with many children who have physical disabilities. If it is present and used, children should never be denied access to this area because of a physical impairment. Such failure of access might lead to increased feelings of rejection, isolation, and incompetence. Take appropriate safety precautions when getting children to the loft, such as lifting them in such a way to prevent back injury. Children with visual impairments may also need to be closely supervised in a loft, but they too must learn to deal with different environmental structures. Climbing can provide a confidence-building experience that will, one hopes, facilitate general mobility around the classroom and community.

Although children do not need extensive props to participate in dramatic play activities, consider the nature and variety of materials and equipment. Factors include children's previous experience with a given setting or role, interests and needs of the children, and any themes or concepts currently being emphasized. For example, nearly all children can relate to a housekeeping area. Appropriate materials for housekeeping include dress-up clothes (men's and women's), dolls, kitchen equipment, utensils, brooms and mops, doll furniture, doll clothes, clay or other material for making "food," and recycled real-life materials such as a telephone. A full-length mirror is important so children can see how they look in different garments. Other possible props include a bed, pillows, tablecloths, and napkins.

The housekeeping materials should be supplemented by items that encourage dramatic play in other areas such as work or adventure (Harms & Clifford, 1980). One such setting is a store where children select and purchase items at a checkout counter. A variety of props should allow children to change the type of store (food for grocery store, books or magazines for bookstore, etc.). Other props and clothing for various familiar occupations are a fire hat, a police badge, or a doctor's stethoscope.

Although some stability or favorite materials are probably desirable, make provisions for varying dramatic play materials in accordance with current classroom themes or recent experiences. For example, if the group recently went on a field trip to a restaurant, make props such as a chef's hat, menus, or aprons available.

Some children will be able to take full advantage of dramatic play. Others, however, will need teacher assistance. Perspective taking is an advanced cognitive attainment that many young children may not be able to understand. However, they can still enjoy dressing up or participating in dramatic play. The teacher may need to encourage the child to participate, suggest ways to become involved, or actually help the child put on clothes or begin to set up. The early childhood literature suggests teachers should observe dramatic play unobtrusively and intervene only when there is a problem or when it is important to expand upon a child-initiated theme or concept. With young children with disabilities, however, the teacher may need to take a more active role. The teacher can become a participant in the center, acting as an appropriate role model and encouraging and facilitating participation as necessary. The possibility of such participation suggests teachers should dress casually and comfortably.

Sand/Water Play Areas　Sand and water play fulfills a number of important functions. It can be an excellent sensory experience, giving children the opportunity to feel and manipulate various textures of materials. Such activity facilitates what Piaget (1963a) refers to as physical knowledge by providing children experience with shape, weight, and quantity. Sand or water play is also enjoyable, particularly for younger children. As with blocks and dramatic play, it can provide a setting that allows numerous opportunities for role playing, social interactions, and the development of language skills.

Sand and water areas are most appropriately placed near a sink and water faucet to encourage easy access and cleanup. A noncarpeted surface is preferable (although not essential) because some spilling is likely to occur. Children should wear plastic aprons to avoid getting wet.

The best apparatus for sand and water play is a table on locking wheels that has a drain. This type of table can be moved outdoors when the weather is suitable and also eases the problem of dumping a heavy tub of water. If such a table is not available, any number of alternatives may be used: a plastic basin, a large tub, or a small animal feeding trough.

Although sand and water are typical substances, many other materials may also be used in setting up such an activity area. For example, a tub full of coarse salt, macaroni noodles, shells, and dried beans of different colors is appealing to young children and provides a different set of textures. Other possibilities include leaves, sawdust, and styrofoam packing materials. Very young children should be supervised when using these materials, however, to prevent their eating or choking on them. Changing tub activities prevents boredom and provides the opportunity to experience a variety of textures. A typical week in the tub activity center might include the following: Monday—water, Tuesday—sand, Wednesday—water with food coloring, Thursday—beans and noodles, and Friday—water with soap suds.

Supplementary materials are important for expanding the sensory feedback from sand and water play. Appropriate materials include cans, sponges, shovels, various floating and sinking objects, boats, mixers, beaters, funnels, squeeze bottles, straws, and buckets. Supplementary materials can also be tied to any concepts or themes being emphasized in the classroom. If a unit on the farm is being presented, small plastic farm animals can encourage generalization of concepts. If some children are working on the color red, all the materials could be red or red food coloring could be placed in the water.

A wide range of objectives may be addressed through guided sand and water play. Children beginning to develop object permanence can be taught to locate objects partially or completely hidden under sand or beans. Children with poor motor coordination can learn to dig, lift, and pour. Older children can be taught to make comparisons using volume and measurement concepts such as empty, full, more, less, and same. Means-ends behavior such as tool use can be taught by using cups and water or spoons and sand.

Sand and water play are appropriate activities for most youngsters with disabilities. Physically impaired children may need special modification of the table to allow for a wheelchair or may need to have the table raised so a prone board may be propped up against it or lowered so a child on a wedge may use it. Some children may initially resist sand and water play because the sensory stimulation is aversive. Getting these children to actively participate in and enjoy sand and water play would be a major teaching accomplishment. A shaping strategy of gradually reinforcing successive approximations to sand and water play may be necessary.

Arts and Crafts Areas Art activities provide the opportunity for creative expression; practice of fine and perceptual motor skills; and the application of language concepts relating to form, shape, color, texture, and spa-

tial relationships. The art area allows children to create products or materials to be used in other activity areas—for example, a sign for the store or a menu for the restaurant.

The art area should be located in a noncarpeted area near a sink to ease the cleanup process. Children should wear smocks to avoid getting clothes wet or stained.

The materials to be included in an art and crafts area will vary, depending upon the age and developmental levels of the children. Harms (1972) suggests the following age-appropriate activities for inclusion in the art area.

18 Months–2½ Years: The child at this age needs simple drawing materials like a soft, thick lead pencil; easel paints in 2 or 3 colors. . . .
2½–3½ Years: The child at this age should have available varied drawing materials including crayons and felt pens; an expanded number of colors as his experience with painting develops; varied sizes and shapes of paper and varied brush sizes; and activities involving finger painting, clay, and salt-flour dough.
3½–4½ Years: Drawing materials should be expanded to include: paint sticks and wet chalk; very large paper and varied size brushes; art activities should include watercolor painting, collage, construction-sculpture, stringing activities, carpentry, sand casting, salt-flour dough mixing from picture recipe, as the child seems ready for these experiences.
4½–5½ Years: Art activities that demand more technical skill should be introduced, such as stitchery, mosaics, and simple block printing. All the basic two- and three-dimensional materials should be included. (Harms, 1972, p. 97)

These suggestions may need to be modified depending upon the severity and type of disabling conditions in a given classroom.

Store materials in an open display shelf to encourage independent use. Some materials should already be set up when children arrive. For example, paper should be on the easels, paints opened and placed on easels, and newspaper or other protective covering on the floor. To avoid competition, either have several small containers or one large container of materials available (Harms, 1972). For example, arguments will arise when there is only one box of crayons. Such conflicts can be avoided by making several boxes available or keeping plenty of crayons for everyone in a large box or tub. Only nontoxic paints and materials should be provided.

The degree of planning and structure in the art center will depend upon the developmental level of the children. Some children will not know how to use any of the materials (paintbrushes, crayons, scissors) and may not learn through simply observing others. The teacher may need to take an active role in instructing basic art area skills, perhaps by frequent repetition of the same type of activity (but using different materials) and initial physical manipulation of the child's hands to assist in performing a skill. An example of equipment used in teaching a child to cut is displayed in Figure 7.1. These scissors have the usual two holes

for the child's fingers and an additional two holes for the teacher's fingers. Initially the teacher will do all of the cutting; the child's fingers are in the holes, however, and she begins to experience the movements required for cutting. Gradually the teacher performs fewer motor movements and allows the child to do more, until the child becomes independent. A similar process of fading teacher assistance can be incorporated with other materials such as crayons or paintbrushes.

Adaptations of materials, procedures, and expectations may need to be made for some physically disabled children. Paintbrush handles can be built up with tape or other material to facilitate handling by children with motor impairments. Other children may need to paint holding the brush in the mouth, with the toes, or perhaps even using a device strapped to the head (a head-pointing device).

Reading/Language Areas   The reading/language arts area gives children the opportunity to relax, be quiet, and be exposed to

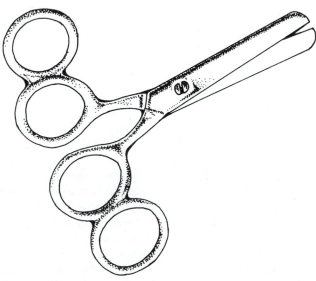

FIGURE 7.1
Double-holed scissors used in teaching

books and other language stimulation materials. Since reading requires concentration, the reading/language area should be located in a quiet section of the room, perhaps next to the small group instructional area. A well-lighted area is essential.

The furnishings in the language center should be inviting and encourage relaxation and quiet involvement. The area should be carpeted and should contain furniture conducive to the intended activities, such as a table, bean bag and other comfortable chairs, and at least one child-sized rocking chair. Display books on an open rack with covers clearly visible at the child's height. Books that are stacked on the shelf are difficult for the child to select and may not be returned to their proper places because there are no obvious empty spaces.

The selection of books for this area should be a function of the age and developmental level of children as well as the relationship of materials to current topics included in the preschool program. Examples of current topics include concept units such as animals or things to ride, holidays such as Thanksgiving or Halloween, and special events such as an upcoming trip to the fire station. Small photo albums with children's pictures from past field trips or other special days may facilitate remembering events and generate talking. Such planning can facilitate skill generalization by exposing children to concepts in a wide variety of contexts and by stimulating language experiences. Although a few favorite books should always be kept in the center, rotation of materials will maintain interest.

Brophy, Good, and Nedler (1975) suggest providing two or more copies of popular books to reduce arguments. Duplicate copies may also facilitate discussion among children as well as noting and matching pictures on similar pages.

Materials other than books should be included in the reading/language area. Some possibilities include a language master, a

tape player, a flannelboard with story pictures, magazines, puppets, felt or magnetic letters, lotto games or picture word cards, and writing materials. One strategy for increasing use of the reading area (since children often prefer to play in more active areas such as housekeeping or blocks) is to conduct story time or other group activities there and leave the materials for children to use. For example, during a discussion of occupations, the teacher may tell a story about a storekeeper using flannelboard pictures and then leave the pictures for retelling or adaptation by the children.

Some adaptations to the reading/language area may need to be made depending upon the type of disabilities experienced by children in the classroom. Visually impaired children may need materials with larger pictures or materials that incorporate simple, clear line drawings rather than many-hued renderings or fuzzy boundaries. Totally blind children will need materials that provide information through other senses. For example, several children's books focus on different textures. "Scratch and sniff" books incorporate smells into the reading experience. Physically disabled children may need adaptive equipment to hold a book, to turn pages (such as a head pointer), or to activate electronic equipment (such as a tape player or a language master).

Materials should be attractive to children. Books should have clear pictures, address familiar topics, and clearly portray sequences. Select books that attempt to be nonsexist and show men and women (or boys and girls) participating in a wide variety of activities, such as the switching of traditional sex-related roles (female doctors, male nurses, female truck drivers, male schoolteachers). Also, books and other materials selected should portray children from a wide variety of cultural and ethnic groups, displaying both similarities and differences. Finally, select materials that picture children with disabling conditions and/or adaptive equip-

ment. Children without disabilities need to
see that persons with disabilities exist outside of the classrooms and children with disabilities need to see that they are not the only
ones who are disabled.

Woodworking Areas   Woodworking provides a setting for practicing many motor
and grasping movements by giving children
the opportunity to constructively use real
tools and wood. Children enjoy the noise
and physical movement involved. As Harms
(1978) suggests, children feel competent and
responsible when working with real tools,
particularly when they have been told by
their parents that the tools may be dangerous. Children can also learn the names and
functions of tools and the concepts of size
and texture.

A woodworking or carpentry area will be
noisy, and should be located in an isolated
section of the room or outdoors. The woodworking area requires several basic components: a tool storage pegboard; a set of low
shelves for tools that cannot be hung; small
containers for accessories such as nails;
boxes or crates for wood storage; and a table
or other work space (Harms, 1981).

Miniature sets of tools purchased in department stores are inappropriate for a carpentry area. Children need real tools to perform activities such as hammering a nail or
sawing wood. Harms (1981) suggests some
basic tools and appropriate sizes.

- A claw hammer weighing between 10 and
  13 ounces
- Some nails (Those with large heads are
  easier to hammer than finishing nails)
- Slotted and Phillips head screwdrivers
  (Short, fat-handled screwdrivers are easier
  for children to use. Rubber grip handles
  may be purchased which make screwdrivers easier to hold without slipping.)
- Screws (Raised, "round head" screws are
  easier to use than flat head screws.)

- Saws weighing less than 12 ounces, 12–15
  inches in length, with 10 teeth per inch
- Hand drills for boring small holes
- Smoothing tools such as rasps, files, and
  sandpaper
- Paintbrush
- Clamps for holding woods

Only soft woods such as pine, fir, cedar, or
balsam should be used.

The woodworking center is potentially
dangerous and no child should use it unless
an adult directly supervises the activity.
Most children will not know how to use the
materials properly, requiring a great deal of
teacher instruction. Limit the number of
children in this area to allow the adult to adequately supervise the activities.

Harms (1978) provides the following strategies for guiding activities within the wood-
working/carpentry area.

1 Young children or children with poor motor skills may need to use tools with a material other than wood. Styrofoam pieces
   can be used for hammering, screwing, and
   sawing.
2 Most children will need help in getting
   nails or screws started.
3 Use the carpentry experience to reinforce
   and expand language skills.
4 Emphasize the process rather than the
   product.
5 Encourage girls as well as boys to use carpentry tools.
6 Provide accessories such as small pieces
   of rug scraps, bottle caps, wrapped wire,
   and rubber bands, which can serve as add-
   ons nailed to wood.

*Activity Areas for Children with Severe
Disabilities*   Independent or semi-independent use of the activity areas is a reasonable
goal for most preschoolers with disabilities.
Children with severe or multiple disabilities
and profoundly retarded children, however,
may need activity areas that address more

basic skills or may need additional supports (such as an adult or adaptive equipment) to help them use materials.

A sensory stimulation activity area can expose children with severe disabilities to a wide variety of experiences. Because these children are not as mobile, they are unable to seek out stimulation or, at best, have limited available experiences. A basic awareness of, sensitivity to, and opportunity to respond to a variety of stimuli are prerequisites to learning more advanced skills and are enjoyable for many children.

Glover and Mesibov (1978) describe strategies for organizing a classroom to provide auditory, visual, tactile, kinesthetic, and gustatory-olfactory stimulation. The auditory stimulation center provides various hearing experiences and includes equipment such as a record or tape player, musical instruments, shakers/rattlers, and paper for crumpling. The visual stimulation center provides exposure to a variety of sights and should be in an easily darkened area. Materials could include a slide projector, flashlight, twinkling Christmas tree or black lights, mobiles, and bright objects such as aluminum pans or red teething rings. The tactile center provides a variety of touching and feeling experiences and includes materials such as various textures of cloth and paper products, cereals or noodles in a tub, finger paints, shaving cream, hand lotion, and foam. The kinesthetic center provides movement experiences and requires equipment such as mats, incline boards, pillows, large balls, and perhaps a waterbed. The gustatory-olfactory area provides exposure to various tastes and smells and should include a wide range of experiences within these sensory modes: sour–sweet, soft–crunchy, wet–dry, salty–not salty, warm–cool, and raw–cooked.

Obviously most activities will require a great deal of teacher involvement, particularly for children with severe motor impairments. Teachers may use a number of strategies to initially set up a center for independent or semi-independent use by severely disabled children. For example, in the auditory or visual stimulation center, a string that activates a sound or visual display could be tied to the child's foot or hand. Or a peer with less severe disabilities or without disabilities could be taught to present various stimuli in a specified manner (Glover & Mesibov, 1978).

Very little research has assessed the benefits of such activities. However, they do make good conceptual sense both from an educational and therapeutic perspective. Dunst (1981) suggests that sensory stimulation should be response contingent as compared to response independent. *Response-contingent stimulation* refers to intervention where the presentation of a given stimulus depends upon a particular behavior performed by the child. Response-contingent stimulation helps the child learn that his behavior can affect his environment in a predictable fashion. A variety of strategies may be used in providing response-contingent stimulation experiences. For example, Watson and Ramey (1972) designed a mobile that could be activated by changes in pressure on the infant's pillow. Any small head movements on this pressure-sensitive pillow would start the mobile moving. Watson and Ramey found that 8-week-old infants without disabilities quickly learned the relationship between head movement and mobile activation. Follow-up data indicated that children who had the mobile in their cribs were more active than those who did not. In addition, numerous displays of pleasure, such as smiling and cooing, were observed in these infants. In a subsequent study with retarded failure-to-thrive infants, Ramey, Starr, Phallas, Whitten, and Reed (1975) found that response-contingent stimulation resulted in significant developmental growth when comparing experimental infants with the control group.

Response-contingent stimulation facilitates the learning of contingency experiences by allowing the child to initially cause a stimulus to occur by making a random movement. Through repeated activations, the child gradually begins to associate movement with stimulus, and learns that she can control the presentation or activation of that stimulus.

Many response-contingent experiences may be devised for children at a variety of developmental levels. One simple setup is to tie a string around the child's foot and connect it to an interesting visual display such as a mobile or a picture or light. A set of bells could be tied to the child's foot, or balls or other bright objects hung so the child could hit them with random movements of his arms. Goldberg (1977) contends that such early contingency experiences are important for enhancing competence motivation in infants and may facilitate predictability and "readability" of children whose signals are unclear. The following guidelines can be used in designing response-contingent stimulation experiences for children with disabilities.

1 Select and arrange a display the child can perceive. A knowledge of the child's sensory abilities is crucial. A visually impaired child will need an auditory or tactile display. A hearing impaired child will need a highly visual or tactile display. The distance between the display and the child should be carefully arranged so the child can perceive the display.

2 Select and arrange a display the child will enjoy and want to perceive again, taking into consideration color, sound, contrast, and other characteristics of objects.

3 Select a behavior or movement you previously observed the child perform, which has a relatively high probability of occurring again. This will depend upon the individual's propensity and ability for movement.

4 Design an appropriate and safe connection between the movement and the stimulus display.

5 Observe the child regularly to determine any increases in the target movement (which would indicate the child may have learned the contingency).

6 Change the display if necessary to make it more appropriate or more appealing to the child.

These guidelines should aid in the identification of appropriate stimulation experiences for individuals in a program. Sayre (1981) describes a variety of automated play units for children with severe motor impairments. Involving parents in planning, designing, and constructing the apparatus for response-contingent experiences may help identify appropriate displays and child behaviors, while giving the parents the feeling that they are contributing to their child's education and development.

Outdoor Play Areas   Every preschool should have an appropriately designed and furnished outdoor play area. Going outdoors provides a break from indoor activities for both adults and children, and has obvious health benefits (sunlight, fresh air), giving children an opportunity for exercise and movement.

Many programs for preschoolers with disabilities, particularly those for children with severe disabilities, have been reluctant to take children outdoors. Reasons include the need for close supervision, an unwillingness to take the time to help children get dressed and undressed, and a fear that the child with a disability may be more likely to get sick. Such attitudes are unfortunate because outdoor activities, unless specifically restricted by the child's doctor or parents, are important. Preschool-age children should go outside at least once in the morning and again in the afternoon if the program is a full day.

A good outdoor play area will provide the opportunity for several types of activities: running, climbing, swinging, games, riding, and object play. Each area should be designed to meet the developmental needs of the children and the demands of the desired activities. A variety of surface areas, such as sand, bark, sawdust or other soft materials should be available in addition to hard areas of concrete or asphalt.

Rules and areas must be clearly delineated. For example, areas appropriate for riding wheeled toys such as tricycles should be identified and limited. Identify areas that are dangerous for running.

Safety is an important consideration in outdoor play. Accidents or injuries may occur because of exposed bolts or sharp edges, improper installation or maintenance of equipment, and inappropriate use of equipment for certain developmental levels (Frost & Henniger, 1979). According to the Consumer Product Safety Commission (1975), the most frequent causes of playground injury are falling from and being struck by a piece of equipment such as a swing. Special precautions should be taken in these areas, increasing the degree of enclosure with the height of the structure. The National Recreation and Park Association (1976), as reported by Frost and Henniger, proposed that structures 4–8 feet high have railings. Those 8–12 feet high should have a protective barrier, with higher structures totally enclosed. The ground surface under climbing equipment should consist of a soft material such as bark to reduce the chance of serious injury. In addition to supervising the outdoor play, the professional should teach children the appropriate ways to use all playground equipment. For further information and examples of playgrounds for exceptional children see Gillet (1978), Jones (1977), and Frost and Klein (1983).

Although playing outside is relaxing and enjoyable, some outdoor activities should be planned. The teacher can use this time to encourage practice of gross motor skills and social interaction or to plan a game or activity.

EVALUATING THE EFFECTS OF ENVIRONMENTS

As with any instructional procedure, teachers and other early intervention specialists should evaluate the effects of environments and environmental changes on children's behavior and development. The evaluative activity would likely involve the following steps.

1 Identify what purposes or outcomes are desired from each activity or activity area. For example, how much time would you want Tashika to spend in the book center and what would you expect her to do while in the center?
2 Periodically review children's engagement, play, levels of learning, and amount of inappropriate or undesirable behavior to see if those purposes/outcomes are being realized. For example, does Tashika look at the books in the center and does she handle them as expected?
3 If the desired behaviors are not occurring, attempt to determine why. For example, the books or other materials in the center may not be interesting for Tashika.
4 Make changes consistent with the possible reasons for not engaging in the desired activity.
5 Evaluate the effects of these changes.

ENVIRONMENTS OTHER THAN CHILD CARE CENTERS

This chapter has focused almost exclusively on considerations in designing, arranging, and using environments in group child care settings such as classrooms and daycare centers. In fact, the general principles and considerations are likely to pertain in other environments as well. Early childhood interventionists should be aware of the variety of environments in which children spend time (see chapter 3) and be able to assess the nature and quality of environments (Bailey, 1989), determine children's skills and needs with respect to environmental supports, and design or alter environments to meet those needs.

An example of the relevance of the preceding considerations for other environments is seen in the hospital. Many infants and young children who have disabilities or who are at risk for disabilities spend time in neonatal intensive care units or pediatric units. Wolke (1987) has described a number of the negative environmental characteristics of neonatal intensive care units, including high noise levels, high and constant light levels with no regular day/night cycle, handling by adults even when sleeping, and the lack of attention to the child's developmental needs. A recent study by Fajardo, Browning, Fisher, and Paton (1990) documents the importance of designing alternative environments that are more sensitive to the special needs of the developing neonate. In this study, low-birthweight, premature infants in the typical neonatal intensive care unit were compared with those placed in an alternative nursery characterized by a definite day/night cycle, indirect lighting, reduced noise, and caretaking that occurred just before feeding and was nondisruptive to sleep states. The study found that the alternative nursery promoted more steady patterns of behavior in children, with longer state durations and fewer state changes per hour. The study clearly demonstrates the impact of the hospital environment on young children's behavior.

SUMMARY

This chapter has addressed issues, principles, considerations, and guidelines for designing and providing environments for young children. This information is important—manipulation of the environment should be considered a teaching strategy in the same way that direct instruction is viewed as intervention. In all cases, early intervention programs should provide physical environments and facilities that are normalized and growth promoting. Although other intervention strategies will likely be necessary for children with disabilities, providing a high-quality environment ought to maximize the effectiveness of other instructional activities and should make early intervention programs enjoyable and secure for both children and adults.

REFERENCES

Alberto, P., Jobes, N., Sizemore, A., & Doran, D. (1980). A comparison of individual and group instruction across response tasks. *Journal of the Association for the Severely Handicapped, 5.* 285–293.

Appleton, T., Clifton, R., & Goldberg, S. (1975). The development of behavioral competence in infancy. In F. Horowitz (Ed.), *Review of child development research.* Chicago: University of Chicago Press.

Apolloni, T., Cooke, S. A., & Cooke, T. P. (1977). Establishing a normal peer as a behavioral model for delayed toddlers. *Perceptual and Motor Skills, 44,* 231–241.

Apolloni, T., & Cooke, T. P. (1978). Integrated programming at the infant, toddler, and preschool levels. In M. F. Guralnick (Ed.), *Early intervention and the integration of handicapped and nonhandicapped children.* Baltimore: University Park Press.

Bailey, D. B. (1989). Assessing environments. In D. B. Bailey & M. Wolery (Eds.), *Assessing infants and preschoolers with handicaps* (pp. 97–118). Columbus, OH: Merrill.

Bailey, D. B., Clifford, R. M., & Harms, T. (1982). Comparison of preschool environments for handicapped and nonhandicapped children. *Topics in Early Childhood Special Education, 2,* 9–20.

Baker, D. B. (1980). Applications of environmental psychology in programming for severely handicapped persons. *Journal of the Association for the Severely Handicapped, 5,* 234–249.

Bender, J. (1978). Large hollow blocks: Relationship of quantity to block-building behaviors. *Young Children, 34,* 17–23.

Blank, M. (1970). Implicit assumption underlying preschool intervention programs. *Journal of Social Issues, 26,* 15–33.

Bradley, R. H., & Caldwell, B. M. (1976). Relation of infant's home environments to mental test performance at fifty-four months: A follow-up study. *Child Development 47,* 1172–1174.

Bredekamp, S. (Ed.). (1986). *Developmentally appropriate practice.* Washington, DC: National Association for the Education of Young Children.

Brophy, J. E., Good, T. L., & Nedler, S. E. (1975). *Teaching in the preschool.* New York: Harper & Row.

Brown, F., Holvoet, J., Guess, D., & Mulligan, M. (1980). The individualized curriculum sequencing model (III): Small group instruction. *Journal of the Association for the Severely Handicapped. 5,* 352–367.

Consumer Product Safety Commission. (1975). *Hazard analysis—playground equipment.* Washington, DC: Consumer Product Safety Commission.

Cybriwsky, C. A., Wolery, M., & Gast, D. L. (1990). Use of constant time delay in teaching preschoolers in a group format. *Journal of Early Intervention, 14*(2), 99–116.

Danoff, J., Breitbart, V., & Barr, E. (1977). *Open for children.* New York: McGraw-Hill.

David, T. B., & Weinstein, C. S. (1987). The built environment and children's development. In C. S. Weinstein & T. G. David (Eds.), *Spaces for children: The built environment and child development* (pp. 3–18). New York: Plenum Press.

DeKlyen, M., & Odom, S. L. (1989). Activity structure and social interactions with peers in developmentally integrated play groups. *Journal of Early Intervention, 13,* 342–352.

DeVellis, R. F. (1977). Learned helplessness in institutions. *Mental Retardation, 15*(5), 10–13.

Doke, L. A. (1975). The organization of day-care environments: Formal versus informal activities. *Child Care Quarterly, 4,* 216–222.

Doke, L. A., & Risley, T. R. (1972). The organization of daycare environments: Required versus optional activities. *Journal of Applied Behavior Analysis, 5,* 405–420.

Dunst, C. J. (1981). Theoretical bases and pragmatic considerations in infant curriculum construction. In J. Anderson & J. Cox (Eds.), *Curriculum materials for high risk and handicapped infants.* Chapel Hill, NC: Technical Assistance Development System.

Elardo, R., Bradley, R., & Caldwell, B. M. (1977). A longitudinal study of the relation of infants' home environments to language development at age three. *Child Development, 48,* 595–603.

Elkind, D. (1976). *Child development and education: A Piagetian perspective.* New York: Oxford University Press.

Fajardo, B., Browning, M., Fisher, D., & Paton, J. (1990). Effect of nursery environment on state regulation in very-low-birthweight premature infants. *Infant Behavior and Development, 13,* 287–303.

Favell, J., Favell, J., & McGinsey, J. F. (1978). Relative effectiveness and efficiency of group vs. individual training of severely retarded persons. *American Journal of Mental Deficiency, 83,* 104–109.

Forman, G. E., & Kuschner, D. S. (1977). *The child's construction of knowledge: Piaget for teaching children.* Monterrey, CA: Brooks/Cole.

Frost, J. L., & Henniger, M. L. (1979). Making playgrounds safe for children and children safe for playgrounds. *Young Children, 34* (9), 23–30.

Frost, J. L., & Kissinger, J. B. (1976). *The young child and the educative process.* New York: Holt, Rinehart & Winston.

Frost, J. L., & Klein, B. L. (1983). *Children's play and playgrounds.* Austin, TX: Playscapes International.

Gillet, P. (1978). Classroom techniques: Retarded children need a special playground. *Education and Training of the Mentally Retarded, 13,* 160–169.

Ginsburg, H., & Opper, S. (1979). *Piaget's theory of intellectual development: An introduction.* Englewood Cliffs, NJ: Prentice-Hall.

Glover, E., & Mesibov, G. B. (1978). An interest center sensory stimulation program for severely and profoundly retarded children. *Education and Training of the Mentally Retarded, 13*, 172–177.

Goldberg, S. (1977). Social competence in infancy: A model of parent-infant interaction. *Merrill-Palmer Quarterly, 23*, 163–177.

Harms, T. (1972). Presenting materials effectively. In H. P. Lewis (Ed.), *Art of the pre-primary child*. Washington, DC: National Art Education Association.

Harms, T. (1978). Creating through carpentry. In D. Cansler (Ed.), *Programs for parents of preschoolers*. Winston-Salem, NC: Kaplan Press.

Harms, T. (1981). *Build and learn: Carpentry guide cards*. Chapel Hill: Frank Porter Graham Child Development Center, University of North Carolina.

Harms, T., & Clifford, R. M. (1980). *Early childhood environment rating scale*. New York: Teachers College Press.

Harms, T., & Cross, L. (1977). *Environmental provisions in day care*. Chapel Hill: Frank Porter Graham Child Development Center, University of North Carolina.

Hart, B. (1982). So that teachers can teach: Assigning roles and responsibilities. *Topics in Early Childhood Special Education, 2*(1), 1–8.

Hildebrand, V. (1975). *Guiding young children*. New York: MacMillan.

Hohmann, M., Banet, B., & Weikart, D. P. (1979). *Young children in action: A manual for preschool educators*. Ypsilanti, MI: High/Scope Educational Research Foundation.

Huston-Stein, A., Friedrich-Cofer, L., & Susman, E. J. (1977). The relation of classroom structure to social behavior, imaginative play, and self-regulation of economically disadvantaged children. *Child Development, 48*, 908–916.

Hutt, C., & Vlazey, M. J. (1966). Differential effects of group density on social behavior. *Nature, 209*, 1371–1372.

Ittelson, W., Proshansky, H., Rivlin, L., & Winkel, G. (1974). *An introduction to environmental psychology*. New York: Holt, Rinehart & Winston.

Johnson, J. E., Ershler, J., & Bell, C. (1980). Play behavior in a discovery-based and a formal-education preschool program. *Child Development, 21*, 271–274.

Jones, M. H. (1977). Physical facilities and environments. In J. Jordon, A. H. Hayden, M. B. Karnes, & M. M. Wood (Eds.), *Early education for exceptional children: A handbook of ideas and exemplary practices*. Reston, VA: Council for Exceptional Children.

Kamii, C., & DeVries, R. (1977). Piaget for early education. In M. C. Day and R. K. Parker (Eds.), *The preschool in action: Exploring early childhood programs* (2nd ed.). Boston: Allyn and Bacon.

Kamii, C., & DeVries, R. (1978). *Physical knowledge in preschool education: Implications of Piaget's theory*. Englewood Cliffs, NJ: Prentice-Hall.

Keith, K. D. (1979). Behavior analysis and the principle of normalization. *AAESPH Review, 4*, 148–151.

Kenowitz, L., Zweibel, S., & Edgar, G. (1979). Determining the least restrictive educational opportunity. In N. G. Haring & D. D. Bricker (Eds.), *Teaching the severely handicapped* (Vol. 3). Columbus, OH: Special Press.

Krantz, P., & Risley, T. R. (1977). Behavior ecology in the classroom. In K. D. O'Leary and S. O'Leary (Eds.), *Classroom management: The successful use of behavior modification*. New York: Permagon Press.

Kreger, K. C. (1971). Compensatory environment programming for the severely retarded behaviorally disturbed. *Mental Retardation, 9*, 29–33.

LeLaurin, K., & Risley, T. R. (1972). The organization of daycare environments: "Zone" versus "man-to-man" staff assignments. *Journal of Applied Behavior Analysis, 5*, 225–232.

Montes, F., & Risley, T. R. (1975). Evaluating traditional day care practices: An empirical approach. *Child Care Quarterly, 4*, 208–215.

Moore, G. T. (1987). The physical environment and cognitive development in child-care centers. In C. S. Weinstein & T. G. David (Eds.), *Spaces for children: The built environment and child development* (pp. 41–72). New York: Plenum Press.

National Association for the Education of Young

Children (1984). *Accreditation criteria and procedures of the National Academy of Early Childhood Programs.* Washington, DC: NAEYC.

National Recreation and Park Association. (1976). *Proposed safety standards for public playground equipment.* Arlington, VA: National Recreation and Park Association.

Olds, A. R. (1979). Designing developmentally optimal classrooms for children with special needs. In S. J. Meisels (Ed.), *Special education and development: Perspectives on young children with special needs.* Baltimore: University Park Press.

Olds, A. R. (1987). Designing settings for infants and toddlers. In C. S. Weinstein & T. G. David (Eds.), *Spaces for Children: The built environment and child development* (pp. 117–138). New York: Plenum Press.

Peck, C. A., Apolloni, T., Cooke, T. P., & Raver, S. A. (1978). Teaching retarded preschoolers to imitate the free-play behavior of nonretarded classmates: Trained and generalized effects. *Journal of Special Education, 12,* 195–207.

Piaget, J. (1952). *The origins of intelligence in children.* New York: International Universities Press.

Piaget, J. (1963a). *The origins of intelligence in children.* New York: Norton.

Piaget, J. (1963b). *Play, dreams, and imitation in childhood.* New York: Norton.

Ramey, C. T., Starr, R. H. Phallas, J., Whitten, C. I., & Reed, V. (1975). Nutrition, response-contingent stimulation, and the maternal deprivation syndrome: Results of an early intervention program. *Merill-Palmer Quarterly, 21,* 45–54.

Risley, T. (1981). *Research on day-care environments.* Paper presented at Frank Porter Graham Child Development Center. University of North Carolina.

Rogers-Warren, A., & Wedel, J. W. (1980). The ecology of preschool classrooms for the handicapped. *New Directions for Exceptional Children, 1,* 1–24.

Sayre, T. (1981). *Play units for the severely handicapped.* Route 2, Box 168, Bostic, North Carolina 28018.

Seligman, M. E. P. (1975). *Helplessness: On depression, development, and death.* San Francisco: W. H. Freeman.

Siegel, R. K. (1977). Stimulus selection and tracking during urination: Autoshaping directed behavior with toilet targets. *Journal of Applied Behavior Analysis, 10,* 255–265.

Skinner, B. F. (1953). *Science and human behavior.* New York: Free Press.

Storm, R. H. & Willis, J. H. (1978). Small group training as an alternative to individual programs for profoundly retarded persons. *American Journal of Mental Deficiency, 83,* 283–288.

Twardosz, S., Cataldo, M. F., & Risley, T. R. (1974). Open environment design for infant and toddler day care. *Journal of Applied Behavior Analysis, 7,* 529–546.

Wachs, T. (1979). Proximal experience and early cognitive intellectual development: The physical environment. *Merrill-Palmer Quarterly, 25,* 3–41.

Watson, J. S., & Ramey, C. T. (1972). Reactions to response-contingent stimulation in early infancy. *Merrill-Palmer Quarterly, 18,* 219–227.

Weisler, A., & McCall, R. B. (1976). Exploration and play: Resume and redirection. *American Psychologist, 31,* 492–508.

Wolfensberger, W. (1972). *The principles of normalization in human services.* Toronto: National Institute on Metal Retardation.

Wolke D. (1987). Environmental neonatology. *Archives of Diseases in Childhood, 62,* 987–988.

8

Promoting Engagement and Mastery

R.A. McWilliam

D.B. Bailey

Engagement has been defined as the amount of time children spend interacting appropriately with their environments (McWilliam, 1991a). The engagement construct is predicated on the theory that time spent in appropriate play is a necessary if not sufficient condition for developmental change (McWilliam, Dunst, & Trivette, 1985). Engagement may be a critical factor for optimal learning; and the key to positive developmental outcomes resulting from engagement may be mastery behavior during engagement. This chapter addresses the historical background of research on engagement and mastery, summarizes current conceptualizations of these terms, and outlines methods for facilitating engagement and mastery behavior.

THE NATURE AND IMPORTANCE OF ENGAGEMENT

The concept that children should spend maximal amounts of time in appropriate behavior has been propounded by (a) educational psychologists concerned with teaching effectiveness; (b) psychologists and special educators concerned with optimal environments for populations as diverse as children in day care, adults in nursing homes, and residents of institutions; and (c) early interventionists concerned with meaningful goals and efficacy indicators.

Time on Task
(Teacher Effectiveness Research)

The focus of the teaching-effectiveness investigators has been on "time on task" in school settings. The earliest studies of how time was spent in schools, in the 1920s, focused on evaluating teacher effectiveness, using class involvement as the outcome. In the 1950s, Bloom (1953) and his colleagues undertook studies to discern students' thought processes during instruction,

by having them recall, later, their thoughts at the time. It was found that college students' thoughts were centered on the task at hand 64 percent of the time during lectures and 55 percent of the time during class discussions. Later studies (Hudgins, 1967; Taylor, 1968), however, found negative correlations between observed attention and student self-reports. A plethora of investigations ensued, reporting high correlations between attention and learning. Carroll's "A Model of School Learning," published in the *Teacher's College Record* in 1963, was the springboard for renewed emphasis on classroom research related to time variables. Based in part on Carroll's ideas that the amount of time students spent on-task while learning languages predicted success, scientists at the Far West Laboratory for Educational Research and Development initiated the concept of "academic learning time (ALT)" (Fisher, Filby, Marliave, Cahen, Dishaw, Moore, & Berliner, 1978). They conducted the Beginning Teacher Evaluation Study (BTES), which demonstrated that elementary students may spend up to 70 percent of their allocated time in seatwork assignments. Teachers whose students were able to achieve more were those who could produce high levels of on-task behavior and low error rates in the children. An important finding from this study was that high levels of "success time, . . . the appropriateness of the task for the student as represented by the student's level of success on that task," (Marliave & Filby, 1985, p. 218) predicted achievement scores better than did either allocated time or engaged time, but all three measures were associated with high achievement. Furthermore, *increases* in success time predicted increases in achievement. Marliave and Filby (1985), two of the authors of the BTES study, concluded that success rate constitutes a measure of task appropriateness. Later, Rich and Ross (1989) found special education students spending similar percentages of time (65.2%) in learning tasks.

Optimal Environments
(Ecological-Behavioral Research)

Independently of the classroom research with school-aged children, Todd Risley and his colleagues at the University of Kansas embarked on a series of studies in the late 1960s and early 1970s that probed the variables that account for high levels of engagement. In this ecological-behavioral research they found that incidental teaching (e.g., Hart & Risley, 1975; 1978; 1980), smooth transitions between activities (e.g., Krantz & Risley, 1974), modified open room arrangements (e.g., Twardosz, Cataldo, & Risley, 1974), accessible toys (Montes & Risley, 1975), and carefully sequenced activities (Krantz & Risley, 1974) produced high levels of engagement. In these studies, engagement was measured by the percentage of children participating in the planned activity. It was thus a group measure of how engaging the activity was. The major contribution of these studies was an increased understanding of the environmental variables affecting engagement in settings less structured than school classrooms. The major drawbacks of these studies were that they focused on group participation and that they (unlike the classroom research) did not seek to establish the relationship of engagement to learning.

Research with Exceptional Infants, Toddlers, and Preschoolers

In more recent years, investigators have addressed the issue of how infants and very young children with disabilities spend time and how this measure affects learning. Krakow and Kopp (1983) found that children with Down Syndrome spent less time engaged with toys than did normally developing subjects and that children who were developmentally delayed with uncertain etiology spent even less time engaged. Research in this area has centered on child attention behavior, active engagement, and mastery motivation.

Attention   Attention consists of looking at or listening to environmental stimuli. The attentiveness of infants, toddlers, and preschoolers has been linked to both learning (Hayes, Ewy, & Watson, 1982) and intelligence (Lewis & Brooks-Gunn, 1981). Attention has been found to vary as a function of prematurity (Landry & Chapieski, 1988; Ruff, 1986a) and of the adult's tone of voice (Santarcangelo & Dyer, 1988); that is, when adults spoke in high-pitched, friendly voices, the infants were more engaged. In play, attentive examination precedes other behaviors with objects and declines sharply as children become familiar with the objects (Ruff, 1986b). The child's attention to the stimulus in operant learning has been found to predict learning of response-contingent behaviors (Hayes et al., 1982), particularly when the response is activated contingently upon the child's fixation (Dunst, 1984). Further, asking children to demonstrate that they are attending through matching or otherwise responding to the salient dimension of stimuli may increase learning (Doyle, Wolery, Gast, Ault, & Wiley, 1990). It has been shown that the interest of kindergartners, particularly of the boys, can be enhanced through performance-contingent rewards (Boggiano, Harckiewicz, Bessette, & Main, 1985). Further, when preschoolers attend to what other children are doing, they subsequently pay more attention to their own activities (Butler, 1989). As an objective for intervention, attention is amenable to shaping; for example, Goetz and Gee (1987), using repeated prompting, taught a 3-year-old with severe mental retardation to increase her visual attention, and the increased attention subsequently led to improved motor skill accuracy. In conclusion, Lewis and Brooks-Gunn (1981) have stated that "accepting attention, within the limitations of what we now know, as an important individual skill that affects other concurrent and subsequent skills takes us closer to understanding how organisms successfully engage their world" (p. 237).

Active Engagement   Dewey, Piaget, Bijou and Baer all stressed that active manipulation of materials is important if learning is to occur. Most studies to date have focused primarily on active engagement with materials, separate from investigations of social play; but current research on engagement includes behavior (by children with disabilities) with both materials and people (McWilliam & Bailey, 1991). Developmental age is one of the variables affecting the extent to which a child engages in active play, with older children spending less time with adults, less time nonengaged, and less time in attentional engagement than younger children (McWilliam & Bailey, 1991). Dunst, McWilliam, and Holbert (1986) also found specific staff assignments and optimal scheduling to be positively related to children's active engagement with materials, whereas the number of adults was inversely related to engagement (i.e., the more adults, the less the active engagement). A child's active engagement with peers was only found to vary (to increase) with the degree of the child's impairment. Active engagement with adults, however, was related to a number of factors—it increased as the curriculum became more individualized; and it decreased as the quality of the physical environment increased, as the number of children in the classroom increased, as the child–adult ratio increased, and as the child's age increased. The setting has also been discovered to have differential impacts on active engagement. Table 8.1 lists some of the key engagement studies, along with the populations studied and the major findings.

Mastery Motivation   Parallel to engagement studies, investigations of *mastery motivation* have been conducted. "Mastery motivation . . . reflects a goal to be achieved,

namely, competence in transactions with and control of one's physical and social environment" (Brockman, Morgan, & Harmon, 1988, p. 268). From Carroll's (1963) early theories, Bloom (1968) developed his model of mastery learning in schools. Drawing on his work and on the "effectance motivation" research of White (1959), others have studied infants' goal-directedness and persistence in challenging tasks. Because of the importance of persistence in this construct, the measurement of duration links this line of research to the engagement literature. In fact, conceptually it is remarkably similar to Carroll's "time-to-learn" research; but mastery investigators have not cited any connection. Some of these mastery studies have included children with disabilities. Almost all the investigations have been conducted in laboratory settings with standardized materials.

This line of research has provided detailed information on how very young children persist in goal-directed behavior. The literature on mastery, however, has not yet led to improvements in instructional practice—for the reasons that (a) what *produces* motivation has not been defined; (b) more attention has been paid to the level of difficulty of the material to be mastered than to the time variable; and (c) the research has focused more on assessment than on intervention. Still, mastery motivation may be a key to what happens *during* engagement that leads to learning.

Competence   As reflected in the definition of mastery motivation provided by Brockman et al. (1988), mastery involves competence in transactions. As notions of "the competent infant" have emerged (e.g., Stone, Smith, & Murphy, 1973), researchers have pursued a line of investigation into aspects of the development of competence in young children—such as *contingent control*, control over the environment, learned by contingent reinforcement (Watson, 1925); *effectance motivation*, the drive to master

TABLE 8.1
Major engagement findings

Study	Population	Findings
Krantz & Risley (1974)	Disadvantaged preschoolers	• Smooth transitions between activities promote engagement.
Twardosz, Cataldo, & Risley (1974)	Disadvantaged preschoolers	• Modified open room arrangements promote engagement.
Montes & Risley (1975)	Disadvantaged preschoolers	• Accessible toys promote engagement.
Hart & Risley (1975; 1978; 1980)	Disadvantaged preschoolers	• Incidental teaching produces high levels of participation.
Krantz & Risley (1974)	Disadvantaged preschoolers	• Carefully sequenced activities promote engagement.
Beginning Teacher Evaluation Study (Fisher, Filby, Maliave, Cahen, Dishaw, Moore, & Berliner, 1978)	Elementary students	• High-achievement students are more engaged & produce few errors. • Success time is more important than engaged or allocated time.
Krakow & Kopp (1983)	Infants & toddlers	• Children with Down syndrome (DS) engage less with toys than normally developing (ND) children, and children with developmental disabilities (DD) (uncertain etiology) are even less engaged.
McWilliam, Trivette, & Dunst (1985)	0–6 children with disabilities	• Program philosophy & activities influence the level & variability of participation.
Dunst, McWilliam, & Holbert (1986)	Programs for children 0–6	• Engagement is associated with program organization, environmental organization, & instruction. • Active engagement with adults is correlated negatively with the physical environment & positively with incidental teaching. • Active engagement with materials is correlated with caregiver elaboration, goal directedness, & appropriate play.
Rich & Ross (1989)	Special ed. students	• Students spend 65.2% of their time in learning tasks.
Bailey, McWilliam, & Ware (1991)	32 normally developing toddlers & preschoolers 16 toddlers & preschoolers with disabilities	• Children with disabilities are more solitary in a same-age group. • Younger children are more nonengaged in mixed-age groups; older children are more nonengaged in same-age groups.
McWilliam & Bailey (1991)	32 normally developing toddlers & preschoolers 16 toddlers & preschoolers with disabilities	• Age, grouping (mixed- vs. same-age), activity structure, & disability status all affect the level of engagement.

challenges (White, 1959); *initiation*, the ability to begin interactions (Sameroff, 1975); *interactive competence*, increasingly differentiated behavior (Dunst & McWilliam, 1988); *social competence*, the ability to engage in interpersonal interactions (Guralnick, 1990); and *mastery motivation*, persistence in goal-directed activities (Yarrow, McQuiston, MacTurk, McCarthy, Klein, & Vietze, 1983). Elkind (1987) has described stages in the history of the competence movement, relating how young children have successively been perceived as "malleable" (Watson, 1925), as having unlimited learning ability (Bruner, 1962), as developing most of their intelligence in the first three years of life and hence being primed to learn early (Bloom, 1964), and as having their intelligence shaped by early experiences (Hunt, 1961). Elkind also refers to the work of Aries (1962), according to whom children were perceived historically as being more competent (e.g., endowed with "wisdom") than we today view them as being. Arriving at the present, Elkind discusses the current "miseducation" of preschoolers. "While the image of childhood competence has served a useful function for low-income children and children with special needs, it has become the rationale for the miseducation of middle-class children both at home and at school" (Elkind, 1987, p. 69). Elkind explains that pushing children to learn and perform before they are developmentally ready is an unhealthy practice. For our purposes in this book, a definition of competence that serves well is Ogbu's (1987) ethnographic notion of "a set of social-emotional, cognitive, and practical skills that are necessary to perform cultural tasks" (p. 157).

Reconceptualization of Engagement

We no longer conceive of engagement as simply the distribution of the child's time across types of behaviors—that is, with adults, with peers, and with materials. The quality of the engagement—what we call mastery—is also important.* Here we offer our revised definition of engagement: *Engagement is the amount of time children spend interacting with the environment at different levels of competence.*

Engagement and its qualitative component, mastery, can be considered as a continuum from nonengagement to sustained engagement. We have identified five levels along this continuum: Level I—nonengagement, Level II—transient engagement, Level III—undifferentiated engagement, Level IV—elaborative engagement, and Level V—sustained engagement. We determine a child's level of engagement by gauging the length of her interactions with people and objects and by assessing the quality of her mastery behavior. The aspects of mastery behavior that we assess are (a) attention to and participation with the environment, (b) appropriateness of behavior, (c) elaboration of behavior, (d) goal-directedness, and (e) persistence. For example, consider two situations in which children are rolling a ball back and forth with an adult. In the first situation the child and the adult are engaged in a reciprocal game in which the child's primary goal is simply to keep the interaction with the adult going. We would credit the child with a particular length of interaction but with little mastery behavior beyond the attentiveness required to keep the game going. In the second situation, however, the child has difficulty rolling the ball and spends much time attempting to put his hands on it to exert a pushing action at every turn. Because of his persistence, we would credit this second

---

*How children spend their time has been found to vary across settings (McWilliam & Bailey, 1991; McWilliam et al., 1985), across social and nonsocial behavior classes (McWilliam & Bailey, 1991), and across mastery levels (MacTurk, Hunter, McCarthy, Vietze, & McQuiston, 1985).

child with a greater degree of mastery behavior, and we would thus see him as being engaged at a higher level.

When we assess the appropriateness of the child's behavior, we must look at the developmental level rather than the chronological age of the child. For example, repetitively banging objects together would be appropriate behavior for a 9-month-old normally developing infant but not for a normally developing 18-month-old. That sort of undifferentiated behavior would be appropriate, however, for the 18-month-old with moderate developmental delays.

When we gauge the length of the child's interactions we must keep in mind that the effect of the interactions is often mediated by the nature of the stimulus. If an adult intermittently speaks to a child who is scribbling with a crayon, and the child responds consistently and appropriately, each interaction might last only five seconds. The total amount of engaged interaction with the adult might be 30 seconds (6 interactions, 5 seconds each) or 1.66 percent of the 30-minute observation period or activity. On the other hand, the adult might approach another child also scribbling with one crayon and play pat-a-cake with the child for five minutes, and then the child might resume her scribbling. The length of interaction in this second case is longer (300 seconds), and it accounts for a greater percentage (16.6%) of the 30-minute activity. But the nature of the stimulus (the adult's behavior) was different for each child—engagement was more intensely elicited with the second child. Both children would thus be evaluated as displaying (Level III) undifferentiated engagement. Neither absolute times nor even percentages, then, can be given for the levels on the engagement continuum. Factors other than time criteria are therefore proposed to define the five levels of engagement. Following are operational definitions for the five levels.

Level I—Nonengagement

The child pays no attention to her surroundings, or she fleetingly looks around without any clear focus of interest. Any interaction with people or objects is short (e.g., 2–3 seconds). There is no evidence of elaboration, goal-directedness, or persistence. Passive nonengagement is only appropriate when the child is deliberately allowed to rest. It is acknowledged that some children require time to escape from stimulation. In general, though, nonengagement is to be avoided, especially in classroom programs. Crying, aggression toward self or others, destructive behavior, self-stimulation, and "misbehavior"—because they are not constructive behaviors—are considered to be forms of nonengagement.

Examples   Jo sits in her travel chair, while all around her children are engaged in free play. Her eye-gaze is often directed at the floor. From time to time, she looks up and around, but not in response to any particular stimulus. Baker is waiting for lunch. He occasionally looks at the teacher and at the other children, but does not appear to be watching or listening to them. He rocks his chair back and forth and squirms more as the wait gets longer. Takeesha holds the scissors that have been placed in her hand, but does not attempt to cut the paper as the other children in the group are doing. When the teacher is not looking, she pokes the scissors into the arm of the child next to her. When she tires of this, she works the scissors into a hole in her jeans, trying to widen the hole. Gary flaps his hands when an adult touches him. If the adult persists with physical contact, Gary hits himself on the side of his head and bites his hand.

Level II—Transient Engagement

The child attends to his surroundings for short durations, but is not really involved in any particular activity. Infants in the first couple of months of life spend much of their time in Level II engagement. There is no elaboration to their actions. Contact with objects and interactions with people are brief. Children displaying transient engagement make no attempt to overcome challenges.

Examples   Thomas walks around the room while the children are supposed to be playing in centers. He stops at centers and picks up objects without really looking at them; he shows no interest in the other children. He walks with deliberation between centers, but does not play with materials or peers when he gets to each center. Esperanza's tiny hands occasionally wrap around the toys in her crib and she brings them to her mouth. When in a convenient position, she seems to look at them. When she drops toys she does not change expression or otherwise indicate any attempt to recover them. She looks at her parents when they speak to her but loses interest quickly. Freddy has finished writing a big F; the other children are still working on their own projects. He looks at their papers and briefly watches them talking. When the teacher asks him if he has finished, he responds, "Uh-huh." He continues to sit quietly. Freddy knows how to write his whole name.

Level III—Undifferentiated Engagement

The child is attentive to her surroundings and participates in the activity. Contact with toys and people is long enough to be considered "play," but the behavior is not elaborated. That is, at each interaction the child plays one way, without expanding on the topography, the physical form, of the behavior. These behaviors may be used to persist somewhat in prolonging the interaction. Although each interaction may be brief, the cumulative duration of the child's engagement is moderately long. When faced with a challenge, the child makes brief attempts to solve the problem.

Examples   Soo Jin (7 months) attends constantly to what's going on around her; she is easily distracted, looking at whatever makes a noise or moves. She will move toward a thing that attracts her attention and then play with the object or person for a short time. Kendrick has severe spastic quadriplegia; he watches the other children and tries to join in anything that is going on. He makes only gross movements with objects, but when his peers move on to other activities, he bangs the toys on his tray and vocalizes loudly, as if to keep the other children nearby. He does not play for very long with any object, either because it falls off his tray or because he gives up playing with it after trying to keep hold of it. Gabi sits with the other children as the teacher reads to a small group. Gabi can speak in whole sentences, but during this particular activity she only gives one-word answers to the teacher's questions. When the teacher asks questions such as, "What else is the bunny doing, Gabi?" she simply shrugs her shoulders.

Level IV—Elaborative Engagement

This level of engagement is characterized by the child's using different behaviors in his interactions with people or objects. Single actions, topographies, or repetitive behaviors are not sufficient. The child tries new ways of playing and communicating. Each interaction is moderately long with considerable cumulative duration of engagement. Behavior is purposeful, and the child persists for moderate durations to overcome challenges.

Examples   Ian is given an ordinary metal saucepan and a wooden spoon. He sits on the floor and bangs on the saucepan for a short while, then turns the saucepan upside down and sits on it. He sees another larger saucepan nearby, fetches it, and tries to put it inside his original one. When that does not work, he succeeds in putting the smaller pan inside the big one. After sitting back and apparently contemplating his achievement, he again tries to put the big pan inside the small one. When that does not work, he nests them correctly again. Maria, who does not walk independently, sits on a chair holding a toy broom, while the other children play with various housekeeping and dress-up clothes nearby. She makes sweeping motions with the broom on the floor. Because of her lack of coordination, she is not able to "sweep" a book on the floor toward her, but she tries as many as ten times. She then reverses the broom, holding the bristles, and uses the handle to pull the book toward her until she can reach down and pick it up. At circle time, Demetrius chooses a song when asked, asks questions about pictures and objects, tells other children to move over, and so on. When the teacher asks what the children did the day before, however, he does not answer. Once someone has answered (e.g., "We played with the bunny rabbit"), he talks about it (e.g., "I held the bunny").

Level V—Sustained Engagement

This level of engagement is seen when the child spends most of her awake time in prolonged goal-directed interactions. When faced with a challenge, she persists, using various strategies, until she solves the problem, which might eventually involve seeking assistance appropriately.

Examples Tara has done her usual rounds of the playground equipment and has come back to the slide. She attempts to go up the slide rather than the ladder, but her dress keeps getting caught under her knees. She turns around and sits on the slide, trying to push herself backwards up the slide. This time her dress gets caught under her feet. She gets off the slide, hitches the dress up

into her panties, gets back on the slide and makes it to the top. Lonnie has been told he has macaroni and cheese and broccoli on his plate. He hates broccoli. Because he is visually impaired, he uses his fork to feel around on the plate to avoid the broccoli. Unfortunately, it was cut up for him, so he cannot readily identify it by touch. He lowers his head to his plate to smell which side the broccoli is on. For the first few bites, he succeeds in getting only macaroni on his fork. Then the dread taste, as he unknowingly puts a piece of broccoli in his mouth. He calls out, "Who likes broccoli?" A child answers, and Lonnie offers his: "Here, take my broccoli off my plate." Carina sits in front of a tape player playing music she likes. The tape player is programmed to stop at variable intervals, but she can restart it by using one of three switches. She can raise her head, activating a mercury switch; she can reach in front and press an Ablenet switch; or she can bend her knee, activating a paddle switch under her tray. Only one switch at a time will restart the music and they are programmed to work in random order. She will sit for as long as allowed, using these various methods to keep her music going.

What causes a low level of engagement? The first cause for the practitioners to consider is the environment. The physical arrangement of the classroom, the appropriateness of the toys and the activities, and the actions of people around the child can affect the level of engagement. Alternatively, the child's impairments may make it difficult for him to attend and participate, to behave appropriately, to elaborate on initial behaviors, to sustain interactions, and to persist in goal-directed schemes. Or the child's low level of engagement may be caused by his temperament or by the fact that he has had little previous experience with the materials and people involved. To facilitate engagement, the interventionist should thus consider making changes in the environment (including teaching methods), choosing goals to circumvent or overcome the child's disabilities, and making adjustments for the child's individual style.

FACILITATING ENGAGEMENT

Given that high levels of engagement are a worthy goal of teaching, valued in regular early education, and, possibly, a critical mediating variable in learning by young children with disabilities, early interventionists should include practices specifically designed to foster this outcome. Generally, center-based programs for normally developing children reflect better early childhood practices than do programs for children with disabilities (Bailey, Harms, & Clifford, 1983). In a study comparing formal programs (characterized by didactic teaching, emphasis on therapy, and no normally developing children) and informal programs (characterized by incidental teaching, emphasis on normal activities, and integration), McWilliam et al. (1985) found that informal programs produced consistently higher levels of engagement. Another study on center-based environments revealed that informal programs such as those in the 1985 study produced more engagement than Head Start classrooms, regular day care centers, or formal programs (Dunst et al., 1986). Related to the issue of classroom structure, least restrictive alternatives in special education, particularly the resource room, have been found to make more in-class learning time available (Rich & Ross, 1989). These studies suggest that the factors contributing to high levels of engagement can be grouped under three headings: (a) the physical environment, (b) the social environment, and (c) the teaching method. We discuss the physical and social environments here and the teaching method later in the chapter.

Physical Environment

The least intrusive and most self-maintaining intervention for promoting engagement is to have a stimulating and responsive physical environment. The room should be organized in a modified open design (Sturmey & Crisp, 1986), entailing clearly delineated zones, separated by low barriers or visual markers. The zones help children remain in individual activities, and the lack of high barriers allows ease of movement during transitions. Such an arrangement has been associated with more goal-directedness and less passivity than more closed environments (Dunst et al., 1986).

Children should have a variety of developmentally appropriate toys and other materials they can manipulate independently. Classrooms should have a variety of types of materials, including those that promote social play, those that promote independent constructive play, and those that promote creativity. Materials should be stored on low shelves, so children can have access to them, and so waiting time and inappropriate behavior are prevented. Placing some toys in sight but out of reach, however, is a technique that has been used to promote spontaneous requests and to provide opportunities for incidental language teaching.

Barren areas of the classroom have been used in traditional early childhood special education classrooms, when the teacher has wanted to ensure that children pay attention to the task at hand. This arrangement works as long as the activity is interesting for every child. An alternative view of "distractibility" is that the child is *otherwise engaged*. The teacher needs to assess whether the child's nonengagement with the activity should be remedied by corrective procedures (i.e., getting the child interested) or by adjusting the activity to the child's new interest. For example, a pile of brightly colored socks are on the floor for the children to sort into colors.

Brian shows no interest in sorting the socks, but goes to the window to watch another class playing outside. Should the teacher redirect Brian to the sock activity or should she get him to point to the children wearing red shirts, those wearing white shirts, and so on? The *deficit view* of Brian would be that he is distractible and should be provided a distraction-free environment and be redirected to the activity. An *engagement approach* would interpret his behavior as otherwise engaged: he found the children playing outside more engaging than the pile of socks. From the engagement point of view, the teacher might employ a *naturalistic* method—providing instruction based on the child's focus of attention, in this case pointing to the children outside. Or the teacher might redirect Brian or change the original activity. If, for some reason, the sock activity represents a high priority for Brian, then even when following the engagement approach, the teacher might direct Brian back to that activity. But more likely the target behavior aimed at in the original activity—in this case the identification of colors—could be addressed in other ways, if not by employing the naturalistic method then by recasting the original activity. Here the children could be directed, say, to *put on* blue socks. Such an approach would have the advantage of using and elaborating on existing engagement.

When the center, zone, or area has many materials, children are more likely to be otherwise engaged. Depending on the purpose of the activity and the goals for the individual child, the teacher can decide which approach to take. High engagement in terms of prolonged attention is more likely to occur when the teaching activity follows the child's interest.

When adults teach small groups of children, it is not uncommon for at least one child to lose interest if she does not receive a fairly high rate of response from the adult.

Because materials can keep children engaged between interactions with adults, it is useful to conduct activities in zones where a variety of materials are available. To maintain some semblance of order, some teachers allow children to play with any materials within the clearly marked zone. It is therefore recommended that all classroom areas have accessible toys and other materials.

Social Environment

The organization of the people in the classroom has an effect on child engagement (Dunst et al., 1986). Assigning staff to zones rather than to individual children has been found to produce higher levels of engagement (LeLaurin & Risley, 1972). Zone assignments prevent a teacher from having to handle situations outside the activity, such as toileting, answering the telephone, or chasing an actively nonengaged child; another adult handles such situations. Zone assignments also ensure that teachers have opportunities to prepare succeeding activities, and downtime during transitions is thus minimized. A second organizational strategy is the pacing of activities. Since young children require a gradual change from a high-energy activity to a quiet one, the schedule should include medium-level activities in between (e.g., outside play, followed by music, then story).

The social environment can be arranged to promote both higher-level functioning within domains and higher levels of engagement. The following seven strategies have been proposed by Ostrosky and Kaiser (1991) to promote communication; these strategies are also applicable for facilitating engagement.

1 Provide interesting materials.
2 Place some objects out of reach to create opportunities for child requests.
3 Provide inadequate portions of objects and foods to create requesting opportunities.

4 Give children choices.

5 Set up situations that require assistance—and therefore child requests.

6 Sabotage situations, cautiously, creating opportunities for the child to indicate there is a problem.

7 Create silly situations that prompt the child's comments.

A study investigating the time children spent with adults, peers, and materials found that children with special needs were more engaged in looking at and listening to adults when they were assigned to mixed-age classes (McWilliam & Bailey, 1991). This study also found that mastery-level engagement with materials was higher for older children when they were in mixed-age groups but higher for younger children when they were in same-age groups.

The level of structure of activities also affects engagement. Structured activities—the adult interacts with the child one-on-one or leads a planned activity—promote engagement with adults, whereas free play promotes engagement with peers and with materials (McWilliam & Bailey, 1991). Whether the child had disabilities affected the influence of free play versus structured activities. Normally developing children were interactively engaged with peers three times as much during free play as they were during structured activities, and they were more engaged with materials during structured activities than during free play. But the pattern was reversed for children with disabilities, who were more engaged with materials during free play and more engaged with peers during structured activities. Nonengagement was higher in structured activities than in free play, with more nonengagement by children with disabilities than by normally developing children.

Thus, the composition of groups in early intervention and the amount of structure in activities can affect engagement. Because all three types of engagement—with adults,

with peers, and with materials—are potentially crucial for young children's development, decisions about groupings should be made with the following conditions in mind: (a) What types of engagement are needed for this child? (b) How old is the child? (c) Does the child have disabilities? These considerations should help determine when same-age rather than mixed-age peer groups should be used and when structured activities rather than free play are recommended. Staff assignments, the organization of peer groupings, and the level of activity structure are aspects of the social environment that can be manipulated to increase engagement.

PLANNING INTERVENTION

Engagement and mastery can be considered as both outcomes and mediating variables. That is, when the intervention team is concerned about the child's overall competence, they can implement strategies to improve engagement and mastery in and of themselves (i.e., as outcomes). On the other hand, improved engagement and mastery might be seen as intermediate stages (i.e., as mediating variables) on the way to attainment of specific functional, developmental skills.

Targeting Competence

Competence goals can be written in terms of engagement types and in terms of mastery.

Engagement Types   In selecting engagement goals, the professional can aim for the child's increasing engagement with adults, with peers, and with materials. This type of intervention consists of expanding the amount of time the child spends interacting appropriately in one or more of these three categories. The goal can be stated at either the molecular level (e.g., "Lisa will talk to and play with adults for five minutes at a time") or the molar level (e.g., "Lisa will talk to and play with adults for a total of thirty minutes during the classroom morning"). *Molecular level goals* are selected when the child's interactions are each shorter than desired; and *molar level goals* are selected when the aim is to increase the overall amount of time spent rather than individual interactions. Engagement-type goals can be appropriate for children at almost any level of development, although increasing the amount of time children spend interacting with peers should be avoided for those under the developmental age of 2 years, since much social interaction would be unexpected at that stage.

Types of Engagement for Targeting Increased Competence
Engagement with adults
Engagement with peers
Engagement with materials

Mastery   Mastery goals address the quality of the child's engagement. The qualitative areas targeted in mastery goals are attentiveness, appropriateness of behavior, elaboration, goal-directedness, and persistence. Table 8.2 displays examples of mastery goals for the five levels of engagement. These are only examples; goals should be selected based on the individual needs and developmental level of the child.

Mastery Areas for Targeting Increased Competence
Attentiveness
Appropriateness of behavior
Elaboration
Goal-directedness
Persistence

Targeting Developmental Skills

Besides being themselves targetable outcomes, engagement and mastery can serve as mediating variables on the way to a child's learning and demonstrating developmental skills. That is, engagement and mastery are psychological processes that affect behavior.

Teachers and parents have noticed, for example, that some children simply do not spend enough time interacting with other children to learn and practice social interaction skills efficiently. Similarly, some children give up so readily when faced with failure that the opportunities to learn a skill are attenuated. When teachers see that problems with engagement and mastery interfere with the child's learning and play, they can plan interventions that include these process variables.

Cognitive Skills   In order for children to learn to solve problems, it is necessary that they spend enough time in interaction with objects, people, and situations (a) to allow them to have the direct experience that will make the particular problem-solving skills meaningful and (b) to allow adults opportunities to teach them when they are interested. Thus, if the team decides that the child is ready to develop object permanence, the plan might be to increase the amount of time she spends playing with objects so that she may learn to find hidden objects. In addition to addressing the type of engagement (in this case, engagement with materials), the professional aiming for the development of the child's cognitive skills may also need to address the quality of the child's engagement (i.e., her mastery behavior). For example, if a child is learning to combine objects in play, the plan might stipulate that she should achieve (Level IV) elaborative engagement during instruction. That is, the teacher first encourages the child to play with the objects in different ways, and then he teaches her how to combine them.

Social and Communication Skills   The development of conventional communication (oral language, sign language, augmentative communication) requires (a) experiences to provide the reasons for communicating and (b) the motivation to communicate (mastery motivation, that is). When working on a

TABLE 8.2
Examples of mastery goals at the five levels of engagement

Engagement Level	Mastery Area	Sample Goal
Nonengagement	Attentiveness	The child will look at people who speak to her 50% of the time.
	Appropriateness	The child will play appropriately for five seconds.
	Elaboration	The child will hold on to an object for 5 seconds (this is the goal for active behavior—a prerequisite to elaboration).
	Goal-directedness	The child will state what toy he wants at the beginning of free play.
	Persistence	The child will try for 5 seconds to get a toy out of a container.
Transient	Attentiveness	The child will watch another child for a minimum of 10 seconds.
	Appropriateness	The child will play appropriately by herself for 3 minutes.
	Elaboration	The child will hold on to an object for 5 seconds (this is the goal for active behavior—a prerequisite to elaboration).
	Goal-directedness	The child will indicate what he is playing with when asked.
	Persistence	The child will indicate she wants help when asked.
Undifferentiated	Attentiveness	The child will maintain appropriate eye contact during interactions.
	Appropriateness	The child will play appropriately during free play for 10 minutes.
	Elaboration	The child will use objects in two ways (e.g., stirring and pretend eating from spoon; rolling car without letting go and letting go).

communication goal, a teacher might include an increase in the amount of time the child spends interacting with adults (i.e., more engagement with adults). If the communication skill requires the child to refer to objects that are not present, to use symbolic language, the intervention plan might include ensuring engagement at the sustained level.

Gross Motor Skills Gross motor skills function primarily to support independence in mobility and positioning. Engagement is fre-

quently a supplementary reason for positioning goals for children with severe physical disabilities. A physical therapist might recommend, for example, that a child spend some time in a prone stander. From an educational standpoint, the intervention plan might call for the child to be engaged (with peers, with objects) while placed in the prone stander. The achievement of a particular engagement level or of mastery behavior might also be important to incorporate in the plan for a child who is learning a specific gross motor skill, such as moving on a riding

TABLE 8.2
continued

Engagement Level	Mastery Area	Sample Goal
	Goal-directedness	The child will use objects, voice, or gestures to get another's attention.
	Persistence	The child will say "more" or otherwise indicate he wants to continue playing.
Elaborative	Attentiveness	(Goals are not usually necessary in this area for children at the elaborative level of engagement.)
	Appropriateness	The child will play using objects in combination 90 percent of the time.
	Elaboration	The child will describe objects using multiple adjectives.
	Goal-directedness	The child will spend 90 percent of the time in purposeful activity during structured activities.
	Persistence	The child will try to solve problems by herself before asking for help.
Sustained	Attentiveness	(Goals are not usually necessary in this area for children at the sustained level of engagement.)
	Appropriateness	The child will talk about past or future events when asked.
	Elaboration	The child will use previously successful strategies to overcome problems in social interactions (e.g., taking another child's favorite toy to him when the other child has refused to play).
	Goal-directedness	The child will spend 90 percent of the time in purposeful activity during free play.
	Persistence	The child will try to make toys work, build structures, or get his own way (appropriately) for 5 minutes.

toy. The plan might call for the child to be engaged at the elaborative level while on the riding toy, because at that level he would be persisting for moderate durations to overcome challenges.

Fine Motor Skills The development of most fine motor skills requires engagement with objects. A child might therefore need to increase the amount of time spent with objects as a first step towards developing the identified skill. The engagement level might be important in the case of an infant who is developing an ability to hold on to objects. In such a case the plan could include intervention aimed at ensuring at least (Level III) undifferentiated engagement, that being the lowest level of engagement at which persistence is evident.

Self-Help Skills To develop daily living skills, the toddler or preschooler requires a level of contact with the environment. If the child does not pay attention when it is time to put on her coat and does not cooperate, the plan can include increasing engagement (i.e., participation) during departure times. Mastery behavior is often important when children are learning self-help skills because of the persistence often required. Thus the teacher and family might plan to work on encouraging a blind child to be engaged at the (Level V) sustained level during meals if he is working on eating with a fork. The child would need to be highly goal-directed (e.g., motivated to have food on the fork at every attempt) and to persist until he is no longer hungry.

Attention to the processes of engagement and mastery can thus help the interventionist focus on the critical components of skill development. Furthermore, addressing these broad-based constructs is more likely to keep the intervention in context, to keep it from becoming too specific (Sparling, 1990). If the child is engaged, particularly at a high level, it is an indication that the activity is meaningful for the child.

TEACHING STRATEGIES

Engagement is best facilitated with *responsive teaching*—that is, with teaching strategies that elaborate on the child's behavior. Although teachers can elicit engagement, using positive reinforcement is considered a more effective technique than adult-directed elicitation—because positive reinforcement increases the likelihood of future self-initiated engagement and mastery. Nevertheless, in the familiar antecedent-behavior-consequence ("ABC") paradigm, both the antecedent and the consequence are important for facilitating engagement. The teacher does have an important role (as antecedent) in establishing optimal conditions for self-initiated engagement; and by taking advantage of the child's engagement, at whatever level, the teacher reinforces in her the idea that her actions are important. In contrast, when teach-

ing *primarily* involves elicitation (prompts, cues, etc.) of desired responses, when the child is interested in something else, (a) the child is less likely to develop a sense of control over the environment, and (b) instruction is more difficult for the teacher.

Most of the guidelines for facilitating engagement consist of techniques that can be incorporated into ordinary classroom routines (see, e.g., Jones & Warren, 1991; McGee, Daly, Izeman, Mann, & Risely, 1991; McWilliam, 1987; Whaley & Bennett, 1991). Some of these guidelines, suggested by Whaley and Bennett (1991), are presented in Box 8.1. Although therapists and educational specialists can probably achieve high levels of engagement during therapy and instruction outside the classroom context, it is possible that generalized engagement may be best achieved by providing therapeutic interventions while the child is engaged in regular classroom routines (McWilliam, 1991b).

Responsive teaching can take many forms, from an almost total absence of adult participation at one extreme to a highly structured schedule of reinforcement at the other extreme. It is thus possible to facilitate engagement by using a variety of theoretical approaches, from discovery-based learning to applied behavior analysis. The continuum of teaching strategies can be thought of in five levels: (a) a responsive environment, (b) participation strategies, (c) responsive elaboration, (d) elicited elaboration, and (e) response-contingent instruction.

Responsive Environment

The least intrusive method for facilitating engagement is to provide space, materials, activities, and people that stimulate a child's attention and active behavior and that reinforce such engagement. The adult's primary role is to organize the environment and provide selective attention.

Teacher attention may be delivered contingent upon appropriate engagement. Selec-

---

BOX 8.1   Guidelines for instructional strategies in the context of daily routines

- Prepare the activity and materials before the children arrive.
- Allow the children to begin play immediately.
- Model appropriate language and desired behavior.
- Use responsive teaching strategies to incorporate children's individual goals into the context of the activity.
- Interact with all the children during the activity.
- Reinforce appropriate or desired behaviors and skills.
- Allow children the opportunity to make choices.
- Encourage children to interact with each other.
- Focus on the acquisition of functional behaviors.

Note: From "Promoting Engagement in Early Childhood Special Education" by K. T. Whaley and T. C. Bennett, 1991, *TEACHING Exceptional Children, 23*(4), pp. 51–54. Copyright 1991 by The Council for Exceptional Children. Reprinted by permission.

---

tive attention involves ignoring the child who leaves the desired activity to pursue another activity and attending to the child when he is in the appropriate place. For this strategy to work, however, the following conditions must be met.

1 The teacher's expectation that the child will participate in the activity must be clear.
2 The child must like teacher attention, or more specifically, teacher attention should be a positive reinforcer.
3 Alternative activities must be less appealing.
4 When the child is appropriately engaged, the teacher must be sure to give him positive attention.

Children need to have begun an activity before the teacher can encourage prolonged engagement. The natural appeal of an activity can set the stage for subsequent involvement. The following strategies may be employed to get children started.

1 *Make the materials appealing.* Colorful toys are better than drab materials. Three-dimensional objects that can be manipulated are often more appealing than pictures or drawings. Toys or materials that provide feedback (noise, visual display, movement) are also good motivators.

2 *Make participation a privilege or a prerequisite for preschoolers rather than a responsibility.* For example, everyone who helps pick up the blocks can have the privilege of coming to story time.

3 *Give the children an immediate role.* For instance, if the story is about farm animals, ask children to choose a toy animal from a box and then sit down and hold the animal in preparation for the story.

4 *Give instructions to begin or prompt initial interactions.* For example, the child who just sits in the block center may need to be told to build something, may need a model, or may need a physical prompt to begin.

5 *Identify children's preferences for materials.* Quiltich, Christopherson, and Risley (1977) described a systematic method for determining preferences for materials by observing the amount of time children play with available toys. Total number of

minutes of child use is determined and then toys are ranked from the most to least used. Quiltich et al. found that environments with high-use toys resulted in higher levels of appropriate engagement with materials than did environments with low-use toys.

Participation Strategies

The second level of responsive teaching involves taking a more active role in ensuring child engagement in the ongoing activity. The term "participation strategies" was coined by Holdgrafer (1987), who listed elaborated repetition and requests for elaboration as intervention strategies, falling under this head. Other "participation" techniques include modeling intermittent reinforcement, question-and-extend, systematic commenting (Jones & Warren, 1991) and scaffolds. Systematic commenting involves the teacher's making observations about the child's behavior, emphasizing the child's communication goals. Scaffolds are the teacher's requests for more information, based on the child's verbalization (e.g., "what's next?"). Question-and-extend involves asking the child a question and then prompting elaboration of her response; the child's responses need not be verbal. Following are guidelines for the professional teaching at this level.

1 *Work towards maximal group participation.* For example, scan the room constantly, helping those children who are not involved in the activity to become involved.
2 *Interact with children to keep them going.* Showing interest in what each child is doing is likely to prolong the activity.
3 *Provide contingent attention primarily to those children who are appropriately participating.* For example, if some children are playing with the materials set out for the organized activity and others are wandering about the room, the teacher might

focus on the first group. This might appear to contradict the first guideline listed here; the teacher needs to find the balance between promoting broad participation and reinforcing appropriate participation.

Responsive Elaboration

The third level of responsive teaching consists of the teacher's using the child's existing behavior for elaboration in the direction of a predetermined goal. In many cases, the goal can be one identified on the child's IFSP or IEP. Included in this level are such techniques as conversational teaching (MacDonald, 1985) and developmental interactive teaching (Bricker & Carlson, 1981). The goals when using responsive elaboration can be to attain (a) greater amounts of time spent engaged, (b) higher levels of engagement, or (c) specific developmental skills (such as the cognitive and other skills we discussed in the section on planning interventions). This level of intervention might be the most generally useful, because it is easily applied with children at different developmental levels, in most contexts, and with most goals. Here we list the key steps for using responsive elaboration.

1 *Provide a stimulating/responsive environment.* A place, toys, and people that can attract the child's attention will set the stage for the teacher to interact with the child in the context of the child's interest.
2 *Ensure child interest.* This step might be accomplished by implementing step 1. Otherwise, the teacher might (a) have to direct the child's attention to the interesting activity, toy, or person, or (b) find another stimulus.
3 *Determine the child's reinforcement preferences.* The teacher can make this determination by watching the child or by trying different reinforcers. What is reinforced at this step is the child's interest. If the child sustains her interest with no

adult involvement, the teacher can move on to the next step. With many children, especially at the younger developmental ages, the adult's participation will be highly reinforcing.

4 *Choose the goals that can be targeted in this interaction.* Multiple goals can be targeted as possible outcomes of a single interaction. For example, both a communication goal and a motor goal could be accomplished in the activity of taking a walk. Communication goals can almost always be combined with other goals. Engagement and mastery goals also are particularly appropriate, alone or in combination with other goals, during all interactions.

5 *Encourage active engagement.* For example, if an infant is holding a noise-making toy, inspecting it, the teacher might show him how to shake it. The emphasis is on active physical or communicative behavior.

6 *Encourage elaboration of active engagement.* For the child learning to communicate, one of the most functional elaborations is the use of language, signs, or communication-board symbols to accompany her active behavior. The emphasis is on a more differentiated response from the child—a more complex skill than at the beginning of the interaction. Elaboration can be either vertical (greater developmental complexity, higher developmental level) or horizontal (more time spent in interaction, more time to practice and learn). Teachers might use the following techniques in encouraging elaboration.

- *Provide nondirective mands.* Once the child is engaged with the object, activity, or person, the teacher might ask, for example, "Can you do this?" If the child shows no interest in trying, at this level the teacher would not persist.
- *Model elaboration with no demands.* If the child is playing with a toy, the

teacher might show him how to do something new with it. If the child imitates, the teacher provides reinforcement. If not, the teacher tries another technique.

- *Pair the child with a peer who can perform the desired skill.* The teacher might both pay attention to the higher-level peer and gently prompt the focal child to imitate the peer.

7 *Encourage approximation of a targeted goal.* The purpose of responsive elaboration is to move the child from existing behavioral repertoires towards the goals targeted for intervention. The interaction ends when the child has made some increment of progress toward at least one of the goals chosen for this interaction.

Elicited Elaboration

The fourth level of responsive teaching involves the adult's taking a more active role in prompting the child to approximate a desired response. The teacher sets the stage for engagement in an activity related to the target goal, observes the child's behavior, and elicits an approximation of that target response. The techniques involved in elicited elaboration can include incidental teaching as described by Warren and Kaiser (1988), the mand-model procedure (Rogers-Warren & Warren, 1980), time delay (Halle, Marshall, & Spradlin, 1979), and the Premack principle (Premack, 1959). Here are some guidelines for elicited elaboration.

1 *Choose a goal appropriate for the context.* The teacher generally chooses a goal from the IFSP or IEP, but might choose one that seems appropriate or necessary at the time. The target behavior should be congruent with the demands of the setting. For example, paying attention at storytime would be appropriate, whereas interacting with peers during storytime might not.

2 *Choose an activity likely to elicit responses in the same behavior class as the target goal.* For example, if the teacher has decided to use free play as a time to teach Noah to put objects into a container, he might be encouraged to play with the blocks and canisters.

3 *Follow active engagement with prompts.* For example, when the child points to an out-of-reach toy she wants, the teacher might say, "What do you want?" If the child continues to point but does not use language, the teacher might say, "The baby? You want the baby?" If the child indicates the affirmative but does not use a word (the target goal), the teacher might say, "Say *baby.*" When the child does say or approximate "baby," the teacher would hand it to her.

A few conditions are necessary for elicited elaboration to work.

1 The child must be capable of producing an approximation acceptable to the adult.

2 The object, activity, or person must be desirable to the child.

3 The teacher must be prepared for the child to change the focus of interest if the desired response is too demanding.

Two "interactive teaching techniques" (p. 49) described by Jones and Warren (1991) exemplify elicited elaboration. Incidental teaching, as they describe it, consists of (a) a child's communicative attempt, (b) the teacher's request for elaboration, and (c) the teacher's reinforcing or modeling the elaboration depending on the child's response. (Note that this version of incidental teaching is more structured than incidental teaching as described earlier.) The mand-model technique (Warren, McQuarter, & Rogers-Warren, 1984) also relies on the child's initial attention to something he wants, but the adult "mands" (instructs) an active communicative attempt. Although these techniques are described for teaching early language, they can also be used for teaching behaviors in other domains.

Response-Contingent Instruction

The fifth level of responsive teaching involves the systematic application of positive reinforcement to desired behavior. It is responsive in the sense that the intervention is contingent upon the display of a particular behavior. Noncontingent instruction, by contrast, involves the provision of stimuli regardless of the child's behavior. Thus, attaching a wind chime via a ribbon to the wrist of a young child with severe disabilities provides contingent reinforcement for arm movements. As the child becomes aware of the effect these movements have on the environment (the sound of the wind chime), he is more likely to move the arm voluntarily to reinstigate the reinforcer. Compare this to wind-up mobiles that are switched on ostensibly to provide stimulation to the child. Although children might attend to new stimuli provided noncontingently, they quickly habituate. Much more effective in terms of establishing and maintaining engagement is response-contingent instruction.

An example of this level of intervention is found at the Walden Learning Center at the University of Massachusetts at Amherst, where teachers promote the engagement of children with autism by differentially dispensing classroom materials (McGee, Daly, Izeman, Mann, & Risley, 1991). Carefully selected sets of individually preferred toys ("hobby boxes," p. 45) are rotated to maintain variety. Some sets are used to secure engagement in chronically nonengaged children, while others are used to prolong engagement. Nonengaged children are redirected to toys after 5 minutes of nonengagement, and preschoolers who are usually engaged receive their hobby boxes as a reward for completing pre-academic work and contingent on their asking for them. As with most response-contingent programs, the systematic application of the hobby box procedures requires the teacher to be well organized.

Higher levels of engagement are likely to be initiated when response-contingent instruction (a) is applied on an appropriate schedule of reinforcement (Baer, 1978) and (b) involves a reinforcer with enough appeal to the child (McWilliam, 1987). For children with very low levels of engagement, a continuous schedule of reinforcement might be appropriate, following which every time the child produces the desired response the reinforcer is provided. For example, Harry rarely looks at people in the environment; every time he does, the adults at home and in the classroom ruffle his hair, which he seems to like. Engagement may need to be elicited if the behavior occurs so seldom that even a continuous schedule of reinforcement does not increase the frequency of the response. Eliciting behavior is the provision of noncontingent reinforcement, but it is always paired with contingent reinforcement. The two stimuli, the one to elicit the response and the one to reinforce it, should be different. Thus, adults call Harry by name (elicitation), and when he looks at them they ruffle his hair (reinforcement). As he becomes more responsive to being called, the adults fade the elicitation; that is, they call him less often or use other forms of the stimulus, such as calling, "Yoo-hoo," or, "Hi there."

Once Harry's rate of looking at adults has increased, the intervention is moved to a *fixed-interval schedule of reinforcement,* in which every second looking response or every third is reinforced. This is a way of fading his dependence on the reinforcer. Once engagement is maintained with fixed-interval reinforcement, a *variable schedule of reinforcement* can be used. Now, the reinforcer is delivered on an unpredictable schedule.

Sometimes Harry's looking behavior is reinforced, sometimes not. This method is used to keep him working at it: persistence is a key factor in higher levels of engagement. Variable schedules are normal in most child care environments.

A particularly useful application of response-contingent instruction (Dunst, Cushing, & Vance, 1985) is to improve the duration of a child's responding, since engagement is defined as the amount of time a child interacts with the environment. *Differential reinforcement* (Allen, Hart, Buell, Harris, & Wolf, 1964) involves the delivery of a stimulus during the time the child produces the desired behavior. For example, 5-year-old Beth does not sit still and attend during teacher-directed activities. Her parents realize the importance of this behavior as Beth approaches entry to kindergarten. She likes the music from television cartoon shows, so the teacher has audiotaped the soundtrack from a number of cartoons. The music is switched on as background noise during the teacher-directed activity, and Beth sits close to the tape player. When she leaves her seat or fiddles around, the teacher uses a remote control device to switch off the music. As Beth realizes the music will only stay on while she's engaged, she spends increasingly longer times in her seat, paying attention. Soon, the teacher will use the music as a reward for 5 minutes of engagement, so Beth will have to be engaged without music for that length of time before the music is switched on. As her engagement improves, the teacher will increase the length of response time prior to delivery of the reinforcer. This method is known as *differential reinforcement of other behavior (DRO)*—reinforcement of behavior other than leaving the seat and fiddling.

Table 8.3 describes the different types of interventions that can be used employing the five levels of teaching structure with the five levels of engagement. The 25 blocks sum-

TABLE 8.3
Purposes of the five levels of responsive teaching for each level of engagement

	I Nonengaged	II Transient	III Undifferentiated	IV Elaborative	V Sustained
Responsive Environment	Ensure objects and people are available	Ensure objects and people elicit attention	Provide a variety of different toys and different forms of social interaction	Provide more complex toys and higher functioning peers	Provide a variety of experiences and opportunities for dramatic play
Participation Strategies	Ensure proximity of materials and people	Offer favorite toys, people, activities	Respond intermittently to actions with objects and social awareness	Encourage sustained interaction with objects and people	Encourage (a) use of pretend-play materials, and (b) sustained pretend-play scenarios
Responsive Elaboration	Respond to and elicit elaborations of fleeting attention and encourage active behavior	Respond to and elicit elaborations of attention, action with objects, and social interactions	Respond to and elicit elaborations of object manipulation, communicative attempts, vocalizations, movement	Respond to and elicit elaborations of constructive, differentiated play and communication	Respond to and elicit sustained pretend play and conversation
Elicited Elaboration	Elicit specific behavior when child is attentive	Respond and elicit action and communication	Respond and elicit elaborations and expansions of communication	Respond and elicit expansions of communication and of pretend play	Respond and elicit expansions of communication and of pretend play
Response-Contingent Instruction	Find discriminative stimuli; eliminate interfering stimuli	Ensure continuous reinforcement schedule	Use changing criterion design or fixed interval schedule of reinforcement	Use variable-interval schedule of reinforcement	Use intermittent schedule of reinforcement

marize the options for teaching strategies that promote optimal engagement. Teachers would be well advised to take a flexible approach in deciding on the teaching strategies to use, because the within-child variability in engagement is enormous. The same child may display transient engagement in some situations and sustained engagement in others, and some situations are more appropriate for intervening with simply a responsive environment and others with elicited elaboration.

Deciding on Appropriate Strategies

Figure 8.1 shows the major factors influencing the professional's decision regarding appropriate strategies: the specificity of the outcome and the child's ability level. These factors should be considered in combination. The figure shows the approximate proportion of time each strategy type would be used, based on this analysis.

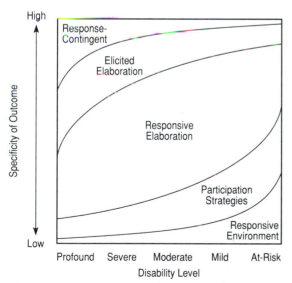

FIGURE 8.1

Factors influencing the decision of which teaching strategies to use

Specificity of the Outcome Generally, the more specific the outcome, the more structured the teaching strategy will be. For example, the target outcome of *participating during circle time*, a low-specificity outcome, might be addressed with a low level of structure, such as a participation strategy (see Table 8.4). On the other hand, *sitting on the carpet square during circle time for two minutes*, a highly specific outcome, might be addressed through a shaping procedure, a highly structured method.

Fuchs and Deno (1991) have articulated the difference between general outcome indicators and specific subskill mastery. *General outcome indicators* focus on the end behavior, include automatic measurement of maintenance and generalization, measure long-term curricular goal performance, and keep the same measurement while specific subskills are taught. *Specific subskill mastery* specifies skill hierarchies, rarely includes a measure of maintenance or generalization, focuses on the short-term objectives, and requires a shift in measurement for each new skill. The intervention team should consider how specific the goal needs to be in order to address the need. Where the goal rests on this continuum between highly specific subskill mastery outcomes and general (low-specificity) outcomes should be considered in tandem with the ability level of the child.

Child's Ability Level The more able the child, the more successful naturalistic teaching methods are likely to be—in general. It stands to reason that children who develop without a high level of specialized intervention are more likely to benefit from nonintrusive teaching strategies than are those who require much assistance. For example, teaching an at-risk infant to raise his or her head might only require a responsive environment, whereas teaching the same skill to an older child with severe learning difficulties and motor coordination problems might require a relatively highly structured teaching strategy.

The specificity level of the outcome and the child's ability level should serve as guidelines, but the least intrusive (i.e., the most normalized and naturalistic) approach possible should be considered first (Bailey & McWilliam, 1991). Clearly, children with severe disabilities can often be taught with relatively unstructured methods. It is, again, the interaction of outcome-specificity and ability level that should guide the selection of a teaching approach for facilitating engagement.

SUMMARY

Engagement and mastery behavior are necessary prerequisites to developmental progress. Unfortunately, many youngsters with disabilities exhibit low levels of persistence and goal-directedness for a variety of reasons. Because infants, toddlers, and preschoolers learn primarily through play and other natural interactions with their environments, engagement is the equivalent of on-task behavior. Optimal physical and social environments provide the foundation for maximal engagement, in terms of both eliciting and reinforcing the child's appropriate responses. The research on engagement has included studies of children's attention, active manipulation of materials, social interactions, and mastery motivation. We now understand that in addition to varying amounts of time spent engaged, children exhibit different levels of engagement. These levels have been defined here as nonengagement, transient engagement, undifferentiated engagement, elaborative engagement, and sustained engagement. A rationale has been presented for planning interventions with an engagement component, either for targeting competence (engagement, mastery) itself or as a complement for targeting developmental skills. Responsive teaching, in which the adult bases interactions on the child's existing engagement, is the preferred instructional mode for enhancing that behavior class. The continuum of responsive teaching strategies consists of providing a responsive environment, using strategies to increase the child's participation in activities (participation strategies), responding to the child to encourage elaborations (responsive elaboration), responding and eliciting elaborations (elicited elaboration), and systematically applying positive reinforcement to desired behavior (response-contingent instruction). Practitioners should decide on the appropriate strategy by gauging the specificity of the desired outcome in relation to the child's level of ability. The methods presented in this chapter are thus designed to facilitate one of the most useful and broadbased goals of early intervention.

REFERENCES

Allen, K.E., Hart, B., Buell, J.S., Harris, F.R., & Wolf, M.M. (1964). Effects of social reinforcement on isolate behavior of a nursery school child. *Child Development, 35,* 511–518.

Aries, P. (1962). *Centuries of childhood.* New York: Knopf.

Baer, D.M. (1978). The behavioral analysis of trouble. In K.E. Allen, V.J. Holm, & R.L. Schieflebusch (Eds.), *Early intervention—A team approach.* Baltimore: University Park Press.

Bailey, D.B., Harms, T., & Clifford, R.M. (1983). Matching changes in preschool environments to desired changes in child behavior. *Journal of the Division for Early Childhood, 7,* 61–68.

Bailey, D.B., & McWilliam, R.A. (1991). Normalizing early intervention. *Topics in Early Childhood Special Education, 10*(2), 33–47.

Bailey, D.B., & McWilliam, R.A., & Ware, W. B. (1991, in preparation). *The effects of same-age versus mixed-age grouping on social behavior in mainstreamed settings.* Chapel Hill, NC: Frank Porter Graham Child Development Center, University of North Carolina at Chapel Hill.

Blasco, P.M., & Bailey, D.B. (1991). Mastery motivation in mainstreamed infants and toddlers. *Journal of Early Intervention.*

Bloom, B.S. (1953). Thought processes in lectures and discussion. *Journal of General Education, 7,* 160–169.

Bloom, B.S. (1964). *Stability and change in human characteristics.* New York: Wiley.

Bloom, B.S. (1968). Learning for mastery. *Evaluation Comment, 1.*

Boggiano, A.K., Harckiewicz, J.M., Bessette, J.M., & Main, D.S. (1985). Increasing children's interest through performance-contingent reward. *Social Cognition, 3,* 400–411.

Bricker, D.D., & Carlson, L. (1980). An intervention approach for communicatively handicapped infants and young children. In D. Bricker (Ed.), *New directions for exceptional children: Language intervention with children* (No. 2). San Francisco: Jossey-Bass.

Brockman, L.M., Morgan, G.A., & Harmon, R.J. (1988). Mastery motivation and developmental delay. In T.D. Wachs & R. Sheehan (Eds.), *Assessment of young developmentally disabled children* (pp. 321–346). New York: Plenum Press.

Bruner, J.S. (1962). *The process of education.* Cambridge, MA: Harvard University Press.

Butler, R. (1989). Interest in the task and interest in peers' work in competitive and noncompetitive conditions: A developmental study. *Child Development, 60,* 562–570.

Carroll, J.B. (1963). A model of school learning. *Teachers College Record, 64,* 723–733.

Doyle, P.M., Wolery, M., Gast, D.L., Ault, M.J., & Wiley, K. (1990). Comparison of constant time delay and a system of least prompts in teaching preschoolers with developmental delays. *Research in Developmental Disabilities, 11,* 1–22.

Dunst, C.J. (1984). Infant visual attention under response-contingent and response-independent conditions. *Journal of Applied Developmental Psychology, 5,* 203–211.

Dunst, C.J., Cushing, P.J., & Vance, S.D. (1985). Response-contingent learning in profoundly handicapped infants: A social systems perspective. *Analysis and Intervention in Developmental Disabilties, 5,* 33–47.

Dunst, C.J., & McWilliam, R.A. (1988). Cognitive assessment of multiply handicapped young children. In T.D. Wachs & R. Sheehan (Eds.), *Assessment of young developmentally disabled children* (pp. 213–238). New York: Plenum Press.

Dunst, C.J., McWilliam R.A., & Holbert, K. (1986). Assessment of preschool classroom environments. *Diagnostique, 11,* 212–232.

Elkind, D. (1987). *Miseducation: Preschoolers at risk.* New York: Knopf.

Fisher, C.W., Filby, N.N., Marliave, R.S., Cahen, L.W., Dishaw, M.M., Moore, J.E., & Berliner, D.C. (1978). *Teaching behaviors, academic learning time, and student achievement.* Technical Report V-1, Final Report of Phase III-B, Beginning Teacher Evaluation Study. San Francisco: Far West Laboratory for Educational Research and Development.

Fuchs, L.S., & Deno, S.L. (1991). Paradigmatic distinctions between instructionally relevant measurement models. *Exceptional Children, 57,* 488–501.

Goetz, L., & Gee, K. (1987). Teaching visual attention in functional contexts: Acquisition and generalization of complex visual motor skills. *Journal of Visual Impairment and Blindness,* March, 115–117.

Guralnick, M.J. (1990). Social competence and early intervention. *Journal of Early Intervention, 14,* 3–14.

Halle, J.W., Marshall, A.M., & Spradlin, J.E. (1979). Time delay: A technique to increase language use and facilitate generalization in retarded children. *Journal of Applied Behavior Analysis, 12,* 431–440.

Hart, B., & Risley, T.R. (1975). Incidental teaching of language in the preschool. *Journal of Applied Behavior Analysis, 8,* 411–420.

Hart, B., & Risley, T.R. (1978). Promoting productive language through incidental teaching. *Education and Urban Society, 10,* 407–429.

Hart, B., & Risley, T.R. (1980). In vivo language

intervention: Unanticipated general effects. *Journal of Applied Behavior Analysis, 13,* 407–432.

Hayes, L.A., Ewy, R.D., & Watson, J.S. (1982). Attention as a predictor of learning in infants. *Journal of Experimental Child Psychology, 34,* 38–45.

Holdgrafer, G. (1987). Getting children to talk: A model of natural adult teaching/child learning strategies for language. *Canadian Journal of Exceptional Children,* Spring.

Hudgins, B.R. (1967). Attending and thinking in the classroom. *Psychology in the Schools, 4,* 211–216.

Hunt, J. McV. (1961). *Intelligence and experience.* New York: Ronald.

Jones, H.A., & Warren, S.F. (1991). Enhancing engagement in early language teaching. *TEACHING Exceptional Children, 23*(4), 48–50.

Krakow, J.B., & Kopp, C.B. (1983). The effects of developmental delay on sustained attention in young children. *Child Development, 54,* 1143–1155.

Krantz, P.J., & Risley, T.R. (1974). Behavioral ecology in the classroom. In K.D. O'Leary & S.G. O'Leary (Eds.), *Classroom management: The successful use of behavior modification* (2nd ed.) (pp. 349–367). New York: Pergamon Press.

Landry, S.H., & Chapieski, M.L. (1988). Visual attention during toy exploration in preterm infants: Effects of medical risk and maternal interactions. *Infant Behavior and Development, 11,* 187–204.

LeLaurin, K., & Risley, T.R. (1972). The organization of day-care environments: "Zone" versus "man-to-man" staff assignments. *Journal of Applied Behavior Analysis, 5,* 225–232.

Lewis, M., & Brooks-Gunn, J. (1981). Attention and intelligence. *Intelligence, 5,* 231–238.

MacDonald, J.D. (1985). Language through conversation: A model for intervention with language delayed persons. In S. Warren & A.K. Rogers-Warren (Eds.), *Teaching functional language.* Baltimore: University Park Press.

MacTurk, R.H., Hunter, F.T., McCarthy, M.E., Vietze, P.M., & McQuiston, S. (1985). Social mastery motivation in Down syndrome and nondelayed infants. *Topics in Early Childhood Special Education, 4*(4), 93–109.

Marliave, R., & Filby, N.N. (1985). Success rate: A measure of task appropriateness. In C.W. Fisher & D.C. Berliner (Eds.), *Perspectives on instructional time* (pp. 217–236). New York: Longman.

McGee, G.G., Daly, T., Izeman, S.G., Mann, L.H., & Risley, T.R. (1991). Use of classroom materials to promote preschool engagement. *TEACHING Exceptional Children, 23*(4), 44–47.

McWilliam, R.A. (1987). Fostering engagement. Unpublished monograph. Technical Assistance Project—Intervention Network, Family, Infant, and Preschool Program, Morganton, NC.

McWilliam, R.A. (1991a). Targeting teaching at children's use of time: Perspectives on preschoolers' engagement. *TEACHING Exceptional Children, 23*(4), 42–43.

McWilliam, R.A. (1991b). Pull-out versus integrated special services: Why are we still debating? *Tribune, 4*(9), 1–3.

McWilliam, R.A., & Bailey, D.B. (1991). Child engagement in infants, toddlers, and preschoolers with developmental disabilities. Chapel Hill: Frank Porter Graham Child Development Center, University of North Carolina. In progress.

McWilliam, R.A., Trivette, C.M., & Dunst, C.J. (1985). Behavior engagement as a measure of the efficacy of early intervention. *Analysis and Intervention in Developmental Disabilities, 5,* 33–45.

Montes, F., & Risley, T.R. (1975). Evaluating traditional day care practices: An empirical approach. *Child Care Quarterly, 4,* 208–215.

Ogbu, J.U. (1987). Cultural influences on plasticity in human development. In J.J. Gallagher & C.T. Ramey (Eds.), *The malleability of children* (pp. 155–170). Baltimore: Paul H. Brookes.

Ostrosky, M.M., & Kaiser, A.P. (1991). Preschool classroom environments that promote communication. *TEACHING Exceptional Children, 23*(4), 6–10.

Premack, D. (1959). Toward empirical behavior laws: I. Positive reinforcement. *Psychological Review, 66,* 219–233.

Quiltich, H.R., Christopherson, E.R., & Risley, T.R. (1977). The evaluation of children's play materials. *Journal of Applied Behavior Analysis, 10,* 501–502.

Rich, H.L., & Ross, S.M. (1989). Students' time on learning tasks in special education. *Exceptional Children, 55,* 508–515.

Rogers-Warren, A.K., & Warren, S.F. (1980). Mands for verbalization: Facilitating the display of newly trained language in children. *Behavior Modification, 4,* 361–382.

Ruff, H.A. (1986a). Attention and organization of behavior in high-risk infants. *Developmental and Behavioral Pediatrics, 7,* 298–301.

Ruff, H.A. (1986b). Components of attention during infants' manipulative exploration. *Child Development, 57,* 105–114.

Sameroff, A.J. (1975). Early influences on development. Fact or fancy? *Merrill-Palmer Quarterly, 18,* 65–79.

Santarcangelo, S., & Dyer, K. (1988). Prosodic aspects of motherese: Effects on gaze and responsiveness in developmentally disabled children. *Journal of Experimental Child Psychology, 46,* 406–418.

Sparling, J.J. (1990). Narrow and broad-spectrum curricula: Two necessary parts of the special child's program. *Infants and Young Children, 1*(4), 1–8.

Stone, L.J., Smith, H.T., & Murphy, L.B. (1973). The competent infant: Research and commentary. New York: Basic Books.

Sturmey, P., & Crisp, T. (1986). Classroom management. In J. Coupe & J. Porter (Eds.), *The education of children with severe learning difficulties: Bridging the gap between theory and practice.* London: Croom Helm.

Taylor, M. (1968). *Intercorrelations among three methods of estimating students' attention.* Report Series 29. Stanford: Stanford Center for Research on Teaching.

Twardosz, S., & Cataldo, M.F., & Risley, T.R. (1974). Open environment design for infant and toddler day care. *Journal of Applied Behavior Anlaysis, 7,* 529–546.

Warren, S.F., & Kaiser, A.P. (1988). Research in early language intervention. In S.L. Odom & M.B. Karnes (Eds.), *Early intervention for infants and children with handicaps: An empirical base* (pp. 89–108). Baltimore: Paul H. Brookes.

Warren, S.F., McQuarter, R.M., & Rogers-Warren, A.K. (1984). The effects of teacher mands and models on the speech of unresponsive language-delayed children. *Journal of Speech and Hearing Disorders, 47,* 42–52.

Watson, J.S. (1925). *Behaviorism.* New York: Norton.

Whaley, K.T., & Bennett, T.C. (1991). Promoting engagement in early childhood special education. *TEACHING Exceptional Children, 23*(4), 51–54.

White, R.W. (1959). Motivation reconsidered: The concept of competence. *Psychological Review, 66,* 297–333.

Yarrow, L.J., McQuiston, S., MacTurk, R.H., McCarthy, M.E., Klein, R.P., & Vietze, P.M. (1983). Assessment of mastery motivation during the first year of life: Contemporaneous and cross-age relationships. *Developmental Psychology, 19,* 159–171.

9

Promoting
Social
Competence

This chapter deals with social competence including what it is and how we as professionals can facilitate its development. While social competence is important for several reasons, two in particular stand out. First, all infants, toddlers, and preschoolers are social beings in a social world. Their actions, lack of actions, and their patterns of responding influence the individuals—family members, professionals, peers—around them. They, in turn, are influenced by the social behavior of the individuals in their environments. Second, social skills and the ability to interact appropriately and adaptively in social situations are critical to how infants and young children are perceived, the enjoyment others derive from them, the reciprocal friendships that develop, where they receive their education, and how they are included in the flow of community life. Thus, promoting social competence is a critical part of the early intervention and early education curriculum.

DEFINITION AND IMPLICATIONS OF SOCIAL COMPETENCE

Social competence has many definitions and descriptions originating from various theoretical perspectives (Bailey & Simeonsson, 1985; Dodge, Pettit, McClaskey, & Brown, 1986; Odom & McConnell, 1985). Guralnick (1990a) suggests that social competence is "the ability of young children to successfully and appropriately select and carry out their interpersonal goals" (p. 4). This definition, like most others, includes two important elements: "The child's *effectiveness* in influencing a peer's social behavior and *appropriateness* given a specific setting, context, and/or culture" (Odom, McConnell, & McEvoy, in press, p. 4).

Impact of Developmental Disabilities

Several assumptions about the definition of social competence and its two common ele-

ments are important. *The presence of developmental disabilities appears to have substantial impact on children's social competence.* The literature identifies several difficulties displayed by children with various developmental delays and disabilities. These include deficits in the ability to engage in group play with peers, use peers as resources, develop and maintain reciprocal friendships, and use the usual process involved in social exchanges (Guralnick, 1990a; Odom, McConnell, & McEvoy, in press). The absence of appropriate and effective social behavior directly affects how peers perceive and accept their classmates with disabilities (Strain, 1985). This assumption has several implications for intervention. First, most young children with developmental delays and disabilities will require intervention to promote their social competence. Second, attaining social competence is a complex process that may require careful intervention plans. Third, the task of promoting social competence must address many different skills, such as those involved in social play, interaction, and friendship formation. Professionals must assess children on a number of skills and plan interventions accordingly. Fourth, the deficits in social competence are likely to be displayed in many different contexts. Thus, the intervention plan must extend beyond early intervention classrooms to include the home and community.

Importance of Context

The social competence of specific social behavior or patterns of behavior is tied directly to the context or situation in which those acts occur. In other words, behaviors or skills that are effective and appropriate in one context may or may not be effective and appropriate in another situation. The skills needed by a preschooler to negotiate a conflict with a peer over ownership of a toy may be quite different from the skills that child needs to negotiate a conflict with his older brother or mother. Similarly, the skills a toddler needs to start an interaction with another toddler may be quite different from the skills needed to keep that interaction going during cooperative play. The implication of this assumption for intervention is fourfold. First, our assessment of the social skills of infants and young children must occur within the contexts in which those skills are needed, that is, various social situations. This requires extensive direct observation of infants and children in social situations (Comfort, 1988; Odom & McConnell, 1989). Second, the goals of intervention designed to promote social competence are likely to be highly varied and specific to particular situations. Although some goals, such as initiating interactions or playing socially, may be important for most young children, the exact nature of the skills that infants and children need are likely to vary depending on the social situations in which each individual lives. Third, our interventions must be designed so that they can be delivered within those contexts. As a result, individuals who interact frequently with the infant or child must be involved in the intervention process (Rosenberg & Robinson, 1988; Strain, 1981). Fourth, because effective and appropriate social behaviors vary from situation to situation, infants and children must learn to discriminate when and under what condition particular behaviors occur. Thus, our task involves teaching young children when particular responses will be effective and appropriate, in addition to teaching particular social behaviors. For example, rough-and-tumble play may be very appropriate and effective in increasing social contact with a father in the backyard, but it likely will not be effective nor appropriate during the family mealtime. Many social situations may vary only slightly in their discriminable features yet they may call for quite different social responses. For example, the strategies a young child can use to initiate interactions with a highly responsive peer may be quite different from the strategies the child must use with a less-responsive peer. Two peers may be of similar size, same gender, and be playing with the same toys; however, engaging in cooperative play with each may require different behaviors and perhaps different levels of persistence. Infants and young children must learn to discriminate between occasions when particular social behaviors will work and be perceived as acceptable and occasions when they will not. Part of our task is to help children learn these discriminations and adjust their behavior accordingly.

Changes in Appropriate Behavior over Time

Not only do various situations dictate the appropriate and effective social behavior, *the social behaviors required of infants and young children change over time.* Effective and appropriate social behaviors for infants are different from those for toddlers, just as effective and appropriate social skills for toddlers are different from those for preschoolers. For example, an infant may coo to maintain attention and interaction from an adult, but cooing may be less effective for toddlers, and quite ineffective for preschoolers. As children develop, they take on more active roles in interactions and more responsibility for starting and maintaining those interactions (Odom, 1983). This assumption holds several implications for intervention. First, our intervention goals must change as children acquire more social competence. As a result, goals related to social competence are probably appropriate for most infants and young children with developmental delays and disabilities. Second, our interventions must be sensitive to changes in children's behavior and be adjusted as children make progress. Third, early attention to social competence is important. While much of the literature on social competence deals with toddlers and preschool children, the social environment of infants is also important

(Rosenberg & Robinson, 1988). Thus, it is important to assist some families in interacting with their infants who have disabilities. This assistance may involve helping family members read the infant's social cues, providing them with consistent and responsive social signals, and helping them engage the child in taking turns.

Complexity of Skills

Further, *the behaviors or abilities that constitute social competence are multiple and complex.* Young children who are rated or identified as being socially competent display a variety of skills. Some of these include sharing frequently with peers, making suggestions to peers about play (called *play organizers*), providing affection and assistance to peers, responding consistently to social initiations from peers, refraining from negative behaviors such as crying or aggression, and displaying well-developed toy play skills (Tremblay, Strain, Hendrickson, & Shores, 1981; Strain, 1985). Other skills include entering peer play groups, extending play activities, and developing a preference for a particular peer that is reciprocated by that peer (i.e., forming friendships) (Odom, McConnell, & McEvoy, in press). It is likely, however, that none of these skills alone will produce high ratings of social competence. For example, being skilled in toy play may set the stage for children to interact with peers; however, unless the toy play is accompanied by play organizers or responsiveness to social initiations, the child may appear socially withdrawn. Thus, professionals must provide intervention on a wide range of social skills that depict social competence. In addition, however, other nonsocial attributes such as being well-dressed, attractive, and having athletic skill also contribute to high ratings of social competence (Strain, 1985). While some of these variables, such as being attractive, are not easily addressed

through intervention, the findings probably indicate that attention to dress, developing motor skills, and being well-groomed are important for young children with disabilities.

Involvement of Skills from Other Domains

In addition, *social competence requires contributions and integration of skills from other domains.* As with most domains of development, social skills involve behaviors from other domains, particularly communication, play, and cognitive skills. For example, deficits in play and communication skills will greatly affect young children's abilities to engage in group play with their peers. Interventions designed to address children's social competence must also address the skills from other areas that impinge on children's social behavior. This requires careful assessment of the child's total behavioral repertoire as well as the use of those skills in social situations.

Attaining social competence is a complex process that is affected negatively by the presence of disabilities. Social competence is related to the various social contexts in which children find themselves, and the skills needed to behave effectively and appropriately vary from situation to situation. The demands and expectations of the social environment change as children get older, requiring more advanced and sophisticated social responses. Social competence is influenced by and must be viewed in light of skills from other domains of development.

The following section of this chapter addresses the issues of caregiver-infant/child interactions because the relationships formed from those interactions are central to children's social competence. The final section of the chapter addresses peer interactions and relationships, and particularly interventions to promote social play, prosocial interactions, and friendship formation.

CAREGIVER-INFANT/CHILD INTERACTIONS AND RELATIONSHIPS

As noted earlier, infants are social beings born into a social world. During the first months of life, a large proportion of the infant's social environment frequently is the family, and a large body of literature addresses the topic of parent-infant (frequently mother-infant) interaction (Marfo, 1988). In this section, the rationale for attending to the parent-infant/child interactions and relationships are described. Infants' interactive behaviors are identified, and issues related to assessment and intervention in parent-infant/child interactions are described. Throughout this section, the term *caregiver-infant/child interaction* is used to depict exchanges that occur between parents or other primary care providers and infants or young children. The term *caregiver* is used rather than *parent* for two reasons. First, many primary caregivers may include guardians, foster parents, or other adults as well as parents. Second, the recommendations frequently are applicable to adults other than parents, especially when the infant is in a group care situation such as day care.

Rationale for Attending to Caregiver-Infant/Child Interactions

Several reasons can be suggested for assessing caregiver-infant/child interactions and relationships. Some of these reasons are based on logic, others on research. Some reasons apply to caregivers and infants generally, and others apply specifically to situations when infants and children have disabilities.

First, *early caregiver-infant/child interactions and relationships may influence children's development.* Most theories of general child development, and particularly of social and emotional development, propose that early caregiver-infant/child relationships influence children's development and behav-

ior (Barnard & Kelly, 1990). These relationships, however, are not uni-directional (i.e., from the caregiver to the infant) nor are they static (i.e., occurring within a stable and unchanging context). In reality, the infant and caregiver influence one another, and subsequent interactions are based on their history of previous interactions (Sameroff & Fiese, 1990). Thus, the social and developmental repertoires of infants and children are constantly changing based on their interactions with the environment as well as on their maturing physiologies.

Second, *secure attachment between caregivers and infants appears to be related to other positive social outcomes.* Attachment is defined as "an affectional tie that one person forms to another specific person or persons, binding them together in space and enduring over time" (Ainsworth, 1973, p. 1). Some characteristics of attachment over the early childhood years are displayed in Box 9.1. The quality of caregiver-infant attachment appears to be related to the sensitivity and responsivity of the caregiver to the infant's signals and cues (Beckwith, 1990). Further, early attachment relationships appear to influence personality development. For example, securely attached infants are likely to "become 2-year-olds who are more enthusiastic, persistent, and likely to elicit and accept their mother's help in problem-solving tasks and show less distress and more positive affect in those tasks than infants who were rated as insecure" (Beckwith, p. 60). Also, higher levels of security in the attachment relationship appear to be related to more cooperative and compliant behaviors (Beckwith). Since attachment appears to be based, at least in part, on the early social exchanges, attention to those interactions to increase the security of the attachment relationship is an important intervention goal. For information on the assessment of attachment, see Teti and Nakagawa (1990).

Third, *disabilities may reduce the infant's capability to engage in rewarding and satis-*

BOX 9.1   Some attainments in the normal development of attachment

Age	Characteristics of Attachment Relationship
0–3 months	Often referred to as the phase of "undiscriminating social responsiveness" (Ainsworth, 1973). Infant uses certain behaviors (visual fixation and tracking, listening, cooing, grasping, crying, smiling) to orient to the environment and test contingencies. Infant is more likely to respond to a human face than to a nonhuman figure but may not be able to discriminate between faces.
2–6 months	Infant responds differentially to familiar and unfamiliar faces. Begins with differentiated smiling and vocalization. Later in this phase, infant cries when attachment figure leaves the room.
7–24 months	Infant actively seeks out proximity and contact with attachment figure. Behaviors include following, approaching, and clinging. Child can take action to secure proximity to attachment figure.
24–36 months	Child still seeks contact but is more likely to be satisfied with looking and verbal communication with attachment figure without requiring physical contact.
36–48 months	Child is more willing to be left for brief periods if left with friendly stranger.
48–60 months	Child finally realizes that there is "a relative invariant in their relationship between parent and child that is not dependent on physical proximity or contact" (Marvin, 1977, p. 39).

Note: From Ainsworth (1973), Bowlby (1969), and Marvin (1977).

---

fying interactions. Over the past two decades, many studies have identified the effects of mental retardation, sensory impairments, and physical disabilities on the infant's capability to engage in caregiver-infant interactions (Hanson, 1984). Examples of such effects include decreased responsiveness to others, less positive affect, delayed or irregular smiling, variable state regulation, fewer initiations, inconsistent responses to others' behavior, and less skill in discriminating the social cues of others (Barnard & Kelly, 1990). Such effects may not be anticipated by families, may interfere with the development of the attachment relationship, and may demand considerable interactive skills on the part of families. Many families appear to react to and learn to interact with

their infants who have disabilities with relatively little assistance and in short order. Other families may require some assistance in reading their infant's cues, waiting for the infant to initiate, and engaging in responsive turn taking (Marfo, 1988).

Fourth, *the presence of disabilities may lead to discomfort and interactive difficulties on the part of caregivers.* From the research literature, it is clear that caregiver-infant/child interactions involving children who are at risk for or display disabilities differ from those involving typically developing children (Barnard & Kelly, 1990; Rosenberg & Robinson, 1988). For example, mothers of infants with disabilities may assume more directive roles during interactions (Cunningham, Reuler, Blackwell, &

Deck, 1981). However, the reasons for the differences in the interactions, the function of the differences, and the extent to which those differences positively or negatively affect the infant are issues of debate (Rosenberg & Robinson, 1988). Nonetheless, some families may be uncomfortable interacting with their infants or may express dissatisfaction from those interactions. The significance of caregiver-infant interactions and the long-term nature of the relationship underscore the importance of helping families become as comfortable and satisfied with the interactions as possible. Further, many variables other than infant-interactive skills (e.g., social support, stress, family functioning) influence caregiver-child interactions and play (Barnard & Kelly, 1990; Dunst & Trivett, 1988). The logic of this rationale is that individuals are more likely to engage in situations or interactions that are comfortable and satisfying. As noted, most caregivers interact appropriately with their infants who have disabilities; however, they may or may not feel comfortable or satisfied. Therefore, in some cases, the interventionist should assist caregivers in finding satisfying and comfortable styles of interacting. In other cases, the interventionist needs to affirm and reassure family members that they are engaging in appropriate and effective interactions.

Fifth, *mutually satisfying interactions may be the base or context from which other interventions occur.* Although infants and young children learn a great deal from their interactions with the inanimate environment (Wachs, 1979), they also learn a great deal from their social environment. Many necessary interventions (e.g., feeding programs, toilet training, communication skills intervention, physical therapy) are conducted or mediated by family members. This rationale suggests that these interventions are more likely to be effective if they are implemented in a context in which caregivers and infants engage in mutually satisfying interaction patterns. In fact, some interventions programs (Bromwich, 1981; MacDonald & Gillette, 1988) are based on the notion that establishing mutually satisfying interaction patterns is a prerequisite or a necessary condition for implementing other interventions designed to promote cognitive and communicative development.

Description of Caregiver-Infant/Child Interactive Behavior

Social and interactive behaviors, like other skills, can be conceptualized as forms and functions (see chapter 5). The forms are the actual behaviors, and the functions are the effects of the behaviors. With interactive behavior, both components are important. The forms are the behaviors displayed by infants or children and caregivers during social interactions, and the functions are the effects of those behaviors on the interactive partners.

Many behaviors by even very young infants appear to result in interactive behavior by caregivers. These include crying; vocalizing and cooing; rapid movement of the arms and legs, reaching, shifts in muscle tone, and general increases and decreases in motor activity; eye contact, gaze, gaze shifts (looking at and then away from the partner); burst-pause episodes or periods of activity followed by brief cessation of the activity (e.g., regular sucking); smiling, scowling, and other facial expressions (Odom, 1983). With many infants, these behaviors are used independently and in combination, and they can occur for varied durations (e.g., extended gaze versus fleeting eye contact) and varying levels of intensity (a slight smile versus a broad and full smile).

However, what is important about these behaviors is their effect on the adult (parent/guardian, therapist, interventionist). These behaviors appear to serve many functions or effects. Some important functions are initiating or starting interactions, responding to the interactive behavior of others, increasing or decreasing the intensity of interactions, sustaining interactions, and terminating or stopping interactions (Musselwhite, 1986).

Two things are important about these forms and functions. First, many of the behaviors can be used to fulfill these functions. For example, an infant can vocalize, cry, increase motor activity, gaze, or smile and as a result, start an interaction. While it may be difficult to determine whether the infant intended to start an interaction, the fact remains that the occurrence of many of these behaviors results in the initiation of interactions. Similarly, several different behaviors can be used to increase the intensity of interactions. For example, increasing motor activity, gazing intently at the partner, and smiling can be used to make the interactions more intense, for example, resulting in more rapid turns or more focused and exaggerated behavior. Each function can be displayed by many different behaviors on the part of the infant and caregiver.

Second, many of the behaviors can be used for multiple functions. For example, whimpering can be used to start an interaction, decrease its intensity, or terminate it. The effect of any of the behaviors depends in large part on the immediate context, or what has just occurred in the interaction, and on the ability of the partner to interpret the infant's behavior and make appropriate adjustments.

Since there are multiple interactive behaviors and multiple interactive functions, the manner in which they are used is important. Several dimensions of interactions can be used to identify high- and low-quality caregiver-infant/child interactions. First, high-quality interactions are characterized by turn taking and reciprocity (Field, 1978). Each partner in the interaction is active and then passive, or is a sender and then a receiver of interactive messages, or is the performer and then the nonperformer. Further, within the turns, it appears that each partner recognizes and responds appropriately to the intent or message of the other. For example, if the infant shifts her gaze and appears to be saying, "Let's slow down a bit," the caregiver appears to understand this, delaying and providing a less salient social response such as a lower tone of vocalization. The behavior of each partner is attuned to and contingent on the behavior of the other (Stern, 1984). Of course, the nature of turns changes over time. Initially, infants tend to assume a more passive role but over time they become more active and assume more control over the course of the interactions and the nature of the turns. On the other hand, low-quality interactions are characterized by failure on the part of at least one partner to allow the other a turn and/or to consistently read and reciprocate the message of the partner.

Second, high-quality interactions are characterized by synchrony, rhythmicity, and smoothness (Brazelton, Koslowski, & Main, 1974; Field, 1978). It appears that the two interactors each understand the other's direction, and each behavior or turn is responded to easily, quickly, and correctly by the partner. In fact, the interactive behavior has been compared to a dance where the partners know the steps and moves. Low-quality interactions are characterized as jerky, out of sync, and irregular.

Third, high-quality interactions are characterized by frequent game playing (Field, 1979; McCollum, 1988), including informal games like "I'm gonna get you," "Peek-a-boo," and "So big." Initially, caregivers tend to initiate and assume the major active role in the games. With the passage of time, the infant or young child begins to initiate the games and assume the role of directing its execution. These games tend to be highly repetitive, or played over and over by the caregiver and infant/child.

Fourth, high-quality interactions appear to be pleasurable. Both parties of the interaction appear to enjoy the interaction; that is, they smile, laugh, and readily repeat sequences. There is an absence of fussy or agitated behavior on the part of the infant or child and an absence of boredom or irritation on the part of the caregiver. Low-quality interactions, however, are not characterized by displays of pleasure and include fussiness or crying, repeated attempts to terminate interaction, and irritation.

Fifth, high-quality interactions are characterized by change over time as caregivers and infants adapt and adjust to one another (Barnard & Kelly, 1990). While much remains to be learned about the nature of this change and the forces that drive it, Sander (1969) proposed a five-stage model of adaptation. He suggested that at each stage, the caregiver and infant adopt different patterns of interacting and different rules that govern those patterns. Rothbart (1984) provided a description of those five stages, as shown in Box 9.2.

Thus, infants and caregivers alike display many behaviors that are used to fulfill multiple functions during the interactions. These behaviors and functions result in high-quality interactions when there is regular turn taking, when the exchange of turns is smooth and predictable, when games are included, when pleasure is expressed by both parties, and when both parties adapt and adjust over

---

BOX 9.2   Developmental issues identified by Sander

Issue	Title	Span of months	Prominent infant behaviors that became coordinated with maternal activities
1	Initial regulation	1–3	Basic infant activities concerned with biological processes related to feeding, sleeping, elimination, postural maintenance, including stimulus needs for quieting and arousal
2	Reciprocal exchange	4–6	Smiling behavior that extends to full motor and vocal involvement in sequences of affectively spontaneous back-and-forth exchanges. Activities such as spoon feeding, dressing become reciprocally coordinated
3	Initiative	7–9	Activities initiated by infant to secure a reciprocal social exchange with mother or to manipulate environment on his/her own selection
4	Focalization	10–13	Activities by which infant determines the availability of mother on his/her specific initiative; tends to focalize need meeting demands on the mother
5	Self-assertion	14–20	Activities in which infant widens the determination of his/her own behavior, often in the face of maternal opposition

Note: From M. K. Rothbart (1984). Social development. In M. J. Hanson (Ed.) *Atypical infant development.* Austin, TX: PRO-ED. (p. 213).

time. Such interactions are thought to facilitate positive caregiver-infant/child relationships, provide each with the feeling of efficacy, and give the young child the building blocks for later peer- and adult-child interactions.

Assessment of Caregiver-Infant/Child Interactions

Assessment of caregiver-infant/child interactions can produce a couple of important types of information. The assessment information can be used to determine whether the interactive patterns are of high quality and appear satisfying to caregivers and whether those patterns appear to provide the infant or child with a facilitating and responsive environment. In situations where caregivers are not satisfied or where the interactions do not appear to promote development, then interventions related to the interaction patterns may be indicated. The assessment information can also be used to get information about the ability of family members to implement other interventions during interactive sequences and about the opportunities for such interventions in those sequences.

However, the professional should be aware that assessing and intervening in caregiver-child interactions should be done with care. The subject of how caregivers interact with their infant or child is quite personal, and some may use their perception of the interaction to judge their adequacy. Simple assessment of the interaction patterns may lead to misinterpretation on the part of the caregivers. They may conclude that (a) they are doing things incorrectly, (b) they are in some way inadequate, or (c) the professional perceives them as not caring for their infant/child. Thus, caution is advised. Clearly, if caregivers express concern about interacting with the infant/child, then professionals should attend to this concern and provide the appropriate assurance and/or assistance.

Assessment of caregiver-infant/child interaction has received a considerable amount of research attention. Barnard and Kelly (1990) suggest that the assessment of interactions for intervention purposes should draw from that research but should be used cautiously. They recommend three guidelines for conducting such assessments: (a) the characteristics and behavior of the infant and caregiver should be considered, (b) the contingent or reciprocal aspects of the interactions should be assessed, and (c) the adaptation of the caregiver and child to one another should be assessed over time. The assessment procedures frequently involve direct observation and/or the use of rating scales. The information that is obtained can be substantially influenced by the setting in which the observation occurs, the length and number of observations, and the activities (e.g., play, diapering, feeding) being observed (Farran, Clark, & Ray, 1990).

Several assessment protocols and observational procedures have been described. Among others, these include the *Greenspan-Lieberman Observation System for Assessment of Caregiver-Infant Interaction during Semi-Structured Play* (Greenspan & Lieberman, 1980); *Interaction Rating Scales* (Clark & Siefer, 1985); *Interpersonal Behavior Construct System* (Kogan, 1980); *Maternal Behavior Rating Scale* (Mahoney, Finger, & Powell, 1985); *Nursing Child Assessment Satellite Training (NCAST) Teaching and Feeding Scales* (Barnard, 1979); *Parent Behavior Progression* (Bromwich, 1981); *Parent-Caregiver Involvement Scale* (Farran, Kasari, Jay, & Comfort, 1986); *Social Interaction Assessment/Intervention* (McCollum, 1984); and *Teaching Skills Inventory* (Rosenberg, Robinson, & Beckman, 1984). Many of these measures were developed for research purposes, but others were developed to assist in the intervention process. Consult Barnard and Kelly (1990), Comfort (1988), Farran et al. (1990), and Rosenberg and Robinson

(1988) for complete discussions of these measures and of the assessment of caregiver-infant/child interactions.

Intervention for Promoting Positive Caregiver-Infant/Child Interactions

As noted earlier, differences have been found in the interactive exchanges between caregivers and their infants with disabilities as compared to caregivers and infants without disabilities. While many of these differences are undoubtedly due to the infant's behavior (e.g., lack of responsiveness, inability to discriminate the social cues of others, lessened positive affect, and less distinct and conventional interactive signals), it is unclear whether the noted differences are necessarily disordered and inappropriate. In fact, in some cases, it may be that families have made appropriate and adaptive adjustments to the interactive behaviors of their infants.

Considerable research correlates the presence of responsive, contingent, and reciprocal behavior on the part of caregivers with positive outcomes of typically developing children (Barnard & Kelly, 1990). The interaction patterns of caregivers and infants and children with disabilities should be characterized by the high-quality dimensions noted earlier. Specifically, the interactions should include (a) turn taking and reciprocity; (b) synchrony, rhythmicity, and smoothness; (c) frequent game playing; (d) displays of pleasure and satisfaction; and (e) adaptation and adjustment over time. Thus, the goal of intervention in relation to caregiver-child interactions is to have these five characteristics typify most of the interactions that occur between caregivers and their infants or young children with developmental delays and disabilities.

Assumptions Related to Intervention with Caregiver-Infant/Child Interactions   Before discussing intervention strategies, we will consider four assumptions that should

guide the use of those intervention strategies. First, *intervention should be designed based on the patterns of responding*. Not all interactions between caregivers and young children will include all the high-quality characteristics listed previously. Isolated exchanges between caregivers and infants or young children may not be reciprocal, may not be rhythmic, may not include game playing, or may not be pleasurable. Thus, observing an unpleasant or nonreciprocal exchange between a caregiver-infant dyad on one occasion does not mean that intervention is warranted. Rather, attention to and intervention with caregiver-infant interactions should occur when these quality characteristics are not typical of the interaction patterns. The basis for determining whether the interaction patterns require changes must be the caregiver's expressions of concern and/or repeated observations and assessments of low-quality interaction patterns.

Second, *the professional should recognize that factors outside the interaction may influence caregiver behavior*. As noted, the amount of stress caregivers experience, the amount of social support they receive, the nature of the caregiving demands, and the expectations they are attempting to meet—sometimes imposed by professionals—all may influence how they interact with their infant. It may be appropriate to focus the intervention on broader issues such as seeking social support, reducing the stress, or easing caregiving demands (Dunst, 1985). Addressing such issues may allow the interaction patterns to become more facilitating and include more high-quality characteristics. If families are highly stressed and have little social support, suggesting ways of altering their caregiver-child interactions may result in increased stress and thus be counterproductive.

Third, *the goal of intervening in caregiver-infant/child interactions is to promote more positive and facilitating caregiver-in-*

fant relationships. Assessment and intervention must be viewed in the broader context of the caregiver-infant/child relationship. While interactions are important elements of that relationship, they probably do not constitute the total picture. An assessment of the caregiver-infant interaction conducted in a clinic in an artificial play session may not provide a valid view of their relationship. The day-in-and-day-out interactions in the home are a better index of the nature of the relationship. Designing interventions to change interaction patterns must be based on extensive contact and observations of the caregiver and child in their natural contexts. Interventions designed with the knowledge of the regular routines of the family are likely to be more sensitive to the caregiver-infant relationship and the other demands on families. As a result, those interventions are more likely to be implemented and produce lasting changes in the relationship.

Fourth, *professionals should establish a supportive relationship with the family before intervening on caregiver-child interactions.* Most interventions will be more readily accepted and implemented when the family views the professional as knowledgeable, caring, and helpful and perceives a need for invention. These perceptions are especially important when the professional is making suggestions about changes in caregiver-infant/child interactions. Appropriate recommendations about changes in caregiver behavior during interactions should be based on extensive observation and information. Usually, such information can be obtained only by interacting with the family on multiple occasions and establishing positive rapport with the family. As noted, caregiver-infant/child interactions are highly personal and families may use such information to judge their adequacy. The professional needs to understand how families view their interactions and how they function before suggesting changes that are likely to be per-

ceived accurately and implemented appropriately. The professional who does not have a trusting and supportive relationship with the family will find it difficult to accomplish these goals.

Guidelines for Implementing Interventions with Caregiver-Infant/Child Interactions

Several intervention programs have been developed to facilitate positive caregiver-child interactions and relationships (Seitz & Provence, 1990). These programs and related issues are discussed in several sources (Affleck, McGrade, McQueeny, & Allen, 1982; Allen, Affleck, McGrade, & McQueeny, 1984; Bromwich, 1981; Mahoney, 1988; Mahoney & Powell, 1988). From these programs and related research, several guidelines can be proposed.

Mahoney and Powell (1986) suggest professionals should assist caregivers in acquiring and using three skills. First, *caregivers must be aware of and understand the developmental functioning of their children.* This skill does not mean that they can state their child's developmental age, but rather that they understand how their child interacts with and acts on the social and physical environment. They should understand how their child initiates social interactions, communicates wants and needs, and manipulates toys and other objects during play. This skill also can involve some level of understanding about sequences of development, for example, that children initially behave as though objects do not exist when they are not perceptually present before they understand that objects exist even when absent. Professionals can serve two important roles: (a) pointing out how the child interacts with people and objects, and (b) explaining how the child's behavior reflects the current level of functioning and what changes can be anticipated in the near future.

Second, *caregivers must be aware of and sensitive to the interests and communicative intents of the child.* This involves the caregivers reading the child's interactive and communicative signals. For example, caregivers need to know what signals the child uses to indicate a desire for an interaction to continue or stop or a request for assistance or to get objects. Caregivers should also recognize what activities and routines the child enjoys, know when the child is hungry or needs caregiving, and realize how the child expresses enjoyment and displeasure. Professionals can help caregivers in observing their children and reading or interpreting their children's interactive and communicative signals. Also, professionals can give caregivers a framework for understanding how new skills will emerge, assist them in providing consistent routines, and help them develop strategies for consoling and comforting distressed children.

Third, Mahoney and Powell (1986) suggest that *caregivers should be responsive to the ongoing behavior of children.* Of particular importance is that caregivers note and respond to children's ongoing focus of attention, follow their lead during play and social interactions, and elaborate and expand the activity and interactions in ways that promote development. Caregivers should respond to child behavior rather than bringing an agenda for teaching particular skills to a given play activity. The professional's role is to help families interpret the activities of children and identify ways to be responsive to the child's lead rather than bringing their own teaching agenda to the interaction or play sequence.

These three strategies proposed by Mahoney and Powell (1986) are consistent with those discussed by Dunst et al. (1987), as described in chapter 6. Specifically, these strategies call for adults to (a) be sensitive to the behavior of the child, (b) view the child's behavior as an intent to interact, (c) be responsive to the child's behavior, (d) encourage the child's ongoing interactions with the social and physical environment, and (e) encourage the child to display more complex

interactions and behaviors. In addition to these general guidelines, Mahoney and Powell (1986) present several specific strategies for promoting children's development in the context of caregiver-child interaction. Among others, these include (a) playing frequently with the child, (b) manipulating objects and engaging in interactions that are similar to the child's, (c) taking short rather than long turns in the interaction, (d) waiting for the child to take a turn so that an even balance of turns exists, (e) imitating the child, (d) decreasing caregivers' mands (non-yes/no commands or requests), (e) increasing the length of turn-taking interactions, and (f) matching the pace of the child's actions. Field (1982) suggests similar strategies including (a) simplifying and slowing down caregivers' behavior, (b) promoting imitation, (c) repeating phrases, (d) pausing or producing silence by the caregiver, and (e) game playing. MacDonald and Gillette (1988) present similar recommendations for promoting interactions and social play that will lead to acquisition and use of communicative goals. A list of recommendations concerning how to promote social play during caregiver-child interactions that can lead to communication skills is presented in Box 9.3. In addition to engaging in these strategies during interactive play sessions, caregivers should be encouraged to make caregiving activities (e.g., diapering, bathing, and feeding) interactive events. As illustrated in Chapter 6, Venn and Wolery (in press) trained caregivers in a mainstreamed day-care program to engage in game playing during diaper-changing routines. When the caregivers engaged in more game playing during diaper changes, the infants became more responsive and initiated more games.

The preceding section describes strategies caregivers can use to promote positive interactions. A legitimate question is, "How does the professional help caregivers do these things?" Several common approaches are used. Of course, the determination of what

BOX 9.3   Strategies for building social play for communication

Strategy	Why It Is Important
Tell yourself you are important	No professional can influence a child as much as a parent who has already taught the child many skills.
Play in routines	Predictable play sequences allow child to learn new things in old, safe context.
Take turns	A give-and-take habit can be used across all learning situations; thus teach a child how to socially use new knowledge.
	Child may learn best from watching and acting, neither alone.
Wait; act once, then wait and show expectation	A delayed child needs considerable time to respond. Waiting also shows you something new from the child.
Imitate actions and sounds	Imitation maintains child's attention and serves as a ready interaction starter. Imitation allows the parent to feel the child's actions and thus to learn more about the child.
Progressive match: Act like child, then add one step	Child learns best from models he can perform.
Be child-like: Play in child's world as the child does	Child can imitate and understand better if you act like her. You can better read intentions if you copy her actions.
Be animated and interesting	Adults must compete with natural distractions and be more interesting than the nearest temptations.
Respond acceptingly to child's contact	A child will stay with you if you accept him.
Show genuine emotions; affection and displeasure. Enjoy playing with the child	Little social learning can proceed if interactions are not personally motivating.

Note: From J. D. MacDonald & Y. Gillette (1988). Communicating partners: A conversational model for building parent-child relationships with handicapped children. In K. Marfo (Ed.), *Parent-child interaction and developmental disabilities: Theory, research, and intervention.* Praeger Publishers, New York, an imprint of Greenwood Publishing Group, Inc., 1988, p. 227. Reprinted with permission; all rights reserved.

needs to be changed should be based on a repeated assessment of the interaction patterns and of the child's current skills and interactive abilities (Dunst & McWilliam, 1988; Field, 1982; McCollum, 1986). After the assessment is completed, the intervention strategies are fairly straightforward. These These involve telling caregivers how to adjust their interaction patterns, showing them how by having the professional demonstrate the change during interactions with the child, watching the caregivers attempt to adjust their behavior in the interactions, and providing feedback. This has been referred to as *interactive coaching* (Field, 1982). Frequently, caregivers wear earphones to hear the professional's suggestions while the interaction occurs. In such instruction, the professional should be careful to emphasize what the caregiver should do rather than what not to do. For example, Brown-Gorton and Wolery (1988) wanted to decrease the frequency with which mothers engaged in manding behaviors, or providing directive commands and questions to the child, during play sessions. The interventionist provided verbal directions to the parents to imitate their child and provided models of verbal and nonverbal imitation. As a result, the mothers increased their imitative behavior and decreased their manding behavior without ever being told to do less manding.

In addition, professionals can videotape themselves and the caregivers interacting with the infant. By reviewing the videotapes with caregivers, the professional can point out the relationship between positive caregiver behavior and the effects on infant behaviors. Such demonstrations frequently are useful in showing caregivers how to change their interactions and read their infants' interactive signals. Videotaping has also been used as a supplement and permanent model of how to complete complex handling procedures for implementing physical therapy goals in caregiver-infant interactions. For example, Woodson (1990) videotaped a physical therapist completing handling procedures with the infant, reviewed the procedures with the parents using a demonstration, observation, and feedback sequence, and then left the videotape with the family, encouraging them to refer to it during the week. As a result, the family implemented the procedures accurately with the child.

Summary of Caregiver-Child/Infant Interactions

When infants or young children have developmental delays or disabilities, caregiver-infant/child interactions are important because they may influence children's development and promote secure attachment that leads to positive social outcomes. Further, the infants' ability to interact may be impaired by the disability, their families may be dissatisfied and uncomfortable with their interactions, and interactions may be the context for implementing other interventions. Infants engage in many different behaviors to fulfill interactive functions, and high-quality interactions are characterized by (a) frequent turn taking and reciprocity; (b) synchrony, rhythmicity, and smoothness; (c) frequent game playing; (e) displays of enjoyment and pleasure; and (e) adjustment and adaptation over time.

The assessment of caregiver-child interactions should be conducted with care and should occur in natural contexts. Interventions to promote positive caregiver-child interactions should be designed only when the patterns of interaction consistently appear to be of low quality, when other factors such as caregiver stress are addressed, when the interventionist understands the caregiver-child relationship in its natural contexts, and when the professional and family have established a supportive relationship. Numerous intervention strategies can promote more positive interaction patterns between families and their offspring.

PEER INTERACTIONS AND RELATIONSHIPS

This section first presents the rationale for promoting child-child interactions and relationships, and then describes two types of social skills: peer interactions and social play. Finally, the section identifies procedures for assessing social skills and describes interventions for increasing child-child interactions and friendships.

Rationale for Focusing on Child-Child Interactions

Among the many rationales for focusing intervention efforts on child-child interaction skills, three are most applicable. First, *peer interaction and relationships are life-long skills that are important for adequate adjustment and development.* Much of the child's schooling will occur in social situations with peers, and most adults work in situations where contact with others is a regular event. The child's ability to interact in appropriate and effective ways with peers will be central to the perceptions others have, the extent of being accepted in social groups, the likelihood of being educated with nondisabled peers, access to community leisure activities, and access to and continued involvement in work opportunities as an adult. Thus, acquisition and use of social skills and interactional abilities is central to a child's adjustment and long-term outcomes. As a result, this is a critical curricular domain in early intervention programs.

Second, *simple contact with peers does not necessarily result in acquisition and use of appropriate and effective social skills.* While it is desirable for children with disabilities to have repeated and sustained contact with their peers who do not have disabilities (Guralnick, 1990b), it is clear from multiple sources that simple contact is not sufficient to produce acceptable social skills. As a result, careful assessment and intervention to promote the acquisition and use of peer interaction and other social skills is needed.

Third, *peer interactions are a useful context for learning other skills.* One of the primary rationales behind the preschool main-

streaming movement is that children with disabilities will be able to learn from their nondisabled peers (Peck & Cooke, 1983). This learning occurs through imitation of peers and through the content of social interactions and social play. However, unless the child with disabilities is attuned to the behavior of peers and is engaged with them meaningfully, such learning is not likely to occur. Further, many useful intervention strategies for social skills (Kohler & Strain, 1990) and communication skills (Goldstein & Ferrell, 1987; Goldstein & Wickstrom, 1986) are peer-mediated interventions. These interventions involve peers directly in promoting skill development of the child with disabilities.

Description of Important Peer Interactions and Social Play Skills

Two major types of social skills appear important for young children and have received considerable research attention. These two types of skills are peer social interactions and social play, and each is described briefly in this section.

Peer Interactions   As with caregiver-infant interactions, peer interactions can be characterized as forms and functions. In fact, many of the forms and functions that are used during caregiver-infant interactions are also used during child-child interactions. Commonly used forms by young children during peer interactions include making vocalizations, using proximity (i.e., getting near a peer), touching a peer or otherwise making appropriate physical contact, giving toys or other materials to peers, receiving toys or other materials from peers (sharing), and looking at peers.

The important functions are securing the peer's attention, initiating interactions, responding to others' initiations, sustaining or maintaining interactions, shifting the focus of interactions, and terminating interactions. In addition to these general functions, there are some specific functions that are valued in our society. These include such things as giving and soliciting affection, giving and soliciting assistance, sharing, and resolving conflicts. These specific functions occur within the context of the general functions. For example, a child may see a peer needing assistance, approach that peer, and provide assistance, thereby initiating an interaction. However, the assistance could also be provided as a response to the initiation of the peer who needs help (i.e., calling to the child and asking for assistance).

As with caregiver-infant interactions, each of these functions can be performed by multiple behaviors. For example, a child can start an interaction by speaking to a peer, moving close to a peer, handing a toy to a peer, or touching a peer. Likewise, frequently a single behavior can be used to fulfill multiple functions. For example, handing a toy to a peer may be used to secure attention, start an interaction, shift the focus of the interaction, or sustain the interaction. Further, the ways in which forms are used to fulfill functions are categorized as positive or negative. For example, touching a peer in a positive way to start an interaction may involve tapping a peer on the leg, putting an arm around a peer, or tickling a peer to start a rough-and-tumble interaction. However, touching a peer in negative ways can also be used to start an interaction. For example, hitting or pinching a peer may be used to start a negative interaction. This variety of important elements has made the development of observational codes a challenging task. However, a set of common definitions for measuring the interactive behavior of young children is shown in Box 9.4.

A socially competent child can effectively and appropriately cause each function to occur and can use multiple behaviors to exercise each function. Over time and with appropriate experiences, children's peer interactions become more complex. This complexity is displayed in a number of ways. The child can use more behaviors to fulfill each function, substituting a different behavior when one behavior is not successful in fulfilling a function. For example, if a child calls to another to initiate an interaction and that is not successful, the child may move closer and touch the peer. The various functions can be sequenced together in longer and more varied chains of interactions. For example, the child can secure a peer's attention, start an interaction, shift the focus of the interaction, and keep that interaction going for multiple turns. The specific functions such as giving assistance and sharing can be used in more varied contexts and in more varied ways. The increased complexity is seen in the ability to interact simultaneously with multiple children at once. Becoming socially competent requires acquisition and use of multiple skills, application of those skills to meet different purposes, use of those skills in varied contexts, and rapid and accurate discrimination of the features of various social situations and appropriate adjustment of behavior based on those discriminations.

Thus, interventions designed to promote social interactions skills must attend to the forms children use, the functions that are performed, the qualitative aspects (i.e., positive and negative) uses of the forms and functions, and the length of the interactions (e.g., number of turns or duration measured in number of seconds). One of the primary differences of caregiver-child and child-child interactions is that the caregiver is assumed to be a competent interactor who can make considerable allowances and adjustments to the interaction. Peers are less able and willing to make allowances and adjustments when the interactive partner is less skilled.

BOX 9.4   Common definitions of child-child interactions

Skill	Description
Social Initiations	
Starting	Nonspecific verbalization or gesture that (a) directs the behavior of another child but does not specify a play activity ("come play"), or (b) is interactive but neither directs nor references a play activity ("What are you doing?").
Sharing	The offering or giving of an object to a peer.
Share Request	Verbal or gestural request to have a peer share play objects or materials.
Play Organizer	Verbalization that both directs the behavior of another child and labels a play activity ("You be the daddy and make us some dinner").
Entry	Verbal or gestural request to join an existing activity of two or more children ("Can I play too?").
Social Responses	
Affirmative Response	Verbal or motor/gestural behavior that indicates agreement to engage in a suggested activity ("O.K., I'll be the daddy") or responds to the form of another initiation (Handing a truck to a peer who requested it).
Alternative Response	Verbalization that suggests an alternative activity ("No, but I'll play house with you instead") or is nonaffirmative but interactive (ignoring content of initiation by peer but converses anyway).
Extended Social Interactions	
Asking Questions	During interaction, asking open-ended questions that are related to content of activity ("Do you want to drive the car now?') or that introduce a new play theme ("Do you want to play blocks now?").
Listening	Attending to interactive peer's verbal or motor/gestural behavior.
Talking About the Same Thing	Engaging in conversation and play behaviors directly related to the ongoing activity, including sociodramatic and unstructured activities.

Note: From: S. R. McConnell, L. A. Sisson, C. A. Cort, & P. S. Strain (1991). Effects of social skills training and contingency management of reciprocal interaction of preschool children with behavioral handicaps. *Journal of Special Education, 24,* (p. 479).

Social Play   Play is an important activity for young children, including those with developmental delays and disabilities. It is beyond the scope of this chapter to discuss toy play, but multiple sources are available (Fewell & Kaminski, 1988; Fewell & Vadasy, 1983; Johnson, Christie, & Yawkey, 1987; Linder, 1990; Musselwhite, 1986). The importance of play is at least twofold. Play provides (a) a means through which children can learn about the animate and inanimate world, and (b) the context for many assessment and intervention activities on other skills. Toy play is probably also important as a prerequisite or necessary skill for engaging in more complex social exchanges around play.

Over the years, attempts have been made to classify the social play of young children. Mueller and Lucas (1975) describe three stages of play for mobile infants and toddlers. These stages focus on objects and describe the development of social interactions. The first stage is called "object-centered contacts" and involves more than one peer attending to or interacting with an object. The contact between children at this point is essentially incidental. The second stage, called "simple and complex contingency interchanges," involves the first peer interactions. Early in this stage simple contingency interchanges occur. The turns tend to involve one initiation and one response, although it may be circular in nature. For example, one child falls down, the other laughs, and the first child falls down again. Later in this stage, the interchanges between children become longer and involve different behaviors. Children begin to take turns but do not exchange roles. For example, Mary looks at Valerie, Valerie smiles, and Mary offers a toy. Valerie takes the toy and shakes it and hands it back to Mary. Mary gets another toy and they repeat the sequence. In the final stage, "complementary interchanges," children begin to engage in reciprocal patterns that may involve reversal of roles. For example, Jimmy chases Daniel and then Daniel chases Jimmy. True interaction and role sharing occur at this stage.

For children 2 years of age and older, a common categorization of social play is Parten's (1932) scale. She suggested that social play emerges through a hierarchical sequence: unoccupied behavior, solitary or independent play, onlooker, parallel play, associative play, and cooperative play. Each

of these categories requires a more advanced level of play than the previous category; for example, solitary play involves toy play and parallel play involves toy play near other children, which may include incidental contact with those children. Also, more advanced social interactions are required at each level. For example, parallel play involves play near other children; however, associative play involves interaction and contact between children. The descriptions of these categories are shown in Box 9.5.

Although these categories describe the sequence of social play development, preschoolers may spend time in each of the categories. For example, a preschooler may play in a cooperative manner with his peers for a short period, and then play near but not with a peer (i.e., parallel play). Later in the day, the child may play by himself away from peers (i.e., independent toy play). Over the course of the preschool years, however, the percent of time spent in each of the categories of play should shift with greater percentages being spent in higher levels of social play. Recent evidence suggests that cooperative sociodramatic play may be most beneficial for learning cognitive, communicative, and social skills (Johnson et al., 1987).

These categories have been used in many studies to assess and describe the social play of young children with disabilities. In addition, these categories have been combined with Smilanksy's (1968) categories of cognitive play (i.e., functional play, constructive play, dramatic play, and play with rules) to describe the nature of the social play (Rubin, Maloni, & Hornung, 1976; see Johnson et al., 1987, for a complete description). Because this system is designed to describe the development of social play, solitary or independent play is devalued. However, such play may be critical for young children with disabilities because it occupies their time, provides them with opportunities to learn

BOX 9.5   Descriptions of Parten's categories of social play

Unoccupied Behavior
The child apparently is not playing, but occupies himself with watching anything that happens to be of momentary interest. When there is nothing exciting taking place, he plays with his own body, gets on and off chairs, just stands around, follows the teacher, or sits in one spot glancing around the room.

Solitary or Independent Play
The child plays alone and independently with toys that are different from those used by the children within speaking distance and makes no effort to get close to other children. He pursues his own activity without reference to what others are doing.

Onlooker
The child spends most of his time watching the other children play. He often talks to the children whom he is observing, asks questions, or gives suggestions, but does not overtly enter into the play himself. This type differs from the unoccupied in that the onlooker is definitely observing particular groups of children rather than anything that happens to be exciting. The child stands or sits within speaking distance of the group so that he can see and hear everything that takes place.

Parallel Activity
The child plays independently, but the activity he chooses naturally brings him among other children. He plays with toys that are like those which the children around him are using, but he plays with the toy as he sees fit, and does not try to influence or modify the activity of the children near him. He plays beside rather than with the other children. There is no attempt to control the coming or going of children in the group.

about the world, and furnishes opportunities to master toys.

Assessment of Peer Interactions and Social Play Skills

Assessment of peer social interactions and social play is a complex process for several reasons. First, social interactions and social play can not be tested directly; thus, naturalistic observation of the child in social contexts or ratings by adults who have observed the child frequently in social contexts are necessary (Odom & McConnell, 1989). Sec-

ond, the conclusions about a child's social skills will depend in large part on the skills of other children in the social environment. For example, a child will appear less skilled if the assessment of social interactions occurs with peers who do not engage in complex social interactions. Likewise, the child's level of social play may appear less advanced if the peers primarily engage in parallel play. Third, the materials in the setting and the structure of the play areas will influence children's social interactions and social play (Odom & Strain, 1984). Fourth, the structure of the activities in which the assessment oc-

Associative Play	The child plays with other children. The conversation concerns the common activity; there is a borrowing and loaning of play material; following one another with trains or wagons; mild attempts to control which children may or may not play in the group. All the members engage in similar if not identical activity; there is no division of labor, and no organization of the activity of several individuals around any material goal or product. The children do not subordinate their individual interests to that of the group; instead, each child acts as he wishes. By his conversation with the other children one can tell that his interest is primarily in his associations, not in his activity. Occasionally, two or three children are engaged in no activity of any duration, but are merely doing whatever happens to draw the attention of any of them.
Cooperative or Organized Supplementary Play	The child plays in a group that is organized for the purpose of making some material product, or of striving to attain some competitive goal, or of dramatizing situations of adult and group life, or of playing formal games. There is a marked sense of belonging or of not belonging to the group. The control of the group situation is in the hands of one or two of the members who direct the activity of the others. The goal as well as the method of attaining it necessitates a division of labor, the taking of different roles by the various group members, and the organization of activity so that the efforts of one child are supplemented by those of another.

Note: From: M. B. Parten (1932). Social participation among preschool children. *Journal of Abnormal and Social Psychology, 27,* 243–269.

curs will influence the amount and nature of social interactions and play (DeKlyen & Odom, 1989). Fifth, the nature of the measures used will influence the extent to which the information is useful in planning interventions. For example, the use of Parten's scale with and without combining it with Smilansky's categories of cognitive play will provide different types of information.

As a result, the professional must carefully plan the assessment activities based on the type of information that is needed. For a complete description of how to design assessments for social interactions and of the types of measures that are available, see Odom and McConnell (1989). For information on designing assessments of toy and social play and for the observation systems available, see Linder (1990) and Wolery and Bailey (1989).

Interventions to Promote Peer Interactions and Social Play Skills

Once assessment information has been collected and analyzed, intervention goals are devised. Intervention goals in peer social interactions and social play are similar to intervention goals in other areas in many respects. First, some goals may focus on teaching new interactive or play skills (i.e., acquisition); others may be related to fluency, maintenance, or generalization of existing skills. Second, acquisition and use of peer-interaction and social-play skills frequently require careful intervention planning because of their complex nature and their immediate and long-term value. Third, the effects of interventions require systematic monitoring to ensure that they are having their intended effects. Fourth, intervention goals for social interaction and play must attend to the child's existing skills in other domains, particularly cognitive and communicative development.

However, intervention goals related to social interactions with peers and social play are unique in at least three respects. First, intervention with both types of skills is dependent on the skills of other children in the environment. For example, it is extremely difficult to teach a child to learn cooperative play if there are no peers in the class who possess cooperative play skills. The professional simply cannot assume the role of peers. The second unique characteristic of intervention with these skills is similar to the first: Setting the occasion for learning opportunities frequently is in the hands of peers rather than the professional. For example, if the goal is to teach a child to respond to the initiations of peers, then the peers must initiate interaction with the child. There may be several peers available who could serve the role of initiator; however, unless they do, the child will not have an opportunity to learn to respond to peers' initiations. Third, social play and peer social interactions are highly variable skills. This variability is caused by the characteristics of the contexts (e.g., physical space, activities, materials) in which social exchanges occur, the skill of peers, the social behavior of peers, the variety of responses that can occur

for any social behavior, and many other factors. Thus, it is difficult to know when a child has acquired or is using the interactive and play behaviors at appropriate levels. As a result, it is difficult to know when the intervention has been successful and thus is no longer needed. One solution is to compare the child's behavior over time to the levels of behavior displayed by typically developing peers in similar contexts (Strain & Kohler, 1988). Because of these unique characteristics, designing interventions for peer social interactions and social play is a challenging proposition. The next section describes various types of interventions that are categorized into three broad groups: ecological or environmental interventions, teacher-mediated interventions, and peer-mediated interventions.

Environmental Interventions for Social Interactions and Play   Chapters 5, 7, and 8 contained information on the effects of materials; effects of particular manipulations of the classroom space, social composition, and activities; and procedures for promoting engagement with and mastery of the environment. Bailey (1989) and Simeonsson (1988) discuss issues related to assessing the effects and adequacy of classroom and home environments. Carta, Sainato, and Greenwood (1988) discuss the use of ecobehavioral assessment to describe and understand the experiences of different children in preschool classrooms. Sainato and Carta (in press) describe the influences of classroom structure on the social competence of young children. The primary conclusions from these sources and related research are (a) many ecological or environmental variables can influence children's engagement, learning, and peer interactions and social play; and (b) the technology for measuring and thus understanding those influences on children generally and on individual children is available (Carta et al., 1988). The recommendation for intervention from these sources is easily stated, but less easily implemented: If particular outcomes are desired for given children, then the environment can and should be structured to produce those outcomes (Bailey, Harms, & Clifford, 1983).

However, two facts about this recommendation should be noted. First, some arrangements of the environment (e.g., materials, physical space, social composition of groups) will produce particular outcomes at the expense of other outcomes. For example, with young children the provision of realistic toys and materials (e.g., clothing for dress-up, dolls, doll furniture, and so forth) will produce more pretend play than materials such as paints, crayons, paper, and puzzles; however, paints, crayons, paper, and puzzles will produce more constructive play (Rubin & Howe, 1985). In practice, the professional may want to produce both pretend social play and constructive play. If this is the case, then different activities and arrangements will be required at different times of the day. While the focus of this chapter is on promoting social competence, other skill areas also are important. Thus, particular arrangements of the environment for promoting social competence may or may not be appropriate for promoting skills in other areas. For example, some activity structures, such as circle time, may produce little social interaction, but may allow children to focus on the critical features of stimuli in preacademic instruction. Second, some of the environmental factors are likely to influence performance differently when combined with different factors. For example, manipulative play on the floor with "social" materials and in the presence of highly social peers is likely to produce more social interaction than manipulative play on the floor with "isolate" materials in the presence of highly social peers.

The following section describes the influences of various ecological factors and is based largely on Sainato and Carta (in press). The specific ecological factors that are discussed include the activity types and structure, physical space, materials and toys, and social composition of groups.

Effects of Activities and Activity Structure on Social Interactions and Play Particular types of activities have been associated with increased or decreased levels of engagement. For example, having optional or required activities produced similar levels of engagement in young children provided they could leave the required activities as soon as they completed their individual tasks (Doke & Risley, 1972). However, if they had to wait for other children to complete their tasks in the required activities, then the levels of engagement were higher in the optional-activities arrangement. Similarly, Doke (1975) compared formal activities (e.g., nursery rhymes, language lessons, story time) with informal activities (blocks, housekeeping, play with manipulative toys). Formal activities involved children being in a specified area and manipulating materials as other children did when led by an adult; informal activities allowed children to use materials as they choose. Children were more engaged during informal activities as compared to formal activities.

The effects of activities and their structure on social behavior as well as engagement have been studied. In one study, children without disabilities were most interactive during free play and least interactive during fine-motor and circle-time activities; children with disabilities were most interactive during snack (Kohl & Beckman, 1984). Similarly, children were most interactive during outdoor play as compared to free-choice center times and story and music times; however, they were more interactive in free-choice center times than during story and music times (Burstein, 1986). In another study, similar results were found: Children with and without disabilities engaged in the most verbal social interactions during free-play and clean-up activities and had the least verbal social interactions during preacademic, story time, language lessons, and fine-motor activities (Odom, Peterson, McConnell, & Ostrosky, 1990). These findings appear to indicate, as logic would suggest, that children will engage in more social interactions during low-structure activities. Structured activities where the teacher leads the activity (e.g., circle time, music, story time) offer fewer opportunities for interactions.

The question then becomes, "Do varying types of free-play activities promote more social interactions and social play?" Two studies suggest an interesting finding. Shores, Hester, and Strain (1976) found that teacher-structured play produced more social interactions than no involvement of the teacher in the play or the teacher participating in the play. DeKlyen and Odom (1989) controlled the amount of teacher interaction during play activities that were rated as high- and low-teacher-structured activities (see Chapter 5 for an explanation of the rating procedure). The activities that involved teachers providing high structure (i.e., teachers identified a theme of play, gave children roles, and set rules) produced more social interactions by children with and without disabilities.

Thus, particular structuring of activities (i.e., formal versus informal, required versus optional) may influence the amount of child engagement. Similarly, less formal activities (e.g., free play and snack) are likely to have higher levels of social interaction than more formal activities (e.g., circle time, story time, music, fine-motor activities). However, if during the low-structure activities such as free play, the teacher identifies a theme of play, sets some rules, and assigns roles, then children are likely to engage in more social interactions than if such structuring does not occur.

Effects of Physical Space on Social Interactions and Play   The effects of space on social behavior, positive and negative, have been proposed for many years (Sainato & Carta, in press; Nordquist, 1978). However, the research is difficult to analyze because the amount of space (square feet per child), the size of the groups, the novelty of the arrangements, the amount and type of materials available, and the existing management systems vary across and sometimes within studies (Sainato & Carta). Crowding has been associated with increases in negative interactions and aggression; however, these effects have not been found if each child has at least 25 square feet of space. More running and rough-and-tumble play may be evident in large spaces (Sainato & Carta). However, when materials and other variables are held constant, more social behavior may occur in smaller spaces if the comparisons provide a large contrast (e.g., 58 square feet per child as compared to 19 square feet per child) (Brown, Fox, & Brady, 1987).

Thus, it appears that less space may be associated with an increased likelihood that particular types of play and social interactions, both positive and negative, will occur; however, this is influenced by several factors. The recommendation to professionals is: If the goal is to increase social contacts and interactions, then restricting the space while keeping materials and group size constant may be appropriate. However, the professional should monitor the level of negative interactions and respond to them appropriately (see chapter 11).

Effects of Materials and Toys on Social Interactions and Play   The effects of toys and materials on children's development have interested researchers for many years. Bradley's (1985) summary of findings from research on this topic was presented in Box 5.3 of chapter 5. In terms of social interactions and play, a couple of findings are pertinent. First, with very young children (e.g.,

1 to 2 years of age), toys may be one of the primary ways to increase social contact. As noted, simple and complex contingency interactions may occur as young children simultaneously focus on a single toy (e.g., a riding toy, slide, or ball). Second, some toys and materials appear to produce more isolated play behavior, while other toys and materials appear to produce more social play behaviors (Quiltich & Risley, 1973; Hendrickson, Strain, Tremblay, & Shores, 1981). Odom and Strain (1984) reviewed the literature on this topic and identified several materials and toys that appeared to have high or low social value; these are presented in Box 9.6. However, teachers can structure the use of low-social-value toys to increase the probability of social interactions and play. For example, puzzles frequently result in isolated play; however, social interactions can be increased by asking two children to complete a single puzzle or asking children to take turns putting in a piece of a single puzzle. Third, the novelty of play materials may influence the amount of social behavior. Novel toys and materials frequently result in explo-

---

BOX 9.6   Play materials of high and low social value

High Social Value	Low Social Value
Balls	Balls
Blocks	Beads
Books	Blackboard
Checkers	Books
Cutting Paper	Clay and Playdough
Dishes	Crayons
Dolls/Doll Corner	Dolls
"Don't Break the Ice"	Gyroscope
"Don't Cook Your Goose"	Paint and Painting
Dress-up Clothes	Paper and Pencils
Hollow Blocks	Parquetry
House Corner	Plasticine
House and Dolls	Pull Toys
Kiddie-Kar	Puzzles
Kitchen Play Equipment	Scissors
Parallel Bars	Shape Templates
Pick-up Sticks	Tinker Toys
Playing Cards	Toy Animals
Puppets	
Record Players	
Sand	
See-Saw	
Trains	
Trucks	
Wagons	

Note: Adapted from S. L. Odom and P. S. Strain (1984). Classroom-based social skills instruction for severely handicapped preschool children. *Topics in Early Childhood Special Education,* 4(3), p. 102.

ration rather than social interactions. Thus, if the goal is to promote social interactions and play, then familiar toys should be used (Odom & Strain).

Thus, while toys and materials may increase children's engagement, not all toys will set the stage for social interactions and social play. Teachers should use toys to encourage young children to make incidental social contacts and exchanges and use familiar toys with high social value to promote increases in interactions and social play.

Effects of Peers on Social Interactions and Play   As noted in the assessment section, the competence and availability of peers are central to the type and nature of social interactions and social play that young children display. Sainato and Carta (in press) describe several findings about the social composition of groups. First, toddlers display more social behavior in small groups of 2 to 4 children than in larger groups. A similar but more tentative finding appears to exist for preschoolers. Second, children appear to engage more often in complex play, dramatic play, and pretend play when with familiar rather than unfamiliar peers. Third, children in same-age groups may engage in more social behavior as compared to mixed-age groups, but more help-giving and assistance-seeking may occur in mixed-age groups. However, grouping children of similar social abilities may result in more social behavior than grouping children by age. Fourth, children's social behavior appears to be influenced by the gender of the peers. Preference for same-gender peers emerges in toddlers, and more cooperative play and positive social behaviors occur in preschoolers during same-gender groupings. However, more aggression also occurs in same-gender groupings. Increases in opposite-gender social behavior can be obtained through teacher reinforcement. Fifth, in mainstreamed settings, typically developing peers appear to prefer and engage in more social interactions with other typically developing peers than with disabled peers. Further, the severity of the disability—mild, moderate, or severe—appears to be correlated with the amount of social contact by typically developing peers, such that decreases in social contact occur as the severity of the disability increases (Guralnick, 1981).

Thus, several factors related to the composition of groups influence children's level and complexity of social interactions and social play. The social composition of classrooms as a whole frequently is beyond the control of the professional. However, within the class, social groupings can be used to promote more social interactions and play. Thus, the professional should attempt to group children based on the desired outcomes and the guidelines from the research on the effects of social groups.

Summary of the Effects of Ecological Interventions   Several ecological variables—activities and activity structures, physical space, materials, and the composition of groups—influence young children's social behavior. It appears that these variables can be used for two purposes. First, they can be used as a primary intervention to increase social exchanges and more complex social play. If the use of these manipulations results in adequate levels of social behavior, then the teacher may have saved considerable time and effort in designing other more complex and costly interventions. Second, when these manipulations do not result in sufficient levels of social behavior, then they should be used as the context in which other social interventions are employed. For example, if teacher- or peer-mediated interventions are planned to increase social play, then such interventions are probably best implemented during teacher-structured free-play activities, in small areas of the classroom, with "social" materials, and with familiar, same-gender, competent peers.

Teacher-Mediated Interventions for Social Interactions and Play Although the environmental manipulations discussed in the previous section require teacher decisions and structuring of the classroom ecology and the peer-mediated interventions described in the following section involve the teacher assisting peers in implementing interventions, some strategies involve direct involvement of the teacher. In this section four types of teacher-mediated strategies are described: teacher attention and reinforcement, teacher prompting, correspondence training, and affection activities (McEvoy, Odom, & McConnell, in press). When using teacher-mediated interventions, the intervention goal should be clearly identified; the steps for implementing the strategy should be determined; and, when possible, these strategies should be used in situations where the environmental factors that promote social behavior are in place. In many cases, understanding the factors that maintain the child's current level of social behavior should also be understood and used in planning interventions (see chapter 11).

Teacher Attention and Reinforcement One of the first studies that demonstrated the effects of manipulating teacher behavior on the social interactions of preschool children was reported by Allen, Hart, Buell, Harris, and Wolf (1964). In this study, a young girl interacted frequently with adults but rarely interacted with her peers. When the teachers ignored her initiations to adults but attended to her when she interacted with peers, there was a dramatic and consistent increase in the frequency of peer interactions. This study is a good example of three important issues. First, the investigators identified a powerful reinforcer for the child—teacher attention. When given a choice, the child sought the attention of teachers rather than peers. Second, the investigators used this information in designing an intervention to increase the child's peer interactions. Recognizing and

using factors such as this in planning interventions increases the likelihood that the intervention will be successful. Third, the investigators understood the child's current skill levels. They noted that although she had the skills for engaging in peer interactions, she rarely used those skills. The intervention they designed may not have been successful if she did not have peer-interaction skills. Since this seminal study, several other studies have documented that teacher attention and reinforcement can increase children's peer interactions and social play (Wusterbarth & Strain, 1980).

The use of teacher attention and other reinforcers should follow several guidelines. First, unless response shaping (see chapter 6) is used, the child must display the target behavior at some level. Generally, reinforcement does not provide information on how to do behaviors, but rather increases the probability that behaviors which already occur at some level will occur more often. Second, powerful reinforcers must be identified. With some children, teacher attention will not be a reinforcer and thus its contingent use is not likely to increase social interactions or social play. As a result, reinforcers such as materials, stickers, "happy faces" and so forth have been used. Third, the reinforcer, as described in chapter 5, must be delivered immediately and contingently. Unfortunately, delivery of teacher reinforcers may frequently interrupt the social interactions and social behavior and thus interfere with the very behaviors the teacher is trying to increase (Strain & Fox, 1981). One solution to this problem is to deliver material reinforcers that can be used to extend children's social play. However, even such reinforcers can interrupt children's social behavior. Another solution is to use tokens that are exchanged for other reinforcers at the end of the play session or later in the day. This is frequently done by placing "happy-face" stickers contingent on certain social behaviors on a board, card, or chart that is visible to the children during the play session (McEvoy et al., in press). Fourth, the reinforcement should be delivered for general and sustained social contact. When reinforcement is delivered for using a particular interactive behavior (e.g., use of play organizers or for social initiations), these behaviors may increase but extended social interactions may not. For example, the child may initiate to one child, be reinforced; initiate to another child, be reinforced; and then initiate to a third child. While the reinforcement clearly may increase the initiations, the general goal of intervention is for children to interact and play socially with their peers for extended durations. Thus, either the reinforcement should be delivered for interactions and interactive behavior generally, or the contingencies must be adjusted so that after the child initiates frequently, reinforcement is only provided if the interaction occurs for extended turns or durations. Finally, the reinforcement scheduled must be thinned so that the interactive and play behaviors are maintained without frequent teacher reinforcement. This involves reinforcing the child for less than every occurrence of the target social behaviors. Such thinning of the reinforcement schedule requires considerable skill on the part of the professional and can take a relatively long time to accomplish (Timm, Strain, & Eilers, 1979). While teacher attention and reinforcement are used frequently, the difficulties noted here (e.g., the need for the child to display the skill, the interruption of interactions, the need to thin the schedule of reinforcement) have caused investigators to search for other strategies.

Teacher Prompts and Reinforcement A commonly used strategy that involves teacher reinforcement is to add the use of prompts for interactive and social play behavior. The advantage of this strategy over teacher reinforcement alone is that the teacher can

cause more behaviors to occur through the use of prompts. However, as discussed in chapter 6, when teacher prompts are used, they also must be faded or children will become dependent upon those prompts.

Frequently the prompts that are used in such studies involve verbal statements and in some cases physical assistance. For example, the child is told at the beginning of the session to play with a particular peer or share a toy with a given peer (Strain & Odom, 1986). If the child does so, reinforcement in the form of teacher praise or tokens are delivered. If the child does not engage in the target behavior, then the prompts are provided when the occasion for successful use of the behavior is likely. In some cases, the prompts are provided and then reinforcement is delivered at the end of the session (Brady et al., 1984). In some studies, verbal prompts are used initially, and if they are ineffective, physical prompts are used. Several studies have documented the effectiveness of teacher prompting and reinforcement in facilitating social interactions and social play (Strain & Odom, 1986; Strain, Shores, & Kerr, 1976; Wolfe, Boyd, & Wolfe, 1983).

A persistent problem in using teacher prompts and reinforcement is the need to fade the use of the prompts. If the prompts are not faded, then the child may only engage in high levels of social interaction and play when the prompts are used. Although there are a number of procedures for fading teacher prompts (see chapter 6), most studies of social behavior have not employed these strategies. However, a model for doing so with adult-child interactions has been studied. Charlop and Walsh (1986) used a time delay procedure to teach young children with autism to make verbalizations of affection to adults. The procedure was effective in teaching the target skills and in removing the need for prompting. Use of such procedures needs further evaluation with social interaction and social play skills. Another way to reduce the reliance on prompts is to provide them only for some children in a group of children who need intervention. When prompts and teacher reinforcement are used for some children, the effects sometimes spill over to other children (Strain et al., 1976), that is, others increase their social behavior without being prompted by the teacher.

Thus, teacher prompting and reinforcement has been effective in teaching social interaction and social play skills. However, the prompts must be faded, and the issues discussed for using reinforcers must be addressed.

Correspondence Training   Correspondence training was described briefly in chapter 6 and is described in detail in chapter 11 (also see Baer, 1990; Paniagua, 1990). Correspondence training is a special case of using teacher reinforcement that avoids some of the problems noted with reinforcement and prompting. In most applications of correspondence training, children are asked about what they will do and are reinforced for describing their behaviors. In some cases, simply reinforcing children for saying what they will do (e.g., "Play with Johnny," "Ask Kisha and Gary to play," "Give toys to Mario and Hoi") results in children doing those behaviors. When this is not successful, the reinforcement is provided when children match their verbal behavior (e.g., "Play with Johnny") to their nonverbal behavior (i.e., during the play time they actually played with Johnny). They are reinforced for a correspondence between their verbal and nonverbal behavior. Because of its relative simplicity and because the intervention does not require the teacher to deliver the reinforcer during play sessions, it is seen as a desirable strategy.

Osnes, Guevremont, and Stokes (1986) used correspondence training to increase the frequency with which two socially withdrawn preschoolers interacted verbally with their peers during play sessions. During baseline, no specific consequences were in effect. During correspondence training, the following procedures were used: (a) immediately before the play session, the children were asked individually what they were going to do and were prompted, if necessary, to say, "I'm going to talk to kids a lot"; (b) the children were then instructed to go play; and (c) after the play session, when the criterion was met, the children selected a reinforcer. If the criterion was not met, they were told no reinforcer was available because they did not talk a lot. These procedures resulted in increased verbal interactions with peers during play for both children. Other studies have also used correspondence training. Rogers-Warren, Warren, and Baer (1977) found that modeling of sharing, reports of sharing experiences, and reinforcement of true reports of sharing resulted in increases in sharing during play periods.

Odom and Watts (in press) extended current research on correspondence training to evaluate its effects combined with visual feedback on the occurrence of generalization of social initiations of preschoolers with autism. They used peer-initiation training, as described in the following section, to increase social interactions in one free-play session. They found increases in initiations during that session, but little generalization occurred to a second free-play period. They then implemented the correspondence training procedure with visual feedback in the second setting. They told the peers to get their partner with autism to play with them, told them that they needed to do this eight times per session, and told them that if they did then they would get a reward. They then asked the peers what they were going to do, and the peers would say, "I am going to get (partner's name) to play with me." During the session, the investigator drew a "happy face" on an index card and showed it to a peer each time the peer got the partner to play with them. This resulted in increases in the second condition *without* teacher prompts to initiate social interactions.

Taken together, these studies indicate that correspondence training may be used (a) with the target children, (b) with the peers in social situations, (c) as a means of increasing particular behaviors, and (d) in combination with other procedures to promote generalization of target social behaviors. The effectiveness of the strategy and the relatively limited effort involved in using it suggest that it is a viable intervention strategy.

Affection Training   Affection training is a specialized training strategy that is usually led by the teacher and thus is considered for this discussion a teacher-mediated strategy (McEvoy, Twardosz, & Bishop, 1990; McEvoy et al., in press). Affection activities are described as follows:

Affection activities are typical preschool games, songs, and activities that have been modified to include varying types or affectionate responses. These activities are conducted during regularly scheduled large or small group activity periods, involve children with and without handicaps, require little teacher training, and are generally fun for the participants. Affection activities begin with the teacher talking to the children about the importance of friendship and the purpose of affection activities. . . . After the initial discussion about the importance of friendship, the teacher begins the activity by asking the children to "greet" each other, usually in an affectionate manner. . . . During the affection activity, the children might sing a typical preschool song such as "If You're Happy and You Know It." However, instead of singing "clap your hands," the children might be instructed to "tickle someone else," "hug a friend," or "smile." . . . Throughout the activity, the teacher reinforces expressions of affection or friendship, even those that are not part of the activity (McEvoy, Twardosz, & Bishop, 1990, p. 161).

McEvoy et al. (1990) recommend that the majority of children taking part in affection

activities be typically developing and that the teacher must strive to keep the activities interesting and fun. To date, the research indicates that children with and without disabilities increase their interactions during affection activities and that most children increase their social interaction during generalization sessions conducted the next day. This strategy has been used successfully with children who were socially isolated (Twardosz, Nordquist, Simon, & Botkin, 1983), children with autism (McEvoy et al., 1988), and children with mental retardation (Brown, Ragland, & Fox, 1988). In some studies (McEvoy et al., 1988), most but not all children showed increased interactions in generalization sessions. For children who have not generalized, the use of instructions to find a friend and praise for increasing interactions have been used.

McEvoy et al. (1990) and Brown, Ragland, and Bishop (1989) describe adaptations of common songs and activities for inclusion in affection training sessions. However, many other activities could be adapted and teachers should feel free to create their own affection training activities. Affection activities can be implemented in short time periods during the day (10 to 15 minutes), frequently involve the entire class or large portions of the class, and appear fun and reinforcing for most students. Thus, the procedure may have wide application in early childhood programs. The relatively high occurrence of generalization that is found with this procedure also speaks for its adoption.

Summary of Teacher-Mediated Interventions for Social Interactions and Play   These four strategies—teacher reinforcement, teacher reinforcement with prompts, correspondence training, and affection activities—provide the professional with several strategies for increasing the peer interaction and social skills of young children with disabilities. Each has been sufficiently studied to recommend their use; however, the cautions noted with each should be addressed. Also, the professional should monitor generalization and maintenance to ensure that such outcomes occur.

Peer-Mediated Interventions for Social Interactions and Play   Because of the difficulties in using and fading teacher prompts and using and thinning teacher reinforcement during social interactions and social play, investigators have moved to use peer-mediated interventions (Kohler & Strain, 1990; Strain, 1981). Peer-mediated interventions are those that involve the use of peers, frequently typically developing peers, to promote social interactions and social play. Kohler and Strain describe four types of peer-mediated strategies: (a) peer management: nonacademic; (b) peer tutoring: academic; (c) modeling; and (d) peers participate in group-oriented contingencies. Each of these types is discussed in the following section with the exception of "peer tutoring: academic."

Peer Management: Nonacademic   Two general types of peer-management procedures have been described: those designed to increase social skills and those designed to produce reductions in peer's problem behaviors. Only the former is described in this chapter. Perhaps the most widely used and more thoroughly researched peer-management strategy is the "Peer Social Initiation Technique" (Strain, Shores, & Timm, 1977). In this strategy, a peer (called a *confederate*) is trained through direct instruction, role playing, prompts, and reinforcement to initiate social interactions with the peer who has disabilities (called the *target* child).

When using the peer social initiation technique, the teacher should identify specific initiations, arrange the environment to promote interaction (as described in the discussion of environmental interventions), provide training to the confederates, and have daily intervention sessions (Strain & Odom,

1986). Confederates frequently are trained to use four types of initiations: delivering play organizers, initiating sharing, providing assistance, and giving affection. Each of these is usually trained in separate daily sessions of about 20 minutes. The first step of training is to select appropriate confederates. Strain and Odom suggest the following criteria: "(a) compliance with requests made by teachers, (b) regular attendance, (c) age-appropriate play skills, (d) no or positive social history with target children, (e) member of the same class as target child, and (f) expressed willingness to participate" (p. 546). The steps for training the confederate to implement the procedure are shown in Box 9.7. During the play sessions when the confederate is to use the initiations with the target child, the teacher provides regular prompts and reinforcement and then reduces the frequency of prompting and reinforcement over time.

Research with this procedure has been used with children who display a variety of disabilities and span a wide age range. No negative effects and some positive effects have been reported for the confederates (Strain & Odom, 1986). In addition, several positive effects have been found for target children. Typically target children increase the frequency of their responses to initiations considerably, some increase their initiations, and some increase the length of social interactions. When generalization settings are integrated to contain nondisabled peers, then the number of responses to initiations and initiations increase as does the length of interactions (Strain & Odom). In some studies, multiple confederates have been trained at once to increase the efficiency of the procedure and decrease the demands on the confederate (Odom, Strain, Krager, & Smith, 1986; McConnell et al., 1991). In addition, this may increase the probability of generalization (McEvoy et al., in press).

Given the effectiveness of the peer social initiation technique, its use in preschool class-

BOX 9.7 Sample script for the peer social initiations technique

Session 1: Introduction to System—Share Initiation—Persistence

TEACHER: "Today you are going to learn how to be a good teacher. Sometimes your friends in your class do not know how to play with other children. You are going to learn how to teach them to play. What are you going to do?"

CHILD RESPONSE: "Teach them to play."

TEACHER: "One way you can get your friend to play with you is to share. How do you get your friend to play with you?"

CHILD RESPONSE: "Share."

TEACHER: "Right! You share. When you share you look at your friend and say, 'Here,' and put a toy in his hand. What do you do?" (Repeat this exercise until the child can repeat these three steps.)

CHILD RESPONSE: "Look at friend and say, 'Here,' and put the toy in his hand."

ADULT MODEL WITH ROLE PLAYER: "Now, watch me. I am going to share with _____ . Tell me if I do it right." (Demonstrate sharing.) "Did I share with _____ ? What did I do?"

CHILD RESPONSE: "Yea! ___ looked at _____ , said 'here _____ ' and put a toy in his hand."

ADULT: "Right. I looked at _____ and said, 'here _____ ' and put a toy in his hand. Now watch me. See if I share with _____ ." (Move to the next activity in the classroom. This time provide a negative example of sharing by leaving out the "put in hand" component. Put the toy beside the role player). "Did I share?" (Correct if necessary and repeat this example if child got it wrong.) "Why not?"

CHILD RESPONSE: "No." "You did not put the toy in _____ 's hand."

ADULT: "That's right. I did not put the toy in _____ 's hand. When I have to look at _____ and say, 'here _____ ' and put the toy in his hand." (Give the child two more positive and two more negative examples of sharing. When they answer incorrectly about sharing, repeat the example. Vary the negative examples by leaving out different components: looking, saying 'here,' putting in hand.)

CHILD PRACTICE WITH ADULTS: "Now _____ , I want you to get _____ to share with you. What do you do when you share?"

CHILD RESPONSE: "Look at _____ and say, 'here _____ ,' and put a toy in his hand."

ADULT: "Now, go get _____ to play with you." (For these practice examples, the role-playing adult should be responsive to the child's sharing.) (To the other confederates:) "Did _____ share with _____ ? What did she/he do?"

CHILD RESPONSE: "Yes/No. Looked at _____ and said, 'here _____ ' and put a toy in his hand."

ADULT: (Move to the next activity.) "Now, _____ . I want you to share with _____ ."

Introduce Persistence

TEACHER: "Sometimes when I play with _____ , he/she does not want to play back. I have to keep on trying. What do I have to do?"

CHILD RESPONSE: "Keep on trying."

TEACHER: "Right, I have to keep on trying. Watch me. I am going to share with _____ . Now I want you to see if I keep on trying." (Role player will be initially unresponsive.) (Teacher should be persistent until child finally responds.) "Did I get _____ to play with me?" **CHILD:** "Yes." **TEACHER:** "Did he want to play?" **CHILD:** "No." **TEACHER:** "What did I do?" **CHILD:** "Keep on trying." **TEACHER:** "Right, I kept on trying. Watch. See if I can get _____ to play with me this time." (Again, the role player should be unresponsive at first. Repeat above questions and correct if necessary. Repeat the example until the child responds correctly.)

Note: From: P. S. Strain, & S. L. Odom (1986). Peer social initiations: Effective intervention for social skills development of exceptional children. *Exceptional Children, 52,* (p. 547).

rooms is recommended. However, teachers should recognize that the procedure requires careful instruction of confederates, frequent teacher prompting of the confederates in the free-play sessions, and frequent reinforcement of the confederates. The prompting and reinforcement can be reduced over time, but this requires careful monitoring.

Peer Modeling   A primary rationale for enrolling children with disabilities in programs designed for typically developing children is that they will imitate their nondisabled peers, learning new and important skills from them. Unfortunately, without specific training, many young children with disabilities do not imitate their peers. Thus, investigators explored several ways to teach young children imitation. Initially, investigators taught children using adult models in structured settings to imitate gross- and fine-motor movements and later speech sounds (Lovass, 1977). In other studies, adult and peer models have been used (Nordquist, 1978) or only peer models have been used (Cooke, Cooke, & Apolloni, 1978; Engel, Richman, & Koegel, 1981). However, two strategies deserve mention: Peer-imitation training, and follow-the leader training.

Peer-imitation training was developed by Cooke and his colleagues (Apolloni & Cooke, 1978; Apolloni, Cooke, & Cooke, 1977; Peck, Apolloni, Cooke, & Raver, 1978). The procedure involves verbal or physical prompts to imitate the behavior of a peer, with adult praise provided for imitative behavior. Prompts are gradually faded as children become more responsive. For example, Peck et al. (1978) investigated the effects of peer-imitation training on three young children with disabilities. The children were placed in a free-play area with three nondisabled peers. Training consisted of 4-minute periods during which the teacher attempted to increase one child's level of imitative behavior. When the child with disabilities was near a peer

model who was engaged in play, the teacher said, "Look! See what she is doing?" and pointed to the peer model, "You do it." If the child imitated the behavior within 5 seconds, the teacher praised the child and gave a pat or a hug. If the child did not imitate, the teacher physically manipulated the child through the behavior and then provided praise. Observations of spontaneous imitation were conducted for 3 minutes after each training period with the teacher out of sight. As each target child began to participate in training, an increase in imitative behavior was observed during the sessions. Further, the effects of training generalized to free-play sessions after the teacher left.

Peer-imitation training employs some desirable features. It is conducted within the natural environment where peer imitation is likely to be beneficial. It is relatively easy to implement because no extensive training of the peer is required. Also, the teacher can implement it for relatively brief periods of time during low-structured activities. Thus, it is not excessively demanding on the part of teachers. Further, the generalized imitation across situations and behaviors noted by Peck et al. (1978) suggests that the procedure produces fairly durable changes in children's behavior. However, it is not clear whether interactional or complex social play skills are subsequently imitated and learned in this manner. Nonetheless, peer-imitation training as described is a useful procedure with young children who have disabilities.

Follow-the-leader training has developed more recently, with less research evidence to support its efficacy. Carr and Darcy (1990) used this technique effectively to establish imitation in young children with autism. Prior to the study, the children displayed simple imitation of adult models. For example, if an adult said, "Do this," when performing a simple behavior such as clapping hands, the children would imitate the clapping. However, they did not imitate more complex chains of behavior. The training occurred in a hallway near the classroom and involved a variety of objects such as boxes, bikes, a jungle gym, a tunnel, a slide, a balance beam, and blocks. A typically developing student served as the model for four young children with autism, but the training was conducted individually. The model cued the target child to observe, performed a complex motor movement such as crawling under a table, and provided an opportunity for the target child to imitate. If the child imitated, praise was provided; if the child did not, prompts were provided. As a result of such training, all four children with autism learned to imitate novel activities.

The follow-the-leader procedure has potential usefulness because it involves complex motor movements and results in generalized imitation. Although the research using this procedure involved fairly structured sessions, the children were free to move about the training area and were not seated, as in previous research (Lovass, 1977). Further research should address whether groups of children can be trained to imitate with this procedure and whether learning to imitate these complex movements results in imitation of complex social play.

Group Contingencies   When children are in groups and when reinforcement is provided to them for their behavior in those groups, then contingencies can be implemented in a number of ways. For example, each child can be reinforced for individual behavior, the group can be reinforced if every member meets some specified criterion, or the group can be reinforced if an individual member meets some specified criterion. The latter two arrangements of reinforcement are called group contingencies.

Group contingencies have a rich research base with older students, and often positive effects that were not trained occur, such as peers helping the target child (Greenwood &

Hops, 1981). Recently, investigators have begun to study the effects of group contingencies on young children's social behavior. In two recent studies (Lefebvre & Strain, 1989; McConnell et al., 1991), children were taught in groups to initiate and respond to peers' initiations. In free-play sessions, various group contingencies were evaluated. In the Lefebvre and Strain study, when group contingencies were in place for the performance of a single triad of children (two typically developing peers and one child with disabilities), the frequency of initiations and responses to peers' initiations increased. In the McConnell et al. study, the rates of the peers' initiations and responses increased, but little change was found for the target child. Taken together, these studies suggest that group contingencies of social interaction may have subtle and specific effects. Thus, when using this strategy, the effects of group contingencies should be monitored carefully and adjusted as needed.

Summary of Peer-Mediated Interventions for Social Interaction and Play   The peer-mediated social skills training, peer modeling, and group contingencies provide a unique set of intervention strategies. Although these strategies are called peer-mediated, the professional should recognize that they require considerable work on the part of the teacher (Kohler & Strain, 1990). This work involves careful monitoring of the implementation and effects of that use.

SUMMARY

Promoting social competence of young children is a complex task, but one for which considerable research has been conducted to guide the professional's practice. In this chapter, we described caregiver-infant/child interactions, including the behaviors infants and children use, the functions those behaviors serve, and the characteristics of high-quality caregiver-infant/child interactions. In addition, we identified issues related to the assessment of caregiver-infant/child interactions. Intervention into those interactions should be done carefully to ensure that families do not misinterpret the professional's intent. When intervention is warranted, a number of intervention strategies can assist in establishing high-quality caregiver-infant/child interactions. In addition, we identified important social skills for young children when interacting and playing with their peers. We identified issues that influence the assessment of peer interactions and social play. In addition, we described three major types of intervention procedures: environmental interventions, teacher-mediated interventions, and peer-mediated interventions.

REFERENCES

Affleck, G., McGrade, B. J., McQueeny, M., & Allen, D. A. (1982). Relationship-focused intervention in developmental disabilities. *Exceptional Children, 49,* 259–261.

Ainsworth, M. D. S. (1973). The development of infant-mother attachment. In B. M. Caldwell & H. Ricciutti (Eds.), *Review of child development research* (pp. 1–94). Chicago: University of Chicago Press.

Allen, D. A., Affleck, G., McGrade, B. J., & McQueeny, M. (1984). Factors in the effectiveness of early childhood intervention for low socioeconomic status families. *Education and Training of the Mentally Retarded, 19,* 254–260.

Allen, K. E., Hart, B., Buell, J. S., Harris, F. R., & Wolf, M. M. (1964). Effects of social reinforcement on isolate behavior of a nursery school child. *Child Development, 35,* 511–518.

Apolloni, T., & Cooke, T. P. (1978). Integrated programming at the infant, toddler, and preschool levels. In M. J. Guralnick (Ed.), *Early intervention and the integration of handi-*

capped and nonhandicapped children. Baltimore: University Park Press.

Apolloni, T., Cooke, S. A., & Cooke, T. P. (1977). Establishing a normal peer as a behavioral model for delayed toddlers. *Perceptual and Motor Skills, 44,* 231–241.

Baer, R. A. (1990). Correspondence training: Review and current issues. *Research in Developmental Disabilities, 11,* 379–393.

Bailey, D. B. (1989). Assessing environments. In D. B. Bailey & M. Wolery (Eds.), *Assessing infants and preschoolers with handicaps* (pp. 97–118). Columbus, OH: Merrill.

Bailey, D. B., & Simeonsson, R. J. (1985). A functional model of social competence. *Topics in Early Childhood Special Education, 4*(4), 20–31.

Bailey, D. B., Harms, T., & Clifford, R. M. (1983). Matching changes in preschool environments to desired changes in child behavior. *Journal of the Division for Early Childhood, 7,* 61–68.

Barnard, K. E. (1979). *Instructor's learning resource manual.* Seattle: NCAST Publications, University of Washington.

Barnard, K. E., & Kelly, J. F. (1990). Assessment of parent-child interaction. In S. J. Meisels & J. P. Shonkoff (Eds.). *Handbook of early childhood intervention* (pp. 278–302). Cambridge: Cambridge University Press.

Beckwith, L. (1990). Adaptive and maladaptive parenting: Implications for intervention. In S. J. Meisels & J. P. Shonkoff (Eds.). *Handbook of early childhood intervention* (pp. 53–77). Cambridge: Cambridge University Press.

Bowlby, J. (1969). *Attachment.* New York: Basic Books.

Bradley, R. H. (1985). Social-cognitive development and toys. *Topics in Early Childhood Special Education, 5*(3), 11–30.

Brady, M. P., Shores, R. E., Gunter, P., McEvoy, M. A., Fox, J. J., & White, C. (1984). Generalization of a severely handicapped adolescent's social integration responses via multiple peers in a classroom setting. *Journal of the Association for Persons with Severe Handicaps, 9,* 278–286.

Brazelton, T. B., Koslowski, B., & Main, M. (1974). The origins of reciprocity: The early mother-infant interaction. In M. Lewis & L. R. Rosenblum (Eds.), *The effect of the infant on its caregiver.* (pp. 49–76). New York: Wiley-Interscience.

Bromwich, R. M. (1981). *Working with parents and infants: An interactional approach.* Baltimore: University Park Press.

Brown, W. H., Fox, J. J., & Brady, M. P. (1987). Effects of spatial density on three- and four-year-old children's socially directed behavior during freeplay: An investigation of a setting factor. *Education and Treatment of Children, 10,* 247–258.

Brown, W. H., Ragland, E. U., Bishop, N. (1989). *A socialization curriculum for preschool programs that integrate children with handicaps.* Peabody College: Vanderbilt University.

Brown, W. H., Ragland, E. U., & Fox, J. J. (1988). Effects of group socialization procedures on the social interactions of preschool children. *Research in Developmental Disabilities, 9,* 359–376.

Brown-Gorton, R., & Wolery, M. (1988). Teaching mothers to imitate their handicapped children: Effects on maternal mands. *Journal of Special Education, 22,* 97–107.

Burstein, N. D. (1986). The effects of classroom organization on mainstreamed preschool children. *Exceptional Children, 52,* 425–434.

Carr, E. G., & Darcy, M. (1990). Setting generality of peer modeling in children with autism. *Journal of Autism and Developmental Disorders, 20,* 45–59.

Carta, J. J., Sainato, D. M., & Greenwood, C. R. (1988). Advances in the ecological assessment of classroom instruction for young children with handicaps. In S. L. Odom & M. B. Karnes (Eds.), *Early intervention for infants and children with handicaps: An empirical base* (pp. 217–239). Baltimore: Paul Brookes.

Charlop, M. H., & Walsh, M. E. (1986). Increasing autistic children's spontaneous verbalizations of affection: An assessment of time delay and peer modeling procedures. *Journal of Applied Behavior Analysis, 19,* 307–314.

Clark, G., & Siefer, R. (1985). Assessment of parents' interactions with their developmentally delay infants. *Infant Mental Health Journal, 6,* 214–225.

Comfort, M. (1988). Assessing parent-child interaction. In D. B. Bailey & R. J. Simeonsson (Eds.), *Family assessment in early intervention* (pp. 65–94). Columbus, OH: Merrill.

Cooke, S. A., Cooke, T. P., & Apolloni, T. (1978). Developing nonretarded toddlers as verbal models for retarded classmates. *Child Study Journal, 8,* 1–8.

Cunningham, C., Reuler, E., Blackwell, J., & Deck, J. (1981). Behavioral and linguistic developments in the interactions of normal and retarded children with their mothers. *Child Development, 52,* 62–70.

DeKlyen, M., & Odom, S. L. (1989). Activity structure and social interactions with peers in developmentally integrated play groups. *Journal of Early Intervention, 13,* 342–352.

Dodge, K. A., Pettit, G. S., McClaskey, C. L., & Brown, M. M. (1986). Social competence in children. *Monographs of the Society for Research in Child Development, 51*(2), Serial No. 213.

Doke, L. A. (1975). The organization of daycare environments: Formal versus informal activities. *Child Care Quarterly, 4,* 216–222.

Doke, L. A., & Risley, T. R. (1972). The organization of daycare environments: Required versus optional activities. *Journal of Applied Behavior Analysis, 5,* 405–420.

Dunst, C. J. (1985). Rethinking early intervention. *Analysis and Intervention in Developmental Disabilities, 5,* 165–201.

Dunst, C. J., Lesko, J. J., Holbert, K. A., Wilson, L. L., Sharpe, K. L., & Liles, R. F. (1987). A systematic approach to infant intervention. *Topics in Early Childhood Special Education, 7*(2), 19–37.

Dunst, C. J., & McWilliam, R. A. (1988). Cognitive assessment of multiply handicapped young children. In T. D. Wachs & R. Sheehan (Eds.), *Assessment of young developmentally disabled children* (pp. 213–238). New York: Plenum.

Dunst, C. J., & Trivett, C. (1988). Determinants of parent and child interactive behavior. In

K. Marfo, (Ed.), *Parent-child interaction and developmental disabilities: Theory, research, and intervention* (pp. 3–31). New York: Praeger.

Egel, A. L., Richman, G. S., & Koegel, R. L. (1981). Normal peer models and autistic children's learning. *Journal of Applied Behavior Analysis, 14*, 3–12.

Farran, D. C., Clark, K. S., & Ray, A. R. (1990). Measures of parent-child interaction. In E. D. Gibbs & D. M. Teti (Eds.), *Interdisciplinary assessment of infants: A guide for early intervention professionals* (pp. 227–247). Baltimore: Paul Brookes.

Farran, D. C., Kasari, C., Jay, S., & Comfort, M. (1986). *Parent/Caregiver Involvement Scale.* Available from Continuing Education, University of North Carolina at Greensboro, Greensboro, NC.

Fewell, R. R., & Kaminski, R. (1988). Play skills development and instruction for young children with handicaps. In S. L. Odom & M. B. Karnes (Eds.), *Early intervention for infants and children with handicaps: An empirical base* (pp. 145–158). Baltimore: Paul Brookes.

Fewell, R. R., & Vadasy, P. F. (1983). *Learning through play.* Allen, TX: DLM Teaching Resources.

Field, T. (1978). The three Rs of infant-adult interactions: Rhythms, repertoires, and responsivity. *Journal of Pediatric Psychology, 3*, 131–136.

Field, T. (1979). Games parents play with normal and high-risk infants. *Child Psychiatry and Human Development, 10*, 41–48.

Field, T. (1982). Interactive coaching for high-risk infants and their parents. In H. A. Moss, R. Hess, & C. Swift (Eds.), *Early intervention programs for infants* (pp. 5–24). New York: Haworth.

Goldstein, H., & Ferrell, D. R. (1987). Augmenting communicative interactions between handicapped and nonhandicapped preschool children. *Journal of Speech and Hearing Disorders, 52*, 200–211.

Goldstein, H., & Wickstrom, S. (1986). Peer intervention effects on communicative interaction among handicapped and nonhandi-

capped preschoolers. *Journal of Applied Behavior Analysis, 19*, 209–214.

Greenspan, S., & Lieberman, A. (1980). Infants, mothers, and their interactions: A quantitative clinical approach to developmental assessment. In *The course of life: Psychoanalytic contributions toward understanding personality development. Vol 1: Infancy and early childhood* (pub. No. ADM 80-786). Washington, DC: U.S. Government Printing Office.

Greenwood, C. R., & Hops, H. (1981). Group-oriented contingencies and peer behavior change. In P. S. Strain (Ed.), *The utilization of classroom peers as behavior change agents* (pp. 327–360). New York: Plenum.

Guralnick, M. J. (1981). The efficacy of integrating handicapped children in early education settings: Research implications. *Topics in Early Childhood Special Education, 1*(1), 57–71.

Guralnick, M. J. (1990a). Social competence and early intervention. *Journal of Early Intervention, 14*, 3–14.

Guralnick, M. J. (1990b). Major accomplishments and future directions in early childhood mainstreaming. *Topics in Early Childhood Special Education, 10*(2), 1–17.

Hanson, M. J. (1984). *Atypical infant development.* Austin, TX: PRO-ED.

Hendrickson, J. M., Strain, P. S., Tremblay, A., & Shores, R. E. (1981). Relationship between toy and material use and the occurrence of social interactive behaviors by normally developing preschool children. *Psychology in the Schools, 18*, 50–55.

Johnson, J. E., Christie, J. F., & Yawkey, T. D. (1987). *Play and early childhood development.* Glenview, IL: Scott, Foresman.

Kogan, K. (1980). Interaction systems between preschool handicapped or developmentally delayed children and their parents. In T. Field, S. Goldberg, D. Stern, & A. Sostek (Eds.), *High-risk infants and children: Adult and peer interactions.* (pp. 227–247). New York: Academic Press.

Kohl, F. L., & Beckman, P. (1984). A comparison of handicapped and nonhandicapped preschoolers' interactions across classroom activities. *Journal of the Division for Early Childhood, 8*, 49–56.

Kohler, F. W., & Strain, P. S. (1990). Peer-assisted interventions: Early promises, notable achievements, and future aspirations. *Clinical Psychology Review, 10*, 441–452.

Lefebvre, D., & Strain, P. S. (1989). Effects of a group contingency on the frequency of special interactions among autistic and non-handicapped preschool children: Making LRE efficacious. *Journal of Early Intervention, 13*, 329–341.

Linder, T. (1990). *Transdisciplinary play-based assessment: A functional approach to working with young children.* Baltimore: Paul Brookes.

Lovass, O. I. (1977). *The autistic child: Language development through behavior modification.* New York: Irvington.

MacDonald, J. D., & Gillette, Y. (1988). Communicating partners: A conversational model for building parent-child relationships with handicapped children. In K. Marfo, (Ed.), *Parent-child interaction and developmental disabilities: Theory, research, and intervention* (pp. 220–241). New York: Praeger.

Mahoney, G. (1988). Enhancing the developmental competence of handicapped infants. In K. Marfo, (Ed.), *Parent-child interaction and developmental disabilities: Theory, research, and intervention* (pp. 203–219). New York: Praeger.

Mahoney, G., Finger, I., & Powell, A. (1985). Relationship of maternal behavioral style to the development of organically impaired mentally retarded infants. *American Journal of Mental Deficiency, 90*, 296–302.

Mahoney, G., & Powell, A. (1986). *The transactional intervention program teacher's guide.* Rock Hill, SC: Center for Excellence in Early Childhood Education.

Mahoney, G., & Powell, A. (1988). Modifying parent-child interaction: Enhancing the development of handicapped children. *Journal of Special Education, 22*, 82–96.

Marfo, K. (1988). *Parent-child interaction and developmental disabilities: Theory, research, and intervention.* New York: Praeger.

Marvin, R. S. (1977). An ethological-cognitive model for the attenuation of mother-child attachment behavior. In T. Alloway, P. Pliner, & L. Krames (Eds.), *Attachment behavior.* New York: Plenum.

McCollum, J. A. (1984). Social interaction between parents and babies: Validation of an intervention procedure. *Child, Care, Health and Development, 10*, 301–315.

McCollum, J. A. (1986). Charting different types of social interaction objectives in parent-infant dyads. *Journal of the Division for Early Childhood, 11*, 28–45.

McCollum, J. A. (1988). Parent playfulness: A case study of infant twins with handicaps. *Child, Care, Health and Development, 14*, 235–253.

McConnell, S. R., Sisson, L. A., Cort, C. A., & Strain, P. S. (1991). Effects of social skills training and contingency management of reciprocal interaction of preschool children with behavioral handicaps. *Journal of Special Education, 24*, 473–495.

McEvoy, M. A., Nordquist, V. M., Twardosz, S., Heckman, K. A., Wehby, J. H., & Denny, R. K. (1988). Promoting autistic children's peer interaction in an integrated early childhood setting using affection activities. *Journal of Applied Behavior Analysis, 21*, 193–200.

McEvoy, M. A., Odom, S. L., & McConnell, S. R. (in press). Strategies for promoting peer social competence of young children with disabilities. In S. L. Odom, S. R. McConnell, M. McEvoy (Eds.), *Peer-related social competence of young children with disabilities.* Baltimore: Paul Brookes.

McEvoy, M. A., Twardosz, S., & Bishop, N. (1990). Affection activities: Procedures for encouraging young children with handicaps to interact with their peers. *Education and Treatment of Children, 13*, 159–167.

Mueller, E., & Lucas, T. (1975). A developmental analysis of peer interaction among toddlers. In M. Lewis & L. A. Rosenblum (Eds.), *Friendship and peer relations.* New York: Wiley.

Musselwhite, C. R. (1986). *Adaptive play for special needs children: Strategies to enhance communication and learning.* Boston: Little, Brown.

Nordquist, V. M. (1978). A behavioral approach to

the analysis of peer interactions. In M. Guralnick (Ed.), *Early intervention and the integration of handicapped and nonhandicapped children* (pp. 53–84). Baltimore: University Park Press.

Odom, S. L. (1983). The development of social interchanges in infancy. In S. G. Garwood & R. R. Fewell (Eds.), *Educating handicapped infants: Issues in development and intervention* (pp. 215–254). Rockville, MD: Aspen.

Odom, S. L., & McConnell, S. R. (1985). A performance-based conceptualization of social competence of handicapped preschool children: Implications for assessment. *Topics in Early Childhood Special Education, 4*(4), 1–19.

Odom, S. L., & McConnell, S. R. (1989). Assessing social interaction skills. In D. B. Bailey & M. Wolery (Eds.), *Assessing infants and preschoolers with handicaps* (pp. 390–427). Columbus, OH: Merrill.

Odom, S. L., McConnell, S. R., & McEvoy, M. A. (in press). Peer-related social competence and its implications for young children with disabilities. In S. L. Odom, S. R. McConnell, & M. McEvoy (Eds.), *Peer-related social competence of young children with disabilities.* Baltimore: Paul Brookes.

Odom, S. L., Peterson, C., McConnell, S. R., & Ostrosky, M. (1990). Ecobehavioral analysis of early education/specialized classroom settings and peer social interaction. *Education and Treatment of Children, 13,* 316–330.

Odom, S. L., & Strain, P. S. (1984). Classroom-based social skills instruction for severely handicapped preschool children. *Topics in Early Childhood Special Education, 4*(3), 97–116.

Odom, S. L., Strain, P. S., Krager, M. A., & Smith, J. D. (1986). Using single and multiple peers to promote social interaction of preschool children with handicaps. *Journal of the Division for Early Childhood, 10,* 53–64.

Odom, S. L., & Watts, E. (in press). Use of correspondence training and visual feedback to promote peer social initiations to young autistic children. *Journal of Special Education.*

Osnes, P. G., Guevremont, D. C., & Stokes, T. F. (1986). If I say I'll talk more, then I will: Correspondence training to increase peer-directed talk by socially withdrawn children. *Behavior Modification, 10,* 287–299.

Paniagua, F. A. (1990). A procedural analysis of correspondence training techniques. *The Behavior Analyst, 13,* 107–119.

Parten, M. B. (1932). Social participation among preschool children. *Journal of Abnormal and Social Psychology, 27,* 243–269.

Peck, C. A., Apolloni, T., Cooke, T. P., & Raver, S. A. (1978). Teaching retarded preschoolers to imitate the free-play behavior of nonretarded classmates: Trained and generalized effects. *Journal of Special Education, 12,* 195–207.

Peck, C. A., & Cooke, T. P. (1983). Benefits of mainstreaming at the early childhood level: How much can we expect? *Analysis and Intervention in Developmental Disabilities, 3,* 1–22.

Quiltich, H., & Risley, T. R. (1973). The effects of play materials on social play. *Journal of Applied Behavior Analysis, 6,* 573–578.

Rogers-Warren, A., Warren, S. F., Baer, D. M. (1977). A component analysis: Modeling, self-reporting, and reinforcement of self-reporting in the development of sharing. *Behavior Modification, 1,* 307–322.

Rosenberg, S. A., & Robinson, C. C. (1988). Interactions of parents with their young handicapped children. In S. L. Odom & M. B. Karnes (Eds.), *Early intervention for infants and children with handicaps: An empirical base* (pp. 159–177). Baltimore: Paul Brookes.

Rosenberg, S., Robinson, C., & Beckman, P. (1984). Teaching skills inventory: A measure of parent performance. *Journal of the Division for Early Childhood, 8,* 107–113.

Rothbart, M. K. (1984). Social development. In M. J. Hanson (Ed.), *Atypical infant development* (pp. 207–236). Austin, TX: PRO-ED.

Rubin, K. H., & Howe, N. (1985). Toys and play behaviors: An overview. *Topics in Early Childhood Special Education, 5*(3), 1–9.

Rubin, K. H., Maloni, T. L., & Hornung, M. (1976). Free play behaviors in middle- and lower-class preschoolers: Parten and Piaget revisited. *Child Development, 47,* 414–419.

Sainato, D. M., & Carta, J. J. (in press). Classroom influences on the development of social competence of young children with disabilities. In S. L. Odom, S. R. McConnell, & M. McEvoy (Eds.), *Peer-related social competence of young children with disabilities*. Baltimore: Paul Brookes.

Sameroff, A. J., & Fiese, B. H. (1990). Transactional regulation and early intervention. In S. J. Meisels & J. P. Shonkoff (Eds.). *Handbook of early childhood intervention* (pp. 119–149). Cambridge: Cambridge University Press.

Sander, L. W. (1969). The longitudinal course of early mother-child interaction: Cross case comparison in a sample of mother-child pairs. In B. M. Foss (Ed.), *Determinants of infant behavior IV*: London: Methuen.

Seitz, V., & Provence, S. (1990). Caregiver-focused models of early intervention. In S. J. Meisels & J. P. Shonkoff (Eds.), *Handbook of early childhood intervention* (pp. 400–427). Cambridge: Cambridge University Press.

Shores, R. E., Hester, P., & Strain, P. S. (1976). The effects of amount and type of teacher-child interaction on child-child interaction during free-play. *Psychology in the Schools, 13*, 171–175.

Simeonsson, R. J. (1988). Assessing family environments. In D. B. Bailey & R. J. Simeonsson (Eds.), *Family assessment in early intervention* (pp. 139–166). Columbus, OH: Merrill.

Smilansky, S. (1968). *The effects of sociodramatic play on disadvantaged children: Preschool children*. New York: Wiley.

Stern, D. N. (1984). Affect attunement. In J. D. Call, E. Galenson, & R. L. Tyson (Eds.), *Frontiers of infant psychiatry*. New York: Basic Books.

Strain, P. S. (Ed.), (1981). *The utilization of classroom peers as behavior change agents*. New York: Plenum.

Strain, P. S. (1985). Social and nonsocial determinants of handicapped preschool children's social competence. *Topics in Early Childhood Special Education, 4*(4), 47–58.

Strain, P. S., & Fox, J. J. (1981). Peer social initiations and the modification of social withdrawal: A review and future perspective. *Journal of Pediatric Psychology, 6*, 417–433.

Strain, P. S., & Kohler, F. W. (1988). Social skill intervention with young children with handicaps. In S. L. Odom & M. B. Karnes (Eds.), *Early intervention for infants and children with handicaps: An empirical base* (pp. 129–143). Baltimore: Paul Brookes.

Strain, P. S., & Odom, S. L. (1986). Peer social initiations: Effective intervention for social skills development of exceptional children. *Exceptional Children, 52*, 543–551.

Strain, P. S., Shores, R. E., & Kerr, M. M. (1976). An experimental analysis of "spillover" effects on the social interaction of behaviorally handicapped preschool children. *Journal of Applied Behavior Analysis, 9*, 31–40.

Strain, P. S., Shores, R. E., & Timm, M. A. (1977). Effects of peer social initiations on the behavior of withdrawn preschool children. *Journal of Applied Behavior Analysis, 10*, 289–298.

Teti, D. M., & Nakagawa, M. (1990). Assessing attachment in infancy: The strange situation and alternate systems. In E. D. Gibbs & D. M. Teti (Eds.), *Interdisciplinary assessment of infants: A guide for early intervention professionals* (pp. 191–214). Baltimore: Paul Brookes.

Timm, M. A., Strain, P. S., & Eilers, P. (1979). Effects of systematic response-dependent fading and thinning procedure on the maintenance of child-child interaction. *Journal of Applied Behavior Analysis, 12*, 308.

Tremblay, A., Strain, P. S., Hendrickson, J. M., & Shores, R. E. (1981). Social interactions of normally developing preschool children: Using normative data for subject selection and target behavior selection. *Behavior Modification, 5*, 237–253.

Twardosz, S., Nordquist, V. M., Simon, R., & Botkin D. (1983). The effect of group affection activities on the interaction of socially isolate children. *Analysis and Intervention in Developmental Disabilities, 3*, 311–338.

Venn, M. L., & Wolery, M. (in press). Increasing day care staff members' interactions during caregiving routines. *Journal of Early Intervention*.

Wachs, T. D. (1979). Proximal experience and early cognitive-intellectual development: The physical environment. *Merrill-Palmer Quarterly, 25*, 3–41.

Wolery, M., & Bailey, D. B. (1989). Assessing play

skills. In D. B. Bailey & M. Wolery (Ed.), *Assessing infants and preschoolers with handicaps* (pp. 428–446). Columbus, OH: Merrill.

Wolfe, V. V., Boyd, L. A., & Wolfe, D. A. (1983). Teaching cooperative play to behavior problem preschool children. *Education and Treatment of Children, 6,* 1–9.

Woodson, C. W. (1990). *Individualized video-taped parent instruction: Teaching an integrated activity to their infants with handicaps.* Unpublished master's thesis. University of Kentucky, Lexington.

Wusterbarth, N. J., & Strain, P. S. (1980). Effects of adult-mediated attention on the social behavior of physically abused and neglected preschool children. *Education and Treatment of Children, 3,* 91–99.

10

Facilitating the Acquisition and Use of Communica- tion Skills

Barry Prizant

Don Bailey

Communication—the process of sharing experiences and relating to others—is central to human interaction. Bobby and Tyrone, two 5-year-olds, are playing in a sandbox. Suddenly, Tyrone says, "Hey, see my castle!" Bobby looks, notices a stick on the top, points to it and asks, "What's that?" Tyrone answers, "That's the flag of the kingdom." Bobby nods and says, "Let's make a road to the castle." Tyrone responds by smoothing over a stretch of sand leading to the castle. Bobby then suggests, "Let's make the road bigger." Both boys extend the road and begin moving their toy cars up and down it. The boys have used the medium of language to engage in and share in an enjoyable activity, to create an imaginary world, and to work toward a common goal.

Jeanie is a 3-year-old who, because of severe motor disabilities, must be fed by her teacher. Her teacher gets the feeding area ready and positions Jeanie for feeding; Jeanie smiles at him, and he says, "You're ready to eat, aren't you, Jeanie?" Jeanie repeats her smile. The teacher presents the first spoonful of oatmeal, one of her favorite foods, and Jeanie takes it, but when he presents another she closes her mouth, her muscles tense, and she attempts to turn her head. He presents the spoon again and she repeats these behaviors. The teacher is puzzled. He puts the spoon back in the bowl and notices the rising steam. He touches the oatmeal and realizes that it is far too hot. Jeanie's nonverbal communication was critical in keeping her from being burned.

Timmy is a 30-month-old toddler who is not yet speaking but who is very active and appears to know exactly what he wants. Timmy's mother brings out three small plastic trucks, places them on the floor, and rolls one truck to Timmy. Timmy laughs and rolls it back, but then he looks toward his toy box, points, and vocalizes. Timmy's mother says "No more toys, we'll play with these trucks now." Timmy responds with a whine, and persists in pointing with a frustrated vocalization. Timmy's mother says with some exasperation, "I don't know what you want." Timmy then gets up, runs to the toy box, pulls out a small man, runs back to the cars and places the man in the driver's seat, and continues to play with the cars. Timmy's mom smiles as she remembers he likes to roll the car with the man in it.

COMMUNICATION

Definitions and Concepts

Communication is the process by which information is transmitted between two or more individuals. Communication involves any behavioral acts, whether intentional or not, that convey information to others about a person's emotional or physiological state, desires, opinions, or perceptions. Thus, in any instance at communication there will be at least one individual who produces the signals and at least one who receives and interprets the signals (Dunst, Lowe, & Bartholomew, 1990). Wetherby and Prizant (1990) propose three requirements that must be met for behavior to be considered a communicative act: (a) it must be comprised of a gesture, vocalization, and/or verbalization; (b) it must be directed toward another person; and (c) it must serve a communicative function. Communicative acts may be oral (e.g., vocalizations, speech), nonoral (e.g., gestures, facial expressions, body posture), or any combination of oral and nonoral behaviors. And communicative acts may be symbolic and based on a formal language system (e.g., speech, American Sign Language), or they may be nonsymbolic (e.g., natural gestures, vocalizations). Communicative acts also vary as to their conventionality or the degree to which their meanings are shared by members of a community.

In the example we have already considered, Tyrone and Bobby were using the mode of speech for communication. *Speech* is defined as the unique sounds and sound combinations produced by movement of the articulators (e.g., tongue, teeth, lips, soft palate) as air passes through the throat and mouth. For sounds to qualify as speech, they must be perceived as meaningful and as representing units of a language system. *Language* is a conventional symbol system used for communication (Lahey, 1988). A symbol system may be comprised of spoken or written words, drawings or printed figures, or manual signs that represent things, ideas, feelings, needs, relationships, and events. Because symbols have an arbitrary relationship with what they represent, successful communication through symbol use can only occur when two or more people have knowledge of the rules governing the meaning of the symbols and the use of the system. In all human languages, there are specific rules that govern the organization and combination of sounds and symbols (i.e., words) and their relationship to meaning. There also are rules governing the use of language and nonverbal behavior in social situations, which determine the effectiveness and social acceptability of particular acts of communication. Children must eventually learn all these rule systems in order to fully participate in the oral-language-based communication of their culture.

The Rule Systems of Language

Oral language is comprised of sounds. *Phonological rules* define the categories of sounds, or phonemes, in a language system. A *phoneme* is the smallest unit of sound that can make a meaningful difference in a language system (Lahey, 1988). For example, "pat" and "bat" differ in meaning because the first sounds are different phonemes in English. Phonological rules also specify the combinations of sounds that can be formed into

words or syllables, and they govern the use of prosodic features including stress, intonation (i.e., patterns of pitch variation), and pause, all of which may differ across languages.

Morphological rules govern the combination of meaningful units in a language system. The smallest unit of meaning is known as a *morpheme*. A morpheme can be a single word and thus stand alone, or it can be attached to a word (i.e., an inflection) at the beginning (i.e., a prefix) or the end (i.e., a suffix). For example, when Tyrone says, "See my castle," the word "my" is a single morpheme that indicates that the castle belongs to Tyrone. When Bobby says, "Let's make the road bigger," he has combined two morphemes in the word "bigger." "Big" refers to something large, and the suffix "-er" refers to a comparison of two things. When morphemes are combined they change the meaning of words (e.g., "hat" vs "hats"; "complete" vs "incomplete") or form new words (e.g., bed + spread = bedspread). Morphological inflections in English carry meaning about verb tense (e.g., past, present), possession, comparison, plurality, and serve other grammatical functions. Morphological rules are a part of the mutually understood language system, and must be learned for language use to be clear and explicit.

The rules that govern the relationship between words and their meaning are *semantic rules*. The study of semantic development is closely related to aspects of cognitive development (McLean & Snyder-McLean, 1978), because the meanings expressed through words and sentences are based on a child's growing knowledge of the world. For example, early semantic functions in single word utterances are based upon the child's first cognitive understandings that objects exist, disappear, and may reappear. Thus, the child's first words include names of familiar objects, noting existence; "all gone" or "bye," noting disappearance; and "more," noting recurrence (Lahey, 1988). When the child first speaks, she speaks about what she already has learned through interactions with objects and people (McLean & Snyder-McLean, 1978).

Syntactic rules are the rules of a language system that determine how words are ordered and combined to create the larger meaningful units we call phrases, clauses, and sentences. If Tyrone had said, "Castle see my," Bobby probably would not have understood what he meant. Bobby may have known the meaning of each word, but this combination of words does not follow the rules of English syntax.

Pragmatics is the study of language and communication in its social context (Bates, 1976). Pragmatic rules address three major areas of communication: (a) purposes, intentions, or functions of communication; (b) rules of conversational and social exchange; and (c) rules governing language and communicative adjustments, relative to different social contexts.

Communicative intentions or purposes describe what a person hopes to accomplish by communicating. When Timmy pointed to the toy box, his mother understood his general intention (i.e., that he was requesting something), but she did not understand his specific intention or purpose (i.e., to get the man to put on his truck). When Tyrone said, "Hey, see my castle," his intention was to call Bobby's attention to the "castle" he made. Bobby looked at the castle; thus, Tyrone's utterance accomplished the intended purpose. When Bobby said, "What's that?" and pointed to the stick, he was requesting information about the stick in the sand, another purpose for communicating. Tyrone responded, "That's the flag of the kingdom," to provide the answer to Bobby's request for information.

When Jeanie's teacher was getting the feeding area ready, Jeanie's smile indicated she wanted to eat. However, after her first bite, her closed mouth, tense muscles, and attempts to turn her head indicated a clear protest. Jeanie's more subtle nonverbal signals required that her teacher pay close attention and interpret her behavior relative to the context of the interaction. For communication to be successful, we must be able on a consistent basis to determine children's intentions or purposes for communicating. Although it is impossible to always know what a child's communicative intentions are, we can infer intentions from communicative behaviors, the context of the interaction, and the child's subsequent reactions.

The second major area governed by pragmatic rules involves conversation and discourse. Here the unit of analysis goes beyond individual sounds, words, sentences, or communicative acts to larger units involving one or more communicative turns between partners. Conversational rules, covering many aspects of communicative exchange, include conventions for (a) initiating, maintaining, and terminating conversations; (b) introducing, maintaining, and switching topics of conversation; and (c) taking and yielding turns. This aspect of communicative competence requires adjusting behavior based on verbal and nonverbal feedback during an interaction. Young children's lack of mastery of conversational rules is easily observed in interactions where frequent topic shifts and conversational interruptions occur. In fact, young children become appropriate conversationalists only long after they acquire the requisite linguistic knowledge for carrying on relatively sophisticated exchanges (Lahey, 1988).

The third major area of pragmatic rules consists of rules of *sociolinguistic sensitivity*, which specify adjustments of communicative style that should be made relative to specific contexts and listeners. These rules encompass a wide range of adjustments including (but not limited to): (a) consistent use of polite (vs. informal) linguistic forms with role superiors or in certain contexts (e.g., at church, in school); (b) use of appropriate vocal volume relative to context (e.g., the playground vs. the library); and (c) adjustment of communicative style relative to speaking context (e.g., when teaching versus chatting informally, or when speaking to a group rather than to an individual).

Pragmatic rules govern verbal and nonverbal behaviors, because appropriate and effective communication goes beyond the spoken word. Acquisition of pragmatic knowledge continues well into the school years. In fact, because there is an infinite variety of social contexts, pragmatic knowledge is acquired across the life span as individuals encounter new social situations.

The field of pragmatics has had a profound influence on work with children with even the most severe disabilities (Prizant & Wetherby, 1989; Warren & Rogers-Warren, 1985), because it specifies the skills and knowledge needed to be an effective and socially appropriate communicator. It also allows for precise description of the purposes of a full range of intentional and unintentional communicative behavior, from infant affect displays, to intentional nonverbal communicative acts, to sophisticated uses of language. Children with disabilities may learn these rule systems more slowly than other children, or they may require special adaptations (e.g., communication boards, speech synthesizers) to communicate effectively. In some cases, children may only be able to learn the rudiments of a symbolic system for communication (e.g., single words rather than phrases or sentences). For children with the most severe cognitive disabilities, symbolic communication may not be an immediate goal, the focus being rather on more concrete means to communicate such as using objects or natural gestures.

LANGUAGE AND COMMUNICATION DEVELOPMENT: AN OVERVIEW

A large body of research has described the sequences in which children develop communication abilities (see Bates, O'Connell, & Shore, 1987; Lahey, 1988; McCormick, 1990b; McLean, 1990; and Owens, 1988 for reviews.) Communication development is closely related to social and cognitive development; communication abilities are first expressed in nonverbal behaviors and then in verbal (symbolic) behaviors; and the complexity and variety of communicative abilities increase as children grow older. The social-affective interactions occurring during infancy form the basis for the social or pragmatic aspects of communication (McLean, 1990). Skills such as initiating, responding to others' initiations, and maintaining interactions are important for developing later conversational skills. Likewise, cognitive knowledge acquired during infancy forms a basis for symbolic behavior (Bates et al., 1979). Sensorimotor knowledge is the essence of what children "know" about their animate and inanimate world, and such knowledge likely influences the meaning aspects of language and communication (McLean & Snyder-McLean, 1978). Sensorimotor knowledge related to the cognitive underpinnings of communication has to do with the relationship of ends to means, causality, schemes for relating to objects (play), and imitation (Bates et al., 1979; Lahey, 1988).

The following brief overview of communication development addresses expressive and receptive development from birth to four years. The greatest detail is provided for the period from birth to two years, because this period includes the most significant transitions and the greatest challenges in communication development faced by young children with disabilities, their caregivers, and early childhood professionals. The reader is urged to consult the reviews just cited for a more detailed account of language and communication development.

Birth to 12 Months

In the first few months of life, an infant's facial expressions, body posture, vocalizations, and even skin color communicate a great deal of information, about comfort, discomfort, or distress, about readiness to engage in interaction, and about interest in objects or events. In the early months, behaviors are primarily reflexive and reactive to internal and external stimuli, and caregivers respond to these infant cues to help regulate the child's level of arousal (Tronick, 1989). Thus, an infant's behavior comes to serve communicative functions when adults interpret and respond to the behavior. Responses may include efforts to comfort the child, provide appropriate levels of stimulation, and provide for tangible needs such as feeding or changing. Caregivers speak with a tone of voice that can heighten the child's interest and that elicits sustained face to face contact. The infant may quiet to a caregiver's voice and touch, and focus on the caregiver's face, creating early joint attentional states and a transactional pattern of affective engagement followed by disengagement (Brazelton & Cramer, 1990).

Between 3 and 8 months, a child makes significant social, cognitive, and motoric gains. Social-affective development is characterized by increased engagement with caregivers, production of more varied and readable behavioral signals, and increased ability to participate in turn-taking sequences, which are thought to provide the foundation for later communicative reciprocity. Cognitive gains result in an increased ability to understand events and their causes, and people and their actions, which leads to greater recognition of contingency relationships. A child actively forms and tests hypotheses about behavior related to outcomes, and

comes to anticipate and initiate events in highly routinized caregiving and play interactions. Increased mobility and interest in exploration provide many opportunities for adults to engage in teaching interactions involving language modeling and mutual engagement with toys. During this period, caregivers clearly are responding to the child's behavior as if it was intentionally communicative, and such contingent responding leads to the child's intentional use of signals to affect the behavior of others (McLean, 1990).

The last 3 months of the first year bring a major new aspect of communication development—the intentional use of communicative signals to have specific preplanned effects on the behavior of others (Bates, 1979). Initially, the child uses primitive gestures and vocalizations to communicate intentions, but by the age of 12 months and continuing into the second year, prelinguistic communicative behaviors begin to become more sophisticated and conventionalized. For example, children first communicate intentionally through gestures and sounds that may be understood primarily by caregivers; but shortly thereafter, conventional gestures such as pointing and showing emerge accompanied by more consistent sound patterns (McLean, 1990). Bruner (1981) indicated that children express three major intentions by the end of the first year:

1 *Behavioral regulation*, including signals to regulate another person's behavior for purposes of requesting objects or actions, rejecting objects, or protesting another person's behavior
2 *Social interaction*, including signals to attract and maintain another's attention to oneself for affiliative purposes, such as greeting, calling, requesting social routines, and requesting comfort
3 *Joint attention*, including signals used to direct another's attention to comment on

interesting objects and events for the purpose of sharing the experience with others

These communicative intentions are initially expressed preverbally and then later through language as it emerges. Many categorical systems have been developed for doc-

umenting early communicative intentions or functions. Box 10.1 presents another classification of the communicative functions served through gestures and/or language.

From early in development, infants orient to sounds and speech in the environment, and by approximately 4 months, they become proficient at localizing auditory stim-

---

BOX 10.1   Taxonomy of early pragmatic functions

Category	Description
Requesting	Solicitation of a service from a listener. Three types of requests are delineated:
	Requests for Objects: Requests are gestures and/or utterances which direct the listener to provide some object for the child; the object is usually out of reach because of some physical or spatial barrier.
	Requests for Action: Requests are gestures and/or utterances which direct the listener to act upon some object in order to make the object move. The child's interest appears to be in the action of an object rather than the object *per se.*
	Requests for Information: Requests are gestures and/or utterances which direct the listener to provide information about an object, action or location.
Protesting	Gestures and/or utterances which express disapproval of an adult action or utterance.
Commenting	Direction of the listener's attention to some observable referent. Two types of comments are delineated:
	Comments on Objects: Comments are gestures and/or utterances which appear to call the listener's attention to some object identified by the child.
	Comments on Action: Comments are gestures and/or utterances which appear to call the listener's attention to the movement of some object rather than the object *per se.*
Greeting	Gestures and/or utterances, subsequent to the entrance of a person into a situation, which express recognition.
Transferring	Primarily a gesture, the intent of which is to place an object in another person's possession.
Showing Off	Gestures and/or utterances that appear to be used to attract attention.
Acknowledging	Gestures and/or utterances which provide notice that the listener's previous utterances or gestures were received.
Answering	A gesture and/or utterance from the child in response to a request for information from a listener.

Note: From "The Communicative Intention Inventory: A System for Observing and Coding Children's Early Intentional Communication" by T. Coggins and R. Carpenter, 1981, *Applied Psycholinguistics, 2,* 235–251. Copyright 1982 by *Applied Psycholinguistics.* Reprinted by permission.

ulation. There is increasing evidence that the infant's auditory system is especially attuned to perceive features of oral language, especially intonational patterns that aid in recognition of familiar voices (Leonard, 1991). By the last few months of the first year, children respond to commonly used ritualized language (e.g., "peek-a-boo") in familiar routines and to some single words with gestural and environmental support.

12 to 24 Months

In the second year, children's communicative signaling becomes more consistent, explicit, readable, and sophisticated, resulting in greater success in communicating and regulating interactions with others. There also is a dramatic increase in the rate of communication. Wetherby, Cain, Yonclas and Walker (1988) found a fivefold increase in the frequency of communicative acts in the child's movement from the preverbal to the multiword stage.

Early in the single-word stage, new-word acquisition is slow and unstable; words may be used inconsistently and may drop out of a child's vocabulary as new words are acquired. Gestures and vocalization still comprise a large proportion of communicative behaviors. Vocabulary increases slowly and steadily until about eighteen months, when two major shifts begin to occur. First, vocabulary begins to expand at a dramatic rate. Second, the child begins to combine two or more words at a time to express more complex meanings.

Throughout this period, there is much continuity in the meanings that the child communicates. The child's emerging words, which begin to appear during the first half of the second year, express meanings similar to those initially expressed nonverbally. Nonverbal behaviors illustrate various semantic functions, as shown in the left-hand portion of Table 10.1. As children begin to speak they express these same functions verbally,

as shown in the right-hand portion of Table 10.1. These and other semantic relationships are later expressed with two-word utterances and still later with two or more words, as shown in Table 10.2 (Lahey, 1988; McLean and Snyder-McLean, 1978). During this period, language use still refers primarily to immediately observable events. Although speech intelligibility may be limited early on, especially to unfamiliar persons, 30 to 40 percent of speech should be intelligible by the time the child is 2 years of age.

Throughout this period, children can respond more consistently to language directed to them with less need for contextual or environmental support. At about 1 year, responses to inhibitions (i.e., "no") and simple familiar actions are observed. By 18 months, the child can locate familiar objects, identify body parts, and follow simple directions. By 24 months, receptive vocabulary has expanded greatly, and the child can respond to words when the object or person is not in the immediate environment. Action words are understood outside of highly routinized utterances, as are two-word semantic relations. The child can also respond to routine questions about actions and about the existence and location of people and objects.

24 to 48 Months

Between 24 and 48 months, the basics of sentence grammar, including morphology (word organization), and syntax (sentence organization), are acquired. Children move from a semantic or meaning base to sentence grammar. Grammatical knowledge and forms that fine tune and modulate meanings are acquired. Due to an expanding vocabulary, use of language is more precise, explicit, and descriptive. A variety of sentence modalities appear allowing for more conventional grammatical means for asking questions and expressing negation. Toward the end of this period, children show increasing politeness in language use. Children begin to communicate about more complex relations such as causality (e.g., "because") and conditionality (e.g., "If . . ., then . . ."). Communication about future and past events increases substantially, and connected narrative discourse emerges as children begin to relate logical sequences of events across many utterances. Speech should be close to 90% intelligible by the end of this period.

Advances in comprehension usually predate achievements in production. Children are increasingly able to understand language about past and future events, and can respond to a wider range of vocabulary. Responses to a variety of question forms—initially "what," "where," and "who," followed by "when" and "why" towards the end of this period—can be observed. Children's greater comprehension and their increased ability to follow meaning in narrative discourse (e.g., in stories) play a major role in their emergence as conversational partners.

Problems Related to Preschool Language and Communication Disorders

Early intervention for young children with communication difficulties is important due to the significant role communication and language play in children's ability to relate

TABLE 10.1

Nonverbal behaviors and one-word statements which express semantic functions

Examples of Nonverbal Behaviors	General Relationship and Function	Single Word Statement	Function/Meaning of Single Word Statements
Child directs attention to object which moves or makes a sudden sound; seeks out desired objects when they are out of sight.	Existence	"there" "uh-oh"	To point out objects— particularly those which startle child
Enjoys repeating actions; indicates desire for more of an object or activity when stopped; enjoys collecting multiple examples of a type of object.	Recurrence	"more"	First to request and later to comment on the recurrence of an activity or object
	Disappearance	"away"	To comment on the disappearance of object which had existed in context
Shows surprise or disappointment if object is not found where expected; indicates that cup is empty.	Nonexistence	"a' gone" "no"**	(same as above) To comment on nonexistence where existence had been expected
	Cessation	"stop"	To comment on the cessation of an activity
Gesturally or physically rejects a toy, food, or activity not desired.	Rejection	"no"*	To protest undesired action or comment on forbidden object (e.g., stove)

TABLE 10.1
continued

Examples of Nonverbal Behaviors	General Relationship and Function	Single Word Statement	Function/Meaning of Single Word Statements
When an object is handed to the child, he looks to the place where it was previously; goes to seek a desired object in the place where it is usually kept; returns object to place from which it was taken.	Location	"up"**	To comment on spatial location
Selects his own cup, coat, shoes, etc. when several are available. Hands an object which belongs to another to that person.	Possession		
Reaches arm up toward adult.	Action	"up"*	To request the action of being picked up
Attempts to perform an action performed by another; participates in alternating, role-exchanged reciprocal play (e.g., ball rolling).	Agency		
Given an object, demonstrates an action typically carried out upon that object (e.g., kicks a ball, pushes a truck, opens a book).	Objective		

*First use of word generally observed.
**Second use of word generally observed.

Note: From *A Transactional Approach to Early Language Training* by J. McLean and L. K. Snyder-McLean, Columbus, Ohio: Charles E. Merrill, 1978. Copyright 1978 by Charles E. Merrill. Reprinted by permission.

socially and to learn from others. Early intervention also may prevent additional difficulties experienced by children and their families (Baker & Cantwell, 1987; Guralnick & Bennett, 1987). Some of these difficulties appear to be closely related to, and possibly to be the result of early language and communication disorders.

First, families of children with communication problems may experience stress related to difficulties in specifying a child's problem. Difficulties in early identification may occur due to the lack of clearly defined criteria for determining communication problems in young children, and the resulting lack of appropriate referrals when a problem is suspected by caregivers (Prizant & Wetherby, 1988). Thus, parents of children with language disorders may experience significant stress due to potential spousal conflict over whether a problem exists, and whether professional guidance should be sought (Gottlieb, 1988). There may be differences of opinion between caregivers as to whether to be concerned about language delays in an otherwise healthy and alert child, especially because there is great variability in the appearance of first words and in the rate of language acquisition even in normally developing children. This problem is more likely to occur when communication and language delays do not coexist with significant physical, sensory, or cognitive disabilities.

Second, the behavior of many preschool children with communication difficulties may pose significant challenges for parents. Based on extensive family interviews, Bristol and Schopler (1984) found major sources of stress included the child's lack of effective communication ability, his lack of response to family members, and the behavior management problems he presented.

Third, a significant relationship has been found between a history of preschool language disorders and later academic problems. Aram and Hall (1989) found that 60 percent

TABLE 10.2

Description and examples of semantic expressions in two- and three-word utterances

Type of Statement	Description	Example and Context
Introducer + Entity	Used to call attention to someone or something. The *introducer word* calls attention to the person, thing, or activity, and the *entity word* names the person, thing, or activity	"This shoe," as the child shows shoe to an adult "It doggie" as the child points to a dog in the yard
More + Entity	Used to request more of something or some activity, or to comment on something or some event that just recurred	"More milk," when child's glass is empty and she wants more milk "Another truck," as child rides in a car and sees another truck pass
Negation + Entity	Used to describe the nonexistence of, reject, or deny something	"No cookie," when child has eaten the cookie (nonexistence) "No cookie," when the child does not want an offered cookie (rejection) "No cookie," when child has cookie but does not want someone else to know it (denial)
Agent + Action	Used to describe someone doing some action or initiating some process	"Doggie eat," as child watches a dog eat "Kitty run" as child watches a kitten run
Action + Object	Used to describe something or someone who is moved or on which (whom) an action or process is initiated	"Drop cookie," as child comments on a dropped cookie "Drink water," as child watches a dog drink from a bowl

TABLE 10.2
continued

Type of Statement	Description	Example and Context
Agent + Object	Used to describe something or someone involved with another thing or person	"Doggie ball," as a child watches a dog play with a ball "Mommy car," as a child watches Mother wash the car
Action + Locative	Used to describe the site of an action or process	"Sit chair," as child climbs up on a chair to sit "Eat table," as child sees parents eating at the table
Entity + Locative	Used to describe the position of someone or something in a given location	"Coat bed," as child goes to get his coat off the bed "Ball box," as child's ball bounces into the box
Possessor + Possession	Used to describe something owned by someone	"My coat," as child takes his coat from the coat rack "Daddy shoe," as the child picks up her father's shoe
Entity + Attribute	Used to describe a quality or quantity of someone or something	"Big shoe," as child picks up father's shoe "Pretty purse," as child looks at mother's purse

Note: These relationships are combined in three-word statements: for example, "Mommy sit chair" is a combination of Agent + Action + Locative.
Source: Semantic relations taken from Coggins and Carpenter (1979).

of children who displayed language disorders at a preschool level required special education placement during later childhood. Similarly, relationships have been found between speech, language, and communication disorders and emotional and behavioral disturbances in children. Various studies have documented co-occurrence rates of 50 to 60 percent for language and communication disorders and emotional/behavioral disorders in children and adolescents (Prizant, Audet, Burke, Hummel, Maher & Theadore, 1990). Stevenson and Richman (1976) found that 59 percent of 3-year-olds with expressive language delays were reported by their parents to have significant behavioral disturbances.

OVERVIEW OF ASSESSMENT

This section provides an overview of the principles, approaches, and domains of communication assessment and describes the importance of involving parents as partners in the assessment process. It is beyond the scope of this chapter to include a comprehensive and detailed discussion of language and communication assessment. The following recent resources provide more in-depth

information on early language and communication assessment: Lahey (1988); Lund
and Duchan (1988); Rossetti (1990); Schuler
(1989); Roberts and Crais (1989) and Richard
and Schiefelbusch (1990).

Principles of Assessment

Communication and language assessment
should be guided by principles that reflect
the complexity and multidimensional nature
of the process of communication. Communication development also is closely related
to other aspects of development, including
cognitive, motor, and socioemotional development. Thus, assessment should address
these relationships. Some basic assessment
principles follow.

Principle # 1   *Assessment is the ongoing
process of gathering information about a
child's communicative behavior across situational contexts over time.* A child's communicative abilities vary greatly as a function
of many factors including the environment
or setting in which a child is observed, the
persons interacting with the child, and the
familiarity of the situation (Lund & Duchan,
1988). Communication assessment should
account for the normal variability observed
in communicative functioning in young children across contexts. This is especially true
for children with delays or identified disabilities, because slower acquisition of communicative abilities, as well as limited generalization, may account for great variability
across contexts (Prizant, 1982).

Thus, assessment ideally involves gathering and coordinating information from a variety of persons who regularly interact with
a child in different contexts. This requires
that assessment be an ongoing process, for
the picture of a child's communicative abilities and needs will not be complete, and indeed may change significantly, as information from different sources helps to fill in the
details.

Principle # 2   *A variety of strategies should
be used for collecting information.* In order to
ascertain a child's communicative strengths
and needs, strategies including direct assessment, naturalistic observation, and interviewing of significant others may be used
(Prizant & Wetherby, 1985). Direct assessment involves interaction with a child, typically using standardized instruments or
checklists or less structured play procedures
to collect a language and communication
sample for later analysis. Naturalistic observation is characterized by nonintrusive data
collection by observing or videotaping a
child in relatively familiar routines and with
familiar persons. Finally, information may
be collected by interviewing significant others who have regular opportunities to observe and interact with a child (Schuler,
Peck, Willard & Theimer, 1989). Each of
these strategies provides qualitatively different information about a child's communicative abilities that may ultimately be integrated to construct a more holistic picture of
a child's communication system. The use of
different assessment strategies also allows
for cross-validation of findings.

Principle # 3   *A variety of instruments or
tools may be used in assessment, and these
should be selected based upon a child's developmental level, the purpose of the assessment, and the assessment strategies to be
used.* For example, a communication interview protocol or developmental checklist focusing on milestones in development may be
used when interviewing caregivers or other familiar persons, and can provide information
for determining eligibility and for planning intervention. An observational checklist may be
used during naturalistic observation or during
direct assessment, and also can provide information regarding eligibility for services and
intervention planning.

In general, more direct and formal communication assessment strategies such as the

use of standardized tests are most appropriate for developmentally advanced preschoolers (e.g., children at conversational language levels or with greater comprehension) and chronologically older preschoolers. Indirect observational approaches are most appropriate for developmentally and chronologically younger children. Roberts and Crais (1989) and Rossetti (1990) provide a detailed listing and discussion of communication assessment instruments.

Videotape is being used with increasing frequency during communication and language assessment. It is especially relevant for early assessment because subtle communicative behaviors including verbal, vocal, and nonverbal elements may need to be documented during a child's interactions with others. The use of videotape also allows the assessor to observe a child's behavior in many contexts without actually being in all those contexts. Videotape can also be used by caregivers as an educational tool and for observing progress over time.

Principle # 4 *Communication assessment must account for unconventional as well as conventional communicative behavior.* For some young children, the acquisition of conventional verbal or nonverbal means of communication is especially difficult. Some children may develop idiosyncratic and even socially unacceptable means of communicating. Idiosyncratic means may include subtle or difficult-to-read behaviors that can only be understood by those who know a child well. Such behavior has been documented in children with multiple handicaps (Yoder, 1989) and children with social-communicative disorders such as autism (Prizant & Wetherby, 1987). Socially unacceptable forms of communication including aggression and tantrumming have been observed in children and adolescents with developmental disabilities (Carr & Durand, 1985; Wetherby & Prutting, 1984). Frameworks and instruments

that document intentional but idiosyncratic or socially unacceptable forms of communication as well as conventional forms of communication are available (Donnellan, Mirenda, Mesaros & Fassbender, 1984; Wetherby & Prizant, 1989, 1990) and provide a more complete picture of a child's communication system. Figure 10.1 presents an observational checklist (Wetherby, 1986) of communicative means and functions based on Bruner's (1981) categorization of communicative intents.

Principle # 5 *Parents or primary caregivers should be considered expert informants about their child's communicative competence.* It is not uncommon for caregivers to report that they observe different patterns or levels of communication in their children than may be observed by professionals during an assessment. Unfortunately, discrepancies between caregiver and professional observations has the potential to lead to misunderstandings. As noted earlier, communication development and competence is naturally variable across contexts, and caregivers have opportunities to observe and interact with their child far more frequently, and in more familiar situations than do professionals. Thus, a general underlying assumption in communication assessment is that caregivers are most knowledgeable about their child's abilities; professionals must refine their interviewing skills (Winton, 1988) and use appropriate techniques and instruments to tap such knowledge (see Schuler et al., 1989).

Principle # 6 *Developmental research on the sequence and processes of language and communication development should provide the framework for assessing a child's communicative abilities.* Familiarity with sequences and processes of communication and language development is essential for at least three reasons. First, although individual differences exist in some aspects of lan-

Child's Name: _____

Date of Sample: ____ / ____ / ____

Context: _____

Communicative Means

Communicative Functions	Preverbal														Verbal					
	Physical Manipulation	Giving	Pointing	Showing	Gaze Shift	Proximity	Head Nod/Head Shake	Facial Expression	Self-injury	Aggression	Tantrum	Crying/Whining	Vocalizing	Other:	Immediate Echo	Delayed Echo	Creative One-word	Creative Multi-word	Other:	Other:
Behavioral Regulation Request Object																				
Request Action																				
Protest																				
Social Interaction Request Social Routine																				
Request Comfort																				
Greeting																				
Calling																				
Request Permission																				
Showing Off																				
Joint Attention Comment																				
Request Information																				
Provide Information																				
Other Functions:																				

FIGURE 10.1

Checklist of communicative functions and means

Note: From "Checklist of Communicative Functions and Means" by A. Wetherby, 1986. Unpublished instrument.

313

guage acquisition, thirty years of research has documented relatively invariant sequences and stages of development (Bates, O'Connell & Shore, 1987), and thus can provide an organizational framework for documenting a child's abilities and development (Lahey, 1988). This framework also helps professionals and caregivers focus on small increments in progress rather than focusing primarily on major change which may take significantly longer periods of time. Second, an intervention plan should be based on a child's current level of ability with developmentally appropriate skills targeted in short- and long-term goals. Of course, goal setting is greatly influenced by a child's functional needs and the caregiver's priorities; however, unless these factors are cast within a developmental framework, goals may be unrealistic. Finally, knowledge of developmental sequences and processes enables professionals and caregivers to model language and communication in daily interactions to facilitate communicative growth.

Principle # 7 *Assessment should always provide direct implications and directions for intervention.* Program planning should be based on ongoing assessment of changes in communication and language behavior. Such documentation provides feedback in evaluating the effectiveness of intervention. Alternative strategies, if needed, can be developed in collaboration with caregivers to address emerging communicative needs within the context of the child's developmental strengths and weaknesses.

Principle # 8 *Assessment should be viewed as a potential form of intervention.* Caregivers' involvement in assessment activities may contribute significantly to their understanding of their child's communicative strengths and needs, which may ultimately benefit their child. Thus, assessment may serve as one form of intervention. For example, caregivers may become more aware of their child's communicative signals and, as

a result, develop interactive strategies that are conducive to sustaining social and communicative exchange. Positive effects of caregiver observation and participation have been documented in early neurobehavioral assessment (Brazelton & Cramer, 1990) and are now being advocated for early communication assessment (Prizant & Wetherby, 1990). Educators and clinicians should plan assessment activities to be supportive of caregiver knowledge and expertise, while at the same time providing caregivers with opportunities to learn about their child's strengths and needs.

Domains of Assessment

Language and communication assessment traditionally has focused on a child's behavior, with an emphasis on the sophistication of communicative means or form (e.g., gestures, sounds, words, multiword utterances), and the level of comprehension of speech (Prizant & Schuler, 1987b). With expanding views of communication development, child-focused assessment concerned primarily with the means of communication is now considered to be only one dimension of a comprehensive communication assessment. (Of course, a comprehensive communication assessment is only one aspect of a multidisciplinary assessment accounting for child and family strengths and needs.) Thus, a comprehensive communication assessment needs to address child abilities in communicative interactions as well as to identify aspects of the behavior of communicative partners that supports or limits successful communicative exchange. Additionally, qualities of learning environments that support or restrict communicative growth need to be identified.

Assessing Child Abilities

An assessment framework delineates specific content areas or domains of a child's communicative behavior that should be assessed to provide a profile of communicative strengths and needs. Some information may be developmental in nature (e.g., developmental level of a child's linguistic comprehension or understanding), while other information may be more qualitative (e.g., frequency of use of nonverbal signals such as communicative gaze in interactions). Box 10.2 presents a generic framework delineating specific content areas. The specific type of information provided in each area will vary according to a child's developmental level of communicative functioning.

Expressive Language and Communication

The primary focus in this domain is documentation of (a) communicative means, or the behaviors by which information is communicated; and (b) communicative functions, or the purposes for which a child communicates (Prizant & Schuler, 1987a). For developmentally young, preintentional children, communicative means may include nonverbal and vocal behaviors involving body posture, facial expression, limb extension, hand gestures, gaze direction and gaze aversion, cry and cooing vocalizations, and intonated vowel and/or babbling vocalizations. These signals may function to inform a receiver of the child's physiological and emotional state, level of alertness, focus of attention, interest in interacting or receiving comfort from other persons, interest in obtaining objects, or desire to have events continue or cease. For developmentally more advanced children who communicate through prelinguistic means, intentional use of idiosyncratic and conventional gestures, as well as vocalizations and emerging word forms (if observed) should be documented. For children using language-based systems including speech, sign language, or graphic systems (e.g., communication boards), range of

---

BOX 10.2   Social-communication assessment framework

I. **Expressive language and communication**
   A. Communicative means (i.e., gestural, vocal, verbal, other)
   B. Communicative functions
   C. Semantic complexity of language and range of vocabulary (if present)
   D. Morphological and syntactic complexity of language (if present)
II. **Receptive language and communication**
   A. Nonlinguistic response strategies
   B. Linguistic comprehension
III. **Speech Production**
   A. Quality of vocal production
   B. Quality of speech production
   C. Oral structure and oral-motor and speech function
IV. **Language-related cognitive abilities**
   A. Symbolic play and object exploration
   B. Attentional capacities
   C. Imitation
V. **Social-affective behavior**
   A. Use of gaze for social referencing
   B. Expression of positive affect
   C. Expression of negative affect

vocabulary and semantic and syntactic complexity as well as communicative functions should be documented. Range of vocabulary refers to the number of different words and word classes (e.g., object words, action words, modifiers or descriptors) children use meaningfully. Semantic complexity refers to the types of semantic functions or meaning categories expressed in language-based systems (see Table 10.2), while syntactic complexity refers to the structural or grammatical complexity of multiword forms for children beyond early language stages. In all the cases just noted, communicative functions should continue to be assessed. It is important to note that as children advance developmentally and are better able to regulate conversational interactions, the purposes for which they communicate may change. Such changes are reflected in the variety of systems that have been developed for documenting communicative intentions and functions (See Chapman, 1981, for a review).

Receptive Language and Communication
A child's ability to receive and respond to communicative signals is the second domain that should be assessed. Initially, a full audiological assessment should be conducted by an audiologist to assess hearing (Roush, 1991). Informal behavioral observation of very young children may also contribute information about a child's functional hearing, including whether a child shows any startle response to loud sounds, localizes or orients to speech or environmental sounds, or can be comforted by a caregiver's voice. At higher levels of ability, children can respond to gestures and vocalizations of others, and with the support of situational cues, comprehend words used in familiar activities and routines. Chapman (1978) has identified such "nonlinguistic response strategies" in young children which can be observed from about 8 months of age. True linguistic comprehension is evidenced when children can comprehend words without situational or nonverbal cues, especially when words refer to persons, objects, and events outside of the immediate environment. Roberts and Crais (1989) provide a detailed discussion of assessment of receptive language and communication.

Speech Production
Many young children with disabilities may not be able to acquire and use speech as a primary mode of communication. This may be due to cognitive impairment, hearing loss, or specific neuromotor speech disorders, such as (a) dysarthria, a paralysis or paresis (i.e., weakness) in the oral musculature often observed in children with cerebral palsy or other identified neurological disorders, or (b) developmental dyspraxia, a dysfunction in the ability to plan the coordinated movements to produce intelligible sequences of speech sounds. Assessment should address the status of speech and vocal production to determine whether an augmentative nonspeech mode of communication may be beneficial. Factors to consider when evaluating the potential for speech include: (a) current level of intelligible speech; (b) ability to imitate a variety of speech sounds; (c) history of problems in chewing or swallowing; (d) abnormal reflexive patterns (e.g., hyperactive gag reflex); and (e) interest in and motivation to use speech. A complete oral function assessment should be conducted by a qualified speech-language pathologist and/or occupational therapist; however, informal observations about vocal control for speech, patterns of chewing and swallowing, and other indicators of oral motor function are also useful.

Language-Related Cognitive Abilities
Communication abilities should be considered in the context of a child's cognitive abilities. For one thing, communication and language development are highly correlated with aspects of cognitive development including

symbolic play and the learning of cause-effect relations (Bates, 1979). By profiling a young child's communicative abilities relative to nonverbal cognitive abilities and capacities, information is provided about the nature of a communication or language delay.

For another thing, communication is the means by which the child expresses her understanding of the world. Thus, the child's language use is a reflection of and is dependent upon her world knowledge. Finally, the choice of augmentative communication systems, which may be influenced by levels of cognitive/representational ability, requires some estimation of cognitive abilities. Westby (1988), Rossetti (1990) and Linder (1990) provide guidelines for assessing language-related cognitive abilities in young children.

Social-Affective Behavior Communicative interactions are regulated by social-affective signals, including facial expression, vocalizations, and other observable behavior. Young children also use gaze to reference, monitor, or signal attention. Some children with social and communicative impairments may have limited use of gaze shifts to regulate interactions, and their emotional states may be difficult to read due to a limited range of expression (Prizant & Wetherby, 1990). Because these signals influence communicative interactions, communication assessment should go beyond consideration of intentional nonverbal and verbal behaviors. This domain of assessment is especially crucial for infants and developmentally young children.

Assessing the Behavior of Communicative Partners

Communicative partners (e.g., parents, other caregivers, educators, therapists) demonstrate a wide range of behavior that may facilitate a child's communicative growth or that in some cases may hinder communicative transactions. In extreme cases, some partners may develop maladaptive interactive styles that are detrimental to the child's communicative and socioemotional development (Field, 1987).

Partners' strengths and weaknesses in supporting communicative interactions may be observed and documented during observations of daily living and play activities. Relevant dimensions of partner style include degree of acceptance of a child's communicative attempts (Duchan, 1989), use of directive versus facilitative styles of interaction (Duchan, 1989; Marfo, 1990), and use of specific strategies such as responding contingently to child behavior, providing appropriate communicative models, maintaining the topics of child initiations, and expanding or elaborating on communicative attempts (Duchan, 1989; Peck, 1989). For example, research has demonstrated that caregivers of children with disabilities tend to be somewhat more directive in interactions, frequently using questions and commands (Clark & Seifer, 1985; Mahoney, 1988; Tiegerman & Siperstein, 1984).

The primary purpose of assessing partner style is to help partners develop an awareness of the strategies they are using. It is important to realize that there is not an optimal or correct communicative style for all children or partners. Factors such as a child's developmental level, extent of disability, attentional capacities, and social motivation must be taken into account. A partner's level of comfort using a particular style and the cultural influences on interactions with young children must also be considered.

The match between a partner's style and a child's ability to participate actively and successfully is of overriding concern. A successful match is predicated on a partner's sensitivity to a child's communicative signals and the child's ability to respond to the partner's overtures; such a match results in a sense of efficacy for both the child and the partner (Dunst, Lowe & Bartholomew, 1990). In one case, the partner's assumption of a more directive style may help keep the child focused and participating actively, while in another case this same style may hinder successful communication. Comfort (1988), Rossetti (1990), Wilcox (1989), Peck (1989) and Duchan (1989) review approaches and strategies for assessing different dimensions of partner-child interaction.

Assessing Learning Contexts

In addition to the interactive factors we have already noted, other situational or contextual factors play an important role in communication development by providing opportunities for young children to participate in communicative interactions. Peck (1989) noted that situational variables exert great influence on the communicative behavior of children and partners. Joint activity routines (JAR's) (Snyder-McLean, Solomonson, McLean, & Sack, 1984) or social routines (McCormick, 1990a), for example, are predictable and repetitive activities requiring active involvement, reciprocal and exchangeable roles, a mutual focus of attention, turn taking, and communicative exchange focused on a common theme or goal. JAR's may be as simple as early mother-child social games such as "peek-a-boo" or songs, but this category also includes more complex activities such as food preparation or social games. The identification of JAR's in a child's daily experiences indicates that there are opportunities for communicative growth.

Peck (1989) and Prizant and Schuler (1987a) also noted that children must have needs to communicate—the need to obtain assistance or desired objects as well as the need to reject or protest in socially acceptable ways. It is from such experiences that children learn to communicate for a wide range of purposes (Prizant & Wetherby, 1988).

Also, opportunities for decision making and choice making have been associated with higher degrees of communicative initiation and spontaneity in older children with disabilities (Peck, 1985; Houghton, Bronicki & Guess, 1987). Such opportunities for children to experience social control are now considered important characteristics of environments that support communicative growth for young children (Theadore, Maher, & Prizant, 1990).

Assessing Communicative Needs

The assessment of communicative needs can be accomplished by interviewing caregivers and by observing the child in everyday situations. Caregivers can identify the communicative skills they feel would be most helpful to their child and family. Specific information may include situations in which a child is frustrated due to limitations in communication or in which the child cannot participate fully because of communicative problems. Caregivers may also be asked to identify their own concerns or needs relative to supporting their child's communicative development. Ecological inventories (Falvey, 1986) can also be used to help determine goals for preschool children. Through observations in a variety of settings, needs can be documented by observing the discrepancy between current abilities and the communicative demands of the different situations.

PRINCIPLES OF INTERVENTION

Strategies to enhance communication and language skills will vary depending upon a child's age, upon his communicative, social, and cognitive functioning, and upon his motor abilities and unique learning style. Other significant factors include family priorities and routines, family supports, and the motivation of caregivers and their ability to make modifications to support communicative growth. The service delivery options available (e.g., home or center-based services) also will influence the types and amounts of services provided (Bailey & Simeonsson, 1988; Prizant & Wetherby, 1988).

Despite this wide range of factors, current literature suggests some generic "best practices" for communication enhancement. The following principles are drawn from the work of Bricker (1989), Bromwich (1990), MacDonald (1989), McCormick (1990a), Prizant and Wetherby (1991), Prizant and Schuler (1987a).

Principle # 1 *Communication enhancement is one dimension of an integrated intervention plan for a child and his or her family.* Communication enhancement should never be viewed as an isolated component of an intervention program. Communication enhancement efforts can be targeted in a wide variety of daily routines, as well as in activities addressing other developmental needs of a child.

Principle # 2 *Successful approaches to communication enhancement are achieved through caregiver–professional partnerships.* Caregiver–professional collaboration is essential to achieve coordination and consistency in communication enhancement efforts. This is especially true for children who spend a significant part of their day in center-based programs. Coordination is needed in the use of an interactive style most conducive to a child's active participation and communicative growth, in developing strategies for arranging learning environments, and in using specific approaches to help a child develop more sophisticated means of communication.

Principle # 3 *Caregivers should be viewed as primary intervention agents.* Language and communication abilities develop in the context of secure and nurturant caregiver–child relationships. Because this climate is

experienced most frequently with primary caregivers, interventions that do not acknowledge the central role of primary caregivers in communication enhancement may have limited effect. To encourage caregivers to participate willingly and voluntarily in such endeavors, they should be respected and supported in setting communication priorities and goals compatible with their values.

Principle # 4 *A child's motivations and preferences should be documented and taken into account in planning activities and strategies for communication enhancement. Less optimal situations for communication enhancement activities should be identified.* Social motivation is a major factor in communication development. Young children communicate to have their needs met, to engage others for social affiliative purposes (i.e., for comfort, for social games), for affective sharing and attunement (Stern, 1985), and for sharing experiences and observations (Wetherby & Prizant, in press). These communicative interactions provide further opportunities for partners to model for children and to expand and elaborate upon children's initiations. However, some children with disabilities may find social interaction and communication to be difficult or even stressful. Educators and clinicians should work with caregivers to identify the most motivating activities and the least stressful contexts in which to target goals. Communicative expectations may be somewhat lower in the more stressful circumstances (e.g., in a context with much distraction, in an unfamiliar environment) or during extenuating circumstances (e.g., while a child is recovering from an illness, when significant changes have occurred in a regular routine causing distress).

McCormick (1990a) discussed three strategies for determining the activities and materials most motivating to a child. A *reinforcement survey* asks caregivers, other familiar people, or the child about favorite activities, toys, peers, and so forth. *Reinforcer sampling* is conducted by allowing a child free access to a variety of materials/toys placed on a display or arranged on the floor of a playroom. Materials/toys chosen by the child may then be listed and incorporated in activities. Finally, *observation of the child in natural routines* provides important information about motivations and preferences. The child's level of attention, her displays of positive affect, and her motivation to interact with others are features that should be observed relative to different activities. The activities of greatest interest may then be targeted for the most intensive communication enhancement efforts.

In addition, patterns in the nature of preferred materials/activities should also be noted (e.g., activities with auditory or visual stimulation, activities such as puzzles or nesting cups requiring visual-spatial judgment, activities with full body movement) in order to direct the choice of future activities and materials. A child's motivations and preferences may change, especially during periods of significant developmental growth. Therefore, educators and clinicians should look for signs of limited interest or boredom, signs such as loss of attention to an activity, restlessness, or interest in other environmental events or materials.

Principle # 5 *Activities should be designed to address a child's developmental strengths and learning style.* Many children with communication needs have uneven profiles of abilities (Wetherby & Prizant, in press) and may demonstrate unique learning styles. For example, it is not uncommon for children with social-communicative impairments to demonstrate relatively strong visual-spatial problem-solving skills and rote memory for events, while at the same time showing weaknesses in language development, imitation skills, and social related-

ness. In planning communication enhancement activities, learning strengths and styles should be taken into account in structuring learning environments, choosing materials and activities, and selecting augmentative communication systems.

Principle # 6 *Communication enhancement efforts should be embedded in naturally occurring events and routines. Didactic activities may be useful for some children, but should occur along with more naturalistic approaches.* Warren and Kaiser (1986; 1988) reviewed research literature on "milieu approaches," a category of intervention strategies that use naturally occurring events as contexts for communication enhancement. In recent years, approaches to language intervention have clearly moved in the direction of milieu approaches and away from more artificial didactic teaching approaches. Milieu approaches are characterized by (a) following the child's attentional focus and interests, and encouraging child-initiated communication; (b) providing and seizing upon naturally occurring opportunities to communicate as opposed to teaching within a repetitive drill format following an adult's agenda; (c) teaching within the context of social interaction and conversational exchange; and (d) using language facilitation strategies that occur naturally in early caregiver–child interactions.

Findings of recent research comparing milieu and didactic language teaching approaches with preschoolers have been mixed. Yoder, Kaiser, and Alpert (1991) found that preschoolers with higher scores on a number of pretreatment variables benefitted the most from a didactic language training program, while those who scored low on pretreatment variables benefitted the most from a milieu approach. These results are in contrast with those of other recent studies. However, Yoder et al. (1991) emphasized the preliminary nature of their findings, and implied that even when didactic approaches are used, milieu approaches also should be used to facilitate generalization.

For very young children, milieu approaches are highly relevant due to their child-centered and developmentally sound principles. Children exposed to milieu approaches (a) experience frequent opportunities for communication enhancement; (b) have potential generalization problems minimized; (c) learn functional communication abilities within relevant and familiar situations; and (d) experience natural reinforcement for social participation and successful communication. For caregivers, the use of naturally occurring routines may ease the burden of feeling the need to set up contrived teaching sessions. With minor modifications in selected daily routines, caregivers can focus on their primary role (i.e., providing for their child's emotional, social, and nutritional needs) while providing facilitative experiences for communicative growth.

Professionals can work closely with caregivers to decide how naturally occurring routines may be modified, and which are best for focusing on communication enhancement. For example, for some families, the level of hectic activity at breakfast time may limit the usefulness of this routine for communication enhancement; however, play time with brother or sister after dinner may be a particularly good time. As with all intervention activities, "goodness of fit" with family lifestyle is a major consideration. This same principle holds for classroom or day care program activities as well.

Principle # 7 *The style of communicative partners is a major intervention consideration.* As communication enhancement approaches have become more focused on interactional variables, the modification of partners' communicative style to be most facilitative of a child's communicative growth

becomes a primary intervention goal (Bromwich, 1990; MacDonald, 1989; Wilcox, 1989). As noted earlier, partners may include any persons who interact regularly with a child. It should be recognized that many caregivers already have strong skills in supporting their child's communication development, and may only need minimal guidance and support. Furthermore, there is no one caregiver style that is most appropriate or successful with all children.

Principle # 8 *Children should have opportunities to learn from peers who can provide positive language and social models.* Recently, attention also has shifted to the facilitative role played by peers who may provide good communicative and conversational models for children with more limited abilities (Goldstein & Strain, 1988; Roberts, Burchinal & Bailey, 1991). The facilitative effects of peer interactions may vary based upon chronological age and developmental and chronological age relationships between a child and his or her peers (Roberts, Burchinal & Bailey, 1991). As a general principle, however, the potential benefits of exposure to other children, especially children without disabilities, can no longer be questioned.

DESIGNING LEARNING ENVIRONMENTS AND ACTIVITIES FOR COMMUNICATION ENHANCEMENT

Clearly, naturally occurring activities and routines are the most desirable contexts for communication enhancement. However, children need to be exposed to learning contexts that facilitate, elicit, and support communication in reciprocal interactions with caregivers and peers. For children who are easily distracted or disorganized by high levels of stimulation, it may initially be necessary to provide communication enhancement activities in contrived contexts with minimal distraction. In such cases, similar activities should occur concurrently in a variety of natural contexts to promote generalization. For many children, however, it may only be necessary to make modifications in naturally occurring activities and routines.

Heightened Structure

The term "structure" does not imply rigidity or inflexibility in activities, but rather the degree of *consistency* and *predictability* across and within activities (Prizant, 1982). Virtually all activities to which children are exposed have some underlying structure (Duchan & Weitzner-Lin, 1987). The event structures invoked by caregivers in a child's first two years create consistent and predictable interactive contexts. Within action-based routines, children learn about the structure of turn taking and communicative reciprocity (Bruner, 1981). Routines may include social games such as "peek a boo" and "hide and seek" or song routines with verbal and gestural components. When exposed repeatedly to interactions within predictable formats, a child is better able to perceive and internalize recurring patterns and is encouraged to take a more active participatory role. Caregivers, on the other hand, develop greater expectations for their children's participation through active communicative signaling during activities with predictable structure (Bruner, 1981; Dunst et al., 1990). In planning approaches to communication enhancement, caregivers can enhance consistency and predictability by clearly marking and highlighting the temporal, spatial, and interactive dimensions.

Temporal Structure   To highlight the temporal aspects of experiences caregivers may employ oral language, visual or object supports, and signs or gestures to mark the sequence of events across activities, the initiation and termination of specific activities, or

even the logical sequence of steps within any one activity. Developing an internalized representation of the passage of time helps children anticipate events, delay gratification, and eventually, communicate about past and future events (Prizant & Wetherby, 1990). Language is an important tool in achieving this goal. Many older children with language learning disabilities demonstrate difficulty in dealing with temporal concepts (Bashir, Wiig, & Abrams, 1987).

Language and nonlanguage supports and adaptations can be helpful in supporting young children's developing sense of time. The caregiver might review a sequence of activities or steps within an activity by using pictures and oral and/or written language both prior to and following the completion of activities; and in this review process the caregiver could clearly mark the salient points of the activities—the initiations (e.g., "time for circle"), the progressions (e.g., "hello time is finished, now time for songs"), the approach of completion (e.g., "one more song and circle time is finished"), and terminations (e.g., "circle time is finished; time to put mats away"). Visual supports, such as photos of activities, and gestures or signs, such as the sign for "finished," can be used along with simple language. The use of various modes provides both simple and complex levels of time representation for children at different levels of comprehension. Doss and Reichle (1991) and Siegel-Causey and Ernst (1989) discuss the use of supports for individuals with severe disabilities.

Spatial Structure   Environments can also be organized to help children associate specific locations with different activities and communicative interactions. Specific activities may be planned to occur in different activity areas, and materials may be located on shelves, cubbies, or cabinets in those areas. Representations including photos or picture communication symbols (Mayer-Johnson,

1981, 1985) may be mounted under shelves or on cabinet doors, so that children through association with them may locate the materials they need (Goossens', 1990). Copies of the photos or picture symbols may be used on choice boards or on individual children's communication boards as well.

Interactive Structure Interactive structure refers to the consistency with which oral language, communicative modes, and interactive strategies are used with and modeled for children. The need for linguistic and interactive modifications is supported by the literature on language development, which has repeatedly documented the adjustments made by caregivers to support their children's communicative growth (Duchan, 1986, 1989; Snow & Ferguson, 1977).

INTERACTIVE-FACILITATIVE STRATEGIES

Interactive-facilitative strategies are ways in which communicative partners spontaneously interact with and respond to young children to support communicative growth. The importance of this dimension of intervention is underscored by (a) the fact that opportunities for communicative growth occur naturally throughout the day, (b) research that has demonstrated that caregivers' style of interaction has an important influence on language and communication development (Mahoney, 1988), and (c) transactional theory, which suggests that with caregivers' appropriate modifications of interactive style, children develop a sense of competence in communication. This growing sense of efficacy results in greater participation in social exchange which in turn reinforces caregivers' sense of competence (Dunst et al., 1990).

Interactive facilitative strategies encompass verbal and nonverbal behavior. Educators and clinicians must work closely with caregivers to discover interactive styles and strategies that will best support children's communicative development, and enable children to communicate intentions independently. Recent literature suggest guidelines for developing interactive-facilitative strategies with young children. The following strategies are adapted from Duchan (1989, 1986), MacDonald (1989), MacDonald and Gillette (1988), and McCormick (1990a).

Accepting Children's Communicative Bids Communicative partners provide children with differential feedback regarding their communicative attempts or bids. Duchan (1989) discussed three categories of response. *Rejection* includes direct (e.g., correcting with disapproval, refusal, or scolding) and indirect negative reactions. Negative reactions may have an adverse impact on communicative growth and motivation, especially if such responses occur frequently or if a child may not understand the reasons for such reactions. Indirect negative reactions include ignoring, making negative corrections, and correcting language forms (e.g., articulation, syntax) while ignoring the child's intent. These reactions are thought to have a detrimental effect as well, because the child is provided with limited and negatively toned feedback regarding the success of the communicative attempt. Duchan indicated that the greater the degree of negative feedback, the less successful the interaction.

In general, conditional and unqualified acceptance are more facilitative of communicative growth (Chapman, Leonard, & Mervis, 1986; Duchan, 1989). *Conditional acceptance* includes corrections that accept and acknowledge a child's attempt and provide positive corrective feedback. For example, if a child calls a pony a "doggie," the partner may respond "that looks like a doggie, it has four legs and a tail, but it's called a pony." Conditional acceptance may also include corrections with explanations. In any case, the child's meaning and intent is acknowledged, and further information is provided in a positive manner.

Unqualified or unconditional acceptance includes positive feedback such as attention, verbal and nonverbal expressions of acceptance (e.g., head nods, "yeah, uh-huh," exact imitations), and expressions of positive affect. Unconditional acceptance is characteristic of very early caregiver–child interactions and helps young children to learn that communication is reciprocal. For more communicatively sophisticated children, however, positive corrective feedback has been shown to be most facilitative of language acquisition (Chapman et al., 1986).

Acceptance of children's communicative attempts depends on the content of the interaction and the individual child's needs. However, the literature suggests that (a) direct and indirect rejection of children's communicative attempts should be avoided; (b) unconditional acceptance may be most effective at early communicative stages because it increases reciprocity in interactions and builds upon early emerging intentional communication, and it may also be effective in encouraging interactions with withdrawn or reticent children; and (c) conditional acceptance involving positive corrective feedback that acknowledges a child's intentions and meanings is most supportive of communication development for children at early language stages.

Adjusting the Degree of Directiveness Another dimension of partner–child interactions is the degree of directiveness in the partner's style (Duchan, 1989; Marfo, 1990). A *directive style* is characterized by adult-selected topics and activities, frequent use of imperatives (commands) and test questions (i.e., asking questions when the answer is known, to test a child's knowledge), and frequent use of physical prompting or forcing of appropriate responses (Clark & Seifer,

1985). A directive style often results in fewer child initiations, less elaborate responses, a limited range of communicative functions, and even conversational reticence or passivity (Duchan, 1989).

The caregiver employing a *facilitative style* follows the child's attentional focus, offers choices within activities, responds to children's intent, models a variety of communicative functions (including commenting on a child's activities), and elaborates upon the topic of communication. When the caregiver employs a more facilitative style, (a) the child is provided with some sense of social control and communicative power which has been found to result in increased initiations and more elaborate communicative attempts (Peck, 1985); (b) the child's attentional focus and motivations are followed, with the result that problems of compliance are reduced and learning may increase; and (c) the child is provided with feedback appropriate to her level of development, feedback that supports her communicative and language development.

Determining whether to use a more facilitative or directive style is a child-specific issue, an issue that must be resolved by observing the effect of partner style on interactions. A good stylistic match should result in (a) increased self-regulation of attention (i.e., the ability to maintain a mutual focus of attention with minimal prompting), (b) active involvement in activities, (c) frequent communicative initiations, (d) more elaborate communicative initiations, and (e) positive affective involvement with the partner. A style is facilitative when these characteristics are observed in the child's behavior. For a highly active and distractible child, a style that promotes a mutual attentional focus and more active involvement, even though it may have some directive qualities (e.g., physical prompting and limit setting), must be viewed as facilitative for that child. This same style, however, may have detrimental effects for a child with a lower activity level and greater attentional regulation. As Marfo (1990) has noted, the *function* of adult directiveness in supporting interactions is of overriding concern, not the presence or absence of features thought to be directive. However, in general, educators and clinicians should attempt to incorporate facilitative features in their interactions and gradually modify style along the facilitativeness–directiveness continuum until an optimal match is found.

Adjusting Language and Social Input The timing and complexity of language and social input may have a dramatic impact on a child's ability to sustain attention to others, to take turns in interactions, and to comprehend others' intentions. At least three features of language input that support children's communicative growth have been documented in literature on mother–child interaction (Snow & Ferguson, 1977).

Simple vocabulary and reduced sentence length—Young children learn word meanings by associating language they hear with persons, objects, and actions in the environment around them. Children also better attend to and are able to process language at or slightly above their level of comprehension.

Exaggerated intonation, slower rate, clear segmentation of speech—Exaggerated intonation heightens attention to speech, and communicates affective information (Fernald, 1985). A slow rate and clear segmentation of speech provides children at early language levels with greater processing time and clearer cues for relating language to events (Prizant & Schuler, 1987b).

Contingent responses and scaffolding—Duchan (1989) noted that by providing information that is within a child's "zone of proximal development" (Wertsch, 1985), educators enable children to constantly build upon their current knowledge base. *Contin-*gent responses, focused on what children are thinking or attending to, support language growth. Examples of such responses are *expansions* (which provide utterances that are slightly more grammatically complete) and *extensions* or *expatiations* (which provide additional information or extend topics while incorporating information from the children's utterances).

Scaffolding (Ninio & Bruner, 1978) occurs when adults provide supports such as modeling and prompting at slightly higher levels of language to enable children to perform at higher levels as independently as possible. Scaffolding also occurs through the use of predictable routines, which enable young children to anticipate and play more active roles. Appropriate scaffolding requires that adults be highly aware of children's current ability levels and that they closely observe children's behavior so to provide appropriate models and minimal assistance.

APPROACHES AND GOALS FOR ENHANCING CHILDREN'S COMMUNICATION ABILITIES

Children at different ability and age levels may require different approaches to communication enhancement. Furthermore, the contexts available for communication enhancement also may differ. Children with more severe disabilities may require special adaptations in communication and language enhancement. Approaches and goals therefore are discussed in reference to these considerations. A basic assumption underlying the following discussion is that professionals are working with caregivers to support caregivers' involvement in determining communication priorities and in implementing communication enhancement approaches with their young children to the best of their abilities.

Communication Enhancement for Developmentally Young or Preintentional Children

For preintentional children functioning up to approximately 8 months developmentally, the overriding communication goal is to develop a joint attentional focus in reciprocal interactions, and eventually, the capacity to produce signals intentionally to affect the behavior of others. This goal is significant because early reciprocity and intentional communication is the foundation for an expressive communication and language system (McLean, 1990). The development of readable, intentional signals occurs in the context of reciprocal play and social interaction involving turn taking and mutual imitation. Therefore, establishing readiness to engage in social exchange and participation in turn taking exchanges and reciprocal play are early priorities.

Bricker and Schiefelbusch (1990) presented a four-phase program for early communication intervention: general readiness; reciprocal actions; social-communicative signals; and symbolic communication. The first three phases are relevant to the developmental period under discussion; they bring the child to the level of prelinguistic intentional communication.

Bricker and Schiefelbusch noted that caregivers and early interventionists must first become sensitive to signals that indicate the child is ready to attend to and engage in social exchange. A child's signals of readiness may include quieting and orienting toward a person who is interacting or speaking with him. More specifically, the early interventionists should observe whether a child uses gaze, body orientation, or body movement to signal readiness for engagement when an adult is positioned directly in front, and they should note the types of daily activities during which these readiness signals occur most frequently (e.g., during changing, feeding,

etc.). The adult may vocalize softly with exaggerated intonation, move closer, and then allow the child an opportunity to respond. Facial expression of positive affect, movement toward the adult, and/or vocalization while maintaining orientation and gaze are all positive signs of readiness for further interaction, and are the earliest forms of social reciprocity. For very young children, such responses are most likely to occur during states of quiet alertness, and they are least likely during states of drowsiness or extreme fussiness. However, speaking in a soft melodic voice, imitating a child's vocalizations, and gently stroking a child may help to induce a state of quiet alertness and help regulate emotional arousal (Brazelton & Cramer, 1990). Tronick (1989) noted that early readable signals of distress or discomfort may function as communicative signals or mutual regulatory behaviors in that these signals induce caregivers to apply strategies to help an infant regulate emotional arousal. Thus, important goals for this first phase of communication enhancement include:

- developing caregiver sensitivity to a child's signals of attention and readiness to engage in reciprocal social exchange
- determining the activities during which a young child is most available for social exchange
- developing strategies (e.g., positioning the child, using specific verbal and nonverbal behaviors) and activities (e.g., daily caregiving routines, toys with interesting sensory effects) that will help a child regulate emotional arousal, orient to persons and events, and be available for social interaction

The second phase discussed by Bricker and Schiefelbusch (1990) involves reciprocal actions and encompasses capacities first observed in the developmental age range from 6 to 12 months. The goal for this phase is to develop the child's capacity to participate actively in dyadic exchange through vocalization and action, and to develop anticipation of events in highly predictable joint action routines. As many researchers (Bruner, 1981; Stern, 1985; Brazelton & Cramer, 1990) have noted, reciprocal activity or joint action routines are organized in logical and predictable ways, so that children anticipate steps in the routines, and eventually engage in reciprocal activity over repeated turns. Initially, each child is able to fill her turn with subtle signals of attention, affect display, and bodily movement, but eventually she will develop more varied and sophisticated behavioral response repertoires. Her behavior will be reinforced by adult imitation and affect attunement.

Imitation of other young children is an important strategy for children at this level because initially the other children are more likely to respond in social exchange with signals from the same behavioral repertoire, and later in this period, can imitate novel behaviors in social interaction (McCormick, 1990b). Enhancement of socioemotional relatedness occurs through affect attunement (Stern, 1985). Affect attunement refers to adults' mirroring the affective displays of young children, not through direct imitation, but through replicating the envelope of intensity of emotional expression, which may occur cross-modally. For example, if a young child works up to a squeal of delight while watching a windup toy, the adult may mirror this behavior and attune to the child's emotional expression by simultaneously vocalizing "Oooh," widening the eyes, and pursing the lips in the same temporal pattern as the child's vocalization. Stern (1985) believes that this cross-modal sharing of affect, this "interaffectivity," is an important dimension of emotional development, because it helps young children relate their own emotional states to observable affect displays of others.

Bricker and Schiefelbusch (1990) discussed cycles in turn taking interactions between infants and caregivers originally identified by Brazelton and his colleagues (see Brazelton & Cramer, 1990, for a recent review). These cycles include: (a) initiation—the child engages in behavior that serves to attract attention; (b) mutual orientation—the adult focuses on the child and establishes shared attention; (c) recognition—the child signals recognition of the shared attentional state; (d) reciprocal play and dialogue—either child or adult initiates action and/or vocalization followed by contingent response by the partner; and (e) disengagement—child averts gaze, loses focus, or focuses on something else in the room, thus terminating the cycle of interaction.

An early goal is to help children engage in cycles of exchange. A few basic guidelines will help children participate optimally. First, a quiet environment will allow most young children to attend best. Intervention activities initially may need to occur in a relatively distraction-free context. Caregivers will need to begin by responding to subtle signals of attention and initiation, and the child will need to be able to focus on the adult's behavior. If a child demonstrates the ability to participate in more naturally busy environments, routines may be introduced in a wider range of contexts. Second, the adult and child should be physically oriented to allow for face to face interaction with minimal need for the child to shift head or trunk position. Physical proximity should also allow the child to avert gaze or otherwise disengage to experience some control of the interaction. Third, when toys are used to engage a child's attention, they should be within easy reach of the adult so that they may be introduced with minimal interruption.

In order for preintentional children to participate in early interactional cycles, adults must modify their behavior based on signals and cues given by young children. It is important that any child behavior directed toward the adult be responded to immediately, and at a level of intensity a child can tolerate. Exaggerated vocal or facial expressions of positive affect may overly arouse some children resulting in gaze aversion and disengagement. Children who are minimally responsive may require intense levels of stimulation. Appropriate levels of response can only be determined by systematically varying response intensity and physical distance and noting a child's reaction. When a child maintains attention, shows interest with widening eyes, or vocally fills the turn in the interaction, the quality and intensity of interaction is appropriate.

Bricker and Schiefelbusch (1990) suggest that once a child can participate over multiple turns consistently, imitative responses to the child should be varied to maintain interest and expand the child's repertoire. Variations may be introduced in the intensity, quality and duration of vocalizations. Objects may be introduced and exchanged in turn-taking sequences, if the child has the requisite motor abilities. Highly predictable social routines with spaces for a child to fill in may be introduced with the expectation that a child will participate more actively. Adults should always be alert for signals of inattention or overstimulation which indicate that the interaction should be terminated until a state of readiness returns. As children demonstrate greater anticipation and participation in social games, and begin to behave in ways that signal their active attempts to keep interactions going, direct work on building intentional communicative acts (i.e., social-communicative signals) can begin (Bricker & Schiefelbusch, 1990).

The Transition to Prelinguistic Intentional Communication

Intentionality is the deliberate pursuit of a goal (Flavell, 1963). For example, a child may reach for a bottle on a shelf, and if it is out of reach, may stand up to obtain it, or if necessary, push a chair over to the shelf and stand on it. Intent to communicate is evidenced when a child uses social means, through vocal and/or gestural signals, directed towards others, to obtain goals. Bates (1979) defined intentional communication as "signaling behavior in which the sender is aware *a priori* of the effect that a signal will have on his listener, and he persists in that behavior until the effect is obtained or failure is clearly indicated" (p. 36). Thus, if the child reaches toward the bottle, vocalizes and looks toward the adult, then shifts his gaze back to the bottle, it can be inferred that signals are being used intentionally to influence another person's behavior.

Most investigators agree that behavioral evidence for communicative intent is observed at approximately 8 to 9 months developmentally (Prizant & Wetherby, 1985; Wetherby & Prizant, 1989). This evidence may include: (a) alternating eye gaze between the goal and a person; (b) persisting in vocal, gestural, and/or verbal signaling until the goal is accomplished or failure is indicated; (c) using a ritualized form of a signal; (d) changing the quality of the signal to accomplish a goal; (e) awaiting a response from the listener; (f) terminating the signal when the goal is met; and (g) displaying satisfaction when the goal is met and dissatisfaction when it is not met (Prizant & Wetherby, 1985). The expression of communicative intent emerges gradually as children observe the effects of their behavior on adults. Through this process children are reinforced for initiations and develop an awareness of contingency and social causality (i.e., that they can act in ways that will influence others). Thus, intervention activities must involve responsive partners reacting consistently to children's behavior as if the behavior was intentionally communicative. This is especially true for children with disabilities, for they need to experience much repetition to associate their behavior with how it affects others. Furthermore, partners' responses need to be immediate, clear, and naturally reinforcing to the child, and should eventually involve prompting and modeling of more conventional and readable signals once intent is clearly established.

Stillman and Battle (1984) described a program developed by Van Dijk for children with dual sensory impairments (i.e., deafness and blindness) that is relevant for children with other communication delays. The program is designed to heighten the child's awareness of her ability to influence others through subtle signaling in simple repetitive movement routines. Gradually, the child is given greater responsibility to signal her desire to have movement activities continue as adults pause during an activity.

The first phase of this program includes resonance activities in which adults move in unison and in direct contact with a child (e.g., rocking together on a mat, playing "row, row, row your boat"). The adult pauses or hesitates at strategic points during the activity and continues only when a child signals for continuation. Early signals may include reenactment strategies (Schuler & Prizant, 1987) in which the child replicates some portion of the routine (e.g., pulling arms to continue "row, row, row your boat"); the child's signal is responded to as an intentional communicative act (e.g., "want more, O.K.") and followed with an immediate continuation. Other signals such as establishing eye contact or smiling or any movements under a child's volitional control may be reinforced by continuation. If necessary, subtle prompting may be used, but the response prompted should be one that the child has the potential to produce independently (e.g., clapping hands).

The next step in the Van Dijk program, called co-active movement, involves the same principles of heightening a child's aware-ness of the effects of signals on others during movement routines. Now, however, activities are conducted at greater physical distances, and movement may take on more of a turn-taking structure rather than occurring simultaneously in order to emphasize the child's independent control and to encourage cognitive distancing. Activities may include alternating jumping movements, or acting on toys that produce interesting sensory effects. Adults respond to children's signals with increasingly greater expectations for more clear or readable signals. During co-active movement activities, more varied signals may be modeled or prompted (e.g., various hand or body movements relevant to the activity, vocalizations) to expand a child's repertoire.

The next step in the program involves the use of natural gestures to signal intentions rather than the more primitive, subtle, or idiosyncratic signals which were responded to earlier. Natural gestures (e.g., reaching, head nods) or even simple signs for "more," "stop," for example, can be modelled and prompted consistently after a child clearly demonstrates the use of signals to affect the partner's behavior.

The Van Dijk approach is, in essence, the use of simply structured joint action routines, in that the emphasis is on developing a child's awareness of communicative reciprocity within highly predictable activities involving mutual participation and a joint focus of attention. This approach, however, places greater emphasis on developing a child's ability to differentiate self from others, and to gradually understand the communicative power of one's behavioral signals. Therefore, it is an excellent framework for moving young children from preintentional communicative signaling, to the intentional use of primitive signals to express intentions, and finally to the use of conventional signals and even early symbolic forms (e.g., protowords, signs) for communication.

Stillman and Battle (1984) and Siegel-Causey and Guess (1989) provide more detailed information on this approach.

Expanding Communicative Competence at a Prelinguistic Level

Children at this level are clearly demonstrating the use of signals to influence the behavior of others. However, signals initially tend to be idiosyncratic and concrete, and they may be produced inconsistently or only in certain contexts (McLean, Snyder-McLean, & Sack, 1983). Thus, for children at early prelinguistic intentional levels, expressive communication goals include: (a) developing more consistent and socially acceptable means for expressing intentions; (b) developing more conventional gestural and vocal means for communication; (c) expanding the range of functions or purposes for communication; and (d) developing repair strategies (i.e., persisting at communication). The ability to initiate communication within reciprocal social interactions and the ability to communicate spontaneously across persons and situations also continue to be high priority goals.

Developing More Consistent and Socially Acceptable Means for Expressing Intentions
Readability of a child's signals depends, in part, on how consistently the symbols are used in daily interactions. Consistency in children's use of communicative signals, in turn, is influenced and reinforced by adults' responsiveness (Dunst et al., 1990). This transactional process is an essential part of prelinguistic communication development. Therefore, children require frequent opportunities to express intent. One strategy is to provide predictable and repetitive activities and caregiving routines that provide opportunities for active communicative signaling by children. Frequent opportunities and needs to communicate may be provided by using antecedent strategies (Prizant & Wetherby, 1988) such as placing desired objects or toys out of reach but still visible to the child, or setting up "Communicative Temptations" (Wetherby & Prizant, 1990), which are designed to entice children to communicate (see Box 10.3).

Developing More Conventional Gestural and Vocal Means for Communication
Children of all cultures develop a repertoire of conventional gestures to communicate a variety of intentions (Bates, 1979). These include: open-handed reach or open hand palm up for requesting; wave for greeting; push away for rejecting or protesting; point for requesting or establishing shared attention to an object or event; giving for requesting action/assistance or establishing shared attention; head nods for affirmation or agreement; and head shakes for rejection or protest (Wetherby & Prizant, 1990).

Children with disabilities may be difficult to "read" because of limited development or use of gestures which are typically acquired between 10 and 24 months. Limited development of conventional gestures may be due to social impairments (conventional gestures are learned through intensive social interaction and observation of others), or motor limitations. In lieu of conventional gestures, concrete gestures (e.g., physically manipulating others, reenacting a part of a routine) or idiosyncratic gestures (i.e., gestures only understood by persons who know a child well) may be used. Concrete and idiosyncratic gestures are acceptable and desirable at early stages of intentional communication, but are less effective than conventional gestures which enable a child to communicate to more persons for more varied purposes at greater distances. Even for children who have acquired a rudimentary language system (i.e., limited speech, signs, or use of a communication board), development of conventional gestures is an important goal because they bring redundancy and clarity to a child's communicative acts and may provide

---

BOX 10.3   Communicative temptations

1 Eat a desired food item in front of the child without offering any to the child.

2 Activate a wind-up toy, let it deactivate, and hand it to the child.

3 Give the child four blocks to drop in a box, one at a time (or use some other action that the child will repeat, such as stacking the blocks or dropping the blocks on the floor), then immediately give the child a small animal figure to drop in the box.

4 Look through a few books with the child.

5 Initiate a familiar and an unfamiliar social game with the child until the child expresses pleasure, then stop the game and wait.

6 Open a jar of bubbles, blow bubbles, then close the jar tightly. Hand the closed jar to the child.

7 Blow up a balloon and slowly deflate it. Hand the deflated balloon to the child or hold the deflated balloon up to your mouth and wait.

8 Hold a food item or toy that the child dislikes out near the child to offer it.

9 Place a desired food item or toy in a clear container that the child cannot open while the child is watching. Put the container in front of the child and wait.

10 Place the child's hands in a cold, wet or sticky substance, such as jello, pudding or paste.

11 Roll a ball to the child. After the child returns the ball three times, immediately roll a rattle or a toy on wheels to the child.

12 Wave and say "bye bye" to a toy upon removing it from the play area. Repeat this for a second and third toy, and do nothing when removing a fourth toy. These four trials should be interspersed throughout the other temptations, rather than be presented in a series.

13 Have the animal greet the child the first time. Repeat this for a second and third time, and do nothing when bringing out the animal for the fourth time. These four trials should also be interspersed when presented.

14 Put an object that makes noise in an opaque bag and shake the bag. Hold up the bag and wait.

15 Engage the child in an activity of interest that necessitates the use of an instrument for completion (e.g., crayon for drawing, spoon for eating, or wand for blowing bubbles). Have a third person come over and take the instrument, go sit on the distant side of the room, while holding the instrument within the child's sight and wait.

Note: From "The Expression of Communicative Intent: Assessment Guidelines" by A. Wetherby and B. Prizant, 1989, *Seminars in Speech and Language,* 10, 77–91. Copyright 1989 by *Seminars in Speech and Language.* Reprinted by permission.

---

a means for repairing communication breakdowns when speech alone is not effective. Furthermore, some conventional gestures (e.g., pointing) are essential in using communication aids such as picture or word boards.

Use of conventional gestures may be developed by frequent modeling of gestures in all activities and by physically prompting of gestures when appropriate. It is important that children have the opportunity to observe others' uses of gestures as well as to experience the immediate success of their own use of communicative gestures. Strategies that may help to foster use of conventional gestures include: (a) engaging in give and take exchanges; (b) commenting on and pointing at pictures and objects; (c) offering desirable and undesirable foods or toys to elicit gestural or vocal requests, or push-away gestures, head shakes or head nods; and (d) modeling and prompting a hand wave for greeting when introducing new toys or when a person enters a room, and when a person leaves or when toys are put away.

The development of conventional vocalizations requires clear modeling of both words and intonation patterns. Although it is not expected that children will clearly imitate and acquire adult forms of words at this stage, sound imitation and approximations of words in highly repetitive routines can be encouraged. As with gestures, adults need to provide clear visible models by being at a child's physical level, encouraging (not coercing) face to face gaze, and producing words slowly, clearly and repetitively in communicative exchanges.

A child's motivation and attention in an activity designed to develop vocalizations is an important determinant of success. Strategies that may heighten a child's attention to speech and foster vocal imitation and approximation include:

- imitating a child's vocalizations and gradually modifying them in a playful turn-taking context
- using short relevant phrases with interesting and simple intonation patterns
- using stereotypic or ritualized utterances in routines (e.g., saying "What's that?" with exaggerated intonation while looking at pictures in a book, "uh-oh" when something falls down, "all done" when completing an activity)
- modeling short utterances in synchrony with body movement during physical games or sensory integration activities
- singing songs with predictable slots for words or sounds to be filled in

With appropriate modeling and opportunities to vocalize and imitate, most children at this level with the requisite oral motor skills should begin to produce varied and frequent vocalizations, with increased imitation of and/or approximation to adult models within highly routinized contexts. Highly limited or restricted vocal production in the presence of clear intentional gestural communication, may indicate motor speech problems requiring an oral motor function evaluation and consideration of an augmentative communication system.

Expanding the Range of Functions or Purposes for Communication   One important aspect of communicative competence is the range of purposes or functions for which a child communicates (Prizant & Wetherby, 1990). Children who communicate for a more narrow range may create fewer opportunities to engage others in social interaction, and the result may be that they have fewer opportunities to learn about the reciprocal nature of communication. For example, a child who communicates primarily to have immediate needs met through requesting or protesting typically has difficulty bringing attention to himself to request social games or comfort from others or bringing attention to events for the purpose of sharing experiences with others. In turn, the transactional impact of a limited range of functions is that communicative partners have less opportunity to model a range of communicative behaviors and expand upon a child's initiations. Therefore, an important goal for children at a prelinguistic intentional communicative level is expansion of the range of functions.

Communicative partners must create needs and opportunities for young children to communicate for a wider variety of purposes, with the provision of intensive modeling, and if necessary, prompting of conventional prelinguistic gestures accompanied by simple language models. The functional breakdown of communicative acts for behavioral regulation, social interaction, and joint attention (Bruner, 1981; Wetherby & Prizant, in press) (see Figure 10.1) is useful because it helps to delineate functions of communication from least social (i.e., behavioral regulation) to most social (i.e., joint attention). Wetherby, Prizant, and Kublin (1989) suggested different characteristics of activities that provide opportunities to elicit and model communicative acts in all three major categories. Activities with these characteristics are appropriate for children at prelinguistic as well as early language levels. Specific activities should be selected by caregivers and professionals based on a child's motivations, needs, and learning strengths. Characteristics of activities for behavioral regulation include opportunities to request food or objects; make choices among alternatives; protest actions, or reject objects or food; request cessation of an activity; and request assistance. Activities for social interaction include opportunities to request social games or routines, or continuation of games or routines; practice greeting behaviors verbally or nonverbally; bring attention to self through calling others or requesting comfort verbally or nonverbally; show off during games (e.g., "hide and seek," "peek-a-boo," dressing up, face painting, "show and tell"). Activities for joint attention include opportunities to give or transfer objects, or to follow another person's focus of attention; use gestures or vocalizations to bring attention to objects or events (e.g., looking at books, going to the zoo, looking out a window onto a busy street); comment on events introducing novelty and change (e.g., taking new toys out of a cloth bag, performing interesting actions on objects); and request information or clarification (for children with higher level abilities).

Developing Repair Strategies (i.e., persisting at communication)

Many factors may interfere with a child's ability to communicate intentions successfully. For example, environmental distractions, the inability to secure a partner's attention, or the production of unclear or unconventional communicative signals (e.g., unintelligible speech, idiosyncratic gestures) may detrimentally influence communication. Therefore, a final generic goal for prelinguistic children is the development of repair strategies, or the ability to persist through repeating or modifying communicative signals when initial communication is unsuccessful. A child who demonstrates limited repair strategies may not realize her communicative potential even though the basic requisite communicative skills are present. Often, such children may appear passive, lethargic, or easily distracted. Intervention strategies to develop the motivation to persist and repair communicative breakdowns are predicated on frequent opportunities for experiencing needs to repair. These opportunities may occur naturally, but also should be provided by partners.

Children must clearly demonstrate intentional goal-directed communication before working on repair strategies. Children at emerging intentional levels should be responded to immediately, even if intent is assigned or imputed, because the purpose is to establish intentional communication. However, with repair strategies, an underlying assumption is that intentional communication is already established, and that persistence in communicating is the next major challenge. Following are some suggestions for developing repair strategies for both prelinguistic children and children in early language stages.

- Use preferred and highly motivating activities that are likely to keep a child interested and focused.
- Begin to require more clear and conventional signals before responding to or imputing intent to subtle or unclear signals. However, acknowledge that you know the child has attempted to communicate by saying "What"? "I don't understand," and

assume a questioning look, with shrugged shoulders, etc.

- If such attempts to elicit a repair do not work, say "Show me" (and extend your hand) or "Say it again," whichever is appropriate to a child's communicative level. If the unsuccessful communicative act involves requesting an object, the object may be presented again and a simple reach may be followed by modeling or the prompting of an appropriate communicative act.

- Requests for repair should never be demanding or withholding or negatively cast through disapproving facial expression on tone of voice. Any initial attempt at persistence should be followed by physical prompting of more appropriate gestures or clear modeling of speech at or slightly above a child's expressive level.

- Opportunities for repair may be set up by (a) delaying responses to initial unclear communicative attempts, (b) intentionally responding incorrectly in a playful manner (e.g., heading to the bathroom when a child signals he wants a drink at the water fountain), or (c) offering undesired foods or items when a child points or reaches in the direction of many items out of reach on a table or shelf. Higher levels of repair may require that a child first secure someone's attention (e.g., tapping someone's arm, calling a name) before that person responds.

Goals for Children at Emerging Language Levels

Children at emerging language levels begin to use conventional words through speech or signs, but still communicate primarily through gestures and vocalizations. The transition from prelinguistic to linguistic communication is a gradual process for normally developing children and a challenge for children with disabilities. The challenge is due, in part, to the greater motor and cognitive de-

mands inherent in oral language use or the use of other symbol systems. Because of motor and cognitive limitations, some children with disabilities will communicate more successfully with nonspeech augmentative communicative means than through speech alone (McCormick & Shane, 1990).

Vocabulary Selection   Although a child typically is exposed to a wide range of vocabulary in daily experiences, decisions must be made regarding the initial vocabulary that will be targeted for an expressive language-based system of communication. When children begin moving into early language stages, they begin to use words to communicate the same meanings for the same purposes as they did through prelinguistic communicative means (Lahey, 1988). One major difference is that communicative partners can now determine the meaning of the child's communication or the content of his attentional focus through emerging language forms. At prelinguistic levels, contextual cues must be relied on to a greater extent. Thus, the acquisition of initial vocabulary or lexical forms signals a child's first step toward a more conventional, explicit, and efficient form of communication. Selection of vocabulary should reflect a child's current level of development as well as addressing functional needs and family priorities.

Some general criteria for initial vocabulary selection, which are relevant for speech or augmentative communication systems, are included in Box 10.4 (Blau, 1983; Lahey, 1988; Lahey & Bloom, 1977).

Lahey (1988) noted that earliest words code basic semantic functions (see #1 in Box 10.4), and that they refer to the existence or presence of objects, events that reoccur, objects that reappear or disappear, people acting on objects, actions that change the location of objects, and personal statements of rejection or possession. Children tend to talk more about objects that are moving or that

---

BOX 10.4   Criteria for initial vocabulary selection

1 Words that express early semantic functions such as nonexistence or disappearance (e.g., "all gone," "no"), recurrence (e.g., "more," "again"), existence (e.g., object labels, "there"), rejection (e.g., "no"), possession (e.g., "mine"), action (e.g., "open"), and locative action (e.g., "up," "out") (see Table 10.1 for a list of early semantic functions).
2 Words to request motivating foods, objects, or activities.
3 Words for routine independent living activities (e.g., eat, drink, sleep/tired, bathroom/potty).
4 Words that can express functions currently expressed through socially unacceptable means (e.g., "no" for rejection/protest, "all done" or "stop" for cessation).
5 Words for expressing agreement or affirmation (e.g., "yes," "O.K.").
6 Names of significant others.
7 Words to request assistance (e.g., "help"), affection or comfort (e.g., "hug," "kiss"), or interaction (e.g., "play").
8 Words for common environments (e.g., home, school, pool).
9 Action words of general application (e.g., "close," "go," "give").
10 Words of attribution (e.g., "hot," "dirty").
11 Words to express feelings or internal states (e.g., "want," "mad," "happy," "scared").

---

are undergoing change, or about objects that they can act on and manipulate, than about objects that are static. The child's earliest words, as we have noted, may serve a variety of communicative purposes or functions (i.e., behavioral regulation, social interaction, and joint attention).

Movement to Early Multiword Utterances

There is no clear evidence that isolated training alone plays a significant role in helping children acquire more advanced linguistic structures that will be used outside of the training context (Fey, 1986; Nelson, 1988). Therefore, appropriate modeling of language and communicative behavior in daily interactions is basic to all successful communication enhancement efforts. At early language levels, it is especially crucial as children begin to associate specific meanings with spoken words and language structures by hearing words and multiword utterances in relation to objects and events they observe.

Alterations in mothers' speech to young children appear to be determined primarily by children's signs of increasing comprehension and readiness for speech production (Chapman, 1988). Thus, appropriate language modeling is crucial for children at early language levels, and it should occur through speech and through any other modality that is an intervention target for a child (e.g., picture board, signs).

There are differing opinions as to the language forms that should be targeted in early multiword utterances. Lahey (1988) advocated focusing on expanding early semantic functions or meanings first expressed through single words (see Table 10.2 for examples). These would include two to three word utterances coding existence (e.g., "this cookie," "that big dog"), nonexistence (e.g., "no cup"), recurrence (e.g., "more drink"), action as part of implied agent–action–object relations (e.g., "eat cookie," "Mommy push"), and locative action (e.g., "Mommy up," "baby [is being put on] chair"). McLean and Snyder-McLean (1978) and MacDonald and Horstmeier (1978) included agent–action (e.g., "Daddy open") and action–object (e.g., "push ball") utterances as priorities. Keogh and Reichle (cf. Reichle & Keogh, 1985) suggested that for children with severe disabilities, initial two word utterances should be in the form of "want + object" because of its specificity and functionality. Clearly, decisions regarding target forms should be based on criteria including (a) meanings and functions a child expresses nonverbally and at a single word level, (b) functional needs and caregiver priorities, (c) child preferences and motivations, and (d) forms that are developmentally appropriate.

Schwartz, Chapman, Terrell, Prelock and Rowan (1985) applied a strategy, referred to as vertical structuring with expansions (Fey, 1986), for helping children with language impairments move from single-word to multiword levels of communication. Eight children with language impairments, ranging in age from 32 to 40 months, with single word vocabularies ranging from 25 to 54 words, were asked questions about pictures or events they observed. When the children produced single word responses, the clinician then asked a question to elicit more specific information, and then followed up by combining the two words in an expanded utterance. For example, if a child said "eat" while watching Mickey Mouse "eating" a cookie, the adult would follow with "Who is eating?" If the child then said "Mickey," the adult's response could be "Yeah, Mickey is eating the big cookie." Schwartz et al. found this strategy to be effective in helping the majority of their normally developing as well as language-impaired subjects move from single-word to multiword utterances. Fey (1986) speculated that such interactions heighten children's attention to early multiword semantic relations.

Another strategy that relies upon the adult's use of questions for eliciting higher language forms is the mand-model technique (Rogers-Warren & Warren, 1980). A mand is a request or an instruction to a child to verbalize. This approach is thus more directive; it has been shown to be effective for increasing language production in children who initiate verbal interaction infrequently (Warren, McQuarter, & Rogers-Warren, 1984). This strategy can be implemented when a child shows a particular interest in an object or materials but has not initiated verbalization. The child may be requested (i.e., manded) to "Tell me what you want," or "Tell me what you want to do." If the child responds appropriately (e.g., "want a drink"), the request may be fulfilled while providing verbal feedback (e.g., "you want a drink? O.K., let's get a cup."). If the child responds with an unclear utterance, does not provide sufficient information, or doesn't respond at all, the adult may provide a model utterance which presumably matches the child's intent, and the child is requested to repeat the model, and then the request is fulfilled.

Children should be given every opportunity to initiate, and adult use of verbal questioning or prompting should occur only after some expectant waiting and pausing. To preclude children from becoming dependent upon question prompts, and ultimately learning to be responders as opposed to initiators, all efforts should be made to provide opportunities for children to initiate verbal communicative acts throughout the day (Fey, 1986; Prizant, 1982). Also, acceptability of a child's response should not be based on grammaticality, or on the correctness of language structure, but should be based on whether the intent is communicated clearly, and whether sufficient information is provided to make the meaning of verbalizations unambiguous. If a child makes grammatical errors, the caregiver can produce appropriate linguistic models in response, while responding to the child's intent.

Individual Differences in Early Language Acquisition

Some children with disabilities begin speaking by producing utterances greater than one or two words in length. These children have been referred to as demonstrating a *gestalt* style of language acquisition characterized by production of language chunks through immediate or delayed repetition in early language stages (Prizant, 1983). These patterns are observed most frequently in children with autism, pervasive developmental disorders (APA, 1987), or visual impairments (Prizant, 1987a), but they may also be observed in a wide range of children with communication difficulties. Gestalt styles have been documented in less extreme forms in a small number of normally developing children (Peters, 1983) who also appear to be relying, to some extent, on rote memory for acquiring and using language forms. The term "language chunks" indicates that even though gestalt learners produce utterances with many words, they may be memorized forms that they perceive as single units. Children demonstrating gestalt styles appear to acquire language through rote memory strategies, and they eventually must learn to "break into" the code of language to be able to develop knowledge of language rules and to generate novel utterances.

The patterns of immediate and delayed repetition observed in gestalt language learners also have been referred to as immediate echolalia and delayed echolalia respectively (Prizant, 1983). Although echolalic speech previously was thought to be a deviant language characteristic that needed to be ignored or extinguished, contemporary approaches recognize that echolalia encompasses a continuum of speech repetition that may serve a variety of communicative functions. Furthermore, for many children, echolalia is now seen as reflecting an extreme version of a gestalt style of language acquisition—that is, as a positive prognostic indicator for movement to more sophisticated language (see Schular & Prizant, 1985, for a review).

The most striking aspect of echolalic behavior is that children appear to be simply repeating language that was spoken to them— they have limited comprehension of the language they are producing. In fact, echolalic children may appear to be far more sophisticated in expressive language abilities than they really are, because of their ability to repeat speech. With delayed echolalia, even long utterances (six to eight words) may be repeated days, weeks, or months after they were originally heard, even though the child's true expressive language level may be at a one to two word utterance stage (Prizant & Rydell, 1984). With both immediate and delayed echolalia, repetitions may be exact, or they may involve changes such as additions or reductions. The term *mitigated echolalia* refers to echoed utterances produced with some changes, and this practice often represents movement from rigid repetition to the emergence of more flexible and creative language (Prizant, 1987a). Here are some guidelines for responding to echolalia (Prizant, 1987a).

Simplify Language Input Although some children may show some comprehension of utterances they are echoing, echolalia frequently occurs when children cannot segment the speech they hear, and when comprehension is limited. Children tend to repeat utterances less, and respond more consistently to speech when it is within their processing capabilities.

Respond to Communicative Intent When immediate or delayed echolalia is produced with communicative intent or purpose, communicative partners should respond to the intent of such utterances and follow up by presenting a simplified model. For example, if a child repeats "Do you want some water?" either immediately or in a delayed manner as a request for water, the adult may respond to the child's intent and follow up with an utterance such as "Oh, you want water. Jimmy wants a drink."

Relate Echoic Utterances to Actions and Objects in the Environment Whenever possible, communicative partners should attempt to emphasize the relationships between echoed speech and environmental referents (i.e., objects, actions, people). Demonstrative gestures (e.g., pointing, touching) and action demonstration may be used by partners to achieve this end. If echoed utterances are not relevant to the context, a child's attention may be redirected through simple language and physical guidance. If echolalia seems to reflect extreme states of high emotional arousal (e.g., distress, great excitement), efforts should be made to calm the child while providing slow, simple, and soothing language input (e.g., "That was a loud noise. Jimmy's scared. Time to relax.").

Deemphasize Correct Pronoun Usage in Early Stages (Fay, 1979) Because of the cognitive-linguistic complexity of pronominal forms, and the concrete learning style of most echolalic children, Fay suggested using proper names in one-to-one interactions with gradual introduction of the I/you distinction. He also suggested the use of peer modeling to help echolalic children with the I/You distinction which is difficult to teach and to learn in direct interactions.

Never Punish or Ignore a Child for Echolalic Behavior Most echolalic behavior has been shown to be intentional and interactive, therefore the challenge faced by com-

municative partners is to help children associate the language they are repeating with objects and events in the environment. Even children who produce highly perseverative and nonfunctional echolalia should be directed to productive learning activities with active involvement. The ultimate challenge is to help echolalic children discover how speech can be used as an effective tool for communication, and to eventually acquire more flexible rule-governed language.

Goals for Children Beyond Emerging Language Levels

Most preschoolers with disabilities have not yet acquired more sophisticated use of language beyond the emerging language stages. Therefore, this section briefly reviews goals and strategies for this level of communication. Many of the strategies discussed in the previous section remain relevant for children at this level.

Goals for children at earlier language stages include the environmentally supported production of language pertaining to immediately observable events (Lahey, 1988). In other words, children will most often use language to communicate about what they observe or what they are doing. Children at early language stages tend to focus on their own actions and activities rather than on those of others. In contrast, as children move beyond two to three word utterances, they communicate increasingly about immediate past and future events and about the activities and actions of others. Such abilities are goals for children at this level. Additional goals include increasing the ability to respond to requests for clarification and to request clarification of others (Fey, Warr-Leeper, Webber, & Disher, 1988) and increasing the frequency of talking and of initiating conversational interaction (Lahey, 1988).

Nelson (1988) presented some "strategies for teaching a first language" for children.

He argued that children will make greater gains when caregivers and teachers challenge them in natural conversational interactions with language that will extend their knowledge. Nelson advocates for rich, varied, and challenging linguistic input based on prior assessment of the child's linguistic system rather than for training specific linguistic structures through "stripping down" language input in contrived training sessions. The following suggestions are relevant for children beyond early multiword utterances and are based (with some adaptations and additions) on Nelson's review of research with normally developing and language-impaired children.

Children should be exposed to a full variety of language structures. There is evidence that for children learning speech or sign language, recasts (expansions or reductions) of children's language that provide structural modifications result in acquisition of new language structures (Baker & Nelson, 1984; Prinz & Masin, 1985). Nelson (1988) suggests that adults should respond 5 percent to 20 percent of the time with "growth-relevant, sentence-specific recasts" (p. 293) including expansions and reductions. Recasts may include a variety of sentence types, such as question forms, negative forms, and complex sentences relevant to a child's language level. Here are two examples of structural recasts.

Child: "Horsey running." (declarative serving a commenting function)

Adult: "Is the horse running to the barn?" (interrogative serving as a request for information)

Child: "Is Daddy coming home in car?" (interrogative serving as a request for information)

Adult: "Daddy's coming home in a train because the car is broken." (Complex sentence form serving the function of providing information)

For children in multiword stages, variability in language styles across communicative partners is desirable, because it is more likely that there will be greater exposure to a variety of structures, vocabulary and functions. This may not be as true, however, for children at very early language stages or for children with more severe disabilities.

To support a child's ability to analyze language input, nonverbal and verbal joint attentional states should be maintained. This may be achieved at verbal levels by following up on the child's topics in conversation and at nonverbal levels by providing consistent cues of attention to the child and to the activity and materials with which the child is involved.

Even if a child is not giving clear evidence of shared attention, provide relevant input—some degree of language processing may occur that is beneficial to linguistic growth. Again, this rule varies somewhat for developmentally younger and more severely disabled children, for whom the need for shared attention and the risk of overstimulation may be greater.

Use scripts and routines to develop discourse and conversational turn-taking skills. Scripts are predictable communicative exchanges typically associated with specific kinds of activities such as circle time or "show and tell." It has been argued that such predictability reduces memory and processing demands for normally developing as well as for communicatively impaired children (Conti-Ramsden & Friel-Patti, 1984; Prizant, 1982). On the other hand, flexibility and variation also are important for the child's linguistic and cognitive growth (Prizant, 1982). Therefore, daily activities should provide a balance between predictable scripted events, which provide opportunities to learn and use specific language forms, and less structured learning opportunities, which may expose children to more varied language forms and interactions.

Strategies for encouraging children to use language about past and future events include reviewing activities upon completion and discussing the sequence of upcoming activities. Picture schedules or photographs may be referred to in order to support such discussions. Communication books with photographs may be exchanged between the home and the center to encourage the use of language about events that are more distant in time and space.

The use of joint activity routines (JAR's) (Snyder-McLean et al., 1984) provides a format and context for encouraging conversational interactions among children. Box 10.5 provides specific information on JAR's. JAR's require communication, interaction, and joint attention in working toward a common goal. The predictable structure of JAR's allows children to use language to problem solve in activities, to direct others' actions to achieve specific end goals, and to predict outcomes of actions. Language concepts of causality (i.e., "because") and conditionality (i.e., "if . . . then . . .") can be modeled and taught in such routines. Pragmatic goals of conversational turn taking and of repairing communication breakdowns by requesting or providing clarification can also be targeted in JAR's.

CONSIDERATIONS FOR CHILDREN WITH MORE SEVERE DISABILITIES

Noonan and Siegel-Causey (1990) identified learning characteristics of children with severe disabilities that must be taken into account when setting goals and objectives and planning communication enhancement activities and strategies. First, such children learn slowly and often fail to notice the relevant features of what is being taught. Second, they do not demonstrate learned skills spontaneously. Third, they do not generalize learned skills to new situations. Although these points are stated somewhat in the extreme, they do reflect the experiences and concerns of many professionals and caregivers. Additional characteristics that have a significant influence on intervention planning include limitations in social skills and social relatedness. Also, due to a greater prevalence and severity of motor and cognitive limitations, augmentative communication must be considered as an important dimension of intervention. Finally, challenging behavior related to communicative limitations is likely to be more of a current and future concern for children with more severe disabilities (Burke, 1990; Prizant & Schuler, 1987b).

Although these children demonstrate significant challenges and limitations, the information we have already presented on assessment and communication enhancement is still applicable. We have been working in this chapter from a broad definition of communication, and we have emphasized the need to describe a child's current communicative status and needs and to focus on developing intervention strategies relative to developmental and functional criteria. When we address the needs of preschool children, the use of chronological-age-appropriate materials and of activities that do not infantilize or stigmatize the individual is not as critical an issue as it is when we address older individuals with severe disabilities. It is more likely that most activities and materials will be both developmentally and chronologically age-appropriate for very young children; however, as children approach school age, greater consideration should be given to the choice of chronological-age-appropriate toys, materials, and activities.

BOX 10.5   Joint activity routines

Critical Elements

1 Obvious unifying theme or purpose
2 Requirement for joint focus and interaction
3 Limited number of clearly delineated roles
4 Exchangeable or reversible roles
5 Logical nonarbitrary sequence
6 Structure for turn taking in predictable sequence
7 Planned repetition
8 Planned for controlled variation

Types of Joint Activity Routines

1 Preparation or fabrication of a specific end product
  e.g., food preparation, product assembly
2 Cooperative turn-taking games or routines
  e.g., songs with spaces to fill, action routines—sports
3 Routines organized around a plot or theme
  e.g., daily living routines—going to a restaurant, doing a wash

Implementing Routines

1 Introduce the concept gradually. Start with simple routines based upon:
  a. motivation and interest
  b. functionality
  c. the likelihood that they already occur or can be scheduled to occur as regular activity
2 Initially, model and prompt to establish routines
  Discuss the purpose or use picture sequence to facilitate understanding.
  Withdraw prompts and support as routines become familiar.
3 Provide structure and repetition until the routine is mastered.
  Add variation after mastery but keep "meaning" or purpose constant.
4 Establish a clear signal for initiation and termination of the routine.
  Provide consistent simple language to mark dynamic aspects of the routine (e.g., actions).

Varying Routines (introducing flexibility)

1 Interrupt or violate routine
2 Omit necessary materials
3 Introduce new materials
4 Initiate old routines in new contexts
5 Introduce new routines in old contexts
6 Initiate the routine then play possum

Note: Adapted from "Structuring Joint Action Routines: A Strategy for Facilitating Communication and Language Development in the Classroom" by L. Snyder-McLean, B. Solomonson, J. McLean, and S. Sack, 1984, *Seminars in Speech and Language, 5,* 213–228.

Special considerations for children with severe disabilities include the need to assure that communication skills will be functional, that generalization is built in to teaching strategies, and that appropriate adaptations are used to enable children to be as independent as possible.

Functional Communication Skills Although the specific skills taught will vary with different children and environments, certain criteria should be followed in establishing priorities for children with severe disabilities. A primary criterion is that communication skills be functional for the child. The term *functional communication skill* includes three components: (a) the ability to communicate for a variety of purposes relevant to an individual's life experiences; (b) the ability to use a variety of means (i.e., verbal and/or nonverbal) to accomplish these purposes effectively; and (c) the ability to initiate and maintain social interactions as a critical dimension of communication (Prizant & Schuler, 1985). This definition emphasizes dimensions of communication enhancement that we have already discussed—such as targeting a range of communicative functions and communicative means, focusing on the child's communicative needs and on family priorities, and planning communication enhancement (to the extent possible) within the context of naturally occurring and reciprocal social interactions.

Facilitating Generalization in Communication With increased emphasis on daily routines and naturally occurring activities, problems of generalization of communication abilities are not as significant as in the case of teaching approaches used in isolated and contrived contexts. McCormick (1990c) reviewed possible explanations for generalization problems associated with direct (didactic) instruction.

1 An emphasis was placed on language structure rather than function.
2 Difficulties in maintaining child interest and attention were more common.
3 Children were taught primarily to respond, and did not use acquired skills in initiated communication.
4 Contexts of training bore little similarity to natural environments.
5 Skills taught were sometimes inappropriate to a child's developmental level.

However, due to some of the special learning limitations and needs of children with severe disabilities, it has been suggested that a combination of didactic and milieu approaches may be most appropriate for these children (Warren & Kaiser, 1988). Given the inherent limitations of didactic approaches, the following procedures for precluding generalization problems have been suggested (McCormick, 1990c; Prizant, 1982; Warren & Rogers-Warren, 1985).

Provide sufficient exemplars—One broad strategy is to provide enough examples of a language concept (e.g., actions, objects, persons) so that the probability of generalized performance is very high. For example, if only the action of opening a door was used in teaching the action concept of "open," the probability of generalization would be less than if a variety of actions involving "opening" were used.

Vary conditions, persons, and situations—In the earlier discussion on designing learning environments, an emphasis was placed on the important role of heightened spatial, temporal, and interactive structure for communication enhancement. For children with severe disabilities, it is essential that variation and flexibility be introduced systematically by varying settings or conditions, persons, and times of activities in order to preclude learning that is specific to particular situations or persons.

Create opportunities and needs for communication and use natural reinforcers—McLean et al. (1983) emphasized the importance of providing many opportunities and needs for communication for children with severe disabilities. Because of the frequency of naturally occurring and motivating instances in carefully planned contexts, children are able to experience multiple learning opportunities for child-initiated communication. Under such conditions, children can also experience the natural reinforcement of successful communication, further precluding the likelihood of generalization problems.

Utilizing Appropriate Adaptations　Adaptations to support successful communication and communication development can take many forms. We have already considered the importance of adapting or modifying environments to foster and support communication. Modifications in interactive style have also been discussed. These first two types of adaptations are important for children with both milder and more severe disabilities. The third major area of adaptations is the use of augmentative communication approaches, which have come to play a major role in communication enhancement efforts for children with more severe communication limitations.

AUGMENTATIVE COMMUNICATION APPROACHES

Due to cognitive, motor, and/or sensory limitations, some children may never learn to speak, or will do so at such a slow rate that speech alone may not be the most effective mode of communication. With these children, some form of augmentative communication should be considered. McCormick and Shane (1990) defined *augmentative communication* broadly as "the total arrangement for supplementing and enhancing an individual's communication. The arrangement includes (a) the communication device or technique, (b) the representational symbol set or system, and (c) the communication skills necessary for effective use of the system" (p. 429).

The term *augmentative communication* implies that this approach augments or supplements a child's developing verbal or vocal skills and is not seen as replacing such skills or as predicting that vocal or verbal skills will not develop. Augmentative approaches currently are far more prevalent for preschoolers, and indeed for all children with limited oral language skills, than they were just a few years ago. This is due to increasing augmentative communication options and commercially available products, a burgeoning research literature demonstrating the effectiveness of augmentative communication approaches for children with various disabling conditions, and increasing evidence that augmentative communication does not inhibit and in some cases may actually support the development of speech (McCormick & Shane, 1990).

Initial attention in the development of augmentative communication approaches focused on selection of devices (e.g., communication boards), systems (e.g., sign language), or symbol sets (e.g., picture communication symbols) for children with primarily physical disabilities (e.g., cerebral palsy) or sensory impairments (e.g., severe to profound hearing loss). Greater emphasis is now being placed on the effective use of devices and systems in interpersonal communication (Reichle, 1991a) for a wide variety of children, and the ways in which environments must be arranged to support augmentative communication (Goossens', 1990). Due to the great proliferation of work in this area in recent years, this section will provide only an overview of considerations and applications of augmentative approaches for young children. More in-depth information is available in recent publications by Reichle, York and Sigafoos (1991), Baumgart, Johnson and Helmstetter (1990), Siegel-Causey and Guess (1989), and McCormick and Shane (1990).

Who Needs Augmentative Communication?

Decision making for augmentative approaches traditionally has been concerned with specifying the cognitive and motor deficits of older children, adolescents, and adults with disabilities that have limited or precluded the development of speech (Reichle, 1991b). For very young children, decisions regarding the introduction of augmentative approaches need to be based upon assessment of current abilities and needs as well as of risk factors that may point to potential barriers to the acquisition of speech later in development. With increasing evidence of the facilitative effects of communication augmentation, there currently is little justification for not introducing an augmentative approach for any child who may not be communicating as effectively as possible through speech or who may be at risk for limited speech development.

Of course, it is critical that caregivers be centrally involved in decisions regarding augmentative communication, for the danger of misunderstandings leading to fragmented approaches is probably greater in this aspect of communication enhancement than in any other. Misunderstandings may occur because caregivers may believe that efforts for speech development are being abandoned or that their child will have no need to learn to speak if another system is used. Most caregivers support a recommendation for introducing an augmentative approach when professionals emphasize (a) that the primary goal is to enable a child to be the most effective communicator possible, a goal that may require a variety of modes of communica-

tion; (b) that vocal and speech development remain an important, if not a primary, target of intervention; (c) that augmentative approaches may support speech development; and (d) that information, support and guidance will be provided to the caregivers to assure a coordinated effort. Finally, the recommendation to introduce an augmentative approach should be just that, and not a predetermined decision that caregivers must be convinced to accept. With caregivers' active participation in the decision-making process, it is more likely that they will "own" the decision and participate actively in augmentative approaches.

Factors to Consider in Selecting Augmentative Systems

Shane (1981) suggested considering specific factors before determining whether a child needs an augmentative communication system. Initially, an evaluation by a developmental team should provide information about a child's current communication, language, motor, oral motor, and cognitive abilities. The persistence of oral reflexes (rooting, biting, or a hyperactive gag reflex) beyond 9 to 12 months of age is strongly related to later speech failure. Also, children who exhibit frequent cessation or blocking of the voice when attempting to vocalize are at risk for speech failure. Laryngeal blocking is particularly common in children with cerebral palsy. In addition, children with significant delays in or problems associated with basic feeding skills (sucking, swallowing, chewing) have a high likelihood of speech failure. Shane suggests that such feeding problems indicate a significant neuromotor problem. The child's age and corresponding physical development are additional factors. Many youngsters may not have the motor skills required to use a particular kind of augmentative system such as signing or using a communication board.

In addition, verbal or vocal imitation appear to be strong predictors of successful speech use. If a child can not imitate vocalizations, or if she demonstrates limited vocal control for producing various sounds, an augmentative communication system should be considered. Response to previous interventions focusing on speech development should also be evaluated to determine the potential for success in acquiring oral communication skills.

The child's level of cognitive development and specific learning strengths are additional considerations. For example, a child who has not demonstrated acquisition or use of abstract representational symbols may be an inappropriate candidate for a system with a high level of representation. However, Reichle and Yoder (1985) were able to teach children with severe disabilities to use black and white graphic symbols even though their level of cognitive functioning predicted an inability to do so. Due to findings like these, current approaches in selecting augmentative systems are based upon predicting a best cognitive and motivational match between a child's abilities and system characteristics and instituting a period of trial teaching with one or more systems, rather than upon making definite decisions on an a priori basis. For example, some children who show particular learning strengths with visual-spatial tasks (e.g., puzzles, visual matching) may succeed with graphic augmentative systems that focus on forms such as line drawings (Mirenda, 1985). Finally, the environment should be evaluated when considering an augmentative communication system. As noted, parents and other significant persons should be actively involved in making decisions about a particular system or systems.

Once it has been decided that a child could benefit from an augmentative mode of communication, a specific strategy must be followed for selecting the system or systems to be introduced, the communicative content

to be included (e.g., vocabulary), and purposes or intents to be targeted. Reichle (1991b) discusses a series of questions that need to be addressed.

1 What reasons does the learner have to communicate?
2 How does the learner currently meet communicative obligations and opportunities?
3 What vocabulary is required to meet communicative obligations and opportunities?
4 What vocabulary is required to meet communicative obligations and opportunities?
5 What communicative intents should be taught?
6 Which communicative mode(s) best matches the learner's abilities and needs? (Reichle, 1991b, p. 40)

Questions 1–4 should be answered by a thorough team assessment. At this point, decisions regarding modes of communication need to be made. The two major modes, other than the vocal, are *graphic* and *gestural*. The choice of communication mode need not be mutually exclusive; a combination of modes may result in the most effective system for a child. For example, a core group of signs and natural gestures may be used in addition to a picture system and emerging speech. Introducing a combination of modes seems to be especially relevant for young children because of the difficulty in determining mode preference for some young children and the rapid developmental changes observed in some youngsters. By systematic modeling and the use of more than one mode, a child's acquisition and performance can be compared among the modes, and subsequent decisions can thus be guided (see Reichle, 1991b, for a discussion of advantages as well as potential disadvantages of using this approach). It is important that educators and clinicians be aware of the characteristics of gestural and graphic modes in order to be able to make informed decisions.

Gestural Modes

Gestural modes include a range of bodily movements, postures, and facial expressions that vary from concrete and primitive to symbolic and language based. Gestural modes (and vocal modes) are referred to as "unaided communication" modes because no additional aids or devices are needed. It is important to recognize that all people use some form of gestural communication that most often accompanies vocal modes. Therefore, it is most desirable to use this natural inclination to provide young children with a richer means to communicate. The gestural mode that has been used most extensively for children falls under the term *sign language*.

Sign Language and Sign Systems Signing is the representation of communicative content through movement and positioning of hands in specific relation to one's body. General use of the term "sign language" is confusing because several different systems are used in different countries, each with a unique vocabulary, syntax, and grammar that often is independent of the native spoken language. *American Sign Language* is the system typically used by deaf and hearing-impaired adults in this country; it is a language in its own right, differing in vocabulary, syntax, and morphology from spoken English (McCormick & Shane, 1990). The unique characteristics of American Sign Language may make it difficult to teach young children with disabilities because it does not have a one-to-one relationship to English. Consequently many educators have turned to sign systems, such as *Signing Exact English*, which do have a direct correspondence between the signs and the spoken words. These systems have been referred to as "manually coded English" because translation between manual, oral, and written forms is easier (Mustonen, Locke, Reichle,

Solbrack & Lindgren, 1991). Another alternative is signs from *Amer-Ind* or *American Indian Sign Language*. These signs appear to be easier to learn and use, they often look like the concepts they represent and are therefore more guessable, and they require gross motor rather than fine motor gestures (Mustonen et al., 1991; Lombardino, Willems, & MacDonald, 1981). Many severely handicapped children may need individually designed manual signs that obviously relate to the functional demands of their environments and that match their individual fine motor skills.

Signs are currently used more often as part of a total communication approach. The term *total communication* refers to the simultaneous use of manual signs, vocalization, and spoken words in communication training. Pairing speech with manual signs in communication training should increase the probability that speech will be understood and used. Speech combined with the manual signing also looks and sounds more "normal" than signing without speech, and may help to form the transitional bridge for children who may eventually move on to speech as the primary mode of communication.

Lombardino et al. (1981) suggested that signing should be considered for children with one or more of the following characteristics:

1 Children who have remained at the single or two-word expressive level for an extended period of time
2 Children whose speech has remained unintelligible for an extended period of time
3 Children having difficulty understanding word reference association through oral language training (e.g., learning that the word "car" stands for the object "car")
4 Children who communicate effectively through gestures and demonstrate no inclination to learn speech
5 Children who are slowly acquiring a vocal

language system but are in need of an immediate interim system of communication

6 Children restricted from adequate speech function because of neurological impairment, oral musculature problems, laryngeal limitations, or sensory deficits. (p. 456)

Signing has several advantages for young children with disabilities. Signs are portable and may form the basis of a linguistic system that corresponds to oral or written language. Signs also are visible—a child can see how they are formed and make comparisons to his own attempts to form the sign. Many signs are iconic; that is, they look like the concepts they represent. Unlike oral language training, sign language training allows for physical prompts or full manipulation to be used to actually form the sign for the child. Numerous studies demonstrate that nonspeaking children with disabilities can learn and use signing as a basic communication system and that in some cases the acquisition of signs may facilitate speech development (McCormick and Shane, 1990; Mustonen et al., 1991).

As for disadvantages, only those children may use sign systems who have adequate motor skills. And the fact that only a very limited portion of the general population understands signs limits communication to specific individuals and contexts. But despite these disadvantages, signs may be an important component of the child's total communication system, and signing may work as a symbol system for children unable to develop oral communication skills at a reasonable rate.

Graphic Modes

Signing has become an important component of augmentative communication approaches for children with fine motor ability adequate for forming the various signs. However, children with mild to severe motor impairments may not have the ability to form signs that would make signing a functional communication mode; also, many children with significant cognitive impairments cannot benefit from sign language because of its representational complexity. Furthermore, Shane (1981) reported that parents and professionals increasingly request other systems even for children who are effective manual communicators because of the limited number of persons who know sign language. Therefore, in recent years, graphic modes of communication have become widely used and accepted even for physically able-bodied children with communication difficulties (Mirenda, 1985). Graphic modes are also referred to as "aided communication modes" because additional devices and materials become an essential part of the child's communication system. Graphic modes include the use of two- or three-dimensional representations to stand for objects and for different concepts (Mustonen, et al., 1991). Mustonen et al. noted that representational and tangible symbols fall under this category.

Representational Symbols Representational symbols include line drawings which may be displayed alongside the written word to expose children to written language. One of the most popular commercially available sets is *Picture Communication Symbols* (Mayer-Johnson, 1981, 1985), black-line 2-inch by 2-inch symbols drawn on white background and representing a wide variety of concepts. These symbols may be reduced in size to increase the number used on a board or in a display, and they may be color coded to classify concepts by conceptual category (e.g., people, actions, objects) or by activity (e.g., washing, eating, etc.).

Blissymbols were originally devised by Charles Bliss in an effort to develop an international symbol system. Blissymbols are black-line drawings that represent concepts or ideas; some look like the object they are designed to represent, and others are more arbitrary. Chapman and Miller (1980) suggested that Blissymbols require cognitive skills at the late preoperational or early concrete operations stage, thus implying that many preschool children with disabilities, especially those with more severe cognitive impairments, would not be good candidates for their use. Blissymbols are used most frequently with children with severe physical disabilities (such as cerebral palsy) who have reached a fairly high cognitive level.

Other graphic representational symbols include photographs, product logos (which may be cut directly from product packaging), and traditional orthography (i.e., printed letters, words, or phrases).

Tangible Symbols   Tangible symbols can be manipulated; their 3-dimensional qualities may provide a more concrete representation of what they stand for. Examples include real objects, object miniatures, parts of objects, and textured symbols (Mustonen et al., 1991). Real objects can be used to represent activities in which similar objects are used or are present (e.g., a toothbrush used to represent a bathroom routine), and these objects may eventually be paired with more abstract representations such as picture communication symbols and then finally faded out altogether (Goossens', 1990). Miniature objects such as refrigerator magnets or objects from doll sets also may be used to represent real objects and activities and can be easily displayed on communication boards with minimal space requirements. Parts of objects provide a space-saving means to use real object representations (e.g., an end section of a bubble wand used to represent a jar of bubbles or an activity using bubbles), and use of parts of objects allows for inclusion of more options on a display or board. Textured symbols include parts of objects with a clearly identified texture (e.g., a piece of rug used to represent nap time) or with an arbitrarily assigned meaning (e.g., a piece of cot-

ton representing a pillow). Tangible symbols are particularly useful for children with severe visual or dual sensory impairments, because the tactile mode of exploration and information processing may be a processing strength for children with these difficulties (see Goetz, Guess, & Stremel-Campbell, 1987, and Siegel-Causey & Guess, 1989, for further information on approaches for children with visual and/or dual sensory impairments).

Mirenda and Locke (1989) found the following hierarchy of ease of learning or "transparency" of graphic and tangible representations with students with cognitive impairments. The order from easiest to most difficult was: actual objects, color photos, black and white photos, miniature objects and picture communication symbols, blissymbols, and written words. Individual differences may of course be observed for some children.

Methods for Displaying and Selecting Symbols

Mustonen et al. (1991) reviewed nonelectronic and electronic methods for displaying and selecting symbols. Nonelectronic methods include communication boards, communication books or communication wallets, and rings that may hold a number of cards. Photos, picture communication symbols, word cards, cutouts from product packaging, and color pictures may be used with any of the methods we have discussed. The use of plastic photo or slide protector sheets for displaying pictures or picture symbols has become popular because of their commercial availability and low cost, and because the quick substitution and addition of pictures that they allow for offers a maximum flexibility as children's needs change. The child may create different displays, representing different contexts, by using the same set of photos or picture symbols. For example, a more comprehensive display in a communication book may be available for table activities while a ring with a limited set of relevant symbols may be used for outdoor activities. Mirenda (1985) and Goossens' (1990) provide other suggestions and guidelines for nonelectronic displays. Children may select items from such displays in various ways—by directed gaze, by reaching, by touching, by pointing, or by handing a picture or card to a receiver.

Electronic displays and devices, initially pioneered for persons with severe physical disabilities who are functioning at higher cognitive levels, are now gaining more widespread acceptance for many children with communication limitations. This is due to their increased durability and compactness, their decreasing cost, and their increasing range of application for children at a variety of cognitive levels. Examples of relevant devices for preschoolers include (a) dedicated units with picture overlays on powerpads that produce speech output or written text, (b) power pads connected to computers and speech synthesizers that produce speech output, printed text, and/or pictures or print on a screen, and (c) devices that systematically scan through a number of choices by means of illumination, or with a rotating clock hand that points to different options on a circular display. With electronic scanning methods, a child must learn to activate a switch; a reliable and discreet motor response is thus required (Mustonen et al., 1991).

Mustonen et al. (1991) have reviewed the advantages of electronic aids. First, many electronic aids have the ability to produce preprogrammed synthesized or natural speech output. This capability allows for communication at a greater distance and does not require that a receiver be looking at a child's communication board. Additionally, the child is able to hear a model of speech production that may provide valuable input for language development. Second, electronic aids have

the ability to produce more sophisticated messages than current language abilities would allow. For example, by simply touching a picture on a power pad, the child may produce a preprogrammed synthesized speech sentence even though he is at a single word level. Third, children who are unable to use direct selection because of physical limitations are allowed by electronic aids to use scanning techniques for selecting items on a display. This is accomplished by custom fitting switches that allow for maximum control in communicative interactions. Finally, unlike nonelectronic picture boards, electronic aids have the ability to program multiple levels of vocabulary or messages for display on a single surface.

Although electronic ("high tech") aids would seem to be the method of choice because of these advantages, a few words of caution are in order (especially for cases involving physically able-bodied young children) so that such aids are not selected prematurely. First, nonelectronic (or "low tech") aids may be more than adequate to meet the needs of some children without the significant expense of electronic aids. Second, electronic and nonelectronic aids should not be viewed as mutually exclusive options. Because some of the skills required may be identical (e.g., touching a picture with an index finger point), nonelectronic aids may provide an initial step toward later implementation (with systematic overlap) of electronic aids. Finally, for very young children, nonelectronic aids may provide the most portable option in a variety of contexts (e.g., outdoor play activities) while electronic aids may be useful in more limited contexts (e.g., table activities). As with all decisions regarding communication enhancement, a child's functional communication needs and current abilities should be the overriding factors in making such determinations. It is beyond the scope of this discussion to review in depth the literature in electronic augmentative communication methods. Recent volumes by Reichle et al. (1991), Silverman (1989), and Blackstone (1989) provide more specific information.

Considerations in Arranging Preschool Environments for Augmentative Communication

Successful implementation of augmentative modes of communication goes beyond the selection of appropriate devices and systems for young children. Environments must be arranged to facilitate and respond to children's use of augmentative communication. Environments must also support transitions to higher level usage of augmentative communication by providing a range of representations. As we have noted, young children are exposed to speech from birth, and most caregivers systematically change the quality and complexity of their language input based on a child's developmental level and responsiveness. Caregivers' finely tuned language input to a child, a child's frequent exposure to other language in the environment, and the child's ability to selectively focus on relevant language in specific contexts are factors seen as crucial to oral language acquisition (Nelson, 1989). But most natural environments do not provide the same degree of intensity as do direct teaching or incidental exposure to augmentative communication; and furthermore, children with disabilities may not have the same selective attentional capacities as normally developing children do for focusing selectively on relevant input. Therefore, helping children to acquire augmentative means must go beyond infrequent teaching episodes. Just as in the case of a child learning oral language, the environment should "bathe" a child in experiences to facilitate acquisition and use of augmentative systems.

Goossens' (1990) believes that frequent problems limiting children's full potential use of augmentative devices include (a) a fragmented approach to designing systems for individual children rather than considering daily activities and routines in the context of day care or classroom settings, and (b) limited modeling by partners of the interactive use of symbols. Goossens' made several suggestions for engineering environments to support interactive augmentative communication.

1 Requesting should be a first expressive goal, and frequent opportunities for choice-making should be provided. Requesting is highly motivating and allows young children to experience the power of communication. The augmentative context should also provide opportunities to reject, and a wide variety of communicative functions should be modeled through "aided language stimulation" (see item #5 following). Furthermore, these opportunities should occur throughout the day—a variety of representations should be available near the location of activities in addition to the child's specific device (e.g., a communication board or book). For children younger than 12 months developmentally, real objects may be the most effective means; for children 12 to 18 months old, photographs may be used; and for children 18 to 24 months old, line drawings or object miniatures may be used.

2 When children receive services in a center-based or classroom setting, the full range of representations should be available to accommodate all children with special needs. In other words, representations should not be determined solely by an individual child's communication system.

3 Lower and higher level representations should be paired to enable children to move to higher level representations. For example, real objects may be paired with photographs on a display in which chil-

dren make choices through manual pointing. For preschool children, an ultimate goal (in addition to speech acquisition) is movement to line drawings and eventually the written word.

4 To the extent possible, each toy or commonly used object available to a child should have a full range of representations (i.e., photos, black and white and colored line drawings, miniature objects) kept with it in a clear plastic photograph pocket so that they are readily available for use.

5 "Aided language stimulation," a teaching approach following which partners provide models of interactive use of augmentative systems, should be provided on an ongoing basis. In general, aided language stimulation involves highlighting pictures or picture symbols on a child's communication display while providing appropriate oral language input. General guidelines for using this approach include (a) using simple utterances about ongoing activities, (b) speaking slowly, (c) commenting about activities rather than using primarily questions or directives, (d) pausing frequently to allow the child to take turns, and (e) expanding upon the child's utterances. The vocabulary used should be relevant to the activity and reflect early semantic functions and relations; but in addition, words should be chosen to reflect the adult's need to model more advanced vocabulary in order to enhance interactive use over time. For a highly distractible child, Goossens' recommends using hand-held lights or noisemakers to bring the child's attention to a target picture.

6 Predictable play routines or caregiving routines should be the primary contexts for facilitating acquisition of augmentative system use, and techniques of cueing, prompting, and fading of cues and prompts should be used systematically.

7 For developmentally older children, larger arrays of vocabulary items should be available for activities involving more complex joint activity routines (e.g., food preparation) and symbolic play. Goossens' (1990) recommends vocabulary sets of up to 36 items for each activity. Increased opportunities for repairing communication breakdowns, using multiword utterances, and using more complex language functions (e.g., requesting information) should also be modeled and encouraged.

Selecting and Using Communication Aids

Teaching a child to use a communication aid requires use of the basic direct and naturalistic teaching approaches. The specific communicative behaviors to be used by a child should be specified. For example, identify the specific symbols, pictures, or other referents the child is to use, and specify the technique by which the child is to select the symbol. The communicative function of a child's behavior should be made immediately clear through the modeling and prompting of appropriate communicative behaviors. For example, a child could be encouraged through modeling and prompting to point to a picture of food or juice and then be immediately presented with food or juice. Likewise the child could be encouraged to point to a picture of a favorite toy and then immediately be allowed to play with that toy. The child's appreciation of the functional consequences of using the communication aid are critical to its subsequent use. In addition, an adult's use of the communication aid along with an appropriate level of speech input should be modeled throughout naturally occurring activities.

In designing and teaching use of communication aids the following points should be remembered.

1 The child must have ready access to a device for it to become a meaningful communication tool. For example, if a com-

munication board is used only in limited activities, the probability of generalization becomes very small. If the board itself is not readily available, the child should always have a means to request the board through gestures, vocalization or verbalization, or other signals (e.g., light or buzzer).

2 The symbol system used on the board should be appropriate to the child's level of cognitive development and learning style.

3 The symbols on the board should represent ideas or wishes the child frequently wants or needs to express.

4 The child should be positioned to facilitate optimal use of the device.

5 The family and other significant persons in the child's environment should find the aid or system acceptable.

WORKING WITH CAREGIVERS TO FACILITATE CHILDREN'S COMMUNICATION DEVELOPMENT

Many approaches for working with caregivers have been discussed in the literature. In general, the evolution of these approaches has paralleled trends in the literature on language intervention and communication enhancement. For example, earlier approaches focused on instructing parents on principles of behavior change using didactic techniques in teaching language skills (e.g., Lovaas, 1981). Caregivers were asked to play the role of teachers or clinicians with their children, and to set up special teaching times at home. In such didactic approaches, parents are given specific predetermined programs to follow which replicate the sequences of objectives and specific activities and procedures used by professionals.

In contrast, approaches for working with caregivers of high-risk infants and toddlers traditionally have focused on interactional issues rather than specific skill training (Bromwich, 1981; Field, 1982). More recently, approaches for working with caregivers of older preschoolers also have become more child-centered and have shifted to helping parents to engage in more successful social interactions that are facilitative of their children's socioemotional and communicative growth (MacDonald, 1989; Mahoney, 1988; Manolson, 1985; McDade & Varnedoe, 1987). These approaches draw heavily from the developmental research literature on mother–child interaction and communication development, as well as from behavioral approaches, and they encourage caregivers to provide more intensive learning experiences using styles and strategies that have been found to be most highly correlated with optimal communication development. One underlying assumption of these approaches is that because caregivers of at-risk and disabled children may develop interactive styles that are not conducive to their children's communication development (Barnard & Kelly, 1990, Marfo, 1990), caregiver interactional style should be a focus of intervention.

Sameroff and Fiese (1900) have noted that within a transactional model of development, goals for working with caregivers include remediation, redefinition, and reeducation. Remediation focuses on helping parents to help their children acquire developmental skills. Acquisition of higher level communication abilities should have the transactional impact of normalizing caregiver–child interaction. Redefinition focuses on assisting caregivers in redefining their perceptions of their children's abilities and needs by helping them to understand their children's developmental strengths and weaknesses. Reeducation involves more direct instruction about principles of raising children and child development.

Most caregiver-directed approaches concerned with communication development address these three general goals of remediation, redefinition and reeducation. More specific goals for working with caregivers in these programs include (a) sensitizing caregivers to their children's level of communication, their specific strategies in communicating, and the specific difficulties they face; (b) informing caregivers about the sequences and processes of language and communication development; (c) helping caregivers develop interactive styles that are responsive to their children and supportive of successful interactions; and (d) helping caregivers to modify daily activities and routines and to develop new activities to support communication development, so to improve their relationships with their young children.

Different models have been reviewed for providing services to caregivers of at-risk infants and toddlers (Seitz & Provence, 1990) and caregivers of developmentally disabled children (Marfo, 1990). Here we present two general models—individual caregiver–child therapy and caregiver educational programs.

Direct Individual Caregiver–Child Therapy Following this model, professionals work directly with a caregiver and his child, often interacting directly with the child, and asking the caregiver to observe and eventually emulate the style that has been modeled. This approach is especially characteristic of the more didactic models that we have discussed, but it is used with less directive, child-centered models. MacDonald (MacDonald, 1989; MacDonald & Gillette, 1988) and Mahoney (1988) provide examples of work with this model which has been shown to be effective in home and clinic-based settings. Such programs are based on the concepts of balanced turn taking and developmental matching. In MacDonald's approach, clinicians or educators work directly with caregivers and their children during play interactions with the goals of identifying (a) communication skills needed by the chil-

dren, (b) problems that interfere with successful interaction, and (c) strategies that caregivers can learn to support their children's development and to resolve interactional problems (MacDonald & Gillette, 1988). The caregiver is taught to follow his child's attentional focus and to take turns that are "progressively matched" to his child's behavior. The "progressive matching" that is central to this approach involves imitating the child's behavior and then providing slightly more advanced models. This approach teaches different interactional strategies geared to a child's abilities through developmental sequences of solo play, social play, preverbal communication, verbal communication, and conversation.

Mahoney's Transactional Intervention Program (TRIP) (Mahoney, 1988) is based upon research which indicated that caregivers of developmentally delayed children tended to dominate interactions and make requests that were developmentally inappropriate for their children's communication levels. Using home visits and videotaping with 34 children with disabilities 2 to 32 months of age, parents were taught the strategies of child-centered communication approaches (e.g., turn taking, interactive matching, reduction of the number of requests, reading and interpreting child behavior, providing developmentally more advanced models). Results of the program indicated that all caregivers made significant changes in interactive style (i.e., to less directive styles) and that outcome levels of child communication and cognitive development were related to the degree of directiveness in caregiver interaction style. That is, children of the least directive parents made the greatest gains.

Interactive coaching (Field, 1982) and interactive guidance (McDonough, 1989) are additional strategies used in the caregiver–child therapy context. These approaches are typically less direct in teaching caregivers specific strategies; and following the belief that direct demonstration with a child may disempower a caregiver who is observing (McDonough, 1989), these approaches may not involve direct interaction between child and professional. Professionals may observe caregiver–child interactions during regular routines or play activities and make suggestions regarding the improvement of communicative and caregiving interactions that caregivers can implement immediately.

Caregiver Educational Programs Educational approaches provide information and support to caregivers, often in a group format, without direct involvement between professional and child. Educational programs may focus on helping caregivers to understand principles of communication development and their role as caregivers in facilitating their children's development of communicative competence.

The Hanen Early Language Parent Program (Manolson, 1985) is a program that uses a group format and adult learning principles (i.e., active involvement and participation, negotiated agenda) to help caregivers to modify their interactive styles and develop strategies to support their children's development. The program typically involves evening meetings with caregivers from 5 to 8 families and periodic home visits over a 3-month period. The content of the program is divided into two parts. The first part focuses on identifying children's communicative abilities and caregivers' patterns of response to their children's communicative attempts, with an emphasis on the importance of caregivers recognizing, acknowledging, and expanding on their children's attempts to communicate. The second part assists caregivers in increasing opportunities for communication within daily routines. Caregivers are asked to keep home diaries and to openly discuss issues with the group. A mutually supportive atmosphere is crucial for caregivers to share their successes and challenges with others. One strategy that is recommended for creating such an atmosphere is the use of parent "graduates" from previous programs as cofacilitators. Modifications of the Hanen Program have been and are being developed to meet the needs of special populations of children and their caregivers (e.g., Girolometto, Ushycky, & Hellman, 1988).

In both caregiver–child therapy approaches and caregiver educational programs, the use of videotapes has become an important tool for reviewing and discussing aspects of communicative interactions that support or that interfere with successful communication. Videotape allows for more objective discussion of the strengths and needs of children and their caregivers and has been demonstrated to be an effective intervention tool (Mahoney & Powell, 1988).

SUMMARY

This chapter has focused on the development of communicative competence by young children with disabilities. We have reviewed the multidimensional and transactional nature of communication development and the significant role played by caregivers. The assessment principles we have presented emphasize the need to gather information about children's nonverbal and verbal communicative abilities over time and in a variety of contexts. Other important aspects of assessment include determining children's communicative needs and evaluating caregiver interactional style and the quality of learning environments.

We have presented principles of communication enhancement with an emphasis on the use of natural routines and activities and on the development of a close working relationship between professionals and caregivers. Suggestions were made for designing learning environments and for modifying professionals' and caregivers' interactive styles to be facilitative of children's communicative development. We have discussed goals and strategies for working with children at the preverbal, the emerging language, and more advanced levels of communicative development. Finally, we have reviewed means for working with children with more severe disabilities—such as using augmentative systems and working directly with caregivers.

REFERENCES

American Psychiatric Association. (1987). *Diagnostic and statistical manual of mental disorders* (3rd ed., rev.). Washington, DC: American Psychiatric Association.

Aram, D., & Hall, N. (1989). Longitudinal follow-up of children with preschool communication disorders: Treatment implications. *School Psychology Review, 18,* 487–501.

Bailey, D., & Simeonsson, R. (1988). Home-based early intervention. In S. Odom & M. Karnes (Eds.), *Early intervention for infants and children with handicaps: An empirical base.* Baltimore: Paul Brookes.

Baker, L., & Cantwell, D. (1987). A prospective psychiatric follow-up of children with speech/language disorders. *Journal of the American Academy of Child and Adolescent Psychiatry, 26,* 546–553.

Baker, N., & Nelson, K. E. (1984). Recasting and related conversational techniques for triggering syntactic advances by young children. *First Language, 5,* 3–22.

Barnard, K., & Kelly, J. (1990). Assessment of parent-child interaction. In S. Meisels & J. Shonkoff (Eds.), *Handbook of early childhood intervention.* Cambridge: Cambridge University Press.

Bashir, A., Wiig, E., & Abrams, J. (1987). Language disorders in childhood and adolescence: Implications for learning and socialization. *Pediatric Annals, 16,* 145–156.

Bates, E. (1976). *Language and context.* New York: Academic Press.

Bates, E. (1979). On the evolution and development of symbols. In E. Bates, T. Benigni, I. Bretherton, L. Camaioni, & V. Volterra, *The emergence of symbols: Cognition and communication in infancy.* New York: Academic Press.

Bates, E. Benigni, T., Bretherton, I., Camaioni, L., & Volterra, V. (1979). *The emergence of symbols: Cognition and communication in infancy.* New York: Academic Press.

Bates, E., O'Connell, B., & Shore, C. (1987). Language and communication in infancy. In J. Osofsky (Ed.), *Handbook of Infant Development* (2nd ed.). New York: Wiley.

Baumgart, D., Johnson, J., & Helmstetter, E. (1990). *Augmentative and alternative communication systems for persons with moderate and severe disabilities.* Baltimore: Paul Brookes.

Blackstone, S. (Ed.). (1989). *Augmentative communication: An introduction.* Rockville, MD: American Speech-Language-Hearing Association.

Blau, A. (1983). Vocabulary selection in augmentative communication: Where do we begin?. In H. Winitz (Ed.), *Treating language disorders: For clinicians by clinicians.* Baltimore: University Park Press.

Brazelton, B., & Cramer, B. (1990). *The earliest relationship.* New York: Addison Wesley.

Bricker, D. (1989). *Early intervention for at-risk infants, toddlers and preschool children.* Palo Alto, CA: VORT Corp.

Bricker, D., & Schiefelbusch, R. (1990). Infants at risk. In L. McCormick and R. Schiefelbusch (Eds.), *Early language intervention.* Columbus, OH: Merrill.

Bristol, M., & Schopler, E. (1984). A developmental perspective on stress and coping in families of autistic children. In J. Blacher (Ed.), *Families of severely handicapped children* (pp. 91–134). New York: Academic Press.

Bromwich, R. (1981). *Working with parents and infants: An interactional approach.* Baltimore: University Park Press.

Bromwich, R. (1990). The interaction approach to early intervention. *Infant Mental Health Journal, 11,* 66–79.

Bruner, J. (1981). The social context of language

acquisition. *Language and Communication, 1,* 155–178.

Burke, G. (1990). Unconventional behavior: A communicative interpretation in children with severe disabilities. *Topics in Language Disorders, 10,* 75–85.

Carr, E., & Durand, V. (1985). The social communicative basis of severe behavior problems in children. In S. Reiss & R. Bootzin (Eds.), *Theoretical issues in behavior therapy.* New York: Academic Press.

Chapman, K., Leonard, L., & Mervis, C. (1986). The effects of feedback on young children's inappropriate word use. *Journal of Child Language, 13,* 101–117.

Chapman, R. (1978). Comprehension strategies in children. In J. Kavanagh & W. Strange (Eds.), *Speech and language in the laboratory, school and clinic.* Cambridge: MIT Press.

Chapman, R. (1981). Exploring children's communicative intents. In J. Miller (Ed.), *Assessing language production in children.* Baltimore: University Park Press.

Chapman, R. (1988). Language acquisition in the young child. In N. Lass, L. McReynolds, J. Northern, & D. Yoder (Eds.), *Handbook of speech-language pathology and audiology.* Toronto: B. C. Decker.

Chapman, R., and Miller, J. (1980). Analyzing language and communication in the child. In R. Schiefelbusch (Ed.), *Nonspeech language intervention.* Baltimore: University Park Press.

Clark, G., & Seifer, R. (1985). Assessment of parents' interactions with their developmentally delayed infants. *Infant Mental Health Journal, 6,* 214–225.

Coggins, T., & Carpenter, R. (1979). Introduction to the area of language development. In M. Cohen & P. Gross (Eds.), *The developmental resource: Behavioral sequences for assessment and program planning.* New York: Grune & Stratton.

Coggins, T., & Carpenter, R. (1981). The communicative intention inventory: A system for observing and coding children's early intentional communication. *Applied Psycholinguistics, 2,* 235–251.

Comfort, M. (1988). Assessing parent-child interaction. In D. Bailey & R. Simeonsson (Eds.),

Family assessment in early intervention. Columbus, OH: Merrill.

Conti-Ramsden, G., & Friel-Patti, S. (1984). Mother-child dialogues: A comparison of normal and language-impaired children. *Journal of Communication Disorders, 17,* 19–35.

Donnellan, A., Mirenda, P., Mesaros, R., & Fassbender, L. (1984). Analyzing the communicative functions of aberrant behavior. *Journal of the Association for Persons with Severe Handicaps, 9,* 201–212.

Doss, S., & Reichle, J. (1991). Using graphic organization aids to promote independent functioning. In J. Reichle, J. York, & J. Sigafoos (Eds.), *Implementing augmentative and alternative communication.* Baltimore: Paul Brookes.

Duchan, J. (1986). Language intervention through sensemaking and fine tuning. In R. Schiefelbusch (Ed.), *Language competence: Assessment and intervention.* Austin, TX: PRO-ED.

Duchan, J. (1989). Evaluating adults' talk to children: Assessing adult attunement. *Seminars in Speech and Language, 10,* 17–27.

Dunst, C., Lowe, L., & Bartholomew, P. (1990). Contingent social responsiveness, family ecology, and infant communicative competence. *National Student Speech, Language, and Hearing Association Journal, 17,* 39–49.

Fay, W. (1979). Personal pronouns and the autistic child. *Journal of Autism and Developmental Disorders, 9,* 247–260.

Fernald, A. (1985). Four-month-old infants prefer to listen to motherese. *Infant Behavior and Development, 10,* 181–195.

Fey, M. (1986). *Language intervention with young children.* San Diego: College-Hill Press.

Fey, M., Warr-Leeper, G., Webber, S., & Disher, L. (1988). Repairing children's repairs: Evaluation and facilitation of children's clarification requests and responses. *Topics in Language Disorders, 8,* 63–84.

Field, T. (1982). Interaction coaching for high-risk infants and their parents. In H. Moss, R. Hess, & C. Swift (Eds.), *Early intervention programs for infants.* Binghamton, NY: Haworth Press.

Field, T. (1987). Affective and interactive disturbances in infants. In J. Osofsky (Ed.), *Handbook of Infant Development* (2nd ed.). New York: Wiley.

Flavell, J. (1963). *The developmental psychology of Jean Piaget.* New York: Van Nostrand.

Girolometto, L., Ushycky, I., & Hellman, J. (1988). Hanen training program for parents of high risk infants. In Proceedings of the symposium *High Risk Infants: Facilitating interaction and communication.* Toronto: Hanen Early Language Resource Centre.

Goetz, L., Guess, D., & Stremel-Campbell, K. (1987). *Innovative program design for individuals with dual sensory impairments.* Baltimore: Paul Brookes.

Goldstein, H., & Strain, P. (1988). Peers as communication intervention agents: Some new strategies and research findings. *Topics in Language Disorders, 9,* 44–57.

Goossens', C. (1990). Engineering the preschool classroom environment for interactive symbolic communication. Workshop presented at Bradley Hospital, E. Providence, Rhode Island, March.

Gottlieb, M. (1988). The response of families to language disorders in the young child. *Seminars in Speech and Language, 9,* 47–53.

Guralnick, M., & Bennett, F. (1987). *The effectiveness of early intervention for at-risk and handicapped children.* New York: Academic Press.

Houghton, J., Bronicki, G., & Guess, D. (1987). Opportunities to express preferences and make choices among students with severe disabilities in classroom settings. *Journal of the Association for Persons with Severe Handicaps, 12,* 18–27.

Lahey, M. (1988). *Language disorders and language development.* New York: Macmillan.

Lahey, M., & Bloom, L. (1977). Planning a first lexicon: Which words to teach first. *Journal of Speech and Hearing Disorders, 42,* 340–350.

Leonard, L. (1991). New trends in the study of early language acquisition. *Asha, 33,* 43–44.

Linder, T. (1990). *Transdisciplinary play-based assessment.* Baltimore: Paul Brookes.

Lombardino, L., Willems, S., & MacDonald, J. (1981). Critical considerations in total communication and an environmental interven-

tion model for the developmentally delayed. *Exceptional Children, 47,* 455–461.

Lovaas, O. (1981). *Teaching developmentally disabled children. The "me" book.* Baltimore: University Park Press.

Lund, N., & Duchan, J. (1988). *Assessing children's language in naturalistic contexts* (2nd ed.). Englewood Cliffs, NJ: Prentice-Hall.

MacDonald, J. (1989). *Becoming partners with children.* San Antonio: Special Press.

MacDonald, J., & Gillette, Y. (1988). Communicating partners: A conversational model for building parent-child relationships with handicapped children. In Marfo, K. (Ed.), *Parent-child interaction and developmental disabilities.* New York: Praeger.

MacDonald, J., & Horstmeier, D. (1978). *Environmental language intervention program.* Columbus, OH: Merrill.

Mahoney, G. (1988). Enhancing the developmental competence of handicapped infants. In Marfo, K. (Ed.), *Parent-child interaction and developmental disabilities.* New York: Praeger.

Mahoney, G., & Powell, A. (1988). Modifying parent–child interaction: Enhancing the development of handicapped children. *Journal of Special Education, 22,* 82–96.

Manolson, A. (1985). *It takes two to talk.* Toronto: Hanen Early Language Resource Centre.

Marfo, K. (1990). Maternal directiveness in interactions with mentally handicapped children: An analytical commentary. *Journal of Child Psychology and Psychiatry, 31,* 531–549.

Mayer-Johnson, R. (1981). *The picture communication symbols.* Salana Beach, CA: Mayer-Johnson.

Mayer-Johnson, R. (1985). *The picture communication symbols: Book two.* Salana Beach, CA: Mayer-Johnson.

McCormick, L. (1990a). Intervention processes and procedures. In L. McCormick & R. Schiefelbusch (Eds.). *Early language intervention.* Columbus, OH: Merrill.

McCormick, L. (1990b). Sequence of language and communication development. In L. McCormick & R. Schiefelbusch (Eds.), *Early language intervention.* Columbus, OH: Merrill.

McCormick, L. (1990c). Developing objectives. In

L. McCormick & R. Schiefelbusch (Eds.). *Early language intervention.* Columbus, OH: Merrill.

McCormick, L., & Shane, H. (1990). Communication system options for students who are nonspeaking. In L. McCormick & R. Schiefelbusch (Eds.), *Early language intervention.* Columbus, OH: Merrill.

McDade, H., & Varnedoe, D. (1987). Training parents to be language facilitators. *Topics in Language Disorders, 7,* 19–30.

McDonough, S. (1989). *Interactive guidance: Treatment of early relationship disturbances.* Paper presented at Child Psychiatry Grand Rounds, Bradley Hospital, E. Providence, RI.

McLean, L. (1990). Communication development in the first two years of life: A transactional process. *Zero to Three, 11,* 13–19.

McLean, J., & Snyder-McLean, L. (1978). *A transactional approach to early language training.* Columbus, OH: Merrill.

McLean, J., Snyder-McLean, L., & Sack, S. (1983). *A transactional approach to early language training: A mediated training program for in-service professionals.* San Antonio: The Psychological Corporation.

Mirenda, P. (1985). Designing pictoral communication systems for physically able-bodied students with severe handicaps. *Augmentative and Alternative Communication, 1,* 58–64.

Mustonen, T., Locke, P., Reichle, J., Solbrack, M., & Lindgren, A. (1991). An overview of augmentative and alternative communication systems. In J. Reichle, J. York, & J. Sigafoos (Eds.), *Implementing augmentative and alternative communication.* Baltimore: Paul Brookes.

Nelson, K. E. (1988). Strategies for first language teaching. In M. Rice & R. Schiefelbusch (Eds.), *The teachability of language.* Baltimore: Paul Brookes.

Ninio, A., & Bruner, J. (1978). The achievements and antecedents of labelling. *Journal of Child Language, 5,* 1–15.

Noonan, M. J., & Siegel-Causey, E. (1990). Special needs of students with severe handicaps. In L. McCormick & R. Schiefelbusch (Eds.), *Early language intervention: An introduc-* tion, 2nd ed. (pp. 383–425). Columbus, OH: Merrill.

Owens, R. (1988). *Language development: An introduction* (2nd ed.). Columbus, OH: Merrill.

Peck, C. (1985). Increasing opportunities for social control by children with autism and severe handicaps. *Journal of the Association for Persons with Severe Handicaps, 10,* 183–193.

Peck, C. (1989). Assessment of social communicative competence: Evaluating environments. *Seminars in Speech and Language, 10,* 1–15.

Peters, A. (1983). *The units of language acquisition.* London: Cambridge University Press.

Prinz, P., & Masin, L. (1985). Lending a helping hand: Linguistic input and sign language acquisition in deaf children. *Applied Psycholinguistics, 6,* 357–370.

Prizant, B. (1982). Speech-language pathologists and autistic children: What is our role? (Part II). *Asha, 24,* 531–537.

Prizant, B. (1983). Language acquisition and communicative behavior in autism: Toward an understanding of the "whole" of it. *Journal of Speech and Hearing Disorders, 48,* 296–307.

Prizant, B. (1987a). Clinical implications of echolalic behavior in autism. In T. Layton (Ed.), *Language and treatment of autistic and developmentally disordered children.* Springfield, IL: Charles Thomas.

Prizant, B. (1987b). Toward an understanding of verbal repetition in the language of visually impaired children. *Australian Journal of Human Communication Disorders, 15,* 79–90.

Prizant, B., Audet, L., Burke, G., Hummel, L., Maher, S., & Theadore, G. (1990). Communication disorders and emotional/behavioral disorders in children. *Journal of Speech and Hearing Disorders, 55,* 179–192.

Prizant, B., & Rydell, P. (1984). An analysis of the functions of delayed echolalia in autistic children. *Journal of Speech and Hearing Research, 27,* 183–192.

Prizant, B., & Schuler, A. (1985). Definition of

functional communication. In *Children and youth with severe handicaps: Effective communication*. Proceedings of conference. Washington, DC: Office of Special Education and Rehabilitative Services.

Prizant, B., & Schuler, A. (1987a). Facilitating communication: Theoretical foundations. In D. Cohen & A. Donnellan (Eds.), *Handbook of autism and pervasive developmental disorders*. New York: Wiley.

Prizant, B., & Schuler, A. (1987b). Facilitating communication: Language approaches. In D. Cohen & A. Donnellan (Eds.), *Handbook of autism and pervasive developmental disorders*. New York: Wiley.

Prizant, B., & Wetherby, A. (1985). Intentional communicative behavior of children with autism: Theoretical and practical issues. *Australian Journal of Human Communication Disorders, 13*, 21–59.

Prizant, B., & Wetherby, A. (1987). Communicative intent: A framework for understanding social-communicative behavior in autism. *Journal of the American Academy of Child and Adolescent Psychiatry, 26*, 472–479.

Prizant, B., & Wetherby, A. (1988). Providing services to children with autism (0–2 years) and their families. *Topics in Language Disorders, 9*, 1–13.

Prizant, B., & Wetherby, A. (1989). Enhancing language and communication in autism: From theory to practice. In G. Dawson (Ed.), *Autism: Nature, diagnosis and treatment*. New York: Guilford.

Prizant, B., & Wetherby, A. (1990). Assessing the communication of infants and toddlers: Integrating a socioemotional perspective. *Zero to Three, 11*, 1–12.

Prizant, B., & Wetherby, A. (1991). Communication in preschool autistic children. In E. Schopler, M. VanBourgondien, & M. Bristol (Eds.), *Preschool issues in autism*. New York: Plenum Press.

Reichle, J. (1991a). Developing communicative exchanges. In J. Reichle, J. York, & J. Sigafoos (Eds.), *Implementing augmentative and alternative communication*. Baltimore: Paul Brookes.

Reichle, J. (1991b). Defining the decisions in-volved in designing and implementing augmentative and alternative communication systems. In J. Reichle, J. York, & J. Sigafoos (Eds.), *Implementing augmentative and alternative communication*. Baltimore: Paul Brookes.

Reichle, J., & Keogh, B. (1985). A selected review of what, when, and how to teach. In S. Warren & A. Rogers-Warren (Eds.), *Teaching functional language* (pp. 25–59). Baltimore: University Park Press.

Reichle, J., & Yoder, D. (1985). Communication board use in severely handicapped learners. *Language, Speech & Hearing in the Schools, 16*, 146–157.

Reichle, J., York, J., & Sigafoos, J. (Eds.). (1991). *Implementing augmentative and alternative communication*. Baltimore: Paul Brookes.

Richard, N., & Schiefelbusch, R. (1990). Assessment. In L. McCormick & R. Schiefelbusch (Eds.), *Early language intervention*. Columbus, OH: Merrill.

Roberts, J., & Crais, E. (1989). Assessing communication skills. In D. Bailey & M. Wolery, *Assessing infants and children with handicaps*. Columbus, OH: Merrill.

Roberts, J., Burchinal, P., & Bailey, D. (1991). Handicapped children's communication in same-aged and mixed-aged settings. Manuscript submitted for publication.

Rogers-Warren, A., & Warren, S. (1980). Mands for generalization: Facilitating the generalization of newly trained language in children. *Behavior Modification, 4*, 230–245.

Rossetti, L. (1990). *Infant-toddler assessment: An interdisciplinary approach*. Boston: College-Hill Press.

Rousch, J. (1991). Early intervention: Expanding the audiologist's role. *Asha, 33*, 47–49.

Sameroff, A. (1987). The social context of development. In N. Eisenburg (Ed.), *Contemporary topics in development*. New York: Wiley.

Sameroff, A., & Fiese, B. (1990). Transactional regulation and early intervention. In S. Meisels & J. Shonkoff (Eds.), *Handbook of early childhood intervention*. Cambridge: Cambridge University Press.

Schuler, A. (1989). *Assessing communicative*

competence (Seminars in Speech and Language, Volume 10). New York: Thieme-Stratton.

Schuler, A., Peck, C., Willard, C., & Thiemer, K. (1989). Assessment of communicative means and functions through interview: Assessing the communicative capabilities of individuals with limited language. *Seminars in Speech and Language, 10,* 51–61.

Schuler, A., & Prizant, B. (1985). Echolalia. In E. Schopler & G. Mesibov (Eds.), *Communication problems in autism.* New York: Plenum Press.

Schuler, A., & Prizant, B. (1987). Facilitating communication: Prelanguage approaches. In D. Cohen & A. Donnellan (Eds.), *Handbook of autism and pervasive developmental disorders.* New York: Wiley.

Schwartz, R., Chapman, K., Terrell, B., Prelock, P., & Rowan, L. (1985). Facilitating word combination in language impaired children through discourse structure. *Journal of Speech and Hearing Disorders, 50,* 31–39.

Seitz, V., & Provence, S. (1990). Caregiver-focused models of early intervention. In S. Meisels & J. Shonkoff (Eds.), *Handbook of early childhood intervention.* Cambridge: Cambridge University Press.

Shane, H. (1981). Decision-making in early augmentative communication system use. In R. L. Schiefelbusch & D. Bricker (Eds.), *Early language: Acquisition and Intervention.* Baltimore: University Park Press.

Siegel-Causey, E., & Ernst, B. (1989). Theoretical orientation and research in nonsymbolic development. In E. Siegel-Causey & D. Guess, *Enhancing non-symbolic communication-interactions among learners with severe disabilities.* Baltimore: Paul Brookes.

Siegel-Causey, E., & Guess, D. (1989). *Enhancing non-symbolic communication interactions among learners with severe disabilities.* Baltimore: Paul Brookes.

Silverman, F. (1989). *Communication for the speechless.* Englewood Cliffs, NJ: Prentice-Hall.

Snow, C., & Ferguson, C. (1977). *Talking to children: Language input and acquisition.* Cambridge: Cambridge University Press.

Snyder-McLean, L., Solomonson, B., McLean, J.,

& Sack, S. (1984). Structuring joint action routines: A strategy for facilitating communication and language development in the classroom. *Seminars in Speech and Language, 5,* 213–228.

Stern, D. (1985). *The interpersonal world of the infant.* New York: Basic Books.

Stillman, R., & Battle, C. (1984). Developing prelanguage communication in the severely handicapped: An interpretation of the Van Dijk method. *Seminars in Speech and Language, 5,* 159–170.

Theadore, G., Maher, S., & Prizant, B. (1990). Early assessment and intervention with emotional and behavioral disorders and communication disorders. *Topics in Language Disorders, 10,* 42–56.

Tiegerman, E., & Siperstein, M. (1984). Individual patterns of interaction in the mother-child dyad: Implications for parent intervention. *Topics in Language Disorders, 5,* 50–61.

Tronick, E. (1989). Emotions and emotional communication in infancy. *American Psychologist, 44,* 112–119.

Warren, S., & Kaiser, A. (1986). Incidental language teaching: A critical review. *Journal of Speech and Hearing Disorders, 51,* 291–299.

Warren, S., & Kaiser, A. (1988). Research in early language intervention. In S. Odom & M. Karnes (Eds.), *Early intervention for infants and children with handicaps: An empirical base.* Baltimore: Paul Brookes.

Warren, S., McQuarter, R., & Rogers-Warren, A. (1984). The effects of mands and models on the speech of unresponsive language-delayed preschool children. *Journal of Speech and Hearing Disorders, 49,* 43–52.

Warren, S., & Rogers-Warren, A. (1985). *Teaching functional language.* Baltimore: University Park Press.

Wetherby, A. (1986). *Checklist of communicative functions and means.* Unpublished instrument.

Wetherby, A., Cain, D., Yonclas, D., & Walker, V. (1988). Analysis of intentional communication of normal children from the prelinguistic to the multi-word stage. *Journal of Speech and Hearing Research, 31,* 240–252.

Wetherby, A., & Prizant, B. (1989). The expression of communicative intent: Assessment guidelines. *Seminars in Speech and Language, 10,* 77–91.

Wetherby, A., & Prizant, B. (1990). *Communication and symbolic behavior scales* (research edition). Chicago: Riverside.

Wetherby, A., & Prizant, B. (in press). Profiling young children's communicative competence. In S. Warren & J. Reichle (Eds.), *Causes and effects in communication disorders.* Baltimore: Paul Brookes.

Wetherby, A., Prizant, B., & Kublin, K. (1989). Assessing communication in infants and toddlers with an eye toward intervention. Short Course presented at the annual convention of the American Speech-Language-Hearing Association, St. Louis, November.

Wetherby, A., & Prutting, C. (1984). Profiles of communicative and cognitive-social abilities in autistic children. *Journal of Speech and Hearing Disorders, 27,* 364–377.

Wertsch, J. (Ed.). (1985). *Culture, communication and cognition: Vygotskian perspectives.* New York: Cambridge University Press.

Westby, C. (1988). Children's play: Reflections of social competence. *Seminars in Speech and Language, 9,* 1–13.

Wilcox, M. J. (1989). Delivering communication-based services to infants, toddlers, and their families: Approaches and models. *Topics in Language Disorders, 10,* 68–79.

Winton, P. (1988). Effective communication between parents and professionals. In D. Bailey, Jr. & R. Simeonsson (Eds.), *Family assessment in early intervention.* Columbus, OH: Merrill.

Yoder, P., Kaiser, A., & Alpert, C. (1991). An exploratory study of the interaction between language teaching methods and child characteristics. *Journal of Speech and Hearing Research, 34,* 155–167.

11

Preventing and Responding to Problem Situations

Mark Wolery

Lucy A. Fleming

In the field of early intervention, the approach to children's problem behavior has undergone considerable reconceptualization in the last 10 to 15 years. In the past, the existence of a problem was sufficient reason to use almost any intervention strategy. Today, the existence of a problem signals a need for an assessment of the child's behavior and its functions; assessment of the contexts in which the behavior occurs; careful analysis of the assessment information; purposeful adjustment of the environment; and, if necessary, a carefully developed intervention based on the assessment data (cf. Cipani, 1989; Gast & Wolery, 1987; Horner et al., 1990; Repp & Singh, 1990; Wolery, Bailey, & Sugai, 1988). Currently, emphasis is placed on a *process* of understanding the factors that set the stage for problem behavior and those that maintain its occurrence. In the first edition of this book, this chapter was titled "Reducing the Occurrence of Inappropriate Behavior"; the title was changed for this edition to: "Preventing and Responding to Problem Situations." This change was made for two reasons. First, it emphasizes the fact that a major task of early educators is to *prevent* the occurrence of problem behavior, and, second, it focuses attention on the contexts or *situations* in which problem behaviors occur.

In this chapter, we list some goals and assumptions related to dealing with problem behaviors, describe a decision model for planning interventions, and discuss interventions for dealing with such responses. We use the designation *"problem" behavior* (rather than, e.g., "challenging," "maladaptive," "aberrant," "disordered," or "inappropriate" behavior) because it conveys a sense that concern exists about the behavior and that a need for change is recognized. The other terms, in our view, do not do this quite as well, although all these terms are used frequently.

GOALS AND ASSUMPTIONS CONCERNING PROBLEM BEHAVIORS

In this section, we review three goals specific to problem situations and behaviors. Then we present seven assumptions related to the process of responding to problem situations.

Goals of Early Intervention for Problem Behaviors and Situations

Goals for early intervention were listed in chapter 2, but here three goals specific to problem behaviors and situations deserve mention. The first goal is *to prevent the occurrence of problem behaviors by teaching adaptive skills and designing environments that promote engagement and prosocial behaviors* (Dunlap, Johnson, & Robbins, 1990). Several rationale for this goal could be stated; here we mention four. First, by focusing on prevention, the professional can redirect intervention time and effort that would have been devoted to behavior change programs toward teaching adaptive and developmental skills. Second, by focusing on prevention, we reduce the stress involved in rearing and educating children who consistently engage in problem behavior. This stress is experienced by families and by teachers who live and work with the children. Third, we decrease the probability that children will acquire patterns of responding that interfere with learning and that could result in behavior disorders and/or more restrictive placements. Fourth, we may decrease the likelihood that children will receive psychotropic medications to control their behavior. Some of these medications have potentially harmful side effects.

The prevention of problem behaviors and situations does *not* mean that children get everything they want and avoid all unpleasant and difficult situations. Rather, it means children are systematically taught the communication skills needed to express their desires (chapter 10) and the social skills (chapter 9) needed to perform adaptively in problematic situations. Also, it means the environment is structured so children are engaged in meaningful and useful activities, experience a high ratio of positive to negative interactions with others, and receive frequent approval and reinforcement for appropriate behavior. In this chapter we describe some preconditions that must be in place before teams use behavior reduction strategies. These preconditions will prevent the occurrence of many situations that lead to problem behaviors. Curricular modifications are described for dealing with problem behaviors, modifications that resulted from studies of cases in which children's problem behaviors were sufficiently severe that intervention was needed. However, some of these modifications have preventive as well as corrective benefits. For example, if a problem behavior is displayed primarily when a child is in instructional programs that are difficult, several curricular modifications are possible. The task could be simplified through partial participation or by restructuring some of the difficult components. The task could remain the same, but more teacher assistance (e.g., a response prompting strategy) could be used to increase success. Also, the child could be reinforced for persisting in attempts to complete difficult tasks as well as for completing the tasks correctly. Further, the child could be taught positive ways of getting teacher assistance. Such curricular modifications can be used to respond to problem behaviors *and* to prevent the occurrence of more severe problem behaviors or the development of additional problem behaviors.

In fairness, it should be noted that this approach to problem situations—attempting to prevent their occurrence—is more demanding for parents and interventionists than other strategies they might choose. For example, it is more difficult to teach social and

communication skills and to ensure that the curriculum is adjusted appropriately than to use a punishment procedure (e.g., time out or overcorrection). However, such effort is justified because using punishment when children are not being taught social and communication skills and when they are experiencing mediocre or poorly designed curricula is basically unfair and inappropriate, and it raises serious ethical questions. Thus, appropriate structuring of the environment and of children's interactions in it requires more work and expertise, but it is more defensible ethically and promotes better outcomes in the long term.

A second goal related to dealing with problem behaviors and situations is *to assist families in dealing with their concerns about their children with problem behaviors.* Parents frequently bring their children to professionals or programs because they perceive their children's behavior as unusual or because their efforts to manage problem behaviors have been frustrating. Assistance provided to families may involve many things. It can be as minor as listening to a parent and confirming that the approach she is using is appropriate. It may also involve helping parents adjust their home environment and their routines for dealing with problematic situations. Or, it may involve assisting them in addressing the severe, life threatening behaviors of their children.

Several rationale exist for helping families deal with the problematic behaviors. First, many families are not adequately prepared to deal with children's problem behavior. They may need assistance in understanding why the behavior is occurring, what maintains it, and how to design the schedule and environment to decrease its occurrence. Second, problem behaviors of children can be stressful and lead to negative outcomes. One father described the problematic behavior of his child as driving a car without brakes; he knew a disaster was likely to happen, but he was powerless to stop it. Such situations may result in excessive punishment, child abuse, or total restriction of the family's social life. By assisting families in dealing with problematic situations, we may lower stress levels and give them alternative ways of responding. Third, by assisting families in dealing with problematic behaviors and situations, we can prevent the development of long-term interaction patterns that are unpleasant, coercive, and debilitating. The outcome of such prevention is that the family system may be strengthened and the child may experience a more growth-promoting home environment. Fourth, by assisting families we can teach/model problem-solving strategies that may be useful in the future. The general public frequently views problem behavior in fairly simplistic ways (e.g., "if he were my child, I'd give him a good whipping"; "he needs to be sat down and told a thing or two"). Unfortunately, prevention and control of problematic behavior are not that simple. They frequently require careful analysis of the context in which the behavior occurs and systematic attempts to design the environment to produce adaptive rather than maladaptive patterns of responding. They also require monitoring to know how well the plan is working. By assisting families in addressing their concerns, we can teach them this process of analyzing the situation, developing a plan, attempting the plan, and determining whether it is successful. This may allow them to learn a style of approaching problem situations that will be useful in the future.

A third goal related to problem situations is *to deal directly with children's problem behaviors in a systematic and proactive manner.* In some cases, attempts at prevention will not be totally successful, or the problem situation will already be well established when the child comes to the attention of professionals. The basic rationale for this goal of dealing directly with the problem be-

haviors is that little justification exists for allowing problem situations to continue if they promote patterns of responding that are harmful to child and family. The early intervention team must deal directly with problem behaviors and situations.

Dealing directly with problem situations requires that the intervention team be skilled *in implementing a behavior reduction process,* a process that includes assessing the behavior, the contexts in which it occurs, and the relationships between the behavior and variables in those contexts; devising an intervention plan that ensures the child is involved in meaningful activities, receives frequent reinforcement for adaptive behaviors, has a high ratio of positive to negative interactions; incorporating specific actions for dealing with the problem behavior/situation; monitoring the effects of the plan; and evaluating the plan on a regular basis (Wolery et al., 1988). We describe this process later in the chapter.

Thus, the goals of early intervention related to problem behavior are to prevent its occurrence, to assist families in dealing with it when it does occur, and to deal directly with it when necessary. These goals represent a comprehensive approach to problem behavior that is integrated with other intervention efforts rather than being a piecemeal or separate part of intervention services. Thus, this chapter does not present a set of procedures that are pulled out to deal with particular situations; rather it treats an integral part of the intervention process.

Assumptions Related to Problem Behaviors/Situations

Here we present seven assumptions about problem behaviors and situations. The process and procedures discussed later in the chapter are based on these assumptions—foundational views from which teams can approach problem behaviors and situations.

The appropriateness/inappropriateness of behavior is, in part, a function of the child's age and developmental level. Infants and toddlers engage in many behaviors that are appropriate for their age but that would not be appropriate for preschoolers. They mouth many objects indiscriminately, engage in repetitive stereotypic movements, rock and flap their hands, pull hair, break objects, throw food, and cry a lot. Again, these behaviors are normal for infants and toddlers, and many of them may serve growth-promoting functions. There are, likewise, many behaviors that are appropriate for 3- and 4-year-old children—for preschoolers, that is—that are not appropriate for older, school-age children. Preschoolers cannot sit still for very long, they frequently interrupt others, they can throw tantrums if they do not get their way, and they love to use "bathroom words." The point here is that one cannot automatically assume that a given behavior is inappropriate without considering the child's age, developmental level, and other aspects of the context in which the behavior occurs. For example, a 6-month old infant cries when he is hungry or wants to be picked up. This behavior is entirely appropriate because crying is the infant's only means of communicating these needs. The adult should respond to most infant crying by picking him up, trying to soothe him, determining whether he is hungry or needs a diaper change, and so forth. For most 4-year-old children, however, crying for food or attention is not appropriate. In this case, the adult should first try to teach the child more appropriate ways to communicate needs.

Not all problem behaviors and situations are of the same importance. Children's problem behavior can come in many different forms (cf. Kerr & Nelson, 1989). *Disruptive behaviors* are those that interrupt, interfere with, and cause disorganization in the flow of activity in the home or center. Examples include failing to comply with rules and directions, making inappropriate noise, touching and interacting inappropriately with others who are engaged in appropriate behaviors, and taking the possessions of peers. *Aggressive behaviors* are responses that involve doing harm or inflicting pain on other persons or attacking others with the intent of doing harm. Examples include hitting, pushing, biting, hair pulling, and kicking. Some descriptions of aggression also include property damage and verbal behavior such as teasing and threatening. Some behaviors are called *self-injurious* and are defined as repetitive acts that result in damage or harm to the performer. Examples include face slapping, self-biting, eye-poking, repeated vomiting, and eating inedible objects (Kerr & Nelson, 1989). Self-injurious behavior does not include acts that result in unintentional injury (i.e., accidents). A similar class of problem behaviors are *stereotypic responses*—"repetitious acts, with invariant topography (form) and no apparent function, they can occur in socially acceptable (e.g., pencil tapping) or unacceptable (e.g., head weaving) forms" (LaGrow & Repp, 1984, p. 595). Examples include rocking, hand flapping, spinning objects, clapping, saliva play, and mouthing objects (LaGrow & Repp, 1984). Still another type of behavior is *social withdrawal*, which includes acts that result in avoidance and escape from social interactions and contact (Kerr & Nelson, 1989).

Each of these types of problem behavior can interfere with children's learning and development; but each type also can be displayed by children without any serious consequence. The seriousness of these behaviors depends a great deal on the age of the child, how often they occur, how long they last, how intense they are, and the conditions under which they occur (Wolery et al., 1988). An occasional push of a peer is not desirable, but it may not be a problem; however, frequent pushing could be. A short temper tantrum when the child is sick or tired is not a problem, but temper tantrums of long duration when the child is well and rested may be. Yelling may be quite acceptable in the outdoors play area but may be problematic when the teacher is reading a story. When determining whether a behavior is problematic, the professional should consider its immediate and long-term outcomes. Sample questions for such deliberations are provided in Box 11.1. These questions are important, as we have just noted, because many of the behaviors of young children do not require special attention while other behaviors require immediate and careful intervention. Most potential problem behaviors of young children can be addressed adequately by providing interesting environments, interacting with children frequently and in positive ways, and reinforcing their adaptive and prosocial behaviors often. The exceptions, the more serious behaviors, should be addressed through the behavior reduction process described later in this chapter.

Children's behavior is lawful but often controlled by multiple factors. This assumption has two elements. First, children's be-

havior follows the principles of nature. We are familiar with natural laws of the physical world. For example, we know that if we drop an object it will fall, and we know that matter changes form if sufficient heat is applied. We also are familiar with how those laws affect us and our behavior. If we drop a heavy object on our toe it will hurt; if we put our hand on a hot stove it will burn. Some laws deal with the relationships between our behavior and our bodies and their physiologies. For example, if we do not eat for several hours, we are likely to be hungry; and if we repeatedly activate certain muscles, they will become fatigued. Other principles deal with relationships between our behavior and the physical and social environment. If we engage in certain behaviors (e.g., taking a walk or shower) we will feel relaxed and refreshed; if we study the correct material sufficiently, we will do well on the test; if we treat other people kindly, many of them will respond with kindness.

Three principles of nature are particularly relevant to problematic behavior. These include the principles of positive reinforcement, negative reinforcement, and stimulus

---

BOX 11.1   Issues related to the seriousness of children's behaviors

1 Does the behavior cause injury to the child or to others?
2 Does the behavior interfere with the learning of the child and of others?
3 Does the behavior present safety risks to the child or others?
4 Is the behavior age-appropriate and likely to be transient?
5 Does the behavior occur at frequencies similar to those for typical peers?
6 Is the behavior a result of skill deficits in other areas?
7 Does the behavior cause others to avoid interacting with the child?
8 Will the behavior be a problem in the next most probable placement?
9 Does the behavior present problems in other situations?

Note: Adapted from *Effective Teaching: Principles and Procedures of Applied Behavior Analysis with Exceptional Students* (p. 354) by M. Wolery, D. B. Bailey, and G. M. Sugai, 1988, Boston: Allyn & Bacon.

control. Specifically, if positive reinforcement contingently follows a behavior, that behavior will likely occur more frequently. If an aversive stimulus is removed contingent upon the occurrence of the behavior, then that behavior will likely occur more frequently. If a given stimulus is present when a particular behavior occurs and reinforcement (positive or negative) is repeatedly and differentially applied to the behavior, then the stimulus will acquire control of that behavior. What do these principles have to do with problem behavior and the manner in which we approach problem situations? The answer is that most behavior problems are learned responses (cf. Carr, 1977). We must understand the relationships between behavior and the factors that set the stage for it and that maintain it, so that we can then modify those factors to produce changes in the behavior. Children sometimes engage in problem behavior because it results in positive reinforcement; in other cases, children engage in problem behavior because it results in negative reinforcement (e.g., escape from aversive situations); in still other cases, children engage in problem behavior in certain situations because those situations have stimulus control (i.e., the stimulus communicates that positive or negative reinforcement is probably available if the problem behavior is displayed).

Much of the time, the positive or negative reinforcement is provided by the environment in the form of adult and peer attention, desirable objects and events, escape from demands and tasks. At other times the reinforcement appears to come from the natural consequences of the behavior itself (Iwata, Vollmer, & Zarcone, 1990); this effect has been referred to as sensory reinforcement or self-stimulation and, more recently as automatic reinforcement. Automatic reinforcement is a preferred designation—because the precise mechanisms may not be clear, and because this description includes the possi-

bility of reinforcement being either positive or negative and does not restrict the effect to physiological (i.e., sensory) processes (Iwata, Pace, Kalsher, Cowdery, & Cataldo, 1990; Iwata, Vollmer, et al., 1990). For example, automatic reinforcement could come because some behavior produces pleasurable sensory feedback, or it could come because the behavior produces relief from aversive stimuli (e.g., a child may sometimes hit her head when she has a severe middle ear infection that is causing pain).

Regardless of whether the reinforcement is external or internal, the major implication for intervention of this assumption is that behavior must be viewed in terms of the effects (functions) it serves. If the function is to receive adult attention, then an intervention could be to teach children more appropriate ways to get attention (Cipani, 1990), to provide attention for appropriate behavior, and to withhold attention for problem behavior. If the function is to provide temporary relief from the pain of a middle ear infection, then treatment of the infection is called for. If the function is to escape from a difficult situation, then the task can be modified or help can be given.

The second part of this assumption is that children's behavior can be controlled by multiple factors. This is illustrated by four different examples. First, two children may display the same behavior, but the factors maintaining it (i.e., the functions or effects of the behavior) may be quite different. One child may behave disruptively to escape difficult tasks, and the second may do so to receive adult attention (Carr & Durand, 1985). Second, some children display multiple problem behaviors, and one may be maintained by one factor while another behavior is maintained by another factor. A child may engage in stereotypic behavior to receive sensory stimulation (automatic reinforcement) and may engage in social withdrawal to escape attention (Repp, Felce, & Barton,

1988). Third, problem behavior may be controlled by more than one factor. A child may not be disruptive in easy tasks but may be disruptive in difficult tasks. The disruptive behavior in difficult tasks may result in both escape from those tasks and attention received from an adult (Carr & Durand, 1985). Fourth, other problem behaviors may be controlled by one factor in some situations and by other factors in other situations. For example, aggressive behavior may be used to get objects (e.g., the child hits a peer to get her toy) in one situation (e.g., when a peer has a desirable toy but the child does not), and aggression may be used in another situation to avoid an aversive stimulus (e.g., the child bites a peer who is annoying him) (Haring & Kennedy, 1990). We present the implications of these multiple possibilities when we describe the next assumption.

Since problem behaviors and situations usually develop over time, some of them get established as interaction patterns or exchanges. *Exchanges* are pervasive patterns that govern how social contact is organized (Kozloff, in press); they are the result of the principles of behavior repeatedly coming into play in social contexts. The notion of exchanges adds an important element to the analysis of children's behavior: Specifically, the environment influences the child's behavior (i.e., through reinforcement and stimulus control), *and* the child's behavior influences the behavior of others, including that of adults (i.e., through reinforcement and stimulus control). Exchanges can be positive (i.e., mutually rewarding and growth promoting), or they can become disordered and interfere with learning and development. Kozloff (in press) has described several different counterproductive exchanges, exchanges that lead to problem situations. Analyzing problem situations in terms of these exchanges is useful for understanding the function of problem behavior, for developing interventions, and for understanding the effect of children's behavior on others. Some counterproductive exchanges are described in Box 11.2.

Interventions should be based on the functions served by problem behaviors and interaction patterns. The second part of the previous assumption (i.e., that children's behavior is potentially controlled by multiple factors and the resulting patterns of exchanges) holds an important implication: the functions and exchanges of problem behaviors should be identified to plan any intervention effectively (Carr, Robinson, Palumbo, 1990; Iwata, Vollmer et al., 1990). We can expand this implication as follows: (a) The same behavior of different children may serve different functions—thus, no single intervention would be effective for all children; (b) different behaviors of the same child may be maintained by different functions—thus, no single intervention may be effective for the multiple behaviors of a single child; (c) the behavior of a single child may serve multiple functions—thus, the intervention strategy must be devised to address all those functions; and (d) the same behavior of the same child may serve different functions when it occurs in different situations—thus, no single intervention may be effective across all situations for a child's behavior. These implications suggest that assessment of behavior problems and situations should be the first step in developing suitable interventions.

Few defensible reasons exist for allowing children to engage consistently in behaviors that impede their learning, interfere with the development of prosocial skills, promote the fluency of antisocial responding, and are age-inappropriate. Rarely, if ever, should problem behaviors continue to exist without intervention (Feldman, 1990; Van Houten et al., 1988). Children's problem behaviors produce minimal, if any, positive outcomes for them. Little benefit results from consistently allowing children to "steal" other children's toys, or from allowing their aggression to result in avoidance of unpleasant tasks, or from allowing their tantrum behavior to interfere with their learning. Children are not better off from having experienced such interactions. Further, as implied in the questions in Box 11.1 and the exchanges in Box 11.2, problem situations can lead to patterns that are maladaptive. Because these patterns may have long-term influences on learning and development, teams have a responsibility to ensure that children are not exposed to situations and exchanges that promote problem behavior. The patterns of responding may begin with relatively innocent and incidental interactions. They are repeated a few times, and soon become relatively durable patterns of behaving. Thus, adults who have contact with children must be aware of the effects of their behavior on children (i.e., ask, "What effect did my behavior produce other than what I wanted it to produce?") and of the effects of children's behavior on them (e.g., "What did his behavior just tell me?"). Thus, interventionists have a responsibility for designing environments that *do not facilitate problem behavior* (Wolery, 1991).

Changing children's behavior is a public matter that requires communication and consultation with families and other professionals. The lack of emphasis in the past on developing interventions based on assessment data resulted in the use of procedures that were considered by many to be excessively aversive, inhumane, and abusive. This issue has resulted in a heated debate about what constitutes right to effective treatment and what constitutes acceptable treatment (Axelrod, 1990; Evans & Meyer, 1985, 1990; Guess, Turnbull, & Helmstetter, 1990; Horner et al., 1990; Lovaas & Favell, 1987; Mulick, 1990; Repp & Singh, 1990). Although the issue is not resolved, two points are pertinent. First, you *may* find yourself in apparent ethical dilemmas related to whether particular procedures should be used. In such cases,

Reamer's (1990) guidelines for resolving ethical dilemmas should be applied (see Chapter 3). Reamer's second guideline suggests that the child's right to basic well-being is more important than a caregiver's right to use or not use a specific strategy. Reamer's fourth and fifth guidelines deal with the responsibility of professionals to obey the regulations and policies of the organizations for which they work or are members. These guidelines apply to the compliance of professionals with the policies of their agencies related to intervention procedures for problem behaviors. A recent review of the special education units in many state departments of education and state mental retardation and developmental disabilities agencies has indicated that many have standards related to using particular procedures, that some procedures are prohibited in some states, and that other states required staff training before certain procedures are used (Morgan, Striefel, Baer, & Percival, 1991). Many professional organizations have made statements on the use of particular procedures (see Singh, Lloyd, & Kendall, 1990). Thus, professionals in early intervention should be aware of the regulations of their agencies and of their professional organizations.

The second point to be made is that it is clear from the debate that changing the problem behavior of children is an issue about which many individuals have diverse but strong feelings and views. As a result, it is foolhardy to engage in the use of most interventions described later in the chapter without consultation with the family and other members of the intervention team. Consulting with others is sound practice in terms of developing better interventions, promoting team cohesiveness, and protecting yourself from unfounded accusations of wrong doing.

Designing interventions to reduce the problem behavior of children should be done for the child's benefit rather than the convenience of the adults. Some behaviors do not

BOX 11.2   Counterproductive exchanges

Rewarded Coercion

Description: Exchanges in which a child performs a problem behavior, and the adult responds by making the child correct the problem. The adult's reaction unwittingly reinforces the child for doing the behavior, and in turn the child's compliance with the adult's reaction reinforces the adult for engaging in the corrective action.

Example: Jamie throws a toy; the teacher looks at him sternly and says, "No throwing"; Jamie does not throw toys for a few minutes; then the sequence is repeated. Jamie is reinforced for throwing by the teacher's attention, and the teacher is reinforced by Jamie's brief interval of no throwing.

Rewarded Threat

Description: Exchanges in which a child displays a mild problem behavior or some other signal that cues the adult that a major problem is in the offing; the adult responds to the mild problem by reinforcing it, and the child's failure to then display the major problem reinforces the adult's response to the mild problem.

Example: It is getting near Terri's bedtime and she wants to avoid going to bed; has a history of tantrum behavior around the bed time routine. When she sees her mother getting up to get the bath ready, Terri whines "drink." The mother responds by giving her a drink of milk, sitting at the table and talking with her while Terri slowly sips her milk. Terri's whining request for milk threatens that a major tantrum is likely; to avoid the tantrum, the mother complies with the request. As a result, Terri is reinforced for whining and delaying the bedtime routine; the mother is reinforced by not having to endure the tantrum and by the pleasant time she has while Terri drinks her milk.

Rewarded Noncompliance

Description: Exchanges in which the adult's requests for reaction on the part of the child are ignored repeatedly and then eventually complied with. The adult is reinforced by the eventual compliance, the child's noncompliance is reinforced by the repeated opportunities to ignore the adult, and/or continued involvement in ongoing activities, and/or delay of the aversive stimulus (i.e., the task involved in the compliance).

Example: Phillip has been playing in the block center but it is nearly time for snack. The teacher says, "Put the blocks away and go to the snack table." Phillip ignores the request and continues to play. In a couple more minutes, the teacher repeats the question, Phillip ignores her, and she is distracted by another child who has fallen and hurt his knee. At last she repeats the request, and Phillip at this point is getting thirsty so he complies. Phillip's ignoring is reinforced by continued opportunities to play, and the teacher's repeated questioning is reinforced because Phillip eventually puts away the blocks.

Mutual Punishment

Description: Exchanges in which each participant inflicts pain on the other and is reinforced by the other's response to pain.

Example: Matthew starts to throw a toy at the window; the teacher grabs his arm; Matthew turns and quickly bites the teacher's hand; the teacher immediately releases Matthew and says, "No biting." Matthew drops the toy and looks at the floor. The teacher is reinforced by her ability to stop Matthew's potentially destructive behavior, and Matthew is reinforced for biting in that it results in release of his arm.

Lack of Opportunities for Desirable Behavior

Description: Exchanges or lack of exchanges in which participation of the child would result in long term benefit, but for some reason the adult does not involve the child.

Example: After lunch time, the children leave their plates, utensils, and napkins on the table and go to the free play area. When they are all in the free play area being supervised by the teaching assistant, the teacher clears the table, throws away the napkins and extra food, puts the utensils in one tray and the plates in another. In this case, the children lost the opportunity to learn independence and responsibility involved in cleaning up after a meal.

Improper Assistance/Prompts

Description: Exchanges in which the adult provides assistance for dependent behavior which reinforces both the child and the adult. The child is reinforced by not being required to expend effort and escaping a difficult task, the adult is reinforced by rapid completion of the task and the compliant response of the child.

Example: Samantha is being toilet trained and is capable of pushing down and pulling up her pants, but it is not easy for her. When she goes into the bathroom, she stands near the toilet and looks at the teacher, the teacher pushes down her pants, and Samantha continues with the routine. This is repeated when she is ready to return to the classroom. Samantha's delay in pushing down her pants cues the teacher to do the behavior and reinforces Samantha's waiting because she avoided the difficult task of pushing her pants down. The teacher was reinforced because he was able to get the pants down quickly and to get Samantha on the toilet before an accident occurred.

Lack of Rewards for Desirable Behavior

Description: Exchanges in which the adult fails (for a number of different reasons) to provide reinforcement for the child's adaptive behavior. The lack of reinforcement results in a weakening of the desirable behavior.

Example: Beth has just completed her first puzzle and is proud of her accomplishment. She takes it over to teacher who says, "No, Beth, we leave the puzzles on the table." The teacher takes the puzzle and puts it away. Beth walks away. This response of the teacher weakens Beth's behaviors of attempting difficult tasks and of sharing her accomplishments with the teacher. The teacher's behavior is reinforced because the classroom stayed orderly (i.e., she rescued the puzzle from being spilled and corrected Beth for doing the wrong thing).

Note: Adapted from *Principles of Developmental-Functional Assessment and Program Planning* by M. Kozloff, in press, Baltimore: Paul Brookes.

interfere with development and learning, but
may annoy, irritate, and embarrass children's parents and teachers. If behaviors do
not lead to antisocial or harmful patterns or
hold other severe negative effects for the
child, then intervention probably should not
be attempted. To ensure that intervention occurs for appropriate reasons, it is wise to
write a rationale for any program to address
behavior problems. That justification should
be based on the good it will do for the child
rather than for the adults in the child's
world.

Thus, to summarize, the goals of intervention in terms of problem behaviors and situations are to prevent their occurrence, assist
families in dealing with them, and to address
them directly when necessary. In meeting
these goals, we should consider the child's
age and development, and we should recognize that some problems are more important
than others, that children's behavior is lawful and potentially controlled by many factors, that interventions should be based on
the functions of problem behaviors, that few
defensible reasons exist for allowing children to develop harmful patterns of responding, and that changing children's behaviors
requires communication with families and
team members.

DECISION MODEL FOR DEALING WITH PROBLEM BEHAVIOR

Decision models are sets of questions and
guidelines for making decisions about
whether to intervene, which intervention
should be used, and whether the intervention has been effective. Several decision
models for addressing problem behaviors exist (e.g., Evans & Meyer, 1985; Foxx, 1982;
Gaylord-Ross, 1980; Lynch, McGuigan, &
Shoemaker, 1983). The steps of the decision
model developed by Wolery et al. (1988) are
displayed in Box 11.3. Each step is described

briefly in the following paragraphs; this discussion is based heavily on Wolery et al.
(1988).

Step # 1: Identify the Problem Situation and State It in a Goal Format

Some problems readily identify themselves;
others such as social withdrawal are less obvious. Teams should periodically review
their students using questions such as these:
(a) Is the child making adequate progress on
objectives? (b) Is the child consistently engaged in the activities? (c) Do others (e.g.,
family members) report problems with the
child? (d) Does the child interact positively
with peers? If a problem appears evident after considering such questions, then the
team should determine if the problem is one
of behavioral excess (occurs too frequently,
lasts too long, has too long a latency, is too
intense), behavioral deficit (occurs too infrequently, does not last long enough, has too
short a latency, and is not done with sufficient force), or inappropriate stimulus control (occurs in the wrong places or at the
wrong times). Also, the team should determine whether the problem behavior is typical for children of that age or developmental
level. Finally, a goal for the intervention
should be written.

Step # 2: Assess the Child and the Environment

The assessment should result in (a) a definition of the behavior, (b) identification of factors and situations that are related to the occurrence of the behavior, (c) identification of
the function and interaction patterns of the
behavior (O'Neill, Horner, Albin, Storey, &
Sprague, 1990), (d) determination of the
child's level of cognitive, communication,
motor, and social skills related to the problem behavior, and (e) identification of adaptive alternative behaviors (Lennox & Miltenberger, 1989). These assessment results are

important for different reasons. The behavior needs precise definition to develop the measurement system. The factors that may be related to the behavior's occurrence need to be identified to plan an appropriate intervention. For example, if the behavior only occurs when the child is hungry, then more frequent feedings would be appropriate; or if the behavior occurs at specific times, then activities scheduled at those times should be altered.

The functions and interaction patterns should be identified to develop a hypothesis about what is causing or maintaining the behavior. O'Neill et al. (1990) have identified two broad types of functions: (a) to obtain desirable events, and (b) to avoid or escape undesirable events. Note that these two

---

BOX 11.3   Steps and sub-steps of the behavior reduction decision model

1 Identify the problem situation and state it in goal format.
  * Determine whether a problem behavior exists and identify its type (e.g., excess, deficit, inappropriate stimulus control).
  * Write a goal statement about the problem.
2 Assess the student and the environment to determine whether a problem situation exists.
  * Define the behavior in the problem situation.
  * Determine whether medical reasons exist for the problem behavior.
  * Identify the function and interaction pattern of the behavior.
  * Determine whether the behavior should be changed.
3 Specify an objective for the intervention.
4 Collect baseline data on the occurrence of the problem behavior in all relevant contexts.
  * Determine what dimension of the behavior will be measured, select an appropriate measurement strategy, and specify the conditions of measurement.
  * Begin data collection, and check the reliability of the data collection.
5 Plan intervention.
  * Ensure the environmental prerequisites are present (i.e., meaningful curriculum activities, frequent reinforcement for adaptive behavior, predictable schedule and consequences for rules violations, choices about activities and reinforcers, high ratio of positive to negative interactions).
  * Determine whether the behavior remains a problem. If a problem remains, select a tentative intervention strategy; develop the specifics of the plan; determine whether plan can be implemented; and determine whether the plan is acceptable to parents, the intervention team, and the agency administration and regulations.
6 Implement the plan and ensure that it is implemented as planned.
7 Monitor child's progress and continue to monitor implementation.
  * Make needed adjustments in the plan.
  * Monitor for the occurrence of positive and negative side effects.
8 Evaluate progress at specific intervals.
  * Make needed adjustments in the plan.
  * Transfer control to all relevant environments.

Note: Adapted from *Effective Teaching: Principles and Procedures of Applied Behavior Analysis with Exceptional Students* by M. Wolery, D. B. Bailey, and G. M. Sugai, 1988, Boston: Allyn & Bacon.

broad classes parallel the two types of reinforcement, positive and negative (Repp & Karsh, 1990). Three sub-types are listed for each of these two types of functions. For obtaining desirable events, the first sub-type is *obtaining internal stimulation* (called automatic reinforcement by Iwata, Vollmer, et al., 1990), which might involve stimulation from rocking, from head weaving, or from cycles of stopping and starting arm flapping. The second sub-type, *obtaining desirable attention*, might come in the form of any positive reinforcement related to attention such as smiles, physical contact (tickling), or even scolding or redirecting the child physically (i.e., things that the adult might not perceive as reinforcers but that may indeed serve as reinforcers). The third sub-type, *obtaining desirable objects and activities*, may be as varied as getting food, toys, or particular activities. The three sub-types of avoiding or escaping events are similar. *Avoiding or escaping internal stimulation* (also called automatic reinforcement by Iwata, Vollmer, et al., 1990) may include temporary displacement of pain caused by sinus and middle ear infections, hunger, and other conditions. *Avoiding undesirable attention* may include all of the stimuli listed for obtaining desirable attention. Different events may have different effects on different children's behavior. A reinforcer for one child may be aversive for another. *Avoiding undesirable tasks and events* may include difficult tasks, changes in routines, interactions with others, or physical contact. Donnellan, Mirenda, Mesaros, and Fassbender (1984) suggest that maladaptive behaviors may fulfill communicative functions. Examples of these are shown in Box 11.4.

BOX 11.4   **Potential communicative functions that may be served by the problem behavior**

Communicative Function	Description	Example of Problem Behavior
Protest/Negation	Behaviors used to communicate that the performer does not want the action or state to continue or to occur.	Toddler cries when told it is time to go to bed. Child bites teacher during instructional session to get it to stop.
Requests (i.e., for any reinforcer such as attention, affection, interaction, assistance, activities, events, or tangible objects)	Behaviors used to communicate that the performer "wants" some reinforcer.	Child grabs and takes peer's toy. Child throws toy to get mother to attend to him. Toddler whines and cries when she cannot get her coat on and crying results in assistance.
Declarations/Comments about stimuli in the environment or about others	Behaviors used to call the attention of another person to some object, activity, event, or person.	Child engages in stereotypic behavior upon seeing a given stimulus (e.g., a spinning top). Child cries when a peer plays with his favorite toy.

The child's developmental level should be considered with respect to the behavior, both globally and within specific domains. For example, a child who does not have a clear understanding of means–ends behavior could not be expected to realize that a particular behavior would hurt another child's feelings.

Alternative (replacement) adaptive behaviors also should be identified. The functions fulfilled by problem behaviors are frequently important. Thus, more adaptive behaviors should be found to take the place of the problem behaviors (Lennox & Miltenberger, 1989). This notion is based on the "fair pair" rule, which states that for every behavior you want to decrease, you should identify one you want to increase (White & Haring, 1980). Ideally, replacement behaviors should require less effort on the part of the child, result in the same reinforcer(s) as the problem behavior, and come under similar stimulus control (Horner, Sprague, O'Brien, & Heathfield, 1990). Selecting replacement behaviors that meet these criteria should lead to more rapid reduction of the problem behavior (because the function is fulfilled more easily) and to successful generalization to other contexts (Horner & Billingsley, 1988).

For completing the assessment, three general strategies are recommended (Lennox & Miltenberger, 1989; O'Neill et al., 1990): (a) interviews with persons who interact frequently with the child, (b) observations of the child in the problem contexts, and (c) direct manipulation of specific variables that may be influencing the behavior. These components should be completed in the order listed; and when the team is confident that the conditions under which the behavior occurs and the function of the behavior are identified, then the assessment activities can stop. O'Neill et al. (1990) present guidelines for conducting such assessments, and they also provide interview forms, observation forms, and guidelines for analyzing the as-

sessment information. These issues also are discussed by Iwata, Vollmer, et al. (1990), Lennox and Miltenberger (1989), and Wolery et al. (1988).

The persons who are interviewed should include the family, professionals who know the child, and individuals who work regularly with the child. The interview should focus on the nature of the problem behavior, the times it occurs, the variables that occur before and after the behavior, and any other information that may identify the function and context of the problem behavior. Some environmental variables to consider are presented in Box 11.5. The perceptions of relevant individuals about the necessity for change also should be addressed.

O'Neill et al. (1990) recommend that observations occur over a period of 2 to 5 days or until the behavior has been observed at least 10 to 15 times. The observation will provide an estimate of how often the behavior occurs, identify situations in which it occurs, and develop a record of what happens before and after each time the behavior occurs.

When the interviews and observations do not provide sufficient information, the child should be observed for a few minutes each day for several days to test factors that are thought to control and not control the behavior's occurrence. During these brief observations, data are collected on the behavior, and the behavior is exposed to conditions that should cause it to occur and to other conditions that should not cause it to occur. For example, if the hypothesis is that attention is maintaining the problem behavior, then under one condition, attention is provided for each occurrence of the problem behavior, and in another condition, attention is not given. If the behavior occurs more frequently when attention is provided, then the assumption (attention maintains the behavior) is supported (cf. O'Neill et al., 1990; Iwata, Dorsey, Slifer, Bauman, & Richman, 1982).

BOX 11.5   Environmental variables that should be addressed in the interview

Type of Variable to Consider
Specific Variables   **Sample Questions about Variables**

Instructional Dimension of Environment

Nature of Materials   • Are materials/activities perceived by students as too
Nature of Activity   immature (e.g., "This is baby stuff")
Nature of Instruction   • Are materials/activities perceived by students as too
Sequence of Activities   gender-specific (e.g., "This is boys/girls' work")?
                                       • Have the same materials/activities been used for sev-
                                          eral days in a row?
                                       • Do materials/activities require skills the student can-
                                          not perform?
                                       • Are materials/activities too easy/difficult for student?
                                       • Are directions for activity clearly understood by
                                          student?
                                       • Is the pace of instruction rapid?
                                       • Does student always have some activity to do?
                                       • Does student receive a high rate of reinforcement or
                                          other positive feedback for correct responses to in-
                                          structional activities?
                                       • What activity preceded the activity where the problem
                                          behavior is displayed?
                                       • What activity immediately follows the activity where
                                          the problem behavior is displayed?

Physical Dimensions of Environment: Noninstructional Variables

Nature of Lighting   • Is the student's area well lighted?
Noise   • Is there a glare from the sun or other lighting?
Heat   • Is student able to see instructional materials (e.g.,
Physical Arrangement   blackboard)?
Time of Day   • Does student appear to be bothered by too much
                                          noise?
                                       • Is student facing stimuli that may be distracting (e.g.,
                                          corridor, window, or other students)?
                                       • Does student appear to react to temperature of the
                                          room?
                                       • Does student appear to react to noise in room?
                                       • Do particular odors appear to affect the student's
                                          behavior?

The assessment activities should produce a precise description of the problem behavior, identification of factors that predict its occurrence, the function it serves, and a replacement behavior. Wolery et al. (1988) suggest that before proceeding, the team should discuss whether the problem behav-

ior should be changed by reviewing the questions listed in Box 11.1.

Step # 3: Specify an Objective

The team should write an objective that will be addressed if an intervention plan is de-

**Type of Variable to Consider
Specific Variables**

                        Sample Questions about Variables

- Does behavior occur at a specific time of day (e.g., after gym, before lunch, etc.)?

Social Dimension of Environment
Number of Other Students
Number of Adults
Behavior of Others Toward Student
Proximity of Others

- Does the number of students in the room/area affect student's behavior?
- Does the number of adults affect student's behavior?
- Does inappropriate behavior occur only in the presence of specific students?
- Does the proximity of adults influence the occurrence of the behavior?
- Does inappropriate behavior occur only in the presence of specific adults?
- Does inappropriate behavior occur only when others have performed a specific behavior?
- Does inappropriate behavior occur only when close to, or away from, specific students?
- Does student behave more/less appropriately when given persons are present/absent?
- Does behavior appear to increase/decrease when other students or adults respond in a specific manner?

Changes in the Environment
Changes in Schedule
Changes in Physical Arrangement
Changes at Home

- Are transition times correlated with the occurrence of the behavior?
- Do disruptions to the schedule appear to increase/decrease the behavior?
- Do changes in the physical arrangement appear to increase/decrease the inappropriate behavior?
- Do specific changes in the student's living environment appear to increase/decrease the occurrence of the inappropriate behavior?

Note: From *Effective Teaching: Principles and Procedures of Applied Behavior Analysis with Exceptional Students* (pp. 360–361) by M. Wolery, D. B. Bailey, and G. M. Sugai, 1988, Boston: Allyn & Bacon. Copyright 1988 by Allyn & Bacon. Reprinted by permission.

veloped. This should include the behavior, conditions, and criterion (see chapter 4).

Step # 4: Collect Baseline Data

This step involves determining whether to measure the frequency, duration, latency, or intensity (or some combination) of the behavior. It also involves selecting an appropriate data collection system (cf. Cooper, Heron, & Heward, 1987; Wolery, 1989; Wolery et al., 1988). It is wise to ensure that two independent observers can consistently record the behavior similarly.

Step # 5: Plan Intervention

Before proceeding with a specific intervention, the team must ensure that certain preconditions are in effect—such as meaningful curriculum activities, frequent reinforcement for adaptive behavior, a predictable schedule and predictable consequences for rules violations, choices about activities and reinforcers, and a high ratio of positive to negative interactions. A meaningful curriculum is one that promotes high child engagement (e.g., 75% or more), learning of useful tasks, and clear presentation of stimuli during direct instruction. Although it is difficult to define "frequent reinforcement," it certainly should be more frequent than the rate at which the problem behavior is being displayed, and probably should be several times that rate. Also, individually determined reinforcers should be used because they may be more effective than commonly used reinforcers (Dyer, 1987). A predictable schedule means that a regular sequence of events transpires throughout the child's day. Although there should be variation within activities, the general sequence should be consistent across days. Also, the rules that are established should receive consistent consequences (Kerr & Nelson, 1989). Children should, to the extent possible, be able to choose activities, materials, and reinforcers. Simply having opportunities to make choices may reduce some behavior problems (Dyer, Dunlap, & Winterling, 1990). Finally, the environment should contain a high ratio of positive to negative interactions. A ratio of at least 4 positive interactions (from the child's perspective) to each negative interaction should exist. The mere presence of these preconditions will prevent problem behavior in many children and will successfully treat the problem behaviors of others. However, regardless of their effects, they are the minimal conditions under which additional interventions should be used.

If the problem behavior persists, then a specialized intervention plan should be developed or selected. The guidelines for making such selections are that the intervention should be (a) based on the function of the behavior; (b) the least intrusive but still *effective* strategy; (c) possible to implement in the needed settings; and (d) acceptable to the family, the intervention team, the administration, and anyone required to use it (Wolery et al., 1988). Specific interventions include medical treatments, curricular and environmental modifications, manipulation of the reinforcement contingencies, and various forms of punishment. These interventions are discussed later in the chapter; however, several options are listed in Box 11.6.

Step # 6: Implement the Plan and Monitor the Implementation

The plan should be implemented, and that implementation should be monitored. If the plan is used incorrectly, then it should be adjusted. This monitoring will ensure that the intervention strategy is given a fair test. The preconditions described in Step #5 also should be monitored, and they should always be in effect when any other intervention strategy is used.

Step # 7: Monitor the Child's Progress and Monitor Implementation

The intervention plan, if successful, should work quite quickly. To determine if it is working, the data collected on the problem behavior are analyzed. The team also should watch for the occurrence of any side effects (i.e., changes in untreated but relevant behaviors). Positive side effects (e.g., increased engagement) should be reinforced, and negative ones (e.g., emotional reactions, withdrawal, etc.) should be monitored. Many of them will be transient, but others may develop into problems of their own.

BOX 11.6   **Potential intervention strategies**

Type of Procedure	Examples
Medical Interventions	Medications
	Surgery
	Dietary changes
Curricular/Environmental Modifications	Change social dimension of the environment
	Change physical arrangement of environment
	Change schedule of activities
	Change the amount and type of materials or activities
	Change instructional methods being used
	Teach responses that fulfill same communicative function currently performed by aberrant behavior
Manipulation of Reinforcement Contingencies	Differential Reinforcement of Other Behaviors (DRO)
	Differential Reinforcement of Incompatible Behaviors (DRI)
	Differential Reinforcement of Low Rate of Behaviors (DRL)
	Contingency contracting
	Token economies
Mildly Intrusive Punishment Procedures	Extinction
	Response cost
Intrusive Punishment Procedures	Timeout
	Overcorrection
	Direct, contingent application of aversive stimuli

Note: From *Effective Teaching: Principles and Procedures of Applied Behavior Analysis with Exceptional Students* (pp. 360–361) by M. Wolery, D.B. Bailey, and G.M. Sugai, 1988, Boston: Allyn & Bacon. Copyright 1988 by Allyn & Bacon. Reprinted by permission.

Step # 8: Evaluate the Progress at Specific Intervals

The team, including the parents, should meet on a regular schedule to discuss the progress of the program. They should decide whether the plan needs to be adjusted and develop plans for transferring the control to all necessary environments. These periodic conferences should continue until the data and the team's judgment indicate that the problem is solved.

Concluding Comment on the Decision Model

At this point, you may be saying, "That's a lot of work." If you are, then you are quite correct. Because of the time and effort involved in the process, it should be entered into only if a behavior problem is severe and if the team can persist in addressing it. Fortunately, the preconditions described under Step #5 will address most behavior problems of young children. The decision model is reserved for serious problems and those that may interfere substantially with learning and development. In the following section, intervention strategies are described.

INTERVENING WITH BEHAVIOR PROBLEMS AND SITUATIONS

Four issues are described in this section. First, we provide information on manipulating general environmental variables and making curricular modifications. Second, we discuss specialized manipulations of reinforcement, including the use of differential reinforcement, correspondence training, and extinction. Third, we address the issue of consulting with families. Finally, we present the conditions under which punishment procedures can be used along with an overview of some punishment procedures.

Environmental and Curricular Interventions

Many interventions manipulate the consequences of the behavior, but curricular interventions generally modify setting or antecedent events or the behavioral responses themselves (Gaylord-Ross, 1982). If behaviors can be controlled by environmental or curricular design without using other procedures, more time can be devoted to promoting developmental and functional skills. Several environmental variables can be manipulated to prevent or reduce problem behavior; these are shown in Table 11.1.

Physical Aspects of the Environment   The physical environment should be designed for maximum comfort of the students and to promote engagement and learning. Teachers frequently state that they have no control over the temperature, lighting, or noise in their classrooms. However, easily implemented modifications can create an appropriate atmosphere for learning in most classrooms (chapter 7).

Lighting is an important variable that potentially influences children's behavior. For example, many parents and teachers dim lights to induce rest or sleep, and many young children sleep more readily with a night light. Although little research has focused on the effects of lighting, environments should be lighted adequately to allow children to interact with the materials/toys. To supplement inadequate lighting, table or floor lamps can be placed around the room. They provide needed light and help define particular learning areas. The suggestion has been made that some types of lighting influence children's activity levels, but such effects, if they exist, tend to be specific to individual children. If all areas of the room are well lighted, teacher scanning (and children's awareness of teacher scanning) will be facilitated. This scanning allows teachers to identify problem situations and address them before they become more problematic.

TABLE 11.1
Variables that can be manipulated to reduce behavior problems

Physical Aspects of the Environment	Social Aspects of the Environment	Aspects of the Curriculum
lighting	number of other children present	rules with consistent consequences
temperature level	proximity of other children	attention to the function of problem behavior
noise level	proximity of adults	choices available to the children about reinforcers and tasks
arrangements of space and materials	amount of interaction with adults	employment of peers as intervention agents
daily routines and scheduling of activities		encouragement of self-management

The *temperature level* in many classrooms is regulated from outside the room and little can be done to change it. However, some evidence suggests that extremes in temperature may influence children's behavior. For example, negative peer interactions appear more likely in hot as compared to cool play areas (Nordquist, 1978). Children who are easily overheated should be allowed to play in cooler areas. A "classroom sweater" should be provided for the child who seems to be always cold. Teachers also should be aware that consistent extreme reactions to temperatures that seem moderate to others may have a medical cause and should be investigated.

Noise levels in classrooms can be moderated by arranging the furniture and activity areas appropriately (cf. chapter 7). Children who have to cross the room to the sink several times during an art activity will make more noise than children who are situated near the sink. In some cases, loud noises are related to the onset of problem behavior. Children with hearing impairments often have difficulty discriminating spoken language from background noise. Hearing aids should be checked daily to ensure that they are mechanically sound and providing the clearest amplification possible.

Particular *arrangements of space and materials* may influence the occurrence of children's behavior problems. For example, reducing the size of play areas leads to increases in social interactions (Rubin & Howe, 1985), but additional restrictions (i.e., crowding) may result in increased aggression (Bailey, Harms, & Clifford, 1983). Reducing the number of materials/toys within a space increases social interactions (Rubin & Howe, 1985), but too few materials lead to disputes between children (Bailey et al., 1983). Thus, the effects of space and materials on children's behavior problems may be complex and may require careful assessment.

Issues involved in the *scheduling of daily routines and activities* were described in chapter 7. However, it is clear that some schedules may present problem situations (O'Neill et al., 1990). Most parents readily recognize that children who have gone too long without rest or without eating tend to become fussy and irritable. Thus, the timing of basic caregiving routines may be related to the occurrence of problem behavior. Similarly, when particular activities, routines, or events are aversive, problem behavior may occur more frequently. Teams should adjust the sequence of those events. For example, tantrum and other resistive behaviors are common at bedtime for children with and without disabilities. Milan, Mitchell, Berger, and Pierson (1981) taught parents to use a chaining and fading procedure called *positive routines* to eliminate the bedtime tantrums of three children with severe emotional disabilities. During pretreatment conditions, after the children were prepared for bed, all interactions stopped and the parents waited for the child to get tired and fall asleep. The time the child fell asleep was recorded every evening for a week. Parents then developed a sequence of pre-bedtime self-care activities. A typical routine included using the toilet, taking a bath, brushing teeth, putting on pajamas, hearing a bedtime story, and getting into bed. This routine was begun every night at the natural sleep baseline time (identified in the pretreatment condition). Children were reinforced for complying with each step of the routine. The starting time for the routine was gradually moved from the natural sleep time to the time the parents preferred. Resistance to bedtime was rapidly eliminated. Using regular activities in a fixed order and reinforcing children for doing those activities established several cooperative responses thus increasing the probability of compliance with the request to go to bed. A similar procedure is called *behavioral momentum* (Mace & Belfiore, 1990; Mace et al., 1988; Mace et al., 1990; Nevin, Mandell, & Atak, 1983). Mace and Belfiore (1990) used behavior momentum to reduce the stereotypic behavior of an adult with se-vere mental retardation. This adult engaged in stereotypic behavior to escape household tasks such as hanging up clothing or helping with the dishes. During training, three com-mands that did not elicit the problem behav-ior and had a high probability of compliance ("Give me five," "Hold my hand," "Give me a hug") were presented immediately before a command that often triggered the prob-lem behavior ("Please hang up your coat"). Compliance with requests about household tasks increased when they were preceded with requests to do brief, highly preferred behaviors.

Social Aspects of the Environment Some children are socially withdrawn when others are present, and others become aggressive or disruptive when they are crowded or con-fined (Bailey et al., 1983). When possible, children should be grouped so that they dis-play the fewest numbers of problem behav-iors. If a child can appropriately interact with one other child but withdraws or be-comes disruptive when more children enter the activity, opportunities for one to one in-teraction should be provided, appropriate behavior should be reinforced, and other children should be added gradually. Simi-larly, two or more children may exhibit prob-lem behaviors when situated near one an-other but behave appropriately when away from each other. The presence of such rela-tionships should be noted in the assessment and addressed in intervention.

Other environmental variables such as the proximity and the amount of interaction with adults can influence children's prob-lem behavior. For example, Brusca, Niemi-nen, Carter, and Repp (1989) found that closer proximity and more adult interaction with children during activities were related to lower percentages of stereotypic behavior. Although some activities appeared to be re-lated to children's problem behavior, spe-cific activities were not related to all chil-dren's problem behavior. In other words, a given activity (e.g., free play or circle time) is not necessarily related to general increases/decreases in problem behavior across chil-dren. "Within activity periods a myriad of factors, including adult and peer interaction, ability to work independently, type of re-sponse required, setting, and task difficulty, all appear to affect the occurrence of stereo-typy" (Brusca et al., 1989, p. 134). Based on experience, such statements are probably true of other problem behaviors. This em-phasizes the importance of understanding the conditions that set the stage for problem behavior and the functions that the behavior serves.

Aspects of the Curriculum Children fre-quently learn appropriate behavior through verbally stated rules. Rules are most effective when accompanied by reasonable rationale (Evans & Meyer, 1985) and consistent con-sequences. Children are more apt to comply with rules that are based on principles of concern for self or others than rules they per-ceive as adult efforts to control them. Often, merely stating the rule before acting upon it is all that is needed. For example, children who are told that an activity is over and it is time for another activity may be less likely to display defiant or fearful responses. This is particularly true with children who are in their first group care experience. Many chil-dren may simply not know how to behave in such settings, and stating rules and respond-ing to rule violations may be sufficient to control problem situations.

Because problem behaviors serve a variety of functions, children may use them to (a) get adult attention or assistance, (b) avoid chal-lenging tasks, or (c) communicate boredom, frustration, or anxiety (Donnellan et al., 1984). Children can learn functionally equiv-alent, yet positive, ways to meet these needs. Verbal and nonverbal communication be-haviors are often established as alternatives to problem behaviors (Carr & Durand, 1985;

Cipani, 1990; Durand & Carr, 1987; Horner, Sprague, O'Brien, & Heathfield, 1990; Steege et al., 1990). For example, Carr and Durand (1985) assessed the behavior of four children with disabilities. They determined that disruptive behavior was displayed by two subjects when teacher attention was infrequent and by the other two subjects when tasks were perceived as too demanding. They taught the children to respond appropriately when their teacher asked, "Do you have any questions?" The children who needed to solicit teacher attention were taught to respond, "Am I doing good work?" The children who needed assistance to perform the task were taught to respond, "I don't understand." Disruptive behavior was effectively reduced in all four children. Cipani (1990) taught two children with severe disabilities

to approach their teacher and say her name in a conversational tone rather than shout across the room when they required assistance. Steege et al. (1990) reduced self-biting in two students with profound mental retardation by teaching them to press a microswitch that activated a recording of "stop" to indicate when a grooming activity became too stressful. Thus, in designing curricular modifications, it is critical to understand the function of the problem behavior. When the function is understood, a number of curricular modifications are frequently possible. In Table 11.2, several curricular modifications are listed for cases in which the function of the behavior is to escape from demands or the difficulties of a task.

Another important curricular modification is allowing children to make choices

TABLE 11.2

Examples of curricular modifications when the function of problem behavior is to escape from tasks/activities

Problem Behavior	Curricular Modification	Sample Reference
aggression disruption property destruction	guide compliance with task	Parrish, Cataldo, Kolko, Neef, & Egel (1986)
tantrums hand mouthing and biting	present repeated trials of task until subject completes task	Mace, Browder, & Lin (1987)
SIB (self-injurious behavior) (arm and hand biting)	eliminate some task requirements	Gaylord-Ross, Weeks, & Lipner (1980)
SIB (finger and wrist biting) aggression frequent crying	select easier task	Weeks & Gaylor-Ross (1981)
SIB (hand mouthing and biting)	increase reinforcement for task completion	Steege, Wacker, Berg, Cigrand, & Cooper (1989)
SIB (head and face hitting) body rocking hand flapping	teach child to request teacher assistance	Durand & Carr (1987)
SIB (head and face slapping, head banging, hand biting, head butting) aggression	teach child to request a break from task engagement	Durand & Kishi (1987)

about reinforcers and tasks (Dyer, 1987; Dyer et al., 1990; Koegel, Dyer, & Bell, 1987; Parsons, Reid, Reynolds, & Bumgarner, 1990). Dyer et al. (1990) used this procedure to reduce the aggressive, disruptive, and self-injurious behaviors of three children with severe disabilities. Functional reinforcers were identified for each child. Pre-academic tasks such as completing a puzzle, sorting objects, and labeling pictures were selected. Two experimental conditions were used. During the no-choice condition, the identified tasks and reinforcers were selected and presented by the teacher according to an independent schedule. When children attempted to choose, they were told, "You have to do this other work now." During the choice condition, tasks were chosen by the children. The children were allowed to change materials if they desired and to select new tasks if they completed a task during a session. Also, children selected reinforcers on a variable-ratio schedule. For all three subjects, the choice condition consistently produced lower levels of problem behavior than the no-choice condition.

Typical peers have often been trained to reinforce desirable behaviors (Hendrickson, Strain, Tremblay, & Shores, 1982; Strain, 1981). They also can serve as intervention agents in programs designed to impact problem behaviors (Carden-Smith & Fowler, 1984; Dougherty, Fowler, & Paine, 1985; Kerr, Strain, & Ragland, 1982; Stern, Fowler, & Kohler, 1988). Carden-Smith and Fowler (1984) decreased the disruptive behaviors of three developmentally delayed children by having peers monitor a token system. The target subjects were identified as the most disruptive in their kindergarten classrooms. All the children (e.g., the 3 target children and their 5 other classmates) were assigned to teams. Team monitors were randomly assigned. Each team was directed to clean an area of the classroom, go as a group to the bathroom, and wait on individual mats

when they returned from the bathroom. At the end of each transition, the team monitors met with the teacher to publicly award points. Each child received one point for participating in each step of the transition appropriately. Children who earned three points were eligible to vote for and participate in an outdoor activity. Children who earned two points could participate but could not help select the activity. Children who earned one point or no points stayed indoors during the activity. Rates of disruptive behavior decreased substantially during the peer monitoring condition.

Teaching Self-Management Skills Self-management is another set of curricular modifications that can reduce the occurrence of problem behaviors. These strategies have had limited use with preschoolers but they have been used successfully to reduce problem behaviors of older children with mild to moderate mental retardation (Baer, Fowler, & Carden-Smith, 1984; Gardner, Cole, Berry, & Nowinski, 1983; Koegel & Koegel, 1990; Matson & Earnhart, 1981; Zohn & Bornstein, 1980). Self-management treatments may include self-monitoring, self-reinforcement, and/or self-instruction components. Self-monitoring occurs when subjects objectively record the frequency of their behavior (Wolery et al., 1988). Koegel and Koegel (1990) used a self-monitoring system with four children with severe disabilities who exhibited self-stimulatory behaviors. Reinforcers were identified for each child. Behaviors were defined and the children were taught to discriminate between their problem behavior and appropriate behavior. Next, an initial self-management interval was chosen. The length of this interval was the average length of time during which the problem behaviors did not occur during pretreatment conditions. Trainers began each interval by saying, "Show me no arm flapping. Ready? Go!" At the end of the interval, the trainer asked, "Did you do any arm flapping?" If no arm flapping had occurred, the subject was prompted to make a mark in a box, he was reinforced, and the next interval began. Prompts to mark the box were faded to an intermittent schedule and then to no prompts being given. Finally, the schedule of reinforcement was thinned by gradually increasing the number of intervals needed to get reinforcers and by increasing the length of the interval.

Self-reinforcement occurs when children give themselves reinforcers when their behavior is at a specified criteria level. In some cases, the students may participate in determining the criteria level for acceptable behavior (Wolery et al., 1988). Baer et al. (1984) used a self-reinforcement procedure to decrease disruptions and off-task behavior exhibited by a child with a severe behavior disorder. During the first condition, the child was required to complete a set of worksheets during an independent work period. He was given a sticker and allowed to participate in recess if a tutor determined that he accurately completed 80 percent of the assigned work. Next, the child was taught to grade his work himself and to determine if he was eligible for the sticker and recess. The schedule for having the tutor check the child's grading was thinned from every task to every six tasks.

Self-instruction occurs when students make statements to themselves that prompt specific behaviors (Wolery et al., 1988). Burgio, Whitman, and Johnson (1980) used a self-instruction package to reduce the off-task behaviors of three children with mental retardation. Self-instruction consisted of teaching the children to (a) ask a task-related question ("What does the teacher want me to do?"), (b) answer the question ("She wants me to do this problem"), (c) provide direction on how to do the task ("First, I need to write down this number"), (d) reinforce

themselves for completing the task ("I did a good job"), (e) provide a cue to ignore distractions ("I hear my friends talking but I'm not going to let them bother me"), and (f) provide direction about how to recognize and deal with unsatisfactory work ("That one is messy. I will be more careful on the next problem").

Thus, several variables related to the environment and curriculum may provide the basis for useful interventions for problem behaviors. The intervention strategy may include the manipulation of environmental factors such as lighting, temperature levels, noise levels, the arrangement of space and materials, the scheduling of routines and activities, and the interactions that occur. Decreases in problem behavior may also result from analyzing the function of the behavior and making appropriate adjustments of the curriculum. Teaching children to manage their own behavior is a useful intervention that may have short- and long-term benefits. Another group of interventions, dealing with manipulation of reinforcement schedules, are described in the next section.

Manipulation of Reinforcement Contingencies

Differential Reinforcement *Differential reinforcement* is used when teaching children desirable behaviors. Reinforcement is provided for skills when they occur at the appropriate times and places, and it is not provided when they do not. Also, as we noted under Step #5 of the behavior reduction decision model, frequent reinforcement for positive behavior is a precondition to using other more intrusive intervention strategies. Differential reinforcement has been used in at least four different and specialized ways as a primary intervention for problem behavior (O'Brien & Repp, 1990): differential reinforcement of (a) other behaviors (DRO), (b) incompatible behaviors (DRI), (c) alternative behaviors (DRA), and (d) low rate behaviors (DRL).

DRO involves delivery of reinforcement if the problem behavior has *not* occurred for a specified length of time. Since reinforcement is given for the behavior *not occurring*, DRO has been referred to as omission training (Cooper et al., 1987). DRO has been used successfully alone (O'Brien & Repp, 1990) and in combination with other interventions (Cooper et al., 1987). Several factors influence the success of DRO: (a) using powerful reinforcers, (b) selecting an appropriate interval that the child must go without doing the problem behavior before receiving reinforcement, (c) using the method consistently, and (d) identifying a schedule for increasing the interval as the problem behavior is controlled.

The procedures described in chapter 5 for selecting reinforcers should be used when planning a DRO program. Selecting the appropriate interval is a critical decision. If the interval is too long, the child will display the problem behavior before the end of the interval and will rarely receive reinforcement. If the interval is too short, the child could receive considerable reinforcement but still display the problem behavior frequently. Repp, Felce, and Barton (1991) found that using the average amount of time between occurrences of the problem behavior as the initial interval was more effective than using an interval twice the length of the average duration between occurrences. The general guideline is for the initial interval to be slightly less than the average duration between episodes of the problem behavior. For example, Phillip's problematic behavior is hitting peers during free play. During a 20-minute session he hits about five times with an average of about 4 minutes between hits. When selecting the interval, his team decided to reinforce him each time he went for 3.5 minutes without hitting.

When using DRO, you must be able to observe the child and keep track of how long it has been since the last behavior occurred. For example, the teacher must watch Phillip during free play and after 3.5 minutes provide him with reinforcement if he has not hit another child. If he hits after 2 minutes, then the interval must be restarted, and reinforcement should be delivered 3.5 minutes after the last hit. Thus, DRO requires careful monitoring.

To avoid having to reinforce the child forever, the length of the delay interval is increased as the behavior comes under control. Usually, small increases occur at first followed by larger increases and sometimes variable lengths of time rather than constant lengths (Cooper et al., 1987; Wolery et al., 1988). For example, after several days of no hitting during free play, Phillip would be required to go 4 minutes without hitting, then 5 minutes, then 7 minutes, and so on until reinforcement is given only at the end of free play. However, if the problem behavior begins to reappear, a shorter interval should be used again.

It is important to note that DRO can be combined with other reinforcement the child receives. For example, Haring and Kennedy (1990) reinforced students for correct responses during instruction *and* for not displaying the problem behavior for specific intervals (i.e., DRO). Generally, DRO is considered a nonaversive procedure, because it does not involve an aversive stimulus. However, recent data have demonstrated that a child for which DRO was successful also emitted a crying response when reinforcement was not delivered because the problem behavior occurred (Cowdery, Iwata, & Pace, 1990). Thus, the DRO strategy produced negative side effects similar to those found with punishment procedures.

In summary, DRO is more complex than it may at first appear. It requires careful planning and use, particularly in relation to selecting and increasing the interval and in administering the reinforcement. When used with multiple problem behaviors, the complexity of the procedure increases. Nonetheless, it has been effective with many problem behaviors (O'Brien & Repp, 1990; Wolery et al., 1988), and it is useful to early intervention teams.

DRI and DRA are similar to one another, but different from DRO. DRI and DRA involve providing reinforcement for the occurrence of an appropriate behavior rather than providing reinforcement at the end of a specific interval of no problem behavior (as with DRO). DRI involves reinforcement of a behavior that is incompatible with the problem behavior. Incompatible means that the child cannot possibly perform both behaviors at the same time. For example, manipulating a toy is incompatible with throwing it, and speaking is incompatible with screaming. DRA involves reinforcement of an appropriate behavior, but one that is not incompatible with the problem behavior. For example, playing with toys is not incompatible with screaming, but if toy play increases, screaming may decrease.

When using DRI/DRA, the team must identify the specific incompatible or alternative behaviors that will be reinforced, select behaviors that are in the child's repertoire, identify a powerful reinforcer, and select a schedule of reinforcement (Cooper et al., 1987; Wolery et al., 1988). Ideally, the incompatible or alternative behavior would meet the criteria specified for replacement behaviors; they would, that is, (a) fulfill the same function as the problem behavior, (b) result in the same reinforcement as the problem behavior, (c) be performed with less effort, and (d) come under the control of the same stimuli (Horner, Sprague, et al., 1990). A continuous reinforcement schedule often is used, and when the problem behavior is under control, the incompatible or alternative behavior is reinforced less often.

DRI and DRA are simpler to use than DRO, because you do not need to keep track of the time interval. Also DRI and DRA may strengthen specific appropriate behaviors that can replace problem behaviors and this strengthening may lead to greater maintenance. Further, these procedures have been used with a number of different behaviors, and as with DRO, can and should be used when more intrusive interventions are employed.

DRL is different from the other differential reinforcement procedures, because the goal is not to eliminate the occurrence of the behavior but to lower its frequency. For example, some children initiate social interactions with adults to such an extent that they do not interact with their peers. Because initiating interactions with adults is appropriate, it should not be eliminated, but to increase interactions with peers its frequency may need to be reduced. With DRL, the reinforcement is provided for reductions in the frequency of the problem behavior.

When using DRL, the team must identify a powerful reinforcer, collect data on the frequency with which the behavior is occurring, identify an acceptable frequency for the behavior, and identify stepwise decreases in that frequency. The reinforcement should initially be presented contingent upon a slight decrease in the occurrence of the behavior. After this criterion is consistently met, the contingency is changed to a lower frequency. When this lower frequency is met consistently, the criterion is again lowered. This continues until the behavior is at the predetermined acceptable frequency.

DRL does not require the child to understand that reinforcement will occur for a lower rate of performance, but such understanding may increase its effectiveness. DRL has been used in two ways (Cooper et al., 1987; Wolery et al., 1988). In one version, the frequency of the behavior must meet the criterion for the entire day or session. In another version, the session or day is divided into intervals, and each interval has a specific criterion. In large part, the team's decision about which version to use should be based on the nature of the behavior, whether it occurs at regular intervals or in spurts, and the situations in which it is problematic. DRL can be used with DRI and DRA.

In summary, the differential reinforcement procedures are positive means of dealing with problem behaviors. They are effective and can reduce the use of punishment procedures. They can be used in centers and in homes and without removing the child from the activity. They do, however, require careful planning and use.

Correspondence Training Besides DRO, DRI, DRA, and DRL, other manipulations of reinforcement will result in changes in children's behavior. One such procedure is known as correspondence training. *Correspondence training* involves reinforcing children for making statements about their behavior and/or reinforcing children for *truthful* statements about their behavior (Baer, 1990; Paniagua, 1990). The assumptions underlying correspondence training are that verbalizations and behavior should match, and that verbal behavior may influence children's actions. In fact, we value individuals whose verbal and nonverbal behavior match; if a person says she will do a particular thing and then does it, she is seen as more reliable and dependable than someone who says one thing but then does another.

Most studies of correspondence training occur in three phases: (a) Children's behavior is measured, (b) the children are reinforced for verbalizations about their behavior, and (c) they are reinforced for matching their verbal and nonverbal behaviors (i.e., for doing what they say) (Baer, 1990). Sometimes, simply reinforcing children for making statements about their nonverbal behavior will change those responses; at other times, no change occurs and reinforcement must be provided for matching what they say

with what they do. For example, prior to free play, the teacher might ask, "What are you going to do?" The child might respond by saying, "Play 'going to the barber.'" If the teacher reinforces the child for this statement, the child may indeed play as he reported. In other cases, he may not, and the reinforcement would need to be delivered for actually doing what he "promises" to do. Interestingly, in some cases, after reinforcement is provided to children for matching what they do with what they say, generalization will occur. That is, statements about behaviors that have not been reinforced for correspondence will result in children doing the behaviors they say they will do. Much of the research on correspondence training has focused on behaviors such as playing with particular toys or in prescribed areas; but in other cases, correspondence training has been used to deal with problem behaviors. Paniagua, Pumariega, and Black (1988) used correspondence training to decrease preschoolers' off-task behaviors, excessive activity, and excessive noise making.

Correspondence training can be used in several different ways (see Paniagua, 1990, for a detailed discussion). Children can be reinforced for their statements about future behaviors. For example, Patricia frequently bites other children during snack time. Before snack, the teacher would ask her what she was going to do, and Patricia would answer (or be prompted to answer), "Drink my juice and eat my cookie; no biting." Children also can be asked and reinforced for their statements about past behaviors (e.g., "What did you do in snack?" "Ate my cookie and drank my juice; no biting"). When children are reinforced *only for their statements*, the arrangements can occur in at least three ways: (a) they are given an opportunity to do the behavior and are reinforced immediately for their statement about it (e.g., they do the behavior, they are asked about it, and they are immediately reinforced), (b) they are reinforced for their statement and then provided the opportunity to do the behavior (e.g., they are asked, reinforced, and allowed to do/not do the behavior), or (c) they are reinforced after the opportunity to do the behavior (e.g., they are asked, provided the opportunity, and then reinforced for their statement regardless of its truthfulness). Sometimes simply reinforcing statements about behavior will produce the desired changes; in other cases, it will not. If it does not, the teacher should reinforce children for matching what they do to what they say.

When children are *reinforced for matching their verbal and nonverbal behavior*, several arrangements also are possible. First, they are allowed opportunities to do the behavior, are asked about it, and are reinforced for *accurate* descriptions. Ronnie frequently throws blocks. His teacher would observe him during play with the blocks. After playing with blocks, the teacher would ask Ronnie whether he threw them. If he reported accurately, then reinforcement would be given; however, if his report was inaccurate, reinforcement would be withheld.

Second, children can be asked what they are going to do, given an opportunity to do it, and reinforced for matching their behavior to their statements. For example, before playing with blocks, the teacher would ask Ronnie how he was going to play with the blocks. He would reply, "Build a road; no throwing," and then he would go to play with the blocks. At the end of the session, the teacher would deliver reinforcement if he built a road and did not throw blocks.

Third, children are asked what they will do, the reinforcer is identified, they are allowed to do what they have said they will do, and reinforcement is given if they do it. For example, Rachel frequently takes other children's toys during free play. Before free play, the teacher would say, "How are you going to get toys you want?" Rachel would say (or be helped to say), "Ask for them."

The teacher would say, "If you ask for toys, then we will read your favorite book" (a reinforcer for Rachel). Rachel would go into the free play area, and the teacher would monitor whether she asks peers for toys or simply takes them. If Rachel asks rather than takes toys, her teacher would read her the book at the end of free play. This procedure is similar to the contingency contracting used with older children (Wolery et al., 1988).

Fourth, reinforcement can be delivered based on the correspondence between intermediate behaviors that lead to the target behavior. For example, Deon frequently runs into peers when he is riding the Big Wheel in the courtyard. When they go outside to play, the teacher would ask him, "How are you going to play on the Big Wheel?" Deon would answer or be prompted to answer. The teacher would then reinforce him for going to the shelter where the Big Wheel is stored, getting it out of the shelter, and moving it to the courtyard (intermediate behaviors). Reinforcement is provided for Deon doing the intermediate behaviors that lead to the target behavior, not for doing the target behavior.

Fifth, reinforcement is delivered for matching the verbal report to the target behavior and for doing the intermediate behaviors. In Deon's case, the reinforcement would be delivered for the intermediate steps involved in getting out the big wheel and for not running into peers when riding the big wheel. The reinforcer also can be identified after the verbal report as was done in the example with Rachel.

A potentially useful application of correspondence training is in extending the control over the behavior to other situations or in maintaining control over problem behavior (Baer, 1990). For example, after reinforcing correspondence between saying and doing on a number of behaviors, reinforcement can be provided only for statements about new behaviors/situations. Sometimes this practice is sufficient to establish generalization. For example, if Ronnie is reinforced for matching his behavior (not throwing) to his statements, and is reinforced for matching his doing and saying about throwing puzzle pieces, and about throwing trucks and cars, reinforcing him for only saying he is not going to throw cookies at snack may be sufficient.

When planning for maintenance, the professional has a choice of two procedures (Baer, 1990). First, requests to make statements about behaviors can be discontinued, and sometimes the behavior change will maintain. Second, after reinforcing a match between saying and doing, the professional can switch to only providing reinforcement for statements about behavior and not any longer for correspondence. Sometimes this procedure will result in maintenance.

Although much of the research with correspondence training deals with doing appropriate behaviors, it is a useful strategy for approaching children's problem behaviors. It is thought to promote self-control; however, the research is not totally clear about whether and how it actually facilitates self-control (Baer, 1990). Regardless of its effects on self-control, it is a desirable intervention because it is simple and requires little effort. Also, the general notion of reinforcing correspondence between saying and doing has appeal. Teaching children to report truthfully about their behavior is desirable, as is teaching children to plan what they are going to do and then to follow through on those plans.

Extinction   *Extinction* is the process of removing reinforcement for a behavior. The assumption underlying extinction is that when the reinforcement for the behavior is removed, then the behavior will no longer occur (Cooper et al., 1987; Wolery et al., 1988). Several issues must be considered when using extinction. First, the reinforcer that is

maintaining the behavior must be identified. Sometimes it is impossible to withhold the reinforcer, and in such cases, extinction would not be an appropriate intervention. For example, if a behavior is maintained by automatic reinforcement or the reaction and attention of peers, then withholding the reinforcement may be impossible or at best impractical. Second, the reinforcer must be withheld each time the behavior occurs. If it is withheld sometimes, but not always, then the behavior will be on an intermittent schedule and will be made more durable. Third, in some instances, withholding the reinforcement may result in an abrupt increase in the problem behavior. This is known as an *extinction burst.* If no reinforcement is provided during the burst, the behavior will eventually decrease. However, teams frequently give in because they think the behavior is getting worse. As a result, extinction is not allowed to work. Fourth, when extinction is used, a replacement behavior must be used that accesses the reinforcer that was previously accessed by the problem behavior. Many individuals equate ignoring with extinction, and when adult attention is the reinforcer, this equation is correct. However, when the reinforcers are something other than adult attention, ignoring the behavior is not extinction and the behavior probably will not decrease.

These specialized uses of reinforcement—differential reinforcement, correspondence training, and extinction—are valuable strategies for addressing problem behaviors. They should be used when the preconditions described earlier are not sufficient to control the problem behavior. However, their use requires careful consideration of many factors.

Assisting Parents in Dealing with Problem Behavior

Much research has been devoted to demonstrating that parents can effectively change the behavior of their children (Friman & Altman, 1990; Friman, Barnard, Altman, & Wolf, 1986; Polster & Dangle, 1984; Wolf, Braukmann, & Ramp, 1987). Training methods include discussions and written materials (Friman et al., 1986; Kelly, Embry, & Baer, 1979), rehearsal and feedback (Van Hasselt, Sisson, & Aach, 1987), *in vivo* modeling (Love, Matson, & West, 1990), and videotaped modeling (Dauz-Williams, Harrison-Elder, & Hill, 1986; O'Dell, Krug, O'Quin, & Kasnetz, 1980; Webster-Stratton, 1985). Data generally show that modeling is more effective than written materials (O'Dell et al., 1982) and that group training formats have some advantages over individual training, advantages such as increased observational learning and cost effectiveness (Christensen, Johnson, Phillips, & Glasgow, 1980). Other variables that influence the success of family training are socioeconomic level (McMahon, Forehand, Griest, & Wells, 1981; Webster-Stratton, 1985), marital stability (Bernal, Klinnert, & Schultz, 1980), single or shared parenthood (Strain, Young, & Horowitz, 1981), parental depression (Griest, Forehand, & Wells, 1981; McMahon et al., 1981), insularity (Wahler, 1980), and the severity of the child's disability (Snell & Beckman-Brindley, 1984).

Egel and Powers (1989) describe a family systems approach to parent behavioral training, an approach that is recommended because it is sensitive to the structure and functioning of the entire family system. This approach builds upon an awareness of three important aspects of family systems. The first aspect is *ecological sensitivity*, which means that a change in one part of the family system will affect other parts of the family system as well as extra-family systems (Egel & Powers, 1989). When introducing changes that will affect parent and child behaviors, professionals should realize that the family has an established ecology and its own history of interactions with other treatment

programs or with its own informal support networks (Rosenberg, Reppucci, & Linney, 1983). Certain behavior change programs, therefore, may not be compatible with the interaction patterns within the family. To ensure that treatment options do not disrupt family ecology, Barber, Barber, and Clark (1983) recommend (a) helping families identify their needs and set priorities about them, (b) having the families select behavioral change targets, (c) considering financial cost and cost of time spent in relation to family resources, and (d) including extra-family members and organizations (e.g., school, church) in support of the treatment.

Family processes constitute the second aspect of family systems that this approach addresses. Family processes are the social and ideological issues that influence families. Such issues as control of decision making, stability of marital and sibling subsystems, the role of cultural and ethnic factors, and the effects of extended family and extra-family networks will have an impact on family training.

Behavioral and ecological interrelationships make up the third significant aspect of family systems. Behavioral interrelationships are the covariations between targeted and nontargeted behaviors that are in the same response class. Changes in one behavior may trigger changes in other behaviors (Neef, Shafer, Egel, Cataldo, & Parrish, 1983). An ecological interrelationship exists when there is goodness-of-fit between the family history and philosophy and the intervention plan. A family's willingness to change, the family members' current skill level in managing their child's behavior (Harris, 1984), their position in the life cycle, and their plans for the future are examples of issues that should be considered when planning and implementing intervention.

Thus, as we noted earlier in this chapter, dealing with children's problem behaviors is not a separate intervention function, but one that should be integrated with the entire intervention effort. The same need for integration holds when families are assisted in dealing with their children's problematic behaviors; the work must be done in the context of the family system (chapter 4) and in the context of the other intervention interactions with the family. This does not mean that specific intervention plans to help families deal with the problem behaviors should be abandoned; rather, it means that such efforts should be developed and implemented in the context of the family's needs and goals.

Punishment Procedures

Defining Punishment   Punishment is something nearly everyone has experienced, and most individuals have strong views about its value and whether it should be used with children. Punishment has many meanings. Most people define it in terms of the actions of the punisher (i.e., spanking, fines, prison terms, grounding, etc.). However, punishment also is a technical term with a precise definition that focuses on its effect on the occurrence of the behavior. Specifically, punishment is a consequence that increases the likelihood that the occurrence of the behavior will be reduced (Cooper et al., 1987; Wolery et al., 1988). It is the opposite of reinforcement; remember that reinforcement is a consequence that increases the likelihood that the behavior will reoccur. As with reinforcement, there are two types of punishment. Type I punishment occurs when the consequence is applied contingent upon a behavior and the occurrence of that behavior decreases. Type II punishment occurs when some reinforcer is removed contingent upon a behavior and the occurrence of that behavior decreases. Throughout the rest of this chapter, we use this technical definition of punishment. As with reinforcers, the stimuli that function as punishing events are indi-

vidually determined; what is a punishing event for one individual may not be so for another, and the punishing power of a stimulus may change over time and across situations.

As we noted earlier, the use of punishment, particularly of procedures that involve aversive stimuli, has been hotly debated. The issue of debate is what constitutes the child's right to effective treatment and what is ethical and humane treatment of children with disabilities. Our position is that the preconditions discussed earlier, the curricular modifications, and the reinforcement procedures will be sufficient for dealing with nearly all of the behavior problems of young children. However, we also recognize that for a small percentage of the young children with disabilities, these procedures may not be sufficient. Therefore, we believe that intervention teams must have the option of using more invasive procedures and, indeed, that they have a responsibility to deal directly with severe, debilitating, and sometimes life-threatening problem behaviors of children. However, before *any* punishment procedure is used, certain additional conditions must be met.

Minimal Conditions for Using Punishment Procedures   The conditions listed here are supplementary to those listed in Step #5 of the decision model. Eleven conditions are mentioned and listed in Box 11.7. These conditions have been discussed elsewhere (Wolery et al., 1988; Wolery & Gast, 1990), and the present discussion is based on these sources. First, *no punishment procedure should be used without employing a decision model.* The rationale for using a decision model is that it will set the occasion for intervention teams to consider issues involved in controlling problem behavior carefully. It does not assure reasoned analysis and judgment, but it should restrict impulsive use of punishment procedures. Several

---

BOX 11.7   Minimal conditions under which punishment procedures should be used

1 A decision model should be used in addressing the problem behavior.
2 The factors that maintain the occurrence of the problem behavior and the function served by the behavior should be identified.
3 Assessment information should be collected and used in planning interventions.
4 Deliberate, comprehensive, and appropriate attempts to teach and reinforce adaptive behavior should occur.
5 Reliable measurement of the problem behavior and reliable implementation of the interventions should occur.
6 Periodic monitoring of the potential side effects of intervention procedures should occur.
7 Maintenance and generalization of the intervention benefits should be programmed.
8 Informed consent by the parents and administrative authorities (including Human Rights Committees) should be secured.
9 Peer Review Committees should examine the intervention plan and make judgments and recommendations about its adequacy.
10 Open implementation of the use of the punishment procedure should occur.
11 Punishment should only be put into effect by a competent team of professionals.

Note: Adapted from *Effective Teaching: Principles and Procedures of Applied Behavior Analysis with Exceptional Children* by M. Wolery, D. B. Bailey, and G. M. Sugai, 1988, Boston: Allyn & Bacon.

---

decision models are used, such as the one described in this chapter and the ones cited earlier. Unfortunately, although the special education units in state departments of education and state mental retardation and developmental disabilities agencies often have guidelines on the use of treatment procedures, those guidelines rarely require the use of decision models (Morgan et al., 1991).

Second, *punishment procedures should not be used until the factors maintaining the occurrence of the problem behavior are identified.* The importance of identifying the function of problem behavior has been described repeatedly in this chapter; specifically, without such information, developing an intervention will be a hit and miss proposition. It may work sometimes, but it will not work always. The procedures used to identify the function of the behavior are discussed in several sources (Iwata, Vollmer, et al., 1990; O'Neill et al., 1990).

Third, *punishment should not be used unless assessment information is employed when planning the intervention.* Assessment activities are completed to devise an intervention plan. Appropriate assessment will result in an abundance of useful information. It should identify the function of the behavior, the places where it occurs, the times it occurs, the events that appear to set the stage for its occurrence, the persons who are available and capable of implementing the procedure, the replacement behaviors, and other relevant information. Collection *and* use of assessment information represents a major advance in the intervention of problem behaviors and situations.

Fourth, *punishment should not be used unless deliberate and appropriate attempts are made to teach and reinforce adaptive behaviors.* As noted above, the "fair pair" rule states that a replacement behavior should be identified and promoted for each behavior that is targeted for reduction. This replacement behavior should fulfill the same function, do so with less effort, result in the same reinforcement as the problem behavior, and come under similar stimulus control (Horner, Sprague, et al., 1990). However, this requirement deals with more than replacement behaviors. It suggests that there should be concentrated attempts to teach and strengthen other adaptive behaviors. This means that the child's entire instructional program and day should be analyzed and made effective before a punishment procedure is employed.

Fifth, *use of punishment requires reliable measurement of the target behavior and of treatment implementation.* The purpose of measurement is to determine what effect, if any, the intervention has on the problem behavior. If measurement is not reliable (i.e., two observers do not consistently agree when the behavior occurs), then the judgments made on the data may not be correct. Before punishment procedures are employed, the behavior must be reliably measured. In addition, the staff members' implementation of the positive interventions must be consistent. If the implementation of those interventions are not consistent, then they cannot be judged as ineffective (they may be effective when implemented correctly and consistently). Also, when a punishment procedure does become necessary, it must be used as planned and that use must be monitored.

Sixth, *use of punishment requires periodic monitoring of the side effects of intervention.* Side effects may be positive (i.e., desirable) or they may be negative (undesirable) (Doke, Wolery, & Sumberg, 1983). Before a punishment procedure is used, the intervention team should determine how they will observe for any potential side effects, what side effects are probable (cf. Wolery et al., 1988), and what will be done to deal with them. When punishment procedures are used, monitoring of side effects is critical because children frequently display emotional

responses (e.g., crying, acting fearful, etc.) and withdraw from the situation and/or the persons involved in the use of the procedure. The positive side effects should be reinforced so that they become durable, and the negative side effects should be monitored to determine if they need intervention.

Seventh, *use of punishment requires programming for maintenance and generalization.* As we noted in chapter 2, one of the goals of early intervention is to produce generalized changes in children's behaviors because maintenance and generalization do not occur automatically. Intervention plans must be designed to promote these goals. When dealing with problem behavior, the goal is to ensure that the reduction of the behavior lasts and extends to all relevant settings, *and* that the replacement behavior maintains and is used in all relevant contexts. The specific interventions for ensuring that these outcomes occur are the procedures used to secure maintenance and generalization of other behaviors (cf. chapter 6).

Eighth, *use of punishment requires informed consent by parents and by administrative authorities. Informed consent* means that the parents and the administrative authorities understand the punishment procedure and have agreed that it is acceptable to use. In many agencies a Human Rights Committee is used to evaluate whether children's rights would be violated by using a punishment procedure. The team should find out whether such approval is required by their agency. Axelrod (1990) states that Human Rights Committees frequently evaluate the clinical appropriateness of intervention plans. He goes on to say that this is inappropriate because their role is to judge whether children's rights are violated—not whether the procedures represent acceptable practice. To evaluate the appropriateness of plans, he suggests the use of Peer Review Committees which are comprised of experts in clinical issues. Barton, Brulle, and Repp (1983) state that the following elements should be included in informed consent.

(a) an accurate description to the client [parents or legal guardian] of the treatment procedure; (b) a description of the data from non-aversive treatment procedures that have been previously implemented (i.e., aversive procedures should be used only after other techniques have failed); (c) a justification for the proposed treatment program; (d) baseline data and recording procedures; (e) the anticipated behavioral outcome and the expected termination date for the program; (f) the qualifications of persons who will be implementing the procedure; and (g) the written consent and review of the Human Rights Committee, if such committee is impaneled. (p. 2)

Ninth, *punishment should not be used without prior peer review of the intervention plan.* A Peer Review Committee should evaluate each intervention plan that includes a punishment procedure (Axelrod, 1990). This committee should include persons who have competencies in many areas, but two areas of competency are critical. Some committee members should have training and expertise in issues related to control of behavior problems, and some should have training and expertise in working with young children with disabilities. This latter set of competencies is necessary because controlling the behavior of young children is different from controlling the behavior of older children. Individuals with these competencies should be able to provide an objective and fair appraisal of the appropriateness of the intervention plan. Further, such individuals should be able to provide unique perspectives on the problem and the intervention and make suggestions for increasing its success. Another function of the Peer Review Committee is to judge the competence of the persons who will be using the intervention. Unfortunately, many agencies, including school districts, do not have Peer Review Committees. In such cases, it is wise to establish such a committee before a punishment procedure is used.

Tenth, *use of punishment requires open implementation.* Open implementation means that family members and relevant professionals should have an opportunity to observe the intervention being implemented, should be able to review the progress of the intervention, and should be allowed to make constructive comments. Open implementation sets the stage for the constructive suggestions of persons not involved in the implementation of the intervention.

Eleventh, *punishment should only be put into effect by a competent team of professionals.* Competence is difficult to define, but at a minimum the persons planning and using the intervention should have specialized training in dealing with problem behaviors. Reading this chapter and discussing the issue in a class session or two are not sufficient training. These activities may provide a foundation for getting more advanced training, but alone they are not adequate.

As we have noted, these eleven conditions must be met before using a punishment procedure. These conditions do not ensure that the procedure will be used appropriately or defensibly; however, they will help restrict the use of such procedures. We recognize that they require a lot of work, are stringent, and are not easily accomplished. However, if followed in good faith, they should minimize the inappropriate use of punishment procedures while allowing the intervention team to retain the punishment option in dealing with severe problem situations.

Description of Punishment Procedures
Given that the intervention team has met all of the preconditions identified in Step #5 of the decision model and all of the minimal conditions listed above, then punishment procedures can be used in severe cases. In this section we describe a few punishment procedures that have been used. The de-

scriptions are brief, and you should consult several sources for more implementation information (e.g., Cooper et al., 1987; Foxx, 1982; Kerr & Nelson, 1989; Repp & Singh, 1990; Wolery et al., 1988).

Response cost involves the loss of a previously earned reinforcer contingent upon the occurrence of the problem behavior. This procedure is analogous to the fines we experience for disregarding traffic laws. Although the procedure has been used extensively with school-age children (e.g., loss of privileges such as recess, or loss of tokens), it has been used less often with preschoolers.

Timeout involves a contingent application of a brief period of time when the child cannot access reinforcers for each occurrence of the problem behavior. Timeout has been implemented in several different forms. For example, children have been required to sit and watch other children play after they have engaged in inappropriate behaviors; this is called *contingent observation* (Porterfield, Herbert-Jackson, & Risley, 1976; White & Bailey, 1990). Another form of timeout is called *the timeout ribbon* (Foxx & Shapiro, 1978; Fee, Matson, & Manikam, 1990). Following this variation, the child wears a ribbon or wrist band that signals that she is eligible to receive reinforcement. If she does the problem behavior, then the ribbon is removed and reinforcement is not provided; however, she can remain in the instructional activity. After a brief period of time, the ribbon is returned to the child and she is then again eligible to receive reinforcement. A third version of timeout is called *exclusionary timeout.* Exclusionary timeout involves removing the child from the activity but keeping him within the room. The procedure often is used by having the child sit in a chair in an isolated part of the classroom. Yet another version is called *movement suppression* (Rolider & Van Houten, 1985). This procedure involves situating the child so that he cannot move (e.g., facing him into a corner

with his arms behind his back) for a brief period of time. Another type is *isolation or seclusion,* which involves removing the child from the activity and putting her in a specially designed timeout room for a given amount of time.

Timeout is an intervention that involves many potential abuses and is restricted by some agencies. A critical factor in the effectiveness of timeout is whether the "timein" environment results in a rich schedule of reinforcement. When timeout works, it does so because the child loses access to reinforcement when he is in timeout. This deprivation means the timein environment should be rich with reinforcement. Unfortunately, sometimes children do not receive sufficient reinforcement when they are not in timeout. In such cases, the procedure may not be effective unless the timein environment is enriched (cf. Solnick, Rincover, & Peterson, 1977). Many steps are involved in using timeout; thus, you should consult the sources cited above before using it. Unfortunately, in our observations of preschool classrooms, we frequently see timeout being used inappropriately.

Overcorrection is a procedure based on the assumption that individuals should be responsible for their actions. There are two types of overcorrection—restitutional overcorrection and positive practice. *Restitutional overcorrection* involves having the individual restore the environment to a condition better than it was at the time the problem behavior occurred. For example, if a child "lost control" and pushed over two chairs and upset a table, then she would be required to pick up the chairs and tables *and* to straighten all the chairs and tables in the room. *Positive practice overcorrection* involves practicing a positive behavior contingent upon the occurrence of an inappropriate behavior. For example, if a child engaged in self-injurious eye poking, then for each eye poke he would be required to practice appropriate arm movements such as moving a toy for two minutes.

When implementing overcorrection, the adult should ensure that the behaviors to be practiced or done while restoring the environment are related to the problem behavior. Each time the child performs the target behavior the adult says, "No (names the behavior)," and applies the overcorrection procedure. Graduated guidance (prompting the child as necessary and removing the prompts when the child does the behaviors) is used to ensure that children do the overcorrection behaviors. Reinforcement should not be allowed during the application of overcorrection, and when the overcorrection is completed, the child should return to his usual activities. Although overcorrection has been effective with many behaviors, it is used infrequently because it involves considerable effort on the part of the adult and is quite intrusive (i.e., the adult frequently must physically guide the child).

Direct contingent application of aversive stimuli is the final punishment procedure to be considered here. This procedure involves the application of some aversive stimulus each time the child engages in the problem behavior. Aversive stimuli are those which individuals attempt to escape from or avoid. They frequently involve pain and/or discomfort. An incredible array of aversive stimuli have been used, including electric shock, water sprays to the face, placing a towel over the face, noxious odors such as ammonia, distasteful substances such as lemon juice, and slaps to the thigh or buttocks. Findings from the use of such stimuli are shown in Box 11.8. These stimuli should only be used as last resort efforts to control serious problem behaviors.

Several punishment procedures exist, but the manner in which they are used determines their effectiveness. However, because they are punishment procedures, their use with young children should occur rarely. If

they are to be used, then the eleven conditions described above should be met prior to their use. The descriptions here do not provide sufficient information for using them; therefore, the cited sources should be consulted.

SUMMARY

The goals of early intervention in relation to problem behaviors are (a) to prevent their occurrence, (b) to assist families in dealing with their children's problem behaviors, and (c) to deal directly with problem behaviors when necessary by planning and implementing appropriate interventions. The approach is based on the following assumptions: (a) children's ages and developmental level should be considered; (b) some problem behaviors are more important than others; (c) behaviors are learned and potentially controlled by many factors; (d) interventions should be based on the functions served by problem behaviors; (e) few defensible reasons exist for allowing children to develop harmful patterns of behaving; (f) changing children's behaviors requires communication with families and team members; and (g) interventions should be implemented for the benefit of children rather than adults. When addressing serious problem behaviors, the professional should use a decision model. The model should include assessment activities, planning of interventions based on the results of the assessment, and careful monitoring of intervention use and the outcomes. Several environmental and curricular modifications can be used to treat children's problem behavior, as can various manipulations of reinforcement. Although several punishment procedures have been used effectively, they should be reserved for severe situations and should only be used if a number of conditions are met. Assisting families in dealing with their children's

---

BOX 11.8   Findings from research on the use of aversive stimuli

Findings	Implications for Practice
Aversiveness of stimuli is individually determined.	Teachers must carefully select the stimuli used as aversive stimuli for each student.
	Teachers must evaluate the stimuli they select as aversive stimuli.
The intensity of the stimulus is related to effectiveness.	Teachers must select the intensity of the aversive stimulus that will be effective, but will not be too harsh.
Side effects may occur.	Teachers should plan for both desirable and undesirable side effects.
	Side effects should be monitored and, when appropriate, treated.
Maintenance of effects is variable.	Teachers should plan for maintenance and teach and reinforce the occurrence of desirable replacement behaviors.
Effectiveness is related to how the aversive stimuli are used.	Teachers should carefully plan the use of aversive stimuli.
	Teachers should periodically check the actual implementation of the aversive stimulus to ensure that it is appropriate.
Use of aversive procedures should be restricted.	Teachers should carefully consider the conditions under which punishment procedures are acceptable and use a decision model when implementing the aversive procedures.

Note: Adapted from *Effective Teaching: Principles and Procedures of Applied Behavior Analysis with Exceptional Children* by M. Wolery, D. B. Bailey, and G. M. Sugai, 1988, Boston: Allyn & Bacon.

---

problem behavior involves considerations of the family as a social unit and the use of well-developed consultation skills.

REFERENCES

Axelrod, S. (1990). Myths that (mis)guide our profession. In A. C. Repp & N. N. Singh (Eds.), *Perspectives on the use of nonaversive and aversive interventions for persons with developmental disabilities* (pp. 59–72). Sycamore, IL: Sycamore.

Baer, M., Fowler, S. A., & Carden-Smith, L. (1984). Using reinforcement and independent grading to promote and maintain task accuracy in a mainstreamed class. *Analysis and Intervention in Developmental Disabilities, 4,* 157–169.

Baer, R. A., (1990). Correspondence training: Review and current issues. *Research in Developmental Disabilities, 11,* 379–393.

Bailey, D. B., Harms, T., & Clifford, R. M. (1983). Matching changes in preschool environments to desired changes in child behavior. *Journal of the Division for Early Childhood, 7,* 61–68.

Barber, K., Barber, M., & Clark, H. B. (1983). Establishing a community oriented group home and ensuring its survival: A case study of failure. *Analysis and Intervention in Developmental Disabilities, 3,* 227–238.

Barton, L. E., Brulle, A. R., & Repp, A. C. (1983). Aversive techniques and the doctrine of the least restrictive alternative. *Exceptional Education Quarterly, 4*(3), 1–8.

Bernal, M. E., Klinnert, M. D., & Schultz, L. A. (1980). Outcome of evaluation of behavioral parent training and client centered parent counseling for children with conduct problems. *Journal of Applied Behavior Analysis, 13,* 677–691.

Brusca, R. M., Nieminen, G. S., Carter, R., & Repp, A. C. (1989). The relationship of staff contact and activity to the stereotypy of children with multiple disabilities. *Journal of the Association of Persons with Severe Handicaps, 14*(2), 127–136.

Burgio, L. D., Whitman, T. L., & Johnson, M. R. (1980). A self-instructional package for increasing attending behavior in educable mentally retarded children. *Journal of Applied Behavior Analysis, 13,* 443–459.

Carden-Smith, L. K., & Fowler, S. A. (1984). Positive peer pressure: The effects of peer monitoring on children's disruptive behavior. *Journal of Applied Behavior Analysis, 17*(2), 213–227.

Carr, E. G. (1977). The motivation of self-injurious behavior: A review of some hypotheses. *Psychological Bulletin, 84,* 800–816.

Carr, E. G., & Durand, M. V. (1985). Reducing behavior problems through functional communication training. *Journal of Applied Behavior Analysis, 18,* 111–126.

Carr, E. G., Robinson, S., & Palumbo, L. W. (1990). The wrong issue: Aversive versus nonaversive treatment. The right issue: Functional versus nonfunctional treatment. In A. C. Repp & N. N. Singh (Eds.), *Perspectives on the use of nonaversive and aversive interventions for persons with developmental disabilities* (pp. 361–379). Sycamore, IL: Sycamore.

Christensen, A., Johnson, S. M., Phillips, S., & Glasgow, R. E. (1980). Cost effectiveness in behavioral family therapy. *Behavior Therapy, 11,* 208–226.

Cipani, E. (Ed.). (1989). *The treatment of severe behavior disorders: Behavior analysis approaches.* Washington, DC: American Association on Mental Retardation.

Cipani, E. (1990). "Excuse me: I'll have . . ." Teaching appropriate attention-getting behavior to young children with severe handicaps. *Mental Retardation, 28,* 29–33.

Cooper, J. O., Heron, T. E., & Heward, W. L. (1987). *Applied behavior analysis.* Columbus, OH: Merrill.

Cowdery, G. E., Iwata, B. A., & Pace, G. M. (1990). Effects and side effects of DRO as treatment for self-injurious behavior. *Journal of Applied Behavior Analysis, 23,* 497–506.

Dauz-Williams, P.A., Harrison-Elder, J.A., & Hill, S. M. (1986). Media approach to family training in behavior management: Two families. *Issues in Comprehensive Pediatric Nursing, 9,* 59–77.

Doke, L. A., Wolery, M., & Sumberg, C. (1983). Effects and side-effects of response contingent ammonia spirits in treating chronic aggression. *Behavior Modification, 7,* 531–556.

Donnellan, A. M., Mirenda, P. L., Mesaros, R. A., & Fassbender, L. L. (1984). Analyzing the communicative functions of aberrant behavior. *Journal of the Association for Persons with Severe Handicaps, 9,* 201–212.

Dougherty, B. S., Fowler, S. A., & Paine, S. C. (1985). The use of peer monitors to reduce negative interaction during recess. *Journal of Applied Behavior Analysis, 18,* 141–153.

Dunlap, G., Johnson, L. F., & Robbins, F. R. (1990). Preventing serious behavior problems through skill development and early intervention. In A. C. Repp & N. N. Singh (Eds.), *Perspectives on the use of nonaversive and aversive interventions for persons with developmental disabilities* (pp. 273–286). Sycamore, IL: Sycamore.

Durand, V. M., & Carr, E. G. (1987). Social influences on self-stimulatory behavior: Analysis and treatment applications. *Journal of Applied Behavior Analysis, 20,* 119–132.

Durand, V. M., & Kishi, G. (1987). Reducing severe behavior problems among persons with dual sensory impairments: An evaluation of a technical assistance model. *Journal of the Association for Persons with Severe Handicaps, 12,* 2–10.

Dyer, K. (1987). The competition of autistic stereotyped behavior with usual and specially assessed reinforcers. *Research in Developmental Disabilities, 8,* 607–626.

Dyer, K., Dunlap, G., & Winterling, V. (1990). Effects of choice making on the serious problem behaviors of students with severe handicaps. *Journal of Applied Behavior Analysis, 23,* 515–524.

Egel, A. L., & Powers, M. D. (1989). Behavioral parent training: A view of the past and suggestions for the future. In E. Cipani (Ed.), *Treatment of severe behavior disorders: Behavior analysis approaches.* Washington, DC: American Association on Mental Retardation.

Evans, I. M., & Meyer, L. (1985). *An educative approach to behavior problems: A practical decision model for interventions with severely handicapped learners.* Baltimore: Paul Brookes.

Evans, I. M., & Meyer, L. (1990). Toward a science in support of meaningful outcomes: A response to Horner et al. *Journal of the Association for Persons with Severe Handicaps, 15,* 133–135.

Fee, V. E., Matson, J. L., & Manikam, R. (1990). A control group outcome study of a nonexclusionary time-out package to improve social skills with preschoolers. *Exceptionality, 1,* 107–121.

Feldman, M. A. (1990). Balancing freedom from harm and right to treatment for persons with developmental disabilities. In A. C. Repp & N. N. Singh (Eds.), *Perspectives on the use of nonaversive and aversive interventions for persons with developmental disabilities* (pp. 261–271). Sycamore, IL: Sycamore.

Foxx, R. M. (1982). *Decreasing behaviors of severely retarded and autistic persons.* Champaign, IL: Research Press.

Foxx, R. M., & Shapiro, S. T. (1978). The timeout ribbon: A nonexclusionary timeout procedure. *Journal of Applied Behavior Analysis, 11,* 125–136.

Friman, P. C., & Altman, K. (1990). Parent use of DRI on high rate disruptive behavior: Direct and collateral benefits. *Research in Developmental Disabilities, 11,* 249–254.

Friman, P. C., Barnard, J. D., Altman, K., & Wolf, M. M. (1986). Parent and teacher use of DRO and DRI to reduce aggressive behavior. *Analysis and Intervention in Developmental Disabilities, 6,* 319–330.

Gast, D. L., & Wolery, M. (1987). Severe maladaptive behaviors. In M. Snell (Ed.), *Systematic instruction of persons with severe handicaps* (3rd ed.) (pp. 300–332). Columbus, OH: Merrill.

Gardner, W. I., Cole, C. L., Berry, D. L., & Nowinski, J. M. (1983). Reduction of disruptive behaviors in mentally retarded adults. *Behavior Modification, 7,* 76–96.

Gaylord-Ross, R. J. (1980). A decision model for the treatment of aberrant behavior in applied settings. In W. Sailor, B. Wilcox, & L. Brown (Eds.), *Methods of instruction for severely handicapped students* (pp. 135–158). Baltimore: Paul Brookes.

Gaylord-Ross, R. J. (1982). Curricular considerations in treating behavior problems of severely handicapped students. *Advances in Learning and Behavioral Disabilities* (Vol. 1), 193–224.

Gaylord-Ross, R. J., Weeks, M., & Lipner, C. (1980). An analysis of antecedent, response, and consequence events in the treatment of self-injurious behavior. *Education and Training of the Mentally Retarded, 15,* 35–42.

Griest, D. L., Forehand, R., & Wells, K. C. (1981). Follow-up assessment of parent behavioral training: An analysis of who will participate. *Child Study Journal, 11,* 221–229.

Guess, D., Turnbull, H. R., & Helmstetter, E. (1990). Science, paradigms, and values: A response to Mulick. *American Journal of Mental Retardation, 95,* 157–163.

Haring, T. G., & Kennedy, C. H. (1990). Contextual control of problem behavior in students with severe disabilities. *Journal of Applied Behavior Analysis, 23,* 235–243.

Harris, S. L. (1984). Intervention planning for the family of the autistic child: A multilevel assessment of the family system. *Journal of Marital and Family Therapy, 10,* 157–166.

Hendrickson, J. M., Strain, P. S., Tremblay, A., & Shores, R. E. (1982). Interactions of behaviorally handicapped children: Functional effects of peer social initiations. *Behavior Modification, 6,* 323–353.

Horner, R. H., & Billingsley, F. F. (1988). The effect of competing behavior on the generalization and maintenance of adaptive behavior in applied settings. In R. H. Horner, G. Dunlap, & R. L. Koegel (Eds.), *Generaliza-*

tion and maintenance: *Lifestyle changes in applied settings* (pp. 197–220). Baltimore: Paul Brookes.

Horner, R. H., Dunlap, G., Koegel, R. L., Carr, E. G., Sailor, W., Anderson, J., Albin, R. W., & O'Neill, R. E. (1990). Towards a technology of "nonaversive" behavioral support. *The Journal of the Association for Persons with Severe Handicaps, 15,* 125–132.

Horner, R. H., Sprague, J. R., O'Brien, M., & Heathfield, L. T. (1990). The role of response efficiency in the reduction of problem behaviors through functional equivalence training: A case study. *Journal of the Association for Persons with Severe Handicaps, 15,* 91–97.

Iwata, B. A., Dorsey, M. F., Slifer, K. J., Bauman, K. E., & Richman, G. S. (1982). Toward a functional analysis of self-injury. *Analysis and Intervention in Developmental Disabilities, 2,* 1–20.

Iwata, B. A., Pace, G. M., Kalsher, M. J., Cowdery, G. E., & Cataldo, M. F. (1990). Experimental analysis and extinction of self-injurious escape behavior. *Journal of Applied Behavior Analysis, 23,* 11–27.

Iwata, B. A., Vollmer, T. R., & Zarcone, J. R. (1990). The experimental (functional) analysis of behavior disorders: Methodology, applications, and limitations. In A. C. Repp & N. N. Singh (Eds.), *Perspectives on the use of nonaversive and aversive interventions for persons with developmental disabilities* (pp. 301–330). Sycamore, IL: Sycamore.

Kelly, M. L., Embry, L. H., & Baer, D. M. (1979). Skills for child management and family support. *Behavior Modification, 3,* 373–396.

Kerr, M. M., & Nelson, C. M. (1989). *Strategies for managing behavior problems in the classroom* (2nd ed.). Columbus, OH: Merrill.

Kerr, M. M., Strain, P. S., & Ragland, E. U. (1982). Teacher-mediated peer feedback treatment of behaviorally handicapped children: An analysis of effects on positive and negative interactions. *Behavior Modification, 6*(2), 277–290.

Koegel, R. L., Dyer, K., & Bell, L. K. (1987). The influence of child-preferred activities on autistic children's social behavior. *Journal*

of Applied Behavior Analysis, 20, 243–252.

Koegel, R. L., & Koegel, L. K. (1990). Extended reductions in stereotypic behavior of students with autism through a self-management treatment package. *Journal of Applied Behavior, 23,* 119–127.

Kozloff, M. (in press). *Principles of developmental-functional assessment and program planning.* Baltimore: Paul Brookes.

LaGrow, S. T., & Repp, A. C. (1984). Stereotypic responding: Review of intervention research. *American Journal of Mental Deficiency, 88,* 595–609.

Lennox, D. B., & Miltenberger, R. G. (1989). Conducting a functional analysis of problem behavior in applied settings. *Journal of the Association for Persons with Severe Handicaps, 14,* 304–311.

Lovaas, O. I., & Favell, J. E. (1987). Protection for clients undergoing aversive/restrictive interventions. *Education and Treatment of Children, 10,* 311–325.

Love, S. R., Matson, J. L., & West, D. (1990). Mothers as effective therapists for autistic children's phobias. *Journal of Applied Behavior Analysis, 23,* 379–385.

Lynch, V., McGuigan, C., & Shoemaker, S. (1983). An introduction to systematic instruction. *British Columbia Journal of Special Education, 7,* 1–13.

Mace, F. C., & Belfiore, P. (1990). Behavioral momentum in the treatment of escape-motivated stereotypy. *Journal of Applied Behavior Analysis, 23,* 507–514.

Mace, F. C., Browder, D. M., & Lin, Y. (1987). Analysis of demand conditions associated with stereotypy. *Journal of Behavior Therapy and Experimental Psychiatry, 18*(1), 25–31.

Mace, F. C., Hock, M. L., Lalli, J. S., West, B. J., Belfiore, P. J., Pinter, E., & Brown, D. K. (1988). Behavioral momentum in the treatment of noncompliance. *Journal of Applied Behavior Analysis, 21,* 123–141.

Mace, F. C., Lalli, J. S., Shea, M. C., Pinter-Lalli, E., West, B. J., Roberts, M., & Nevin, J. A. (1990). The momentum of human behavior in a natural setting. *Journal of the Experimental Analysis of Behavior, 54,* 163–172.

Matson, J., & Earnhart, T. (1981). Programming treatment effects to the natural environment: A procedure for training institutionalized retarded adults. *Behavior Modification, 5*(1), 27–37.

McMahon, R. J., Forehand, R., Griest, D. L., & Wells, K. C. (1981). Who drops out of treatment during parent behavior training? *Behavioral Counseling Quarterly, 1*, 79–85.

Milan, M. A., Mitchell, Z. P., Berger, M. I., & Pierson, D. F. (1981). Positive routines: A rapid alternative to extinction or elimination of bedtime tantrum behavior. *Child Behavior Therapy, 3*(1), 13–25.

Morgan, R. L., Striefel, S., Baer, R., & Percival, G. (1991). Regulatory behavioral procedures for individuals with handicaps: Review of state department standards. *Research in Developmental Disabilities, 12*, 63–85.

Mulick, J. A. (1990). The ideology and science of punishment in mental retardation. *American Journal of Mental Retardation, 95*, 142–156.

Neef, N. A., Shafer, M. S., Egel, A. L., Cataldo, M. F., & Parrish, J. M. (1983). The class specific effects of compliance training with "Do" and "Don't" requests. *Journal of Applied Behavior Analysis, 16*, 81–99.

Nevin, J. A., Mandell, C., & Atak, J. R. (1983). The analysis of behavior momentum. *Journal of the Experimental Analysis of Behavior, 39*, 49–59.

Nordquist, V. M. (1978). A behavioral approach to the analysis of peer interaction. In M. Guralnick (Ed.), *Early intervention and the integration of handicapped and nonhandicapped children* (pp. 53–84). Baltimore: University Park Press.

O'Brien, S., & Repp, A. C. (1990). Reinforcement-based reductive procedures: A review of 20 years of their use with persons with severe and profound retardation. *The Journal of the Association for Persons with Severe Handicaps, 15*, 148–159.

O'Dell, S. L., Krug, W. W., O'Quin, J. A., & Kasnetz, M. (1980). Media assisted parent training: A further analysis. *The Behavior Therapist, 3*, 19–21.

O'Dell, S. L., O'Quin, J. A., Alford, B. A., O'Briant, A. L., Bradlyn, A. S., & Giebenhain, J. E. (1982). Predicting the acquisition of parenting skills via four training methods. *Behavior Therapy, 13*, 194–208.

O'Neill, R. E., Horner, R. H., Albin, R. W., Storey, K., & Sprague, J. R. (1990). *Functional analysis of problem behavior: A practical assessment guide.* Sycamore, IL: Sycamore.

Paniagua, F. A. (1990). A procedural analysis of correspondence training techniques. *The Behavior Analyst, 13*, 107–119.

Paniagua, F. A., Pumariega, A. J., & Black, S. A. (1988). Clinical effects of correspondence training in the management of hyperactive children. *Behavioral Residential Treatment, 3*, 19–40.

Parrish, J. M., Cataldo, M. F., Kolko, D. J., Neef, N. A., & Egel, A. L. (1986). Experimental analysis of response covariation among compliant and inappropriate behaviors. *Journal of Applied Behavior Analysis, 19*, 241–254.

Parsons, M. B., Reid, D. H., Reynolds, J., & Bumgarner, M. (1990). Effects of chosen versus assigned jobs on the work performance of persons with severe handicaps. *Journal of Applied Behavior Analysis, 23*, 253–258.

Polster, R. A., & Dangle, R. F. (1984). *Parent training: Foundations of research and practice.* New York: Guilford Press.

Porterfield, J. K., Herbert-Jackson, E., & Risley, T. R. (1976). Contingent observation: An effective and acceptable procedure for reducing disruptive behavior in young children in a group setting. *Journal of Applied Behavior Analysis, 9*, 55–64.

Reamer, F. G. (1990). *Ethical dilemmas in social service.* New York: Columbia University Press.

Repp, A. C., Felce, D., & Barton, L. E. (1988). Basing the treatment of stereotypic and self-injurious behaviors on hypotheses of their causes. *Journal of Applied Behavior Analysis, 21*, 281–289.

Repp, A. C., Felce, D., & Barton, L. E. (1991). The effects of initial interval size on the efficacy of DRO schedules of reinforcement. *Exceptional Children, 57*, 417–425.

Repp, A. C., & Karsh, K. G. (1990). A taxonomic approach to the nonaversive treatment of maladaptive behavior of persons with developmental disabilities. In A. C. Repp & N. N. Singh (Eds.), *Perspectives on the use of nonaversive and aversive interventions for persons with developmental disabilities* (pp. 331–347). Sycamore, IL: Sycamore.

Repp, A. C., & Singh, N. N. (Eds.). (1990). *Perspectives on the use of nonaversive and aversive interventions for persons with developmental disabilities.* Sycamore, IL: Sycamore.

Rolider, A., & Van Houten, R. (1985). Movement suppression time-out for undesirable behavior in psychotic and severely developmentally delayed children. *Journal of Applied Behavior Analysis, 18,* 275–288.

Rosenberg, M. S., Reppucci, N. D., & Linney, J. A. (1983). Issues in the implementation of human service programs: Examples from a parent training project for high-risk families. *Analysis and Intervention in Developmental Disabilities, 3,* 215–225.

Rubin, K. H., & Howe, N. (1985). Toys and play behaviors: An overview. *Topics in Early Childhood Special Education, 5*(3), 1–9.

Sheridan, S. M. (1990). Behavior consultation with parents and teachers: Delivering treatment for socially withdrawn children at home and school. *School Psychology Review, 19*(1), 33–52.

Singh, N. N., Lloyd, J. W., & Kendall, K. A. (1990). Nonaversive and aversive interventions: Issues. In A. C. Repp & N. N. Singh (Eds.), *Perspectives on the use of nonaversive and aversive interventions for persons with developmental disabilities* (pp. 3–16). Sycamore, IL: Sycamore.

Snell, M. E., & Beckman-Brindley, S. (1984). Family involvement in intervention with children having severe handicaps. *Journal of the Association for Persons with Severe Handicaps, 9,* 231–230.

Solnick, J. V., Rincover, A., & Peterson, C. R. (1977). Some determinants of the reinforcing and punishing effects of timeout. *Journal of Applied Behavior Analysis, 10,* 415–424.

Steege, M. W., Wacker, D. P., Berg, W. K., Cigrand, K. K., & Cooper, L. J. (1989). The use of behavioral assessment to prescribe and evaluate treatments for severely handicapped children. *Journal of Applied Behavior Analysis, 22*(1), 23–33.

Steege, M. W., Wacker, D. P., Cigrand, K. C., Berg, W. K., Novak, C. G., Reimers, T. M., Sasso,

G. M., & DeRaad, A. (1990). Use of negative reinforcement in the treatment of self-injurious behavior. *Journal of Applied Behavior Analysis, 23,* 459–467.

Stern, G. W., Fowler, S. A., & Kohler, F. W. (1988). A comparison of two intervention roles: Peer monitor and point earner. *Journal of Applied Behavior Analysis, 21,* 103–109.

Strain, P. S. (1981). Modification of sociometric status and social interaction with mainstreamed mild developmentally disabled children. *Analysis and Intervention in Developmental Disabilities, 1,* 157–169.

Strain, P. S., Young, C., & Horowitz, J. (1981). Generalized behavior change during oppositional child training: An examination of child and family demographic variables. *Behavior Modification, 5,* 15–26.

Van Hasselt, V. B., Sisson, L. A., & Aach, S. R. (1987). Parent training to increase compliance in a young multihandicapped child. *Journal of Behavior Therapy and Experimental Psychiatry, 18*(3), 275–283.

Van Houten, R., Axelrod, S., Bailey, J. S., Favell, J. E., Foxx, R. M., Iwata, B. A., & Lovaas, O. I. (1988). The right to effective behavioral treatment. *Journal of Applied Behavior Analysis, 21,* 381–384.

Wahler, R. G. (1980). The insular mother: Her problems in parent-child treatment. *Journal of Applied Behavior Analysis, 13,* 207–219.

Webster-Stratton, C. (1985). Modification of mother's behaviors and attitudes through a videotape modeling group discussion. *Behavior Therapy, 12,* 634–642.

Weeks, M., & Gaylord-Ross, R. (1981). Task difficulty and aberrant behavior in severely handicapped students. *Journal of Applied Behavior Analysis, 14,* 449–463.

White, A. G., & Bailey, J. S. (1990). Reducing disruptive behaviors of elementary physical education students with sit and watch. *Journal of Applied Behavior Analysis, 23,* 353–359.

White, O. R., & Haring, N. G. (1980). *Exceptional teaching* (2nd ed.). Columbus, OH: Merrill.

Wolery, M. (1989). Using direct observation in assessment. In D. B. Bailey & M. Wolery (Eds.), *Assessing infants and preschoolers with handicaps* (pp. 64–96). Columbus, OH: Merrill.

Wolery, M. (1991). Basic behavior management techniques. In E. Cipani (Ed.), *A guide for developing language competence in preschool children with severe and moderate handicaps* (pp. 43–67). Springfield, IL: Charles C. Thomas.

Wolery, M., Bailey, D. B., & Sugai, G. M. (1988). *Effective teaching: Principles and procedures of applied behavior analysis with exceptional students.* Boston: Allyn and Bacon.

Wolery, M., & Gast, D. L. (1990). Reframing the debate: Finding middle ground and defining the role of social validation. In A. C. Repp & N. N. Singh (Eds.), *The use of non-aversive and aversive interventions for persons with developmental disabilities* (pp. 129–143). Sycamore, IL: Sycamore.

Wolf, M. M., Braukmann, C. J., & Ramp, K. A. (1987). Serious delinquent behavior as part of a significantly handicapping condition: Cures and supportive environments. *Journal of Applied Behavior Analysis, 20,* 347–359.

Zohn, C., & Bornstein, P. (1980). Self-monitoring of work performance with mentally retarded adults: Effects upon work productivity, work quality, and on-task behavior. *Mental Retardation, 18,* 19–25.

12

Facilitating Motor Skills

Dale Scalise-Smith

Don Bailey

Motor skills such as locomotion (moving independently from one place to another), reaching, grasping, and maintaining one's body position and orientation in relation to objects in the environment allow children to master, control, and interact with the environment. Motor skills also affect a child's ability to perform behaviors in other developmental areas. For example, speaking involves precise movements of the lip and tongue muscles; a social skill such as play frequently involves movement of objects; a self-help skill such as dressing involves reaching, grasping, and removing clothing; a cognitive skill such as object permanence is usually demonstrated by performing certain motor behaviors.

Many young children with disabilities demonstrate motor delays and deficits (Bigge, 1991). In children with severe physical disabilities, the treatment of motor deficits and delays will be a major portion of the early intervention curriculum, requiring a team effort by teachers, physical therapists, occupational therapists, and/or physical educators. Team members should understand each others' language; thus, the techniques and terms used by occupational and physical therapists and physical educators are discussed in this chapter.

This chapter contains traditional and contemporary concepts concerning motor development and intervention, as well as sections addressing major areas of motor development, including postural control and motor learning; locomotion and other gross motor skills; and fine motor skills. The theoretical assumptions and practices underlying motor development and its facilitation have undergone dramatic changes in the past five years. The following section is thus devoted to a description of how these assumptions evolved, how they compare with prior assumptions, and implications for practice.

CONCEPTS IN MOTOR DEVELOPMENT

Traditional Views of Motor Development

Principles of motor development as described by developmental theorists (Gesell, 1940; Gesell, 1945; McGraw, 1943) have been the cornerstone for the study of child development. Much of the research by Gesell (1940; 1945) and McGraw (1943) documented the sequential progression of motor skills and the timing of developmental tasks, with extensive descriptions of motor skills. These early developmentalists attempted to link observed motor behaviors to the maturation of the central nervous system. This neuromaturational model, based on work by Coghill (1929), has been the theoretical foundation for infant development until recently.

Coghill (1929) studied neural and behavioral maturation in salamanders. He reported that the neural maturation of this species was tightly linked to movement behaviors. As the nervous system matured, the motor skills became more complex. McGraw's (1943) work in motor development used this neuromaturational model to explain changes in the motor system as they related to changes in the central nervous system.

Gesell's (1940) detailed descriptions of motor skill development, based on neuro-anatomical, physiological, and behavioral changes, have guided many assumptions about development. Some of the major assumptions include: (a) movement occurs in a cephalo-caudal direction (e.g., control of the head occurs prior to trunk control), (b) movement occurs in a proximal-to-distal progression (e.g., muscle control develops at the shoulder prior to the hand and fingers), (c) progression of one motor skill results in regression of other motor skills (e.g., as ball throwing develops, coordination of running patterns may appear more awkward and less refined), (d) motor milestones are invariant in sequence (e.g., creeping occurs before walking), (e) progression of motor skills occurs from gross to fine (e.g., gross-raking grasp develops before isolated-pincer grasp), and (f) development of motor control progresses from reflexive to voluntary (e.g., grasp occurs initially as a reflexive movement and progresses to voluntarily opening and closing the hand).

Early developmentalists also approached the study of infant behavior with the perspective that the infant is passive and only responds when a stimulus is introduced. This perspective suggests that, early in development, the infant's movements are reflexive. Traditional concepts of motor development based on reflexive-to-voluntary control of motor skills evolved from the early work of Sherrington (1906) and Jackson (1932). These researchers proposed a hierarchical model of central nervous system (CNS) control. This model of CNS control predicted that as higher centers develop, they exert control over the lower centers, and as the primitive reflexes become integrated, voluntary movement develops.

The hierarchical model of CNS organization was the theoretical foundation for the neurophysiological approaches developed during the 1950s to treat patients with CNS dysfunction. Neurodevelopmental treatment (NDT) is one neurophysiological approach often used in the treatment of children with cerebral palsy. This neurophysiological approach is based on four primary goals of treatment: (a) normalizing muscle tone; (b) inhibiting spasticity; (c) inhibiting primitive reflexes; and (d) facilitating normal movement patterns through proprioceptive inputs (Bobath, 1980). Abnormal muscle tone and spasticity have been thought to be major factors which influenced movement patterns and which proponents of NDT felt must be inhibited before focusing on development of normal motor skills. A major problem with

this approach, however, is that normalizing muscle tone and inhibiting spasticity is temporary and does not facilitate the development of functional motor skills (Gordon, 1987). While some physical therapists believe that qualitative changes in a child's movement can be seen when implementing an NDT approach, little research is available to support or refute this claim (Girolami, 1987; Horn, 1991). Consequently NDT and other neurophysiological approaches to treatment have become highly controversial.

Current Concepts in Motor Development

Although the maturational and hierarchical concepts of motor development offer some explanation for changes in motor behaviors, they cannot fully account for the truly complex behaviors seen in even the youngest infant. Neural maturation may explain broad concepts such as the general sequence of motor development, but within this development we see a wide range of variability. Consequently contemporary researchers in motor development are evaluating the interactive nature of different subsystems with the environment, using a dynamic systems model (Heriza, 1991; Thelan, 1985). Two recent theories dominate current thinking about motor development: dynamic systems theory and motor programs. These theories are briefly discussed to introduce the reader to contemporary concepts in motor development and motor control and their implications for treatment of children with motor disabilities.

Dynamic Systems Theory Current concepts in motor control suggest that dynamic systems theory may help explain concepts in development not well explained by more traditional models. Dynamic systems theory assumes that the human organism functions as a system, which in turn is comprised of many subsystems. Among the many subsystems most directly relevant to motor behavior and development are the neuromuscular, musculoskeletal, sensory, cognitive, and vestibular subsystems. Dynamic systems theory hypothesizes that subsystems interact with each other in an ongoing series of transactions. In this interaction, each subsystem both influences and is influenced by others to produce coordinated movements. Concepts of dynamic systems theory that may help explain why motor skills do not progress along a developmental timeline, as earlier developmentalists suggested, demonstrate that: (a) one developmental task may progress while another task regresses; (b) a small change in the system may result in large changes in behavior; (c) a developmental task moves through periods of stability and instability; and (d) new behaviors emerge that had not been previously observed (Giuliani, 1991).

The first major concept underlying dynamic systems theory is that a child may exhibit progression of one developmental task with regression of another developmental task. Gesell (1945) suggested that development progresses in a nonlinear fashion such that infants exhibit progress in one skill area with the regression of another skill. New concepts in motor control suggest that rather than being related to changes in the CNS, progression-regression of skills in development may be related to changes among multiple subsystems including sensory, musculoskeletal, cognitive, and environmental (Thelan, 1985). This progression-regression in development is thought to be due to dynamic interaction of the subsystems rather than being tied purely to the CNS. One example of progression and regression may be seen with gross motor and expressive language development. A child who is already able to run and just beginning to speak may demonstrate an apparent regression in motor skills as expressive language increases. This

regression occurs temporarily with the progression of expressive language.

The second major concept underlying dynamic systems theory is that small changes to the system may produce large changes in behavior. Studies by Thelan, Fisher, and Ridley-Johnson (1984), which investigated stepping responses in young infants, provide some evidence that large changes in a child's behavior may be seen when only small changes are applied to the system. These researchers applied a small weight to an infant's leg, and the infant stopped stepping. By adding this small weight, the investigators found that the infant decreased the number of steps walked. This experiment simulated weight gain in the child as would typically occur across time but controlled for developmental changes by measuring stepping over one session with different weights. The application of a weight to a child's leg provides one example of how a small change in the system can produce a large change in behavior.

A third major concept underlying dynamic systems theory is that children exhibit periods of stability and instability within a task across time. Stability and instability in development result from the interaction of many subsystems within the body. The period of stability and instability refers to changes in a motor behavior, such as stepping, as other variables enter into the equation. Kamm, Thelan, and Jensen (1990) and Heriza (1991) described this stability/instability (also referred to as organization/disorganization/reorganization) seen in infants' stepping patterns across time. These researchers observed periods where the stepping movements were tightly linked and predictable (organized) during "reflexive" stepping, to periods of disorganization as the infant's weight increased and the stepping behavior decreased, and finally a reorganization of the stepping behavior with the emergence of mature patterns observed in young infants cruising along furniture.

A fourth major concept is the emergence of behaviors not previously observed. One example is the child who is unable to sit independently when placed on the floor but can momentarily maintain sitting independently when placed on a bench. Sitting on the floor may not be an optimal condition to facilitate the behavior to occur, but the bench is a more precarious position and may facilitate the emergence of behaviors not previously seen.

Evaluating the influence of the sensory, musculoskeletal, neuromuscular, vestibular, and cognitive systems on development of motor skills across time can provide teachers and therapists alike with an idea of how different subsystems may have more or less impact at different points in development. For example, children with visual impairments also exhibit delays in motor development, since infants and young children utilize vision to maintain upright control in sitting and standing, as demonstrated in the research of Butterworth and Hicks (1977), Forssberg and Nashner (1982), and Lee and Aronson (1974). The visual system has an important role in development of motor skills in infants and young children, but it is only one of the many subsystems in the human organism that influence motor development. Each subsystem plays a different role at various points in development, and the subsystems continuously interact with one another.

Motor Programs   Although dynamic systems theory can provide a theoretical framework for some concepts in development, it is by no means the only perspective to consider in motor development. The concept of motor programs provides yet another framework from which we can evaluate changes in motor behaviors.

Motor programs may be defined as centrally stored commands, located in the CNS, which provide information about how to execute a task. The movement plan may not necessarily be "hard-wired" or permanent in the CNS. Instead, it may be modifiable depending on the environment and the interaction of other subsystems.

Motor programs appear to have components which are either variant or invariant. In an example of throwing a ball, we can see that the force, or how hard the ball is thrown, and speed, or how fast the ball is thrown, are variant characteristics of throwing, but the coordination or pattern of the arm movement in throwing remains relatively fixed or invariant (Brooks, 1986; Schmidt, 1988).

The plan or execution of the task may be carried out using feedback, either intrinsically or extrinsically generated, or may be carried out in a "feedforward" manner (Brooks, 1986). Feedback provides input for modifying and adapting the program to meet the needs of the entire system. A feedforward concept implies that well-learned, rapid, automatic movements can be executed without information from various subsystems. Feedback is available and utilized by the system but not until after the movement is completed.

Some researchers (Brooks, 1986; Jejka & Kelso, 1989) from either a motor program or dynamic systems theory have argued that these concepts are incompatible. As Schmidt (1989) has suggested, however, motor programming may be the CNS component within dynamic system theory. The interaction between these two concepts may contribute to our understanding of motor development better than either concept alone. Within the concept of the dynamic systems theory, the motor program model may provide a framework from which the CNS control may be explained.

Some of the key concepts differentiating traditional and contemporary models of motor development are displayed in Table 12.1. Using a model that incorporates both motor program and dynamic systems perspectives, perhaps we can devise more effective and efficient treatments for children with motor impairments and move toward more functional skills. This approach may be more beneficial than being concerned about facilitating "normal" patterns of movement or inhibiting primitive reflexes, as more traditional treatments have suggested. As educators, therapists, and parents, the ultimate

TABLE 12.1
Traditional vs. contemporary models for working with children who have cerebral palsy

Hierarchical (Traditional) Theoretical Framework	Systems (Contemporary) Theoretical Framework
• Top-down control of CNS • Higher centers of CNS control lower centers • Separation of reflexive and voluntary movement • Development of proceeds cephalocaudally	• Interaction between subsystems controls the behavior to achieve motor task • No one subsystem has ultimate control over other subsystems • Development proceeds in cephaloid and caudal regions simultaneously
Underlying Concepts in Treatment	**Underlying Concepts in Treatment**
• Facilitate normal movement patterns with proprioceptive inputs • Modify the CNS from the experience of normal movement patterns • Fractionalize movements by breaking up abnormal synergies • Inhibit abnormal muscle tone and primitive reflexes • Prevent the CNS from learning abnormal movement patterns	• Practice tasks • Teach motor problem-solving (i.e., adaptability to contexts) • Learn strategies to coordinate efficient, effective behaviors • Develop effective compensations for limitations in movement • Utilize musculoskeletal and environmental constraints
Clinical Findings	**Clinical Findings**
• Abnormal muscle tone results from a lesion to the higher center in the CNS • Children exhibit primitive reflexes, which inhibit voluntary movement • Stereotypical patterns of movement • At-risk for orthopedic deformities resulting from limitations in range of motion	• Muscle weakness restricts voluntary movement • Muscle tone not considered • Musculoskeletal changes not a result of CNS damage • Reflexes accepted and encouraged if voluntary movement is restricted (e.g., rolling using asymmetrical tonic neck reflex)
Problems	**Problems**
• No carryover to functional activities • Patients are passive • Does not take musculoskeletal or environment variables into consideration • Inhibition of primitive reflexes does not release normal movements	• Hard to quantify efficient, effective compensations • Less "hands on," too "cognitive" • Difficult to retrain anticipatory control and use prior experience • Hard to provide the time-consuming practice of skills

goal is attaining functional independence so that the child can maximize growth potential in all areas of development.

Innate Motor Behaviors

Innate motor behaviors are comprised of primitive and postural reflexes. Initially infants were thought to exhibit only primitive reflexes or stereotypic responses. Brazelton (1984) and Fiorentino (1972) have provided detailed descriptions of these developmental reflexes.

The infant's response is tightly linked to the stimulus, leading some early researchers to suggest that the infant is a passive being acted upon by the environment. Brazelton (1984), however, has shown that these responses may be influenced by other subsystems, such as state, sensory, or musculoskeletal subsystems. He described newborn infants as competent beings, who are not acted upon by the environment as in a stimulus-response type paradigm, but rather are highly interactive, complex beings. His work demonstrated that infants are capable of complex facial movements in imitation of adult faces and can auditorially and visually track people and objects. These purposeful, voluntary behaviors, seen at birth or shortly thereafter, are very different from the stereotypic responses described by earlier developmentalists.

Additionally, studies by deVries, Visser, and Prechtl (1982; 1985) and Sparling et al. (1990) support the idea that the newborn infant is a competent being capable of complex, voluntary behaviors, given the appropriate environment. For example, the hand-to-mouth behavior described by Brazelton (1984) as a self-calming behavior in newborns has been observed in fetuses during ultrasound (Sparling et al., 1990).

Als and Brazelton (1981) have suggested that innate motor behaviors are not stimulus-

dependent but may also be dependent on the infant's behavioral state as well as environmental factors. For example, a sucking reflex is elicited by placing a breast or synthetic nipple in an infant's mouth. If the infant has just been fed and is drowsy when the stimulus is introduced, however, the infant may not suck. This does not infer that the infant's sucking reflex is abnormal; more likely it means that this response is not purely reflexive and may be more accurately referred to as an innate motor behavior. These innate motor behaviors are not solely linked to the CNS maturation, as traditionally thought, but are a result of the interaction and interdependence of intrinsic and extrinsic variables.

Research by Thelan (1983; 1985) and Thelan and Cooke (1987) supports the premise that infants may be capable of a variety of behaviors, but the behaviors may not be available to the infant because of the constraints of the environment. One example of this is the stepping reflex, a reflexive behavior (stimulus-response, or S-R) which is elicited when an infant is held in a standing position with the feet on a firm surface. The earlier developmentalists suggested that this reflex disappeared and later re-emerged within the first year of life as voluntary walking. This reflexive-to-voluntary movement was thought to be related to the maturation of the CNS, as discussed earlier. By changing the environment, Thelan found that the capability to produce the stepping reflex was still present, but as the infant gained weight he no longer produced that behavior when placed in standing. Thelan varied the context, for example, by placing the child in water or on a treadmill, and found that the stepping response had not disappeared or been integrated but that the infant still had the capability of producing the response under certain conditions.

DeVries, Visser, and Prechtl (1982; 1985) and Sparling et al. (1990) have conducted studies of fetal movement using ultrasound. They reported that by 16 weeks of age a fetus has demonstrated a variety of behaviors that are complex, very refined, and not restricted to the stereotypic responses described by Hooker and Humphrey (1954). The earlier proposal of developmental progression based upon maturation of the nervous system is clearly refuted by the refined, complex movements described by these researchers in 16-week fetuses. The fetus demonstrated many behaviors which did not appear to be elicited nor responded to in S-R reflexive movements. Rather these behaviors were assumed by the researchers to be purposeful movements. The fetuses exhibited hand-to-mouth behaviors similar to self-calming behaviors seen in newborn infants. This complex movement, demonstrating good motor control to move the hand accurately towards the mouth, is just one example of the capabilities of the fetus and consequently the newborn. Changes in the environment from uterine to extra-uterine life, with changes in gravitational forces, result in changes in the motor behaviors.

Although the concept of infants being dependent on reflexes (stereotypic responses) early in life, with no purposeful, voluntary movements has been questioned, the idea of innate motor behaviors is still supported. Contemporary researchers acknowledge the existence of reflexes but limit the importance of these behaviors to identifying the intactness of the neural circuitry. Evaluating reflexes or innate motor behaviors such as sucking or stepping shows they are indicators of the state of the CNS but do not provide information about the ability to control movement.

Developmental Milestones

Early developmentalists have documented the sequence of normal motor development (McGraw, 1943; Gesell, 1945; Bayley, 1969). The problem lies in understanding how these movements develop and how we can maximize development of motor skills in children at-risk for or with diagnosed motor dysfunction (Heriza, 1991).

Assessment in infants and children has typically been based upon key motor milestones identified as markers for normal motor development, such as those in Table 12.2. Motor milestones assess only the end-product rather than the process that children use to attain the skill. Perhaps as important as the actual attainment of the motor milestone is how the movement changes, as well as the functional importance of the movement.

The change in focus of physical therapy from a neurodevelopmental approach facilitating motor development to a functional, task-oriented approach significantly influences our view of motor development. Current perspectives emphasize the identification of motor skills that are important to developing functional independence in infants and young children, with consideration for the environmental, sensory, cognitive, musculoskeletal, and neural subsystems. An example of the emphasis of contemporary physical therapists in treating infants and young children may be seen in changing the focus from normalizing gait or walking patterns to developing functional walking patterns (Bobath, 1967; Gordon, 1987). Traditional therapists using an NDT approach attempted to facilitate a normal walking pattern by placing their hands on a patient's hips or shoulders as key points of control in the body. The problem lies in that the treatment effects disappear when the therapist's hands are removed. Moving towards a functional, task-oriented approach of motor development, therapists focus on developing an efficient and effective movement pattern, more directly addressing the individual needs of the child.

TABLE 12.2
Normal sequences of gross motor skills

Age	Sample Locomotion Skills	Examples of Other Gross Motor Skills
0–6 months	Chin up Chest up Rolls over Sits with support	
6–12 months	Sits alone Moves to all-fours position Crawls Creeps Walks when led Pulls to stand	Bangs large objects Attempts to throw
12–18 months	Stands independently Walks independently Walks up steps with help Sits self in chair Begins stiff running	Rolls ball
18–24 months	Runs well Climbs steps independently, but one foot at a time Jumps from bottom step	Throws ball overhand
2–3 years	Jumps Walks backwards Walks on tiptoes	Catches large ball with arms straight out Kicks ball forward Begins to pedal tricycle
3–4 years	More fluent running Walks straight line Stands on one foot (1–2 seconds) Hops Skips on one foot	Rides tricycle well Throws, maintaining balance Catches bounced ball
4–5 years	Skips, alternating feet Running or standing broad jumps Marches Walks backward heel-to-toe Jumps over 10″-high object	Throws overhand well Turns somersault

Dynamic Postural Control

A key component to early development of movement is postural control. Postural control is defined as the ability to maintain an upright posture by maintaining or returning the center of mass over the base of support (Horak, 1987). Obviously, postural control is a consideration when working with children with motor dysfunction, since this component is key to developing motor skills.

Researchers have suggested that development of postural control is dependent upon the activation of two or more muscles in a consistent sequence (Harbourne & Giuliani, 1988). These consistent sequencing of muscles, identified as postural synergies, are thought to be well-developed in infants and young children (Harbourne & Giuliani, 1988; Shumway-Cook & Woollacott, 1985). The investigators proposed that these synergies contribute to the acquisition of skills requiring postural control, such as sitting or walking.

The importance of postural control in motor development is apparent. Children with motor dysfunction exhibit delays in development of postural control that impairs their ability to perform functional tasks such as sitting or walking. Just as we alter the surface and conditions to vary their experience and develop postural control in normal infants, we also must provide varied experiences for children with motor impairments.

MOTOR DEVELOPMENT IN CHILDREN WITH SPECIAL NEEDS

Earlier we discussed the interaction between intrinsic and extrinsic subsystems and how these may impact development. These interactions can probably best be seen in development of children with special needs. In this section, we will review motor functioning of children with different diagnoses, including: mental retardation, Down syndrome, cerebral palsy, spina bifida, visual impairments, and other diseases.

Mental Retardation

The first milestones parents and professionals observe in infants are in motor development and consequently can be early indicators of problems. Motor delay may be one of the first signs that lead to a diagnosis of mental retardation, although not all children

who are mentally retarded (Capute, Shapiro, & Palmer, 1981) have delays in motor development.

Motor problems in children who have mental retardation remain largely unexplored (Bradley, 1989). Delays in motor development may be related to factors such as the level of cognitive impairment, access to physical games or activities, biomechanical limitations, delayed postural responses, or a variety of other factors yet to be identified.

Down Syndrome

Children with Down syndrome are one group whose delayed motor development has been studied. Shumway-Cook and Woollacott (1985) evaluated postural responses in standing among children with Down syndrome. The researchers found that when children with Down syndrome were displaced they exhibited delayed and poorly organized muscle responses, decreased postural sway, and difficulty resolving sensory conflicts during sway-rotation perturbations. The muscle responses were similar to those of normal children and adults, but the timing of the muscle responses was slower. These investigators suggest that difficulties with postural control may be related to centrally organized responses, not necessarily to hypotonia, which has often been cited as the major problem in motor development of children with Down syndrome (Shumway-Cook & Woollacott, 1985). Additional research is necessary to investigate more closely the primary locus of postural control problems in children with Down syndrome and how we can maximize their motor skill development.

Cerebral Palsy

Cerebral palsy may be identified as a composite of movement and postural control disorders resulting from a nonprogressive insult to the immature central nervous system (Shumway-Cook & Woollacott, 1985). Types of cerebral palsy are generally classified according to location and clinical symptoms, as summarized in Table 12.3.

Traditional treatment for decreasing spasticity in children with cerebral palsy, using a neurodevelopmental approach, was to inhibit abnormal reflexes and normalize muscle tone through facilitation techniques, such as hand placement at key points on the body. Spasticity has been identified as one of the symptoms that impairs the functional abilities of children with cerebral palsy and as such has been a primary target of therapists.

"Spasticity is a velocity-dependent increase in the tonic stretch reflex with exaggerated tendon jerks resulting from hyperexcitability of the stretch reflex" (Duncan & Badke, 1987).

Current theories of motor control suggest that muscle weakness, not spasticity, is one of the primary problems of children with cerebral palsy. Muscle strength is defined as the ability of a muscle to produce and grade tension through a coordinated movement (Smidt & Rogers, 1982). Children with cerebral palsy reportedly have muscle atrophy,

TABLE 12.3

Cerebral palsy classified by types of motor involvement and the area of the body affected

Type	Motor Involvement
Spastic	Characterized by loss of voluntary motor control; frequent co-contractions: muscles used in flexion and extension contract at the same time resulting in tense, jerky movements which are poorly controlled. The posture may be fixed and rigid when the child is startled. Limb deformities are possible as children grow older.
Athetosis	Characterized by involuntary, purposeless limb movements; fluctuating muscle tone affects deliberate muscle extensions resulting in writhing, irregular movements; throat and diaphragm muscles frequently involved, producing drooling and labored speech.
Ataxia	Characterized by balance problems, staggering gait, slurred speech, poor depth perception, and poor gross and fine motor movements.
Rigidity	Characterized by extreme stiffness and appears to be severe spasticity; difficult for child to bend limbs, and when bent they tend to stay in that position.
Tremor	Characterized by shakiness of limbs; shakiness frequently only present during intentional movements; limb movements are small and rhythmic.
Mixed	Characterized by more than one of the above types.

Area of Body Affected with Motor Involvement

Monoplegia	Only one limb of the body has paralysis.
Hemiplegia	Limbs on one side are affected; frequently, trunk muscles are also affected.
Paraplegia	Lower limbs (legs) are affected, but arms are not.
Diplegia	All limbs are affected with paralysis, but the legs are more seriously affected than the arms.
Quadriplegia	All four limbs are affected with paralysis.

Note: From Cross, D. P. (1981). "Physical disabilities." In A. E. Blackhurst & W. H. Berdine (Eds.), *An Introduction to Special Education.* Boston: Little, Brown.

which is more related to their limitations in functioning than spasticity (Milner-Brown & Penn, 1979). Muscle atrophy coupled with changes in musculoskeletal tissues may be a more accurate assessment of the limitations in movement than spasticity.

Contemporary concepts in working with children who have cerebral palsy include evaluating muscle strength, functional motor skill level, postural control, mobility, and range of motion. Using this functional approach in evaluating children with cerebral palsy can help us better determine how to assist them in maximizing their productivity and independence in society.

Myelomeningocele (Spina Bifida)

Spina bifida occurs in 1 in every 1,000 live births, second only to Down syndrome in birth defects (Myers, 1984). The diagnosis of spina bifida is usually made at birth by the external sac containing the meninges and the spinal cord identified on the infant's back. Generally the opening is in the lumbar or low-back region, but the lesion can be located at any point along the spine (Tappit-Emas, 1989).

Spina bifida affects the neuromuscular, musculoskeletal, and genitourinary systems (Morrissey, 1978). Children primarily have difficulty with movement and sensation in their lower extremities as well as hydrocephalus.

Working with children who have spina bifida should include evaluating muscle strength through manual muscle tests, functional motor skill level, postural control, mobility, and range of motion. Using a functional approach to evaluating children with spina bifida enhances their potential for productivity and independence in society.

Visual Impairments

Children rely heavily on their visual system to maintain upright control (Butterworth &

Hicks, 1977; Forssberg & Nashner, 1982; Lee & Aronson, 1974). The results of these studies suggest that children use visual input to guide themselves throughout much of their motor development. We often use visual cues to motivate children to reach for or move to obtain an object.

Without the sensory input, children with visual impairments are resistant to move and explore within their environment, thus exhibiting delays in motor development. By giving appropriate assistance and external support, parents and professionals can facilitate motor development in children with visual impairments.

Other Diseases

Many other diseases that result in physical impairments, such as muscular dystrophy, scoliosis (curvature of the spine), kyphosis, clubfoot, poliomyelitis, juvenile rheumatoid arthritis, hip dislocations, and Legg-Perthes disease, influence a child's motor performance. Medical conditions may also affect motor performance or restrict the type of intensity of movement and activity. These include cystic fibrosis, hemophilia, diabetes, and heart disease/defects. For information regarding these disorders, the reader may refer to Tecklin (1989) and Batshaw and Perret (1986). Teachers are not expected to be thoroughly knowledgeable concerning the description, etiology, diagnosis, treatment, and effects of these conditions. When working with a child with a specific diagnosis, however, they should increase their general knowledge about the diagnosis through medical personnel and reference sources. Additional sources for information include the child's family and physicians.

Motor development is influenced not only by orthopedic and neurological impairments but also by medical diagnosis. Despite the variability in motor impairments we must somehow evaluate progress or changes in a child's motor skill level. Gross motor development in all children is generally based on milestones attained by normally developing children. The expectation is not that children with motor impairments attain all motor skills seen in normal children or that the skills occur in a similar sequence. Rather, changes in motor development are grossly gauged by development of normal infants and children.

PLANNING AND IMPLEMENTING TREATMENT STRATEGIES IN GROSS AND FINE MOTOR DEVELOPMENT

Although children's disabilities are each unique, general suggestions can be made regarding motor learning and motor skill assessment, positioning techniques, adaptive equipment, and fine motor skill assessment in children with disabilities. Each of the following sections will provide guidelines for maximizing a child's functional independence utilizing motor learning and positioning techniques, as well as adaptive equipment.

Motor Learning in Motor Skill Acquisition

Educators working with infants and young children may ask, "What problems do children face in controlling their movements to carry out a functional task?" We know that children are not passive beings within their environment but rather active participants who must constantly solve problems about moving within their environment. Development of motor skills occurs out of a need to solve specific motor problems in the environment. A primary function for all professionals working with infants and young children is to identify functional motor skills that a child can and cannot perform. After determining their motor strengths and needs, we can determine how to facilitate development of these skills.

Educators understand how important learning is to a child's cognitive development; learning is not only a cognitive task but is also related to development of motor skills. Motor learning is a relatively permanent change in a motor behavior (Schmidt, 1988). Stallings (1973) has defined motor learning as an improvement in a motor skill as a result of experience rather than maturation. As we examine these definitions, we see that practice or experience appears to be a major factor in developing proficiency in a motor skill.

As children practice motor skills throughout their daily activities, the environmental context is often changing. Typically young children walk along tiled and carpeted floors, grass, rocks, and uneven outdoor surfaces, providing them with a variety of situations on which to develop proficiency in walking. Again, practice is the key, but we may also vary the conditions of the practice so that children walk over different surfaces, maintaining upright postural control. Given opportunities for practice under a variety of conditions, children develop what Schmidt (1988) has defined as a schema, which is viewed as concepts or relationships that develop as a result of experience. As children learn about the rules of performing a task, they use practice to identify and encode correct and incorrect motor responses. Identifying correct and incorrect responses provides the child with information about which parameters of movement result in successful performance of a motor task.

Motor learning, which provides one possible explanation for how skills are developed and maintained over time, is important for understanding skill development in infants and children. Factors that are important to motor learning and assist professionals in promoting development of motor skills include: (a) prompts or encouragement to perform a behavior; (b) assistance in performing a behavior; (c) practice of the skill;

(d) variability of the practice; and (e) feedback about performance and outcome of the skill.

Infants and young children typically will practice a task such as walking as a part of their play. Although most children learn motor skills through day-to-day experience, children with motor delays may not have the opportunity to practice motor skills without external support. Given external support either through hands-on assistance from an adult or through adaptive equipment, children then have the opportunity to practice the motor skills.

Assessing Movement Skills

In the assessment of movement, the teacher should initially evaluate the child's abilities, then determine the presence and quality of functional movements. Finally, the teacher should assess the environmental opportunities and expectations for the child's movement within the indoor and outdoor areas. A detailed overview of motor assessment procedures is provided by Smith (1989). The following discussion presents some important considerations in this process.

Assessing Developmental Skills   Assessment of developmental levels of motor performance specifies the existence and extent of motor delays, helps interpret the child's abilities, and plan an instructional program for the child. The child is compared with children who do not have motor delays by means of broad checklists, criterion-referenced tests, and norm-referenced tests. For example, instruments such as the Bayley Scales of Infant Development (Bayley, 1969), the Battelle Developmental Inventory (Newborg, Stock, Wnek, Guidubaldi, & Svinicki, 1984), and the Hawaii Early Learning Profile (Furuno et al., 1979) each have sections for assessing gross and fine motor skills.

The Movement Assessment of Infants (Chandler, Andrews, & Swanson, 1980) and the Peabody Developmental Motor Scale (PDMS) (Folio & DuBose, 1974) are examples of measures that are totally devoted to motor assessment. The PDMS has separate scales that assess fine and gross motor skills from birth to 7 years. The gross motor scale has 170 items, and the fine motor scale has 112. Each item is rated on a 1–5 scale where 1 is scored when the child needs total manipulation by the examiner and 5 when the child performs the behavior without assistance. The scale was standardized nationally on a population of 617 children. The PDMS yields age scores, differential motor quotients, T scores, and Z scores. Programmed activities translate assessment data into instructional activities.

Assessing Functional Movements   When assessing functional movements, the result of the movement is important, rather than the form. For example, locomotion, or the ability to get from place A to place B, is a functional skill with the result of arriving at point B. To get from A to B, one might use a variety of forms, such as rolling, creeping, walking unassisted or with crutches, using a wheelchair, or perhaps asking someone to help them get to B.

When determining whether a child's form is functional, observe several dimensions of behavior, including accuracy, duration, endurance, fluency, and flexibility. Accuracy refers to the child's ability to use any behavior to consistently achieve the desired goal, such as moving 15 feet. Duration is the length of time a behavior lasts. For example, one might be interested in how long a child could maintain a given position. Endurance is the ability to repeat a behavior a number of times without stopping. For example, in locomotion, a child most likely repeats a small behavior a number of times, having the strength to take several steps, make several crawling movements, or roll over and over. Fluency or speed measures whether the child can perform the behavior fast enough to be useful. In the example of locomotion, the teacher would be interested in whether the child can use a given method (creeping) fast enough to reach a desired goal within a reasonable time period. Flexibility refers to the variety of accurate and fluent forms a child uses to accomplish a given result; such a child will have more adaptive and functional responses than the child with only one form.

In motor performance, a variety of skills are considered functional. These skills include locomotion, reaching/grasping (procurement of objects), moving grasped objects, maintenance of position, shifts in position without loss of balance, and maintenance of balance during locomotion.

Assessing Environmental Demands and Opportunities The opportunities available in the environment for functional movement are important in assessment. Does the child have opportunities to use existing functional motor skills and learn new ones? Determine whether opportunities for movement are built into the schedule, if children are given time for movement during transitions between activities, and whether activities used to teach skills from other developmental areas include movement.

Another aspect of measuring the environment involves determining whether movements are expected and demanded. In this context, movement is demanded when the environment is structured to set the occasion for movement, reinforce movement when it occurs, and prompt its occurrence when it does not. More than simply providing the opportunity for movement, the teacher expects, accepts, encourages, and reacts to movement as though it is the intended, usual, and desired response. For example, Joe has the ability to locomote, but does not do so quickly. When Joe is done with his snack, he has the opportunity to go to the free play area. If Joe sits in his chair and asks the teacher to carry him to the free play area

and the teacher complies, movement is not expected or demanded in this situation. However, if the teacher verbally cues Joe to find something fun to play with and physically assists him in getting out of his chair and into his locomotion position, then the teacher expects and demands movement from Joe.

Facilitating Movement

When designing environments to encourage and facilitate movement skills, teachers should consider children and movement when equipping and arranging the classroom and provide abundant opportunities for those skills. Issues related to equipping and arranging the preschool environment to facilitate skill development were discussed in Chapter 7. Child-sized equipment should be used, and the environment should be structured to stimulate and allow movement.

When selecting child-sized equipment, the teacher should remember that not all children are the same size. Chairs should allow children to place their feet comfortably on the floor. If the chairs are too tall, blocks or small wooden platforms can be placed on the floor in front of the chairs. Tables should be about as high as the children's elbows when children are seated.

As described in Chapter 7, activity areas in the classroom should be arranged to allow for easy movement. Some areas should invite gross motor movements. In activity areas, place materials at eye level and make them easily accessible to children. Consider safety when structuring the home and school environment for movement. Wolinsky and Walker (1973) provide a checklist for parents of preschoolers with disabilities to evaluate the safety of their homes. Many items on the checklist can also be adapted for the classroom.

Provide abundant opportunities for movement. For most children, acquisition and refinement of movement skills occur throughout the preschool years. Thus, opportunities for activities involving movement are appropriate and important for most preschool children with disabilities. In implementing this guideline, the teacher should consider that movement is a high-probability behavior for preschool children. Their play frequently involves movement of objects. Teachers should use this propensity for movement as a reinforcer, for example, giving the opportunity for movement contingent on children's successful completion of other adaptive behaviors (Homme, DeBaca, Devine, Steinhorst, & Rickert, 1963).

The teachers should also be aware that movement and the training of specific movements should be embedded into training activities to reach other skills. Training children to perform specific movements can easily be accomplished by making the movements a part of another activity. This practice not only facilitates acquisition of specific movements but can facilitate acquisition of behaviors from other developmental areas. For example, in training children to label objects receptively, Janssen and Guess (1978) found that allowing the children to functionally move the objects as a consequence for correct labeling resulted in faster acquisition of labels. Similarly, training children in social skills such as taking turns, sharing, and participating in a group can be accomplished naturally through movement activities. For example, rolling or throwing a ball between two or three children and sliding on a playground slide can provide opportunities to teach turn-taking and sharing. Preschool teachers frequently use songs involving actions to teach social skills such as participating in a group and cognitive skills such as spatial relationships.

In addition, the teacher should provide a variety of structured (teacher-directed) and unstructured (child-directed) opportunities for movement. Schedule time each day for outdoor, gross motor, and play activities.

Some activities will need to be structured to facilitate acquisition of specific skills. However, time should also be allowed for children to engage in self-directed activities to practice previously learned behaviors that are apt to have more reinforcement value than structured activities. When using either structured or unstructured activities, the teacher may be an observer or participant, extending the child's play or attempting to induce cognitive conflict as described in Chapter 7. When activities involve gross motor behaviors, children's participation can be increased by adult participation. The teacher can also model a variety of new behaviors and thus increase the types of children's movements. However, the teacher should avoid wearing easily damaged and unsafe shoes, clothing, and jewelry when participating in active behaviors.

At other times the teacher may systematically observe the children playing. Such observation allows excellent opportunities for assessing and monitoring child-child interactions, communicative behaviors, and motor performance.

Teaching Functional Motor Skills

Skills such as walking, running, hopping, jumping, catching and throwing balls, and riding tricycles are common preschool gross motor behaviors. As a result, teachers of preschoolers frequently attempt to teach these skills. Several issues should be considered when attempting to teach such behaviors.

As suggested before, consult with a physical or occupational therapist. Therapists may provide essential information for teaching major steps in a new skill.

Still another issue to be considered is that skills selected for training should be functional, that is, they should serve a useful purpose in the child's life and improve control of the environment. Behaviors such as proficient locomotion and head control are more functional than standing on one foot or jumping from an 8-inch platform. Teachers should be sure to select functional target behaviors when evaluating curricula that accompany developmental checklists.

Also, maintenance and generalization of gross motor behaviors do not necessarily occur. For example, two of the subjects in the O'Brien, Azrin, and Bugle (1972) study did not maintain walking as a means of locomotion after the training was complete. Reintroduction of the contingencies for walking resulted in maintenance. Generalization of sitting in positions other than the reverse tailor position occurred for some subjects, but not for all, in the Bragg et al. (1975) study. Thus, teachers should be sure they enhance behaviors that will be expected and reinforced in other situations. To accomplish maintenance and generalization of gross motor behaviors, teachers should work with parents in selecting skills to be developed and then expecting and reinforcing those skills in other situations.

Finally, when possible, motor skills should be facilitated in a game format (Russo, 1979). The game format increases the likelihood of maintenance and generalization, incorporates the target motor skill into a variety of other motor behaviors, promotes opportunities for social interactions, and increases the probability that children will acquire behaviors for recreational and leisure time activities.

Positioning Techniques and Principles

Positioning refers to the use of appropriate body positions to ensure that the child is in an optimal position for learning and participating in classroom activities. Although positioning techniques must be specific to the child, several general guidelines are important. One guideline is to provide stability for the child, allowing the child to relax and focus attention toward an activity, such as listening to a story or participating in group activities. Adults, unlike equipment, can constantly modify the amount and location of the support to maximize a child's function and at the same time develop strength, for example, in the trunk.

Varying the child's position, if the child cannot do so alone, provides different perspectives on the activity and improves strength and endurance in many different positions, much like a child without physical limitations. Unless there is a medical rationale, positioning should allow the child to maximize independent functioning and adapt to the task at hand. The teacher should also consult with a therapist regarding lifting and carrying children for both the child's and the teacher's safety.

Adaptive Equipment

Adaptive equipment for positioning, mobility, and activities of daily living plays an important role in the lives of infants and children with physical disabilities. Introducing equipment at an early age can significantly reduce deformities, enhance motor development, and facilitate social and cognitive development (Bergan, 1982). While encouraging independence in children with disabilities, much the same as with children without physical disabilities, their learning within the class or group activity is greatly enhanced.

In encouraging independence and development of motor skills in young children with disabilities, it is important to realize that no one piece of equipment can meet all the child's therapeutic and functional needs. Children may require one type of equipment that provides postural support to perform an activity sitting or standing and another type that may assist in independent mobility.

With rapid technological advances in adaptive equipment available to infants and children with physical disabilities, teachers often have a more difficult time selecting the appropriate equipment. A therapist familiar with the individual needs of the child should be consulted in selecting adaptive equipment. Considerations include the particular strengths and needs of the child, which should be evaluated prior to ordering equipment, including muscle strength and motor skill level; social, psychological, and financial impact on the child and family; and durability and life expectancy of the equipment. Therapists can fit the equipment to the child and assist the teacher in identifying the purpose of a given piece of equipment and how to use it within a classroom, according to a child's needs and family priorities.

Evaluating a child for different types of adaptive equipment requires evaluating the static (stationary) and dynamic (changing) posture of the child. One example of variability in dynamic and static posture is in sitting. Static postural control in sitting can be addressed using equipment such as a Kinder-chair[1] or a floor sitter,[2] but dynamic postural control in sitting is more appropriately addressed using a dynamic posture chair.[2]

Equipment that is often seen in a classroom with a child who is physically impaired includes wedges, sidelyers, prone standers, and modified chairs. The wedge, pictured in Figure 12.1, may be purchased or constructed from high-density foam or wood covered with padding. The purpose of the wedge is to provide support at the trunk and free the upper extremities for other activities, improve neck strength, and encourage midline activities. The child should be positioned on the wedge so that the arms and shoulders are over the edge (see Figure 12.1).

Sidelyers are often used with young children or older children with moderate to severe impairments in motor development (Figure 12.2). The sidelyer is used to provide an alternative to sitting, prone, or supine positions. Sidelyers can be purchased with elaborate pieces that are easily modified for different children's needs or made by the therapist and/or family. Sidelying encourages neutral alignment of the head, trunk, and extremities; playing in the midline; and free movement of the child's hands to play with or manipulate objects.

Static standing devices or prone standers are often used with children who require assistance in maintaining upright standing (Figure 12.3). Support is provided at the trunk, buttocks, and legs or modified to meet a child's needs.

The goal of the prone stander is to allow weight bearing in the lower extremities while continuing to participate in classroom activities. Through lower extremity weight bearing, the child receives physiologic benefits as well as social/emotional and perceptual benefits of being upright.

The importance of sitting as a functional posture is apparent, although the seating devices used with children who have disabilities do not always enhance function. Modified seating devices are important to developing and maximizing functional independence.

Throughout school, sitting is an important posture for many classroom activities. While evaluating the needs of the child, considerations must be made regarding when and for what activities the chair will be used, how the chair will fit into the environment, and the ease of assisting the child moving into and out of the chair. A chair should be fitted to the child considering range of motion, muscle strength, and level of functional independence. These criteria must be used for all seating devices, whether static seating devices or wheelchairs. Figures 12.4 and 12.5 show examples of modified chairs.

---

[1]Kaye Products, Inc., 535 Dimmocks Mill Rd., Hillsborough, NC 27278.

[2]J.A. Preston Corp., 60 Page Road, Clifton, NJ 07012.

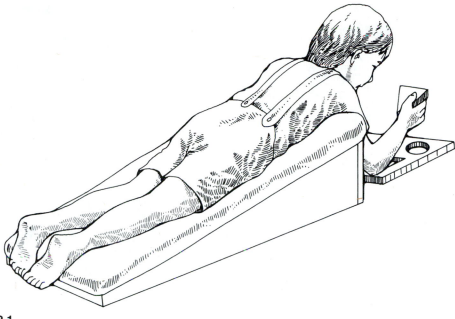

FIGURE 12.1
Example of a Wedge

Mobility for a child with physical disabilities is a concern for family and professionals. Wheelchair design can range from a power chair, which the child maneuvers within the environment, to a manual chair propelled by a child or adult (Figures 12.6– 12.8). The purpose of the wheelchair is to provide mobility for a person unable to function within the environment. A physical therapist can best assess the child's needs and identify the most appropriate chair to meet the child's and family's needs.

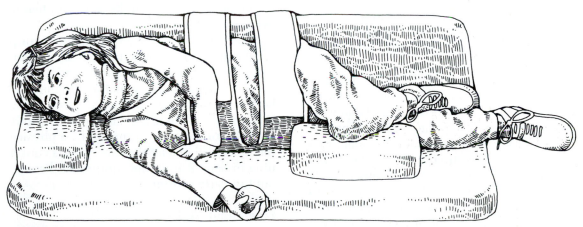

FIGURE 12.2
Example of a Sidelyer

FIGURE 12.3
Example of a Prone Stander

FIGURE 12.4
Example of a Modified Chair

Assistive devices that may aid a child in ambulation or working include rollator walkers or walkers with wheels, non-rolling walkers, and crutches, either axillary or lofstrand (Figures 12.9–12.12). The purpose of these assistive devices is to provide postural support in the upright position and allow the child to move through the environment.

Lower-extremity orthoses, also identified as braces and splinting, may also be necessary for children with physical impairments (Figures 12.13 and 12.14). The decision to use an orthosis should be based on the physical therapy assessment of range of motion, muscle strength, and alignment of the lower extremity.

The devices used may vary from the more traditional metal upright, to a molded plastic splint worn in the shoe providing support to the foot, ankle, and, if necessary, the knee. Additional orthoses are available and may be recommended based on the physical therapy assessment.

Selecting and purchasing adaptive equipment can be an overwhelming and time-consuming process. Professionals and parents should jointly decide which equipment can best meet the needs of the child and fit the lifestyle of the home and classroom. Periodic re-evaluation of the equipment by a physical therapist will ensure that the child is continuing to benefit from the equipment throughout the daily routine.

Fine Motor Skills

Fine motor skills, particularly those required for accurate and efficient use of the hands

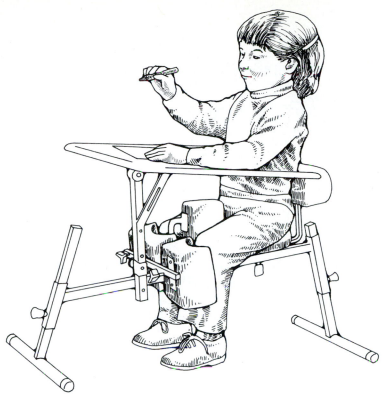

FIGURE 12.5
Example of a Modified Chair

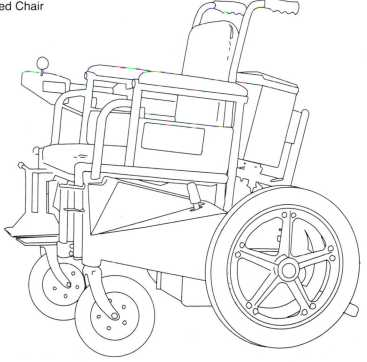

FIGURE 12.6
Example of a Wheelchair

427

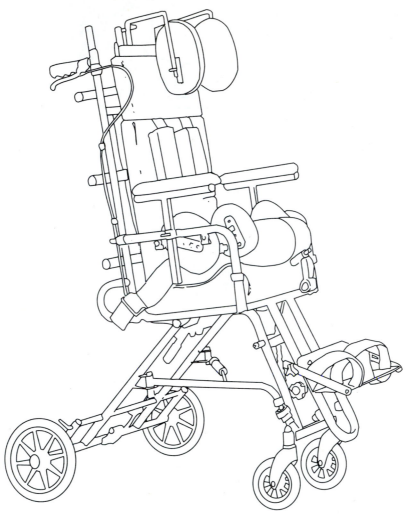

FIGURE 12.7
Example of a Wheelchair

and fingers, develop in a relatively predictable fashion.

The development sequence of grasp patterns is displayed in Figure 12.15 (p. 432). At birth, infants exhibit a *reflexive-palmar grasp*. This grasp is stimulated when an object comes in contact with the palm and involves closing the fingers around the object. The thumb may wrap around the object in the same or opposite direction as the fingers. However, the thumb is not important in this grasp and is not used in opposition (Livingston & Chandler, 1977).

The *ulnar-palmer grasp* and all subsequent grasps are volitional rather than reflexive; that is, the child can use them in the absence of direct object stimulation. The little finger and ring finger and on occasion the middle finger are used to secure the object against the palm. The thumb is not used in opposition to the fingers (Livingston & Chandler, 1977). The ulnar-palmar grasp is some-

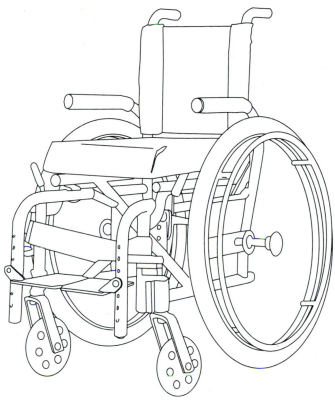

FIGURE 12.8
Example of a Wheelchair

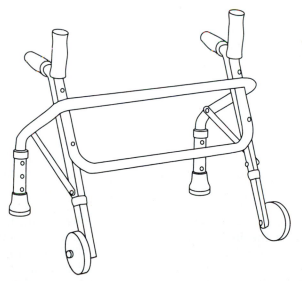

FIGURE 12.9
Example of Assistive Device for Walking

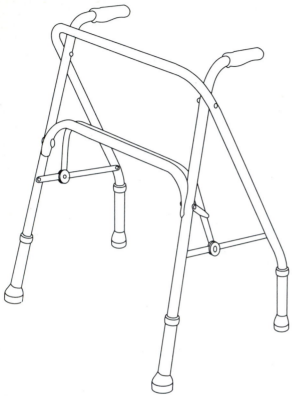

FIGURE 12.10
Example of Assistive Device for Walking

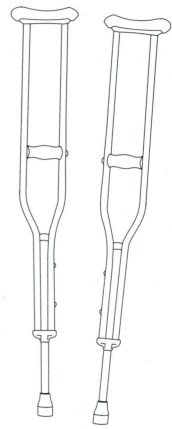

FIGURE 12.11
Example of Assistive Device for Walking

times called the *dagger grasp* because the manipulandum, the grasped and manipulated object, protrudes from the ulnar side of the hand like a dagger (Molloy, 1972).

In the *radial-palmar grasp*, the index and middle fingers hold the manipulandum against the palm of the hand (Livingston & Chandler, 1977) and the thumb may be used. This grasp is also called the *shovel grasp* because the manipulandum may protrude from the radial side of the hand like the head of a shovel (Molloy, 1972).

The *scissors grasp* involves the thumb in opposition to the side of the index finger. The point of contact on the index finger is usually farther out (more distal) toward the end of the finger than the radial-digital grasp (Livingston & Chandler, 1977; Molloy, 1972).

The *radial-digital grasp* involves the thumb used in opposition to the middle and index fingers, frequently at the base of the fingers (Cohen & Gross, 1979). The movement of the manipulandum away from the palm of the hand as in the radial-palmar grasp indicates the proximal-to-distal direction of development.

The *pincer grasp* involves picking up small objects with the thumb in opposition to the ends of the index and/or the middle fingers. The child must rest an arm on a surface. The neat or fine pincer grasp develops later and does not require resting the arm on a surface.

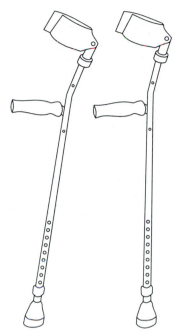

FIGURE 12.12
Example of Assistive Device for Walking

FIGURE 12.13
Example of Braces

The development of grasp patterns is accomplished in normally developing children within the first year of life (Cohen & Gross, 1979). However, the ability to use these grasps is refined throughout the preschool years. The strength, speed, and coordination of these grasp patterns increases as children grow older.

Selecting Materials for Fine Motor Training

Nearly every preschool program has a variety of materials frequently referred to as "fine motor materials" or as "manipulative toys." Common examples are puzzles, blocks, shape-sorting toys, clay, peg boards, form boards, crayons, threading and stacking toys, nesting cups, and construction sets. Often, time is devoted to these materials without careful consideration of the objectives, child's needs, or the sequences through which children can meet the objectives. Teachers should clearly

identify the purposes for which they use manipulative toys, including facilitating grasp acquisition and refinement (proficiency); eye-hand coordination; specific arm movements while maintaining grasps on objects; independent play; persistence at tasks (see Chap-

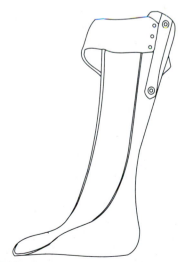

FIGURE 12.14
Example of Braces

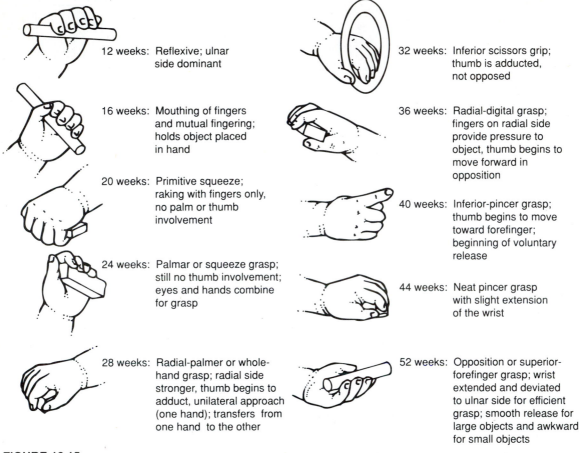

12 weeks: Reflexive; ulnar side dominant

16 weeks: Mouthing of fingers and mutual fingering; holds object placed in hand

20 weeks: Primitive squeeze; raking with fingers only, no palm or thumb involvement

24 weeks: Palmar or squeeze grasp; still no thumb involvement; eyes and hands combine for grasp

28 weeks: Radial-palmer or whole-hand grasp; radial side stronger, thumb begins to adduct, unilateral approach (one hand); transfers from one hand to the other

32 weeks: Inferior scissors grip; thumb is adducted, not opposed

36 weeks: Radial-digital grasp; fingers on radial side provide pressure to object, thumb begins to move forward in opposition

40 weeks: Inferior-pincer grasp; thumb begins to move toward forefinger; beginning of voluntary release

44 weeks: Neat pincer grasp with slight extension of the wrist

52 weeks: Opposition or superior-forefinger grasp; wrist extended and deviated to ulnar side for efficient grasp; smooth release for large objects and awkward for small objects

FIGURE 12.15
Fine Motor Skills: Grasp Patterns

ter 7); social skills such as turn-taking; and cognitive skills such as part-whole relationships, size, form, and color relationships, and problem-solving.

Many manipulative materials can be used to assist children in developing and practicing proficient grasping. An assessment of the child's functional grasps should be done by comparing grasps to the sequence of grasps in Figure 12.15. Materials should then be provided to stimulate the use of the given target grasp, with emphasis on grasping a variety of objects, rather than one or two.

When children begin to use a pincer grasp proficiently, present functional activities such as fastening clothing and opening milk cartons. In addition, more time should be spent on activities to develop proficiency in using pencils, such as coloring and painting. Milone and Wasylyk (1981) describe the grasps and strokes necessary for painting.

When using manipulative toys to teach eye-hand coordination, the teacher should remember that eye-hand coordination means the eyes guide the hands and the hands in turn guide the eyes. Thus, to facilitate this mutual guiding and following, the teacher should be sure the child looks at the toys while manipulating them. Many children manipulate toys in a haphazard manner without looking at what their hands are doing and thus do not learn eye-hand coordination. Toys that require progressively more eye-hand coordination should be used as children acquire this skill. The eyes also guide other movements of the body such as reaching, tool use, foot movements, and locomotion. DeOreo and William (1980) describe the relationships between vision and motor skills.

If training is to stimulate arm movements, select toys that produce a result when moved. For example, a mobile produces an interesting sight when touched. A toy hammer produces a sound and the object pounded may move or change form. Several arm movements are needed to facilitate functional manipulation of objects in the environment. These are hand-to-mouth movement, slapping, pushing, shaking, poking, pulling, and wrist rotation. In addition, grasped objects frequently must be held while the movement occurs and some movements must be performed with both arms at the same time (Molloy, 1972). Select materials that stimulate the targeted arm movement.

Finally, materials and skills used in fine motor training should be functional. Skills should be taught when the child has acquired the necessary developmental precursors. However, at issue is whether the materials used in teaching should be real or artificial. For example, when teaching a basic self-help task such as buttoning a shirt, should the teacher use an artificial aid such as a buttoning board? Or should realistic materials such as buttons and an enlarged buttonhole be employed? The child may not generalize from the buttoning board to the real task; thus training using the artificial materials may be more lengthy than necessary. It is also difficult to approximate real

task conditions of buttoning by using a board, particularly since relative positions of persons and materials will be different. Therefore, the more efficient instructional strategy would be to use the real materials, modifying them to the needs of each child. Artificial materials should be used sparingly.

Another example related to the training of functional motor skills is in the area of writing. Many teachers require children to draw certain shapes in preparation for writing letters. A common shape included on many assessment tools is a rectangle with diagonal lines connecting the corners. This skill alone is not very functional since children are never asked to draw that shape in the real world (except when taking a test!). This skill is taught because it is on the tests and because it is assumed to be good practice for teaching writing. But why not go ahead and begin simple letter writing, which can be simpler and more functional? Given the limited amount of teaching time coupled with children's developmental delays, teachers should focus on developmentally appropriate yet functional skills.

Direct Instruction of Skills

Although children learn many motor skills through day-to-day experience, many children with disabilities will need direct instruction to learn or refine those skills. The direct instruction process in teaching fine motor skills is similar to that used in teaching other skills. An appropriate skill is targeted, expected levels of performance are specified, and instruction begins. Teachers often provide assistance, either through physical prompts and manipulations or cues or models.

SUMMARY

This chapter has described traditional and contemporary concepts in motor development and the impact contemporary concepts may have on evaluating and working with children who have motor impairments. The areas of primary concern in motor development include innate motor behaviors, motor milestones, postural control, and motor learning.

Reflexes allow us to evaluate the status of the nervous system and the continuity of the neural circuitry, but they do not address the dynamic nature of development. With current treatment based on functional tasks rather than inhibiting abnormal motor responses, the importance of evaluating reflexes is diminished.

Using motor learning by varying the task, environment, and practice is essential for developing and improving motor skills in children with motor impairments. The importance of teaching functional motor skills that will maximize a child's independence was discussed throughout the chapter. Finally, the importance of consulting with therapists

when developing instructional programs was emphasized.

Two case studies are included at the end of the chapter to give examples of how some techniques might be used to help facilitate motor skills. Also, a glossary of special terms is provided in Box 12.1.

CASE HISTORY

Tammy is a 2-year-old girl who has had a history of seizures since 3 months of age. She has up to 20 seizures per day which doctors have been unsuccessful at controlling through medication. She has a history of respiratory infections but is currently healthy. Her family has recently moved from a rural location to a larger metropolitan area. Tammy's mother is currently 6 months pregnant and concerned that she will soon be unable to carry Tammy. Tammy is receiving physical therapy 2 times per week at an early intervention program.

BOX 12.1   Glossary of terms

Feedback: Sensory information that is contingent on having produced a movement.

Feedforward: Sending information ahead of time to ready a part of the system for incoming sensory feedback or for a future motor command.

Gait: A manner of walking, stepping, or running.

Hypertonia: Increased muscle tone; stiffness in the muscles.

Hypotonia: Decreased muscle tone; floppy muscles.

Muscle Synergy: Activation of two or more muscles in a consistent sequence.

Muscle Tone: The normal state of tension or firmness of the muscles.

Musculoskeletal System: Muscles, bones, cartilage, ligament, and tendons that interact to produce a movement.

Neuromuscular System: Muscles and nerves that interact to produce a movement.

Proprioception: Sensory information about the movement and position of the extremities without input from the visual system.

Range of motion: Displacement of a body part through an arc of movement.

Spasticity: Increased resistance to passive movement.

Vestibular System: Receptors in the inner ear that are sensitive to the orientation of the head with respect to gravity, rotation of the head, and balance.

Current Status

Tammy rolls across the room to attain desired objects. Rolling is currently her only means of independent mobility. She is able to sit with minimal support but cannot sit independently. Joint and muscle range of motion are within normal limits in both arms. In the lower extremities, she has tightness in her heelcords, hip, and knee flexor muscles. Her trunk and extremities are mildly hypotonic. Muscle strength is decreased in the trunk and legs.

Focus of Physical Therapy

Problem #1: Tammy's mom expressed concern over carrying Tammy after her new sibling arrives. Rolling is her only means of independent mobility.

Possible Solutions:

a. A modified stroller or pogon buggy will provide Tammy's family with a means of moving her within the environment without physically stressing family members. These pieces of equipment are visually attractive to family members while giving Tammy support and safe transportation.

b. A wheelchair is less appealing than a stroller or pogon buggy but may provide a better seating device and ultimately a long-term piece of adaptive equipment.

Problem #2: Tightness in heelcords, hip, and knee flexors

Solutions:

a. Molded plastic ankle-foot orthoses (AFO's) for both lower extremities will provide passive range-of-motion stretching and functional alignment of the involved joints.

b. Positioning suggestions for Tammy's family, including using the prone stander or while supported at a low table to stretch the muscles in her lower extremities.

c. Range-of-motion exercises to decrease tightness in her ankles, knees, and hips will passively move her lower extremities through her current arc of motion and gradually increase motion at all joints.

Problem #3: Decreased muscle strength in both lower extremities and trunk

Solution:

a. Tammy will receive physical therapy 2 times per week to improve muscle strength in her trunk and legs. The therapist will position Tammy to maximize her independent movement against gravity.

b. A modified seating device will support Tammy during feeding, fine motor, and cognitive activities. The modified seating device will maximize support while providing a safe, functional seating device.

c. A home exercise program, requested by Tammy's family, devised to improve her muscle strength through positioning and exercises. Tammy's physical therapy is limited to 2 times per week but her needs are 24 hours per day, 7 days per week. Her family can provide daily exercise programs to maximize her strength and functional outcome.

CASE HISTORY

Peter is a 10-month-old boy who had an uncomplicated birth and neonatal course. At 4 months of age, Peter's family realized he was not smiling, focusing on, or following faces or brightly colored objects. Subsequently he was diagnosed as having a severe visual impairment.

Current Status

Peter props on his elbows but does not prop on extended arms or get on hands or knees. He sits when supported but is unable to sit independently. He rolls towards sound (i.e., a musical toy) or his family talking to him. He is extremely cautious about movement and becomes extremely anxious if placed in prone. Joint and muscle range of motion are within normal limits in all extremities and trunk. His muscle tone is generally hypotonic. Muscle strength is decreased in Peter's neck and trunk.

Focus of Intervention

Problem #1: Peter is unable to sit independently.

Solution

a. Weekly physical therapy to develop postural control in sitting on multi-texture surfaces. Altering the texture and surface level to more closely resemble the experiences of children without visual impairment provide children with visual impairments more typical experiences.

b. Suggestions for his day-care center to carry out activities that would facilitate sitting, development. Varying the level of trunk support and increasing the time spent in sitting will improve Peter's strength, endurance, and motor development.

Problem #2: Peter is anxious when placed in standing and will not take any steps.

Solution

a. Use sturdy furniture for support to encourage standing and auditory stimuli to facilitate cruising along furniture. Most children without visual impairments can utilize vision and are more adventuresome than children with visual impairments.

b. Use alternative environments. For example, use water to encourage walking while providing different levels of support. Water will require less strength, since body weight is less with support from the water to provide stability and decrease anxiety.

Problem #3: Peter's muscle strength is decreased and tone hypotonic in his trunk.

Solution:

a. Adaptive equipment provides support and can be gradually reduced as strength increases. Adaptive equipment can be used for safe positioning, as well as to increase muscle strength and endurance.

b. Use auditory stimuli to motivate and facilitate trunk extension and improve muscle strength. Visual stimuli are highly motivating for normally developing children but alternatives are needed for infants with visual impairments.

c. Use home programs to encourage trunk extension through play (e.g., airplane or horse games sitting on an adult's legs). Encourage motor skill development through parent-child interaction and improve strength in the extremities and trunk.

REFERENCES

Als, H., & Brazelton, T. B. (1981). A new model for assessing the behavioral organization in preterm and full-term infants. *Journal of the American Academy of Child Psychiatry, 20*, 239–263.

Batshaw, N. L., & Perret, Y. M. (1986). *Children with handicaps: A medical primer* (2nd ed.). Baltimore: Paul H. Brookes.

Bayley, N. (1969). *Bayley scales of infant development.* New York: Psychological Corporation.

Bergan, A. (1982). *Positioning the client with central nervous system deficits: The wheelchair and other adapted equipment.* New York: Valhalla Press.

Bigge, K. L. (1991). *Teaching individuals with physical and multiple disabilities.* Columbus, OH: Merrill.

Bobath, K. (1980). *A neurophysiological basis for the treatment of cerebral palsy.* Philadelphia: J. B. Lippincott.

Bradley, N. S. (1989). *Physical therapy course 581–318: Applied neurology.* Unpublished manuscript, McGill University, Montreal, Quebec, Canada.

Bragg, J. H., Houser, C., & Schumaker, J. (1975). Behavior modifications: Effects on reverse tailor sittings in children with cerebral palsy. *Physical Therapy, 55*, 860–868.

Brazelton, T. B. (1984). *Neonatal Behavioral Assessment Scale.* Philadelphia: J.B. Lippincott.

Brooks, V. B. (1986). *The neural basis of motor control.* New York: Oxford University Press.

Butterworth, G., & Hicks, L. (1977). Visual proprioception and postural stability in infancy. A developmental study. *Perception, 6,* 255–262.

Capute, A. J., Shapiro, B. K. Palmer, F. B. (1981). Spectrum of developmental disabilities. Continuum of motor dysfunction. *Orthopedic Clinics of North America, 12,* 3–22.

Chandler, L. S., Andrews, M. S., & Swanson, M. W. (1980). *Movement assessment of infants.* Rolling Bay, WA: Authors.

Coghill, G. E. (1929). *Anatomy and the problems of behavior.* New York: Hafner.

Cohen, M., & Gross, P. (1979). *The developmental resource: Behavioral sequences for assessment and program planning* (Vol. 1). New York: Grune & Stratton.

Cross, D. P. (1981). Physical disabilities. In A. E. Blackhurst & W. H. Berdine (Eds.), *An introduction to special education.* Boston: Little, Brown.

DeOreo, K., & William, H. G. (1980). Characteristics of visual perception. In C. B. Corbin (Ed.), *A textbook of motor development.* Dubuque, IA: William C. Brown.

deVries, J. I. P., Visser, G. H. A., Prechtl, H. F. R. (1982). The emergence of fetal behavior: 1. Qualitative aspects. *Early Human Development, 7,* 301–311.

deVries, J. I. P., Visser, G. H. A., Prechtl, H. F. R. (1985). The emergence of fetal behavior: 2. Quantitative aspects. *Early Human Development, 12,* 99–120.

Duncan, P. W., & Badke, M. B. (1987). Determinants of abnormal motor control. In P. W. Duncan and M. B. Badke (Eds.), *Stroke rehabilitation: The recovery of motor control* (pp. 135–159). Chicago: Yearbook Medical Publishers.

Fiorentino, M. (1972). *Reflex testing methods for evaluating CNS development.* Springfield, IL: Charles E. Thomas.

Folio, R., & DuBose, R. F. (1974). *Peabody Developmental Motor Scales* (rev. experimental ed.). Nashville: Institute on Mental Retardation and Intellectual Development.

Forssberg, H., Nashner, L. M. (1982). Ontogenetic development of postural control in man: Adaptation to altered support and visual conditions. *Journal of Neuroscience, 2*(5), 545–552.

Furuno, S., O'Reilly, K. A., Hosaka, C. M., Inatsuka, T. T., Allman, T. L., & Zeisloft, B. (1979). *The Hawaii Early Learning Profile.* Palo Alto, CA: Vort.

Gesell, A. (1940). *The first five years of life.* New York: Harper.

Gesell, A. (1945). *The embryology of behavior:* New York: Harper.

Girolami, G. (1987). *Evaluating the effect of a neurodevelopmental treatment physical therapy program to improve motor control of high risk pre-term infants.* Unpublished master's thesis, University of North Carolina at Chapel Hill, Chapel Hill, NC.

Giuliani, C. A. (1991). Current theoretical issues in motor control. *Proceedings of the II Step Conference,* Norman, OK.

Gordon, J. (1987). Assumptions underlying physical therapy intervention: Theoretical and historical perspectives. In J. Carr, R. Shepard, J. Gordon, A. Gentile, & J. Held (Eds.), *Movement Science* (pp. 1–30). Rockville, MD: Aspen Press.

Harbourne, R. T., & Giuliani, C. A. (1988). A kinematic and electromyographic analysis of sitting posture in infants. Unpublished master's thesis, University of North Carolina at Chapel Hill, Chapel Hill, NC.

Heriza, C. B. (1991). Implications of a dynamical systems approach to understanding infant kicking behavior. *Physical Therapy, 71*(3), 222–235.

Homme, L. E., DeBaca, P. C., Devine, J. V., Steinhorst, R., & Rickert, E. J. (1968). Use of the Premack principle in controlling the behavior of nursery school children. *Journal of the Experimental Analysis of Behavior, 6,* 544.

Hooker, D., & Humphrey, T. (1954). Some results and deductions from a study of the development of human fetal behavior. *Gazette of Medicine,* Port. 7, 189–197.

Horak, F. (1987). Clinical measurement of postural control in adults. *Physical Therapy, 67*(12), 1881–1885.

Horn, E. M. (1991). Basic motor skills instruction for children with neuromotor delays: A critical review. *The Journal of Special Education, 25*(2), 168–197.

Jackson, J. H. (1932). Relations of different divisions of the central nervous system to one another and to parts of the body. In J. Taylor (Ed.). *Selected Writings of John Hughlings Jackson.* London, Hodder, and Stoughton Ltd.

Janssen, C., & Guess, D. (1978). Use of function as a consequence in training receptive labeling to severely and profoundly retarded individuals. AAESPH Review, 3, 246–258.

Jejka, J. J., & Kelso, J. A. S. (1989). The dynamic pattern approach to coordinated behavior: A tutorial review. In S. A. Wallace (Ed.), *Perspectives on the Coordination of Movement* (pp. 2–45). New York: Elsevier Science Publishers.

Kamm, K., Thelan, E., & Jensen, J. L. (1990). A dynamical systems approach to motor development. *Physical Therapy, 70*(12), 17–29.

Lee, D. N., & Aronson, E. (1974). Visual proprioceptive control of standing in human infants. *Perception and Psychophysics, 15,* 529–532.

Livingston, S. S., & Chandler, L. S. (1977). Fine motor development and skill development. In N. G. Haring (Ed.), *The experimental education training program.* Seattle: Experimental Education Unit.

McGraw, M. B. (1943). *Neuromuscular maturation of the human infant* (2nd ed.). New York: Hafner.

Milner-Brown, H. S., & Penn, R. (1979). Pathological mechanisms in cerebral palsy. *Journal of Neurosurgery and Psychology, 42,* 606–618.

Milone, M. N., & Waslylyk, T. M. (1981). Handwriting in special education. *Teaching Exceptional Children, 14,* 58–61.

Molloy, J. S. (1972). *Trainable children: Curriculum and procedures.* New York: John Day.

Morrissey, R. T. (1978). Spina bifida: A new rehabilitation problem. *Orthopedic Clinics of North America, 9,* 379–389.

Myers, G. J. (1984). Myelomeningocele: The medical aspects. *Pediatric Clinics of North America, 31,* 165–175.

Newborg, J., Stock, J. R., Wnek, L., Guidubaldi, J., & Svinicki, J. (1984). *Battelle Developmental Inventory.* Allen, TX: DLM Teaching Resources.

O'Brien, F., Azrin, N. H., & Bugle, C. (1972). Training profoundly retarded children to stop crawling. *Journal of Applied Behavior Analysis, 5,* 131–137.

Russo, L. M. (1979). Fun stuff: Having a ball. *Exceptional Parent, 9,* 55–58.

Schmidt, R. A. (1988). *Motor learning and motor control* (2nd ed.). Champaign, IL: Human Kinetics.

Schmidt, R. A. (1989). Motor and action perspectives on motor behavior. In O. G. Meijer & K. Roth (Eds.), *Complex motor behavior: The motor-action controversy* (pp. 3–44). New York: Elsevier Science Publishers.

Sherrington, C. S. (1906). *The integrated action of the nervous system.* London: Constable.

Shumway-Cook, A., & Woollacott, M. H. (1985). The growth of stability: Postural control from a developmental perspective. *Journal of Motor Behavior, 17,* 131–147.

Smidt, G. L., & Rogers, M. W. (1982). Factors contributing to the regulation and clinical assessment of muscular strength. *Physical Therapy, 62,* 1283–1290.

Smith, P. D. (1989). Assessing motor skills. In D. Bailey & M. Wolery, (Eds.), *Assessing infants and preschoolers with handicaps* (pp. 301–338). Columbus: Merrill.

Sparling, J. W., Wilhelm, I. J., McLeod, A. M., Green, S., Katz, V., & Huntington, G. S. (1990). The study of fetal movement. *Physical and Occupational Therapy in Pediatrics, 10*(1), 43–46.

Stallings, L. M. (1973). *Motor skills, development, and learning.* Dubuque, IA: W. C. Brown.

Tappit-Emas, E. (1989). Spina bifida. In J. S. Tecklin (Ed.), *Pediatric physical therapy* (pp. 106–140). Philadelphia: J. P. Lippincott.

Tecklin, J. S. (1989). Pulmonary disorders in infants and children and their physical therapy management. In J. S. Tecklin (Ed.), *Pediatric physical therapy* (pp. 141–172). Philadelphia: J. P. Lippincott.

Thelan, E. (1983). Learning to walk is still an "old" problem: A reply to Zelazo. *Journal of Motor Behavior, 15,* 139–161.

Thelan, E. (1985). Developmental origins of motor

coordination: Leg movements in human infants. *Developmental Psychobiology, 18*(1), 1–22.

Thelan, E. & Cooke, D. W. (1987). Relationship between newborn stepping and later walking: A new interpretation. *Developmental Medicine and Child Neurology, 29,* 380–393.

Thelan, E., Fisher, D. M., & Ridley-Johnson, R. (1984). The relationship between physical growth and a newborn reflex. *Infant Behavior and Development, 7,* 479–493.

Wolinsky, G., & Walker, S. (1973). A home safety inventory for parents of preschool handicapped children. *Teaching Exceptional Children, 6,* 82–86.

Feeding and Nutritional Issues

Martha L. Venn

Ariane Holcombe

Mark Wolery

Feeding and mealtimes are unique routines that fulfill important functions and require a number of varied skills. Adequate intake of nutrients is central to maintaining life and good health, and feeding is a lifelong activity that addresses basic universal human and bodily needs. Feeding is, however, much more than a simple means for receiving adequate nutrition. In our culture eating is a social activity that serves many necessary functions. Meals, for example, are treated as recreational and leisure activities, and they are used for conducting business, for maintaining ethnic identity, and for celebrating important events. Meals also have unique family functions. We use meals as the context for ensuring communication between family members, for strengthening social interactions and relationships, for passing on important information to our children, and for building family cohesion and unity. For these reasons, mealtimes are occasions that can serve families with salient cues for judging their adequacy and worth.

When infants and young children have developmental delays and disabilities, their feeding skills may also lag behind the usual course of development. Children with disabilities may experience problems that interfere with adequate nutrient intake; that require excessive demands on parents' skills, time, and effort; and that set the stage for negative interactions and counterproductive exchanges to develop. As a result, eating, self-feeding, and mealtimes may be high-priority issues for many families of infants and young children with disabilities, and they may be critical curricular areas for early intervention personnel.

In this chapter, we describe many issues related to feeding and nutrition. We begin with a discussion of four general statements about feeding and then describe the developmental course of early feeding behaviors and the effects of different disabilities. We then present procedures and guidelines for addressing feeding problems and for teaching feeding skills. The chapter concludes with a discussion of nutritional issues.

GENERAL STATEMENTS ABOUT THE FEEDING PROCESS

In this section, four foundational statements about early intervention and feeding are made. The *feeding process*, as described in this chapter, involves caregiver behaviors related to ensuring adequate nutrition intake, the abilities and skills of infants and young children related to food and liquid intake, the gradual teaching of children to feed themselves independently, and all the interventions necessary to accomplish adequate nutritional intake and conformity with societal expectations for mealtime routines.

Family and Professional Roles in the Feeding Process are Critical

In the past, early services and activities related to the feeding process were delivered through variations of the "medical model." The professional assumed the role of "expert" and deliverer of prescriptive information. Families assumed the roles of receiving information and following advice. Parents often became passive recipients of information rather than active partners in their children's programs, and dependency on early intervention and health-care professionals was promoted (Bazyk, 1990; Dunst, Trivette, & Deal, 1988). In this situation, parents were at risk for developing a sense of helplessness about their caregiving abilities (Dunst et al., 1988).

As the field matured, professionals came to recognize the importance of family involvement in the education of children. This recognition was operationalized in P.L. 94–142, which provided a legal mandate to include parent participation in planning and delivering services to eligible children with disabilities. Unfortunately, in practice, professionals still maintained control of much of the decision making about intervention and the delivery of services. Two new roles, however, were created for parents—the role of teacher/therapist and the role of nominal team member. As a result, parents frequently were overburdened with responsibilities and spoken and unspoken expectations by professionals. This situation gave rise to compliance/noncompliance issues related to "following through" on home programs (Bazyk, 1990).

Fortunately, the field also recognized, through the persistence of vocal families (cf. Winton & Turnbull, 1981), the inadequacies of this approach. As a result, a shift in perspective occurred. Importance has been placed on providing interventions that are ecologically sensitive (chapter 6) and family-focused (Bailey & Simeonsson, 1988), interventions that are designed to promote family strength and well-being (Dunst et al., 1988). Working from this new perspective, professionals seek to build intervention services on an identification of family needs and family members' perceptions of their needs, an understanding of family structure and of the roles played by various family members, a knowledge of the support and resources that are available, and an appreciation of family goals and aspirations. The new perspective has been operationalized in P.L. 99–457, particularly in the sections of the law dealing with infants and toddlers.

The roles of families and professionals have shifted. As we indicated in chapter 4, the role of the family in assessment activities has expanded to involve more active participation in the collection and use of relevant information. The family's role in intervention also has changed. Families are more active in deciding what interventions should be used *and* in determining the role they will play in the implementation of those inter-

ventions. The role of the professional, of necessity, has shifted from primary decision maker to participant in a joint decision-making process. Professionals have shifted from directing to supporting family behavior, from making prescriptions to attempting to fit recommendations to realities.

These role shifts are particularly important in feeding programs. This importance occurs because unlike most other areas of the curriculum, we cannot avoid it. We can delay or avoid teaching specific dressing skills, addressing particular social competencies, or working on particular physical and communication skills. But the feeding program is one area of the curriculum that we cannot avoid. Feeding must occur daily, and intervention in the feeding process cannot be delayed. Because parents are responsible for many feeding activities, they can use their day-to-day experiences to provide valuable insight into their children's strengths and needs and into their own concerns about feeding (Morris & Klein, 1987). Further, the shifting roles of professionals and families are important because, as we have noted, feeding and mealtime routines are occasions families may use for judging the adequacy of their parenting skills and of their family in general.

The Feeding Process Fills Many Functions

The most basic function fulfilled by feeding is the ensuring of adequate nutritional intake. Several different disabilities and conditions—for example, very low birth weight, sensory impairments, Down syndrome, neuromotor impairments, Prader-Willi syndrome, psychosocial dwarfism, metabolic conditions, and combinations of sensory, physical, and intellectual impairments—may negatively affect feeding routines and adequate nutrient intake. Thus, nutritional intake is a critical issue in the assessment and intervention of many infants and young children with disabilities (Morris & Klein, 1987; Ore-love & Sobsey, 1987; Solis, Chustz, McCarty, & Stotko, 1989; Snell, 1987). Nutritional problems common in infants and young children with disabilities include poor growth and failure to thrive, overweight and obesity, constipation, medication-nutrient interactions, malnutrition due to multiple separate and interactive factors, iron-deficiency anemia, and food allergies (Brizee, Sophos, & McLaughlin, 1990; Pipes, 1983; Werner, 1987).

As we have noted, feeding and mealtimes fulfill cultural and familial functions. Families of infants with disabilities may face immediate and unavoidable issues related to feeding. Infants spend a large portion of their awake time feeding, and their feeding is inherently interactional. Besides providing life-sustaining nutrition, the feeding activity promotes parent–infant interaction and attachment, builds a sense of trust, creates opportunities for contingent sensory input and feedback, and develops early communicative interactions between infant and caregiver (Gorga, 1989; Kleinert, 1990). The teaching of self-feeding skills provides an opportunity for promoting independence and social competencies (Morris & Klein, 1987; Snell, 1987). Mealtimes present opportunities for carrying on meaningful conversations, increasing social interactions, and facilitating the development of cognitive skills (Jewett & Clark, 1979).

The Process of Feeding Is a Longitudinal Endeavor

Like many other skills that comprise the early childhood curriculum, feeding, self-feeding, and mealtime behaviors are learned throughout the early childhood years. With young infants, intervention may focus on ensuring that adequate nutrition is being secured and on helping the parent read and respond appropriately to the infant's cues related to feeding. With older infants, it may involve determining the types and consistency of foods that should be fed, assessing oral motor functioning, and helping parents engage in mutually satisfying interactions related to feeding. With toddlers, intervention may involve selecting foods that are appropriate for the child's oral abilities, assisting families in allowing more independence in feeding, and integrating the child's feeding with the mealtime routines of other family members. With preschoolers, it may involve teaching self-feeding behaviors, teaching the social expectations related to feeding skills, establishing good eating habits, and helping families establish mealtime routines that are growth promoting and pleasant. Thus, intervention teams must be skilled in dealing with a wide range of feeding behaviors, issues, and problems. Teams must be skilled in assessing infants and young children and providing instruction related to feeding and mealtime behaviors; and they must be skilled in assisting families to identify their concerns and take action to deal with them. It is likely that most infants, toddlers, and preschoolers will have some objectives in their individualized plans that deal with feeding and mealtime behaviors.

The Feeding Process Requires a Team Effort

The needs of the family in relation to feeding change as the infant becomes a toddler and then a young child. "The complex nature of this process emphasizes the importance of professionals being well-informed about public policy, available community services, and discipline-specific areas of expertise" (Dunn, 1989, p. 718). In any case in which such feeding and nutritional needs, difficulties, and changes are addressed, several professionals will come to play important team roles in the problem-solving and intervention process. Initially, parents—perhaps along with the early interventionist—may develop concern over some feeding/nutritional issue. Often this is the first step of the problem-solving and intervention process. After careful observations, parent reports, and initial screenings, the second step of the process should be a formal referral by the early interventionist to one or more of the specialists on the program staff. Specialists who may be consulted on feeding issues include occupational therapists, speech-language pathologists, physical therapists, nutritionists, pediatricians, and dentists. The roles of these specialists may, at times, overlap. It is important to remember that each member of the professional team provides a specific expertise in the feeding process. An occupational therapist can provide information on oral-motor functioning, self-feeding readiness, and interventions that will promote typical oral motor patterns (Pipes, 1983). A speech-language pathologist will be able to provide much of the same knowledge as the occupational therapist. In addition, the speech therapist may have a broad base of knowledge in regard to oral-motor development. The physical therapist can provide information related to proper positioning and adaptive equipment. Another possible team member is the nutritionist. The nutritionist can provide team members and parents with a knowledge of appropriate foods and of combinations of foods that will facilitate growth and development in infants and young children. Although many early intervention programs do not have a nutritionist on staff, local public health departments frequently employ such professionals. A pediatrician addresses such issues as overall health, food allergies, tube feeding, and surgical options for disabilities (e.g., cleft lip and cleft palate). A pediatric dentist may be consulted for infants and children with oral structure malformations (Morris & Klein, 1987) and should be consulted regularly for dental examinations.

In summary, early intervention with feeding and mealtime behaviors involves a recognition of some important issues. Families should determine their roles in feeding and should be active participants in the assessment of feeding and in the determination of feeding interventions. Feeding and mealtime routines fulfill many functions including ensuring adequate nutrient intake; promoting parent–child interactions and relationships; and teaching other important cognitive, social, and communicative behaviors. Because the feeding process is longitudinal, team members should be skilled in dealing with the many different issues related to the development of feeding behavior. Finally, the development of adequate feeding and mealtime behaviors is a team endeavor that requires careful coordination of the efforts of various professionals.

DEVELOPMENT OF THE ORAL MOTOR MECHANISM

The oral motor mechanism includes the mouth, its muscles, and the related movements. In this section we present a description of the normal sequences of oral motor movements. We understand these movement patterns on the basis of two developmental principles that operate simultaneously. The first principle: *With increased maturation, the oral reflexes become integrated.* Reflexes are automatic, stereotypic responses to particular environmental stimuli. For example, if you stick your finger down your mouth you will gag. That gag is a reflex; you do not have to think about doing it and trying to stop it probably will not keep it from occurring. The presence and pressure of your finger is the stimulus. Infants with typical development display several oral motor reflexes. Integration means that over time greater stimulation is required to produce the reflex and that the reflex does not occur as frequently when the stimulus is presented.

The second developmental principle has been referred to as the orthogenetic principle (Werner, 1957): *Development proceeds by differentiation and hierarchical integration.* The term *differentiation* refers to the separate use of the component parts of a behavior or muscle group. For example, initially the infant's tongue, lips, and jaw all appear to work as a unit rather than as separate parts. But as differentiation occurs, each part (i.e., the tongue, the lips, and the jaw) all come to move separately. You can probably clinch your jaw, move your tongue about on the inside of your mouth, and/or move your lips. Thus, your oral motor mechanism is differentiated. *Integration*, as it is understood in the orthogenetic principle, is different from the integration of the reflexes that we have just described. Under the orthogenetic principle, integration refers to the combining of the movements of differentiated behavior to form new more complex responses, and to the combining of responses into a hierarchy of progressively more complex skills. For example, you can use the differentiation of the oral mechanism to make different speech sounds, to chew, to bite, to whistle, and to suck.

Understanding these two principles will assist you in understanding the changes that we now describe in the development of children's feeding behavior. In the following paragraphs, the sequences of feeding behaviors are described for typically developing infants and young children. You should be aware that these sequences may not be relevant teaching sequences. When you see deviations, delayed development, and abnormal patterns of the oral mechanism, you should follow a simple guideline that will be presented repeatedly in this chapter: *Seek assistance from a qualified speech-language pathologist, occupational therapist, or other specialist.* While this general recommendation

to seek assistance from other professionals is relevant for many areas of development, it is particularly so for the development of feeding and eating skills. Use of inappropriate procedures or failure to use appropriate procedures may compound feeding problems and the stress and difficulties that families experience related to feeding. This leads to another general guideline, one that is presented throughout this chapter and this book—*much of the task of the early intervention professional is to reduce family stress and increase their sense of competence and self-sufficiency.*

Birth to 1 Month

At this age, infants' primary movements in regard to feeding are reflexive and appear to be designed to promote survival. The reflexes include rooting, suckle-swallow, and gag. In typically developing infants, the rooting reflex is present from birth until the infant is 3 to 4 months of age and is observed as the infant turns toward the source of food. It is activated by providing stimulation to the corners of the mouth and to the upper and lower lips. The first pattern to be developed by the infant is the suckle-swallow in which the tongue moves rhythmically forwards and backwards (Morris & Klein, 1987). This is activated by placing an external object (e.g. nipple) in the infant's mouth. The gag reflex serves to protect the infant from choking and is activated when a piece of food (or another object) is placed on the back of the tongue. This reflex may occur easily until the infant is able to tolerate stimulation on the back of the tongue.

The suckle-swallow is the most common source of feeding difficulty in children with developmental delays (Connor, Williamson, & Siepp, 1978). If the infant does not display a suckle-swallow reflex, abnormal eating behaviors (e.g. tongue thrust and jaw thrust) may develop (Copeland & Kimmel, 1989).

Tongue thrust is defined as "a forceful protrusion of the tongue from the mouth" (Morris, 1977, p. 159). "The tongue often appears thick or bunched during the thrust" (Morris, 1977, p. 159). Campbell (1990) defines jaw thrust as "a strong downward depression of the jaw accompanied by forward movement and increased postural tone" (p. 34). Problems which may affect the child's ability to suckle-swallow include respiratory problems which may alter breathing (Bazyk, 1990), poor breath control, or the lack of coordination of the tongue and lips (Mills & Hedges, 1983). If a child has suckle-swallow difficulties it is recommended that a referral be made to a qualified speech-language pathologist, occupational therapist, or physician for physical and oral structure examination. This examination may lead to the ascertaining of the cause of the difficulty and the development of recommendations concerning feeding (Connor et al., 1978).

2 to 3 Months

The infant still uses a suckle-swallow during this phase, with about three sucks before a swallow. The suck becomes both rhythmic and efficient, enabling the infant to consume approximately 8 ounces of liquid in 20 to 30 minutes (Morris & Klein, 1987). In the immature infant, short sucking bursts are followed by swallows which are arrhythmical (Solis et al., 1989). If the infant is fed pureed foods during this stage of development, coughing, choking, and gagging may occur. The caregiver will observe that motor movements (e.g., the opening of the mouth in anticipation of being fed) are used by infants at this age to express eating desires (Copeland & Kimmel, 1989).

4 to 6 Months

The child should begin eating in an upright position when she is 4 to 6 months old. Typically developing infants at this age recognize the bottle, open their mouths for the spoon, and may show food preferences. Reflexes have become integrated so that the infant is allowed to exhibit a strong suck, to coordinate and stabilize jaw movements without slowing, and to control the tongue and jaw. Tongue thrusting in response to the removal of a spoon or cup is considered normal for infants up to this age (Copeland & Kimmel, 1989). Drinking from a cup may be introduced at this time although the caregiver should attend closely to the child's drinking pattern. If the child does not have a coordinated suck and swallow, coughing and choking may occur while drinking as the result of a rapid flow of liquid (Morris & Klein, 1987).

7 to 9 Months

Finger feeding begins when the infant is 7 to 9 months old. The child frequently can transfer foods from the center to the side of the mouth, with the jaw and tongue exhibiting an up and down motion (e.g., munching). The upper lip becomes more active during this period and should close on the spoon or cup. In addition, the infant typically holds his own bottle or cup.

10 to 15 Months

A normally developing child will finger feed, begin to exhibit a rotary chewing pattern, bite through food, and drink from a cup by the time she is 15 months old. "Rotary movements in chewing involve the interaction of the jaw muscles which open and close the mouth and those which pull the jaw in a lateral or sideways direction" (Morris, 1977, p. 120). Self-feeding is emerging at this time, although it may be messy while the child is developing better lip closure. Choking and coughing should seldom occur, because the child now exhibits coordinated sucking sequences (Morris & Klein, 1987).

A controlled biting pattern emerges when the child is 10 to 12 months old. At this stage the child will be able to bite soft foods but will not have the strength to bite hard foods (e.g., meat). The ability to bite hard foods does not arrive until the child is approximately 21 months old.

The early interventionist should be aware of several problems related to biting. The child may exhibit a tonic bite reflex—a sudden tense bite with poor release. The tonic bite reflex is often seen in children who are tactilely defensive (Morris & Klein, 1987). It is activated by sensory stimulation to the teeth and gums. A rubber coated spoon with a flat bowl will allow the caregiver to feed the child without touching the teeth and gums. Interventionists are warned against placing their fingers in the mouth of a child with a strong bite reflex. If the child does bite on an object and cannot release the bite, do not attempt to pull the object from the child's mouth because this action will generally stimulate the reflex rather than allowing the object to be removed from the mouth. Instead, wait several seconds to allow the child an opportunity to relax the bite. If the waiting is not effective, then try applying slight pressure with your finger to the muscles at the back of the jaw while tilting the head forwards.

Another problem in regard to bite is the prolonged use of a phasic bite—that is, a reflexive bite and release pattern (Morris & Klein, 1987). The phasic bite is a stage of normal development in 5- to 6-month-old infants, but it is not considered a functional bite. This bite does not allow for the prolonged contraction of oral muscles that is needed to bite through hard or thick foods. If the child is using the phasic bite past the time he is 6 months old, the physician or qualified occupational therapist should be consulted.

15 to 24 Months

During this phase self-feeding skills are refined as a result of coordinated tongue and jaw movements. The child exhibits movement of the tongue independent of the jaw. Strong lip closure allows the child to drink and chew with little spillage from the mouth by the time she is 15 months old. Good rotary chewing enables the child to eat most solid food with a variety of textures. It is recommended that lumpy and chopped foods be introduced into the child's diet prior to the introduction of foods that require chewing. This will give the child experience with a variety of textures and stimulate the beginning of chewing patterns. By the time the child is 24 months old, a controlled bite should be established and the child should be able to hold a small cup with one hand and use an up and down sucking pattern to drink liquid.

The early interventionist is cautioned to beware of biting problems related to chewing, problems such as tonic bite, jaw thrust, and choking or gagging when foods that require chewing are placed in the child's mouth (Morris & Klein, 1987). Once chewing has become established the interventionist should observe whether the child is able to move food from the center to the side of the mouth and from the side to the center. Suspicion of chewing difficulties during the feeding routines should alert the interventionist to consult an occupational or physical therapist.

Severe choking is a frightening event for the infant or young child and for caregivers and other family members. An episode of choking can result in loss of air supply which in turn can produce brain injury and death. All individuals who feed infants and young children should know what to do when choking occurs. In Box 13.1 we present some guidance regarding choking.

ISSUES AND EFFECTS OF VARIOUS DISABILITIES

The development of feeding skills is complex and occurs over time. This development can be influenced negatively by a number of factors including different disabling conditions. Feeding issues and problems can also present a number of difficulties for families. We discuss these issues in the following paragraphs.

"An increasing number of critically ill and immature infants survive today due to recent advances in neonatology" (Bazyk, 1990, p. 1070). Risk factors associated with prematurity present a highly complex set of special needs and problems (Solis et al., 1989) addressed by physicians, nurses, occupational therapists, physical therapists, feeding specialists, caregivers, and early interventionists.

One of the earliest issues that should be addressed through the team approach is the impact of disabilities on feeding skill development, which begins with the newborn and may continue through the preschool years. As we have noted, support for the family should continue over time, through each feeding accomplishment and past each roadblock that occurs as infants grow into toddlers and then into preschoolers.

For caregivers, a series of stressors are not only focused on the feeding of their infants but also on their own perceptions of their parenting skills. In our culture, mothers frequently assume responsibility for meeting the feeding and nutritional needs of infants, either by breast-feeding or bottle feeding. "When an infant is difficult to feed, it is often traumatic for the family, strong feelings of inadequacy, helplessness and failure may arise" (Morris, 1977, p. 108). These same feelings may reoccur when mothers take their infants in for routine medical follow-up appointments and the medical staff measure weight gain over time. "Even when there is objective evidence that the child's feeding problems are unrelated to issues of mothering, often there is a nagging inner voice that tells us that if we were smart enough, or creative enough, or persistent enough, our child would be able to eat" (Morris & Klein, 1987, p. 319). Another family stressor may include the amount of time required to feed infants who are premature or disabled (Case-Smith, Cooper, & Scala, 1989; Morris, 1977). Morris (1977) reported that it is common for a single feeding to last 1½ to 2 hours and then be repeated four to six times a day. Such a schedule consumes the majority of a mother's time. This can be a frustrating and exhausting experience for the entire family.

In this section, we describe five types of disabilities that early interventionists may encounter—low birth weight infants, infants fed by tubes, infants with cleft lip/palate, infants with neuromotor impairments, and infants with Down syndrome—and we identify the associated potential feeding difficulties. For more extensive information see Morris and Klein (1987) and Semmler (1989).

Low Birth Weight Infants

The birth of a premature infant and the transition from the Neonatal Intensive Care Unit to the home is a sensitive period for the family. The infant's ability to consume food and to suck, swallow, and chew are affected by the immaturity of the central nervous system (Solis et al., 1989). Case-Smith et al. (1989) reported that infants with manifestations of central nervous system insults differed from nonstressed premature infants particularly in the temporal organization of rhythmical oral motor patterns. Premature infants "neurological immaturity, abnormal muscle tone, depressed oral reflexes, and overall weak

---

BOX 13.1   Guidelines for treating the choking child

"In children under the age of 6 years, aspiration of a foreign body is the leading cause of accidental death occurring at home" (Torrey, 1983, p. 751). There is a great deal of controversy regarding the most appropriate method of intervention for a choking child. The methods suggested most frequently in the medical literature are back blows (Torrey, 1983) and the Heimlich maneuver (Heimlich, 1982). Proponents of the use of back blows suggest that "back blows generate higher and faster pressure pulses, which might be more effective in dislodging a foreign body than the longer pulse resulting from abdominal or chest thrusts" (Torrey, 1983, p. 752). In contrast, those who recommend the Heimlich maneuver state that the use back blows results in a higher rate of internal damage than the use of the Heimlich maneuver (Heimlich, 1982).

Barkin and Rosen (1990) suggest that for children, and particularly for infants, a "combination of maneuvers may be more effective than any single method" (p. 646). They go on to add that "these methods of intervention are under constant reevaluation" (p. 646). Therefore it is suggested that agencies adopt program policies regarding choking emergencies. These policies should be made with the input of local medical professionals and be reevaluated periodically to reflect current "best practice." Although there is not a common consensus concerning the best intervention with a choking infant/child, there are some general guidelines which should be followed. These guidelines are divided into two categories (Don'ts and Do's) and are listed below.

Definite Don'ts

• *Don't pat the child on the back.* When someone is choking it is almost instinctive to lightly pat that person on the back as if you were burping a baby. This intervention is not suggested because it causes inhalation which may lead to aspiration or cause the object to become securely lodged in the throat (Heimlich, 1982; Mueller, 1975; Torrey, 1983).

---

and irritable state can decrease the quality of their oral-motor skills and the quantity of their intake" (Morris & Klein, 1987, p. 311). Common feeding problems that arise in the premature infant include (a) weak rooting reflexes due to abnormal muscle tone, (b) weak sucking which may result in longer feeding routines, (c) unorganized suck-swallow patterns, (d) aspiration problems, and (e) poor weight gain as a result of fatigue which may be attributable to inefficient sucking patterns (Case-Smith et al., 1989; Connor et al., 1978; Morris & Klein, 1987; Solis et al., 1989).

Infants Fed by Tubes

For some infants, feeding must occur through the use of a tube due to a variety of problems such as an inability to suck or swallow (Morris & Klein, 1987), congenital anomalies (Fee, Charney, & Robertson, 1988), cardiac defects (Bazyk, 1990), severe cleft lip and/ or palate (Shelly, Cowlishaw, & Galloway, 1989), and anatomical problems (Morris & Klein, 1987). Infants born under 34 weeks of gestation are often tube fed due to an undeveloped respiratory system (Bazyk, 1990).

Shelly et al. (1989) state four purposes for tube feedings: "(a) to ensure proper and adequate nourishment when an alternative feeding method is impossible or contraindicated, (b) to prevent aspiration and abdominal distention, (c) to conserve calories, which may be important for a preterm infant, and (d) to instill feedings and medications

- *Don't turn the child upside down.* If the foreign body is loose in the trachea and causing only partial obstruction of the airway, turning the child upside down may cause the object to slip between the vocal cords and completely obstruct the airway (Heimlich, 1982; Passy & McMaster, 1977).
- *Don't use the Heimlich maneuver without training on infants and children.* Without training specific to infants and children, use of the Heimlich maneuver may result in liver lacerations and damage to other internal organs (Torrey, 1983).
- *Don't use chest thrust.* This method is not recommended because it is impossible to know at what pressure the chest will be crushed. Asserting too much pressure may result in damage to the lungs, spleen, and heart (Heimlich, 1982).

Definite Do's

- *Attend to the child's breathing.* Before selecting the appropriate intervention you should know if the child is breathing partially or not at all.
- *Keep the child and others calm.* If the child is still breathing, he may be able to dislodge the object without assistance. Your obvious anxiety may alarm the child thus causing the object to become firmly lodged.
- *Establish program policy on what method to use in the event of a choking emergency.* Individual programs should gain advice from local medical professionals concerning the most appropriate intervention for dealing with infants and children who are choking.
- *Receive training related to infants and children in the selected method of intervention by trained professionals.* All staff members should be trained in the selected method of intervention. It is important that this training focus on the specific characteristics of infants and children. In addition, it is suggested that all staff members be trained in infant/child cardio-pulmonary resuscitation (CPR).

For additional information regarding choking see Barkin and Rosen (1990) and Whaley and Wong (1987).

safely and efficiently" (p. 162). The tube can be inserted through the infant's nostrils, mouth, or abdomen. A tube inserted through the nostrils that passes to the stomach is called a nasogastric (NG) tube. An oral gastric (OG) tube passes through the mouth to the stomach, and a gastrostomy tube (G) is placed through the abdominal wall into the stomach (Morris & Klein, 1987; Shelly et al., 1989) Tube-fed infants show an array of characteristics, including respiratory difficulties, disorganized and arrhythmical sucking patterns, swallowing disorders, and abnormal or aversive responses to oral stimulation (Morris & Klein, 1987).

"A critical, or sensitive, period in infancy exists wherein the failure to introduce liquid or solid foods by mouth may result in future feeding problems" (Bazyk, 1990; p. 1071). Infants fed with a nasogastric or oral gastric tube are particularly at risk for later oral motor problems (Bazyk, 1990; Moore & Greene, 1985; Morris & Klein, 1987). Feeding problems which specifically affect the infant include (a) the loss of small sucking and swallowing movements that may have been present but due to lack of stimulation and practice diminish; (b) an overall lack of sensory stimulation to the mouth that normally developing infants receive from the breast or bottle, spoon, cup, fingers, and toys (Morris & Klein, 1987); and (c) the inability to discriminate between a variety of tastes and food textures (Bazyk, 1990). Infants fed with a gastrostomy tube should be referred to an occupational therapist for the purpose of building pleasant oral motor experiences and potentially limiting the negative effects of extended tube feedings.

When the infant is deemed stabilized, the physician may recommend the transfer to oral feeding. A feeding specialist or occupational therapist is generally consulted for oral-motor and feeding intervention (Bazyk, 1990; Morris & Klein, 1987). Transition times from tube feeding to oral feeding can range from a few days to several weeks, although for some infants the transition to oral feeding may never occur (Bazyk, 1990). Bazyk (1990) reported that premature infants with no medical complications were able to make the transition to oral feeding within 3 to 6 days, while the length of transition for infants with fetal alcohol syndrome ranged from 10 to 14 months.

The effects on the family when the infant is fed through a tube are multiple. Parents are the primary caretakers after the infant is discharged from the hospital. Due to the complexities of tube feeding, families must become proficient and knowledgeable in maintaining the equipment, preparing the child for feeding, inserting the tube properly, feeding the infant, and recognizing common tube-feeding problems (Moore & Greene, 1985; Shelly et al., 1989). Common problems associated with tube feedings and potential causes and solutions are shown in Table 13.1. The early interventionist is advised to consult a qualified physician and/or nurse immediately when problems with tube feedings arise.

Cleft Palate/Lip

Infants born with a cleft palate/lip may be subject to immediate feeding problems. Morris and Klein (1987) define a cleft as a separation of parts of the mouth usually joined together during the early weeks of fetal development. The cleft can occur on one side

or both sides of the upper lip and may or may not extend into the nasal cavity (Morris & Klein, 1987). Cleft palate may occur in the bony hard palate or in the soft palate of the back of the mouth. Cleft lips and palate do not necessarily occur together, but both are structural abnormalities affecting the face and oral-motor development. Surgery to close the cleft palate/lip is usually done within the first months after birth.

Infants born with cleft palate/lip may not be at a high risk for severe oral-motor and feeding problems (Orelove & Sobsey, 1987), but some infants will experience a variety of feeding difficulties (Morris & Klein, 1987). Characteristics of feeding problems associated with cleft palate/lip are (a) inability to maintain a strong suck; (b) inefficient sucking and swallowing reflexes; and (c) collection of food on the roof of the mouth with expulsion of food through the nose resulting in choking, coughing, spitting, and/or vomiting (Morris & Klein, 1987; Orelove & Sobsey, 1987).

For parents of infants with cleft palate/lip, important issues to be addressed by professionals include feeding positions for presenting the breast or bottle, choosing the appropriate feeding equipment (nipples, spoons, etc), feeding techniques appropriate for each infant, and knowledge of how to make the transition from liquids to textured foods (Morris & Klein, 1987). Because these infants may go through numerous surgeries to repair the cleft palate/lip, it is important for parents to be aware of specific nutritional needs and feeding procedures during these times. For parents of an older child with a cleft palate/lip, attention to problems such as missing or displaced teeth (Orelove & Sobsey, 1987), prominent dental arches (Morris & Klein, 1987), development of mature chewing patterns (Orelove & Sobsey, 1987; Morris & Klein, 1987), and speech difficulties should be addressed by the appropriate professionals.

TABLE 13.1
Common tube feeding problems

Problems	Possible Causes	Possible Solutions
Diarrhea	Too rapid feeding	Slow feeding
	Too concentrated formula	Dilute with water or Pedialyte (consult with physician or nutritionist)
	Intolerance to formula	Formula change
	Medications	
	Malabsorption	
	Bacterial overgrowth	
Cramping	Cold formula	Room temperature formula
	Tube in wrong place	Reposition
	Too fast feeding	Slow feeding
Constipation	Inadequate fluid	Use more water to rinse and with medicine
	Lack of fluid in diet	Increase fluids or prune juice (*consult physician first*)
	Lack of activity	
Vomiting	Too rapid feedings	Slow feeding
	Tube too large	Use smaller-size tube
	Improper tube placement	Reposition
	Large residual in stomach	
	Formula too concentrated	
	Medications given with feedings	
Nausea	During feeding may indicate delayed gastric emptying	Stop feeding; resume when nausea stops
	Stomach distention	
	Too cold formula	
Reflux	Large residual in stomach	Elevate head before, during, and 30 minutes after feeding, or as suggested by results of a pH probe evaluation for reflux. Place the child in prone position.
	Physiologic problem	Thicken feedings (add baby rice cereal to feeds)
		Use a reflux harness
		Medications prescribed by physician

Note: From "Instructions for Nasogastric, Oral Gastric, and Gastrostomy Tube Feedings" by D. L. Shelly, M. Cowlishaw, and J. Galloway, 1989, in *A Guide to Care and Management of Very Low Birth Weight Infants* (pp. 161–174), Ed. by Caryl Semmler, Ph.D., OTR. Copyright 1989 by Therapy Skill Builders, a division of Communication Skill Builders, Inc., P.O. Box 42050, Tucson, AZ 85733. Reprinted by permission.

Infants with Neuromotor Impairments

Infants with cerebral palsy have abnormalities in muscle tone, which may be exhibited through hypotonia during the newborn period and may gradually move to a state of spasticity (Logigian, 1989). Due to hypotonicity, these infants exhibit weak or absent rooting, sucking, and swallowing reflexes (Copeland & Kimmel, 1989; Logigian, 1989). By the time these infants reach the age of 4 to 5 months, abnormal oral-motor patterns become more pronounced (Laverdure, 1989) and little independent control may be exhibited over head movement, with the result that the sucking pattern does not develop normally (Copeland & Kimmel, 1989).

Infants with cerebral palsy have decreased growth and decreased caloric and nutrient intake (Fee et al., 1988), possibly as a result of inefficient sucking patterns, increased feeding times, and reduced feeding intake (Morris & Klein, 1987). An ineffective or poorly coordinated swallow can produce recurrent aspiration, pneumonia, and other medically threatening conditions (Laverdure, 1989). Clinical evidence of aspiration includes a wet, gurgling vocal quality with feeding; coughing and sputtering; frequent respiratory illness; and weak, breathy vocalizations and cries (Fee et al., 1988). When aspiration problems are suspected, the child's physician should be contacted. The physician is best qualified to assess the complex process of swallowing through use of a barium swallow or other radiological procedures. These procedures evaluate three phases of swallowing: oral, pharyngeal, and esophageal (Fee et al., 1988).

Common feeding problems associated with infants and children with cerebral palsy include (a) jaw thrust; (b) tonic-bite reflex; (c) tongue thrust; (d) tongue retraction; (e) nasal regurgitation; (f) lack of mouth, head, and body control; (g) poor sitting balance; (h) difficulty bending the hips enough to reach forward; (i) poor hand-eye coordination; and (j) difficulty holding things and taking them to the mouth (Copeland & Kimmel, 1989; Fraser, 1987; Laverdure, 1989; Morris & Klein, 1987; Werner, 1987). The inability of the infant to hold and bring food to its mouth hinders the development of independent feeding skills such as finger feeding.

Infants and children with cerebral palsy often exhibit signs of tactile defensiveness or hypersensitivity to stimulation on the face and/or mouth (Laverdure, 1989). "Tactile defensiveness can be described as hyperexcit-

able, often hypertonic with exaggerated responses and a remarkably low threshold to sensory stimulation" (Larson, 1982; p. 591). Hypersensitivity to tactile stimulation in and around the mouth inhibits hand to mouth behaviors, such as finger feeding, mouthing of toys, and experiencing different food textures and changes in food temperatures (Laverdure, 1989). Feeding infants with neurological disabilities becomes even more difficult and challenging for caregivers because tactile stimulation to the mouth may result in increased muscle tone, jaw thrust or bite, lip and tongue retraction, and abnormal gag reflexes (Laverdure, 1989).

Infants with Down Syndrome

Children with Down syndrome often exhibit low muscle tone resulting in weak control of the oral musculature. Low tone does not allow for the normal thin, cupped position of the tongue which is a prerequisite for efficient sucking (Morris & Klein, 1987). Low tone in the cheeks and lips reduces strength, control, and flexibility during feeding and may result in weak and unsuccessful attempts at eating (Orelove & Sobsey, 1987). In addition low tone causes the mouth to hang open which may cause the child to drool excessively and hinder the child's ability to establish a firm lip closure on the nipple (Copeland & Kimmel, 1989).

Clearly different conditions affect the development of independent eating skills and play a major role in the way the feeder interacts with the child. Issues related to independent feeding for infants and young children include the ability to control the rate of eating and the size of the spoonfuls. These issues influence children's ability to feel safe, to prepare the mouth to swallow food and to breathe in a rhythmically coordinated fashion. Feeding too fast and/or too much can decrease a child's confidence and increase the fear of mealtimes (Morris & Klein,

1987). Considerations for feeding the infant or young child include (a) preparing the child for mealtime, (b) developing a consistent feeding routine, (c) telling the child the food is approaching or touching a specific area of the mouth as a signal that food is approaching, (d) watching for signs of readiness to eat, (e) pacing the feeding, and (f) noting when the child is full. The professionals should be sensitive to temperature preferences, and encourage the child to help during feeding by holding on to the bottle or spoon and thus building independent feeding skills (Morris & Klein, 1987).

PROMOTING SELF-FEEDING SKILLS

In this section, we describe procedures for teaching self-feeding, discuss a number of issues that should be addressed in planning self-feeding programs, and suggest some early intervention guidelines.

Physical, cognitive, and sensory impairments may prevent the child with disabilities from acquiring self-feeding skills as naturally as does the child with typical development. The child with disabilities may need the use of adaptive equipment, special positioning, and/or direct instruction to acquire independent feeding skills. Although initially it may require less time and energy for the caregiver to feed the child, this does not promote independence or facilitate successful integration into future environments; thus, teaching self-feeding is a desirable activity for most young children with disabilities. It is important to note that if the child is not able to gain complete independence in self-feeding, partial participation is a desirable goal (see Box 6.5).

Before targeting self-feeding as an intervention goal, the professional should consider several factors. First, an assessment should be conducted that involves all relevant team members (Wolery & Smith, 1989).

Members of disciplines such as occupational therapy, physical therapy, and speech-language pathology can provide useful information concerning self-feeding goals. The assessment should cover the child's feeding history, the concerns of family members related to feeding, the family's current method of feeding the child, the development of the child's oral-motor mechanism, the positioning of the child for feeding, the child's volitional behaviors (e.g., hand to mouth behavior), adaptive equipment needs, and the child's grasp of objects and use of objects as tools. As we have noted throughout the chapter, this assessment is best conducted by a team of relevant professionals. The involvement of multiple team members is particularly critical with children who have physical disabilities, children who have a history of feeding problems, and children for whom concern exists about their nutritional intake.

When, based on this assessment, the team determines that self-feeding is a legitimate goal, then the instructional plan should be developed. The full plan will have several components. It should identify the target behaviors, the adaptive equipment that will be used, the design of the feeding environment, any specialized positioning issues, the individuals who will carry out the instruction and the training they will need, the meals that will serve as instructional feeding sessions, the reinforcers that will be used, and the appropriate instructional strategies. These component issues are discussed in the following paragraphs.

Identification of the Target Behaviors

Self-feeding involves many different skills. To be a competent self-feeder, the child must learn to use several different response chains and to use them as they are needed. The critical response chains involve use of the cup, spoon, fork, knife, and napkin. Within any given meal, each of these separate response chains may be used several times. However, in initial self-feeding instruction, only one or two response chains are taught. Generally, it makes sense to teach spoon use and cup use first. When these two chains are acquired, then use of the fork and/or napkin can be taught. Use of knives is usually taught last.

Five guidelines should be followed when teaching the response chains involved in self-feeding. First, *identify the steps in the response chain to be taught.* Although eating with a spoon or drinking from a cup seem like simple skills to us, they really involve several different movements that may present major learning challenges. For example, using a spoon includes the following behaviors: (a) grasping the spoon firmly, (b) dipping the spoon into the food to fill it, (c) lifting the spoon so that the food stays in it, (d) moving the spoon to the mouth, (e) inserting the spoon in the mouth, (f) taking the food off the spoon, (g) moving the spoon out of the mouth, (h) moving the spoon back down to the table, (i) releasing the spoon or holding on to it while chewing and swallowing the food. Depending upon the child's motor control and entry level skill on these steps, all or part of this response chain may be targeted. With Andrea you may want to begin instruction with the entire response chain, and with David you may only teach moving a filled spoon to his mouth, inserting it in his mouth, and removing it. However, before instruction begins, you must clearly identify which steps of the chain you will teach. This is usually accomplished through task analysis as described in chapter 4. The number and types of steps included in the task analysis will vary depending upon the child's abilities and the amount of assistance needed.

Second, *use total task sequencing when teaching self-feeding* (Kayser, Billingsley, & Neel, 1986). To ensure that the skill becomes useful to the child, it is wise to involve him in the entire response chain of the skill you are teaching. For example, if you are initially going to teach David to move a filled spoon to his mouth, insert it, and then remove it, you should use partial participation in the remaining steps. You would use full physical prompts on grasping the spoon (i.e., put the spoon in his hand, and put your hand over his), dipping it into the food, and lifting it, and then you would implement your instructional strategy (discussed later) for the target steps. As he moves the spoon out of the mouth, you would again use the full physical manipulation to move the spoon down to the table. This use of partial participation on steps that are not targeted for initial instruction will help establish the entire response chain as a coordinated movement. Such instruction is preferred to your filling the spoon by yourself and then having him grasp it and move it to his mouth.

Third, *use foods that are appropriate to the chain being taught.* We always want to use foods that will ensure adequate nutrition and foods that are preferred by the child. The rationale for using foods that will ensure adequate nutrition is obvious—it will promote better health. The rationale for using preferred foods is that they are likely to be reinforcers which will act to increase children's motivation to participate in the feeding instruction. We recognize that these two general recommendations may not be compatible; that is, the highly preferred foods may not be those that are of high nutritional value. In such cases, both types of foods can be present during instruction, and bites of them can be alternated. Also, the foods that will ensure adequate nutritional intake can be provided at meals that are not used for instruction. However, in terms of this guideline, foods should be used that will increase the likelihood of success. For example, when teaching a child to use a spoon, the interventionist should use foods that stick to the spoon (e.g., mashed potatoes) rather than slippery foods (e.g., sliced peaches, soups).

Likewise, when teaching a child to spear with a fork, the interventionists should cut the foods into bite-size pieces that can be easily speared. Hard food such as some meats will be difficult for the child with weak spearing movements to get on the fork. Similarly, when teaching children to cut with a knife, the interventionist should use foods that are easily cut. As the child becomes more skilled in performing each of these chains, then more difficult foods should be gradually introduced.

Fourth, *teach the child to use all needed response chains.* In eating most meals, we may use our cup, spoon, fork, knife, and napkin several times throughout the meal. We may do each of these response chains in a variety of sequences. For example, we may take a drink from the cup, use the fork or spoon for a few bites, and then use our napkin. At this point, we may use our spoon or fork, cut something with our knife, then take a drink, and then use our napkin. Rarely do we use only one response chain for the entire meal. Thus, we may need to teach children to use these response chains in a number of different orders. Usually, this teaching is accomplished by providing verbal prompts, or others if necessary, to cue children to use particular chains. Such instruction frequently occurs after the child has learned to use the separate response chains fluently.

Fifth, *teach the child an appropriate pace of eating.* The appropriate pace of eating is important socially and nutritionally. Ideally, a moderate pace of self-feeding allows time for adequate chewing of food, passing food to others, and participating in conversation or other social interactions during the meal. Problems with the pace of eating can occur at either end of the continuum; some children will eat too fast and others will eat too slowly. To prevent these problems, initial instruction should be presented at a moderate pace. Frequently, when children are being taught to use the spoon, instruction is pro-

vided too rapidly and a pattern of rapid spoon use is encouraged. Thus, a moderate pace of eating should be employed. However, when problems in pace exist, verbal prompts and reinforcement for adjustments are frequently useful. Also, providing smaller portions may slow the pace of eating. Closely related to the pace of eating is the size of the load the child puts on the spoon. Usually the child will put too much on the spoon. Teaching more precise dipping and filling of the spoon and cutting foods into bite-size pieces will solve this problem.

Equipment

Equipment should be selected to match the individual needs of the child. A physical therapist and occupational therapist are important team members to consult regarding appropriate equipment. Adaptive equipment is available for cups, bowls, and spoons. Examples are shown in Figure 13.1. Adaptive equipment for positioning is discussed later.

When selecting a cup, the interventionist should look for several things. The child should be able to drink from the cup without having to tilt the head back. A cup can be adapted by cutting out a U shape on one side of the cup. The child drinks from the opposite side of the cut out edge. "The design of a properly constructed cut-out cup allows the cup to be tipped to reach liquid in the bottom without simultaneously tipping back the child's head" (Morris & Klein, 1987, p. 369). In addition, the child's ability to hold the cup should be considered. Cups are available with handles for the child who has sufficient grasp. If a child has a weak grasp or poor control, then a cup with two handles will allow for greater control. Once the child has a strong grasp and wrist control, she will be able to grasp the cup and drink with one hand. If the interventionist wants to readily determine the amount of liquid consumed, a clear plastic cup should be selected. *Caution*

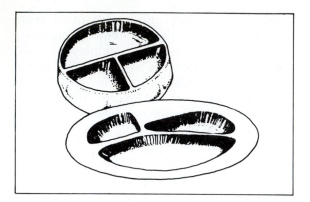

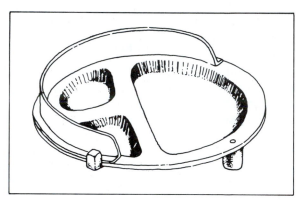

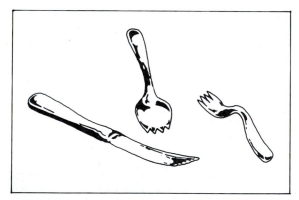

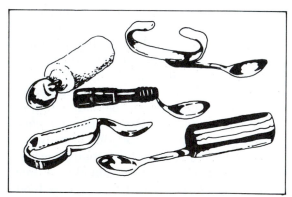

FIGURE 13.1
Adaptive equipment for eating

is advised against the use of styrofoam and thin plastic cups which may be easily eaten or shattered.

Bowls and plates can be adapted, for example, by raising and curving the sides. The raised side assists children in filling the spoon with food. Children can scoop the spoon into the food and move it against the side of the bowl and lift. The raised side keeps food on the spoon and gives the child a subtle cue to lift the spoon. This allows a smooth filling pattern to develop. Many children have difficulty filling their spoons, and adapting the plate can sometimes solve this problem. Another adaption is a suction cup or plastic on the bottom of the bowl to prevent sliding while the child is filling the spoon. Such bowl adaptations are particularly useful for the child who makes rapid and strong movements with the spoon or who may push the bowl with her free hand. Another adaptation of some bowls is a container within the bowl for warm/hot water that can be used to keep food warm during feeding. Those bowls are helpful for maintaining the temperature of food and may be useful with children who require long feeding sessions.

The size of the child's mouth, oral sensitivity, tonic bite reflex, and grasp should all be considered when selecting a spoon (Morris & Klein, 1987). The selected spoon should match the size of the child's mouth; usually spoons with small bowls should be used. Also, the spoon should have a flat bowl to allow for the removal of food by the upper lip. For the child who is orally sensitive or has a tonic bite reflex, spoons are available in nonbreakable plastic or plastic-coated metal. These spoons are less likely to activate the bite reflex. If a child has a weak grasp, foam may be wrapped around the handle or a velcro strap may be added. In addition, spoons are available with angles and swivels to compensate for a lack of wrist control. *Caution is given against the use of thin plastic spoons which will shatter easily if the child bites down.*

The rationale for the use of these adaptive devices is to facilitate the acquisition of self-feeding skills. For children with severe handicaps, adaptive equipment may always need to be used. For other children, once certain skills have been acquired (e.g. wrist control, strong grasp, fluid hand movements) the adaptive equipment should be faded. The interventionist should begin to fade the use of the adaptive equipment only after the child is proficient at self-feeding.

Environment

It is important *"to create an environment in which the child is alerted to the feeding process rather than to environmental sensory variables"* (Morris & Klein, 1987, p. 141). In creating a calm environment we increase the child's feelings of security in relation to the feeding process rather than setting the occasion for a stressful event. In addition, the child is able to focus on the feeding routine rather than the distractions. The quality of the environment can affect the positioning of the child during the feeding routine. If a child is easily distracted or has high tone, distractions and stress should be minimized during the initial phase of instruction to prevent any distress which may increase the tone of the child (Morris & Klein, 1987). To reduce stress that may be associated with the feeding routine, an attempt should be made to minimize distractions such as excess noise, interruptions by other children, and bright lights.

Minimizing distractions will not be necessary for all children with disabilities. Many children can receive instruction in an integrated setting during the usual family and preschool mealtimes. Integrated into these settings, the children are able to observe family members and peers modeling self-feeding skills.

Positioning

The child's positioning should allow for a sufficient amount of support. Proper support will fulfill at least two purposes. First, it will allow the child to use his oral motor structures to make the movements required in taking food from the spoon, munching, chewing, and swallowing. These movements are best accomplished with most children when they are in flexed positions and when movements into extension patterns is avoided. To illustrate, sit in a chair, arch your back, move your arms out to the side, and tilt your head back. When you are in this position, try to swallow or chew something. As you can see, going *into extension* interferes with your ability to use your oral musculature appropriately.

Second, proper support will allow for adequate movements of the arms and head, movements that are necessary for self-feeding. To obtain such movement, appropriate alignment of the spine is necessary (Campbell, 1987). In addition, proper positioning should allow the child to have trunk control, shoulder control, and head control to normalized muscle tone (Campbell, 1987; Morris & Klein, 1987). Additional support may be needed if the child is weak in any one or all of these areas. Children with low muscle tone may need more upper body support than other children. Similarly, children with high muscle tone may need support. For example, a child who has weak head control may need to be fed with her chair tilted back about 10 to 20 degrees (Campbell, 1987). This position provides sufficient support for the head and prevents neck extension. Several versions of adaptive wheelchairs exist for providing adequate support for self-feeding to children with physical disabilities. Consultation with a physical or occupational therapist to identify and evaluate various positions is necessary. Generally, however, children should be seated upright. The feet should be secure rather than dangling. The hips should be flexed to prevent patterns of extension. Straps are sometimes used to provide additional trunk support, and towel rolls or foam rubber also can be employed to provide support for the trunk (Campbell, 1987).

Although children with physical disabilities present particular challenges in positioning during self-feeding, positioning of young children without disabilities also is important. Proper positioning for most children is to be seated in a child-sized chair with a back. The child's feet should touch the floor; if they do not, then a foot stool or

large cardboard blocks should be placed under them. The height of the table is also important. When the child is seated, she should be able to place her forearms on the table with her arms at her sides.

Instructors

Before instruction is initiated, a decision must be made regarding who will conduct the training. Each trainer should be trained (if necessary) to implement the selected instructional strategy reliably before instruction begins. Family members as well as staff members may be included as instructors.

The instructor's position in relation to the child during the feeding routine is important. When teaching a child to spoon-feed, the trainer should sit slightly behind the shoulder of the child's dominant arm. This should allow the instructor to prompt normal arm movements and sufficiently see oral motor movements.

Target Meals

The most appropriate time for instruction in self-feeding skills is during the natural feeding routines. Instruction may occur during established meal times, during snack times, or at both times. If sufficient nutrient consumption is an issue, the interventionist may select snack time as the targeted routine for self-feeding instruction, thus assuring adequate nutrient intake during meals. When the child is able to self-feed during the snack, he should then be allowed to self-feed during mealtimes. If generalization of self-feeding to the meal routines does not occur, the interventionist should be prepared for continued instruction during the meal routine. One means of ensuring generalization is to provide instruction across all meal routines when possible.

When snack time is selected as the only target routine, the number of instructional sessions that can occur in a day may be limited to one or two. Instruction across both snacks and meals will give opportunity for a greater number of instructional sessions each day, and this increase may facilitate a more rapid acquisition of the self-feeding skill.

Although teaching self-feeding at natural times (i.e., when the child is hungry) is recommended, two qualifications are necessary. First, when the child initially is learning to self-feed, the process may be slower than when an adult feeds the child. Thus, if the child is extremely hungry, she may become upset or frustrated with the slower pace of feeding. To prevent this, the adult can feed her a small portion of food at the beginning of the meal and use the remainder of the meal to teach self-feeding. Second, as the meal progresses and child becomes full, there may be decreased motivation to participate in the self-feeding activity. Such times (i.e., the ends of meals) may not be ideal self-feeding times. A solution to this problem is to use a number of small meals for feeding.

Azrin and Armstrong (1973) used a "mini-meal" approach to increase the opportunities for training self-feeding skills each day. In this approach each meal was divided into three mini-meals for a total of nine meal routines per day. The mini-meal approach was effective in training 11 adults with mental handicaps to self-feed. Stimbert, Minor, and McCoy (1977) replicated the mini-meal procedure and trained six children with mental disabilities to spoon feed. In this study six mini-meals were implemented each day for 15 minutes each. Again, the procedure was effective in increasing self-feeding behaviors. Although the mini-meal procedure is fairly time-intensive, the procedure's effectiveness may outweigh the instructor time involved.

Reinforcement

A strong reinforcer is critical to any instructional strategy. When feeding, you have a built-in primary reinforcer (i.e., food and liquids) for some children; but it should be noted that all children do not find food and drinks reinforcing. To take advantage of the primary reinforcement value that food has for some children, the instructor should select foods and drinks that the child likes. It will be difficult to get a child to take a second bite of something he does not enjoy eating. If necessary, small edibles (e.g., mini marshmallows, small bits of crackers or cookies, or pieces of fruit cocktail) may be used as reinforcers following each trial.

Another consideration when using food as a reinforcer is satiation. Primary reinforcers are frequently affected by satiation (Wolery, Bailey, & Sugai, 1988). By the end of the session the food may lose reinforcing value because the child is no longer hungry or no longer desires the food. Thus, instruction may best occur during the middle parts of the meal or by using the mini-meals we have just described.

For children who do not find food reinforcing, an alternate reinforcer must be selected (see chapter 5). When selecting a reinforcer other than food, the interventionist should keep the feeding routine in mind. If reinforcement is to be delivered after every trial, you would not want to select a reinforcer that might break up the flow of the feeding routine. Regardless of the reinforcer selected, it should be paired with verbal praise and then thinned as the child has acquired the selected skill. Also, as we have indicated, it may be helpful to alternate preferred foods with those the child does not prefer.

Instructional Strategies

As we indicated in chapter 6, the early interventionist can choose from among a number of instructional strategies. The stimulus modification procedures and response prompting procedures are well-suited for teaching self-feeding. The stimulus modifications involve the adaptations of equipment (spoons, cups, and bowls) that we have described and can also involve such techniques as mashing food or cutting it into bite-size pieces.

The response prompting procedures, again as we described them in chapter 6, involve providing a stimulus (i.e., the self-feeding situation), using teacher assistance (prompts) to support the child in doing the behavior, allowing the child to respond, providing reinforcement (in the case of self-feeding it is usually the food), and fading or removing the teacher assistance (Wolery, Ault, & Doyle, in press; Wolery et al., 1988). Several response prompting procedures have been used to teach self-feeding. Wilson, Reid, Phillips, and Burgio (1984) used the system of least prompts. This approach involved providing the child with a hierarchy of prompts on each feeding trial. The trial began with the presentation of the opportunity to perform independently and then a series of additional, more intrusive prompts were presented if needed. Collins, Gast, Wolery, Holcombe, and Leatherby (1991) used constant time delay to teach utensil, cup, and napkin use to young children with severe disabilities. Albin (1977) taught spoon use with verbal and physical prompts and a 2-second delay and graduated guidance. Azrin and Armstrong (1973) and Stimbert et al. (1977) used graduated guidance with the minimeals to teach self-feeding.

In addition to systematic means of removing prompts, other procedures have been used extensively in the teaching of self-feeding behaviors. For example, modeling, physical guidance, and error correction have been used to teach utensil use (Nelson, Cone, & Hanson, 1975); modeling, verbal instruction, and physical guidance have been used to teach spoon, cup, and napkin use (Sisson & Dixon, 1986); modeling, verbal instruction, and physical guidance have been used to teach spoon and cup use (Matson, Taras, Sevin, Love, & Fridley, 1990); physical guidance has been used alone to teach spoon use (Song & Gandhi, 1974); and response shaping with an adaptive device has been used to teach cup use (Petersen & Ottenbacher, 1986).

In all of these cases, some method (frequently unspecified) was used to fade the models, the verbal instructions, and the physical prompts. Graduated guidance has been a useful means of fading prompts. As we described this technique in chapter 6, graduated guidance involves providing the amount of assistance needed to initiate the behavior, immediately removing the assistance as soon as the child does the behavior, and immediately providing the needed assistance when the child stops doing the behavior or when she begins to move in the wrong direction. Graduated guidance also frequently involves "shadowing," a technique in which the adult keeps his hands near the child's hands as the child does the behavior. Thus, if assistance is needed it can be instantly provided. Graduated guidance is particularly well suited for self-feeding behaviors for two reasons. First, it has been used successfully with a variety of chained responses, and self-feeding behaviors are chained responses. Second, by removing and then instantly providing assistance as appropriate, the procedure can reduce the spills and accidents that are frequently involved in self-feeding. To illustrate the use of graduated guidance and the issues we have just described, we discuss an example case in the following paragraphs.

The intervention team determined that a high-priority goal for Drew was to teach him to use a spoon and to use a cup. Before instruction began, the team members addressed the issues described earlier. They identified precisely the behaviors he would be taught by conducting a task analysis. They determined that no adaptive equipment would be necessary beyond a suction plate that would stay in place while he learned self-feeding. Because he is not easily distracted, they decided to teach him right at the table with other children. However, they decided to seat him at the end of the table to give the teacher room to implement the training; and they also decided to use the mini-meal approach and to have some of his meals occur with only Drew and his teacher present. The physical therapist on the team decided that no specialized positioning would be required beyond seating Drew in a child-size chair and table with his feet supported. In terms of instructors, the teacher and Drew's mother were identified to implement the training. His teacher taught his mother how to use the graduated guidance procedure, and she arranged for her to provide Drew with three small meals in the afternoon and evening: One is given as soon as he gets home from the center at 2:00 pm, another at 5:00 before the family eats, and the third at 7:30 before his bath and bedtime. The team determined that the mother would feed Drew a small meal in the morning and that the teacher would provide him with a small meal soon after he gets to school and one at 11:30 when the other children eat. Because he likes a variety of foods, they decided to give him some choices before most meals, and they decided not to use any additional reinforcers beyond the food and liquids to be consumed and praise for correct spoon and cup use.

So at each meal, Drew is given some choices of foods and liquids. After he has made a choice, the food is prepared, he is positioned, and the plate and cup are placed in front of him. The teacher puts the spoon at the side of the plate, and says, "Let's see you eat." Initially she takes his hand, places it on the spoon, scoops some food, and moves it to his mouth. At any point where he appears

to be doing the correct movements, she fades her physical prompts in two ways. First, she provides less and less pressure on his hand, moving from a firm hold, to a hold with less pressure, to simply resting her hand on his, and finally to shadowing. Second, she moves her hand up his arm from his hand to his wrist, to his forearm, and to his elbow. However, at any point where he needs more assistance, she moves the hand down his arm and applies the pressure that is needed. This method of prompting allows her to provide the assistance he needs and to remove it gradually but quickly, and it allows Drew to use natural movement patterns. After a few times of using the spoon, she asks him if he wants to drink and applies the same procedure to cup use. Although graduated guidance as described here encourages rapid learning, it is dependent upon the teacher and mother to be very attentive to the fading of prompts. Unlike some of the other response prompting procedures, the removal of prompts is highly dependent upon the adult's making rapid judgments about when to release and when to apply the prompts.

In summary, a number of issues must be addressed when teaching children to feed themselves. These include conducting an appropriate assessment, identifying the response chains and the behaviors of those chains that are to be taught, adapting equipment as necessary, considering the effects of the environment on the child's behavior, positioning the child appropriately, selecting and training the adults who will provide the instruction, identifying the meals that will be the focus of instruction, selecting appropriate reinforcers, and using effective instructional strategies. As with other intervention plans, the effects of these decisions should be monitored and adjusted as instruction is provided (see chapter 5). When the child has acquired the targeted self-feeding behaviors, then the focus of instruction during mealtimes should be shifted to teaching social, communicative, and cognitive skills. The following section on designing mealtime environments addresses this issue.

DESIGNING MEALTIME ENVIRONMENTS

Once the child has acquired self-feeding behaviors, the focus of the mealtime should turn to integrating social, communicative, and cognitive skills. Active child involvement in the meal and snack routines also is important. For example, children should be given the opportunity to select the preferred food or drink items and serve themselves. Mealtimes should be pleasant and not viewed simply as means for providing nourishment; providing nourishment is a primary rationale for meals and snacks, but it should not be the only objective for mealtime routines. In the following paragraphs, we list additional objectives for mealtime routines.

Bailey, Harms, and Clifford (1983) identified seven differences in the mealtime routines between programs serving typical children and programs serving children with disabilities. The following suggestions for the preparation of the mealtime environment are taken from the results of their research and from Wolery and Smith (1989). The reader is cautioned that the following paragraphs represent general suggestions. If at any time these suggestions interfere with nutritional consumption or self-feeding behaviors, modifications in the program should be made immediately.

Involve Children in Mealtime Preparation Children should be given an active role in the preparation of snacks and meals. They should be encouraged to help with table preparation (e.g., by laying out mats, plates, napkins, cups, and utensils) and with food preparation (e.g., by obtaining food items from the refrigerator or shelves and placing them on the table).

Allow Children to Make Choices Meal routines can be used to give the child the opportunity to make choices. This is particularly important for toddlers and younger children. The ability to make choices involves a knowledge of the choices available and a preference from the items available. Children can make choices between such things as food items, drink items, and the color of cups.

Allow Children to Serve Themselves Equipment should be used that allows children the opportunity to serve themselves. For example, child-size pitchers should be used rather than adult pitchers. If individual milk cartons are used children should be taught how to open the cartons and then be given the opportunity to open the cartons and pour the milk themselves. By following a family-style approach to meals (the food is in serving dishes on the table) rather than a cafeteria or restaurant style (e.g., the adults serve the children), the teacher can engage children naturally in the performance of a variety of social and self-help skills such as requesting, passing food, and serving food.

Promote Social Interactions of Child with Child Frequently during mealtime routines it is the case that there are few social interactions or that interactions revolve primarily around the teacher. Often in such cases the intention is to rush children through the meal so that other "more important" instruction can be conducted. It is important to understand that bringing about social interactions of child with child is a valued goal in the educational process. Children should be encouraged to interact with one another during the routine, and positive communicative interactions should be facilitated. The quality of the mealtime environment will thus be enhanced.

Teach Other Concepts in Addition to Self-care Behaviors

As we mentioned in the previous paragraph, mealtime routines are often viewed only as times for providing nourishment to children. But when the provision of nourishment is the only objective of the mealtime routine, valuable naturalistic instructional opportunities are overlooked. Cognitive skills such as identifying the color of the foods and cups, counting the number of food items desired, and classifying the foods into categories can be embedded quite naturally into the mealtime routines. Mealtime routines allow an opportunity for language instruction—for example, through requesting and through increasing the number of word utterances.

Involve Children in Postmeal Clean-up Activities

In addition to helping to prepare the meal, children should also be encouraged to clean up after the meal. Clean-up activities might include putting away leftover food and drink items, throwing away trash, and wiping the table. Bailey et al. (1983) suggest that motor skills such as "picking up, putting in, sweeping, wiping, putting lids on, and stacking" (p. 22) can be taught during child participation in clean-up activities.

Encourage Appropriate Postmeal Hygiene

Postmeal hygiene should include hand washing (which should occur both before and after the mealtime routine) and toothbrushing. This occasion provides an opportunity for instruction in proper toothbrushing, and instructor supervision can take place as needed. Each child should be provided with her own toothbrush. As with mealtime preparation, children should be allowed to access the toothbrushing materials (e.g., toothbrush and toothpaste) independently, based on their own skills.

NUTRITION

Nutritional issues for infants and children with disabilities must be explored in conjunction with self-feeding issues. Children with disabilities appear to be at a greater risk for nutritional deficits than their typical peers (Connor et al., 1978; Orelove & Sobsey, 1987; Solis et al., 1989). Wolery and Smith (1989) provide a list of factors that may put the child at risk for inadequate nutrition. Nutritional problems common in infants and children with disabilities include poor growth or failure to thrive, overweight and obesity, feeding problems, constipation, drug-nutrient interactions (Brizee et al., 1990), malnutrition, iron-deficiency anemia, and food allergies (Pipes, 1983; Werner, 1987). The following section addresses nutritional screening, breast- and bottle-feeding issues, progressing from liquids to solids (dietary consumption), vitamins and minerals, and some common nutritional problems in infants and children with disabilities.

Nutritional Screening

Nutritional screenings can lead to early identification of infants and children with disabilities who are at risk for nutritional problems. Infants with feeding problems that inhibit consumption of liquids and foods are at high risk for not being able to access the nutrients necessary for growth and development. Growth rate and nutritional status should be closely monitored. "If left untreated, severe nutritional problems may exacerbate or even cause developmental disabilities" (Brizee et al., 1990, p. 10). Nutritional screenings should be an integral part of the initial assessment process, especially for infants with disabilities.

When concerns are raised, nutritional screenings can be conducted by any of the intervention team members—by medical professionals (physicians, nurses), nutritionists, feeding specialists, therapists (occupational therapist, physical therapist, speech-language pathologist), early interventionists, paraprofessional health care workers, and/or caregivers (Brizee et al., 1990). Screening of nutritional status can be used to identify infants and children at risk for nutritional problems. Brizee et al. (1990) recommend three ways to gather information: "(a) interviewing caregivers; (b) gathering current data (height, weight, weight for height, and hemacrit) and observing general appearance of hair, teeth, gums, and skin; and (c) reviewing medical/health records" (p. 11).

The caregiver interview can provide information on infant dietary intake (e.g., whether the infant is breast- or formula-fed), the types of foods consumed, the amount consumed per feeding, vitamin and mineral supplements that are used, special medical problems associated with feedings (e.g., vomiting), and difficulties that are experienced with bottles and nipples. The interview can also provide the early interventionist the opportunity to gather information on caregiver behavior during feeding (e.g., whether feeding is a difficult experience for the caregiver), on the components of the feeding routine (e.g., how is the routine set up, whether the caregiver is able to read the infant's hunger and satiation cues), and on the caregiver's positioning and handling of the infant during feeding.

Gathering current medical data and observing general appearances can provide the early interventionist information on growth status. Such data collection and observation can take place during routine physical examinations by the physician or nurse. If the caregiver and/or early interventionist is concerned about possible growth problems, the family's pediatrician should be contacted. By integrating both the information gathered by the early interventionist and the medical information, more informed decisions can be made by the team. If after initial screenings are conducted further assessment information is required, a formal nutritional assessment should be sought. For nutritional assessment and planning, a registered dietician (RD) should be consulted. When access to a registered dietician is limited or nonexistent, a pediatrician or a pediatric nurse with nutritional training is the qualified person from whom to seek information (Brizee et al., 1990). Because nutritional assessments can be costly and time consuming (Pipes, 1983), it is important for professionals to know how to access financial support through various state and federal programs for families. Assessment of nutrition, monitoring of nutritional problems, nutritional counseling, and location of funding sources if needed should be included in the individualized programs for infants and children who are at risk for feeding problems (Brizee et al., 1990; Hayman, 1983; Solis et al., 1989).

The nutritional assessment usually begins with information about the child's intake. The caregiver may be asked to keep a 3- to 7-day log of everything the child eats. Several things should be recorded—an exact description of the food and liquid that is consumed, the amount of food and liquid consumed, the method of food preparation, and a description of supplementary foods such as condiments and between-meal snacks (Pipes, 1983). The role of the interventionist in nutritional issues is threefold: (a) identifying children who are at risk for nutritional problems and making appropriate referrals, (b) assisting families in collecting information needed by the nutritionist, and (c) assisting families in acting on the recommendations of nutritional experts (Wolery & Smith, 1989).

Issues Related to Breast-fed Versus Bottle-fed Infants

The American Academy of Pediatrics Committee on Nutrition (1985) has advocated breast-feeding as the optimal method for providing nutrition to the full-term infant. Breast milk is thought to provide all the necessary nutrients required for growth and development in healthy infants during the first 4 to 6 months of life (Anderson, 1985; Barness, 1985; Pereira & Barbosa, 1988; Whaley & Wong, 1987). There is, however, debate within the medical community surrounding issues related to the use of breast- versus bottle-feeding particularly with premature infants. Also, early interventionists should recognize that while some mothers have very positive views of breast-feeding, others may not enjoy the experience, may find it frustrating, or may not be able to breast-feed because of employment demands. In general, early interventionists should help families adapt to the method of feeding that best fits their own lifestyles and preferences.

Researchers have identified differences between the breast milk from mothers who delivered prematurely and that from mothers who delivered at term (Anderson, 1985; Pereira & Barbosa, 1988; Solis et al., 1989). Pre-term breast milk has higher levels of sodium and protein than full-term breast milk. This finding raises the issue whether preterm breast milk may be preferred for premature infants over breast milk donated by mothers who have been breast-feeding for a few months (Pereira & Barbosa, 1988). However, Anderson (1985) suggests that research findings have not clearly demonstrated that breast-feeding the premature infant with its mother's milk meets all the necessary nutrient requirements for a premature infant. Two preferred methods of feeding a premature infant are (a) the breast milk from the infant's own mother with appropriate nutrient supplements and (b) special low-birthweight infant formulas (Anderson, 1985). Either of these choices of feeding is preferred over donated "mature" breast milk.

With advances in the development of commercially prepared formulas, infant formulas are now similar to premature and mature breast milk (Pereira & Barbosa, 1988). Supplementary nutrients and/or vitamins may be required in addition to breast milk or formula. Some formula companies are developing mineral fortification mixtures to be added to the mother's breast milk before feeding (Anderson, 1985). The determination regarding the use of supplements should be made by the medical staff, but the interventionists may wish to raise the question with them. For infants who are not growing and developing it may be necessary to provide nutrients through tube-feedings.

The mother and infant may encounter several problems when choosing to breast-feed. An inability of the infant to maintain a strong suck may hinder access of the breast milk. In addition, the infant may tire easily, with a consequent reduction of the amount of milk consumed. Oral hypersensitivity and a tonic bite reflex may result in discomfort for the mother (Morris & Klein, 1987). For these reasons the monitoring of the nutritional status of premature infants and infants with feeding problems should be an ongoing process.

Progressing from Liquids to Solids

We present the following guidelines for progressing from liquids to solids. It is important to note that these are only guidelines and that age spans may overlap. Specific recommendations should be made dependent upon the infant's disability, feeding behaviors, and other problems.

Birth to 6 Months Breast milk, infant formulas, or special formulas are considered to meet the nutrient needs of infants (Anderson, 1985; American Academy of Pediatrics Committee on Nutrition, 1985; Morris & Klein, 1987; Whaley & Wong, 1987). Infants usually are fed six to eight times a day or on demand (Morris & Klein, 1987; Whaley &

Wong, 1987). Vitamin supplements may or may not be required.

5 to 8 Months   Breast milk, infant formulas, or special formulas should be continued. Solids should be introduced to the infant's diet. Iron-fortified infant cereals are usually introduced first. Rice cereal is the easiest of the infant cereals to digest and has less allergenic potential (Whaley & Wong, 1987). Usually cereal should be mixed with breast milk, infant formula, fruit juices, or water rather than cow's milk, because infants may be sensitive or allergic to cow's milk. Strained, pureed, or mashed vegetables and fruits can be introduced into the infant's diet. According to Rothenberg, Hitchcock, Harrison, and Graham (1981) guidelines for an infant's daily menu could include the following servings (an average serving for a six month old is 3 to 6 tablespoons): "2 protein foods, 2–3 cereal, grain; 5 fruit/vegetable (including 1 juice, 1 dark green or yellow vegetable); 3–4 milk (approximately 24–32 oz. of breast milk or formula)" (p. 68). In Table 13.2 we present a list of guidelines for introducing solid foods.

9 Months   When the child is around nine months of age, egg yolks (hard-boiled, soft-boiled, or poached) can be introduced. Avoid introducing the egg white to the infant's diet until around the end of the first year to avoid allergic reactions (Whaley & Wong, 1987). Meat, poultry, and fish should be prepared by broiling, boiling, steaming, or poaching and then mashing or straining. Initially, raw foods should not be used because of the difficulty in digestion and because they may be more allergenic (Rothenberg et al., 1981). Fatty meats should be avoided. An alternative to meats is hard cheese. Processed

TABLE 13.2
Guidelines for introducing solid foods

Age	Food	Instructions
4–6 months	Iron fortified baby cereal	Start with 1–2 teaspoons rice cereal mixed with formula or water. Increase gradually. Other cereals may be added later.
	Strained or pureed vegetables and fruits	Start with 1–2 teaspoons and increase gradually. Introduce *one* new fruit or vegetable every 2–4 days (watch for allergic reactions).
	Strained or pureed meats, beans, or egg yolks	Start with 1–2 teaspoons and increase gradually. Avoid vegetable-meat combination dinners because of small protein content. Avoid egg white as it may cause allergic reactions.
5–8 months	Orange juice	1–2 teaspoons diluted with water. Increase gradually.
6–7 months	Whole eggs	Start with 1/4 cooked egg and increase gradually.
8 months	Cottage cheese, mashed potatoes, soups, zwieback	Start with 1–2 teaspoons.

Note: From *Parentmaking: A Practical Guide for Teaching Parent Classes About Babies and Toddlers* by B. A. Rothenberg, S. L. Hitchcock, M. L. Harrison, and M. S. Graham, 1981, Menlo Park, CA: Banister Press. Copyright 1981 by Banister Press. Reprinted by permission.

cheeses are usually too mushy for infants. Plain yogurt and legumes (peas, beans) also should be offered.

10 to 12 Months Breast milk or infant formula is still recommended. All the foods already mentioned should continue as a part of the infant's dietary consumption. In addition, finger foods can be introduced— firmly cooked vegetables, raw pieces of fruit, pieces of hard cheese, cold cereals (Cheerios), graham crackers, diced meats. Caution should be taken in cutting up finger foods to prevent possible choking. Examples of finger foods are presented in Box 13.2.

13 Months to 3 Years During this period the infant may or may not be weaned from the breast or the bottle. Vitamin fortified milk (regular, low-fat, or evaporated) can be introduced into the diet. If the infant cannot tolerate cow milk, soy milk may be substituted. As with any nutritional concern or problem, the pediatrician should be consulted first. Connor et al. (1978) state that for a child to stay healthy, at least one food from each of the following seven food groups should be consumed: (a) yellow and green leafy vegetables; (b) citrus fruits, tomatoes, raw cabbages, and salad greens; (c) non citrus fruits, potatoes, and vegetables not included in the first group; (d) milk, cheese, and other milk products; (e) meat, poultry, fish, eggs, nuts, dried beans, and peas; (f) bread, whole-grain or enriched flour, and cereals; and (g) butter, fortified margarine, or vegetable oils (p. 64). In this listing, three food groups have been added to the original four basic food groups to ensure that the fat, vitamins, and minerals required by the body are met (Connor et al., 1978). Basic nutrients, their importance, identified food sources, daily requirements, and potential health problems associated with vitamin deficiencies or excesses are presented in Table 13.3 (p. 472).

Common Nutritional Problems for Infants/Children with Disabilities

The caloric intake needs of infants for proper growth range from 100 calories per kilogram (approximately 50 calories per pound of body weight) to 120 calories per kilogram daily (American Academy of Pediatrics, 1985; Connor et al., 1978; Pereira & Barbosa, 1988). Although, caloric intake needs for premature infants have not been clearly established, it is estimated to range from 114 calories/kg to 181 calories/kg daily (Pereira & Barbosa, 1988). The American Academy of Pediatrics Committee on Nutrition (1985) recommends for proper growth a daily caloric intake of 120 calories per kilogram for premature infants. Infants with disabilities may require greater caloric intake than typical infants. Connor et al. (1978) found that for proper weight gain and growth, infants with disabilities need a caloric intake that is 10 to 25 percent higher than that for typical infants.

Inadequate caloric intake may be evidenced in infants and children with disabilities. Several factors associated with caloric intake problems are: (a) chronic diarrhea, (b) constipation, (c) grastroesophageal reflux, (d) food intolerance and allergies, and (e) side effects from medications (Connor et al., 1978; Fee et al., 1988; Levene, Tudehope, & Thearle, 1987; Morris & Klein, 1987; Orelove & Sobsey, 1987).

Chronic Diarrhea Diarrhea is characterized by frequent loose bowel movements. Breast-fed infants often begin by having frequent stools that should not be confused with diarrhea (Levene et al., 1987). Infants with cystic fibrosis, failure to thrive, or central nervous system impairments are prone to chronic diarrhea (Connor et al., 1978; Levene et al., 1987). Management of chronic diarrhea should include evaluation of both caregiver and infant factors: for the caregiver, evaluation of the mother's diet (if she is

---

BOX 13.2   Finger foods

Breakfast

Cereal—Cheerios

Eggs—soft-boiled or poached, tossed with
    cubes of buttered toast
    —scrambled semi-firm (with milk to
    make fluffy)
    —hard-boiled and diced

Bread with yogurt, cottage cheese, peanut butter, etc.

Pancakes or French toast—cut into strips (no syrup)

Fruit breads (heavy, not crumbly) cut into sticks (oatmeal, banana, etc.)

Fruit—melon or orange, sliced or cut into eighths, strawberries (after 9 months), peach, plum, canned fruit (drained and dried to remove syrup and to make less slippery)

Lunch & Dinner

Protein

Chicken or turkey—slivered or diced

Roast beef, etc.—diced

Fish—cooked and flaked
    —canned tuna or salmon (drained)

Chicken livers—steamed (do not overcook)

Hot dogs, link sausage—note the additives

Hamburger—cut into small pieces (ground veal, ground beef, etc.)

Pureed meats—spread on bread to make small sandwiches

Cottage cheese—large curd

Cheese—grated or sliced or sticks
    —casseroles such as macaroni and
    cheese
    —melted on bread under broiler, cut
    into quarters

Peanut butter—spread on toast, bread, or crackers

Tofu—cut into pieces

Vegetables

Carrots, peas, green beans, beets, asparagus tips, celery, broccoli, zucchini, cucumber—steamed until tender, not mushy

Potatoes, sweet potatoes, yams—baked or boiled and diced

Cherry tomatoes—cut in half (after 9 months)

Pickles—sweet or dill

Fruits

Apples, pears—grated or very thinly sliced

Avocado—diced

Peaches, pears, nectarines, plums, bananas, grapes, apricots—fresh or canned, peeled and diced.

Starches

Rice (brown or converted)—can be cooked in chicken or beef broth instead of water

Macaroni—different shapes and sizes add interest

Noodles—(whole wheat and vegetable as well as egg)

Beans—baked, lima, kidney, or garbanzo

Potatoes—small pieces

Bread—bread sticks, crackers, zwieback, teething biscuits, etc.

Note: From *Parentmaking: A Practical Handbook for Teaching Parent Classes About Babies and Toddlers* by B. A. Rothenberg, S. L. Hitchcock, M. L. Harrison, and M. S. Graham, 1981, Menlo Park, CA: Banister Press. Copyright 1981 by Banister Press. Reprinted by permission.

---

breast-feeding), evaluation of formula mixtures, and determination of correct feeding requirements; for the infant, determination regarding possible infections (bacterial, viral, or nonspecific) and evaluation for sugar intolerance. Antibacterial medications can be prescribed to treat infections, but anti-diarrhea medications are not recommended during the newborn stage (Levene et al., 1987).

Evaluation and treatment of chronic diarrhea requires the supervision of a physician. Dehydration and secondary infections are potentially serious problems related to chronic diarrhea (Connor et al., 1978). If chronic diarrhea persists, parenteral treatment (tube-feeding) may be advocated.

Constipation   Constipation is characterized by hard, dry bowel movements. Infants and children with neuromuscular disabilities are prone to chronic constipation. Morris and Klein (1987) identify six possible causes for constipation: "(a) muscle inactivity; (b) muscle tone imbalance; (c) insufficient liquid intake; (d) insufficient fiber or texture in the diet; (e) poor or inactive positioning during and after meals; and (f) food or chemical sensitivities and allergies" (p. 184).

Evaluation of chronic constipation should be brought to the attention of a physician and/or nutritionist. Potential dietary solutions may include increasing daily fluid intakes; making dietary fluid changes (adding prune juice or orange juice); and adding more fiber (Levene et al., 1987; Morris & Klein, 1987). Foods high in fiber are whole-grain breads, high-fiber cereals, uncooked vegetables and fruits, nuts, sweet potatoes, cabbage, spinach, broccoli, dried peas and beans, and unprocessed bran (Morris & Klein, 1987). The physician may recommend the use of mild laxatives, glycerine suppositories, or enemas to be used on a limited basis (Levene et al., 1987). Such treatments should not be used without direction from a physician.

Food Intolerance and Allergies   "An allergy is an adaptive response of the immune system designed to protect the individual from a substance that the body perceives as dangerous to its welfare" (Morris & Klein, 1987, p. 185). Food intolerances, which are more global, include any adverse reactions to food (Whaley & Wong, 1987). Symptoms of food allergies may include outward signs of runny nose, wheezing, hives, skin rashes, or increases in muscle tone, decreases in muscle tone, increases in incoordination,

irritability, hyperactivity, sleep disorders, headaches, and fatigue (Morris & Klein, 1987). Gastrointestinal problems that may be associated with allergies are indigestion, cramps, reflux, and colic.

Infants are susceptible to food allergies due to the immaturity of the intestinal tract and the exposure to many new foods (Whaley & Wong, 1987). Typical foods that may cause allergic reactions in infants and children are displayed in Box 13.3 (p. 476).

Evaluation and determination of food allergies and food intolerances should be conducted by an allergist. The allergist or nutritionist can also provide appropriate nutritional counseling regarding dietary substitutions.

Side Effects of Medications   Medication side effects can produce nutritional problems in infants and children with disabilities. Side effects are possible from medications for seizures, from tranquilizers, from laxatives, from antibiotics, or from diuretics (Morris & Klein, 1987; Orelove & Sobsey, 1987). Anticonvulsant medicine side effects include stomach lining irritation and interference with vitamin absorption and overall nutrient absorption (Orelove & Sobsey, 1987). Weight gain can be adversely affected by medication side effects. Tranquilizers may reduce caloric requirements and increase caloric intake, thus raising the potential for obesity (Orelove & Sobsey, 1987). Diuretics and antibiotics decrease the body's ability to absorb the mineral zinc. "Deficiencies in zinc can contribute to a reduced appetite and hypersensitivity or hyposensitivity to taste" (Morris & Klein, 1987; p. 187).

Evaluation of the potential side effects of drug therapy should be conducted by the pediatrician. A pharmacist can also be consulted to provide valuable information on medication side effects. A nutritionist can make assessments and provide nutritional counseling and dietary suggestions to help minimize drug-nutrient problems (Orelove &

TABLE 13.3
Basic nutrients and their importance

Nutrient	Nutritional Importance	Food Sources	Daily Requirement	Effects of Deficiency
Protein	Promotes growth and repair of body tissues; supplies energy; helps fight infections; forms an important part of blood, enzymes, and hormones to regulate body functions.	Lean meats; poultry; fish; shellfish; eggs; milk; cheese; dry beans and peas; nuts; peanut butter; bread; and cereals.	2.5–3.5 g/kg/per day 6 months—2 servings (3–6 tablespoons) per day 13 months—2 servings (1/4 to 1/3 cup) per day	Impedes growth and development; does not provide the infant/child with the necessary vitamins and nutrients listed below; places the child at risk for health problems
Carbo-hydrates (Starches and sugars)	Supply energy; spare protein for body building and repair; also necessary for bulk and proper elimination.	Breads; cereals; grits; corn; rice; potatoes; macaroni and noodles; bananas; sugar; honey; syrup; jam; jelly; molasses.	6 months—2–3 cereal, grain servings 13 months—4 or more servings per day	Same as above
Fats	Supply concentrated energy; improve taste of food; help body use other nutrients; help maintain temperature; lubricate intestinal tract.	Butter; margarine; whole milk; ice cream; cheese; egg yolk; shortening; lard; puddings; salad oils.	4–6 g/kg/per day	Same as above
Calcium	Builds sturdy bones and teeth; helps blood clot; helps to keep nerves, muscles, and heart healthy; aids in healing wounds; helps fight infections.	Milk; ice cream; cheese; cottage cheese; kale; collards; mustard and turnip greens; salmon; sardines; egg yolk; sunlight.	All ages, 10μ g (400 IU)	Rickets Note: Human milk does not contain enough Vitamin D to prevent rickets.
Iodine	Helps thyroid gland work properly in regulating energy.	Iodized salt; salt-water fish and shellfish	Specific recommendations not available	Enlarged thyroid

Mineral/Vitamin	Function	Sources	Amount	Deficiency
Iron	Necessary to form hemoglobin (red substance in blood) which carries oxygen from lungs to body cells.	Liver; heart; kidneys; oysters; lean meats; egg yolk; clams; whole-grain and enriched cereals; dry beans; molasses; raisins, and other dried fruits; dark green leafy vegetables.	Breast milk provides sufficient iron for an infant to 6–9 months of age. Pre-term infants—4 mg of iron daily up to age of 9–12 months.	Anemia
Sodium	Preserves water balance in body; helps the body absorb glucose.	Table salt; meat; fish; poultry; eggs; olives; numerous prepared foods	2.5 to 3.5 kg/per day	Dehydration; hypotension; convulsions; muscle cramps; intracranial hemorrhage.
Potassium	Keeps nerves and muscles healthy; helps to maintain fluid balance.	Meat; fish; bran; bananas; citrus fruits; dried fruits; peanut butter; cereals; potatoes.	2.5 to 3.5 kg/per day	Muscular weakness; lethargy; kidney and respiratory failure.
Phosphorous	Essential (with calcium) for bones and teeth; helps fat work in the body; aids enzymes used in energy metabolism.	Milk; ice cream; cheese; meat; poultry; whole-grain cereals; dry beans and peas; fish; nuts; carbonated beverages.	1.0 to 1.5 kg/per day	Weakness; bone pain. Note: For newborns discourage use of whole cow's milk in order to preserve calcium-to-phosphorus ratio.
Magnesium	A must for strong bones and teeth; helps muscle contraction; aids in transmitting nerve impulses; aids production of proteins.	Cereals; dry beans; meats; milk; nuts; soy beans; green leafy vegetables (uncooked); tea; cocoa; raisins.	0.6 kg/per day	Tremors, spasms, irregular heartbeat; muscular weakness; convulsions.
Vitamin A	Helps maintain eyesight, especially in dim light; aids normal growth and development of skin, bones, and teeth; promotes growth; helps to resist infection.	Liver; broccoli; turnips; carrots; sweet potatoes; winter squash; apricots; butter; fortified margarine; egg yolk; fish liver oils; cantaloupe; milk and nonskimmed milk products.	Infants—300μ g	Night blindness, poor growth; impaired resistance to infection; defective tooth enamel.

TABLE 13.3
Continued

Nutrient	Nutritional Importance	Food Sources	Daily Requirement	Effects of Deficiency
Thiamine Vitamin B-1	Helps body cells obtain energy from food; needed for healthy nervous system; promotes good appetite and digestion.	Pork; lean meats; poultry; fish; liver; dry beans and peas; egg yolk; whole-grain and enriched cereals and breads; soybeans.	Infants—0.5 mg/1,000 kcal	Restlessness, cardiac failure, hoarseness; gastrointestinal problems (constipation); convulsions and coma (in infants).
Riboflavin Vitamin B-2	Helps body use protein, fats, and carbohydrates for energy and for building tissues; aids in maintaining eyesight; maintains healthy skin.	Milk; cheese; liver; kidneys; heart; eggs; green leafy vegetables; enriched cereals and breads; yeast.	Infants—0.6 mg/1,000 kcal.	Poor growth; burning, itching, tearing of the eyes; skin problems (dermatitis); delayed wound healing and tissue repair.
Niacin	Required for healthy nervous system, skin, and digestive tract; aids energy production in cells.	Lean meats; poultry; fish; dark green vegetables; whole-grain and enriched cereals and breads; peanuts; peanut butter.	6.6 mg/1,000 kcal	Dermatitis, gastrointestinal problems (diarrhea)
Vitamin C (Ascorbic Acid)	Aids in building the materials that hold cells together; helps in healing wounds and resisting infection; needed for healthy teeth, gums, and blood vessels; increases absorption of iron for hemoglobin formation; essential for collagen formation.	Citrus fruits; strawberries; cantaloupe; tomatoes; potatoes; Brussels sprouts; raw cabbage; broccoli; green and sweet red peppers.	Infants—35mg	Scurvy; signs of anemia; gum problems (bleeding); irritability; dry skin; decreased wound healing; increased susceptibility to infection.

Vitamin	Function	Food sources	Dosage	Deficiency
Vitamin D	Helps body use calcium and phosphorus to build strong bones and teeth.	Fortified milk; fish-liver oils; egg yolk; liver; salmon; tuna. Direct sunlight also produces Vitamin D.	All ages—10μ g (400 IU)	Rickets
Vitamin B-6	Aids body to use protein and maintain normal hemoglobin in blood; needed for formation of antibodies.	Meats; wheat germ; liver; kidney; whole-grain cereals (wheat and corn); soybeans; peanuts.	Infants 0.2 to 0.3 mg	Scaly dermatitis, weight loss; anemia; poor growth; irritability; convulsions.
Vitamin B-12	A necessity for producing red blood cells and for building new proteins in the body; needed for normal functioning of nervous tissue.	Meats; liver; kidneys; fish; eggs; milk; cheese (no vegetable source known).	All ages—1–2μ g	Anemia, neurological deterioration (spinal cord deterioration); lemon yellow tinge to skin.
Vitamin E	Function is not clearly understood, although it is thought to help form red blood cells, muscle, and other tissue.	Wheat-germ oil; salad oils; whole grains; green leafy vegetables; nuts; dry beans and peas; margarine.	Infants—4mg	Hemolytic anemia in premature infants; otherwise no clear-cut deficiency syndrome known in man.
Vitamin K	Promotes normal blood clotting	Green leafy vegetables; cauliflower; tomatoes; egg yolk; liver; pork; cheese; soybean oil.	Newborn—single dose of 1 mg; thereafter, 5μ g/day for older infants	Hyperbilirubinemia in infants; hemorrhage.

Note: Adapted from *Pediatric Nutrition Handbook* by the American Academy of Pediatrics Committee on Nutrition, 1985, Elk Grove Village, IL: American Academy of Pediatrics; *Program Guide for Infants and Young Children With Developmental Disabilities* by F. P. Connor, G. G. Williamson, and J. M. Siepp, 1978, New York: Teachers College Press; *Parentmaking: A Practical Guide for Teaching Parent Classes About Babies and Toddlers* by B. A. Rothenberg, S. L. Hitchcock, M. L. Harrison, and M. S. Graham, 1981, Menlo Park, CA: Banister Press; and *Nursing Care of Infants and Children* by L. F. Whaley and D. L. Wong, 1987, St. Louis: C. V. Mosby.

BOX 13.3   Hyperallergenic foods

Food	Sources
Milk	Ice cream, butter, margarine, yogurt, cheese, pudding, baked goods, wieners, bologna, canned creamed soups, instant breakfast drinks, powdered milk drinks, mild chocolate
Eggs	Mayonnaise, creamy salad dressing, baked goods, egg noodles, some cake icing, meringue, custard, pancakes, french toast, root beer
Wheat	Almost all baked goods, wieners, bologna, pressed or chopped cold cuts, gravy, pasta, some canned soups
Peanuts, legumes	Peanut butter or oil, legumes, such as beans, peas, lentils (peanuts are a legume, not a nut)
Nuts	Chocolate, baked goods, cherry soda (may be flavored with a nut extract)
Fish or shellfish	Cod liver oil, pizza with anchovies, Caesar salad dressing, any food fried in same oil as fish
Chocolate	Cola beverages, cocoa, chocolate-flavored drinks
Buckwheat	Some cereals, pancakes
Pork, chicken	Bacon, wieners, sausage, pork fat, chicken broth
Strawberries, melon, pineapple	Gelatin, syrups
Corn	Popcorn, cereal, muffins, cornstarch, corn meal
Citrus fruits	Orange, lemon, lime, grapefruit, any of these in drinks, gelatin, juice, or medicines
Tomatoes	Juice, some vegetable soups, spaghetti, pizza sauce, and catsup
Spices	Chili, pepper, vinegar, cinnamon

Note: From *Nursing Care of Infants and Children* (p. 610) by L. F. Whaley and D. L. Wong, 1991, St. Louis: C. V. Mosby. Copyright 1991 by C. V. Mosby. Reprinted by permission.

Sobsey, 1987). Common medication-nutrient interactions are displayed in Box 13.4.

Gastroesophageal Reflux   Gastroesophageal reflux is more commonly referred to as vomiting after the ingestion of liquids or foods. It is often seen in premature infants, infants and children with neurological impairments, and failure-to-thrive infants (Fee et al., 1988; Levene et al., 1987). Barium swallow procedures are used to document the presence of gastroesophageal reflux (Fee et al., 1988).

Evaluation and treatment should be conducted by the pediatrician or appropriate medical professional. Treatment may include positioning changes, thickening of feedings, dietary changes, use of medications, and surgery (Fee et al., 1988; Levene et al., 1987; Morris & Klein, 1987).

BOX 13.4   **Drug-nutrient interactions with medications commonly used for children with developmental disabilities**

Drug	Effect(s) on nutrients
Anticonvulsants Phenobarbital Primidone Carbamazepine Phenytoin	Altered metabolism of vitamin D and calcium leading to bone demineralization and rickets in severe cases. Effects are worse with multiple anticonvulsants. Altered metabolism of folic acid leading to deficiency with phenytoin alone and in combination with other anticonvulsants. Effects are worse with multiple anticonvulsants.
Laxatives containing mineral oil	Reduced absorption of fat-soluble vitamins: A, D, E, and K.
Stimulants Methylphenidate hydrochloride Dextroamphetamine Pemoline Imipramine hydrochloride	Depressed appetite leading to inadequate food intake and reduced rate of weight gain and linear growth.
Diuretics Furosemide Spironolactone Triamterene Thiazides	Increased excretion of certain minerals: potassium, calcium, magnesium. The mineral(s) affected depend on the particular diuretic.

Note: From "Nutrition Issues in Developmental Disabilities" by L. S. Brizee, C. M. Sophos, and J. F. McLaughlin, 1990, *Infants and Young Children, 2* (3), 10–21. Copyright 1990 by *Infants and Young Children.* Reprinted by permission.

SUMMARY

Feeding fulfills life support and other adaptive and social functions. The roles of and the relationships between family members and professionals from different disciplines are critical when feeding problems exist. To address feeding issues in infants and young children, professionals should understand the development of the oral-motor mechanism and the effects of different disabilities on feeding and eating behaviors and skills. When self-feeding skills are to be promoted, the behaviors to be taught must be identified through assessment, any necessary adaptive equipment should be selected, a plan should be developed for using the facilitating dimensions of the environment and controlling the impeding dimensions, the proper positioning for the child should be determined, the persons providing the instruction should be identified and trained, the feeding times (meals) during which instruction will occur should be identified, reinforcers should be selected, and effective instructional strategies should be chosen. Interventionists should carefully attend to factors related to making mealtimes enjoyable, normative, and growth promoting. Many infants and young children with disabilities may be at risk for inadequate nutritional intake. Thus, interventionists may be involved in conducting or planning nutrition screenings, assisting families in making determinations about breast- and bottle-feeding, promoting the progression from liquids to solid foods, and addressing common nutritional problems.

REFERENCES

Albin, J. (1977). Some variables influencing the maintenance of acquired self-feeding behavior in profoundly retarded children. *Mental Retardation, 15,* 49–52.

The American Academy of Pediatrics Committee on Nutrition (1985). *Pediatric Nutrition Handbook.* Elk Grove Village, IL.: American Academy of Pediatrics.

Anderson, G. H. (1985). Human milk feeding. *Pediatric Clinics of North America, 32*(2), 335–353.

Azrin, N. H., & Armstrong, P. M. (1973). The "mini-meal": A method for teaching eating skills to the profoundly retarded. *Mental Retardation, 11,* 9–13.

Bailey, D. B., Harms, T., & Clifford, R. M. (1983). Social and educational aspects of mealtimes for handicapped and nonhandicapped preschoolers. *Topics in Early Childhood Special Education, 3*(2), 19–32.

Bailey, D. B., & Simeonsson, R. J. (1988). *Family assessment in early intervention.* Columbus, OH: Merrill.

Barkin, R. M., & Rosen, P. (1990). *Emergency pediatrics: A guide to ambulatory care.* St. Louis: C. V. Mosby.

Barness, L. A. (1985). Infant feeding: Formula, solids. *Pediatric Clinics of North America, 32*(2), 355–362.

Bazyk, S. (1990). Factors associated with the transition to oral feeding in infants fed by nasogastric tubes. *American Journal of Occupational Therapy, 43*(11), 723–728.

Brizee, L. S. Sophos, C. M., & McLaughlin, J. F. (1990). Nutrition issues in developmental disabilities. *Infants and Young Children, 2*(3), 10–21.

Campbell, P. H. (1987). Physical management and handling procedures with students with movement dysfunction. In M. E. Snell (Ed.), *Systematic instruction of persons with severe handicaps* (pp. 174–187). Columbus, OH: Merrill.

Campbell, P. H. (1990). *Promoting Posture and Movement Skills.* Lexington, KY: Interdisciplinary Human Development Institute-University of Kentucky.

Case-Smith, J., Cooper, P., & Scala, V. (1989). Feeding efficiency of premature neonates. *American Journal of Occupational Therapy, 43*(4), 245–250.

Collins, B. C., Gast, D. L., Wolery, M., Holcombe, A., & Leatherby, J. G. (1991). Using constant time delay to teach self-feeding to young students with severe/profound handicaps: Evidence of limited effectiveness. *Journal of Developmental and Physical Disabilities, 3,* 157–179.

Connor, F. P., Williamson, G. G., & Siepp, J. M. (1978). *Program guide for infants and toddlers with neuromotor and other developmental disabilities.* New York: Teachers College Press.

Copeland, M. E., & Kimmel, J. R. (1989). *Evaluation and management of infants and young children with developmental disabilities.* Baltimore: Paul Brookes.

Dunn, W. (1989). Occupational therapy in early intervention: New perspectives create greater possibilities. *The American Journal of Occupational Therapy, 43*(11), 717–721.

Dunst, C., Trivette, C., & Deal, A. (1988). *Enabling and empowering families.* Cambridge, MA: Brookline Books.

Fee, M. A., Charney, E. B., & Robertson, W. W. (1988). Nutritional assessment of the young child with cerebral palsy. *Infants and Young Children, 1*(1), 33–40.

Fraser, B. A. (1987). *Physical management of multiple handicaps.* Baltimore: Paul Brookes.

Gorga, D. (1989). Occupational therapy treatment practices with infants in early intervention. *American Journal of Occupational Therapy, 43*(11), 731–736.

Hayman, L. (1983). Nutritional assessment of handicapped preschoolers. *Topics in Early Childhood Special Education, 3*(2), 9–17.

Heimlich, H. J. (1982). First aid for choking children: Back blows and chest thrusts cause complications and death. *Pediatrics, 70*(1), 120–125.

Jewett, J., & Clark, H. B. (1979). Teaching preschoolers to use appropriate dinnertime conversation: An analysis of generalization from school to home. *Behavior Therapy, 10,* 589–605.

Kayser, J. E., Billingsley, F. F., & Neel, R. S. (1986). A comparison of in-context and traditional instructional approaches: Total task, single trial versus backward chaining, multiple trials. *Journal of the Association for Persons with Severe Handicaps, 11,* 28–38.

Kleinert, J. (1990). *Communication and infancy: Assessment and Intervention.* Lexington, KY: University of Kentucky, Interdisciplinary Human Development Institute.

Larson, K. (1982). The sensory history of developmentally delayed children with and without tactile defensiveness. *American Journal of Occupational Therapy, 36*(9), 590–596.

Laverdure, P. (1989). Oral motor skills. In M. K. Logigian & J. D. Ward (Eds.), *Pediatric rehabilitation: A team approach for therapists* (pp. 48–61). Boston: Little, Brown.

Levene, M., Tudehope, D., & Thearle, J. (1987). *Essentials of neonatal medicine.* Edinbourgh, England: Blackwell Scientific Publications.

Logigian, M. K. (1989). Cerebral palsy. In M. K. Logigian & J. D. Ward (Eds.), *Pediatric rehabilitation: A team approach for therapists* (pp. 23–30). Boston: Little, Brown.

Matson, J. L., Taras, M. E., Sevin, J. A., Love, S. R., & Fridley, D. (1990). Teaching self-help skills to autistic and mentally retarded children. *Research in Developmental Disabilities, 11,* 361–378.

Mueller, H. (1975). Feeding. In N. R. Finnie (Ed.), *Handling the young cerebral palsied child at home* (pp. 113–132). New York: Dutton.

Mills, Y. L., & Hedges, C. A. (1983). The feeding process and the nutritional needs of handicapped infants and preschoolers. *Topics in Early Childhood Special Education, 3*(2), 33–42.

Moore, M. C., & Greene, H. L. (1985). Tube feeding of infants and children. *Pediatric Clinics of North America, 32*(2), 401–417.

Morris, S. (1977). *Program guidelines for children with feeding problems.* Edison, NJ: Childcraft Educational Corporation.

Morris, S., & Klein, M. D. (1987). *Pre-feeding skills: A comprehensive resource for feeding development.* Tuscon, Arizona: Therapy Skill Builders.

Nelson, G. L., Cone, J. D., & Hanson, C. R. (1975). Training correct utensil use in retarded children: Modeling vs. physical guidance. *American Journal of Mental Deficiency, 80,* 114–122.

Orelove, F. P., & Sobsey, D. (1987). *Educating children with multiple disabilities: A transdisciplinary approach.* Baltimore: Paul Brookes.

Passy, V., & McMaster, W. C. (1977). Foreign bodies in the throat, nose and ear. *Journal of Hospital Medicine, 13*(8), 8–11.

Pereira, G. R., & Barbosa, N. M. M. (1988). Controversies in Neonatal Nutrition. *Pediatric Clinics of North America, 33*(1), 65–89.

Petersen, P., & Ottenbacher, K. (1986). Use of applied behavioral techniques and an adaptive device to teach lip closure to severely handicapped children. *American Journal of Mental Deficiency, 90,* 535–539.

Pipes, P. L. (1983). Health care professionals. In S. G. Garwood & R. R. Fewell (Eds.), *Educating handicapped infants* (pp. 323–342). Rockville, MD: Aspen Systems.

Rothenberg, B. A., Hitchcock, S. L., Harrison, M. L., & Graham, M. S. (1981). *Parentmaking: A practical guide for teaching parent classes about babies and toddlers.* Menlo Park, CA: Banister Press.

Semmler, C. (Ed.). (1989). *Neonatal network guide to very low birth weight infants.* Tucson, AZ: Therapy Skill Builders.

Shelly, D., Cowlishaw, M., & Galloway, J. (1989). Instructions for nasogastric, oral gastric, and gastrostomy tube feedings. In C. Semmler (Ed.), *Neonatal Network Guide to Very Low Birth Weight Infants* (pp. 161–174). Tucson, AZ: Therapy Skill Builders.

Sisson, L. A., & Dixon, M. J. (1986). A behavioral approach to the training and assessment of feeding skills in multihandicapped children. *Applied Research in Mental Retardation, 7,* 149–163.

Snell, M. E. (1987). *Systematic instruction of persons with severe handicaps*. Columbus, OH: Merrill.

Solis, D., Chustz, L., McCarty, C., & Stotko, L. (1989). Nutrition and feeding screening: A practical guide. In C. Semmler (Ed.), *Neonatal Network Guide to Very Low Birth Weight Infants* (pp. 136–160). Tucson, AZ: Therapy Skill Builders.

Song, A. Y., & Gandhi, R. (1974). An analysis of behavior during the acquisition and maintenance phases of self spoon-feeding skills of profound retardates. *Mental Retardation, 12*, 25–28.

Stimbert, V. E., Minor, J. W., & McCoy, J. F. (1977). Intensive feeding training with retarded children. *Behavior Modification, 1*, 517–529.

Torrey, S. B. (1983). The choking child: A life-threatening emergency. *Clinical Pediatrics, 22*(11), 751–754.

Werner, D. B. (1957). The concept of development from a comparative and organismic point of view. In D. B. Harris (Ed.), *The concept of development* (pp. 125–148). Minneapolis: University of Minnesota Press.

Werner, D. B. (1987). *Disabled village children*. Palo Alto, CA: The Hesperian Foundation.

Whaley, L. F., & Wong, D. L. (1991). *Nursing care of infants and children*. St. Louis: C. V. Mosby.

Wilson, P. G., Reid, D. H., Phillips, J. F., & Burgio, L. D. (1984). Normalization of institutional mealtimes for profoundly retarded persons: Effects and noneffects of teaching family-style dining. *Journal of Applied Behavior Analysis, 17*, 189–201.

Winton, P. J., & Turnbull, A. P. (1981). Parent involvement as viewed by parents of preschool handicapped children. *Topics in Early Childhood Special Education, 1*, 11–19.

Wolery, M., Ault, M. J., & Doyle, P. M. (in press). *Teaching students with moderate and severe disabilities: Use of response prompting strategies*. White Plains, NY: Longman.

Wolery, M., Bailey, D. B., & Sugai, G. (1988). *Effective teaching: Principles and procedures of applied behavior analysis with exceptional students*. Boston: Allyn & Bacon.

Wolery, M., & Smith, P. (1989). Assessing self-care skills. In D. B. Bailey & M. Wolery (Eds.), *Assessing infants and preschoolers with handicaps*. (pp. 447–477). Columbus, OH: Merrill.

14

Teaching Toileting and Adaptive Skills

This chapter focuses on selected self-care and adaptive skills. Self-care skills are behaviors that result in independent functioning, are basic to maintaining life, deal with bodily functions, and involve adopting cultural practices in doing so. Adaptive skills are similar in that they result in independence and promote children's "fit" in their homes and communities. Chapter 13 addressed eating and self-feeding. In this chapter the self-care skills of toileting, dressing and undressing, and grooming are described and procedures and issues involved in teaching them are included. In addition, we address certain skills that allow children to function adaptively in the home and the community. The chapter begins with a discussion of some general characteristics of self-care skills, then toileting and dressing/grooming skills are treated separately. In the final portion of the chapter, we describe selected adaptive skills and illustrate procedures for their instruction.

CHARACTERISTICS OF SELF-CARE SKILLS

In this section, general characteristics of self-care skills are described, and implications for instruction are noted. These characteristics are included to provide foundational information for planning and implementing instruction of these skills.

Self-Care Skills Are Acquired Throughout the Preschool Period   As we noted in chapter 13, feeding and eating skills are important to infants, to toddlers, and to preschoolers. Toileting and dressing skills are similar to these skills in that parts of these behaviors are learned throughout the preschool period. A young child may learn to toilet when she is taken to the bathroom, but to be truly independent, she must engage in the entire toileting routine—a sequence that includes recognizing when she needs to toilet, manag-

ing clothing, toileting, wiping, washing her hands, and returning to the appropriate activities. Acquiring and becoming fluent in doing all of these skills requires a long time. It is the same for dressing skills: The infant or toddler begins by cooperating with an adult who dresses/undresses him; learns to anticipate and participate while being dressed/undressed, pushing his arm through a sleeve, for example; eventually is able to take off and put on some garments; and concludes with unsupervised dressing/undressing.

Because the self-care skill acquisitions occur throughout the preschool period, three major implications follow for the intervention team. First, team members should realize that most young children with disabilities will need instruction on some self-care skills. Although the focus with infants may reside primarily in eating and feeding (chapter 13), most toddlers and preschoolers will have objectives for toileting and dressing/undressing. Second, teams must be competent in assessing and teaching a broad range of self-care skills (Browder, 1987; Wolery & Smith, 1989). Interventionists must know how to teach these skills and to promote their use. Third, teams must be aware of the prerequisite skills and sequences involved in learning these skills. Since these abilities are acquired throughout the preschool period, they are not all learned at once. Teams must be aware of the sequences through which they are most appropriately taught.

Most Self-Care Skills Are Chained Responses   As we noted in chapter 5, some of the skills we teach are discrete responses, and others consist of a sequence or series of discrete behaviors that are put together to perform a particular function or more complex skill. Toileting, dressing/undressing, and grooming skills fit in this latter category. To be useful to children, these skills involve performing several different behaviors in certain orders to meet larger goals. Putting on pants involves grasping the pants in the correct alignment (i.e., so the front of the pants are in the front), putting one leg in, putting a second leg in, pulling the pants up the legs and over the buttocks, and fastening the pants. It may also involve stringing a belt through the pant loops and buckling it. All of these separate behaviors must be performed in the correct order. Thus, two things are learned: the basic requirements of each step, and the sequence in which steps should occur.

The implication of this characteristic for instruction is that teams must be competent in assessing and teaching behaviors in response chains. In designing instructional programs teachers must assess children's abilities to perform the steps and to put these steps together in meaningful chains. Then in addition to teaching the response chains, team members must be competent to monitor the effects of the teaching.

Self-Care Skills Are Best Taught When They Are Needed   Many skills should be taught when they are needed; this is particularly important in teaching self-care skills. Toileting can only be taught when the child has a need to urinate or defecate. Washing one's hands does not make sense when the hands are clean; putting on and taking off clothing is meaningless except when it fulfills some need for getting dressed or undressed. Thus, the timing and context in which these skills are taught is critical to their instruction.

Two major implications follow from this characteristic of self-care skills. Many of the "natural" times for teaching these skills occur in homes. Thus, parents may need to be involved in the instruction. Not only must the intervention team members be able to teach these skills; they must also be able to help other adults teach them. Carrying out this training task requires attention to the routines that exist within the home and to the skills of families in providing instruction. This part of the interventionist's work

carries with it the recognition that the natural times for doing these skills (e.g., when getting dressed in the morning) may not be the ideal teaching times. The demands of getting children awake, fed, dressed, and off to school or child care settings can be considerable. These demands, coupled with the demands on the caregiver to look after other children and perhaps to get himself ready for work, may very well make the teaching of dressing skills difficult and of low priority. Teams must accommodate to these realities when assisting families in teaching self-care skills. The second implication, then, of this characteristic of self-care skills—that they are best taught when they are needed—is that teams may need to make adaptations in the schedule (of the home or center) to increase the need for using these skills. As described in chapter 13, one method of increasing the number of opportunities to teach self-feeding is to provide several small meals rather than three or four large meals. Similar adjustments can be made to increase the need to toilet and dress/undress. As described later, some toilet training methods involve increased liquid intake to increase the need to urinate. With dressing and undressing, the schedule can be adapted to increase the opportunities for teaching. For example, the child can change clothing (or some article of clothing) when she goes out to play, when she comes in from play, when she gets ready to paint and after painting, before and after taking naps, during toileting routines, and at other times of the day. Thus, teams must not only be skilled in teaching these skills and helping others teach them, but they must be creative in designing times when such instruction can occur.

Self-Care Skills Occur Within Routines that Are Performed on a Regular but Low-Frequency Basis   Unlike many of the other skills we teach, self-care skills are needed throughout the child's life. From their first day of life, infants toilet, are dressed/undressed, are bathed, and must be fed. These routines do not stop with infancy. Despite occurring daily over the course of a lifetime, these routines do not occur many times per day. Children may only need to toilet a few times per day, and they may need to change clothing only once or twice a day. When these skills are needed, they frequently occur in routines. Routines, as described in chapter 6, are events that must be completed on a regular basis and frequently involve response chains.

Several implications result from this characteristic of self-care skills. First, teams must be skilled in assessing and teaching skills when they are needed. As we have noted, this may involve assisting families in providing such instruction and it may involve adapting the schedule to create additional occasions for teaching. Second, teams must teach children to know when skills should be performed. Children need to anticipate and know when the routine should be initiated. For example, many young children who have recently been toilet trained have accidents because they become involved in play and do not recognize that they need to urinate. When they do recognize it, it is too late to get to the bathroom or to call for assistance in getting to the bathroom. Third, teams should establish routines that are natural and predictable. Resistance to learning dressing and undressing can occur when children perceive instruction as interruptions of their ongoing activities and play. Thus, the times when dressing/undressing and grooming skills are taught should be established as regular and predictable routines. For example, brushing teeth should occur after eating and it should be incorporated into the schedule as a usual activity following eating. The washing-hands routine should regularly follow toileting and precede eating. By establishing such routines and teaching within them, instruction can be made more natural, and appropriate hygiene practices can be established. Fourth, chil-

dren's independence within routines should be promoted. For example, the routine of toileting involves getting to the bathroom, taking care of clothing, toileting, and returning to the ongoing activities. As much as possible, children's independence should be encouraged through the *entire* routine not just while urinating in the toilet. The promotion of independence may involve having the child signal others for help (e.g., in wiping, fastening clothing, adjusting the temperature of the water when washing hands), and it may involve adapting the routines through partial participation (cf. Box 6.5). Finally, these routines should involve frequent positive interactions. To keep the routines from becoming mechanical and being perceived as chores, teams should engage children in positive social interactions during the performance of routines. This can be accomplished by making routines gamelike, by providing enthusiastic praise for the performance of the steps in the routines, and by calling attention to children's accomplishments (e.g., "Go show Daddy how shiny you got your teeth.").

To Be Useful, Self-Care Skills Must Be Performed Fluently, Maintained by Natural Consequences, and Performed in Varied Situations Self-care skills, like most skills, must be conceptualized in terms of the learning hierarchy. As described in chapter 5, the hierarchy includes acquisition, fluency, maintenance, and generalization. For the dressing skill to be useful, for example, the child must learn to dress quickly, to do so without someone watching, and to do so when necessary. Learning to put on a shirt is one thing, learning to do it rapidly and without monitoring is quite another.

The major implication of this characteristic is that teams must be competent in facilitating acquisition, in promoting fluent performance, in understanding what contingencies will maintain performance, and in facilitating use of skills in all relevant environments. As described in early chapters, promoting acquisition involves ensuring a motivated learner and providing assistance and feedback for the process of learning the basic requirements of tasks. Fluency is promoted by a motivated learner practicing the skills on a regular basis. Maintenance is promoted by thinning the schedule of reinforcement for doing the skills and by using naturally occurring consequences. Generalization is promoted by using a variety of materials (e.g., different types of clothing), teaching in varied contexts, and delaying and thinning reinforcement schedules. One of the primary means of accomplishing such instruction is to ensure that acquired skills are needed. This involves communication with families to identify skills they value. For example, teams can teach children to dress and undress, but if families do not allow children to dress, then the likelihood of maintenance and generalization is reduced.

Summary   Self-care skills are important behaviors for children to learn, and they require special instructional competencies. Because they are acquired throughout the preschool period, most children in early intervention programs will have objectives in this area. These skills involve response chains that require acquisition of the specific behaviors and of the sequences for putting those behaviors together. These skills should be taught when they are needed—doing so involves helping parents provide or support instruction, and it involves adapting the environment to ensure that sufficient occasions are provided that call for these skills. These skills involve routines that occur on a regular basis but do not occur many times each day. Thus, teams must be fluent in teaching within the context of routines. Finally, these skills must be established at fluent levels, maintained by natural contingencies, and generalized to all needed contexts. Instruction must address all phases of the performance hierarchy.

TOILET TRAINING

In this section, we describe some unique aspects of toileting and toilet training. The rationale for early intervention teams being involved in toilet training also is provided. The goals for toilet training are presented so that teams can establish realistic objectives for children in relation to toileting. Finally, guidelines and procedures for toilet training are presented.

Unique Aspects of Toileting and Toilet Training

Toileting is a unique skill for at least three reasons. First, *it is a major developmental accomplishment*. It is an accomplishment that signals to others that children are becoming competent and independent persons. In early childhood, the accomplishment of being toilet trained is rivaled in importance only by the first words, the first steps, and going to school for the first time. It is the type of event that causes parents to phone grandparents with the good news. It is a cause for family celebration. As such, it is important to families with children who have disabilities. Usually, children with disabilities are toilet trained later than children with typical development. This delay in toileting success may cause stress for the family, and having younger siblings who are toilet trained before the child with disabilities may be one of those critical events families face in their development (Bailey, 1988). Thus, toilet training may be a high-priority goal of the individualized programs of many children, and early intervention teams must recognize its importance and ensure that the family is assisted in meeting this goal.

Second, *toileting is a skill that has major physical requirements but also involves several learned responses*. To be toilet trained, children must have the physical capacity to hold their urine and feces and release it in large quantities. If children do not have the physical capabilities, toilet training may be unsuccessful and frustrating. However, having these capabilities will not ensure that independent toileting will occur. In fact, many middle-aged adults who live in residential institutions for persons with mental retardation have the physical capabilities for independent toileting but have never been toilet trained (Foxx & Azrin, 1973). Toilet training involves learning when and where to urinate and defecate. It involves discriminating when the bladder or bowel is full, acting on that discrimination by getting to the bathroom, and then releasing the waste when appropriately situated at the toilet. Thus, unlike most other skills, toileting involves children attending to stimuli from their bodies and controlling their bodily functions. When the child can perform this routine successfully, he has earned a major sense of accomplishment; however, during training, accidents may lead to disappointment, frustration, and emotional reactions. Toileting also involves the child's learning appropriate ways to request the use of the bathroom and other skills such as the management of clothing and the washing of hands. Thus, team members must be aware of the child's physiological development, must respond to his accomplishments and accidents appropriately, and must understand how to teach him the skills involved in conforming with societal expectations.

Third, *toileting is a unique skill because it is largely under the control of children.* With most skills, we can set the occasion for their occurrence and do so repeatedly. For example, if we are teaching a child to walk, we can stand her in a supported position, move back a couple steps, and call to her to come. We can repeat this process several times in rapid succession. Or if we are teaching the child to use more elaborate language, we can structure the environment to cause her to talk and then respond to her in ways that will cause more talking. If we are teach-

ing the child to interact, we can put her with social peers and provide the peers with training to help get her to interact. It is much more difficult to set the occasion for the child to toilet. We can give her increased liquids to make her urinate more, but this process will take time. When the child has the need to toilet, we must immediately identify the need and use it for instruction—because once the need is gone, training cannot occur again until the child needs to toilet again. Again, with many skills we can provide response prompts that will cause behaviors to occur. With toileting there are few prompts we can provide that will cause urination or defecation. Thus, toileting is to a large extent dependent upon the child's initiation of the behavior. This fact, coupled with the importance that may be assigned to it by families, sets the stage for a variety of interaction patterns. Although toileting should be viewed as a skill to be learned and taught, intervention teams must recognize that it is also a skill that sets the stage for negative interaction patterns between children and parents. The child and family can get into a power struggle over toileting that results in the child purposefully having accidents, and in disappointment, frustration, and scolding on the part of families. Such events can quickly develop into counterproductive exchanges and patterns of interacting (see Box 11.2, p. 372). Thus, when conducting toilet training programs, intervention teams should monitor interactions and ensure that negative exchanges do not develop. When such patterns do begin to develop, team members must be aware of procedures for assisting families in breaking those patterns and establishing more productive exchanges.

The Rationale for Toilet Training

From a family perspective, good reasons exist for establishing independent toileting skills. First, children who are toilet trained are simply more independent than those who are not. As we noted in chapter 2, promoting independence is a major goal of early intervention programs. Second, by teaching toileting skills, the regular and enduring caregiving demands of changing diapers is eliminated. The caregiving demands of young children can be stressful for parents of children with and without disabilities; however, the demands are usually thought to be more intense and to occur over greater lengths of time when the children have disabilities (Dyson & Fewell, 1986). When the child independently toilets, a major caregiving demand is reduced. Although most parents get used to changing diapers, few would say that it is the highlight of their day, and few would choose to do so if it was not necessary. Third, the expense of using diapers is also eliminated. Purchasing disposable diapers or washing reusable diapers is an expensive proposition. Toilet training is one of the few skills children learn that has immediate economic benefits for families. This economic benefit also exists for center-based programs that supply diapers for children. Fourth, independent toileting may result in more normalized interactions and placements. Being toilet trained rather than wearing diapers makes children appear less discrepant from their typical peers. Frequently, one of the most salient cues that a child in a mainstreamed program has disabilities is his being the only child with diapers. This situation engenders questions such as, "Why does Nina wear diapers?" and "Is Allicia still a baby 'cause she wears diapers?" Further, when children wear diapers and have bowel movements that produce salient odors, other children may avoid interacting with them and/or make comments (e.g., "Joey stinks again."). In addition, some child care programs require children to be toilet trained before they are enrolled. While publicly funded programs cannot have such requirements, private after-school care or other child-care programs that may be needed by the family and may allow access to typically developing peers can and frequently do have such requirements (Berk & Berk, 1982). Thus, being toilet trained may result in more interactions with peers and greater access to more placement options.

At this point, you may be asking, "Isn't toilet training a family task?" The answer is, "Yes and no." "Yes" because families should be intimately involved in all toilet training endeavors. While it is possible to have children toilet trained in centers but not at home, this is not a desirable situation. Teams should involve families in deciding whether to initiate training, when to do so, what the role of families in training will be, and which methods to use. Families also should be involved in supporting the toilet training activities of professionals. Such joint decision making and support cannot be secured without purposeful communication with families. But the answer is "no" because toileting is no more a family responsibility than training in communication or social skills. By the mandate of the individualized appropriate education provision of the Individuals with Disabilities Act, toilet training is a legitimate educational endeavor (Snell, 1980). Thus, early intervention professionals are likely to engage in toilet training activities and assist families in implementing such activities. In the next section, the goals for toilet training are described.

Goals of Toilet Training

For most young children with disabilities, the goals or outcomes of early intervention related to toilet training can occur on three progressively more complex and independent levels (Wolery & Smith, 1989). The most basic level of toilet training involves children urinating and defecating in the toilet when taken on a regular schedule. This level does not involve substantial independence; in fact, if the adults do not take the child to the toilet, then accidents occur. However, this level is preferred over no control. It may avoid the use of diapers and allows the child to remain dry and unsoiled. It can eliminate the repeated and unpleasant task of changing children's diapers. The child at the intermediate level of toilet training anticipates the need to toilet and communicates that need to an adult. The adult then can get the child to the bathroom and assist the child in managing clothing, wiping, and washing hands after toileting. This level of training places on the child the responsibility for initiating the toileting behaviors. The adults may provide reminders or ask questions, but the child is sufficiently independent to know when toileting is needed. The child who has achieved the most advanced level of toilet training anticipates when to toilet, moves independently to the toilet (in safe environments) or communicates the need to adults, manages her clothing without assistance, toilets, washes her hands, and returns to the ongoing activities. This most independent level of training is reached only after considerable time. The level that is appropriate for each child depends in large part on the child's skills in other areas, particularly in dressing/undressing, in communicating, and in moving independently. However, each level builds upon the other. Although achievement of the third level is most desirable, attainment of either of the other levels is a legitimate outcome of training and a worthy reason for celebrating success.

A fourth goal of toilet training deals with children for whom standard toilet training is physically impossible due to paralysis or to other conditions that preclude usual toileting functions. With such children, the goal is to assist them in being as independent as possible in managing their waste products and to design procedures to allow them to do this with dignity. Consultation with medical professionals is necessary when addressing this goal.

General Guidelines for Teaching Toileting Skills

To achieve the goals for toilet training, teams should follow several general guidelines.

Assess Children's Readiness for Toilet Training   As with other skills in the early childhood curriculum, intervention planning and instruction should follow careful assessment (see chapter 4). Assessment of toileting skills has been addressed in other sources (Campbell, 1977; Orelove & Sobsey, 1987; Snell, 1987; Wolery & Smith, 1989). With typically developing children, chronological age of 2 years or 2.5 years is a good predictor of readiness for toilet training, and children who are 2.5 to 3 years old are more easily trained; however, successful toilet training has been reported for children as young as 1 year old (Smeets, Lancioni, Ball, & Oliva, 1985). Sullivan-Bolyai (1986) states that

the age at which a child can be trained will vary depending upon his physical and emotional development. This includes local conditioning of reflex sphincter control (about nine months of age); completion of myelination of pyrimidal tracts (12 to 18 months of age), and emotional maturity, which allows the child to want to control bowel and bladder function (18 months to 3 years of age). (p. 79)

With children who have disabilities (particularly those with physical or central nervous system disabilities), chronological age may not be a good indication of readiness. Thus, three issues deserve consideration. First, children should have the prerequisite skills for toileting before toilet training is initiated. The prerequisite skills include bladder control (i.e., the ability to hold urine as represented by regular periods of dryness), the ability to release urine in large amounts, and the ability to assume an appropriate sitting position on the toilet (a particularly significant prerequisite for young and physically involved children). An additional prerequisite is freedom from medical conditions (e.g., urinary tract infections) (Wolery & Smith, 1989). The second issue concerns the presence of a number of supplementary skills, "desirable" skills that can increase the success of toilet training. A list of the prerequisite and desirable skills and a summary of methods for assessing their presence are presented in Box 14.1. The third issue concerns convenience—toilet training should only be initiated when it is convenient for families. Thus, times near vacations, visits from relatives, or other unusual events that consume a family's attention are poor times to initiate toilet training. Toilet training, even if initiated at a center, will require follow-through by parents. This means that they must be free to attend to children's needs and implement the training procedures.

Initiate Training on Daytime Rather than Nighttime Toileting   Although being dry during the day and being dry during the night are both desirable outcomes, toilet training should be initiated during the day. Children with typical development frequently are dry during the day for a year or two before being able to stay dry at night. This is because they are more alert and aware of their bodily sensations during the day. Thus, daytime training is the major toilet training activity of early intervention teams. Generally, it is appropriate to use diapers during the night for children who are being trained or for those who have just been toilet trained. Later in the chapter, procedures for addressing persistent nighttime accidents are described.

Begin Training with Bladder Rather than Bowel Control   Although children sometimes physically can control their bowel functions before their bladder functions, there are some good reasons to focus training

on urination. First, children urinate more often than they defecate. As a result, we have more opportunities to teach toileting skills, to reinforce them, and to use correction procedures (if they are employed). Children will more quickly learn skills that are performed and reinforced several times per day than those that are performed and reinforced three or four times per day. Thus, to ensure rapid acquisition of toileting behaviors, we focus initially on training bladder control. Second, the number of times that children urinate can be increased more easily (i.e., through additional intake of liquids) than can the number of bowel movements. Thus, if the usual liquid intake does not provide sufficient opportunities for training, the number of opportunities can be easily increased for urination but not for defecation. Third, urination should be the focus of training because urination and defecation may occur at approximately the same time. If we train children to urinate in the toilet, it is likely that some bowel movements will incidentally occur while children are on the toilet. In such cases, the adult should reinforce this occurrence. If training focused on bowel movements, fewer opportunities for the two types of elimination to co-occur would happen, and children would require additional training for bladder control. However, some children show definite signs of bowel movements. They become less active, they quiet, and they assume a strained facial expression. When you observe such behavior during the course of training, it is wise to take the child to the toilet and see if a bowel movement occurs. If it does, reinforcement should be provided.

Begin Training with Children Sitting on the Toilet   Although boys will eventually learn to urinate while standing, it is wise to initiate training with boys sitting on the toilet. This is true for several reasons. First, during initial training, children may not urinate

---

BOX 14.1   Prerequisite and desirable skills for toilet training

Type of Skill/Factors	Summary of Measurement Procedures
Prerequisite Factors	
Bladder control	Direct observation using a time-sample recording system to note when child urinates, defecates, and takes in liquid and food
Releases urine in large amounts at once	Direct observation using anecdotal recording about whether diaper is soaked
Sitting position on toilet	Direct observation and consultation with physical or occupational therapist to identify appropriate position
Free of interfering medical conditions	Review of medical records, interviews with parents, and knowledge of child; consultation with physician on questionable cases
Desirable Factors	
Reinforcer identification	Direct observation, interviews with parents, and use of reinforcer menu
Instructional control	Direct observation using event recording to assess compliance with adult requests, and direct observation using event recording to determine frequency of interfering behaviors
Awareness of elimination and/or discomfort	Direct observation using anecdotal recording and parent interviews about changes in child behavior related to toileting
Sitting on toilet	Direct observation timing the duration of sitting on the toilet
Parent involvement	Interview with parents to explain procedures, solicit participation, and determine ability to implement training program
Requesting skills*	Direct observation using anecdotal recording to determine presence of requesting function
Clothing management,** locomotion, and hygiene	Direct observation using event sampling to assess clothing management skills and ability to move to bathroom

---

*Assessed only if second level of toilet training outcomes is targeted.

**Assessed only if third level of toilet training outcomes is targeted.

Note: From "Assessing Self-Care Skills" by M. Wolery and P. D. Smith, 1989, in *Assessing Infants and Preschoolers with Handicaps* (pp. 447–477), Ed. by D. B. Bailey and M. Wolery, Columbus, OH: Merrill. Copyright 1989 by Macmillan Publishing. Reprinted by permission.

---

quickly when taken to the toilet. They may need to be there a few minutes. It is simply easier to keep them sitting while you wait for the urine to come than it is to try to keep them standing in front of the toilet. Second, young boys have notoriously poor control of the direction of their urine flow. If they are standing near the toilet, they may turn as they begin to urinate, and the urine may hit the floor, the trainer, or anything else in its range. By having boys seated, such occurrences can be avoided. However, even when boys are seated their urine may not flow into the toilet; thus, you are urged to stand to the side while they are sitting waiting to urinate. Some potty seats have shields to control this problem, but these are not completely successful, and because children with disabilities are usually older than typical children when they are toilet trained, their legs are bigger and are often scratched in getting up and sitting down when the shield is on the seat. Finally, children should be seated during toilet training to control for the possibility mentioned above that bowel movements may occur at approximately the same time as urination.

Initiate Training in all Relevant Environments Some young children spend time in multiple settings each day. They may attend a specialized or mainstreamed program in the morning, go to a family day care in the afternoon, go to clinic (e.g., for therapy), and then return to their homes. Although occasionally toilet training in one setting will result in improvements in other settings (cf. Richmond, 1983; Sadler & Merkert, 1977), this usually is not the case. Dunlap, Koegel, and Koegel (1984) studied this issue. They included four children with autism between the ages of 5 and 7 years. Each child spent time in four to six environments (including family outings) on a regular basis. During baseline one child did not receive any specific toilet training, two received training in one setting, and one child received training in two settings. During baseline, the training involved frequent trips to the toilet, reinforcement for using the toilet, reinforcement for being dry when off the toilet, immediate detection of accidents (2 children wore electronic moisture sensing devices), positive practice overcorrection for accidents (explained later), and physical guidance to engage in positive practice. However, none of the children were consistently dry on half of the measured days. As a result, a continuity

of training procedure was implemented. This involved designating one person to coordinate efforts and contact trainers in other settings. Written instructions accompanied the child to promote consistent implementation. Frequent telephone contacts between the coordinator and others occurred. As a result of this effort, all children showed substantial improvements. This included the one child who had no previous toilet training experience, and three children who had experienced long but unsuccessful toilet training. This study argues strongly for involving families in toilet training decisions, providing training in all settings where the child spends time, and ensuring that the same procedures are being used across different settings and trainers.

Teach the Child to Communicate the Need to Use the Bathroom in the Later Stages of Toilet Training To be truly independent in toileting, children should be able to move to the bathroom when they need to go. Ideally, classrooms and homes would be designed to allow this to occur. However, some home and classroom arrangements do not allow this freedom, and when children are in the community with their families such freedom is undesirable for young children. Therefore, children should be taught to communicate to adults when they need to use the bathroom.

The words and/or signals used in teaching children to indicate the need to toilet should be selected with the family. Different families use different words to describe toileting functions, and the adults who provide training should be sensitive to those words and/or signals and try to use them consistently.

It should be in the later stages of toilet training that children are taught to indicate the need to toilet. In the initial stages, they may have no awareness of the need to toilet and hence no reason to communicate. However, during initial stages of training, adults should use the words and/or signals that will be expected later, to begin to build an association between the words and signals and the toileting routine. As we have noted, sometimes children begin to anticipate the need to toilet and they display unique behaviors (e.g., quieting, grabbing their crotch area, crossing their legs). These occasions are ideal times to teach the communicative signals; however, it is also important to move the child rapidly to the bathroom at such times.

Teach All the Skills Involved in the Toilet Training Routine As noted earlier, toileting is a routine that involves many skills other than urinating and defecating in the toilet. To ensure that children become maximally independent, all the skills involved in the toileting routine should be taught. A listing of skills frequently included in a toileting routine are listed in Box 14.2. However, it is important to recognize that some of these be-

haviors may be impossible for some young children. In such cases, use of partial participation is appropriate. This is particularly important in terms of the clothing children wear. Pants with difficult fasteners, tight fitting clothing, and body suits are difficult for young children (and sometimes adults) to manage. During toilet training, it is wise to use elastic waist-band pants that can be pushed down easily.

Maintain Records of Toileting Success and of Accidents During Training The records that are maintained on children's toilet training will vary slightly depending upon the method used. However, they are maintained to identify times when children are successful and times when accidents occur regularly. The recordkeeping can be as simple as recording on a sheet near the toilet when

---

BOX 14.2   Behaviors of many toilet training routines

1 Child recognizes a bodily sensation that indicates the need to toilet.
2 Child communicates the need to an adult or leaves the current area and moves (walks, moves wheelchair) directly to the bathroom.
3 Upon entering the bathroom, the child moves to the toilet, and may need to transfer from wheel chair to toilet.
4 Child unfastens clothing as necessary.
5 Child adjusts clothing for toileting, pushes down underwear.
6 Child sits on toilet.
7 Child maintains sitting balance on toilet waiting for urination/defecation.
8 Child eliminates urine or feces.
9 Child wipes self until clean as necessary.
10 Child disposes of toilet tissue.
11 Child gets off toilet.
12 Child flushes toilet.
13 Child pulls up underwear and adjusts other clothing as necessary.
14 Child approaches the sink, turns on the water and adjusts water temperature as necessary.
15 Child washes hands using soap.
16 Child drys hands and disposes of towel as appropriate.
17 Child returns to the ongoing activity.

The adult can provide assistance on steps that cannot be accomplished independently, but may need to teach the child to signal when assistance is needed.

children were taken and when they urinated in the toilet. Records can also be more complex and include a listing of the food and liquid intake (Fredericks, Baldwin, Grove, & Moore, 1975). The records should be maintained in all settings in which the child regularly spends time. These records will help maintain consistency in the toileting regime and will serve to ensure that toileting skills are being demonstrated when and where they are needed.

Before initiating toilet training, teams should determine whether children display the prerequisite and desirable skills, and whether it is a convenient time for the family. Toilet training should focus on daytime training, should initially focus on bladder rather than bowel control, and should occur in all relevant settings. Training should begin with children sitting on the toilet rather than standing near it, and as training progresses, children should be taught to signal that they need to use the bathroom. While conducting toilet training, all of the skills involved in the toileting routines should be taught. Finally, records should be maintained to ensure that success and generalization are occurring.

Methods of Toilet Training

At least three major methods exist for teaching children toileting skills. These methods can be used by professionals and by families. When the methods are used by professionals, families should be active decision makers about when and how the training is conducted, and should support appropriate toileting behaviors at home. When the methods are used by families, chances of success are increased if consultation and assistance are provided by the intervention team.

Schedule Method   The schedule method, as the name implies, involves taking children to the toilet on some schedule. At least two versions of the schedule method exist. The first involves taking children to the toilet at regular intervals (e.g., every hour). The second version involves taking children to the toilet near times when they are likely to urinate. The second version requires the identification of times when children regularly urinate (i.e., wet their diapers) under usual conditions of liquid intake.

With both versions of the schedule method, the child is required to sit on the toilet for a designated number of minutes (e.g., 5 to 10 minutes) or less if she urinates or defecates. If urination or defecation occur, the child is reinforced heavily and removed from the toilet. If neither occurs, then the child is removed from the toilet at the end of the time interval and returned to the ongoing activities. Two types of data are usually maintained: the time the child is taken is recorded, and the results (urination, defecation, both, neither) are recorded.

The schedule method, based on parent report, has been used with typical children and frequently is effective. Experience with children who have disabilities also suggests that the schedule method is used frequently. Sometimes it is effective; however, it is clear that it takes a long time and that many trips to the toilet may not result in urination and/or defecation. Thus, for many young children with disabilities, it is not the recommended practice.

Distributed Practice Method—Improved Schedule Procedure   This method was developed by Fredericks et al. (1975) to minimize the effort expended by the adult during toilet training. It is similar to the schedule method, but has some useful improvements. The procedure involves the following steps.

1. *Collect baseline data on the child's patterns of urination and defecation.* Fredericks et al. recommend collecting data each half hour of the child's entire waking day for at least 14 consecutive days. At each half-hour interval, the adult checks whether the

child is dry, whether urination or defecation has occurred, where (toilet or in pants) any voiding occurred, and what food/liquids and how much of each were consumed by the child during the past half hour. This data should be collected in all environments in which the child spends time (home, school, family daycare, etc.). A timer can be used to cue the adult to collect the data.

2. *Analyze the data to identify patterns of urination and defecation.* In this method, unlike the traditional schedule method, training is implemented initially only at the two most probable times when the child will urinate. Thus, the data from the 14 days are scrutinized to identify the two times each day when the child most consistently urinates. These two times will later be used for instruction. If the data are erratic and do not reveal two times per day when the child is consistently wet, then toilet training should be delayed or data collection should continue for another 2-week period.

3. *Select reinforcers for use in the toilet training program.* Fredericks et al. recommend that a powerful reinforcer be identified and used only for toilet training. As we indicated in chapter 5, reinforcers can be identified by interviews, observation, and reinforcer preference tests. When multiple strong reinforcers are available, it is wise to use a powerful reinforcer only for the toilet training program. This restriction will reduce the possibility that the reinforcer will lose its power. Letting children select the reinforcer each day also is a useful practice.

4. *Implement toilet training at the two identified times using the identified reinforcers.* As we have indicated, training is initially implemented only at the two times when the child is most likely to urinate. When the first time comes around, the adult says, "Let's go potty," and takes the child to the toilet. The child is seated on the toilet for 10 minutes. If the child urinates, then he is removed from the toilet and reinforcement is provided. If the child does not urinate, then he is allowed off the toilet for 5 minutes and put back on it for an additional 5 minutes. If urination occurs, reinforcement is provided; if it does not, the child is returned to the usual activities. This procedure is repeated at the second time that was identified for toilet training each day. Data are collected only on whether urination occurs at these two times per day. The baseline data collection is suspended when training is initiated.

5. *Collect and use the data on the child's performance during toilet training.* When training is initiated, data are recorded only at the two times the child is taken to the toilet. These data are used to determine when to extend the training to other times of the day. When the child urinates at 50 percent of the two times taken over a 2-week period, the adult should continue the training *and* begin to collect more baseline data as described in step 1. This additional data collection is done to identify other times when the training could be implemented.

6. *Expand training to other periods of the day.* When the child urinates at 75 percent of the original two training times over a 2-week period, then training should be expanded to include a third and possibly a fourth daily training time. These additional times of training are identified through the expanded data collection that was initiated as described in step 5. The training (as described in step 3) continues at the original two times and now commences at the one or two additional new training times. This process of providing training at selected times, collecting additional data when success is shown at those times, and expanding the training to new times is continued until the child is consistently dry throughout the day.

7. *Teach the child to communicate the need to toilet.* When the child is urinating at 75 percent of the times that he is taken to the toilet and is dry throughout the day, he is taught to communicate the need to toilet.

Throughout training, the adult has used the words or signals that will be taught at the beginning of each training time. To teach the child to communicate the need to toilet, the adult models the words and/or signal (e.g., the adult says "Go potty" or makes the manual sign of a "t"). The child is trained to imitate the model, and once imitation is occurring on a regular basis, the trainer asks the child, "Where do you need to go?" The child is taught to reply, "Go potty," or to use whatever signal has been selected. Over time, the child is given the responsibility for indicating whether he needs to toilet. As we mentioned earlier, the words or signals should be selected in consultation with the family, and all adults involved in the training process should use the same words and/or signals.

The Fredericks et al. (1975) procedure relies heavily on the use of positive reinforcement. Accidents are responded to in a matter-of-fact manner without scolding or punishment. If accidents occur after the child is toilet trained, prompts (e.g., "Do you need to potty?") should be added throughout the day. These prompts are then gradually removed. If accidents persist, a change is made in the reinforcer for correct toileting. If this change is not successful, then differential reinforcement (DRO) as described in chapter 11 is used. Initially, the child is reinforced for going a reasonable amount of time without accidents (e.g., for 1 hour). At the end of each hour, if no accident has occurred, the child is reinforced. This interval is slowly increased (e.g., by 15-minute increments) until reinforcement is provided only at the end of the day for having no accidents.

This procedure has several positive benefits. It increases the probability of urination in the toilet because the child is taken only at times when it is highly likely that urination will occur. It also relies heavily on positive reinforcement, which can reduce the possibility of negative and counterproductive exchanges developing between the child

and the parent or teacher. The demands on the adult are relatively minimal because the procedure involves taking the child to the toilet only at selected times. The procedure is relatively simple and does not require excessive training of parents. The interventionist can review the records and make decisions about when to reinstate the baseline data collection, when to expand training, and which times are the best teaching times. However, the process will require several weeks to complete. When this time frame is acceptable, then use of the procedure is highly recommended.

Massed Practice or Rapid Method Foxx and Azrin developed the massed practice method (Azrin & Foxx, 1971; Foxx & Azrin, 1973) for persons with retardation who were living in residential institutions (Fox & Azrin, 1973). Later it was adapted to create the "less-than-a-day" method for young children with typical development (Azrin & Foxx, 1974). Although the two methods are different from one another, their basic structure is similar. The rapid method establishes self-initiated, independent toileting within a short time period. Independent toileting means that without assistance the child will move to the bathroom, take down her pants, urinate and/or defecate, wipe, flush the toilet (or empty the bowl, if a potty chair is used, and flush it), pull up her own pants, and wash her hands. This process was accomplished with adults who had retardation in 4-5 days of intensive training and with young children who had typical development in 4-5 hours. The training occurs throughout the day and lasts for several hours (4–8) per day. It generally requires one teacher for one or two children. Other basic components are as follows:

1 The amount of liquid the child drinks during training is increased substantially. This increase produces an increase in the number of times the child needs to urinate

and thereby increases the number of opportunities to implement training and provide reinforcement for correct toileting. About 1 cup of fluids per hour is recommended for young children. Thompson and Hanson (1983) describe precautions related to providing children with increased liquids.

2   The child is seated on the toilet for a set period of time. Ten minutes is recommended for the young child. The child is then allowed off the toilet for a set period of time (e.g., 15 minutes). The amount of time off the toilet increases after each urination in the toilet.

3   The child is reinforced immediately for urinating in the toilet. Reinforcement frequently includes presenting praise, liquids, and edibles. When appropriate, salty edibles are used to increase the child's desire to drink more fluids. The child also is reinforced for engaging in play when off the toilet, for sitting on the toilet, and for managing clothing.

4   The child is reinforced on a regular basis (e.g., every 10 minutes) for staying dry when off the toilet. This involves the adult having the child touch his/her crotch area and feeling the dry pants, and then providing reinforcement for "being dry."

5   Graduated guidance is used to prompt the child to move to the toilet, manage clothing, flush, and so forth. As with other graduated guidance programs, the prompts are provided only as necessary and are removed quickly when the child performs the correct behavior.

6   Prompts to move to the toilet are decreased as training progresses. This transfers the need to move to the toilet from the adult to the child's recognition of her full bladder.

7   When accidents occur, the adult does four things. First, the child is verbally reprimanded for wetting (e.g., "No, don't wet your pants."). Second, positive practice

overcorrection is provided that involves having the child move to the toilet, take down the pants, sit on the toilet for 1 or 2 seconds, stand up, pull up the pants, and move to another part of the room. This is repeated several times in rapid succession. Third, opportunities are provided for the child to feel her wet pants. Fourth, at the end of the positive practice, the child is required to take off the wet pants and to wash them under running water and to clean any urine that is on the floor (restitutional overcorrection). As described in chapter 11, overcorrection is a punishment procedure. It may result in crying, tantrums, and other emotional reactions. Frequently, graduated guidance is required to ensure that the child does the positive practice and restitutional behaviors. Therefore, this procedure should be implemented consistently, correctly, and with care, and it should only be used when rapid toilet training is critical.

8   During maintenance, the child is regularly reinforced for staying dry, and the consequences of accidents remain essentially the same except that the opportunities for feeling wet pants may be eliminated.

Frequently, with the rapid method, a urine sensing device is placed on children's pants. The device will sound an alarm when the child begins to urinate. Thus, the adult has a signal about when accidents occur. If the device is not used, then the adult must keep a watchful eye on the child's pants to detect accidents and to respond as soon as they occur. Usually, training is conducted with the child wearing only training pants. Training can be successful with or without the alarm device (Williams & Sloop, 1978).

The "less-than-a-day" procedure for typically developing children includes verbal rehearsal of the toileting sequence. It also includes having the child "toilet train" a doll that wets. Also, a "friends who care" list is devised and their names are used during verbal reinforcement (e.g., "Grandma [Santa Claus, Big Sister, etc.] will be so proud of you for using the toilet.") (Azrin & Foxx, 1974).

Variations of this rapid method have been tried with similar success using children older than preschoolers (Smith, 1979; Williams & Sloop, 1978). Also, Butler (1976a) assisted a mother in using the Foxx and Azrin (1973) procedure to toilet train a 4.5-year-old boy with spina bifida meningocele. The number of accidents was significantly reduced, although the training did not control the dribbling that is characteristic of spina bifida children. Saddler and Merkert (1977) compared the Foxx and Azrin (1973) method to a traditional schedule method in a day treatment center. The subjects were 15 children (7 to 12 years old) with severe to profound mental retardation. The Foxx and Azrin method resulted in quicker toilet training and generalization to homes for some children. However, considerable time was required by the staff members, who questioned whether the Foxx and Azrin method was worth the time and effort.

Perhaps the most significant study related to the rapid method for preschoolers was conducted by Richmond (1983). Four preschool children (32 to 46 months of age) who were developmentally functioning at about the 12-month level participated. They were enrolled in a specialized program for preschoolers with developmental retardation for about 4.5 hours per day. All children were ambulatory; they had minimal expressive language, but they did follow some verbal directions. There were six children in the class and two adults. As in many preschool centers, children did not have free access to the bathroom. Before training, records were maintained of accidents. Children were taken to the toilet every hour; if they urinated, they were praised; if accidents occurred, they were changed and cleaned. Before training, they were averaging more than one accident per day. Training occurred for 4 weeks and included the following procedures. For the first week, children were taken to the toilet every 15 minutes; for the second week they were taken every 30 minutes; for the third week they were taken every hour; and during the fourth week, they were taken every 2 hours. They were given dry pants checks before each time they were taken to the toilet. If they urinated in the toilet, they were praised and given liquid to drink to increase the frequency of urination. If accidents occurred, the children received a "brief reprimand and simple correction (i.e., the child was responsible for getting a clean set of clothes, removing the dirty clothes, washing necessary body areas, disposing of dirty clothes, and dressing)" (p. 200). Throughout training, they were taught to indicate the need to use the toilet by using a method similar to that described above for the distributed practice procedure. At least 4 weeks of posttraining data were collected. Toileting accidents, while not totally eliminated, were substantially decreased—down to 2.0, 1.4, 0.9, and 0.6 accidents per week for the subjects respectively. This study indicates that the requirements of the rapid method (e.g., conducting training all day long, using overcorrection, using urine sensing devices on children's clothing) can be modified considerably. No replications of this study have been found, but this initial success suggests that further studies are warranted.

A few studies (Butler, 1976b; Matson, 1975; Matson & Ollendick, 1977) have investigated the ability of parents to use the *Toilet Training in Less Than a Day* book (Azrin & Foxx, 1974). Several findings are apparent. As reported by Azrin and Foxx (1974), children over 25 or 26 months of age are more quickly trained than younger children (Butler, 1976b; Matson & Ollendick, 1977). Also, some children, perhaps 20 to 30 percent, stop wetting the bed as a result of the training. Tantrum and avoidance behavior occur during positive practice (Butler, 1976b; Matson, 1975; Matson & Ollendick, 1977). Parents using the book without consultation or supervision from a professional are less likely to be successful than those who do receive consultation (Matson & Ollendick, 1977). Thus, the intervention team should be available to help families who plan to use the book to toilet train their children. Our own experience suggests that parents should read both books (Azrin & Foxx, 1974; Foxx & Azrin, 1973) and discuss the procedure thoroughly before deciding to use it. Also, the procedure appears to work best when the interventionist conducts the first part of the training in the home, and then after 2 or 3 hours trains a parent to do the procedure. When this is done, the family can follow through with the procedure at home and the interventionist can ensure generalization to the center. Other rapid methods have been developed (see Bettison, 1982; Lancioni & Ceccarani, 1981; Mahoney, Van Wagenen, & Meyerson, 1971), and Snell (1987) provides an overview of these procedures. However, the Foxx and Azrin approach is the most common.

When selecting a procedure, the team (including the family) should determine whether training must be completed rapidly or whether it can move at a slower pace. If rapid training is necessary, then a rapid training procedure should be selected. If slower acquisition is acceptable, then the distributed practice procedure should be adopted. However, this decision must be made with the realization of the commitment involved. With the rapid method, a heavy commitment of time and effort is required over a short period of time (e.g., 1 to 5 days). With the distributed procedure, less intense commitment is required (a few minutes each day), but the commitment occurs over several weeks. In most cases, the schedule method should be avoided.

Assisting Children Who Have Disabilities that Interfere with the Toileting Process
Children with conditions such as spina bifida, spinal cord trauma, Hirschsprung's disease and others may have paralysis that interferes with toileting functions. These conditions are called neurogenic bowels and bladders and they can interfere with the function of the bladder and bowel and with the child's brain receiving sensations that the bowels or bladder are full (Sullivan-Bolyai, 1986). Although surgical diversions such as colostomies for bowel function and ileostomies for bladder function have been used, they are not treatments of choice (Sullivan-Bolyai, 1986; Tarnowski, & Drabman, 1987). Management of toileting function through other means is recommended.

For bowel control, a diet that prevents both constipation and diarrhea should be provided. In addition, a regular regime of attempting to defecate should be established (Sullivan-Bolyai, 1986). As with the toilet training of other children, establishing a secure sitting position on the toilet is necessary. When on the toilet, the child is instructed to bend forward and strain (Sullivan-Bolyai, 1986). In addition to regular attempts to defecate, the use of suppositories, enemas, and digital stimulation may be necessary (Sullivan-Bolyai, 1986). Two guidelines should be followed: (a) consultation and supervision by medical personnel is necessary; and (b) over time, the responsibility for management should be shifted from the caregiver to the child.

For children with neurogenic bladders, a recurring problem is lack of total emptying of the bladder, which leads to urinary tract infections and potentially to kidney damage. Thus, procedures are needed to ensure regular and complete voiding. Another problem with some children with neurogenic bladders is dribbling (i.e., leakage of small amounts of urine). To prevent leakage on clothing, to eliminate odor, and to avoid the use of diapers, "incontinent pants" are recommended. These can be purchased at local medical supply outlets. Also, with young boys, external penile appliances for the collection of urine can be used (Sullivan-Bolyai, 1986).

For the emptying of the bladder, children should be taken to the toilet on a regular schedule (e.g., every 2 to 3 hours). While sitting, the child should be instructed to strain. This may be successful with some children. In addition, some medications have been used, but these carry the possibility of negative side effects (Sullivan-Bolyai, 1986). An alternative is clean intermittent catheterization (CIC). Regular catheterization has increased periods of dryness, decreased urinary tract infections, and avoided the use of surgical diversions (Neef, Parrish, Hannigan, Page, & Iwata, 1989; Tarnowski & Drabman, 1987).

CIC involves insertion of a catheter into the urethral opening. With young children, the catheterization is conducted by nurses and other caregiving staff as well as by teachers and parents several times per day. Older children are taught to perform the procedure themselves. Hannigan (1979) taught four children (5 years of age) with myelodysplasia to perform the catheterization procedure. The instructional procedures included the use of anatomically correct dolls; that is, children learned to perform the CIC procedure on the dolls. However, all of the children in Hannigan's study had cognitive development within normal limits. Neef et al. (1989) taught the CIC procedure to two girls (one 4 years old and one 8 years old) with myelomeningocele. The younger child had normal cognitive functioning, and the older child had borderline intellectual performance. The training was conducted while the children were in the hospital for a few days. The procedure was broken into four components which are displayed in Box

14.3. The training, conducted in individual sessions, included verbal directions, models, point prompts, and, when necessary, physical guidance. Children were taught to perform the catheterization on dolls. Praise was employed for completion of correct steps. Children also were assessed on their ability to apply the procedure to themselves. Both children were successful; however, the younger child required direct training on steps of inserting the catheter when applied to herself. Parents were contacted 3 months after training, and reported that both children were regularly performing the self-catheterization. Tarnowski and Drabman (1987) also taught two 6-year-old boys self-catheterization procedures. Both boys displayed mild mental retardation (i.e., WISC-R Full Scale IQ scores of 61 and 63). Prior to the study, the staff or parents had completed the catheterization. Training involved general verbal directions, specific verbal prompts, verbal prompts with models, and verbal description with physical guidance. Praise was delivered for completed steps of the procedure and the schedule was thinned as children became proficient. In addition, a "star chart" was used to deliver tokens for correct performance, and backup reinforcers were available. At a result, both children learned the self-catheterization procedure with assistance available from adults for pushing the inserted catheter the last 1 to 2 inches.

In summary, these studies show promising results for teaching young children with neurogenic bladders to engage in independent care of their toileting routines. However, a few statements are necessary. First, the training was conducted in hospitals by trained staff. Thus, teaching self-catheterization using these procedure is *not recommended* without vigilant supervision from appropriate medical staff. Second, the children who participated in these studies all had normal upper extremity movements and

---

BOX 14.3 Component steps of self-catheterization

1. Preparation
   1.1 Obtains silk catheter, paper towel, mirror, and urine container (if toilet is not used) from storage.
   1.2 Washes complete surface of hands with soap and water so that no dirt or residue is visible, and dries.
   1.3 Rinses alcohol from catheter with running water, without contact between catheter and sink (if catheter contacts nonsanitary surface, rewashes with soap and water).
   1.4 Places catheter on paper towel.
   1.5 Removes underclothes and frees garment from at least one leg.
   1.6 Sits on chair or toilet with legs spread apart at least 90°.
2. Mirror placement and adjustment
   2.1 Places mirror in front of self on chair or toilet seat.
   2.2 Positions mirror with red mark facing self.
   2.3 Applies pressure to top of compact to secure suction cup.
   2.4 Opens compact mirror.
   2.5 Adjusts angle of mirror.
   2.6 Rests mirror on stand.
3. Catheter insertion and removal
   3.1 Lifts clitoris to expose urinary meatus and/or moves finger downward between labia to urinary opening and separates labia by spreading index finger and middle finger in opposite directions while applying pressure against labia.
   3.2 Holds labia apart until catheter is inserted.

3.3 Grasps catheter between tip and 2 in. from end of pincer grasp.
3.4 Looks in mirror at urinary opening.
3.5 Touches genital area with appropriate end of catheter for insertion.
3.6 Inserts catheter into urinary opening.
3.7 Uses hand to assist in insertion of catheter.
3.8 Places free end of catheter in container or toilet.
3.9 Pushes catheter upward until urine starts to flow (or past marked point on catheter for training purposes if bladder is nonfunctional).
3.10 Holds catheter in place until urine stops flowing (or for at least 5 s for training purposes if bladder is nonfunctional)
3.11 Withdraws catheter.
4. Clean-up
   4.1 Closes mirror.
   4.2 Releases suction in mirror.
   4.3 Removes mirror.
   4.4 Puts on underclothes.
   4.5 Washes catheter with soap and water inside (water flows through catheter) and outside.
   4.6 Returns mirror and catheter to appropriate storage.
   4.7 Empties container into toilet and flushes toilet.
   4.8 Disposes of container and used paper materials in appropriate trash receptacle.
   4.9 Washes all surfaces of hands with soap and water so that no dirt or residue is visible, and dries.

Note: From "Teaching Self-Catheterization Skills to Children with Neurogenic Bladder Complications" by N. A. Neef, J. M. Parrish, K. F. Hannigan, T. J. Page, and B. A. Iwata, 1989, *Journal of Applied Behavior Analysis, 22,* 237–243. Copyright 1989 by *Journal of Applied Behavior Analysis.* Reprinted by permission.

well-developed hand and finger control. These children also had well-developed cognitive skills (e.g., only mild mental retardation or normal intelligence). Third, some steps of the CIC procedure can result in injury; thus, simulated training with dolls (as in Neef et al., 1989) and/or adult assistance (as in Tarnowski & Drabman, 1987) would appear to be important training components. Fourth, even when the actual insertion of the catheter is conducted by staff or parents, children should be taught to perform the other steps of the CIC procedure (e.g., preparation and clean-up steps as shown in Box 14.3). Fifth, the intervention team must ensure that medical staff provide adequate training to families related to toileting children with neurogenic bladders and bowels.

Nighttime Toilet Training

Most children acquire nighttime toileting control (i.e., sleeping through the night without wetting) in the months that follow acquisition of daytime bladder control. However, for some children, bed wetting persists. This problem is known as nocturnal enuresis; daytime wetting is known as diurnal enuresis. There are two types of enuresis: If the subject has never experienced extended periods of dryness, the condition is called *primary enuresis*; if the wetting follows a period of dryness that lasted at least a year, the condition is called secondary enuresis (Houts & Mellon, 1989). The diagnosis of nocturnal enuresis should not be made before the child is 5 years of age (Houts & Mellon, 1989). The role of intervention teams in addressing nocturnal enuresis should be to provide information and assistance to parents. Because many parents come to early intervention personnel for advice even after their children have entered the elementary-school years, this issue is discussed briefly here.

Prevalence of Nocturnal Enuresis The prevalence of primary nocturnal enuresis decreases in the nondisabled population as age increases. About 12 to 17 percent of the 5-year-old children wet the bed at least once per month (many do so as frequently as 5 to 7 times per week). By the time the children reach eighteen years of age, only 1 to 3 percent wet the bed at least once per month. Boys are more prone to have nocturnal enuresis than girls (Houts & Mellon, 1989). Much higher rates of nocturnal enuresis appear to occur for adults with mental retardation, with estimates ranging between 41.5 percent (Smith, 1981) and 70 percent (Azrin, Sneed, & Foxx, 1973). Prevalence figures could not be found for school-age children with disabilities.

Potential Causes of Nocturnal Enuresis Several causes have been explored (see Houts & Mellon, 1989 for a review). Urinary tract infections, some diseases (e.g., nephritis and diabetes), and physical defects can cause enuresis. Thus, medical consultation is warranted prior to use of other treatments. Other causes that have been proposed are emotional factors, sleep factors, and the failure to learn to attend and respond to a full bladder when sleeping. When children are free of medical problems, enuresis is often approached as a learning problem.

Treatments for Nocturnal Enuresis Several treatments have been proposed for dealing with nocturnal enuresis. *Medications*, particularly imipramine hydrochloride (Tofranil), have been used. Houts and Mellon (1989) state, however, that medications stop the enuresis while the children take them (in about 50% of the children treated with Tofranil), *but* do not produce lasting cures. Except for a small percentage, most children resume wetting after medication is discontinued. Further, Tofranil "produces numerous side effects. Among its physical effects are increased heart rate (sometimes accompanied by irregular heartbeat), muscle tremor, profuse sweating, increased blood pressure, loss of appetite, and retention of urine" (Houts & Mellon, 1989, p. 66). Reported cases of Tofranil poisoning also have occurred.

Another treatment is the use of a *urine alarm system*. This is a relatively old and standard method of treatment (Mower & Mower, 1938). Originally the system involved a disposable fiber sheet between two foil sheets that were placed under the child's bed sheets and connected to the alarm. When the child urinates, the moisture completes an electrical circuit between the two foil sheets and sounds the alarm, awaking the parent or child. The parent then gets up and ensures that the child moves to the toilet and urinates. Currently, a small absorbent strip can be used to replace the foil sheets; this strip fits in the child's pants. Estimates of initial success vary from 75 percent (Doleys, 1977) to approximately 84 percent (Sloop, 1974). However, many families stop using it before the enuresis is controlled (Arzin & Besalel, 1979), and relapses are common when the procedure is withdrawn (Taylor & Turner, 1975). "Single parents who have problems of their own, as well as couples with marital problems, have been less successful than families without such problems" (Houts & Mellon, 1989, p. 67). It has been somewhat successful with institutionalized persons with retardation, and increasing fluid intake, providing reprimands for wetting, changing the bed when wet, and delivering reinforcement for staying dry throughout the night appear to increase its effectiveness (Smith, 1981).

Fredericks et al. (1975) describe a *four-phase procedure*. Each phase, unless successful, is used for 10 days. Phase I involves having the child go to the bathroom before bedtime and providing reinforcement if the child stays dry. Phase II involves reducing liquid intake for two hours before the child goes to bed and providing reinforcement if he stays dry. Phase III involves the same procedures as Phase II with the addition of awakening the child at the parents' bedtime. Phase IV involves determining when the child usually wets and gradually moving the awakening in the direction of that time. As with the day time procedure described by these authors, this nighttime procedure relies heavily on reinforcement.

Azrin, Sneed, and Foxx (1973, 1974) developed a *dry-bed training* procedure similar to their daytime rapid method (described earlier in this chapter). It involves the use of the urine alarm, increased liquid intake, practice getting up and going to the bathroom, hourly awakenings to urinate, verbal rehearsal of procedures, reinforcement for staying dry, and overcorrection for accidents. Overcorrection involves the child changing the bed sheets and practicing getting up and going to the bathroom 20 times. This procedure has been successful with adults who have retardation (Azrin et al., 1973) and with nondisabled children (Azrin et al., 1974). The procedure is less effective when used without the alarm (Azrin & Thienes, 1978) and in some cases ineffective (Bollard & Nettelbeck, 1981; Nettelbeck & Langeluddecke, 1979). When compared to use of the urine alarm alone, it is superior (Bollard & Nettelbeck, 1981), and it is effective when administered by parents (Bollard & Nettelbeck, 1981; Bollard & Woodroffe, 1977). Azrin and Besalel (1979) described the procedures with some changes in a manual for parents. The changes are the addition of retention control during the day and hourly awakenings only until one o'clock in the morning. Evaluation of the parent manual resulted in considerable success (Azrin & Besalel, 1979); however, relapse rates for this procedure are similar to those for the urine alarm system (Houts & Mellon, 1989).

Another procedure, *retention control*, is based on the notion that the bladders of enuretic children are smaller (Muellner, 1960). The capacity of the bladder can be increased by waiting before urinating, attempting to hold more urine, and being reinforced for waiting and holding (Doleys, Ciminero, Tollison, Williams, & Wells, 1977). Unfortunately, increasing the bladder capacity does not necessarily change toileting behaviors (Doleys, 1977). Thus, the procedure is a weak treatment, although it is used with other treatments (e.g., urine alarm, dry-bed training). Its real function may be to provide children with salient sensations of a full bladder.

A final procedure, *full spectrum home training*, was developed by Houts and Liebert (1984). The procedure includes the urine alarm system, retention control, cleanliness training, and overlearning (Houts & Mellon, 1989). In addition, it includes a family support agreement (a behavioral contract between the professional and the parents), meetings of the parents and with the professional, and telephone contacts. The traditional urine alarm or the strip-in-the-pants alarm is used. The retention control procedure, called self-control training, is conducted daily.

The child begins by drinking a large glass of water. If the child feels the need to urinate, the child tells the parent of this, and the parent instructs the child to postpone going to the bathroom for 3 minutes. If the child can wait 3 minutes and then use the toilet, the child is given a nickel. When the child completes a holding goal, the next day a new goal of 3 minutes longer is set and the reward increases by a nickel for each new goal. This part of the training is completed when the child successfully completes a 45-minute goal in step-by-step fashion." (Houts & Mellon, 1989, p. 71)

The cleanliness training involves having the child remake the bed each time the alarm sounds. A wall chart also is used to note dry and wet nights. The overlearning involves increased liquid intake 15 minutes prior to bedtime. It is implemented after 14 consecutive dry nights. Initially, children drink 4 ounces of fluid every night at this time until they can remain dry for two consecutive nights. The amount of liquids is then increased by 2 ounces every night until the criterion of two consecutive dry nights is again achieved. This process is repeated until a maximum amount is reached. The maximum amount equals one ounce for each year of age plus 2 ounces (e.g., for a 10-year-old child it would be 10 ounces plus 2 for a total of 12 ounces of fluid). If the procedure is not effective, nightly wakenings are employed. The child is awakened 3 hours after going to bed. For each dry night, the child is awakened 0.5 hours earlier (e.g., 2.5 hours after going to bed); this process continues then until no awakening is needed.

Although all of these procedures have reports of success, none have proven completely free from relapses. The urine alarm and the full spectrum training procedures are the treatments of choice. However, with all of these procedures, consultation from professionals is necessary. None of these procedures would be used with children who have not attained daytime control, and none are appropriate for children younger than 5 years of age. Finally, most of these procedures have been used with typical children; their application with young children who have disabilities awaits further research.

Summary of Toilet Training

Toileting is a unique skill. Several rationale exist for toilet training, including promoting independence, decreasing the demands on and expense for families, and increasing access to normalized interactions and placements. We have discussed several guidelines and described several methods for both day and nighttime toilet training. Careful attention to these guidelines and methods, constant communication, and the participation of parents are factors critical to toilet training success.

TEACHING DRESSING/UNDRESSING AND GROOMING SKILLS

Dressing/undressing and grooming skills are different from one another, but they are similar in terms of their instruction. They are acquired over time; they are chained skills; they should be taught when needed; they occur within routines; and acquisition, fluency, maintenance, and generalization must be promoted if they are to be useful to children. When acquired and generalized, they result in increased independence, a sense of accomplishment, and decreased demands for parental caregiving. Further, physical appearance or attractiveness (the quality of which may be influenced by dress and grooming) may set the stage for more social interactions with peers and higher positive ratings by peers (Strain, 1985). In this section, we describe the goals of dressing/undressing and grooming skills, general sequences of acquisition, prerequisite behaviors, general guidelines, and instructional procedures.

Goals of Dressing/Undressing and Grooming Skills

General goals for dressing/undressing and grooming skills involve the achievement of progressively more independence in the completion of relevant routines. The *first level* of training calls for cooperation with the adult who dresses/undresses, bathes, or otherwise grooms the child. For example, the child lets adults dress her without crying, squirming, or resisting. The *second level* calls for the child to anticipate specific steps within the routine and assume some responsibility for those steps—for example, pushing the arm through the sleeve of a shirt, or

protruding the head when the adult wipes her nose. The *third level* calls for independent completion of some steps of the routine. For example, after the legs are inserted in the pants, the child would pull them up over the legs and buttocks; or the child might put on the pants, but the adult would fasten them; or the child might brush her teeth after the adult has put toothpaste on the brush. The *fourth level* calls for independence within the routine, but supervision from the adult. For example, the child would put on her clothing with the adult watching and maintaining attention to the task. The *fifth level* calls for unsupervised independent performance of the entire routine. In some routines (e.g., adjusting the water when bathing, fastening small buttons, and selecting matching clothing), the fifth level may not be attained during the preschool period.

General Sequences and Skills

Children learn to dress over a period of a number of years. The order in which they learn to take off, put on, and fasten various items of clothing varies depending upon the construction of the clothing, their experience, and their motor abilities. Cohen and Gross (1979) provide detailed sequences and age levels for each item of clothing. When they reach 7 to 12 months of age, children begin to anticipate dressing sequences by holding out their arms or sticking out their feet. By the end of the second year, children begin to find and push their arms through armholes as well as lift their feet to go into the legs of pants. At approximately 1 year, children pull off loose pullover shirts and sometimes push down wet or soiled pants. During the first part of the second year they take off socks and shoes, and during the second half of that year, they take off their coats and other front-opening garments. During the third year, they learn to put on socks, shoes, pants, and front-opening garments.

Skills such as buttoning, zipping, and snapping are learned during the third year, while lacing and tying shoes are learned from the fourth to sixth years.

In terms of grooming (Cohen & Gross, 1979), infants show definite reactions to the bath during the first few months of life. In the second year, they attempt to help in bathing, during the fourth year they can wash and dry themselves with verbal direction and some assistance, and they continue to need supervision during the fifth year. They show interest in washing their hands and face during the second year, and can wash and dry their hands and face unaided during the third and fourth year, but they typically will get their clothing wet until the fifth or sixth year. They usually begin to brush their teeth during the third year, but they may not get their teeth clean until the fourth or fifth year. Although they may allow their hair to be combed/brushed from infancy and as toddlers may hold the hand of the brushing adult, they usually cannot brush/comb their hair unaided until the fifth year.

Prerequisite Behaviors

Prerequisite skills for dressing/undressing and grooming may vary slightly for the specific routine being taught, but we can identify three general prerequisite skills (Wolery & Smith, 1989): (a) the maintenance of balance in the positions used to complete the dressing/undressing and grooming sequences, including the ability to adjust the position as the skill is performed; (b) the ability to move at least one arm volitionally and accurately; and (c) a strong grasp that can be maintained while moving the arms (an effective pincer grasp is required for fastening skills). Two other preconditions are desirable. First, the child should be under instructional control, meaning that reinforcers are identified, problem behavior is infrequent, and the child complies with requests

he understands. Second, the child should be imitative. While the child who is not imitative or under instructional control can be taught these skills, learning is more rapid and instruction is delivered more easily and pleasantly if these two preconditions are in force. Procedures for assessing dressing and grooming skills are described by Wolery and Smith (1989).

General Guidelines

Several general guidelines can be identified for teaching dressing/undressing and grooming skills. These guidelines provide the basis for structuring instruction and making decisions about it. Some of the guidelines are similar to those that we described for toileting; others are not.

Teach at Natural Times When Skills Are Needed Teaching skills at natural times (i.e., when there is a reason to engage in the skill) means that families may need to provide the instruction, that classroom routines may need to be adapted, and that rapid methods may be needed. Parents of young children with handicaps ranked toileting and eating skills as more important than dressing but ranked dressing as the second most difficult self-care skill to teach (Lance & Koch, 1973). Thus, parents may need assistance in teaching such skills. A widely practiced procedure for accomplishing such training in homes is to describe the strategies to be used to the family, demonstrate the strategies, watch the parents try it, provide feedback on their performance, have the parents do it for a week or so and perhaps collect data on it, and then review the progress the next week (Shearer & Shearer, 1977).

However, this procedure requires the parents to work either from memory of the model or from written instructions. It also requires parents to collect data on child performance. An alternative was evaluated with four parents of infants with severe disabilities in a weekly home visiting program (Woodson, 1990). In this study, mothers were taught complex skills for handling their infants with severe handicaps. The interventionist visited the home weekly and provided a model of the behavior, and observed and prompted (physically and verbally) the parent in implementing the procedure. In addition, a video of the interventionist performing the teaching procedure with the infant was left in the home for review. Thus, a model was always available to the family. To eliminate parental data collection but develop a record of performance by the parent and child, the parents videotaped their teaching each day. These tapes were reviewed by the interventionist at home visits and later scored in the office. This procedure resulted in rapid acquisition of complex skills for all four parents across all skills taught.

Parents may not be the only "teachers" available in the home; older siblings may also serve as instructors. A study illustrating this approach is shown in Box 14.4. When parents and siblings are engaged in training self-care and other skills, several cautions are in order. First, they should be willing participants. Some family members may not want to engage in teaching, and others may have such excessive demands on their time and energy that teaching is an added burden. Second, the instruction should be structured to fit into daily routines rather than creating artificial teaching sessions. Third, attention should be given to the effects of the instruction on the parent–child interaction patterns

---

BOX 14.4   Use of siblings in teaching self-care skills

Swenson-Pierce, Kohl, and Egel (1987) used a brother or sister of children with moderate to severe mental retardation to teach skills such as making a sandwich, making a sack lunch, and making a bed. The siblings were trained to use the system of least prompts and to praise the correct performance of the children with disabilities. The training for the typical peers included: "(a) an explanation of their role as an instructional agent, (b) an overview and discussion of the system of increased prompting and social praise, (c) an overview and discussion of the task analysis for Task 1, (d) a period of role playing where the instructor portrayed the sibling with a handicap, and (e) a period of in vivo instruction accompanied by instructor feedback" (p. 54).

After receiving this training, the typical siblings taught their brother/sister with mental retardation specific skills. The instructor was gradually removed from the training session. In addition, the siblings with typical development also were observed teaching their sibling another skill that was not taught to them by the instructor.

In all three cases, the siblings without disabilities were successful in teaching their brother/sister with mental retardation to do both tasks. Interestingly, "the siblings indicated that they enjoyed participating in the study and that it did not interfere significantly with their personal time" (p. 58). Two of them said they used their new instructional skills with other tasks.

This study indicates that with careful training, siblings can be taught to provide self-care instruction to their brothers and sisters who have disabilities.

Note: Adapted from "Siblings as Home Trainers: A Strategy for Teaching Domestic Skills to Children" by A. Swenson-Pierce, F. L. Kohl, and A. L. Egel, 1987, *Journal of the Association for Persons with Severe Handicaps, 12,* 53–60.

and relationships. Teaching can be made to be fun, mutually satisfying, and rewarding for both the parent and child; or it can be stressful and unpleasant for all concerned. Fourth, the guidelines and strategies described later in this chapter are relevant to home as well as classroom applications. Fifth, attention should be given to promoting generalization of the instructional skills learned by family members. Cordisco, Strain, and Depew (1988) describe an intensive family training program that included group training of parents, and then individual training in two home settings. Data also were collected in a third setting. Only one of three participating parents generalized the acquired skills to the third setting without specific programming.

In cases where family involvement in training is minimal, teams must assume the responsibility for teaching high-priority self-care skills. Generally, as we explain later, this can be accomplished by following the guidelines and instructional strategies that follow and by adapting classroom routines. However, an alternative is the intensive method developed originally for teaching adults with profound mental retardation to dress themselves (Azrin, Schaeffer & Wesolowski, 1976). This method involves graduated guidance, total task sequencing, and sessions of 2 to 3 hours in duration. The procedure requires use of powerful reinforcers because of the duration of the daily sessions and because the tasks are not taught in the context of a routine. As a result, this procedure is recommended only in cases where particular skills must be established rapidly.

Teach Using Total-task Instruction Most dressing/undressing and grooming skills are comprised of a series of behaviors sequenced together to form a more complex (chained) skill. When teaching such tasks, the professional has at least three options: forward chaining, backward chaining, and total-task instruction. Forward chaining involves teach-

ing the first step in the sequence first, and when it is acquired, teaching the second step, and so on until the entire chain is learned. Backward chaining involves teaching the last step first, and then the next to the last step, and so on until the entire chain is learned. The advantage of backward over forward chaining is that the child can receive the natural reinforcer for independent performance at the end of the sequence. Total-task instruction involves teaching all steps of the task at once. Thus, when teaching chained tasks, you must decide which of these three procedures to use. In addition, you must decide whether to use single or multiple trials of the chain. Current findings on this issue are: (a) total-task instruction with single trials results in more rapid learning than multiple-trial backward chaining (Kayser, Billingsley, & Neel, 1986); (b) total-task instruction results in more rapid learning than forward chaining (McDonnell & McFarland, 1988); (c) total-task instruction has been successful with multiple trials each session (Schoen, Lentz, & Suppa, 1988); and (d) total-task instruction has been successful with single trials each session (Wolery, Ault, Gast, Doyle, & Griffen, 1990; Griffen, Wolery & Schuster, in press). Based on this research, the general recommendation is to use total-task instruction with single or, if necessary, multiple trials.

Teach in Accordance with Sequences of Difficulty Some tasks are more difficult than others, and the level of difficulty should be recognized when teaching dressing/undressing. Here we make four points related to level of difficulty. First, *taking off clothing is frequently easier than putting on clothing.* As a result, you should teach children to undress before teaching them to dress. This does not mean that children are taught to take off all their clothing before teaching them to put on any clothing; rather, when teaching a child to manage any given garment, the child should first be taught to take it off and then be taught to put it on. Second, *loose-fitting garments are easier to put on and take off than tight-fitting garments.* Your instruction should begin with clothing that is loose. After children become fluent in dressing/undressing with loose-fitting garments, teach them to put on and take off tight-fitting garments. If instruction is being provided at school, the teacher should ask the parents to furnish a loose-fitting set of clothing to keep in the classroom. These clothes can be used for dressing instruction and as a spare outfit when toileting and other accidents occur. Third, *some sequences are easier than others.* Most clothing can be put on or taken off using a variety of sequences. Four sequences for taking off a pullover shirt are listed in Box 14.5. Each of these sequences fulfills the same function (i.e., the shirt is taken off). The specific sequence used is less important than the final result. This also applies to many grooming skills. Therefore, you should be flexible as to the sequence used. If a child's physical disabilities or preferences suggest than one sequence is easier than another, then the easier sequence should be taught. Fourth, *putting on and taking off clothing are usually easier than fasteners.* Fastening maneuvers such as buttoning, snapping, zipping, lacing, buckling, and tying frequently require a well-developed pincer grasp and considerable finger strength. They are difficult to perform. One approach for dealing with this difficulty is to use clothing that does not require fasteners, such as elastic-waist-band pants, slip-on shoes, and pullover shirts. Thus, teams should recommend to parents that they purchase such clothing. As the child gets older and has more finger control and strength, the fastening maneuvers can be taught more easily and quickly. Another approach is to teach these fastening skills with adapted materials (Edgar, Maser, & Haring, 1977). For example, large buttons on vests are used, and progressively smaller buttons are introduced as chil-

dren can manage the larger ones. When doing this you must use realistic adaptations, and ensure that children acquire and practice them in real alignment with their bodies (e.g., when the objective is learning to tie a shoe the toe should be facing away from the child's body).

Teach Using Adaptations and Partial Participation as Needed When teaching in routines, it is likely that some steps will be impossible for children to complete at this time and that some will be dangerous (e.g., adjusting water temperature). Partial participation (see Box 6.5 for guidelines) should be used. A nicely detailed example of partial participation with toothbrushing is provided by Snell, Lewis, and Houghton (1989). In addition, clothing and grooming appliances can be adapted. For example, velcro fasteners are easier to manipulate than buttons (Michaelis, 1979). Other adaptations of clothing include the sewing of reinforcements into garments to reduce wear caused by braces. Suggestions and directions for making adaptations and drawings of various adaptations are described by Hoffman (1979); Bare, Boettke, and Waggoner (1962); Kernaleguen (1978); and Werner (1987). When designing adaptations, the interventionist should take care to minimize the extent to which the adaptation makes the child look different from his non-disabled peers.

Teach to Maximize Acquisition, Fluency, Maintenance, Generalization, and Unsupervised Responding *Acquisition* of dressing/undressing and grooming skills is accomplished by careful task analysis and definition of the target steps, application of the guidelines we have listed, use of effective instructional procedures (described in the next section), and modification of instruction when it is not working (Wolery, Ault, & Doyle, in press). *Fluency* in the use of these skills is probably best promoted by a combination of three procedures (Wolery, Bai-

BOX 14.5   Sample sequences for taking off a pullover shirt

Sequence	Steps in the Sequence
Crossed-Arm Method	1 Child crosses both arms in front of his trunk
	2 Child grasps bottom of shirt with each hand
	3 Child raises both arms flexing at the elbows and pulling shirt off trunk
	4 Child extends both arms over head and pulls shirt off neck and head
	5 Child grasps opposite sleeve with one hand and pulls shirt off first arm
	6 Child grasps other sleeve with other hand and pulls shirt off arm
Elbow-Tuck Method	1 Child crosses dominant arm across trunk
	2 Child grasps bottom of shirt with dominant hand
	3 Child pulls bottom of shirt away from trunk
	4 Child flexes nondominant arm and tucks elbow into trunk
	5 Child pulls bottom of shirt over nondominant elbow
	6 Child raises dominant elbow over head, while maintaining grasp of bottom of shirt with the dominant hand
	7 Child extends dominant arm up and away from body pulling the shirt off the nondominant arm and head
	8 Child grasps sleeve of dominant arm with nondominant hand and pulls shirt off dominant arm
One-Arm-at-a-Time Method	1 Child grasps end of sleeve of nondominant arm with dominant hand
	2 Child extends dominant arm, while maintaining grasp of sleeve end and flexes nondominant arm pulling the sleeve off the nondominant arm
	3 Child drops nondominant arm under shirt and out the bottom
	4 Child grasps bottom of shirt on nondominant side and pulls it up over nondominant shoulder
	5 Child repeats process with dominant sleeve
	6 Child grasps shirt and pulls over head
One-Arm-over-the-Back Method	1 Child raises dominant arm, flexed at elbow, over the shoulder
	2 Child places thumb of dominant hand inside of the shirt at the collar
	3 Child gathers back of shirt into grasp of dominant hand
	4 Child flexes neck forward and pulls shirt off head by extending dominant arm at elbow
	5 Child pulls or shakes shirt off arms

Note: From "Assessing Self-Care Skills" by M. Wolery and P. D. Smith, 1989, in *Assessing Infants and Preschoolers with Handicaps* (pp. 447–477), Ed. by D. B. Bailey and M. Wolery, Columbus, OH: Merrill. Copyright 1989 by Macmillan Publishing. Reprinted by permission.

ley, & Sugai, 1988). First, the environment should be structured so that multiple brief periods of practice are required. These may be single trials on the skills, but several opportunities should be provided throughout the day. Second, reinforcement can be provided for completing all the steps of the skill in progressively shorter amounts of time. Third, performance of the skill can be made into a game; for example, have the child "race" against a timer. *Maintenance* of these skills is promoted by ensuring that the skills are needed regularly in the child's day, by systematically providing less reinforcement over time, by providing reinforcement only at the end of a sequence, and by using natural reinforcers. (e.g., entry into the next activity). Also, by systematically inserting a delay between the behavior and its feedback (reinforcers and corrective feedback), the trainer can enhance maintenance (Dunlap, Koegel, Johnson, & O'Neill, 1987). *Generalization* of these skills is facilitated by using multiple materials (e.g., teaching dressing with several shirts) selected through general case programming, by using multiple trainers (teachers and family members), by ensuring that the skills are required in all relevant settings, and by using self-control procedures (Horner, Dunlap, & Koegel, 1988). In addition, correspondence training (reinforcement for truthfully reporting on behavior) has been used to ensure that adolescents with disabilities completed self-care routines (Paniagua, 1985).

As we noted earlier, an ultimate goal of self-care skill instruction is performance of the routines in unsupervised conditions. For example, ideally a parent could wake up a child, interact with him for a couple minutes, and tell him to get dressed and come to the kitchen to eat. If the child can do this without the adult in the room, then this is a mark of true independence and simplifies the lives of other family members. Although

we have found no research that has addressed this issue with the self-care skills of preschoolers, there is some guidance from the research literature on establishing such responding. Dunlap and Johnson (1985) compared the effects of predictable supervision and unpredictable supervision on the on-task and correct-task behavior of children with severe handicaps. In the predictable supervision condition, the adult was present for the first part of the session and absent for the last part; in the unpredictable condition, the adult was intermittently and randomly present and absent. The results indicate that under the unpredictable supervision condition children had higher rates of on-task and correct-task performance. The possible implication for teaching self-care skills is that when fading supervision, the adult should use intermittent and random absences from the setting rather than predictable absences. In a related study, a subject's responding was measured in a training task and three generalization tasks. In the training task, the adult initially reinforced the subject for every response. When a high rate of responding was established, the adult thinned the reinforcement schedule. When the subject was being reinforced on the average of every eighth response, the adult moved near the door. At this point, the adult began to step out of and back into the room; the length of the absences increased and the reinforcement schedule continued to be thinned. Finally, the adult remained outside of the room and reinforced the subject only after the session. This thinning and fading procedure resulted in the high level of performance in the training task being maintained and generalized to the other tasks. The potential implication of this study for teaching children unsupervised self-care tasks is that the reinforcement probably should be thinned gradually and that the adult should be absent for progressively longer intervals of time. It should be noted that the adult's absence in this study was on an intermittent and random schedule rather than on a predictable schedule.

Instructional Strategies

Several of the response prompting strategies described in chapter 6 can be used for teaching independent dressing/undressing and grooming skills. These include most-to-least prompting (Sisson, Kilwein, & Van Hasselt, 1988), graduated guidance (Schoen et al., 1988), and the system of least prompts (see Doyle, Wolery, Ault, & Gast, 1988 for a review). Tasks similar to these have also been taught with progressive time delay (Snell, 1982) and constant time delay (Schoen & Sivil, 1989; Wolery et al., 1990). Any of these procedures may be effective. Physical prompts with and without accompanying verbal prompts, models with and without verbal prompts, and verbal prompts have also been used. When children imitate others readily, models and verbal prompts are recommended; when children do not imitate,

---

BOX 14.6   Teaching face washing and drinking from a fountain with most-to-least assistance

Schoen, Lentz, and Suppa (1988) taught four preschool children with Down syndrome to wash their faces and to get a drink from a fountain using most-to-least prompts and graduated guidance. The most-to-least prompting procedure, also called decreasing assistance, is described here.

Face washing was task analyzed into the following steps "(1) orients self to sink, (2) touches faucet, (3) turns on water, (4) obtains soap, (5) wets hands, (6) lathers, (7) returns soap, (8) washes face, (9) rinses, (10) turns off water, (11) touches towel, and (12) wipes face." (p. 351). Before instruction, each child was assessed to identify the steps they could do independently, and none of them could do any of these steps.

During instruction, the teacher gave a verbal direction (e.g., "Wash your face."), and immediately provided a full physical prompt. This involved the teacher placing his/her hands over the child's and guiding the child's actions. After the child performed the steps with this level of assistance, the teacher faded the physical prompts. At the second level, the teacher gave the task direction and modeled the steps of the task analysis. After two successful assisted trials at this level, the prompts were again faded. The teacher gave the task direction and then provided verbal prompts until the child performed independently. Errors resulted in an increase in the level of assistance provided. At all prompt levels, praise was provided for each correct step.

During training, each child being taught was paired with another child who could not wash his/her face independently and who did not receive instruction. This child simply observed the instruction.

As a result of this training, the subjects who were taught to wash their faces learned to do so independently. However, a more important finding of this study was that the observer-peers also learned, without direct instruction, to wash their faces.

Note: Adapted from "An Examination of Two Prompt Fading Procedures and Opportunities to Observe in Teaching Handicapped Preschoolers Self-Help Skills" by S. F. Schoen, F. E. Lentz, and R. J. Suppa, 1988, *Journal of the Division for Early Childhood, 12,* 349–358.

512   Chapter 14

physical prompts are necessary. An example of a study teaching dressing skills with the most-to-least procedure is described in Box 14.6.

When such skills are being taught, data collection can be problematic. For example, if you simply collect data on whether the child does or does not complete the task correctly, you will not be able to identify problems with particular steps of the behavior. Haring and Kennedy (1988) have devised a system for collecting and presenting such data; and this system has been adapted for use with the time delay procedure as well (Ault, Gast, Wolery, & Doyle, in press). The system allows you to graph the percentage of steps on which the child is independent on a standard line graph (Figure 14.1), and

also allows the data to be displayed on each step of the task. We have found this procedure helpful in identifying steps on which children are having difficulty, steps where independence is easily established, and patterns of responding that require modifications of instruction.

Summary of Dressing/Undressing and Grooming Skills

Several good reasons exist for teaching dressing/undressing and grooming skills. The ultimate goal of teaching these skills is to promote independent performance that occurs with minimal supervision. Assessment procedures exist for identifying which skills to teach, and the prerequisites for

FIGURE 14.1

Data collection and graphing form for chained tasks (e.g., putting on pants).

Note: Adapted from "Units of Analysis in Task-Analytic Research" by T. G. Haring and C. H. Kennedy, 1988, *Journal of Applied Behavior Analysis, 21,* 207–215. Copyright 1988 by *Journal of Applied Behavioral Analysis.* Adapted by permission. Also adapted from "A Data Collection and Graphing Method for Use in Teaching Chained Tasks with the Constant Time Delay Procedure" by M. J. Ault, D. L. Gast, M. Wolery, and P. M. Doyle, in press, *Teaching Exceptional Children.* Copyright 1991 by Council for Exceptional Children.

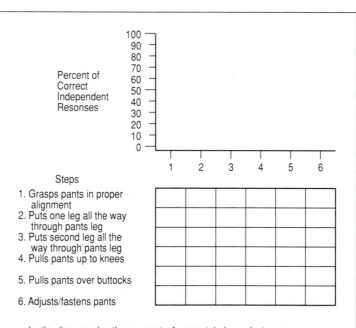

teaching these skills are known. Several general guidelines should be followed when implementing instruction on these skills. Teaching should occur when the skill is needed, and this may involve teaching family members to provide the instruction. Total-task instruction is probably the best way to teach the sequences of these skills. Several sequences of difficulty exist, and instruction should be organized to account for them. Adaptations and partial participation should be used when necessary. Instruction should be designed to address the phases of the performance hierarchy and to teach unsupervised responding.

ADAPTIVE SKILLS

One of the goals of early intervention, as described in chapter 2, is to prepare children for living in normalized environments. As a result, they need many skills that can best be characterized as adaptive skills. Adaptive skills are those which promote independence and facilitate children's "fit" into their unique ecologies. In identifying and teaching such skills, the views and desires of families are critical issues. Families should know best where their children have skill deficits or response patterns that interfere with their fit in the family ecology. Thus, it is nearly impossible to identify all the skills that would facilitate children's adaptation to their unique ecologies. But in this section—to show the breadth of the skills that may be needed, and to suggest models for devising instruction—we describe four studies that are examples of teaching adaptive skills.

Making a Snack

An adaptive skill closely related to self-care skills is making snacks and food preparation. Food preparation is a valuable skill for older children with disabilities because it may promote independent living and provide job opportunities (Schuster, 1988). Further, cooking activities frequently occur in preschool classrooms for typically developing children. Schoen and Sivil (1989) taught preschool children with moderate to severe disabilities to make a sandwich. They compared the system of least prompts and constant time delay. The skill was task analyzed and the procedures were systematically implemented. The results indicated that each of the children learned to make the snack without assistance regardless of the procedure that was used; however, the constant time delay procedure resulted in more rapid learning. Interestingly in this study, another young child with disabilities also watched each child being taught to make the snack. The observer was told to watch, was praised for watching the instruction, and was assessed daily on her own ability to make a sandwich. As a result, the observer also learned to make sandwiches. An implication of this study is that the inclusion of observers when teaching adaptive and self-care skills may result in learning by the child being taught and by the child who observes.

Eating in a Restaurant

As noted in chapter 13, eating is a social event as well as a means of obtaining adequate nutrition. Going out to eat is also an event that reduces meal preparation activities, is used to celebrate accomplishments, and is a leisure activity. In addition, it can be a time when families interact and communicate positively. However, taking young children to a restaurant can be a challenging and draining experience. Advice manuals for parents have been successful in making going to a restaurant more pleasant (Bauman, Reiss, Rogers, & Bailey, 1983), but only in cases in which parents acquired such a manual, read it, understand it, and apply its recommendations. An alternative was evaluated by Green, Hardison, and Greene (1984). Specifically, they compared the use of two types of placemats. Traditionally available placemats that included games such as tic-tac-toe, mazes, and riddles were compared to "Table-Talk" placemats that had drawings and written suggestions for conservations and activities. For example, one placemat had a picture of two dogs eating at a table and another dog serving them. The caption asked, "What would a restaurant for dogs be like? Do you suppose they would have people bags instead of doggie bags?" (p. 500). During a 26-minute premeal time at the table, a number of behaviors were measured including discussions about food, social and educational comments, material interaction, coercive comments by parents, distracting comments by children, and disruptive behavior by children. Four two-parent families with at least one child between the ages of 3 and 5 participated in the study. More social and educational comments were made with the Table-Talk placemats than with the traditional placemats or with no placemats. Also, there was less disruptive behavior, fewer distracting comments by children, and fewer coercive comments by parents, when the Table-Talk placemats were used. This study illustrates that simple changes in the environmental design (i.e., the types of placemats) can set the stage for more positive interactions, more adaptive behavior, and more pleasant mealtime experiences. Assisting parents in making such environmental arrangements in the home and in the community is clearly an interesting and useful role of early intervention teams.

Using Seat Belts

Young children frequently spend large amounts of time being transported in cars. Data indicate clearly that use of seat belts can substantially reduce fatalities, injuries, and hospital costs when accidents occur (Lehman & Geller, 1990). The promotion of

seat belt use has included the provision of incentives (e.g., stickers) for children who are buckled upon arrival at school; however, Lehman and Geller (1990) provide an alternative. They collected data on the number of kindergarten-age children who arrived at school wearing seat belts. The kindergarten teacher then introduced a story about "Buckie Buckle" that included a young boy named Buckie Buckle who went for rides with different people (father, mother, and other relatives). There were several scenarios in the story, and each one included Buckie using his seat belt and the driver giving a standard reason for not wearing a seat belt. The drivers were subsequently injured when the car crashed. This story was developed into a skit in which each child had a part and which was presented to the parents and other students in the school. Each time Buckie buckled his seat belt, he said, "I love my buckle buckled" and the audience was cued to say this with him. A coloring book of the story was used. After the skit, the number of children arriving at school with seat belts buckled increased considerably and was higher than initial data collection on a three-month follow-up. Interestingly, some parents who observed the skit also increased their use of seat belts. Although no children with known disabilities participated, the study provides a model for how activities within preschools may influence adaptive responding outside of the classroom.

Resisting the Lures of Strangers

Abduction of children is a major social problem. Data from the National Center for Missing and Exploited Children (April, 1990) for the period from June 1984 to March 1990 indicate that 24,655 children in the United States were reported as missing. Over half of these children were abducted, with about three-fourths being abducted by family members. Of those abducted by non-family members, about 37 percent of those located were found dead. As young children are normalized into community environments, the risk of abduction is increased. Although a number of studies have taught typically developing children to resist abduction (Miltenberger & Thiesse-Duffy, 1988; Poche, Yoder, & Miltenberger, 1988), only one study to our knowledge has addressed this issue with preschool children who have disabilities.

Gast, Collins, Wolery, and Jones (in press) taught four preschool children with disabilities through the use of simulation and *in vivo* instruction to resist the lures of strangers. Multiple examples of three types of lures were used: (a) general (e.g., "Would you like to go for a walk?"), (b) authority ("Your mother said for you to go with me."), and (c) incentive ("Would you like some candy?"). Children were first taught using constant time delay in the preschool classroom. The correct response was to say "No" within 3 seconds and turn and walk at least 5 feet toward the teacher within 3 seconds. Daily probe trials occurred outside the preschool classroom in the community. One of 26 different individuals who were unknown to the children approached the child each day and offered one of the three lures. Children quickly acquired the responses in the classroom setting, but did not generalize to novel community settings until constant time delay instruction was provided in selected community sites. Maintenance of the skill also was demonstrated. This study illustrates that a safety behavior of resisting the lures of strangers can be taught to preschool children with disabilities. However, it also illustrates that teaching such adaptive skills in the classroom may not be sufficient to ensure generalization. Thus, at a minimum, such adaptive skills should be assessed for generalization in appropriate community situations. If generalization does not occur, then procedures for facilitating its occurrence are needed.

Summary of Adaptive Skills

These four studies on different adaptive skills illustrate that a number of possible interventions can be used to teach skills that will allow children to function more adaptively and safely in the community. Acquisition of such skills may decrease caregiving demands on parents (e.g., the making-the-snack study), may lead to more pleasant and growth-promoting interchanges (e.g., the eating-in-the-restaurant study), and may lead to greater safety (e.g., the seat-belt and resisting-the-lures-of-strangers studies). To accomplish these skills, investigators used response prompting procedures (the snack and lure studies), activity-based events in the classroom (the seat-belt study), and environmental arrangements (the restaurant study). Thus, the technology and models for addressing important, family-identified adaptive skills are available.

SUMMARY

The teaching of toileting, dressing/undressing, grooming, and adaptive skills is an important early intervention endeavor. When conducting such instruction, teams should understand the unique characteristics of these skills. In addition, they should comply with the guidelines for teaching them, particularly giving attention to the role of families and their participation in the instruction. A variety of methods exist for establishing these important skills, and the selection and modification of these methods are important considerations.

REFERENCES

Ault, M. J., Gast, D. L., Wolery, M., & Doyle, P. M. (in press). A data collection and graphing method for use in teaching chained tasks with the constant time delay procedure. *Teaching Exceptional Children.*

Azrin, N. H., & Besalel, V. A. (1979). *A parent's guide to bedwetting control: A step-by-step method*. New York: Simon & Schuster.

Azrin, N. H., & Foxx, R. M. (1971). A rapid method of toilet training the institutionalized retarded. *Journal of Applied Behavior Analysis, 4*, 89–99.

Azrin, N. H., & Foxx, R. M. (1974). *Toilet training in less than a day*. New York: Simon & Schuster.

Azrin, N. H., Schaeffer, R. M., & Wesolowski, M. D. (1976). A rapid method of teaching profoundly retarded persons to dress. *Mental Retardation, 14*(6), 29–33.

Azrin, N. H., Sneed, T. J., & Foxx, R. M. (1973). Dry bed: A rapid method of eliminating bedwetting (enuresis) of the retarded. *Behavior Research and Therapy, 11*, 427–434.

Azrin, N. H., Sneed, T. J., & Foxx, R. M. (1974). Dry bed training: Rapid elimination of childhood enuresis. *Behavior Research and Therapy, 12*, 147–156.

Azrin, N. H., & Thienes, P. M. (1978). Rapid elimination of enuresis by intensive learning without a conditioning apparatus. *Behavior Therapy, 9*, 324–354.

Bailey, D. B. (1988). Assessing critical events. In D. B. Bailey & R. J. Simeonsson (Eds.), *Family assessment in early intervention* (pp. 119–138). Columbus, OH: Merrill.

Bare, C., Boettke, E., & Waggoner, N. (1962). *Self-help clothing for handicapped children*. Chicago: National Society for Crippled Children and Adults.

Bauman, K. E., Reiss, M. L., Rogers, R. W., & Bailey, J. S. (1983). Dining out with children: Effectiveness of a parent advice package on premeal inappropriate behavior. *Journal of Applied Behavior Analysis, 16*, 55–68.

Berk, H. J., & Berk, M. L. (1982). A survey of day care centers and their services for handicapped children. *Child Care Quarterly, 11*(3), 211–214.

Bettison, S. (1982). *Toileting training to independence for the handicapped: A manual for trainers*. Springfield, IL: Charles C. Thomas.

Bollard, J., & Nettelbeck, T. (1981). A comparison of dry-bed training and standard urine-alarm conditioning treatment of childhood bedwetting. *Behavior Research and Therapy, 19*, 215–226.

Bollard, J., & Woodroffe, P. (1977). The effect of parent-administered dry-bed training on nocturnal enuresis in children. *Behavior Research and Therapy, 15*, 159–165.

Browder, D. M. (1987). *Assessment of individuals with severe handicaps: An applied behavior approach to life skills assessment*. Baltimore: Paul Brookes.

Butler, J. F. (1976a). Toilet training a child with spina bifida. *Journal of Behavior Therapy and Experimental Psychiatry, 7*, 63–65.

Butler, J. F. (1976b). The toilet training success of parents after reading *Toilet training in less than a day*. *Behavior Therapy, 7*, 185–191.

Campbell, P. H. (1977). Daily living skills. In N. G. Haring (Ed.), *Developing effective individualized educational programs for severely handicapped children and youth*. Washington, DC: Bureau of Education for the Handicapped.

Cohen, M. A., & Gross, P. J. (1979). *The developmental resource: Behavioral sequences for assessment and program planning* (Vol. 1). New York: Grune & Stratton.

Cordisco, L. K., Strain, P. S., & Depew, N. (1988). Assessment for generalization of parenting skills in home settings. *Journal of the Association for Persons with Severe Handicaps, 13*, 202–210.

Doleys, D. M. (1977). Behavioral treatments for nocturnal enuresis in children: A review of the recent literature. *Psychological Bulletin, 84*, 30–54.

Doleys, D. M., Ciminero, A. R., Tollison, J. W., Williams, C. L., & Wells, K. C. (1977). Dry-bed training and retention control training—a comparison. *Behavior Therapy, 8*, 541–548.

Doyle, P. M., Wolery, M., Ault, M. J., & Gast, D. L. (1988). System of least prompts: A review of procedural parameters. *Journal of the Association for Persons with Severe Handicaps, 13*, 28–40.

Dunlap, G., & Johnson, J. (1985). Increasing the independent responding of autistic children with unpredictable supervision. *Journal of Applied Behavior Analysis, 18*, 227–236.

Dunlap, G., Koegel, R. L., Johnson, J., & O'Neill, R. E. (1987). Maintaining performance of autistic clients in community settings with delayed contingencies. *Journal of Applied Behavior Analysis, 20,* 185–191.

Dunlap, G., Koegel, R. L., & Koegel, L. K. (1984). Continuity of treatment: Toilet training in multiple community settings. *Journal of the Association for Persons with Severe Handicaps, 9,* 134–141.

Dyson, L., & Fewell, R. R. (1986). Stress and adaptation in parents of young handicapped and nonhandicapped children: A comparative study. *Journal of the Division of Early Childhood, 10*(1), 25–34.

Edgar, E., Maser, J. T., & Haring, N. G. (1977). Button up: A systematic approach for teaching children to fasten. *Teaching Exceptional Children, 9,* 104–105.

Foxx, R. M., & Azrin, N. H. (1973). *Toilet training the retarded: A rapid program for day and nighttime independent toileting.* Champaign, IL: Research Press.

Fredericks, H. D., Baldwin, V., Grove, D. N., & Moore, W. G. (1975). *Toilet training the handicapped child.* Monmouth, OR: Teaching Research.

Gast, D. L., Collins, B. C., Wolery, M., & Jones, R. (in press). Teaching children with developmental delays to respond to the lures of strangers. *Exceptional Children.*

Green, R. B., Hardison, W. L., & Greene, B. F. (1984). Turning the table on advice programs for parents: Using placemats to enhance family interaction at restaurants. *Journal of Applied Behavior Analysis, 17,* 497–508.

Griffen, A. K., Wolery, M., & Schuster, J. W. (in press). Triadic instruction of chained food preparation responses: Acquisition and observational learning. *Journal of Applied Behavior Analysis.*

Hannigan, K. F. (1979). Teaching intermittent self-catheterization to young children with myelodysplasia. *Developmental Medicine and Child Neurology, 21,* 365–368.

Haring, T. G., & Kennedy, C. H. (1988). Units of analysis in task-analytic research. *Journal of Applied Behavior Analysis, 21,* 207–215.

Hoffman, A. M. (1979). *Clothing for the handicapped, the aged, and other people with special needs.* Springfield, IL: Charles C. Thomas.

Horner, R. H., Dunlap, G., & Koegel, R. L. (Eds.).

(1988). *Generalization and maintenance: Life-style changes in applied settings.* Baltimore: Paul Brookes.

Houts, A. C., & Liebert, R. M. (1984). *Bedwetting: A guide for parents and children.* Springfield, IL: Charles C. Thomas.

Houts, A. C., & Mellon, M. W. (1989). Home-based treatment for primary enuresis. In C. E. Schaefer & J. M. Briesmeister (Eds.), *Handbook of parent training: Parents of co-therapists for children's behavior problems,* New York: John Wiley.

Kayser, J. E., Billingsley, F. F., & Neel, R. S. (1986). A comparison of in-context and traditional instructional approaches: Total task, single trial versus backward chaining multiple trials. *Journal of the Association for Persons with Severe Handicaps, 11,* 28–38.

Kernaleguen, A. (1978). *Clothing designs for the handicapped.* Edmonton: University of Alberta Press.

Lance, W. D., & Koch, A. C. (1973). Parents as teachers: Self-help skills for young handicapped children. *Mental Retardation, 11,* 3–4.

Lancioni, G. E., & Ceccarani, P. S. (1981). Teaching independent toileting within the normal daily program: Two studies with profoundly retarded children. *Behavior Research of Severe Development Disabilities, 2,* 79–96.

Lehman, G. R., & Geller, E. S. (1990). Participative education for children: An effective approach to increase safety belt use. *Journal of Applied Behavior Analysis, 23,* 219–225.

Mahoney, K., Van Wagenen, R. K., & Meyerson, L. (1971). Toilet training of normal and retarded children. *Journal of Applied Behavior Analysis, 4,* 173–181.

Matson, J. L. (1975). Some practical considerations for using the Foxx and Azrin method of toilet training. *Psychological Reports, 37,* 350.

Matson, J. L., & Ollendick, T. H. (1977). Issues in toilet training normal children. *Behavior Therapy, 8,* 549–553.

McDonnell, J., & McFarland, S. (1988). Comparison of forward and concurrent chaining strategies in teaching laundromat skills to students with severe handicaps. *Research in Developmental Disabilities, 9,* 177–194.

Michaelis, C. T. (1979). Why can't Johnny look

nice, too? Revisited. *The Exceptional Parent, 9,* 9–14.

Miltenberger, R. G., & Thiesse-Duffy, E. (1988). Evaluation of home based programs for teaching personal safety skills to children. *Journal of Applied Behavior Analysis, 21,* 81–87.

Mowrer, O. H., & Mowrer, W. M. (1938). Enuresis: A method for its study and treatment. *American Journal of Orthopsychiatry, 8,* 336–359.

Muellner, S. R. (1960). Development of urinary control in children. *Journal of the American Medical Association, 172,* 1256–1261.

National Center for Missing and Exploited Children (April, 1990). Arlington, VA.

Neef, N. A., Parrish, J. M., Hannigan, K. F., Page, T. J., & Iwata, B. A. (1989). Teaching self-catheterization skills to children with neurogenic bladder complications. *Journal of Applied Behavior Analysis, 22,* 237–243.

Nettelbeck, T., & Langeluddecke, P. (1979). Dry-bed training without an enuresis machine. *Behavior Research and Therapy, 17,* 403–404.

Orelove, F. P., & Sobsey, D. (1987). *Educating children with multiple disabilities: A transdisciplinary approach.* Baltimore: Paul Brookes.

Paniagua, F. A. (1985). Development of self-care skills and helping behaviors of adolescents in a group home through correspondence training. *Journal of Behavior Therapy and Experimental Psychiatry, 16,* 237–244.

Poche, C., Yoder, P., & Miltenberger, R. (1988). Teaching self-protection to children using television techniques. *Journal of Applied Behavior Analysis, 21,* 253–261.

Richmond, G. (1983). Shaping bladder and bowel continence in developmentally retarded preschool children. *Journal of Autism and Developmental Disorders, 13,* 197–204.

Sadler, O. W., & Merkert, F. (1977). Evaluating the Foxx-Azrin toilet training procedure for the retarded children in a day training center. *Behavior Therapy, 8,* 499–500.

Schoen, S. F., Lentz, F. E., & Suppa, R. J. (1988). An examination of two prompt fading procedures and opportunities to observe in teaching handicapped preschoolers self-help skills. *Journal of the Division for Early Childhood, 12,* 349–358.

Schoen, S. F., & Sivil, E. O. (1989). A comparison of procedures in teaching self-help skills: Increasing assistance, time delay, and observational learning. *Journal of Autism and Developmental Disorders, 19,* 57–72.

Schuster, J. W. (1988). Cooking instruction with persons labeled mentally retarded: A review of literature. *Education and Training in Mental Retardation, 23,* 43–50.

Shearer, M. S., & Shearer, D. E. (1977). Parent involvement. In J. B. Jordan, A. H. Hayden, M. B. Karnes, M. M. Wood (Eds.), *Early childhood education for exceptional children.* Reston, VA: Council for Exceptional Children.

Sisson, L. A., Kilwein, M. L., & Van Hasselt, V. B. (1988). A graduated guidance procedure for teaching self-dressing skills to multihandicapped children. *Research in Developmental Disabilities, 9,* 419–432.

Sloop, E. W. (1974). *Conditioning treatment of nocturnal enuresis among the institutionalized.* Unpublished doctoral dissertation. Florida State University.

Smeets, P. M., Lancioni, G. E., Ball, T. S., & Oliva, D. S. (1985). Shaping self-initiated toileting in infants. *Journal of Applied Behavior Analysis, 18,* 303–308.

Smith, L. J. (1981). Training severely and profoundly mentally handicapped noturnal enuretics. *Behavior Research and Therapy, 19,* 67–74.

Smith, P. S. (1979). A comparison of different methods of toilet training the mentally handicapped. *Behavior Research and Therapy, 17,* 33–43.

Snell, M. E. (1980). Does toilet training belong in the public schools? A review of toilet training research. *Education Unlimited, 2,* 53–58.

Snell, M. E. (1982). Analysis of time delay procedures in teaching daily living skills to retarded adults. *Analysis and Intervention in Developmental Disabilities, 2,* 139–155.

Snell, M. E. (Ed.). (1987). *Systematic instruction of persons with severe handicaps* (3rd ed.). Columbus, OH: Merrill.

Snell, M. E., Lewis, A. P., & Houghton, A. (1989). Acquisition and maintenance of toothbrushing skills by students with cerebral palsy and mental retardation. *Journal of the As-*

sociation for Persons with Severe Handicaps, 14, 216–226.

Strain, P. S. (1985). Social and nonsocial determinants of handicapped preschool children's social competence. *Topics in Early Childhood Special Education, 4*(4), 47–58.

Sullivan-Bolyai, S. (1986). Practical aspects of toilet training the child with a physical disability. *Issues in Comprehensive Pediatric Nursing, 9*, 79–96.

Swenson-Pierce, A., Kohl, F. L., & Egel, A. L. (1987). Siblings as home trainers: A strategy for teaching domestic skills to children. *Journal of the Association for Persons with Severe Handicaps, 12*, 53–60.

Tarnowski, K. J., & Drabman, R. S. (1987). Teaching intermittent self-catheterization skills to mentally retarded children. *Research in Developmental Disabilities, 8*, 521–529.

Taylor, P. D., & Turner, R. K. (1975). A clinical trial of continuous, intermittent, and overlearning "bell and pad" treatments for nocturnal enuresis. *Behavior Research and Therapy, 13*, 281–293.

Thompson, T., & Hanson, R. (1983). Overhydration: Precautions when treating urinary incontinence. *Mental Retardation, 21*, 139–143.

Werner, D. (1987). *Disabled village children: A guide for community health workers, reha-* bilitation workers, and families. Palo Alto, CA: Hesperian Foundation.

Williams, F. E., & Sloop, E. W. (1978). Success with a shortened Foxx-Azrin toilet training program. *Education and Training of the Mentally Retarded, 13*, 399–402.

Wolery, M., Ault, M. J., & Doyle, P. M. (in press). *Teaching students with moderate and severe disabilities: Use of response prompting procedures.* White Plains, NY: Longman.

Wolery, M., Ault, M. J., Gast, D. L., Doyle, P. M., & Griffen, A. K. (1990). Comparison of constant time delay and the system of least prompts in teaching chained tasks. *Education and Training in Mental Retardation, 25*, 243–257.

Wolery, M., Bailey, D. B., & Sugai, G. M. (1988). *Effective teaching: Principles and procedures of applied behavior analysis with exceptional students.* Boston: Allyn and Bacon.

Wolery, M., & Smith, P. D. (1989). Assessing self-care skills. In D. B. Bailey & M. Wolery (Eds.), *Assessing infants and preschoolers with handicaps* (pp. 447–477). Columbus, OH: Merrill.

Woodson, C. W. (1990). *Individualized videotaped parent instruction: Teaching an integrated activity to their infant with handicaps.* Unpublished masters thesis. University of Kentucky, Lexington.

15

Promoting Functional Cognitive Skills

Mark Wolery

Ruth Ashworth Wolery

Terms that describe cognitive skills—cognition, intelligence, literacy, information processing, concept development—mean many things to many people. Unlike some of the other skill areas described in this text that are easily identified (e.g., social skills, toileting, communication), cognitive skills are less easily recognized. We can easily see when two children are playing cooperatively, when a father and child are communicating, or when a child is eating or toileting; however, it is less obvious when children are engaging in "intelligent" behavior, processing information, remembering, forming concepts, or doing cognitive acts. The task of defining and measuring the intelligence or cognition of infants and young children in precise ways has plagued researchers for many years (Goodman, 1990; Neisworth & Bagnato, in press). This difficulty in defining and assessing leads to further difficulties in planning intervention programs to promote its development. However, these difficulties do not diminish the value we place on cognitive skills. To paraphrase Neisworth and Bagnato (in press), which of us would choose to have less rather than more intelligence? Which of us would choose to have less rather than more ability to think clearly, note obtuse relationships between variables, solve problems effectively and efficiently? Which of us would choose to be less rather than more able to learn rapidly, recall facts and principles we learned in the past, or understand order where chaos is apparent? The point is that although this skill area presents difficulties in definition, measurement, and intervention, as individuals and as society, we value it.

This chapter addresses "functional" cognitive skills. The first section of the chapter describes an overview of these skills and assumptions related to intervention with them. The second section addresses the cognitive skills of infants (i.e., sensorimotor capabilities). The last three sections discuss preschool cognitive skills, including skills commonly identified as important for young children with typical development, preacademic skills, and early literacy skills. Each section includes related instructional strategies and guidelines.

DESCRIPTION OF FUNCTIONAL COGNITIVE SKILLS

Cognitive skills include attending to stimuli, noting similarities and differences between stimuli, cross-modal perception, remembering, thinking, reasoning, problem-solving, and many similar abilities (Harris, 1983). It is beyond the scope of a single chapter to describe all the skills related to cognition. In fact, professionals disagree about what skills should be included in a comprehensive discussion. Similarly, it is impossible to identify all the interventions that may promote children's development of those skills. Nonetheless, teachers and families of infants and young children with disabilities and developmental delays are concerned at some level about how to interact with and teach their children so that they will be perceived as more rather than less intelligent, better rather than less able to face the demands of their unique environments, and more rather than less successful in subsequent schooling.

The decision of which cognitive skills to address in this chapter relied on a statement Piaget (1963) made nearly 30 years ago, "Intelligence is an adaptation" (p. 3). Piaget borrowed the term *adaptation* from biology to refer to the processes by which young children organize and construct their knowledge of the world. In defining functional cognitive skills, we further extend Piaget's definition to include the degree to which children perform adaptively in their environments. That is, what groups of cognitive skills allow children to function in more advanced and functional ways? What skills constitute the cognitive content of the infant and early childhood curriculum?

The functional cognitive skill we have chosen to describe in this chapter are skills that result in important achievements for infants and children that influence their adaptation in the world. For infants, we describe sensorimotor skills, which are based on Piaget's formulation of early cognitive development and on subsequent research. The important achievement derived from this set of skills is the primitive ability to symbolize or think (Ginsburg & Opper, 1979). For preschoolers, we describe three groups of cognitive skills that result in major achievements. First, we address skills that are frequently identified as important for typically developing children. The major accomplishment resulting from these skills is they enable children to participate broadly in later schooling and in the community. Second, we address preacademic skills, which are those specific abilities that allow access to purposeful instruction in academics. Third, we describe early literacy skills. These are the abilities that result in being ready to learn written communication and reading. Before discussing the skills themselves, however, we note the following six assumptions about the skills and related intervention strategies.

The first assumption is that children's abilities in cognitive skills are assessed through their performance of behaviors in other domains. Almost by definition, cognitive skills are generally unobservable. We infer that they exist, or are present in a child, when that child performs some motor act or communicative behavior or responds socially in reliable ways. This assumption holds two important implications for intervention with cognitive skills. First, if children have deficits in motor, communication, and social domains, then our ability to understand their cognitive abilities is diminished. Frequently this leads us to underestimate children's

abilities. Therefore, with children who have delays and disabilities across domains, our assumptions about their cognitive abilities should be held lightly. In short, they may know much more about the world and how it operates than they appear to know. We must continually observe their interactions with the world and make adjustments in our conclusions about what they know. Second, the objectives for children's cognitive skills will likely include behaviors from other domains. Thus, the behaviors children use to indicate they have learned a concept or an operation may represent other developmental areas, some of which may be primary areas of disability. We must be flexible in terms of the behaviors we use to infer that children have or do not have a particular cognitive skill.

The second assumption is that children's cognitive skills overlap and interact with skills in other areas. As noted throughout this text and as others have argued (Berkeley & Ludlow, in press), we use developmental domains as a means to think and communicate about children's behavior. However, most skills that offer value to young children have their roots in several different domains. Two general implications exist. First, many behaviors of young children that can be identified as cognitive skills also can be classified as motor, social, or communicative behavior. For example, Natasha is a young child attempting to put a block on a boat at the water table. She looks at her friend, Alex, who also is at the water table, and says, "Look." She tries to put the block on the boat, but the boat scoots away and she drops the block in the water. She retrieves the block and the boat and tries again with the same result. She again retrieves both objects, holds the boat with one hand and puts the block on the boat with the other hand, but when she lets go of the block it slips off into the water. She again retrieves both objects and takes them out of the water, she holds the boat and puts the block back on top of it, but when she moves them to the water, the block falls off again. At this point she appears a bit disgusted, looks up, and calls to her teacher for help. How can we best describe her behavior? Is it cognitive, social, or communicative? There are certainly cognitive components, such as recognizing that boats can be used to hold objects, that two objects can be combined in play, and that if one solution is not successful another should be attempted, and her behavior is certainly goal-directed. There also are social components, such as calling her peer's attention to her behavior, persisting in her efforts, and seeking assistance from the teacher. There are communicative components as well, speaking to Alex and requesting help from the teacher. In reality, her behavior includes all three components and cannot be neatly subdivided. As professionals, we must understand children's abilities in all domains to plan appropriate intervention activities for young children in the domain of cognitive development. The second implication of this assumption is that children's abilities and advances in some areas will influence their abilities and advances in other areas. For example, the nature of children's play with toys may both influence and be influenced by their cognitive abilities (Bradley, 1985). Again, as professionals we must understand children's abilities across domains and across skill areas within domains to plan the most effective intervention programs for them.

The third assumption is that children's cognitive skills are a collection of many different skills. In the past, intelligence was seen as a "thing" and as a unitary construct, but nearly everyone would now agree that it is comprised of many different skills. Cognitive skills, like other areas of development, include several different abilities that can be measured in various ways (Sattler, 1988). Thus, when asked, "Which of your children is the brightest?" a mother can legitimately answer, "All of them." One child may be more advanced in one area of cognitive skills, another in some other area, and a third in yet another area. The result is that we must then identify the separate skills and be able to measure them reliably. However, as noted elsewhere (Goodman, 1990; Neisworth & Bagnato, in press), this has not been accomplished with complete satisfaction. Nonetheless, the implications for intervention are twofold. First, we must understand children's cognitive development in many different areas (Uzgiris & Hunt, 1987). Second, we must plan and implement interventions across those areas.

The fourth assumption is that children's cognitive skills are teachable behaviors. Because cognitive skills are not easily measured and children are thought to contribute substantially to the construction of their own knowledge of the world, some individuals have concluded that cognitive skills cannot be taught (Kamii & Devries, 1977, 1978). Such a conclusion flies in the face of logic, research, and experience. Nearly all theorists would maintain that cognitive abilities result from interactions with the social and nonsocial world and that the environment in which those interactions occur greatly influences children's cognitive development (Bijou & Baer, 1978; Flavell, 1982; Hunt, 1960, 1987; Piaget, 1963; Wachs, 1979). It follows that, at least at the extremes, those interactions could be organized in ways that promote or retard children's cognitive development. Further, there is clear evidence that the quality of home environments influences children's cognitive outcomes (Bradley & Caldwell, 1984; Henry, 1990). Finally, there is a large body of research indicating that discrete behaviors that are otherwise classified as cognitive can be taught to a variety of children with disabilities (Mercer & Snell, 1977; Wolery, Ault, & Doyle, in press).

Much of the debate on the extent to which cognitive skills are teachable rests with the definition of teaching. Teaching should be defined broadly as manipulations of the environment. These manipulations include organizing the schedule, the aspects of the physical space, the social composition and behavior of the group, the selection and use of toys and materials, and the interactions of children with their peers and the adults in their environments (see chapters 5 and 6). When defined in this way, it is clear that some ways of organizing the environment promote cognitive development, while others do not; some ways of teaching produce changes in cognitive behavior, while others do not. This view does not diminish the role of children in their cognitive development, but recognizes that the environment provides opportunities for and encourages or discourages children's acquisition and use of their cognitive abilities. An implication of this assumption for intervention is that we must view teaching broadly when attempting to promote children's cognitive development. It is clear from experience that no single organization of the environment is sufficient for all children or for any given child. Thus, the manner in which the environment is organized must be matched to the child's current development and needs. Further, teachers must alter that arrangement as children learn and as their needs change. Finally, as with other skills that are teachable, it is instructive to remember the learning/performance hierarchy described in chapter 5: acquisition, fluency, maintenance, and generalization. For example, if our goal is to teach a child to try another solution when one is not successful, then we must first focus on their acquisition of this type of responding. However, we cannot say that they have learned it until they demonstrate that they can quickly try another viable solution (fluency), or until they continue to do it after we have stopped teaching it (mainte-nance), or until they have demonstrated the ability to discard unsuccessful solutions and select alternatives for many different types of problems and in different contexts (generalization).

The fifth assumption is that children's cognitive abilities should be viewed from a longitudinal perspective. Since early interventionists deal with infants and young children, many of the skills we teach require a longitudinal perspective. That is, we are teaching skills that will be refined throughout children's schooling. For example, in the social domain, we teach interactive and social play skills. However, we clearly recognize that learning to initiate interactions, engage in several interactive turns, and play cooperatively with peers is only the beginning of true social skills. As children enter the elementary years, these skills form the base for learning more complex and intricate social exchanges. Similarly, the cognitive skills that are the focus of the infant and preschool curriculum are the base for acquiring other conceptual knowledge of the world and academic skills. In terms of implications for intervention, we should teach skills that will form the basis for understanding the world broadly, adapting to specific demands of children's environments, and preparing children to benefit from instructional experiences in the general education program.

The sixth and final assumption about functional cognitive skills is that many of the cognitive skills that are important for young children are best taught when there is a reason to learn them. We readily recognize that children learn to locomote (crawl, walk, and so forth) when there is a reason to move from one place to another. We also realize that children learn communication skills more quickly if they have a message and a receptive person with whom to communicate. Similarly, children learn to initiate interactions more readily when they have a reason to start an interaction with a peer. Cognitive skills are similar. Children more readily learn about how the world is organized and operates if they have a reason to do so. Learning that objects can be ordered by size is more readily accomplished, for example, when a child is motivated to place a series of cylinders in a block with different-sized holes. The primary implication of this assumption for intervention is that our interventions should be designed to build upon children's current interests and activities. This requires careful observation of their current abilities and behavior. It also requires presenting them with opportunities to test, confirm, refute, and modify their current conceptualizations of nature. For example, if the goal is to have children become aware of print and learn that print can communicate meaning, then we must structure the environment to meet that goal. Simply having books available is not sufficient. We must design experiences for children to interact with print and recognize that print has meaning. We can provide examples to show that some displays of print have different meanings from others, for example, that the logo of one fast-food restaurant may mean a place to get a hamburger, but a logo from another may mean a place to get a pizza.

SENSORIMOTOR SKILLS IN INFANTS

Sensorimotor skills are those behaviors acquired during infancy and thought to be precursors to basic thinking and conceptual development. According to Piaget (1963), these skills begin as reflexes but quickly become motor schemes, or patterns of behavior, which in turn become mental schemes, or internal strategies for responding. By the end of the sensorimotor stage, at about 2 years of age, the infant has acquired a primitive ability to symbolize or mentally represent (Phillips, 1975). This accomplishment

is considered the crowning achievement of the sensorimotor period.

Description of Sensorimotor Skills

In this section, we initially describe six sensorimotor skills: Means-ends (purposeful problem-solving), object permanence, spatial relations, causality, imitation (gestural and vocal), and schemes for relating to objects (play). We then list five "interactive competencies" that appear to parallel the development of sensorimotor stages. Each of the sensorimotor skills develops in a logical progression from motor movements to manipulations of mental representations or symbols. Some of the steps are shown in Table 15.1. These steps are ordinal. Each higher step in the skill is more complex than the previous steps, and the more complex steps incorporate or integrate the less complex steps. The less complex steps must be learned first because they make up, in part, the more complex steps. Because of these two characteristics, the steps of the sensorimotor skills have been used as the content or sequence of the curriculum for infants with disabilities (Brassell & Dunst, 1976, 1978).

Since sensorimotor skills represent a sequence from simple motor movements to mental representations, there are some similarities across skills. For example, the most complex step of each skill involves primitive symbolic ability. Piaget (1963) grouped these similarities into six substages of the sensorimotor period (see Table 15.1, left-hand column). The relationship between the sensorimotor skills (vertical) and sensorimotor substages (horizontal) is one of ascending complexity. The first substage represents the lowest level of development; the sixth, the most complex. The simplest steps of the vertical sensorimotor skills are at the base of Table 15.1 near the first substage. The most complex steps of each skill are at the top of the sixth substage. Procedures for assessing and teaching the sensorimotor skills rather than the sensorimotor substages are described because children do not acquire all the skills of a given substage at the same time (Dunst, Brassell, & Rheingrover, 1981).

Means-Ends Behavior (purposeful problem-solving)   Means-ends behavior involves purposeful problem-solving using both objects and people. This behavior involves the ability of children to separate the procedures, or means, for solving a problem from the goal, or ends, of the solved problem. It begins with a simple reflexive response to external stimuli and evolves into repeating a behavior to make an interesting event last (e.g., hitting a mobile again to keep it moving), then discovering through trial and error that a given solution will solve a particular problem (e.g., learning that a stick can be used to obtain an object that is otherwise out of reach), and finally inventing or mentally figuring out the solution to a given problem without using trial and error. For example, a child would learn not to attempt stacking a solid disk on a pole, although it might be mixed with disks that have holes. The animate or social aspects of means-ends behavior involve discovering and using people to solve problems. A child may use gestures at first and vocalizations later to request some behavior, or solution, from others. For example, a child might laugh and make eye contact to get her mother to repeat an interesting game, or she might lead her father to the sink to get a drink of water.

Object Permanence   Object permanence involves the ability of children to realize that objects exist even when they cannot hear, see, or touch the objects. Objects, in this case, refer to physical things and social entities, or people. For sighted children, object permanence begins with the ability to fixate visually on something and then follow or

track it as it moves, disappears, and then reappears. The next level involves searching for an object after seeing someone hide it, and progresses later to searching for an object without seeing it hidden. For blind children, the beginning steps of object permanence may be demonstrated by the ability to locate an auditory signal and then follow it as it moves. Social-object permanence, or person permanence, involves "the child's recognition that his or her primary caregivers are stable entities who react predictably in response to the child's attempts to signal a desire to be attended to, cared for, picked up, etc." (Dunst, 1981, p. 46). This skill would progress from recognition of the caregivers to expectations that they would behave in a predictable manner.

Spatial Relationships   Spatial relationships involve the recognition of an object's position in space as well as the recognition of one object's location in relation to another. Initially, infants do not appear to be aware of spatial relationships. Later they begin to track moving objects visually and through auditory signals, act on objects as though they have a given location, and rotate objects in relation to the spatial orientation. For example, if presented a bottle with the nipple turned away, infants will turn the nipple toward the mouth and suck it. Finally, infants begin to recognize the spatial relationship between two objects without testing the relationship with their own body. For example, a child may go around a barrier to retrieve an object, rather than attempting to go through it. Mental representation of space is manifested by recognition of the absence of some object, usually in a given location. For example, a child may notice that a certain chair is missing from a room without having observed someone removing it. The social component of spatial relations deals with the infant's position in relation to objects, or the

TABLE 15.1
Stages of sensorimotor skill development

Stage (Age in Months)	Domains of Sensorimotor Development						
	Purposeful Problem-solving	Object Permanence	Spatial Relationships	Causality	Vocal Imitation	Gestural Imitation	Play
I Use of reflexes (0–1)	Shows only reflexive reactions in response to external stimuli	No active search for objects vanishing from sight	Shows no signs of appreciation of spatial relationships between objects	Shows no signs of understanding causal relationships	Cries on hearing another infant cry (vocal contagion)	Shows no signs of imitation in movements he/she performs	Shows no signs of intentional play behavior
II Primary circular reactions (1–4)	Shows first acquired adaptations, coordination of two behavioral schemes (e.g., hand-mouth coordination)	Attempts to maintain visual contact with objects moving outside the visual field	Reacts to external stimuli as representing independent spatial fields (e.g., visual, auditory) rather than as a spatial nexus	Shows signs of pre-causal understanding (e.g., places thumb in the mouth to suck on it)	Repeats sound just produced following adult imitation of the sound	Repeats movements just made following adult imitation of the action	Produces primary circular reactions repeatedly in an enjoyable manner
III Secondary circular reactions (4–8)	Develops procedures for making interesting sights last: repeats actions to maintain the reinforcing consequences produced by the action	Reinstates visual contact with objects by (a) anticipating the terminal position of a moving object, and (b) removing a cloth placed over his/her face. Retrieves a partially hidden object	Shows signs of understanding relationships between self and external events (e.g., follows trajectory of rapidly falling objects)	Uses "phenomenalistic procedures" (e.g., generalized excitement) as a causal action to have an adult repeat an interesting spectacle	Imitates sounds already in his/her repertoire	Imitates simple gestures already in his/her repertoire that are *visible* to self	Repeats interesting actions applied to familiar objects

Stage							
IV Coordination of secondary circular reactions (8–12)	Serializes two heretofore separate behaviors in goal-directed sequences	Secures objects seen hidden under, behind, etc., a single barrier	Rotates and examines objects with signs of appreciation of their three-dimensional attributes, size, shape, weight, etc.	Touches adult's hands to have that person instigate or continue an interesting game or action	Imitates novel sounds but only ones that are similar to those he/she already produces	Imitates (a) self-movements that are *invisible* (e.g., sticking out the tongue), and (b) novel movements comprised of actions familiar to self	During problem-solving sequences, he/she abandons the terminus in favor of playing with the means. Applies appropriate social actions to different objects (ritualization)
V Tertiary circular reactions (12–18)	Discovers novel *means behavior* needed to obtain a desired goal	Secures objects hidden through a series of *visible* displacements	Combines and relates objects in different spatial configurations (e.g., places blocks in a cup)	Hands an object to an adult to have that person repeat or instigate a desired action	Imitates novel sound patterns and words that he/she has not previously heard	Imitates novel movements that he/she cannot see self perform (i.e., *invisible* gestures) and that he/she has not previously performed	Begins to use one object (e.g., doll cup) as a substitute for another (e.g., adult-size cup) during play with objects (adaptative play)
VI Representation and foresight (18–24)	Invents *means behavior*, via internal thought processes, needed to obtain a desired goal	Recreates sequence of displacements to secure objects; secures objects hidden through a sequence of *invisible* displacements	Manifests the ability to "represent" the nature of spatial relationships that exist between objects, and between objects and self	Shows capacity to (a) infer a cause, given only its effect, and (b) foresee an effect, given a cause	Imitates complex verbalizations. Reproduces previously heard sounds and words from memory; deferred imitation	Imitates complex motor movements. Reproduces previously observed actions from memory; deferred imitation	Uses one object as a "signifier" for another (e.g., a box for a doll bed). Symbolically enacts an event without having ordinarily used objects present (symbolic play)

Note. From *A Clinical and Educational Manual for Use with the Uzgiris and Hunt Scales of Infant Psychological Development* (p. 2) by C. J. Dunst, 1980, Baltimore: University Park Press. Copyright 1980 by University Park Press. Reprinted by permission.

position of other persons in relation to physical objects or the infant.

Causality Causality refers to the recognition of causes for interesting events, particularly the realization that behavior can produce changes in objects. Initially, infants show no awareness of causal relationships. Later they begin to realize that performing a given action can cause interesting events to occur (dropping things produces interesting sounds regardless of what is dropped); that getting an adult's attention can result in the adult making interesting things occur (patting a mother's hand to get her to reactivate a toy); that giving the adult a toy communicates the desire to have it reactivated more than simply touching the adult; and finally mentally inferring what will cause an event to occur. For example, the child may push or pull on the key of a wind-up toy to get it to work although no one activated the toy. The social component of causality involves the infant's ability to realize that other people can cause important things to occur, for example, recognizing a parent as the person who provides nourishment.

Imitation Imitation involves the ability to match or copy the verbal (vocal) and motor (gestural) behavior of others. Initially, infants will sporadically repeat vocal behaviors that are in their repertoire if the model performs similar behaviors. For example, infants will vocalize in response to their mother's vocalization. The sounds they produce probably will not be identical but will be of the same class (i.e., vocal behavior). Later, if a child makes a vocalization and the caregiver repeats it, then the child will repeat that sound. Occasionally, a child will even repeat a sound made in the past, but not recently. This skill then progresses to imitating novel sounds or patterns. In gestural imitation, children generally first imitate familiar behaviors that are visible, then familiar actions that are not visible, and later unfamiliar or novel actions that are not visible. The final step in the sequence of imitation is deferred or representational imitation, in which children see or hear a model perform a behavior, and can display that same behavior at a later time.

Schemes for Relating to Objects (play) Schemes for relating to objects involve the ability to perform various behaviors on a variety of objects. These behaviors frequently are thought of as play and exploratory behaviors. Initially, children repeatedly produce enjoyable movements, such as sucking on fingers. Intermediate levels involve repeating actions with familiar objects (shaking a rattle, a bottle, mother's keys); beginning to manipulate different objects in different ways (shaking a rattle and pushing a ball); beginning to use objects to imitate an adult's use (rocking a doll, drinking from a toy cup); and using two objects together (pounding with a hammer, stirring with a spoon). Finally, they begin to use objects in a pretend fashion, for example, using a chair as a car and pretending to drive it or using a toy banana as a telephone. The social component of schemes for relating to objects, or social play, involves the ability to use objects in socially meaningful ways and engage in behaviors depicting social situations. For example, a child is engaged in social play when rolling a toy truck on the floor and making a motorlike sound, or when picking up a purse and waving, "Bye, bye."

Sensory Organization Responses Sensory organization responses (Robinson & Robinson, 1978) occur during the early steps of many sensorimotor skills. These are *visual fixation*—the ability to visually focus on an object or person; *sound localization*—the ability to identify, usually by turning the head, the source and direction of auditory stimuli; *visual and auditory tracking*—the ability to follow, usually by moving the eyes or head, sensory stimuli as they move from one location to another; *grasp mainte-nance*—the ability to hold an object for 30 or more seconds away from support; and *sen-sory-directed reaching and grasping*—the ability to note either through vision or hearing the presence and location of an object, reach for it based on sensory information, and grasp it. These behaviors may be a large part of the sensorimotor curriculum of neonates and children who are profoundly disabled. Proficient execution of these responses will facilitate development of the more complex sensorimotor skills.

Interactive Competencies   The sensorimotor skills described in this section develop as a result of children's maturing biological systems and their interactions with the animate and inanimate environment. Dunst and McWilliam (1988) describe five levels of interactive competencies, as listed in Table 15.2. These interactive competencies describe a sequence through which interactions with the environment, primarily the social environment, progress. These competencies roughly parallel the development of the sensorimotor skills.

Rationale for Assessing and Teaching Sensorimotor Skills

At least four factors provide a rationale for promoting the sensorimotor development of infants and young children with disabilities. First, considerable evidence indicates that individuals with mental retardation of various levels acquire these skills in a similar sequence as typically developing infants (Weisz & Zigler, 1979). Thus, the sequences of these skills may describe the natural order of difficulty. Second, some of the sensorimotor skills have functional value in their own right. For example, the skill of learning schemes for relating to objects (play) is a legitimate and useful skill for young children with disabilities. Imitation is useful because it allows children to learn additional skills

from others. Third, some sensorimotor skills are prerequisites to other skills. Specifically, the primitive ability to symbolize is central to many other conceptual tasks. Fourth, the sequences of sensorimotor skills appear to describe a means of measuring the child's progress toward acquisition of the ability to symbolize. Promoting the development of these skills is one of the most defensible means of teaching infants and young children "to think."

Assessing Sensorimotor Skills

Although several measures of sensorimotor performance exist, the most widely used is the *Ordinal Scales of Psychological Development* (Uzgiris & Hunt, 1975) and Dunst's (1980) adaptation of those scales. These scales assess each sensorimotor skill in a flexible and appropriate manner, and they can be used reliably. For additional information on the assessment of sensorimotor skills, see Dunst (1980); Dunst, Holbert, and Wilson (1990); Dunst and McWilliam (1988); and Langley (1989).

Promoting Acquisition and Use of Sensorimotor Skills

Cognitive-Linguistic Model   Perhaps the most comprehensive curriculum for addressing the sensorimotor skills is Dunst's (1981) *Cognitive-linguistic curriculum*, in which Dunst proposes a three-dimensional model of intervention. The first dimension of the model involves three phases of interventions that deal with progressively more complex and advanced sensorimotor abilities. The second dimension involves two general types of sensorimotor abilities included in each intervention phase: (a) psychological abilities, which deal with the infant's knowledge of the inanimate world, or of objects and their relationships, and (b) psychosocial abilities, which deal with the infant's knowledge of the animate or social world, or

TABLE 15.2
A developmental model of interactive competencies

Level	Interactive Type	Definition	Function	Examples
I	Attentional interactions	The capacity to attend to and discriminate between stimuli	Provides a basis for establishing selective attention to salient and consequently reinforcing features of the environment	1. Smiling on seeing a familiar person 2. Anticipatory feeding response
II	Contingency interactions	The use of simple, undifferentiated forms of behavior to initiate and sustain control over reinforcing consequences	Provides a basis for the infant to learn about his or her own capabilities as well as the propensities of social and nonsocial objects	1. Simple lap games (e.g., "so-big") 2. Swiping at a mobile
III	Differentiated interactions	The coordination and regulation of behavior that reflects elaboration and progress toward conventionalization	Provides the infant with a set of behaviors that permit adaptations to environmental demands and expectations, especially social standards	1. Nonverbal gestures (point, give, etc.) 2. Independent cup drinking

knowledge of and interactions with people. The third dimension deals with the context of intervention. Dunst recommends that, to the extent possible, intervention strategies should be implemented within the naturally occurring interactions of the infant's day. This model covers the entire sensorimotor stage, or roughly the first 2 years of development.

For each intervention phase in the model, Dunst (1981) describes its major goal, identifies the cognitive skills involved, and lists

intervention objectives and activities to ensure acquisition of those skills. Phase I, *Facilitating the Development of Response-Contingent Behaviors*, corresponds with the first three substages of the sensorimotor period (see Table 15.1). The major goal of this phase "is to facilitate the infant's ability to understand the relationship between his or her own behavior and the consequences of these behaviors" (Dunst, 1981, p. 60). This means that infants learn that their behavior can have specific consequences, particularly

TABLE 15.2
continued

Level	Interactive Type	Definition	Function	Examples
IV	Encoded interactions	The use of conventionalized forms of behavior that are context-bound and that depend on referents as a basis for evoking the behaviors	Provides the child with a set of "rule-governed" behaviors that permit increased "balance of power" (independence) favoring the developing child	1. Verbal or nonverbal communication (e.g., sign language, communication board) 2. Helping "set" a table
V	Symbolic interactions	The use of conventionalized forms of behavior (language, pretend play, sign language, drawings, etc.) to "capture, preserve, invent, and communicate information" (Wolf & Gardner, 1981, p. 209)	Provides the child with a set of behaviors that permit recollections of previous occurrences, requests for future occurrences, and construction of novel forms of "rule-governed" behavior	1. Communicating "want drink" in the absence of reference-giving cues 2. Role-taking (e.g., enacting part of a previously heard story)

Note. From: Cognitive Assessment of Multiply Handicapped Young Children (p. 216) by C. J. Dunst and R. A. McWilliam in T. D. Wachs & R. Sheehan (Eds.), *Assessment of Young Developmentally Disabled Children*, 1988, New York: Plenum. Copyright © 1988 by Plenum Press. Reprinted by permission.

reinforcing ones, on the environment, that they can use their behavior to cause things to occur. For example, a smile will result in attention from the caregiver and shaking a rattle will result in sound. During Phase I, there are two types of psychological behaviors: manual, or those dealing with the hands, such as reaching, grasping, pulling, batting, and others; and nonmanual, or those dealing with other parts of the body, such as kicking their legs or rolling over to look at an interesting object. The three types of psychoso-cial behaviors in Phase I are: social contingency actions, or behaviors used to initiate and maintain social interactions, such as smiling, changes in body tone and activity; vocalizations, or behaviors used during social interactions, such as cooing and babbling; and artificially mediated contingency interactions, or behaviors that result in a caregiver providing a reinforcing response, such as an infant smiling resulting in the caregiver tickling the infant, or an infant reaching toward the adult resulting in the adult taking the infant's hand, shaking it quickly, and vocalizing to the child. In all Phase I behaviors, the intent is for infants to learn that their behavior produces effects on objects or people in their environment.

Phase II of Dunst's (1981) model, *Facilitating the Development of Differentiated Sensorimotor Abilities*, corresponds with the fourth and fifth substages of the sensorimotor period (see Table 15.1). The major goal of this phase "is to develop a wide variety of both social and nonsocial differentiated sensorimotor behaviors considered to be the precursors for symbolic play . . . representational problem-solving . . . the semantic aspects of language . . . and the communicative aspects of language (Dunst, p. 44). These skills have two important characteristics. First, infants now modify their behavior based on the outcomes of their actions. For example, an infant may be standing on the floor trying to reach a toy on top of a table, but is not tall enough to reach it. The child would recognize that continued reaching will not result in obtaining the toy and then decide to climb up on a chair near the table to get it. Second, infants recognize that two or more sequences of behavior are equally effective in achieving some goal. For example, a child who wants something that is out of reach can stand near the object, point toward it, and look expectantly at an adult; or the child could grab the caregiver's hand and lead him over to the desired object. During Phase II, "the five categories of psychological cognitive behaviors are object permanence, means-ends abilities, spatial relationships, operational causality, and schemes for relating to objects (nonsocial play)" (Dunst, 1981, p. 45). The six psychosocial cognitive behaviors in Phase II are person permanence, or recognizing that caregivers are stable and predictable entities; gestural imitation, or copying the motor movements of others; vocal imitation, or copying the verbal behavior of others; social causality, or recognizing that

other people affect the child; nonverbal communication, or using gestures and objects to send specific messages to others; and social play, or playing with objects in socially meaningful ways.

The third intervention phase of Dunst's (1981) model, Phase III, *Facilitating the Acquisition of Early Cognitive-Linguistic Abilities*, corresponds to the sixth substage of the sensorimotor period (see Table 15.1). The primary goal of this phase "is to develop cognitive and linguistic skills that are *symbolically* based, *semantically* organized, and used for *communicative* purposes" (Dunst, p. 44). Three major strategies are used at this phase: cognition, semantics, and communication. The types of behavior in the cognition strategies are "representational problem-solving and symbolic play" (p. 46). The semantic language behaviors are "spatial locatives, body parts, receptive language, and expressive language" (p. 47). The communicative behaviors are "nonverbal and vocal-verbal communicative acts" (p. 47).

In each phase, Dunst (1981) presents several different objectives and activities as well as matrices that show how each objective or activity relates to each sensorimotor skill. His model represents an integrated and comprehensive intervention program based on sound empirical and logical sources.

General Guidelines for Promoting Sensorimotor Skills

In addition to the cognitive-linguistic model, four general guidelines for intervention in the sensorimotor area can be proposed. *Instruction should be horizontal as well as vertical.* Vertical instruction occurs when emphasis is placed on accelerating children's attainment of a sequence of skills, such as the sequences of sensorimotor skills presented in Table 15.1. In vertical instruction, teachers attempt to teach progressively more advanced skills. While this approach is needed, attention should also be given to horizontal instruction. Horizontal instruction refers to teaching children to perform a given behavior in a variety of situations. Rather than focusing exclusively on teaching progressively more complex skills, children are taught to perform a given skill in different stimulus conditions, with different objects, in a variety of settings, and with different persons. Horizontal instruction also involves teaching children multiple activities or behaviors or multiple variations of each sensorimotor skill at each phase of intervention. The primary rationale for teaching horizontally is to avoid establishing skills that are not useful to the child and that are not well generalized. When teaching sensorimotor skills, we should teach children to perform more than one sensorimotor skill at a time. Various sensorimotor skills appear to be independent of one another, and training on one sensorimotor skill produces little if any generalization to others. Ideally, a variety of sensorimotor skills should be taught within the same activity.

Instruction should involve functional skills in functional contexts. For a skill to be functional, children must need the skill in their natural environment, and they should receive reinforcement, ideally natural reinforcement, when they perform the skill. Thus, determining whether a skill is functional requires an analysis of the child's natural environment. Those skills that would result in the greatest adaptation and competence within the child's environment should be taught. In some cases, we may need to adapt the natural environment so that the sensorimotor skills will be needed and responded to appropriately. For example, if we teach children to explore at school, we may also need to assist families in setting limits and allowing exploration at home. The intent is to allow children to have more control over the environment and to facilitate their communicative interactions in the environment. If a family anticipates and responds to a child's needs without problem-solving

or communicative behavior from the child, then we may help the family identify appropriate times to withhold satisfying the child's needs to encourage the desired communicative or problem-solving behavior. Functional skills are best taught when and where they are needed, such as during the caregiving routines of feeding and bathing, play interactions, or ongoing activities of the home or child-care center.

The natural contexts in which children acquire sensorimotor and other cognitive skills often include play with toys, other objects, and other persons. Bradley (1985) proposed a model for describing the potential effects of play materials, the resulting interactions (transactions), and the subsequent effects on social-cognitive development, as displayed in Figure 15.1. The first column shows five possibilities of the initiating functions of toys or objects. A toy may set the stage for an adult to initiate an interaction, arouse the child's curiosity, present a challenge for the child to master, set the stage for the child to initiate an interaction with the adult, or serve as a prop in pretend social play. The next two columns show potential responses of the participant to the initial function of the toy or object. The result is enhanced social-cognitive development, as shown in the last column. This schematic is especially useful in helping professionals understand the potential effects of toys in setting the stage for promoting sensorimotor development, whether social or nonsocial. An important point is that the adult often follows the lead of the child in responding to and interacting with the toy.

Instruction should be provided on animate and inanimate components of sensorimotor skills. As noted in the cognitive-linguistic model, the sensorimotor skills include both object-related knowledge and knowledge of the social world. Because of the overriding importance of social skills and interactions in schooling and the broader

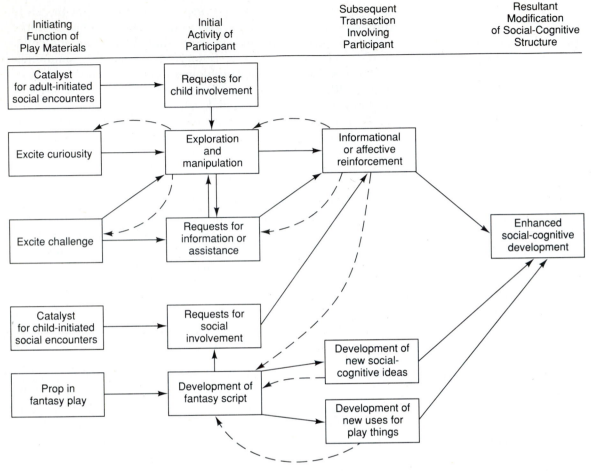

FIGURE 15.1

Bradley's Model for Social-Cognitive Development in Play

Note. From: Social-cognitive development and toys by R. H. Bradley, 1985, *Topics in Early Childhood Special Education, 5,* p. 26.

community, the social components of the sensorimotor skills are particularly important (see chapter 9). To promote these social components and the interactive competencies noted in Table 15.2, Dunst et al. (1987) propose five general guidelines, as listed in Box 15.1. These were also described in chapter 6.

Instruction should involve adapting activities for children with sensory or physical disabilities. Children with disabilities appear to develop sensorimotor skills in a se-

quence similar to that of typically developing children. Not all children with disabilities will perform or learn each step of all sensorimotor skills. Some children may have a disability such as blindness, deafness, or cerebral palsy that will prevent them from performing certain steps of the sensorimotor skills. Certain disabilities may affect both acquisition and demonstration of the skills. We must be aware of this not only during instruction but also during assessment activities.

BOX 15.1   Intervention strategies for sensorimotor skills and interactive competencies

1 *Being sensitive to the child's behavior.* Paying attention to and focusing on what elicits and maintains the child's attention sets the occasion for interactive episodes.

2 *Reading the child's behavior as intents to interact.* Interpreting the child's attentional capabilities as intents to interact with the social and nonsocial environment sets the occasion for responding to the child's initiations.

3 *Responding to the child's initiations.* Structuring the nonsocial environment in a way that produces reinforcing consequences in response to child initiations, as well as consistently responding to social bids, provides a high level of contingency experience for the child.

4 *Encouraging ongoing child initiations.* Teaching episodes that emphasize a high level of child-initiated interactions, as opposed to those that are adult directed, are more likely to lead to a greater display of child competence.

5 *Supporting and encouraging competence.* Interactive episodes that emphasize encouragement and support on behalf of the child's attempt to further his or her competence are more likely to lead to elaboration and conventionalization in the child's behavior.

Note. From A Systemic Approach to Infant Intervention by C. J. Dunst, J. J. Lesko, K. A. Holbert, L. L. Wilson, K. L. Sharpe, and R. F. Liles, 1987, *Topics in Early Childhood Special Education, 7,* (pp. 29–30). Copyright © PRO-ED, Inc.

Teachers should use three guidelines when deciding whether to adapt a given step or activity. First, children should not be expected to perform physically impossible skills. Second, if the skill results in functional behavior, then adaptations should be devised. Third, if the skill does not lead to immediate functional behavior, then consider teaching other sensorimotor skills that do not require adaptation. An example of a skill sequence for children with blindness, deafness, or physical disabilities is shown in Box 15.2.

COGNITIVE SKILLS IDENTIFIED FOR TYPICALLY DEVELOPING PRESCHOOL CHILDREN

After the sensorimotor period, young children continue to acquire a great deal of knowledge about how the animate and the inanimate world is structured and operates (Flavell, 1982). In this section, we describe the skills that are frequently thought to be important in the preschool cognitive domain for typically developing children. The implication is that the skills and strategies used to teach these skills are probably also important for many children with disabilities.

Description of Commonly Identified Preschool Cognitive Skills

Perhaps no area of the early childhood curriculum is as poorly identified and described as the cognitive portion of the curriculum after the sensorimotor period. Referring to children of this age, Flavell (1982) says, "the poor 3-year-old . . . gets labeled as 'preoperational' (even at times 'preconceptual'), and all too often our description of her thinking has been little more than a dreary litany of her wrong answers to concrete-operations tests" (p. 48). From the child's perspective, however, there are many exciting and wonderful things to figure out and to master. During this time, children begin to develop mental templates that tell them how specific

BOX 15.2   Adaptation of a sensorimotor skill

Objective: Child will retrieve object hidden under/behind one barrier, 5 of 5 opportunities

Unadapted Sequence	Adaptation for Blind Child	Adaptation for Deaf Child	Adaptation for Physically Disabled Child*
Visually fixates on object	Makes body movement in response to sounds	None necessary	None necessary
Visually tracks slow-moving object	Makes a differential response when sound moves close to or farther away from child	None necessary	None necessary
Turns head to maintain tracking when object goes out of visual field	Moves or vocalizes when interesting sound stops	None necessary	Attempts movement or vocalizes when object leaves visual field
Looks at point of reappearance when tracked object goes behind barrier	Differentially responds when sound stops and starts in different location	None necessary	None necessary
Secures object when partially hidden by barrier or screen	Reaches for object making sound; reaches for object when sound is quieter or less frequent	None necessary	Demonstrates increase in tone when shown partially hidden object; vocalizes when teacher reaches for object
Secures object from behind screen	Reaches for object when sound stops	None necessary	Does not show surprise when hidden object is uncovered; shows anticipation when adult starts to uncover object as compared to when adult removes another screen

*Assumes physically disabled child has sensory systems intact and is unable to move arms and legs (e.g., quadriplegic)

routines and repeatedly occurring events should work; they have a more refined sense of causality than infants; and their perceptions of objects in space appear to be based on relationships between objects, as adults think, rather than in relation to themselves, as infants appear to think (Flavell). Further, they appear to learn that many things in the world can be classified and that some classifications are broader than others. For example, dogs are animals, but peas are not; there are more animals than dogs and more vegetables than peas. In addition, preschool children have more complex representational skills than infants. This is seen in their vastly improved language skills, their drawings and pretend play, their initial use of language to control their own behavior, and their understanding of how the world is quantified and can be counted (Flavell). In short, there are many things learned by 3-, 4-, and 5-year-old children that make them quite different in their cognitive abilities from infants and toddlers.

The question remains, however, "What is the content of the cognitive portion of the curriculum for typically developing preschoolers?" This question is important for two reasons. First, many young children with disabilities will be enrolled in programs designed for typically developing children. Thus, understanding the content of that curriculum and the instructional strategies that are used may assist professionals to develop successful mainstreamed programs. Second, understanding the content for typically developing children may provide clues as to appropriate content for children with developmental delays and disabilities.

Uniform agreement does not exist on the content of the cognitive curriculum for preschoolers with typical development. However, two sources provide detailed information: (a) the joint policy statement of the National Association for the Education of Young Children (NAEYC) and the National Association of Early Childhood Specialists in State Departments of Education (NAECS/SDE) (1990) and (b) the *Cognitively Oriented Curriculum* (Hohmann, Banet, & Weikart, 1979). The NAEYC-NAECS/SDE policy statement outlines the types of curriculum practices that should guide the development and operation of child-care programs for young children. The document identifies a list of sample skill areas that are important for young children. These were presented in chapter 5 (Box 5.1). Although these skills are only samples, they cover many of the types

of skills deemed important by regular early childhood educators. In addition, NAEYC presents the following recommendation concerning the cognitive development of 4- and 5-year-old children:

Children develop understanding of concepts about themselves, others, and the world around them through observation, interaction with people and real objects, and seeking solutions to concrete problems. Learning about math, science, social studies, health, and other content areas are all integrated through meaningful activities such as those when children build with blocks; measure sand, water, or ingredients for cooking; observe changes in the environment; work with wood and tools; sort objects for a purpose; explore animals, plants, water, wheels, and gears; sing and listen to music from various cultures; and draw, paint, and work with clay. Routines are followed that help children keep themselves healthy and safe (Bredekamp, 1987, p. 56).

The *Cognitively Oriented Curriculum* developed by the High Scope Project represents another attempt to identify and describe the cognitive component of the regular preschool curriculum. This model has been evaluated extensively and found effective with children from economically disadvantaged homes. Further, this model has been widely disseminated throughout the nation.

The curriculum contains 50 key experiences divided into eight categories, as displayed in Box 15.3. It is important to note that the key experiences "are not goals to 'attain' and check off but are more like vitamins and other nutrients: their repeated presence in many different forms is important for good 'intellectual nutrition'" (Hohmann et al., 1979, p. 6).

Educational Practices with Typically Developing Children

Both the NAEYC (Bredekamp, 1987, in press) and the *Cognitively Oriented Curriculum* (Hohmann et al., 1979) describe instructional

---

BOX 15.3   Key experiences from the cognitively oriented curriculum

Category	Key Experiences

Active Learning
    Exploring with all the senses
    Discovering relations through direct experience
    Manipulating, transforming, and combining materials
    Choosing materials, activities, and purposes
    Acquiring skills with tools and equipment
    Using the large muscles
    Taking care of one's own needs
Language
    Talking with others about personally meaningful experiences
    Describing objects, events, and their relations
    Expressing feelings in words
    Having one's own words written down and read back
    Having fun with language
Experiencing and Representing
    Recognizing objects by sound, touch, taste, and smell
    Imitating actions and sounds
    Relating models, photographs, and pictures to real places and things
    Role playing
    Making models
    Making drawings and paintings
    Observing that spoken words can be written down and read back
Classification
    Investigating and describing the attributes of things
    Noticing and describing how things are the same and how they are different (sorting and
        matching)
    Using and describing objects in different ways
    Talking about the characteristics something does not possess or the class it does not belong
        to
    Holding more than one attribute in mind at a time
    Distinguishing between "some" and "all"

---

guidelines to promote children's cognitive development. The following recommendations of NAEYC are called "developmentally appropriate practice" (DAP) guidelines: (a) activities should be integrated across developmental domains; (b) children's interests and progress should be identified through teacher observation; (c) teachers should prepare the environment to facilitate children's active exploration and interaction; (d) "learning activities and materials should be concrete, real, and relevant to the lives of young children" (p. 4); (e) a wide range of interesting activities should be provided; and (f) the complexity and challenge of activities should increase as children understand the skills involved (Bredekamp, 1987). The roles of teachers and caregivers include being responsive to children, providing opportunities for communication, supporting

Category	Key Experiences

Seriation
   Making comparisons
   Arranging several things in order and describing their relationships
   Fitting one ordered set of objects to another through trial and error
Number
   Comparing amounts
   Arranging two sets of objects in one-to-one correspondence
   Counting objects
Spatial Relations
   Fitting things together and taking them apart
   Rearranging and reshaping objects
   Observing and describing things from different spatial viewpoints
   Experiencing and describing the relative positions, directions, and the distances of things
   Experiencing and representing one's own body
   Learning to locate things in the classroom, school, and neighborhood
   Interpreting representations of spatial relations in drawings, pictures, and photographs
   Distinguishing and describing shapes
Time
   Stopping and starting an action on signal
   Experiencing and describing different rates of speed
   Experiencing and comparing time intervals
   Observing seasonal changes
   Observing that clocks and calendars are used to mark the passage of time
   Anticipating future events verbally and making appropriate preparations
   Planning and completing what one has planned
   Describing and representing past events
   Using conventional time units in talking about past and future events
   Noticing, describing, and representing the order of events

Note. From: *Young children in action* by M. Hohmann, B. Banet, and D. P. Weikart, 1979, Ypsilanti, MI: High/Scope Educational Research Foundation.

children's success in completing tasks, reducing stress experienced by children, engaging in accepting behaviors that promote self-esteem, promoting the development of self control, and providing opportunities for increased independence (Bredekamp, 1987).

Although NAEYC explicitly calls for adaptation and inclusion of children with a range of developmental abilities, the effects of using DAP with children who have dis-

abilities has not received adequate research. As a result, recommendations about their use should be guarded (Carta, Atwater, Schwartz, & McConnell, 1991; Wolery, Strain, & Bailey, in press). A particular concern is whether the DAP guidelines have focused sufficiently on outcomes to ensure that young children with disabilities will acquire and use important cognitive skills. As described by Wolery, Strain, and Bailey, however, it is likely that programs that follow the DAP guidelines serve as a good context in which intervention for young children with disabilities can be conducted.

The *Cognitively Oriented Curriculum* also includes suggestions for the use of the key experiences listed in Box 15.3. First, the key experiences are not presented as sequences nor as separate skill clusters. In fact, Hohmann et al. (1979) recommend that they be integrated into activities and that multiple key experiences may occur within in a single activity. "All preschool learning activities should be built upon active experiences with objects. These active experiences are extended through language and through nonverbal representation . . . Concrete, active experience is examined and elaborated through language and nonverbal representation; it is not replaced by symbolic modes." (Hohmann et al., 1979, p. 5). Second, each of the key experiences can be accomplished through many different activities. Thus, no prescribed activity occurs with each key experience. Third, general sequences (i.e., from concrete to abstract, simple to complex, and here-and-now to remote-in-time-and-space) should be used to implement the activities for the key experiences. Fourth, the key experiences should occur many times throughout the year; they are not goals that should be mastered, but experiences that are beneficial to children's cognitive development.

The following four intervention strategies are used in the context of having an established range of interesting activities and helping children plan their participation in those activities.

1 Establishing and maintaining a secure and comfortable atmosphere by (a) setting limits on child behavior, (b) providing justifications for saying "No," and (c) addressing difficult situations as they arise.
2 Encouraging children's interactions, play, and language by (a) watching children and noting what they are doing and then joining in their play, (b) retaining a perspective on the child's intent when joining a child's activity, (c) touching children to communicate acceptance and support of their efforts, (d) carrying on conversations with children about what they are doing, (e) encouraging children to talk with one another, (f) providing sufficient time for children to complete their projects, and (g) refraining from talking about children when they are present.
3 Assisting children in making decisions and choices by (a) providing several options of activities and materials, (b) assisting children in understanding the options, (c) including choices throughout the day, (d) restating children's choices when they have made them, and (e) refraining from giving choices when no option really exists.
4 Assisting children in solving problems and being independent by (a) refraining from doing for children what they can do for themselves, and (b) allowing children to experience the natural consequences of their mistakes.

The role of the teacher or caregiver in implementing this curriculum is also described by Hohmann et al. (1979). Specifically, caregivers should provide an array of activities and materials that are interesting and inviting from which children can select; ask children "to plan, in some way, what they are going to do and how they are going to do it" (p. 6); and use questions and suggestions to ensure that the key experiences set the stage for children to think and develop language and social skills.

As with the DAP approach, it is unclear the extent to which these intervention strategies and caregiver roles are likely to help children with a range of disabilities acquire and use important cognitive skills. Such children may require more purposeful planning, careful structuring of activities and materials, systematic monitoring of their progress, and intensive interventions focused on producing specific and identified outcomes (Wolery, Strain, & Bailey, in press). However, these suggestions await further, more controlled research.

In the meantime, the benefits of mainstreaming in other domains, such as the social domain, argue for the inclusion of children with disabilities in preschool programs using DAP and/or the *Cognitively Oriented Curriculum*. It is important, however, that the needs of the children with disabilities be carefully identified and that an individualized plan is developed to ensure that those needs are addressed (Wolery & Fleming, in press). In chapter 6 (Table 6.1), 10 tests for evaluating individualized curriculum endeavors in mainstreamed settings were proposed. These tests can be used as a heuristic method for evaluating whether children's needs are being identified, intervention goals are being addressed, and intervention strategies are being used correctly and having the desired effects.

PREPARING PRESCHOOL CHILDREN FOR ACADEMIC SKILLS

A standard recommendation for teaching young children with disabilities is to retain a longitudinal perspective. This perspective involves ensuring that the skills taught hold current and future value in children's natural environments and preparing children for the next most probable educational placement (Fowler, Schwartz, & Atwater, 1991; Salisbury & Vincent, 1990). Many, if not most, young children with developmental delays and disabilities will spend several years after their preschool experiences receiving instruction in academic settings (i.e., schools) and often continue to learn academic skills. Professionals voice a common concern about the preschool cognitive curriculum: What do we need to do to get chil-

dren ready for academic instruction? This question prompts three other questions:

> Is it legitimate to prepare children for academic instruction?
>
> What is readiness, and what does it mean for practice?
>
> What are academic skills and what are their characteristics?

The answers to these questions are addressed in the following section.

Legitimacy of Preparing Young Children with Disabilities for Academic Instruction

In answering the question, "Is it legitimate to prepare preschool children with disabilities for academic instruction?" it is helpful to analyze the assumptions and implications of the question. One assumption is that an established curriculum exists in the elementary program. The question asks whether we should prepare children to benefit from that curriculum. On one hand, the answer should be a resounding, "No!" Children should not be prepared to fit some established and fixed curriculum; rather, they should be provided with a curriculum in preschool and elementary school that is tailored and designed to address their needs as defined by their families and other intervention team members.

In practice, children's needs exist on a continuum of importance, and addressing one need may create other needs. For example, a family may determine that a primary goal is to have their child educated with typically developing peers during the elementary years. Although such a goal requires placement in the general education classroom, it does not require that the child experience the same curriculum as his typically developing classmates. However, to de-emphasize differences and increase the possibility of acceptance by peers and of remaining in general education classrooms over subsequent years, it may be desirable to ensure that the child can participate in and learn from the general education curriculum, with adaptations as necessary. This line of reasoning and events then suggests a positive answer to the question of whether there is merit in preparing children for the academic curriculum of elementary school.

Further, it is important to note that societal forces, such as the goals stated in the *America 2000: An Education Strategy* (1991) report, may increase the value placed on academic performance. Children with disabilities are not likely to be immune from those forces if they are in the general education program. For a description of such societal forces and their effects on mainstreaming, especially at the preschool level, see Strain (in press). While we may worry about the effects of such forces on the quality of instruction for children with disabilities, the forces are nonetheless real, powerful, and pervasive. The implication is that young children with disabilities may require preparation for an elementary school curriculum that places heavy emphasis on academics, values the competent performance of academic skills, and holds the educational system accountable for all children learning these skills effectively.

Another potential conclusion that may be drawn from this question is that preparing children for the elementary school academic curriculum means using the instructional procedures employed with older children. However, as will become apparent in the following section on early literacy, this is not the case. In fact, a primary motivating force for NAEYC to develop a statement about appropriate practice for young children is the widespread practice of applying instructional procedures employed with elementary-aged children to preschoolers. Instruction that requires young children to sit still and engage in extensive paper and pencil tasks is clearly inappropriate for most preschool children. It ignores their propensity

to move, their interest in how things work, the value of play, and many of the important preschool cognitive skills described in the previous section. Thus, the task of the professional in early education is to use instructional strategies that are appropriate to children's developmental levels to teach skills that prepare them for learning in the academic curriculum.

For many young children with developmental delays and disabilities, a primary goal of their early childhood education program is to reduce the likelihood that they will require specialized services during the remainder of their schooling. For such children, the answer clearly is that they need to be prepared for the elementary school curriculum, and should be given everything possible to increase the likelihood of success in that curriculum. For whatever reason, if it is determined that given children will participate in the academic portion of the elementary school curriculum, then the task becomes getting them ready for that academic experience.

Conceptualizations of Readiness

Readiness is the state of being prepared to learn a skill or benefit from a particular experience, such as academic instruction. Two conceptualizations of readiness are the maturational perspective and the learning-theory perspective (Wolery & Brookfield-Norman, 1988). Both have advocates, both have some appearance of truth, and both have potential weaknesses.

The *maturational perspective*, popularized by Gesell and his colleagues (1940), views genetic factors and physiological maturation as the primary determinants of readiness. Experience plays a minimal role, but biology plays a primary role in determining when a child will begin to walk, speak, read, write, or compute. This perspective would predict that certain types of learning, such as walking or reading, will occur at certain stages or points in biological development. At certain stages or periods, the child is "primed for" and sensitive to developing new skills (Havighurst, 1972). This quickly leads to age-based recommendations about when children should be taught particular skills, for example, that children should not be taught to read until they are 6 year old.

At first blush, this may appear to be the case. Many typically developing children begin to crawl at around 6 months of age and begin to walk at about 1 year of age. At around 20 months, a virtual explosion occurs in the number of words children say. On closer examination, however, it is clear that these age-based predictions or standards are highly suspect. For example, for children who are within normal limits cognitively and physically, the age when they learn to walk may vary from 8 to 16 months. Tremendous variability exists in children as to when they acquired particular developmental milestones.

This variability suggests that the maturational perspective of readiness does not predict children's performance with reliable accuracy. It is clear that biological forces influence children's performance and learning, but their experiences also influence when children learn particular skills. More recent data suggest that, although some stages of neurobiological development do appear primed for particular types of learning, experience may influence the development of neurobiological systems, particularly the sensory systems (Anastasiow, 1990).

There are three primary weaknesses to the maturational perspective of readiness. First, as noted, it does not account for the wide range of variability that children display. The variability across children is so substantial that it cannot be ignored. Even children with the same home environments, parents, and diagnoses (e.g., Down syndrome) show tremendous differences in their rate of de-

velopment and the nature and frequency of their interactions with inanimate and social environments. Second, the maturational view of readiness leads to inappropriate recommendations about which skills are needed to get children ready to learn particular skills. This point is well illustrated in the following quotation from Anderson, Hiebert, Scott, and Wilkinson (1985).

In the past, under the belief that it would develop readiness for reading, kindergarten children were taught to hop and skip, cut with scissors, name the colors, and tell the difference between circles and squares. These may be worthwhile activities for four- and five-year-olds, but skill in doing them has a negligible relationship with learning to read . . . There are schools, nonetheless, that still use reading readiness checklists that assess kicking a ball, skipping, or hopping. Thus, reading instruction is delayed for some children because they have failed to master physical skills or other skills with a doubtful relationship to reading (p. 29).

The weakness lies in giving tasks to children who, for one reason or another, are thought not to be ready for a particular type of instruction or experience, when these tasks, at best, will not assist them in "becoming ready" and, at worst, are a waste of time because of their meaningless nature. A third weakness of this view is that it leads to incorrect causal explanations for a child's lack of learning. For example, statements may be made that a child is not performing some skill, such as speaking, reading, or staying dry at night, *because* she is not ready to do so. Such causal statements are often followed with the recommendation to "wait and see." As a result, the child may not receive the experiences or interventions that would lead to skill acquisition or use. Another potential result is dampening the hope or expectation that the child is able to learn the skill in question or leading to the conclusion that one can do nothing but wait.

In the *learning-theory perspective*, readiness is defined as "the state wherein children are capable of performing the prerequisite behaviors necessary for doing more complex or advanced skills" (Wolery & Brookfield-Norman, 1988, p. 112). This view has been popularized by proponents of the behavioral persuasion (e.g., Bijou, Baer, Skinner, and others). In this conceptualization, each behavior or complex task can be analyzed into component parts and prerequisite behaviors or skills. Children are thought to be ready to learn a more advanced skill when they can fluently perform all the prerequisite behaviors. This perspective gives considerable weight to the role of experience in learning the prerequisite skills. The contributions of the biological system are recognized but given less emphasis.

The learning-theory perspective of readiness has substantial appeal to interventionists. It implies that any child can learn to do anything if the skills are sufficiently sequenced, or task-analyzed, and the prerequisite skills or behaviors are known and acquired. In fact, there is considerable support for the use of this perspective in the education of individuals with mental retardation, particularly those with moderate to severe mental retardation (Snell, 1987; Wolery, Ault, & Doyle, in press). There are many examples where complex skills were at first thought to be impossible for children to learn, but then made possible when those skills were task-analyzed, the prerequisite behaviors were established, and the components of the task analysis were taught.

There are two primary weaknesses to this perspective of readiness. First, this view is based on the assumption that the relevant prerequisite behaviors can be identified. Depending on the complexity of the task, this weakness may be overcome. However, a poorly conducted task analysis and failure to identify the relevant prerequisite behaviors can have any of three undersirable out-comes: (a) the instruction focuses on meaningless tasks, (b) the sequence of instruction is inappropriate, or (c) the child does not learn the skill. For many skills, the prerequisite behaviors are not readily obvious. For example, the two prerequisite behaviors for learning to read a sentence of words are the ability to imitate orally each of the words in the sentence and the ability to match each word to itself, or identity match, indicating that the child can visually discriminate one word from another. In fact, these two prerequisite skills are all that is required, given that deliverable reinforcers exist and effective instructional procedures are used. Further, the task analysis for learning to read the sentence might be learning to read the first word, then the second, then the third, and so on until all words in the sentence are read independently. The child is then taught to say the words in sequence. However, this approach to reading may result in tremendously slow acquisition for several reasons. It does not take into account children's existing language or their understanding of language. A child who can orally express the sentence and would use it in daily speech will learn to read it much more rapidly than a child who does not understand its meaning and does not yet use the words in the sentence in daily speech. The approach does not account for a child's understanding that print can be used to deduce meaning. It fails to account for the prior knowledge that the child brings to the instruction or even why the child might need or want to read that particular sentence. All of these factors influence children's ability to learn such tasks and the speed with which they will learn them. Identifying the relevant prerequisite behaviors and conducting a task analysis to account for all the other factors that influence performance are critical steps in the learning-theory perspective of readiness.

The second weakness of this approach is that it is based on the assumption that adequate time exists for learning all the prerequisite behaviors and all the steps of the task analysis. The axiom that "anything can be taught to anyone given it is broken into small enough steps"is a hopeful statement and one that may well be true. In practice, however, many skills must be broken into many steps, and there may not be enough hours in the day, or days in a life, to get them all taught. This does not mean that such instruction should be avoided. It means that choices must be made about what is most important to learn.

On the other hand, there are many examples of curricula that have carefully analyzed the skills, considered the influences of other important forces, and correctly identified the relevant prerequisite behaviors. A prime example would be the cognitive-linguistic model (Dunst, 1981) for early sensorimotor development described earlier in this chapter. Such curricula are based on (a) careful analysis of the relevant skills, (b) clear empirical support for the sequences that are proposed and for the identified prerequisite behaviors, and (c) comprehensive analysis of the factors that influence children's learning of the skills in question.

From an interventionist perspective, the learning-theory conceptualization of readiness seems more defensible than the maturational view. It results in taking action rather than waiting, and it provides options for instruction rather than a lack of options. When we know the demands and supports in children's environments, understand their current skills, and determine the factors that affect their performance, this perspective can lead to meaningful instruction and efficient acquisition of skills.

Academic Skills and Their Characteristics

The primary academic skills include reading, writing, and mathematics. Reading is "the process of constructing meaning from written texts" (Anderson et al., 1985, p. 7). The intent is to derive meaning from the text rather than simply to decode or say the words. Writing can be defined as an expressive form of language that conveys meaning through graphic representation. Again, the purpose is to convey meaning to some audience. Mathematics deal with the analysis of quantity or amount. It involves the operations for computing and judgments about amount, time, monetary value, and many other types of measurement. Although not necessarily taught directly at the preschool level, these skills have their roots in children's early experiences. Children's early experiences influence the ease and skill with which they can later learn these content areas. These skills share four characteristics that influence how the skills are taught (Wolery & Brookfield-Norman, 1988).

First, *preacademic and academic skills are means rather than ends*. These skills are used for particular functions or purposes rather than for their own performance. Reading is used to get information and for relaxation and pleasure, writing is used to communicate messages, and mathematics is used to solve practical problems.

Two implications of this characteristic are important for instruction. First, to be used as means, these skills must be performed fluently. Second, achieving the end is most important, followed by having some means to meet the end efficiently. The specific behaviors used in the means are least important. For example, being able to understand the meaning of a given note is much more important than being able to read each word correctly and orally without error. Further, given recent technological advances, many traditional means for performing these behaviors may become obsolete. For example, learning to use a hand calculator may be more important than being able to perform particular mathematical functions with a paper and pencil (Horton, 1985). Using a microcomputer to write messages may be a more appropriate goal than learning to write with pencils. Using reading machines may help a child learn to deduce meaning from print more effectively than traditional methods.

Second, *the forms used to perform preacademic and academic skills are less important than the discriminations and relationships involved.* Many academic skills involve discriminations among stimuli and subsequent relationships with meaning. What is important is that children can make the discriminations and associations correctly, rather than the manner in which they show us that they made those discriminations. When presented with a simple addition problem (2 + 1 = _____), children could show they know the right answer in many ways. They may say "three," write *3* or *three*, point to a *3* from a choice of other numerals, select three objects, or answer "yes" or "no" when presented with a series of numbers. All these behaviors show that children are making the correct discriminations and noting the appropriate relationships. The presence of the knowledge in children is important, not how they demonstrate that knowledge.

The implications for instruction are threefold. First, the acquisition of knowledge is more important than the method of demonstrating knowledge. Thus, the instruction should be aimed primarily at ensuring that children acquire knowledge of the world and recognize the relationships of symbols to that knowledge, rather than the forms they use to demonstrate the existence of that knowledge. Second, when teaching preacademic and academic skills, we should be flexible about which behaviors children use to show us they have knowledge. Physical and sensory disabilities, lack of well-developed speech, and lack of manual dexterity may all interfere with the performance of behaviors that are traditionally used to demonstrate that some knowledge exists. Profes-

sionals should seek to identify the easiest modes possible for children to show their knowledge. Third, when possible, we should encourage and teach children multiple ways of showing their knowledge. This allows for an increase in the likelihood of generalization across different situations.

Third, *most preacademic and academic skills must be highly generalized across stimulus formats.* To be useful, nearly all the skills children learn must be generalized across materials, settings, and persons. This is true of both preacademic and academic skills. For example, children must learn that meaningful print may occur in many different forms and stimulus displays—on signs, in books, on a computer screen—and that all objects can be counted and measured. Thus, children must learn to apply these skills across many different stimulus variations. General case programming (Albin & Horner, 1988), as described in chapter 5, is useful for selecting the types of stimuli and the responses to use in teaching preacademic and academic skills.

An implication for instruction is that children should be taught to use preacademic and academic skills across many different stimulus formats. Priority should be given to formats that are found in the natural environment and that will be used extensively in the next most probable educational placement. Another implication is that generalization must be assessed and found to occur across various formats before instruction is said to be successful.

Fourth, *preacademic and academic skills are discrete responses that occur in a variety of response chains.* Many chained responses, such as eating with a spoon, putting on a coat, or taking a bath, involve steps that are performed in a consistent order. Although the order of steps may vary from child to child (Wolery & Smith, 1989), each child uses the same order fairly consistently once it is learned. This is not the case with preacademic and academic skills. With such skills, the response chains are highly fluid and variable.

One implication for instruction is that children need to be taught to combine and recombine many different, discrete responses into many different response chains. This is particularly important in prereading, reading, and writing. A second implication is that most preacademic and academic skills are meaningless outside of being performed in response chains. While a few words (e.g., signs on bathrooms, exit signs) are functional when used alone, nearly all others will be meaningful only when sequenced with other words.

Summary of Preparing Preschool Children for Academic Skills

Preparing children for the academic portion of the elementary school curriculum is a defensible practice for many young children who have developmental delays and disabilities. We should base the decision about their readiness for such instruction on a careful analysis of the skills involved, the prerequisites to those skills, the factors that influence performance on those skills, the demand and supports in their environment, and the usefulness of those skills immediately and later when they enter the elementary school program. When teaching preacademic skills, professionals should keep the characteristics of those skills in mind as well as the implications of those characteristics for instruction.

The next section addresses the issue of early literacy. To emphasize an earlier point, the preacademic instruction of young children with developmental delays and disabilities should differ from the traditional instruction provided to elementary-aged children. Preparing children for academic instruction at the later elementary school level requires that we attend to how young children learn,

their propensity to move and act on the environment, their language skills, and their engagement with a range of activities that will allow them to acquire the broad sets of conceptual skills identified earlier in this chapter.

EARLY LITERACY SKILLS IN PRESCHOOL CHILDREN

In this section, the historical roots of the early literacy movement are identified. General conclusions from this research with typically developing children are listed and implications are drawn for intervention with children who have developmental delays and disabilities. In addition, taxonomies of children's early literacy behavior, and strategies for promoting its development are described.

Historical Perspective of Early Literacy

Prior to 1920, educators generally believed that literacy development did not begin until children encountered formal instruction upon entry into elementary school. In the 1920s professionals began to consider kindergarten and preschool years as a time of preparation for later schooling. At this point, the concept of reading readiness was introduced. Since Gesell's maturational theory of child development (Gesell et al., 1940) was prominent at that time, readiness was conceptualized as described for the maturational perspective. This position was further buttressed by Morphett and Washburne (1931) who tested 141 beginning first-graders on the *Detroit First Grade Intelligence Test* and the *Stanford-Binet Intelligence Test* in September, 1928. Children's mental ages were calculated from these measures, and 6 months later they assessed children's progress on the reading curriculum. Based on the results, they concluded that children should not be taught to read until they reach a mental age of 6 years, 6 months (Witty & Kopel, 1939). However, as early as the 1930s this assumption was being questioned, particularly because gifted children were reading well before that age and were often learning to read without formal instruction (Witty & Kopel). Nonetheless, publishing houses began developing and selling reading-readiness tests, reading-readiness workbooks, and basal reading series.

The compensatory education movement in the 1960s stimulated intervention research and practice. As a result, prerequisite skills for reading instruction were identified and proposed. These were often considered to be letter-naming and visual, auditory, and perceptual skills (Katims, 1991). About the same time, research in cognition and in child language led investigators to begin studying young children's acquisition of reading and writing. Early researchers such as Marie Clay, Ken and Yetta Goodman, and Dolores Durkin demonstrated that children's early writing and reading experiences begin well before any formal instruction was provided (Durkin, 1980). More recently, investigators such as Teale, Sulzby, Ferreiro, McCormick, Mason, Taylor, Bissex, Harste, Woodward, Burke, and others have continued to study children's early acquisition of literacy and variables that affect it.

Descriptions and Assumptions of Early Literacy

Vygotsky (1978) defines literacy as part of a "unified historical line" of the development of symbolism from speech, through play and drawing, to reading and writing. Koppenhaver, Coleman, Kalman, and Yoder (1991) identified four major conclusions from the early literacy research with typically developing children. These are described below with implications for intervention.

First, *literacy is a continuous process beginning at birth.* As noted, children do not begin acquiring skills needed for learning to read and write when they enter school. As with expressive language, literacy development appears to be a continuous process that begins soon after birth and continues throughout childhood. Many young children, even in the first and second year of life, have experiences with books and with symbols such as signs and logos (e.g., pointing to the baby on the infant cereal box and saying, "baby" or "cereal"). Likewise, many may also have observed people reading and writing. Early literacy development in children is thought to have its roots in their early use of nonverbal (gestures) and verbal (words) symbols. Subsequently, they begin to mark on paper with crayons or pencils and ascribe meaning to those symbols. The use of symbols allows children to represent experiences, feelings, ideas, and even imaginary worlds (McLane & McNamee, 1991).

The primary implication of this conclusion for young children with developmental delays and disabilities is that the curriculum should include experiences related to early literacy. While early intervention programs frequently focus on promoting language and communication development, including speaking, listening, and carrying on conversations (see chapter 10), emphasis on other literacy skills is often absent. Later in this section, strategies are provided to include such experiences in the curriculum.

Second, *"reading, writing, speaking, and listening abilities develop concurrently and interrelatedly, rather than sequentially"* (Koppenhaver et al., 1991, p. 5). Each of these abilities (i.e., reading, writing, speaking, and listening) is composed of many subskills that are acquired and refined over a period of several years. Two issues are currently clear. First, these skills are acquired and refined concurrently. In other words, children learn to speak and listen and learn about reading and writing simultaneously, rather than first acquiring speaking and listening skills, followed by reading, then by writing. Second, the performance of one skill influences the development of others (i.e., they are interrelated). When children speak to others while drawing (a precursor of writing), their speech describes their drawing, and they appear to learn that they can draw what they are saying (Dyson, 1986). Early writing experience also has positive effects on other skills. "It helps children develop their concept of words . . . it promotes their ability to segment words phonemically, as well as their knowledge of letter-sound mapping, spelling, and decoding" (Teale & Martinez, 1989, p. 181). Some children learn to read before formal reading instruction has occurred. Typically, these children have been read to often by their parents or others (Sulzby, 1985). Based on this finding, it appears that young children's literacy acquisition involves a transition from oral language to written language (Sulzby, 1985).

Thus, in terms of implications for the preschool cognitive curriculum for young children with developmental delays, two statements can be made: (a) young children should have experiences in each of these skills (i.e., listening, speaking, reading, and writing), and (b) those experiences should be related to one another. For example, children should be encouraged to talk about their drawings and other art work; they should listen to stories read by adults, and that experience should include opportunities to ask and answer questions about the stories; and they should have opportunities for people to write what they are saying.

Third, *the functions of literacy are as integral to literacy learning as the forms*" (Koppenhaver et al., 1991, p. 6). *Functions* as used here refers to the reasons or purposes for which writing and reading are conducted. A fundamental early literacy concept is that writing is done for reasons and that reading is done for reasons (Teale & Martinez, 1989). In most cases, these reasons are

social (e.g., writing or drawing to communicate a message to another person) or are integral parts of daily routines (e.g., making a shopping list, reading a television guide to find a desired program). Children learn from observation and experience that reading and writing can help us do things that are important in our lives. Learning that reading and writing have purposes (i.e., functions) is as important and perhaps more basic than learning the forms of writing and reading—to write letters correctly and neatly or name words correctly (i.e., oral reading of words). When children engage in pretend reading and writing, they demonstrate that they believe such behaviors are functional and meaningful. With experience, children begin to recognize that written language has meaning, just as spoken language has meaning. For example, Juan observes his father writing and asks, "What does that say?" Katrina makes some marks on the paper, tells her mother what it says, asks her mother to read it, and says she is going to read it to her brother.

The implications of this conclusion for the cognitive portion of the preschool curriculum are that (a) children should have opportunities to observe adults reading and writing for purposes, and (b) children's participation in early literacy activities should be done with clear purposes in mind. For example, children might be encouraged to draw and scribble to make invitations for their parents to come to an end-of-the-year picnic, even though they do not write words; or they can be asked to make a list before a shopping trip. Their reading experiences should also have clear purposes, such as reading a picture receipe book to make cookies for snack.

Fourth, *children learn written language through active engagement with their world*" (Koppenhaver et al., 1991, p. 7). Learning about the functions of writing, reading, and other early literacy skills does not appear to occur as a result of passive observation. Rather, children are active and interactive with books and writing instruments. Children request reading of favorite stories to the extent that they begin to anticipate each part of the story, point to pictures as each event occurs in the story, and finish the sentence if the adult pauses. Further, questioning by adults about stories, drawings, and environmental print is an important part of making the process interactive.

The major implication of this conclusion is that simply supplying literacy stimuli in the environment and making books and writing instruments available are not sufficient to promote children's development of early literacy skills. The intervention requires action by the child and interaction with adults and must involve integrating literacy activities into children's play sequences and activity areas.

Taxonomies of Early Literacy Skills

Literacy development can be described as occurring through some general sequences; however, children progress through those sequences in a variety of ways and at a wide range of ages (Sulzby & Teale, 1985). In this section, various ways of classifying children's early literacy accomplishments are described. Whether these classifications can be used to assess the literacy behaviors and plan interventions for promoting their development in young children with developmental disabilities and delays is open to question. However, these taxonomies clearly provide a framework for understanding children's literacy behaviors.

Goodman (1986) identified five "roots of literacy;" these are:

1 *Print awareness in situational contexts.* This is seen when young children recognize familiar environmental print in context. Examples are "K-Mart," "McDonald's," and "Cheerios."

2 *Print awareness in connected discourse.* This is seen in the following example. Jennifer's grandmother reads her a book one morning. Later in the day, Jennifer is playing outside and calls to her father, "I read a book, Daddy." Jennifer has two large leaves lying flat on the palm of each hand. When her father sits down next to her, she begins to "read." Jennifer's story contains some of the same features as the one read to her by her grandmother, and her voice resembles the dramatic inflection used by her grandmother (McLane & McNamee, 1991).

3 *Use of functions and forms of writing.* Examples of this are observed in young children who seem to think they can write even though they cannot read. For example, 3-year-old Timmy scribbles on a piece of paper, gives it to his mother, and says, "It says, 'I love you, Mommy'." Five-year-old Steven makes a sign to put over his fort. The sign says, "NO GULZ ULD" ("no girls allowed"). Therefore, proportional to their functional experiences with writing, they use forms of writing to serve certain functions.

4 *Use of oral language to talk about written language.* Examples of this occur when young children use terms like *read*, *write*, and *draw*, which are general descriptors of the literacy activities, but they may not know words such as *letter*, *word*, *number* and may not be able to identify reliably letters or numerals.

5 *Metacognitive and metalinguistic awareness of print.* Examples of this occur when children can analyze and explain the process of language itself—to talk about language as if it were an object of study.

This classification provides some information on how children use language to interact with literacy activities and experiences.

Being aware of print is critical to beginning reading instruction. McCormick and

Mason (1986) present a three-stage hierarchy. First, children learn the *functions of print*. At this stage, children become aware of words, but that awareness is highly contextualized. They can recognize *stop* on a stop sign, the names of stores, signs, labels, and other print that is highly related to some environmental context. They may not know these words when they are printed in a different format or are presented out of context. Second, children learn the *forms of print*. As children learn words in the first step of the hierarchy (functions of print) and letters, they attend more to the form of the words. For example, they learn that the same words can occur in different contexts and that some letters have consistent sounds. They begin to learn letter-sound relationships. Third, children learn the *coordination of the form and function of print*. This occurs "through extensive experiences in reading" (McCormick & Mason, p. 92). They notice that recombining letter patterns with different letters can be used to form new words (e.g., changing the *b* in *boy* to a *t* will make it *toy*). Using information about how letters form words and how they relate to sounds allows children to attend less to each word and focus more on meaning.

Similarly, investigators have attempted to classify children's early writing (Clay, 1975; Sulzby & Teale, 1985). Sulzby (1986) identified six categories of written products: (a) writing in the form of drawings; (b) writing in the form of scribbling; (c) writing letter-like forms; (d) writing "well-learned units," in which the child takes a word she knows how to spell, such as her name, and reorders the letters to form new words or uses letter sequences from the alphabet as new words; (e) writing using "invented spellings," which are attempts to use one letter per phoneme of words, although not necessarily a perfect one-to-one correspondence; and (f) writing using conventional spellings and letters. This hierarchy shows the use of letters and other symbols in increasingly correct and complex or conventional ways. However, Sulzby and Teale indicate that this is not a fixed hierarchy. As children master more and more of these steps, they continue to use all of them. "The same child may use scribble for one story, letter strings for another, write his name conventionally, and write a list of words in a mix of conventional and invented spellings" (Sulzby & Teale, p. 10). However, this sequence clearly shows the value of early scribbling, drawing, and making letter-like forms. Young children who initiate such forms of writing should probably be encouraged to continue making such products. Teachers should ask them to read their scribbles to ensure that children relate them to meaning.

Intervention Strategies for Early Literacy

Although a large amount of descriptive research has dealt with typically developing children, intervention research is less common (Teale & Sulzby, 1986). Almost no research has dealt with young children with developmental delays and disabilities (see Katims, 1991, for an exception). Thus, the following recommendations for interventions are based on data from typically developing children, logic, and experience.

Intervention in Early Literacy Is More Than Exposure Although typically developing children benefit to some degree from simply being exposed to books, writing instruments, and adults who model reading and writing behavior, they must be actively involved with literacy experiences to derive substantial benefit from them. For children with developmental delays and disabilities, we conclude that mere exposure to books, writing materials, and adults who read and write will be insufficient for establishing early literacy skills. Merely being exposed to an environment that is rich with literacy opportunities will not be sufficient for all children to become literate.

It appears necessary to structure the environment so that young children with disabilities have opportunities to interact with print in a variety of ways. Teachers should provide special spaces and materials in early childhood classrooms that promote literacy development (Strickland & Morrow, 1988). However, the interventions must go beyond providing materials and environmental structuring. When planning for literacy experiences, it is important to keep in mind the functions of writing—to send messages, control behavior, as with a shopping list, and express feeling—and the functions of reading—to get information and have a context for interacting with others, as in reading a story or listening to one being read.

Early Literacy Intervention Requires Promoting Language Development   Many children with developmental delays and disabilities will have delayed or disordered language development. Because the use of language is central to early literacy accomplishments, intervention in language is a necessity for most children. Although intervention in the communication domain was described in chapter 10, three general guidelines are provided here. First, communication should be integrated into as many activities as possible. Snack activities, circle-time activities, low-structure activities such as free play, and arts-and-crafts activities are important times for providing communicative opportunities and prompting language behaviors. Second, adults can increase children's communicative exchanges by responding to their language attempts and providing interesting events and activities that "give them something to talk about." Third, structured play sessions should be used to promote increases in peer interactions that include communicative exchanges. For example, DeKlyen and Odom (1989) found that play activities

such as "doctor," "shoe store," "hair salon," and "camping" were dramatic play themes that promote interactions between peers (see chapter 5).

Play and Activity Areas Should Be Structured to Promote Literacy Experiences
Many of the activity areas that are commonly found in preschool programs (e.g., block area, housekeeping area, fine-motor/manipulative area, dress-up area) can be either devoid of or rich with literacy stimuli. Neuman and Roskos (1990) examined play areas as a context for literacy. First, they recommend labeling all areas with words and pictures that depict the activities that occur within each area. Mobiles hung at eye level can contain signs that identify each area. Second, equipment can be identified by labels that have writing on them (e.g., chairs with children's names, tables with the word *table* or *puzzle table*, gross motor equipment such as slides or jungle gyms with labels. Third, after the physical environment is enriched in this way, they recommend adding "literacy props" to further increase the likelihood that literacy-based experiences will occur. For example, the block and truck area could be enriched by designing a gas station and auto repair area. Advertisements could be hung for getting your car fixed, numbers could be affixed for prices of gas, receipts for sales and service could be available with writing instruments for completing them (Morrow & Rand, 1991). Examples of props recommended by Neuman and Roskos are shown in Box 15.4. Fourth, specially designed literacy-enriched play areas may set the stage for children to engage in literacy experiences. Examples of such areas would be a book or library area, post office, kitchen with added literary props, and offices such as a doctor's office. They suggest that all areas be clearly defined, with literacy enrichment areas clustered as far from noisier areas as possible.

BOX 15.4   Examples of literacy props for enriching play/activity areas

Literacy props used to enrich play centers

Play center	Literacy props	Play center	Literacy props
Kitchen	Books to read to dolls/animals		Clipboards
	Telephone books		Post-it™ notes/address labels
	A real telephone		Note cards
	Emergency number decals		Large plastic clips
	Cookbook		Pens, pencils, markers
	Blank recipe cards		Trays
	Labeled recipe boxes	Post office	Envelopes of various sizes
	Small plaques/decorative		Assorted forms
	magnets		Stationery
	Personal stationery		Pens, pencils, markers
	Food coupons		Stickers, stars, stamps, stamp
	Grocery store ads/fliers		pads
	Play money		Post Office mailbox
	Empty grocery containers		A tote bag for mail
	Small message board		Computer/address labels
	Calendars of various types		Large plastic clips
	Notepads of assorted sizes		Calendars of various sizes
	Pens, pencils, markers		Small drawer trays
	Large plastic clips		Posters/signs about mailing
Office	Calendars of various types	Library	Library book return cards
	Appointment book		Stamps for marking books
	Message pads		A wide variety of children's
	Signs (e.g., open/closed)		books
	Books, pamphlets, magazines		Bookmarks
	File folders		Pens, pencils, markers
	Racks for filing papers		Paper of assorted sizes
	In/out trays		A sign-in/sign-out sheet
	Index cards		Stickers
	Business cards		Alphabetized index cards
	Assorted forms		Telephone
	Play money		Telephone books
	Ledger sheets		Calendars of various types
	Typewriter or computer		Posters of children's books
	keyboard		File folders

Note. From: Play, Print, and Purpose: Enriching Play Environments for Literacy Development by S. B. Neuman and K. Roskos, 1990, *The Reading Teacher, 44,* (p. 217). Reprinted with permission of Susan B. Neuman and the International Reading Association.

***Play/Activity Areas Can Include Unit-Theme
Literacy Materials/Props***   In addition to
having the usual play/activity areas and separate literacy areas, the classroom should
also contain areas that are related to unit
themes that are being taught. Strickland and
Morrow (1989) suggest that such theme-
based play/activity areas can contain rich literacy stimuli. For example, during a unit on
animals, they suggest designing a veterinar-
ian's office. Literacy props may include magazines and posters in the waiting room; prescription pads and note paper in the doctor's
room; and an office with a phone, a phone
book, and appointment books. During a unit
on foods or the community, they suggest a
restaurant area with literacy props such as
menus, a chalkboard for the daily specials,
order pads, a cash register, money, a telephone, activity placemats, and even recipes
or a cookbook for the chef. Supermarket
areas and newspaper offices are other literacy areas they suggest.

***Library/Book Areas Should Be Structured
to Promote Literacy Experiences***   A classroom library collection should contain a variety of books. Katims (1990) selected a
collection of classic children's literature including poems, fairy tales, picture books, alphabet books, fables, informational books,
holiday books, and narratives. Books with elements of repetition (phrases repeated throughout) and prediction (allowing children to
predict what will come next such as repetitive text or rhyme) are especially suited to
the beginning reader (Rhodes, 1981). Alphabet and counting books also are good selections because they contain sequences (sequence books). Concept books, dealing with
shapes or numbers, for example, should be
included in the library. Concept books with
environmental print, allowing children to
see a connection between reading books and
the words in their environment, make good
choices for the library (Lamme, 1987). The

library area should be attractive in design.
When possible, teachers may want to deco-
rate the library, for example, with pillows,
rugs, and a lamp. A listening station with
books and cassette recordings of the book
contribute to a well-equipped classroom library. Strickland and Morrow (1988) suggest
slide viewers with story wheels. A selection
of books recommended for preschool classroom libraries is presented in Box 15.5.

***Teachers Should Encourage Children's Use
of a Writing Center***   A writing center in the
early childhood classroom is an important
part of a print-rich environment. Strickland
and Morrow (1988) suggest an area with a table and chairs. Writing materials should include paper in various sizes, kinds, and
colors and a variety of pens, pencils, markers, and crayons. Some children may want or
need to use a word processor or typewriter,
if available. Small chalkboards and colored
chalk also should be available. Book-making
material such as blank books should be included as well as a variety of pictures and
magazines to stimulate ideas for both writing
and illustrating. Since children need to share
their written work, an "author's bulletin
board" should be in or near the writing center. Equally important are mailboxes and a
message board where children display their
writing.

   "Author's Chair" is a time set aside for
children to read to an audience something
they have written. This is an important part
of the writing center, but it usually requires
careful teacher monitoring. It often works
best if the teacher sets aside a special time of
the day and allows a few children to be "Authors of the Day." This could occur at circle
time or at other times such as the beginning
of nap time.

   In addition to structuring the environment to facilitate literacy development, there
are many literacy enrichment strategies that
teachers of young children with develop-

mental delays and disabilities should use. These are described in the following paragraphs.

Adults Should Read Aloud to Children

Anderson et al. (1985) state that reading aloud has been shown to be the "single most important activity for building the knowledge required for eventual success in reading" (p. 23). Yet studies have found that this practice is not common in most classrooms (Lapointe, 1986; Morrow, 1982). Trelease (1989) suggests that the "keys to read-aloud's success are also part of its liability: It is fun, it is simple, and it is cheap"(p. 89). Given the limited budgets of most preschool programs, these are desirable characteristics of effective interventions. However, Trelease says with a degree of irony that if the strategy were difficult to implement and expensive, then it might be taken more seriously and used more frequently.

When implementing read-aloud strategies, teachers should consider several factors. First, as Trelease (1989) puts it, "Listening comprehension comes before reading comprehension. If a child has never heard a word, he or she will never say the word. And if you have neither heard it nor said it, it is highly unlikely you will be able to read and write it" (p. 204). If listening comprehension is similar to receptive language, then young children can understand stories that they cannot read. Therefore, stories that are read aloud should be rich with language. Gertsen and Dimino (1990) cite an excellent example of a language-rich story from Routman (1988), comparing the richness of language in an unabridged selection of children's literature to a version adapted for use in a basal reading series. The original version was:

A long time ago there was an old man. His name was Peter, and he lived in an old, old house.

The bed creaked. The floor squeaked. Outside, the wind blew the leaves through the trees.
The leaves fell on the roof. Swish. Swish.
The tea kettle whistled. Hiss. Hiss.
'Too noisy.' said Peter.

The adapted version was:

Peter was an old man who lived in an old, old house. There was too much noise in Peter's house. The bed made noise, the door made noise, and the window made noise. Peter didn't like all that noise.

Children will more likely enjoy and benefit from the original, language-rich version, which allows them to create mental images of the content. However, this does not mean that only language-enriched stories should be read to children. Some children's books use very simple and repetitive language, yet they are regularly enjoyed by children.

Adults Should Engage in Shared Reading

Shared reading is a read-aloud strategy used with small groups of children. In shared reading, the adult shares a book with a child or small group of children by pointing to the words as they are read (Doake, 1985; Holdaway, 1979). Predictable books that use patterned language (phrases repeated throughout the book) such as Martin's *Brown Bear, Brown Bear* (1983) work best for this strategy. Teachers interact with children by not only pointing to the words as they are read, but also asking prediction questions ("What do you think will happen next?") and encouraging participation such as joining in on refrains, making appropriate sound effects, and moving or clapping to the rhythm. As children repeatedly hear the words and see the print, they begin to make connections between printed words and oral language.

Teachers Should Use Dramatic Play to Reenact Stories

Dramatic play is a natural extension of listening to stories and an excel-

---

BOX 15.5   Suggested books for the classroom library

Predictable Pattern Books for Shared Reading

Most Predictable

Althea	*Can You Moo?* London: Dinosaur Press, 1981.
Carle, Eric	*What's for Lunch?* New York: Putnam, 1982.
Duke, Kate	*Guinea Pig ABC.* New York: Dutton, 1982.
Duke, Kate	*Guinea Pigs Far and Near.* New York: Dutton, 1984.
Gibbons, Gail	*Trucks.* New York: Crowell, 1981.
Ginsburg, Mirra	*Kittens from One to Ten.* New York: Crown, 1980.
Hands, Hargrave	*Bunny Sees.* London: Walker, 1985.
Hands, Hargrave	*Duckling Sees.* London: Walker, 1985.
Hands, Hargrave	*Little Goat Sees.* London: Walker, 1985.
Hands, Hargrave	*Little Lamb Sees.* London: Walker, 1985.
Hands, Hargrave	*Puppy Sees.* London: Walker, 1985.
Hawkins, Colin, & Jacqui Hawkins	*Old Mother Hubbard.* New York: Putnam, 1985.
Hill, Eric	*Where's Spot?* New York: Putnam, 1980.
Langstaff, John	*Oh A-Hunting We Will Go.* New York: Atheneum, 1984.
Lobel, Arnold	*On Market Street.* Toronto: Scholastic, 1981.
Parish, Peggy	*I Can, Can You?* New York: Greenwillow, 1980.
Prater, John	*On Friday Something Funny Happened.* London: Puffin, 1985.
Rockwell, Anne	*Planes.* New York: Dutton, 1985.
Rose, Gerald	*Trouble in the Ark.* London: Bodley Head, 1985.
Tafuri, Nancy	*Have You Seen My Duckling?* New York: Greenwillow, 1984.
Watanabe, Shigeo	*Hallo, How Are You?* New York: Penguin Books, 1979.
Wildsmith, Brian	*Cat on the Mat.* Toronto: Oxford, 1982.
Wildsmith, Brian	*Toot Toot.* London: Oxford, 1984.
Ziefert, Harriet	*Where Is My Dinner?* New York: Putnam, 1985.
Ziefert, Harriet	*Where Is My Family?* New York: Putnam, 1985.
Ziefert, Harriet	*Where Is My Friend?* New York: Putnam, 1985.

Very Predictable

Bayer, Jane	*A, My Name Is Alice.* New York: Dutton, 1984.
Ginsburg, Mirra	*Across the Stream.* New York: Puffin, 1985.
Goss, Janet L., & Jerome Harste	*It Didn't Frighten Me.* Worthington, OH: Willowisp, 1985.
Hill, Eric	*Spot Goes to the Beach.* New York: Putnam, 1985.
Hines, Anna Grossnickle	*Come to the Meadow.* Boston, MA: Houghton Mifflin, 1984.
Hooper, Meredith	*Seven Eggs.* London: Patrick Hardy, 1985.
Luton, Mildred	*Little Chick's Mothers: And All the Others.* New York: Viking, 1983.
Rockwell, Anne	*Boats.* New York: Dutton, 1982.
Roffey, Maureen	*Home Sweet Home.* London: Bodley Head, 1983.
Roffey, Maureen	*Look, There's My Hat.* London: Bodley Head, 1984.

Predictable

Allen, Pamela	*Who Sank the Boat?* London: Hamish Hamilton, 1982.
Bauer, Caroline Feller	*My Mom Travels a Lot.* New York: Warne, 1981.
Bayley, Nicola	*Spider Cat.* London: Walker, 1984.
Brett, Jan	*Annie and the Wild Animals.* Boston, MA: Houghton Mifflin, 1985.
Brown, Ruth	*If at First You Do Not See.* London: Anderson, 1985.
Brown, Ruth	*The Big Sneeze.* New York: Lothrop, Lee and Shepard, 1985.
Chase, Edith Newlin & Barbara Reid	*The New Baby Calf.* Toronto: Scholastic, 1984.
Degen, Bruce	*Jamberry.* New York: Harper & Row, 1983.
Duke, Kate	*Seven Froggies Went to School.* New York: Dutton, 1985.
Grindley, Sally	*Knock, Knock, Who's There?* London: Hamish Hamilton, 1985.
Lobel, Arnold	*The Rose in My Garden.* New York: Greenwillow, 1984.
Mayer, Mercer	*Just Grandma and Me.* Racine, WI: Golden Books, 1983.
Murphy, Jill	*Peace at Last.* New York: Dial, 1980.
Stinson, Kathy	*Big or Little?* Toronto: Annick, 1984.
Szekeres, Cyndy	*Puppy Too Small.* Racine, WI: Golden Books, 1984.
Wood, Audrey	*Quick as a Cricket.* Purton, England: Child's Play (International), 1982.
Wood, Audrey	*The Napping House.* New York: Harcourt Brace Jovanovich, 1984.
Zolotow, Charlotte	*Some Things Go Together.* New York: Crowell, 1983.

Note. From: *The Administrator's Guide to Whole Language* (pp. 170–172) by G. Heald-Taylor, 1989, Katonah, NY: Richard C. Owens.

lent method of encouraging oral language development. Many children enjoy acting out stories or making and using puppets to portray characters in stories. In another extension of dramatic play, students dress up and pretend to be a favorite storybook character. Such role-playing can occur while the story is being read or after hearing the story.

Teachers Should Encourage the Use of Shared Writing Following the reading of pattern or predictable books, teachers engage the students in a shared writing activity. The children are encouraged to experiment with language by creating a new shared story, based on the familiar story.

Teachers Should Assist Families in Promoting Children's Literacy Development Children's literacy development is most likely to be enhanced if both the preschool program and the child's family work together in providing literacy experiences. As with teachers, parents should model reading and writing activities and actively encourage children's participation in those activities. A number of suggestions for helping families integrate literacy experiences into their ongoing activities of daily life are presented in Box 15.6.

The Role of the Teacher in Promoting Literacy Experiences

As stated earlier, simply placing children in literacy rich environments will probably not result in their learning to read. There are, however, many things a teacher can and should do to facilitate literacy development. Special times should be established each day for teachers to read aloud to children. Observations of a kindergarten classroom with a good library and a teacher who read aloud daily indicated that during free time children were three times more likely to select and look at familiar books, than unfamiliar books (Martinez & Teale, 1988). Likewise, children were two times more likely to select a somewhat familiar book over the unfamiliar books. Familiar books were ones the teacher had read aloud many times, somewhat familiar books had been read aloud only once, and unfamiliar books had not been read to the class. Katims (1990, 1991) reported similar findings from a replication of Martinez and Teale. These findings and others that support reading to children underscore the importance of teachers planning times each day for reading aloud to children.

In addition to structuring a literacy-rich environment and planning a daily read-aloud program, the teacher must ensure that children are engaging in and benefiting from that environment and reading. Vygotsky (1962) describes a zone of proximity, or "proximal development," as the area between what a learner already knows (i.e., prior knowledge) and what the learner can learn or do next with assistance. In language acquisition research, scaffolding is an instructional strategy used to facilitate communication slightly beyond children's actual ability level. For example, a young child says, "Mommy, birdie!" When the mother replies, "Yes, there's a bird outside on the fence, isn't there?" She is providing a literacy scaffold (Boyle & Peregoy, 1990). Teachers should use scaffolding strategies in addition to good questioning strategies when interacting with young children. Simply responding to a young child's use of language with "Yes, I see" is just not sufficient.

The final role the teacher plays in literacy development is evaluating. Despite an enriched environment, a daily read-aloud program with follow-up activities, and effective use of literacy scaffolding, some children could still "slip through the cracks." The direct observation systems for monitoring children's development were discussed in chapter 5. Some literacy goals will be in the area of writing, and permanent products can be used to document progress. However, since these products are usually sent home, it is wise to develop a system to record goals and progress for writing behavior. A recording system is also necessary for prereading literacy goals, such as spending time in the book area, showing interest in favorite books, retelling familiar stories, and recognizing environmental print.

Summary of Early Literacy Skills

Children begin learning reading and writing soon after they are born, and these skills are learned simultaneously with speaking and listening. Children's early literacy competence is related to understanding the functions of reading and writing and developing an awareness of these skills. This is accomplished by allowing children to observe adults reading and writing and by offering them multiple experiences facilitated by adults with literacy materials and activities.

DESCRIPTION AND INSTRUCTION OF PREACADEMIC SKILLS

Definition and Listing of Preacademic Skills

In the previous section, strategies were identified for ensuring that young children, in-

BOX 15.6   Suggestions to families for promoting early literacy

Activity	Suggestions

When reading aloud to your child:

1 Whenever possible, let your child sit on your lap while you read aloud.
2 Start reading when the child is an infant. The child will become accustomed to the rhythmic sound of your reading voice.
3 When children are between 6 months and 1 year of age, select books with colorful illustrations and rhythmic text.
4 Read the same stories over and over. Studies show that the books children select for themselves are likely to be books they have heard more than once. Follow print with your finger and encourage your child to read along with you when text is repetitive or predictable.
5 Ask children to tell you what is happening in the story and what they think might happen next.
6 Point out things like title, author, and illustrator each time you read a book. And it's fine to go ahead and use words like *title* and *author*!
7 Visit the public library regularly and get different books. Place books throughout the house.

In the home:

1 Open and read mail in front of children. Be sure they observe you responding to mail. If you write letters, give your children paper and markers and get them to write a letter, too.
2 Read labels to children. They soon begin to recognize cereal boxes and canned drinks. Be aware of all the labeling in your home and attempt to point these out to children when appropriate.
3 Before going food shopping, allow your child to talk to you about what food and household items will be purchased. When appropriate, let your child help you look through the food section of the newspaper and make a list. Make a small grocery list for your child.
4 Watch Educational Television shows like *Sesame Street* with your child. Ask your child to explain to you some of the things that take place on the show.
5 Show your child how you use the television guide and the weather map in the newspaper. Show your child how you use a cookbook and recipes when preparing foods. Be sure your child observes you reading for pleasure.

In the community:

1 At the supermarket, let children help you find food on your list, and you help them find the food on their lists. If you use coupons, involve children in helping find the items at the grocery store.
2 Point out environmental print to your child. Examples are store signs, road signs, billboards, and letters and numbers on license tags and the names of cars.
3 In a restaurant, make sure your child notices the menu, the print on paper products, the labels on trash bins, and any print that might be on table mats or tables.

Many times it is also possible to incorporate specific preacademic training into some of these literacy activities. When your child sees the K-Mart sign and says, "My name has a K, too," not only would you praise your child for being so smart, you might also provide additional information such as "Burger King also has a K in its name." At other times, you may want to point out to your child that the *T* in *Tide* is the same letter and/or sound as the *T* in his name, *Tommy*.

TABLE 15.3
Proposed preacademic behaviors for prereading instruction

Preacademic Skill	Description	Relationship to Academic Skill	Usefulness to Nonacademic Children*
Well-developed language system (at least receptive language) (Smith, 1977)	Child demonstrates ability to understand what is being communicated to her/him	Allows child to determine meaning in what will be read	Student can use language for communication with others
Predict future events (Smith, 1977)	Child answers questions about what will happen next	Allows child to anticipate what will occur in text being read and thus adds meaning	Allows child to engage in more complex communicative exchanges
Awareness of print, books, and purpose of reading (McCormick, 1983; Wiseman, 1984)	Child demonstrates understanding that environmental print is symbolic and provides information	Allows child to approach print as though it is symbolic; thus, it is something from which information can be obtained	Allows child to be aware of environmental signs and symbols
Auditory discrimination of relevant phonetic sounds (Neisworth, Willoughby-Herb, Bagnato, Cartwright, & Laub, 1980; Palardy, 1984)	Child indicates that different but similar sounds are not the same	Foundation skill for learning that sounds are related to specific symbols	Minimal
Auditory blending of phonetic sounds (Cohen & Gross, 1979)	Child combines phonemes to produce words	Foundation for combining sounds to form words	Minimal
Auditory segmentation of series of phonetic sounds (Allan, 1982; Cohen & Gross, 1979)	Child separates phonemes or syllables within a word (presented auditorily)	Foundation for letter/ sound training	Minimal

cluding those with developmental delays and disabilities, have experiences that will prepare them to learn academic skills and function in a literate world. The skills involved and the strategies recommended seem legitimate for nearly all young children; however, in some cases more direct instruction of preacademic skills may be warranted. In this section, we identify some of those skills and discuss strategies for teaching them. An important caution should be provided. *The strategies described in this section should be used in the context of a preschool program that implements the early literacy practices described in the previous section.*

Preacademic skills, as used here, refer to skills that, on the basis of logic and/or empirical evidence, are needed before pur-

TABLE 15.3
continued

Preacademic Skill	Description	Relationship to Academic Skill	Usefulness to Nonacademic Children*
Visual discrimination of letters/words (Palardy, 1984)	Child indicates that different but similar letters/words are not the same	Allows child to learn skill needed for associating graphic symbols with referent	Allows child to learn important useful words needed in community
Matching letters/words (Brigance, 1978; Cohen & Gross, 1979)	Child indicates that same letters/words are the same	Allows child to learn skills needed for associating graphic symbols with referent	Allows child to learn important useful words needed in community
Letter/word recognition and identification (Brigance, 1978; Cohen & Gross, 1979)	Child indicates letter/word when named by another, or names letter/word when asked	Allows child to learn that given graphic symbol has specific name, and in the case of words, specific meaning	Allows child to respond to words in community
Sound/letter match, recognition, and identification (Brigance, 1978; Neisworth et al., 1980)	Child indicates letter associated with given sound or indicates sound associated with given letter	Allows child to attempt new words and learn their meaning	Minimal
Left-to-right sequence, top-to-bottom sequence, and front-to-back sequence (Neisworth et al., 1980)	Child interacts with sequenced materials using these sequences	Allows child to approach print as a source of information	May allow child to "read" picture books

*Usefulness to nonacademic children refers to the possible utility of the preacademic skill for children with whom later academic instruction in reading would be inappropriate; these statements indicate the potential usefulness of the skill despite the possibility that the child may never use reading to obtain information.

Note. From (Pre)Academic Instruction for Handicapped Preschool Children (p. 114) by M. Wolery and J. Brookfield-Norman, 1988. In S. L. Odom & M. B. Karnes (Eds.), *Early Intervention for Infants and Children with Handicaps: An Empirical Base,* Baltimore: Paul Brookes.

poseful instruction in reading, writing, and mathematics is provided at the initial first-grade level (Wolery & Brookfield-Norman, 1988). Thus, these skills are the prerequisite and precursor behaviors that may make subsequent instruction on academic skills more successful. Tables 15.3, 15.4, and 15.5 present a series of proposed preacademic behaviors for reading, writing, and math, respectively.

Although each skill does not have empirical evidence of being a prerequisite, expe-

TABLE 15.4
Proposed preacademic behaviors for prewriting instruction

Preacademic Skill	Description	Relationship to Academic Skill	Usefulness to Nonacademic Children*
Grasps writing instrument and scribbles (LeMay, Griffin, & Sanford, 1977; Neisworth et al., 1980)	Child produces marks on paper with writing instrument	Allows child to learn that the writing instrument will produce marks	Minimal
Holds writing instrument with fingers and scribbles (Fredericks et al., 1976; Neisworth et al., 1980)	Child produces marks on paper with writing instrument	Allows child to learn that the writing instrument will produce marks	Minimal
Imitates specific strokes (e.g., circular, vertical, horizontal, diagonal) in isolation (Fredericks et al., 1976; Neisworth et al., 1980)	Child imitates another person making specific marks	Allows child to learn skill that will be used in forming letters or words	Minimal
Traces or copies from two-dimensional model specific strokes in isolation (Fredericks et al., 1976; Neisworth et al., 1980)	Child produces strokes that match a two-dimensional model	Allows child to learn skill that will be used in forming letters	Minimal
Imitates, traces, copies from models (live or two-dimensional) that combine strokes to form letters (Haring, et al., 1981; LeMay et al., 1977)	Child produces combined strokes needed to print letters or numerals	Allows child to produce forms that can be labeled as letters or numerals	Minimal
Prints letters or numerals without model (Cohen & Gross, 1979; Fredericks et al., 1976)	Child produces letters or numerals without model	Allows child to produce letters without model; thus, will be useful for writing	Minimal
Prints combinations of letters using left-to-right sequence (Cohen & Gross, 1979)	Child produces letters to form words by moving from left to right	Allows child to print words	Minimal

Usefulness to nonacademic children refers to the possible utility of the preacademic skill for children with whom later academic instruction in writing would be inappropriate; these statements indicate the potential usefulness of the skill despite the possibility that the child may never use writing to communicate.

Note. From (Pre)Academic Instruction for Handicapped Preschool Children (p. 115) by M. Wolery and J. Brookfield-Norman, 1988, in S. L. Odom & M. B. Karnes (Eds.), *Early Intervention for Infants and Children with Handicaps: An Empirical Base,* Baltimore: Paul Brookes.

TABLE 15.5
Proposed preacademic behaviors for premath instruction

Preacademic Skill	Description	Relationship to Academic Skill	Usefulness to Nonacademic Children*
Rote counting (Baroody & Price, 1983; Fredericks et al., 1976)	Child verbally says numerals in sequence	Serves as a basis for counting objects	Minimal
Rational counting (Clements, 1984; Tawney, Knapp, O'Reilly, & Pratt, 1979)	Child counts objects, enumerating each object once and stopping at last object	Allows child to count objects and use counting to solve problems requiring counting	Allows child to count objects in real situations
Cardinal counting (Baroody & Snyder, 1983; Clements, 1984)	Child demonstrates that the last number counted in a set is the number of items in that set (i.e., responds correctly to "How many?")	Serves as foundation for working with numerals to solve computation problems	Allows child to determine how many objects, etc., are in a set
Matches/compares sets (Baroody & Snyder, 1983; Cohen & Gross, 1979; Tawney et al., 1979)	Child identifies sets of objects as same, more, or less	Allows child to make judgments about amount in computation problems	Allows child to make judgments of objects in sets
Recognizes and names numerals (Cohen & Gross, 1979; Fredericks et al., 1976; Neisworth et al., 1980)	Child responds correctly to "Show me (the numeral named)" and "what is this?" (numeral shown)	Provides foundation for using numerals in computation problems	Minimal
Matches numeral to set and correct number of objects to numeral (Cohen & Gross, 1979; Neisworth et al., 1980)	Child places correct numeral on set with correct number of objects; places correct number of objects on numeral	Foundation for using numerals to represent amount	Allows child to use numerals for solving everyday problems dealing with amount (e.g., recipes, directions)

Usefulness to nonacademic children refers to the possible utility of the preacademic skill for children with whom later academic instruction in math would be inappropriate; these statements indicate the potential usefulness of the skill despite the possibility that the child may never use math for computation or problem-solving.

Note. From (Pre)Academic Instruction for Handicapped Preschool Children (p. 116) by M. Wolery and J. Brookfield-Norman, 1988, in S. L. Odom & M. B. Karnes (Eds.), *Early Intervention for Infants and Children with Handicaps: An Empirical Base,* Baltimore: Paul Brookes.

rience and logic suggest that they are useful skills in preparing children for academic instruction. The skills are not necessarily presented in order of importance or in a sequence for instruction. In fact, many of the listed skills include a long sequence of subskills. Thus, simultaneous instruction on multiple skills from this list is probably the most defensible practice. For example, the preacademic reading list (Table 15.3) includes a well-developed language system and an awareness of print. Both of these skills probably should be taught throughout children's preschool experiences. Also, the strategies described in this section are not the only ones for promoting acquisition and use of these skills. In fact, many of the strategies described in the previous section on early literacy may result in these skills being learned. Probably the most efficient means of teaching these skills is the use of the strategies described in this section embedded in the contexts of literacy-rich homes and preschool classrooms.

Instruction of Preacademic Skills

Several issues are involved in planning and providing supplementary instruction on preacademic skills. *The team must first decide whether supplementary preacademic skill instruction is necessary.* This decision is an individualized decision made by the child's intervention team, including the family. Factors that should be weighed in the decision to conduct supplementary preacademic instruction include the child's next most probable placement and the demands, curriculum, and instructional strategies used in that placement; children's interest in learning these skills; and the usefulness of the skill in other contexts (i.e., beyond its value in preparing children for academic instruction). In Tables 15.3 to 15.5, the right-hand column lists some of the potential benefits of learning the respective skills despite the fact that the child may never, or not

in the near future, experience academic instruction.

If a determination is made that supplementary instruction on preacademic skills is necessary, then *the team must decide on the nature of that instruction.* Specifically, the team must select the skills to be taught (see chapter 4), determine how learning opportunities will be structured and provided (see chapter 6), select instructional strategies (see chapter 6), and develop a monitoring system for evaluating the progress (see chapter 5). In addition, the team should clearly discriminate between the knowledge being taught and the manner in which children will demonstrate that knowledge (Wolery & Brookfield-Norman, 1988).

Learning opportunities for supplementary instruction on preacademic behaviors can be provided in many ways. In part, it depends on the skill being taught. For discrete responses, at least three options exist: (a) embedding the skill in other instructional activities, (b) providing trials during transitions, and (c) using direct instructional sessions. Embedding instruction on preacademic type behaviors is illustrated by two studies. Kincaid and Weisberg (1978) had a classroom that used tokens as part of the classroom management system. Each day, children met with a teacher and exchanged tokens for back-up reinforcers. Letters were written on each token. During the exchange process, the teacher taught children to recognize the letters written on the tokens. In a study conducted during the ongoing circle time in a Head Start program that included children with developmental delays, the teacher used a simultaneous prompting procedure to teach children to read names of children in the class (Wolery, Fleming, Venn, Domjancic, & Thornton, 1991). These trials were interspersed throughout other circle-time activities (e.g., reviewing the calendar, doing finger plays, reviewing who was present) and all children in the circle-time activity responded chorally (i.e., in unison).

The trials were not presented one after the other, but were distributed throughout the activity. The children with developmental delays acquired these names quickly.

In addition to embedding instruction in other activities, learning opportunities can be provided during transitions. For example, Wolery, Doyle, Gast, Ault, and Lichtenberg (1991) used transition-based teaching to present single trials during in-class transitions on a number of preacademic behaviors to young children with a variety of developmental delays. When an activity was completed and before children moved to the next activity, the teachers secured a child's attention, presented the target stimulus, and provided the child with an opportunity to respond. After this single trial, children progressed with the transitions. This procedure resulted in rapid learning of the target skills; in fact, the efficiency of the procedure was about equal to one-to-one instructional sessions using progressive time delay with the same teacher and children.

The third option for presenting supplemental instruction on preacademic behaviors is conducting direct instructional sessions. Although these can be one-to-one sessions, the preferred method is to conduct small-group sessions (e.g., two to five children). The steps for planning and implementing small-group instructional sessions was presented in chapter 6 (Box 6.8). Small-group instructional sessions have been used to teach preschoolers with developmental delays and disabilities a variety of preacademic skills, such as receptively identifying symbols (Wolery, Holcombe, Werts, & Cipolloni, 1991), naming numerals and reading number words (Holcombe, Wolery, Werts, & Hrenkevich, 1991), reading functional words (Alig-Cybriwsky, Wolery, & Gast, 1990), and naming the value of coins (Wolery, Werts, Holcombe, Billings, & Vassilaros, in press). These sessions were relatively brief (e.g., 4 to 10 minutes), used response prompting procedures such as constant time de-lay or the simultaneous prompting procedure (chapter 6, Box 6.2), used fast-paced instruction, involved presentation of multiple target stimuli to children in each session, and resulted in children acquiring criterion-level performance, involved children making relatively few errors, and resulted in high levels of reinforcement and positive teacher-child exchanges.

Selecting instructional strategies for supplemental instruction of preacademic behaviors should follow the guidelines identified in chapter 6. However, several considerations are important. First, the strategies selected should result in rapid acquisition with few errors. The response-prompting procedures such as constant and progressive time delay and simultaneous prompting meet this criterion (Wolery, Ault, & Doyle, in press; Wolery, Holcombe, et al., in press). Second, the strategies should be used as described. Generally teachers require relatively little training to use these strategies effectively. However, the implementation of these strategies should be monitored and incorrect or inconsistent use should be rectified. Third, children should be assessed to ensure that they can perform the prerequisite skills related to the target behaviors. For example, if visual stimuli are used, then children should be able to match samples of these stimuli to other identical examples of the stimuli. Fourth, children should be allowed to choose reinforcers for correct responses. Fifth, children's performance should be monitored to ensure that they are acquiring the desired skills (chapter 5; Wolery, Ault, & Doyle, in press).

In summary, children should experience literacy-rich environments and interactions with the adults in their lives. Given this context, teams may decide that in certain situations supplemental instruction on some of the preacademic behaviors is necessary. When this instruction is provided, it should be planned and implemented as described.

SUMMARY

Cognitive skills for infants and young children with disabilities constitute an important curricular domain. For infants, this domain primarily involves sensorimotor skills and interactive competencies. These skills are best taught during the ongoing interactions that infants have with objects or toys and people in their environments. At the preschool level, children should be taught the skills that are seen as important for their nondisabled peers, should experience a preschool classroom that has numerous choices of activities and materials, and should have adults who are responsive to their behavior and attempt to expand it through questioning and joint participation in play. For many preschoolers with developmental delays and disabilities, the cognitive portion of the preschool curriculum should prepare them for academic instruction during the elementary school years. This preparation should include a preschool environment that contains books and other literacy stimuli and should involve frequent reading to children and other literacy-related activities. For some children, however, supplemental instruction on preacademic behaviors may be needed. When this need exists, the team should purposefully plan the instruction to promote acquisition and use of those skills.

REFERENCES

Albin, R. W., & Horner, R. H. (1988). Generalization with precision. In R. H. Horner, G. Dunlap, & R. L. Koegel (Eds.), *Generalization and maintenance: Life-style changes in applied settings* (pp. 99–120). Baltimore: Paul Brookes.

Alig-Cybriwsky, C., Wolery, M., & Gast, D. L. (1990). Use of a constant time delay procedure in teaching preschoolers in a group format. *Journal of Early Intervention, 14,* 99–116.

Allan, K. K. (1982). The development of young children's metalinguistic understanding of the word. *Journal of Educational Research, 76,* 89–92.

America 2000: An Education Strategy. (1991). Washington, DC: U.S. Department of Education.

Anastasiow, N. J. (1990). Implications of the neurobiological model for early intervention. In S. J. Meisels, & J. P. Shonkoff (Eds.), *Handbook of early childhood intervention.* Cambridge: Cambridge Press.

Anderson, R. C., Hiebert, E. H., Scott, J. A., & Wilkinson, I. A. G. (1985). *Becoming a nation of readers: The report of the commission on reading.* Washington, DC: The National Institute of Education.

Baroody, A. J., & Price, J. (1983). The development of the number-word sequence in the counting of 3-year-olds. *Journal for Research in Mathematics Education, 14,* 361–367.

Baroody, A. J., & Snyder, P. M. (1983). A cognitive analysis of basic arithmetic abilities of TMR children. *Education and Training in Mental Retardation, 18,* 253–259.

Berkeley, T. R., & Ludlow, B. L. (in press). Developmental domains: The mother of all inventions; or the subterranean early development blues. *Topics in Early Childhood Special Education.*

Bijou, S. W., & Baer, D. M. (1978). *Behavior analysis of child development.* Englewood Cliffs, NJ: Prentice-Hall.

Boyle, O. E., & Peregoy, S. F. (1990). Literacy scaffolds: Strategies for first- and second-language readers and writers. *The Reading Teacher, 44,* 194–200.

Bradley, R. H. (1985). Social-cognitive development and toys. *Topics in Early Childhood Special Education.* 5(3), 11–29.

Bradley, R. H., & Caldwell, B. M. (1984). The relation of infants' home environment to achievement test performance in first grade: A follow-up study. *Child Development, 55,* 803–809.

Brassell, W. R., & Dunst, C. J. (1976). Comparison of two procedures for fostering the development of the object construct. *American Journal of Mental Deficiency, 80,* 523–528.

Brassell, W. R., & Dunst, C. J. (1978). Fostering the object construct: Large-scale intervention with handicapped infants. *American Journal of Mental Deficiency, 82*, 507–510.

Brigance, A. H. (1978). *Inventory of early development.* Woburn, MA: Curriculum Associates.

Bredekamp, S. (Ed.) (1987). *Developmentally appropriate practice in early childhood programs serving children from birth through age 8.* Washington, DC: National Association for the Education of Young Children.

Bredekamp, S. (in press). *Appropriate curriculum and assessment in program serving children, 3 through 8 years of age.* Washington, DC: National Association for the Education of Young Children.

Carta, J. J., Schwartz, I. S., Atwater, J. B., & McConnell, S. R. (1991). Developmentally appropriate practice: Appraising its usefulness for young children with disabilities. *Topics in Early Childhood Special Education, 11*(1), 1–20.

Clay, M. M. (1975). *What did I write?* Auckland, New Zealand: Heinemann Educational Books.

Clements, D. H. (1984). Training effects on the development and generalization of Piagetian logical operations and knowledge of number. *Journal of Educational Psychology, 76,* 766–776.

Cohen, M. A., & Gross, P. J. (1979). *The developmental resource: Behavioral sequences for assessment and program planning* (Vol. 2). New York: Grune & Stratton.

DeKlyen, M., & Odom, S. L. (1989). Activity structure and social interactions with peers in developmentally integrated play groups. *Journal of Early Intervention, 13,* 342–352.

Doake, D. (1985). Reading-like behavior: Its role in learning to read. In A. Jaggar & M. T. Smith-Burke (Eds.), *Observing the language learner* (pp. 82–98). Newark, DE: International Reading Association.

Dunst, C. J. (1980). *A clinical and educational manual for use with the Uzgiris and Hunt Scales of infant psychological development.* Baltimore: University Park Press.

Dunst, C. J. (1981). *Infant learning: A cognitive-linguistic intervention strategy.* Allen, TX: Teaching Resources/DLM.

Dunst, C. J., Brassell, W. A., & Rheingrover, R. M. (1981). Structural and organisational features of sensorimotor intelligence among retarded infants and toddlers. *British Journal of Educational Psychology, 51,* 133–143.

Dunst, C. J., Holbert, K. A., & Wilson, L. L. (1990). Strategies for assessing infant sensorimotor interactive competencies. In E. D. Gibbs & D. M. Teti (Eds.), *Interdisciplinary assessment of infants: A guide for early intervention professionals* (pp. 91–112). Baltimore: Paul Brookes.

Dunst, C. J., Lesko, J. J., Holbert, K. A., Wilson, L. L., Sharpe, K. L., & Liles, R. F. (1987). A systematic approach to infant intervention. *Topics in Early Childhood Special Education, 7*(2), 19–37.

Dunst, C. J., & McWilliam, R. A. (1988). Cognitive assessment of multiply handicapped young children. In T. D. Wachs & R. Sheehan (Eds.), *Assessment of developmentally disabled children* (pp. 213–238). New York: Plenum Press.

Durkin, D. (1980). *Teaching young children to read* (3rd ed.). Boston: Allyn & Bacon.

Dyson, A. H. (1986). Transitions and tensions: Interrelationships between drawing, talking, and dictating of young children. *Research in the Teaching of English, 20,* 379–409.

Flavell, J. H. (1982). *Cognitive development* (2nd ed.). Englewood Cliffs, NJ: Prentice-Hall.

Fowler, S. A., Schwartz, I., & Atwater, J. (1991). Perspective on the transition from preschool to kindergarten from children with disabilities and their families. *Exceptional Children, 58,* 136–145.

Fredericks, H. D., Riggs, C., Furey, T., Grove, D., Moore, W., McDonnell, J., Jordan, E., Hanson, W., Baldwin, V., & Wadlow, M. (1976). *The teaching research curriculum for moderately and severely handicapped.* Springfield, IL: Charles C. Thomas.

Gertsen, R., & Dimino, J. (1990). Reading instruction for at-risk students implications of current research. *Oregon School Study Council, 33*(5), 1–30.

Gesell, A., Halverson, H. M., Thompson, H., Ilg, F. L., Castner, B. M., Ames, L. B., & Amatruda, C. S. (1940). *The first five years of life: The preschool years.* New York: Harper & Row.

Ginsburg, H., & Opper, S. (1979). *Piaget's theory of intellectual development* (2nd ed.). Englewood Cliffs, NJ: Prentice-Hall.

Goodman, J. F. (1990). Infant intelligence: Do we, can we, should we assess it? In C. Reynolds & R. Kamphaus (Eds.), *Handbook of psychological and educational measurement of children.* New York: Guilford.

Goodman, Y. (1986). Children coming to know literacy. In W. Teale and E. Sulzby (Eds.), *Emerging literacy* (pp. 1–14). Norwood, NJ: Ablex.

Haring, N. G., White, O. R., Edgar, E. B., Affleck, J. Q., Hayden, A. H., Munson, R. G., & Bendersky, M. (Eds.) (1981). *Uniform performance assessment system.* Columbus, OH: Merrill.

Harris, P. L. (1983). Infant cognition. In P. H. Mussen (Ed.), *Handbook of child psychology.* (pp. 689–787, 4th ed.). New York: John Wiley.

Havighurst, R. J. (1972). *Developmental tasks and education* (3rd ed.). White Plains, NY: Longman.

Heald-Taylor, G. (1989). *The administrator's guide to whole language.* Katonah, NY: Richard C. Owens.

Henry, M. (1990). More than just play: The significance of mutually directed adult-child activity. *Early Child Development and Care, 60,* 35–51.

Hohmann, M., Banet, B., & Weikart, D. P. (1979). *Young children in action.* Ypsilanti, MI: High/Scope Educational Research Foundation.

Holcombe, A., Wolery, M., Werts, M. G., & Hrenkevich, P. (1991). *Increasing the efficiency of future learning by manipulating current instruction.* Manuscript submitted for publication.

Holdaway, D. (1979). *The foundations of literacy.* Portsmouth, NH: Heinmann.

Horton, S. (1985). Computational rates of educable mentally retarded adolescents with and without calculators in comparison to normals. *Education and Training of the Mentally Retarded, 20,* 14–24.

Hunt, J. McV. (1960). Experience and the development of motivation: Some reinterpretations. *Child Development, 31,* 489–504.

Hunt, J. McV. (1987). The effects of differing kinds of experience in early rearing conditions. In I. C. Uzgiris, & J. McV. Hunt (Eds.), *Infant performance and experience* (pp. 39–97). Urbana: University of Illinois Press.

Kamii, C., & Devries, R. (1977). Piaget for early education. In M. C. Day & P. K. Parker (Eds.), *The preschool in action: Exploring early childhood programs* (2nd ed.). Boston: Allyn & Bacon.

Kamii, C., & Devries, R. (1978). *Physical knowledge in preschool education: Implications of Piaget's theory.* Englewood Cliffs, NJ: Prentice-Hall.

Katims, D. S. (1990, April). *Project I.E.P. (Intervention for Early Progress): An emergent literacy approach to early childhood special education.* Paper presented at the 11th Annual International Conference of the Young Adult Institute on Developmental Disabilities, New York.

Katims, D. S. (1991). Emergent literacy in early childhood special education: Curriculum and instruction. *Topics in Early Childhood Special Education, 11*(1), 69–84.

Kincaid, M. S., & Weisberg, P. (1978). Alphabet letters as tokens: Training preschool children in letter recognition and labeling during a token exchange period. *Journal of Applied Behavior Analysis, 11,* 199. Abstract.

Koppenhaver, D. A., Coleman, P. P., Kalman, S. L., & Yoder, D. E. (1991). *The implications of emergent literacy research for children with developmental disabilities.* Manuscript submitted for publication.

Lamme, L. L. (1987). Children's literature: The natural way to learn to read. In B. E. Callinan (Ed.), *Children's literature in the reading program.* Newark, DE: International Reading Association.

Langley, M. B. (1989). Assessing infant cognitive development. In D. B. Bailey & M. Wolery (Eds.), *Assessing infants and preschoolers with handicaps,* Columbus, OH: Merrill.

Lapointe, A. (1986). The state of instruction in reading and writing in the U.S. elementary schools. *Phi Delta Kappan, 68,* 135–138.

LeMay, D. W., Griffin, P. M., & Sanford, A. R. (1977). *Learning accomplishment profile—Diagnostic edition.* Chapel Hill, NC: Chapel Hill Training and Outreach Project.

Martin, B., Jr. (1983). *Brown bear, brown bear.* New York: Holt, Rinehart, & Winston.

Martinez, M., & Teale, W. H. (1988). Reading in a kindergarten classroom library. *The Reading Teacher, 41,* 568–572.

McCormick, C. E., & Mason, J. M. (1986). Intervention procedures for increasing children's interest in and knowledge about reading. In W. H. Teale & E. Sulzby (Eds.). *Emergent Literacy* (pp. 90–114). Norwood, NJ: Ablex.

McCormick, S. (1983). Reading aloud to preschoolers age 3–6: A review of the research. *Reading Horizons, 24*(1), 7–11.

McLane, J. B., & McNamee, G. D. (1991). The beginnings of literacy. *Zero to Three, 12,* 1–8.

Mercer, C. D., & Snell, M. E. (1977). *Learning theory research in mental retardation: Implications for teaching.* Columbus, OH: Merrill.

Morphett, M. V., & Washburne, C. (1931). When should children begin to read? *Elementary School Journal, 41,* 496–503.

Morrow, L. M. (1982). Relationships between literature programs, library corner designs, and children's use of literature. *The Journal of Educational Research, 75*(6), 339–344.

Morrow, L. M., & Rand, M. K. (1991). Promoting literacy during play by designing early childhood classroom environment. *The Reading Teacher, 44,* 396–402.

National Association for the Education of Young Children and the National Association of Early Childhood Specialists in State Departments of Education (1990). *Policy statement.* Washington, DC: National Association for the Education of Young Children.

Neisworth, J. T., & Bagnato, S. J. (in press). Case against intelligence testing in early intervention. *Topics in Early Childhood Special Education.*

Neisworth, J. T., Willoughby-Herb, S. J., Bagnato, S. J., Cartwright, C. A., & Laub, K. W. (1980). *Individualized education for preschool exceptional children.* Rockville, MD: Aspen.

Neuman, S. B., & Roskos, K. (1990). Play, print, and purpose: Enriching play environments for literacy development. *The Reading Teacher, 44*(3), 214–221.

Palardy, J. M. (1984). Some thoughts on systematic reading readiness instruction. *Reading Horizons, 24,*167–171.

Phillips, J. L. (1975). *The origins of intellect: Piaget's theory.* (2nd ed.). San Francisco: W. H. Freeman.

Piaget, J. (1963). *The origins of intelligence in children.* New York: Norton.

Rhodes, L. K. (1981). I can read! Predictable books as resources for reading and writing instruction. *The Reading Teacher, 34,* 511–518.

Robinson, C. C., & Robinson, J. H. (1978). Sensorimotor functions and cognitive development. In M. E. Snell (Ed.), *Systematic instruction of the moderately and severely handicapped.* Columbus, OH: Merrill.

Routman, R. (1988). *Transitions: From literature to literacy.* Portsmouth, NH: Heinmann.

Salisbury, C. L., & Vincent, L. J. (1990). Criterion of the next environment and best practices: Mainstreaming and integration 10 years later. *Topics in Early Childhood Special Education, 10*(2), 78–89.

Sattler, J. M. (1988). *Assessment of children* (3rd ed.). San Diego, CA: Sattler.

Smith, F. (1977). Making sense of reading—and of reading instruction. *Harvard Education Review, 47,* 386–395.

Snell, M. E. (1987). *Systematic instruction of persons with severe handicaps.* Columbus, OH: Merrill.

Strain, P. S. (in press). Integration in context of broader social policy issues. In C. A. Peck, S. L. Odom, & D. Bricker (Eds.), *Integrating young children with disabilities into community programs: From research to implementation.* Baltimore: Paul Brookes.

Strickland, D. S., & Morrow, L. M. (1988). Creating a print rich environment. *The Reading Teacher, 42*(3), 156–157.

Strickland, D. S., & Morrow, L. M. (1989). Environments rich in print promote literacy behavior during play. *The Reading Teacher, 43,* 178–179.

Sulzby, E. (1985). Children's emergent reading of favorite storybooks: A developmental study. *Reading Research Quarterly, 20*(4), 458–481.

Sulzby, E. (1986). Writing and reading: Signs of oral and written language organization in the young child. In W. H. Teale & E. Sulzby (Eds.), *Emergent literacy* (pp. 50–89). Norwood, NJ: Ablex.

Sulzby, E., & Teale, W. H. (1985). Writing development in early childhood. *Educational Horizons, 64,*8–12.

Tawney, J. W., Knapp, D. S., O'Rielly, C. D., & Pratt, S. S. (1979). *Programmed environment curriculum.* Columbus, OH: Merrill.

Teale, W. H., & Martinez, M. G. (1989). Connecting writing: Fostering emergent literacy in kindergarten children. In J. M. Mason (Ed.), *Reading and writing connections* (pp. 177–198). Boston: Allyn & Bacon.

Teale, W. H., & Sulzby, E. (Eds.), (1986). *Emergent literacy.* Norwood, NJ: Ablex.

Trelease, J. (1989). Jim Trelease speaks on reading aloud to children. *The Reading Teacher, 43*(3), 200–206.

Uzgiris, I. C., & Hunt, J. McV. (1975). *Assessment in infancy: Ordinal scales of psychological development.* Urbana: University of Illinois Press.

Uzgiris, I. C., & Hunt, J. McV. (1987). *Infant performance and experience.* Urbana: University of Illinois Press.

Vygotsky, L. S. (1962). *Thought and language.* Cambridge, MA: MIT Press.

Vygotsky, L. S. (1978). *Mind in society: The development of higher psychological processes.* Cambridge, MA: Harvard University Press.

Wachs, T. D. (1979). Proximal experience and early cognitive-intellectual development: The physical environment. *Merrill-Palmer Quarterly, 25,* 3–41.

Weisz, J. R., & Zigler, E. (1979). Cognitive development in retarded and nonretarded persons: Piagetian tests of the similar sequence hypothesis. *Psychological Bulletin, 86,* 831–851.

Wiseman, D. L. (1984). Helping children take early steps toward reading and writing. *The Reading Teacher, 37,* 340–344.

Witty, P., & Kopel, D. (1939). *Reading and the education process.* Boston: Ginn.

Wolery, M., Ault, M. J., & Doyle, P. M. (in press). *Teaching students with moderate and severe disabilities: Use of response-prompting procedures.* White Plains, NY: Longman.

Wolery, M., & Brookfield-Norman, J. (1988). (Pre) academic instruction for handicapped preschool children. In S. L. Odom and M. B. Karnes (Eds.), *Early intervention for infants and children with handicaps: An empirical base* (pp. 109–128). Baltimore: Paul Brookes.

Wolery, M., Doyle, P. M., Gast, D. L., Ault, M. J., & Lichtenberg, S. (1991). *Comparison of progressive time delay and transition-based teaching.* Manuscript submitted for publication.

Wolery, M., & Fleming, L. A. (in press). Implementing individualized curriculum in integrated settings. In C. A. Peck, S. L. Odom, & D. Bricker (Eds.), *Integrating young children with disabilities into community programs: From research to implementation.* Baltimore: Paul Brookes.

Wolery, M., Fleming, L. A., Venn, M. L., Domjancic, C. M., & Thornton, C. (1991). *Effects of simultaneous prompting during circle time.* Manuscript submitted for publication.

Wolery, M., Holcombe, A., Cybriwsky, C. A., Doyle, P. M., Schuster, J. W., Ault, M. J., & Gast, D. L. (in press). Constant time delay with discrete responses: A review of effectiveness and demographic, procedural, and methodological parameters. *Research in Developmental Disabilities.*

Wolery, M., Holcombe, A., Werts, M. G., & Cipolloni, R. M. (1991). *Effects of simultaneous prompting and instructive feedback.* Manuscript submitted for publication.

Wolery, M., & Smith, P. D. (1989). Assessing self-care skills. In D. B. Bailey & M. Wolery (Eds.), *Assessing infants and preschoolers with handicaps* (pp. 447–477).

Wolery, M., Strain, P. S., & Bailey, D. B. (in press). Applying the developmentally appropriate practice framework to children with special needs. In S. Bredekamp (Ed.), *Guidelines for appropriate curriculum content and assessment in programs serving children ages 3 through 8.* Washington, DC: National Association for the Education of Young Children.

Wolery, M., Werts, M. G., Holcombe, A., Billings, S. S., & Vassilaros, M. A. (in press). Comparison of simultaneous and alternating presentation of nontarget information. *Journal of Behavioral Education.*

Index

Transdisciplinary play-based model, 116
Transition, prelinguistic to linguistic communication, 334–37
Transition-based teaching, 166
Transitions, 77–80, 183–84
  guidelines for, 184
Trelease, J., 557
Tremblay, A., 260, 281, 386
Treusch, N., 49
Trivette, C. M., 28, 55, 84, 85, 121, 230, 233, 263, 442
Trohanis, P. L., 13, 17, 87
Tronick, E., 304, 326
Tube feeding, 450–53
Tudehope, D., 469
Turn taking cycles, 327
  guidelines, 327–28
Turnbull, A. P., 48, 50, 77, 88, 443
Turnbull, H. R., 48, 50, 88, 371
Turner, R. K., 502
Twardosz, S., 210, 231, 232, 286

Udell, T., 135
Unqualified or unconditional acceptance, 324
Upshur, C. C., 53
Urwin, C. A., 15
Ushycky, I., 354
Uzgiris, I. C., 531

Vadasy, P. F., 274
Van Biervplet, A., 181
Vance, S. D., 249
Van Dijk program, 329
Van Haitsma, K., 84
Van Hasseh, V. B., 393, 511
Van Houten, R., 370, 398
Van Wagenen, R. K., 498
Varnedoe, D., 352
Vassilaros, M. A., 172, 184, 567
Venn, M., 50, 172, 183, 184, 269, 566
Vertical instruction, 534–35
Vietze, P. M., 234
Vincent, L. J., 80, 106, 117, 543
Violation of expectancy, 165
Visser, G. H. A., 413
Vlazey, M. J., 201
Vocabulary selection, 334
  criteria for, 335
Vollmer, T. R., 369, 370, 376, 377, 395
Von Bertalanffy, L. V., 64
Vygotsky, L. S., 550, 560

Wachs, T. D., 55, 104, 130, 137, 138, 200, 202, 263, 524, 533
Wacker, D. P., 385
Waggoner, N., 508

Walker, D., 7
Walker, L., 44, 79
Walker, S., 135, 421
Walker, V., 306
Walsh, M. E., 284
Ware, W. B., 110, 233
Warner, J., 150
Warren, R., 84
Warren, S. F., 47, 169, 185, 244, 246–48, 285, 303, 320, 336, 342
Warr-Leeper, G., 338
Washburne, C., 549
Washington, V., 7, 34
Wasik, B. H., 89
Waslglyk, T. M., 432
Watson, J. S., 221, 231, 233, 234
Watts, E., 285
Webber, S., 338
Webster-Stratton, C., 393
Wedel, J. W., 210
Wedge, 424–25
Weeks, M., 385
Weeldreyer, J. C., 106
Weikart, D. P., 8, 205, 206, 539, 541
Weil, M., 82
Weiner, B. J., 41
Weinhouse, E., 44
Weinstein, C. S., 199
Weinzierl, C., 184
Weisberg, P., 566
Weisler, A., 202
Weisner, T. S., 65
Weisz, J. R., 531
Wells, K. C., 393, 503
Werner, D. B., 444, 445, 454, 465, 508
Werts, M. G., 172, 181, 184, 567
Wertsch, J., 325
Wesolowski, M. D., 507
West, D., 393
Westby, C., 19, 317
Wetherby, A., 300, 303, 306, 309, 311–14, 317–20, 322, 328, 330–33
Whaley, L. F., 244, 245, 451, 467, 468, 471, 475, 476
Wheelchairs, 424, 426–29
White, C., 24
White, O. R., 10, 47, 149, 152, 155, 377
White, R. W., 25, 71, 232, 234
Whitman, B. Y., 21
Whitman, T. L., 387
Whitten, C. I., 221
Whole interval system, 152
Wickstrom, S., 168, 272
Widerstrom, A. H., 55
Wigg, E., 322
Wilcox, M. J., 318, 321
Wiles, D. L., 81
Wiley, K., 186, 231
Wilkinson, I. A. G., 545

Willard, C., 311
Willems, S., 346
William, H. C., 433
Williams, C. L., 503
Williams, F. E., 497
Williamson, G. G., 446, 475
Willis, J. H., 204
Willoughby-Herb, S. J., 104
Wilson, L. L., 531, 537
Wilson, P. G., 121, 462
Winkel, G., 201
Winterling, V., 140, 165, 380
Winton, P. J., 19, 36, 37, 39, 77, 79, 110, 113, 312, 443
Witty, P., 550
Wnek, L., 104, 420
Wolery, M., 11, 47, 50, 55, 56, 101, 104, 116, 123, 129, 130, 141–45, 149, 151, 152, 163, 166, 167, 170–72, 179, 181, 183, 184, 186–89, 205, 231, 269, 271, 277, 364, 366–68, 371, 375, 377, 398, 400, 453, 461, 462, 464–66, 482, 488–90, 505, 507–9, 511, 512, 515, 524, 541, 543, 544, 546, 547, 549, 563–67
Wolf, M. M., 101, 123, 249, 283, 393
Wolfe, D. A., 284
Wolfe, V. V., 284
Wolfensberger, W., 47, 48, 199
Wolinsky, G., 135, 421
Wolke, D., 14, 224
Wong, D. L., 451, 467, 468, 471, 475, 476
Woodroffe, P., 502
Woodson, C. W., 271, 506
Woolacott, M. H., 416
Wusterbarth, N. J., 283
Wyne, M. D., 37

Yajniki, G. G., 81
Yarrow, L. J., 234
Yawkey, T. D., 274
Yeates, K. O., 64
Yoder, D., 77, 345, 550
Yoder, P. J., 40, 70, 136, 164, 312, 320, 515
Yogman, M. W., 24
Yonclas, D., 306
York, J., 51, 344
Young, C., 393

Zarcone, J. R., 369
Zelman, J. G., 104
Zero reject, 4
Zigler, E., 7, 36, 531
Zipper, I. N., 82
Zohn, C., 386
Zone of proximal development, 560
Zone procedure, 209
Zweibel, S., 204